Edo and Paris

Edo
AND
Paris

*Urban Life and the State
in the Early Modern Era*

EDITED BY
JAMES L. MCCLAIN, JOHN M. MERRIMAN,
AND UGAWA KAORU

CORNELL UNIVERSITY PRESS
Ithaca and London

Cornell University Press gratefully acknowledges
a grant from the Japan Foundation that aided in
bringing this book to production.

The costs of publishing this book have been defrayed in part by the 1996 Hiromi
Arisawa Memorial Award from the Books on Japan Fund with respect to the cloth
edition of this volume and *"Rich Nation, Strong Army": National Security and the
Technological Transformation of Japan,* by Richard J. Samuels, published by Cornell
University Press. The award is financed by the Japan Foundation from generous
donations contributed by Japanese individuals and companies.

First published 1994 by Cornell University Press.
First printing, Cornell Paperbacks, 1997.

Printed in the United States of America

♾ The paper in this book meets the minimum requirements of the American
National Standard for Information Sciences—Permanence of Paper for Printed
Library Materials, ANSI Z39.48-1984.

Library of Congress Cataloging-in-Publication Data

Edo and Paris : urban life and the state in the early modern era / edited by
  James L. McClain, John Merriman, and Ugawa Kaoru.
      p.   cm.
    Entry words also in Japanese.
    Includes bibliographical references and index.
    ISBN 0-8014-2987-0 (alk. paper)
    ISBN 0-8014-8183-X (pbk.: alk. paper)
      1. Tokyo (Japan)—History—1600–1868. 2. Paris (France)—
    History—17th century. 3. Paris (France)—History—18th century.
    I. McClain, James L., 1944– . II. Merriman, John M. III. Ugawa,
    Kaoru, 1931– .
    DS896.62.E34 1994
    952'.135025—dc20   94-14462

Cloth printing   10 9 8 7 6 5 4 3 2 1

Paperback printing   10 9 8 7 6 5 4 3 2 1

In celebration
of the scholarship of
JOHN W. HALL
and
NISHIYAMA MATSUNOSUKE

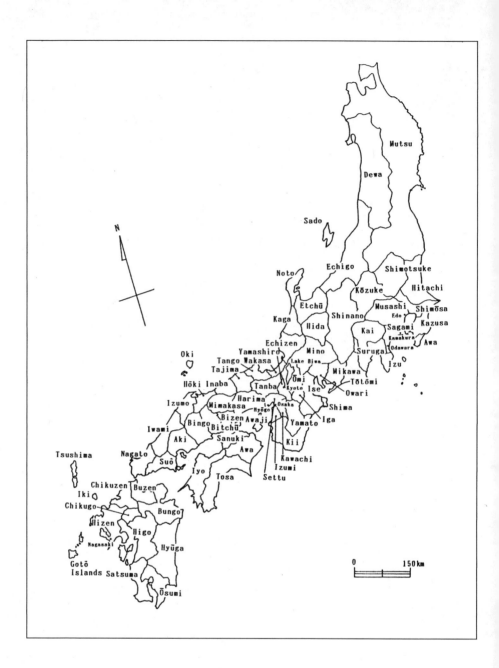

The traditional provinces of Japan.

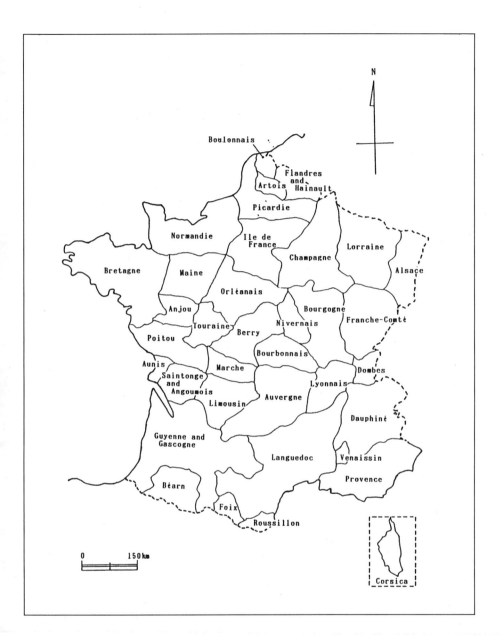

The major regions of France.

Contents

Maps and Illustrations

Figures and Tables

Preface

In the early summer of 1990, four hundred years after Tokugawa Ieyasu first marched into Edo, nearly fifty scholars from East and West gathered in Tokyo to explore the relationship between the emergence of the early-modern state in Japan and France and the evolution of Edo and Paris as the political capitals of shogun and king. This volume is a product of that gathering.

As historians interested in cities and in France and Japan, we long had been intrigued by the apparent parallels between those two societies in the early-modern period. During the late sixteenth and early seventeenth centuries, political leaders emerged to lay ideological claim to a new basis of authority in each country. On opposite sides of the globe, the Bourbon kings and the Tokugawa shoguns alike struggled to translate their conceptions of power into a new centralism that would garner for themselves unprecedented control over the people and institutions of their countries, and each promoted the growth of a capital city that reflected the enhanced powers of its political master and stood unrivaled in its part of the world. The state became as omnipresent in Japan as it did in France, and the quest for absolute power in each nation became intimately caught up in the growth of an administrative capital.

The parallels continued even inside the capital cities. Louis XIV redesigned Paris by turning ancient ramparts into boulevards and erecting triumphal arches, all heavy with statuary and medallions glorifying the Sun King's achievements. In Japan, Ieyasu's sprawling castle, which served as administrative headquarters as well as military fortress, dominated the heart of Edo, and his shogunate claimed the ultimate right to decide all land use within the city. Each of the rulers endeavored to bring all city residents more directly under his administrative control. In the new city of Edo, Ieyasu and his successors had to create an urban bureaucracy where none had existed before, whereas in Paris, long since established, the Bourbons' task was to cut away at older, competing prerogatives claimed by the aristocracy, church, and bourgeoisie. The new political elites even attempted to shape the style and texture of cultural life. In Paris the Sun King added to his glory by founding the Opéra and the Comédie-Française; the Tokugawa shoguns, more fearful of the theater's impact on public morality, enchained kabuki in a tight weave of restrictions. The points of comparison between statemaking and urbanism seemed to us to be almost startling, and certainly worthy of systematic exploration.

A preliminary workshop held in New York under the auspices of the Social Science Research Council provided an opportunity for us to consult with Roger Chartier, John W. Hall, William W. Kelly, and Charles Tilly. There deliberations focused on clarifying the areas of possible inquiry and on identifying scholars who might help to broaden our understanding of state-making and urbanism in France and Japan. Those discussions prompted us to invite to a symposium in Tokyo specialists who would pursue similar topics in respect to France and Japan, Paris and Edo. This procedure, we anticipated, would have two benefits. We could look forward to essays that would enrich the existing scholarship on each national culture; at the same time, we could hope to develop a set of empirical findings, questions, and conceptual approaches that could more clearly define the similarities, as well as the disjunctions, in regard to political power and urban developments in Japan and France, thus expanding our knowledge of what was common and what was culturally specific about the early-modern experience in two geographically separated societies.

Within this context, we mapped out two broad areas of inquiry. The first we called "the city from above"—an examination of the ways in which the new forms of state authority in France and Japan influenced the general direction of urbanization during the early-modern period. Thus we were interested in discovering the components of state power and in learning how the Bourbon kings and the Tokugawa shoguns implemented their authority within an urban setting. For one thing, we wanted to understand how they came to see their capitals as reflections of their worldly authority and so built anew or physically reorganized their cities to reflect the imperatives of power. Moreover, we wished to encourage an exploration of attempts by French kings and Japanese shoguns to impose cultural values and lifestyles on the urban populations; of state attitudes toward policing and dissidence; and of the ways in which the growth of Edo and Paris influenced government attitudes toward provisioning and the urban economy.

The second area of inquiry focused on "the city from below"—an investigation of the role of urban commoners in the emergence of Edo and Paris. Literature that appeared in the decade or so before our symposium made it clear that the residents of the early-modern capitals contributed to the evolution and shaping of urban institutions, and we wished to understand better the exact nature and significance of that process. We sought to learn more about how ordinary people perceived their roles, however modest, in urban political life; how they helped to call into being new economic institutions; how they enlivened the urban cultural scene; and why they sometimes acquiesced in the imposition of new statist powers and at other times resisted their political masters. In sum, we sought a thorough discussion of how the everyday activities of urban merchants and artisans shaped the urban experience and the nature of political authority.

The scholars who convened in Tokyo addressed these issues in depth, and we present their essays, revised and augmented, in this volume. Their contributions focus on the period from the 1590s, when the Bourbons and Tokugawa rose to power, until the 1780s and 1790s, when the monarchy fell and the collapse of the Kansei reforms marked the beginning of several difficult decades that culminated in the Meiji Restoration. An introductory overview seeks to provide a context for the essays and outlines the main themes pursued by the individual authors. The remaining chapters are grouped according to five topics: governance, space, provisioning, culture, and resistance. Within each of those categories, the essays discuss the issues of power and urbanism, the city from above and the city from below. But equally significant are the rich interconnections that span the subdivisions and tie the essays together into an integrated whole. Issues concerned with provisioning, for instance, cannot be disentangled from the matter of governance, and all essays, in one form or another, touch upon the question of resistance by urban commoners to state power. Edo and Paris—each city owed its identity to a complex intersection of interests that flowed from above and welled up from below, and the nuances of that process touched on every aspect of the human experience in the two cities.

We thank all the persons who participated in the symposium. Ogi Shinzō opened the proceedings with a keynote speech that elaborated the themes we proposed to investigate. In addition to the essays included here, Meera Viswanathan and Yoshiwara Ken'ichirō presented papers titled "The Question of Realism in Paris and Edo Theater" and "Social Organization and Political Control in Edo." Karasawa Tatsuyuki, Gary Leupp, Sakada Toshio, and Constantine Vaporis helped to prepare translations of conference drafts, thus facilitating discussion. Hasegawa Teruo, Ninomiya Hiroyuki, Takazawa Norie, and Paul Waley, as well as Leupp and Vaporis, delivered comments on various of the presentations, and many members of the audience joined in debate, offering valuable insights and observations that found their way into the revised essays.

James L. McClain translated for publication the contributions by Hatano Jun, Hayashi Reiko, Katō Takashi, and Takeuchi Makoto. John M. Merriman translated from French the contribution by Roger Chartier and Steven L. Kaplan's study of the "false workers" of the faubourg Saint-Antoine (chapter 15), which originally appeared in *Annales E.S.C.* (1988). We appreciate permission to include it in our volume.

In the essays that follow, the dates of events in France follow the Gregorian calendar; dates for events in Japan are given according to the imperially proclaimed era year and the subsequent month and day of the lunar calendar, with a conversion of the era year to the nearest corresponding Western year. That is, an event that occurred in the third lunar month of

Kyōhō 3 is cited as taking place in the Third Month of 1718. Unfortunately, premodern Japanese lunar-based years were not exactly coterminous with Western solar-based years, so events that fell in the final two months of a Japanese year might find their equivalent dates in the following Western year. Since Tokugawa Ieyasu, for instance, was born on the twenty-sixth day of the Twelfth Month of Tenbun 11, the year of his birth often is given as 1542, whereas the exact correspondence is 31 January 1543. We provide both Western and Japanese dates of important events.

Japanese is romanized according to the Hepburn system. Names take their native form: surname follows given name for Westerners, surname precedes personal name for Japanese (except for persons writing in English). Since this volume is intended for both specialists and interested general readers, the editors have tried to provide translations for technical terminology wherever possible. All works with Japanese titles cited in the notes were published in Tokyo unless another place is named.

Finally, we thank the people and institutions that made the symposium possible. The Thomas J. Watson Jr. Institute for International Studies at Brown and the Tokyo Municipal Government provided generous support. We are also grateful for grants from the Department of East Asian Studies at Brown University and the Nomura Foundation for the Arts and Sciences (Nomura Gakugei Zaidan).

Hatano Jun, in addition to contributing an original illustration for his own chapter, kindly prepared all of the maps of Edo, the maps of France and Japan that appear at the front of the volume, and the map of Edobashi at the end of the eighteenth century.

Julia Emlen of the Watson Institute deserves special thanks for help in making travel arrangements, as do Andrew Bell, Betty Y. Chung, Elizabeth Dougherty, and Lisa E. Hartmann for their assistance in preparing the manuscript for publication. We also wish to convey our deep appreciation to Roger Haydon of Cornell University Press for invaluable advice, always given in a kindly manner.

Sendai, Japan   JAMES L. McCLAIN

Balazuc, France   JOHN M. MERRIMAN

Tokyo, Japan   UGAWA KAORU

Chronology

BOURBON KINGS		TOKUGAWA SHOGUNS	
Henry IV, reigned	1589–1610	Ieyasu, ruled	1603–1605
		Hidetada	1605–1623
Louis XIII	1610–1643	Iemitsu	1623–1651
Louis XIV	1643–1715	Ietsuna	1651–1680
		Tsunayoshi	1680–1709
		Ienobu	1709–1712
		Ietsugu	1713–1716
Louis XV	1715–1774	Yoshimune	1716–1745
		Ieshige	1745–1760
		Ieharu	1760–1786
Louis XVI	1774–1789	Ienari	1787–1837
		Ieyoshi	1837–1853
		Iesada	1853–1858
		Iemochi[a]	1859–1866
		Yoshinobu[b]	1867–1868

[a] Appointed shogun on Ansei 5.12.1 (4 January 1859)
[b] Appointed shogun on Keiō 2.12.5 (10 January 1867); left office on Keiō 3.12.9 (3 January 1878)

1589/Tenshō 17

Henry of Navarre advances his claim to the crown, arousing the opposition of the Catholic League

1590/Tenshō 18

Hideyoshi wins a major victory against the Hōjō daimyo of Odawara, achieves military hegemony; Hideyoshi transfers Ieyasu to the Kantō; Ieyasu enters Edo (8.1); Ieyasu is said to have authorized construction of bridges (8.18), instructed Taruya Tōzaemon and Naraya Ichiemon to oversee the affairs of merchants and artisans (Eighth Month), and

ordered the platting of residential districts for merchants and artisans
(9.1)

1594/Bunroku 3
Henry of Navarre is crowned in Chartres as Henry IV, first in the line of
Bourbon kings (February); Henry enters Paris in triumph (22 March); the
crown levies municipal taxes to pay for street lighting

1600/Keichō 5
Ieyasu is victorious at Sekigahara, begins to accept oaths of loyalty from
daimyo (Ninth Month)

1603/Keichō 8
Tokugawa Ieyasu is appointed shogun (2.12); Ieyasu begins the practice
of granting to daimyo residential land in Edo (Second Month); the
shogunate authorizes construction of a bridge at Nihonbashi (3.3); Henry
IV authorizes construction of the Place Royale, an indication of the
crown's intention to clean up the ruins of the siege of 1589–1594 and to
impose a new royal design on Paris

1605/Keichō 10
Ieyasu retires as shogun and is succeeded by Hidetada (4.16);
construction of a hall of worship at Zōjōji is completed; houses of
prostitution are transferred away from Yanagi-chō to make space
available for the expansion of Edo Castle

1607/Keichō 12
Izumo no Okuni is said to have performed kabuki dances in Edo Castle
(2.20); the donjon is completed at Edo Castle (Ninth Month); royal edict
prohibits timber framing on houses fronting streets and calls on
Parisians to tear down portions of their residences that project into the
street; Henry orders work to begin on the Place Dauphine

1609/Keichō 14
The crown orders owners of vacant lots or houses standing in ruin
inside of the Paris city walls to rebuild in six months or risk having their
land auctioned off

1614/Keichō 19
A statue of Henry IV is erected at the Pont-Neuf, overlooking the Place
Dauphine

1615/Genna 1
The shogunate issues "Regulations concerning Warrior Households"
(*buke shohatto*) (7.7) and "Regulations concerning the Emperor and
Court" (*kinchū narabi ni kuge shohatto*) (7.17); Genna era begins 7.13

1617/Genna 3
Ieyasu is deified as "Great August Illuminator of the East, Buddha
Incarnate" (Tōshō Daigongen) (2.21); the shogunate authorizes
construction of a mausoleum at Nikkō for Ieyasu (Third Month); the
government declares that only samurai may wear swords; by this year,
the prostitution district at Yoshiwara is reported to be flourishing "more
than ever before"

1622/Genna 8

The project at the former palace of Queen Marguerite extends land speculation in subdivision projects beyond the old city walls of Paris

1623/Genna 9

The shogunate decrees that masterless samurai, merchants, and artisans may not live on daimyo's estates (2.15); Hidetada retires as shogun (7.27); first senior councilors (*rōjū*) are appointed

1626/Kan'ei 3

Construction of Tōshōgū shrine at Ueno is completed (9.3); contracts for prostitutes are limited to ten years (Tenth Month); Parlement decrees that no new religious orders may be established in Paris

1629/Kan'ei 6

The shogunate orders formation of *tsuji ban'ya* guardhouses in samurai neighborhoods (Third Month); traditionally given as the date when the shogunate banned women's kabuki, although women appear on stage as late as 1646 (Tenth Month); the king makes establishment of new religious orders contingent on issuance of royal letters of patent

1631/Kan'ei 8

The shogunate adopts the practice of appointing two ("north" and "south") city magistrates (*machi bugyō*) (10.5); the shogunate issues restrictions on samurai's clothing and housing (11.5); the crown erects thirty-one markers to define the territorial limits of Paris and prohibits new construction beyond those limits

1632/Kan'ei 9

Iemitsu constructs the Taitokuin mausoleum for his predecessor, Hidetada, who dies on 1.24; Iemitsu revises the "Regulations concerning Warrior Households" of 1615 and issues "Regulations concerning Vassals" (*shoshi hatto*) (9.29); Iemitsu begins to appoint commissioners of building (*sakuji bugyō*) and inspectors general (*ōmetsuke*) on a regular basis (Twelfth Month)

1633/Kan'ei 10

Iemitsu makes first appointments of junior councilors (3.26); the shogunate announces regulations governing inheritance among merchants and artisans (8.13)

1634/Kan'ei 11

Iemitsu begins to reconstruct Nikkō Tōshōgū, the mausoleum of Ieyasu, and refurbishes Zōjōji in Edo; senior councilors assume the responsibility for overseeing the affairs of daimyo and their retinues in Edo

1635/Kan'ei 12

The "Regulations concerning Warrior Households" and "Regulations concerning Vassals" are revised (6.21); the shogunate announces that the system of alternate residence (*sankin kōtai*) is to be enforced for all "outside lords" (*tozama daimyō*); commissioners of shrines and temples (*jisha bugyō*) are appointed regularly from this year (11.9); the shogunate defines the duties of the city magistrates, commissioners of shrines and temples, and commissioners of finance (*kanja bugyō*)

1637/Kan'ei 14
Iemitsu begins to reconstruct the donjon tower of Edo Castle and several of the residential enclosures (8.15)

1639/Kan'ei 16
A statue of Louis XIII is erected at the Place Royale

1642/Kan'ei 19
A royal edict orders the artisans and merchants of the faubourg Saint-Antoine to incorporate; the shogunate instructs "allied lords" (*fudai daimyō*) to comply with the requirements of the alternate residence system (5.9)

1643/Kan'ei 20
The crown undertakes a cadastral survey of Paris in order to support a tax levy to repay the canon of Notre-Dame for the development of the Ile Saint-Louis; the shogunate orders sixteen daimyo to organize firefighting brigades

1645/Shōhō 2
The city magistrates prohibit the employment of women dancers and the mixing of the sexes on stage (10.23)

1648/Keian 1
The Keian era begins on 2.15; the shogunate issues a major legal code regulating the lives of Edo's commoners (Second Month); the Fronde begins

1652/Jōō 1
Boys' kabuki is banned (6.27); the Jōō era begins on 9.18; Louis XIV retakes Paris

1655/Meireki 1
The Meireki era begins on 4.13; the shogunate issues the *Edo machijū sadamegaki,* a legal code governing the behavior of merchants and artisans (10.13)

1657/Meireki 3
Two great fires destroy large portions of Edo and together with a snowstorm leave more than 100,000 persons dead (1.18–19); the crown assumes administrative responsibility for the Hôpital Général; the workers in the faubourg Saint-Antoine are granted an exemption from the guild system

1658/Manji 1
The Manji era begins on 7.23; the shogunate organizes four all-samurai, all-Edo firefighting squads (9.8)

1661/Kanbun 1
The Kanbun era begins on 4.25; construction commences at Versailles; Asai Ryōi publishes his *Tōkaidō meishoki* ("Account of Famous Places along the Tōkaidō Highway") and *Musashi abumi* ("The Musashi Stir Up")

1662/Kanbun 2
Asai publishes *Edo meishoki* ("Account of Famous Places in Edo")

1663/Kanbun 3
  The shogunate orders guards at the *tsuji ban'ya* not to engage in
  commercial activities

1666/Kanbun 6
  Louis XIV establishes a ministerial *conseil de police*

1667/Kanbun 7
  Louis XIV appoints a lieutenant general of police for Paris (March); the
  monarch orders that the Cour des Miracles, traditional haven of
  pickpockets and thieves, be cleaned out; the city provides five thousand
  lanterns to light the streets of Paris; in the wake of the great London
  fire, the crown reissues the building codes of 1607 and more rigorously
  enforces injunctions against building in wood (permitted only for
  bridges and for houses inside courtyards)

1670/Kanbun 10
  Louis XIV orders that the walls of Paris be torn down; the king
  authorizes work to begin on the Invalides

1671/Kanbun 11
  Louis XIV ceases to reside in Paris

1672/Kanbun 12
  Kawamura Zuiken completes development of coastal shipping circuits
  around Japan

1673/Enpō 1
  The Mitsui family opens the Echigoya in Edo (Eighth Month); Enpō era
  begins 9.21; Louis XIV grants the Opéra a monopoly on musical
  productions

1674/Enpō 2
  Louis XIV suppresses nineteen seigneurial and corporate autonomous
  enclaves in an attempt to bring administrative regularity to Paris; Louis
  renews the decree of 1631 forbidding new construction outside the city
  walls

1677/Enpō 5
  Edo suzume ("The Edoite Sparrow"), the first guidebook to Edo actually
  to be published in that city, appears; Invalides opens with a capacity of
  six thousand patients

1680/Enpō 8
  Louis XIV authorizes the establishment of the Comédie-Française

1683/Tenna 3
  Louis XIV puts the budgets and borrowing power of municipalities
  under the tutelage of the intendants

1684/Jōkyō 1
  The Jōkyō era begins 2.21; Louis XIV locks up the prostitutes of Paris

1687/Jōkyō 4
  Kokyōgaeri no Edo-banashi ("A Chat about Edo with One Who'd Settled
  There but Is Going Home") is published

1690/Genroku 3
> Louis XIV puts all hospitals under the Grand Bureau, headed by the archbishop of Paris, the president of the sovereign courts, the provost of merchants, and the lieutenant general of police

1692/Genroku 5
> The shogunate revises the "Regulations concerning Warrior Households" (Seventh Month); Louis XIV creates hereditary mayorships (*maires*) with powers greater than those of elected city councils

1694/Genroku 7
> Merchants in Edo form the "organization of ten associations of wholesalers" (*tokumidoiya*); Osaka merchants join together in the "organization of twenty-four associations of wholesalers" (*nijūshikumidoiya*)

1695/Genroku 8
> Shogunate completes a census of the commoner population of Edo (353,588 persons)

1700/Genroku 13
> The conseil de commerce is established to coordinate the interests of merchant oligarchies all over France; the population of Paris reaches 510,000

1716/Kyōhō 1
> The Kyōhō era begins on 6.22; Yoshimune is appointed shogun on 8.13 and soon launches what become known as the Kyōhō reforms

1718/Kyōhō 3
> City magistrates order neighborhood chiefs to organize squads of commoner firefighters (Twelfth Month)

1720/Kyōhō 5
> The shogunate creates the *i-ro-ha* structure of commoner firefighters

1722/Kyōhō 7
> The infirmary–convalescent center (*yōjōsho*) opens at Koishikawa (12.7; 13 January 1723); the shogunate lifts the ban on importing Western books, except those dealing with Christianity

1724/Kyōhō 9
> The shogunate orders merchants who handle oil, rice, and other commodities to form protective associations

1726/Kyōhō 11
> The shogunate requires Edo wholesalers specializing in any of fifteen products, including rice and lamp oil, to submit account books and price lists (Fourth Month)

1733/Kyōhō 18
> Edo commoners riot for the first time (1.26)

1742/Kanpō 2
> The shogunate compiles the *kujikata osadamegaki*, a codification of its legal codes and procedures (Fourth Month)

1745/Enkyō 2
    Jurisdiction over the merchant and artisan quarters is transferred from the commissioners of shrines and temples to the city magistrates (intercalary 12.15; 5 February 1746)

1764/Meiwa 1
    Controller General Laverdy begins municipal reforms; little theaters emerge as the principal attractions of the boulevards of Paris; the Meiwa era begins on 6.22

1767/Meiwa 4
    Entertainers begin to perform regularly at Edobashi

1771/Meiwa 8
    The crown reestablishes venal municipal offices

1772/An'ei 1
    Tanuma Okitsugu is appointed as a senior councilor (1.15); the great Kōjin-zaka Fire destroys large portions of Edo (2.19); the An'ei era begins 11.16

1781/Tenmei 1
    Paris begins to install street lighting; the Tenmei period begins on 4.2

1786/Tenmei 6
    Tanuma is ousted as senior councilor (8.27)

1787/Tenmei 7
    Riots sweep Edo (5.20–24); Matsudaira Sadanobu is appointed as senior councilor, launches what become known as the Kansei reforms (6.19)

1789/Kansei 1
    The Kansei era begins on 1.25; the French Revolution begins

1790/Kansei 2
    Workhouses (*ninsoku yoseba*) open at Ishikawajima (2.19); the neighborhood chiefs are divided into seventeen groups (10.6)

1792/Kansei 4
    The city savings association (*machi kaisho*) opens (5.19)

1793/Kansei 5
    Matsudaira Sadanobu, author of the Kansei reforms, is removed from office (Seventh Month)

Edo and Paris

1

Edo and Paris

Cities and Power

JAMES L. MCCLAIN AND JOHN M. MERRIMAN

On 30 August 1590, with the summer heat beating down on the great Kantō plain, Tokugawa Ieyasu for the first time marched into Edo, a small fishing village at the innermost recess of Edo Bay. Not four years later, on 22 March 1594, Henry of Navarre, newly crowned as Henry IV and first in the line of Bourbon monarchs, fought his way into a Paris still gripped by winter's chill and ousted the forces of the intransigent Catholic League. Although fighting continued in the provinces, for all intents and purposes the Wars of Religion were over. Paris had been considered France's capital from at least the fourteenth century, and such was its importance, both real and symbolic, that Henry could secure his kingship only by seizing the city. In France, Paris was the political center, and on the other side of the globe, Edo soon would become so.

In 1590 Ieyasu helped his mentor, Toyotomi Hideyoshi, smash their opponents entrenched at Odawara Castle on the southern end of the Kantō plain, thus securing for Hideyoshi military hegemony over Japan's regional lords, the daimyo, who within the year acknowledged Hideyoshi's supremacy by submitting oaths of allegiance to him and receiving in return documents of enfeoffment. To reward Ieyasu for his military service, Hideyoshi granted to the head of the Tokugawa family several provinces in the Kantō region, to rule as his own independent domain. As the historic homeland of the samurai estate and the most extensive rice-producing region in Japan, the Kantō proved to be an ideal base from which to contend for national leadership. Ultimately, from his seat of power in Edo, Ieyasu succeeded Hideyoshi, won appointment as shogun, and went on to fashion a system of governance that made the Tokugawa family the undisputed, de facto rulers of all of Japan.

In Paris, too, Henry and his Bourbon successors gathered power unto

We thank William Beik, Colin Jones, and Charles Tilly for their comments on a draft of this chapter.

themselves. In doing so, they profited from the accomplishments of their predecessors, especially the Valois line of kings, who had won the right to raise a standing army and to levy annually a direct tax known as the *taille*. The Valois kings also confirmed Paris's identity as seat of royal power: in 1528 François I (r. 1515–1547), who until then had preferred life in the Loire Valley, wrote to municipal authorities that he had decided to reside "henceforth" in and around "his good town of Paris."[1] By then the royal presence loomed so large, in fact, that when François sought loans to continue a foreign war, a leading noble of Paris assured the king that "we do not wish to dispute or minimize your power; that would be a sacrilege, and we know very well that you are above the law."[2]

The Bourbon kings—especially Henry, Louis XIII, and Louis XIV, monarchs whose reigns spanned the seventeenth century—built on the royal legacy and further expanded state power by taming the aristocrats, regulating merchants, and harnessing the independence of the provinces. During the reign of Louis XIII (1610–1643), Armand Jean Du Plessis de Richelieu (1585–1642), the king's chief minister, prepared the fiscal foundations of absolutism, forced the surrender of Protestant forces at La Rochelle in 1628, ordered the destruction of Huguenot fortresses, and shaped a new alliance between church and state, affirming their mutually supportive relationship. At the height of Bourbon glory, Louis XIV could not only boast that he was above the law, he even asserted that he constituted the very embodiment of state authority ("L'Etat, c'est moi," he is said to have exclaimed), and he further claimed to stand as God's representative on earth, the Sun King.

In Japan and in France in the seventeenth and eighteenth centuries, state power and administrative capitals grew together, for only from the urban center could claimants to national hegemony hope to spread their authority over the rest of the nation. A city of 250,000 residents in 1594, Paris more than doubled its population during the next century as it became the largest metropolis in Europe. A humble village in 1590, Edo in 1700 had twice again the population of Paris, and in all likelihood was the world's most populous city. The Tokugawa shoguns and the Bourbon kings, Edo and Paris, cities and power: burgeoning urban growth and the expansion of state power colored the early-modern period in Japan and France.

THE POLITIES

Pretensions to Absolutism

Both the Tokugawa shoguns and Bourbons kings have been called absolute rulers. Admittedly, neither Ieyasu nor Henry IV possessed a blueprint for absolutism when he settled in his city in the 1590s, and neither family would ever accumulate in reality as much power as it claimed in theory. But both

1. R. J. Knecht, *Francis I* (Cambridge: Cambridge University Press, 1988), p. 253.
2. Eugene F. Rice, Jr., *The Foundation of Early Modern Europe, 1460–1559* (New York: Norton, 1970), p. 93.

shogun and king strove to control as much as was possible. By the final decades of the seventeenth century, when the process of state building had run its course in France and in Japan, the shogun and king embraced in principle and often exercised in practice an unprecedented degree of power. Each hegemon asserted the supreme right to proclaim laws, levy taxes, and adjudicate disputes. Each ruler presided over a bureaucracy that carried out the details of governance, and each state enjoyed a monopoly on the legitimate use of physical force, the better to impose its will. Neither autocrat, neither state, as we shall see, ever went unchallenged in its exercise of authority, but each had brought together a concentration of governing powers unseen in its country's history until that time.

The impulse toward centralization burst forth from the crucible of warfare.[3] Several decades before Ieyasu was born, the great Ōnin War (1467–1477) touched off a maelstrom of violence that brought considerable destruction to Kyoto, the home of the aristocracy and the emperor, who as a descendant of the Sun Goddess, the most influential figure in Japan's pantheon of deities, served as the traditional fount of political legitimacy. With the old ruling center no longer capable of asserting authority outside of the confines of the imperial capital, the Japanese countryside in the late fifteenth and early sixteenth centuries fractured into dozens and then into innumerable domains, each controlled by a military lord, or daimyo, and his band of samurai followers. From the middle of the sixteenth century, Japan began to put itself back together again. Large daimyo conquered small, the weak submitted to the strong, and in nearly ceaseless military campaigns that spanned the final decades of the sixteenth century, Oda Nobunaga (1534–1582) and Toyotomi Hideyoshi (1537–1598) brought their opponents to their knees. The process reached its climax in 1590, when Hideyoshi carried his banners into eastern Japan.

Tokugawa Ieyasu (1543–1616) rose to power in this vortex of war. The Tokugawa family traced its origins back to a small village in eastern Japan, but it later moved to the province of Mikawa, where by the middle of the sixteenth century it had carved out a domain of its own. After Ieyasu became the head of the Tokugawa house, he had the good fortune to ally himself with Nobunaga and Hideyoshi, a maneuver that provided him with new opportunities to expand the territories under his military sway. By 1565 Ieyasu had made all of Mikawa his; in 1570 he added neighboring Tōtōmi; by the middle of the next decade he controlled parts or all of five provinces; and Ieyasu's move to the Kantō in 1590 made him the single most powerful daimyo in all of Japan. When Hideyoshi died in 1598, Ieyasu stood poised to succeed him as the leader of the country's military estate. Yet, for all of Ieyasu's wealth, armed strength, and distinguished warrior pedigree, sev-

---

3. Scholars as different in their approaches as Lewis Mumford and Charles Tilly have written about the close connection between warfare and the growth of political absolutism: Charles Tilly, *Coercion, Capital, and European States* (Oxford: Basil Blackwell, 1990); Lewis Mumford, *The City in History: Its Origins, Its Transformations, and Its Prospects* (London: Secker & Warburg, 1966), pp. 360–63.

eral lords in western Japan were not about to accept Tokugawa suzerainty without a struggle. In the autumn of 1600 Ieyasu and his allies put 70,000 troops in the field at Sekigahara and took the measure of their opponents from the west. Three years later, the emperor appointed Ieyasu as shogun.

The title was an ancient one. From the eighth century, the emperor bestowed it from time to time on court nobles who led military expeditions against insurgents and indigenous peoples on the northern frontier. During the medieval period, appointments to the post were made on a regular basis, warrior families came to monopolize the office, and the duties were redefined so that the shogun's principal responsibilities were to supervise the warrior estate, ensure domestic peace, and protect Japan from outside threats. During the seventeenth century, the Tokugawa shoguns expanded the responsibilities of the position, claiming new rights over taxation, lawmaking, and judicial authority. In practice, they came to function as heads of state, in theory accountable to no one except the emperor. They also continued to police the samurai, and they discharged their obligation to safeguard the nation by severing most links with the outside world. During the opening decades of the seventeenth century, the Tokugawa shoguns prohibited Christianity and restricted foreign commerce to Chinese and Dutch traders at Nagasaki, thus ushering in the Pax Tokugawa, two centuries of peace under a warrior government.

After Henry IV marched into Paris, he, too, had to put a country back together. The series of religious wars that had divided France from 1562 culminated in the assassination of Henry III in 1589. An intense civil war ensued between extremists of the Catholic League on the one hand and the proponents of the Protestant heir, Henry of Navarre, on the other, during which the League, supported by Spain, seized control of the city of Paris. Henry's conversion to Catholicism split his religious enemies and opened up for him an avenue to the throne. But even then succession was not secure until Henry had marched into Paris and made it his: "Only now," he exclaimed when he arrived in the city, "am I the King of France."[4] Like Ieyasu after his appointment as shogun, Henry stood ready to extend state power. Unlike the Tokugawa, who found peace by secluding Japan from most international contacts, however, Henry and the other Bourbons ruled over a country that was situated at the strategic heart of an entire continent. With neighbors on all sides who could not be ignored, the Bourbons found it impossible to avoid foreign entanglements. Indeed, they had troops in the field for more than half of the period from 1660 to 1789, and the number of men under arms grew from 50,000–80,000 in 1600 to more than 300,000 by the middle of the next century.

The Horizontal Extension of Power

Statemaking in Japan and France had a horizontal component, as shogun and king sought to extend authority over elite rivals. Varying historical cir-

4. Henry Kamen, *European Society, 1500–1700* (London: Unwin Hyman, 1990), p. 19.

cumstances led the two rulers to choose somewhat different tactics, each devising his own mix of sheer force, ominous intimidation, seductive patronage, and timely compromise. Toward the sovereign emperor and the aristocracy in Kyoto, for instance, Ieyasu and his successors acted with appropriate deference, granting them sustenance lands and rebuilding long-neglected palaces. But the shoguns also stationed a military governor in the ancient imperial capital, garrisoned the newly constructed Nijō Castle, and in 1615 authorized the seventeen-clause "Regulations concerning the Emperor and Court," which confined the emperor and nobility to a life of ceremonial and artistic pursuits. The same blend of coercion and patronage characterized the shogun's relationship with the Buddhist religious establishment. In bloody fighting in the latter half of the sixteenth century, Nobunaga and Hideyoshi had destroyed the armed regiments maintained by influential sects and deprived the temples of their landed wealth. The policy of the Tokugawa shoguns was to keep the church fiscally dependent upon government and isolated from secular affairs. Thus the shogun's officials endowed important shrines and temples with landholdings sufficient to sustain them as religious centers, but in 1615 the government also announced a code that restricted priests to purely religious and ritual activities, and twenty years later it placed religious institutions under the careful purview of the commissioners of shrines and temples.

In France the Bourbons had to deal with an international church that was in some ways outside their control, and they could not tame the religious establishment to the same degree as the Tokugawa shoguns. Henry IV, for instance, had to ask the pope to accept his conversion, and he was compelled to permit the Jesuit order to operate freely in France. Still, the monarchy frequently was able to manipulate the crown-church relationship to its own advantage. In this context, Henry's conversion to Catholicism put the king at the center of a century of struggle committed to containing—and eventually to eliminating—Protestants, who, thanks to the Edict of Nantes (1598), continued to occupy major enclaves of religious and political autonomy within the kingdom even after Henry took Paris. The Bourbons' role as protector of the faith permitted them to exploit sources of religious patronage in a manner that expanded their secular power in other ways as well. By the Concordat of Bologna of 1516, the French crown had obtained virtual control over the appointment of bishops and other high ecclesiastical officials. Henceforth kings could maintain at least nominal fidelity to Rome while exercising royal prerogatives that amounted to the existence of a French, Gallican church. It was an alliance that the Bourbons mined to good advantage: Louis XIV postured as God's representative on this planet, charged with keeping order, and successive Bourbon monarchs meddled in the affairs of France's clergy and increasingly leaned on the religious establishment for special grants and loans.

With the nobles the Bourbons hammered out a set of compromises that offered advantages to each side. From the aristocrats the crown expected obedience (nobles had to give up their private armies) as well as continued and unquestioning acknowledgment of the legitimacy of the Bourbon monarchy. In return the king confirmed the nobles' privileges: titles, appointments, lands, exemptions from most direct taxes. In addition, Louis XIV flattered the aristocratic tradition by portraying himself as the first seigneur and *gentilhomme* of the realm. But such a benign attitude masked another side of royal authority, for retribution could await the noble reluctant to honor the wishes of the crown. What the king could give he could also take away, and Louis XIV aggressively asserted the right to monitor the legitimacy of all titles and even to confiscate aristocratic estates.

If the Bourbons had to negotiate a mutually beneficial relationship with the nobles of France, the Tokugawa shoguns faced a similar problem with the approximately 280 daimyo who, after the climactic Battle of Sekigahara, remained as regional lords. The Tokugawa tolerated the existence of those potential rivals while imposing as much control over them as possible. From every one of these daimyo, for instance, the successive Tokugawa shoguns expected an oath of loyalty, in return for which they bestowed upon the lord a document of enfeoffment, and the shogun's government reserved the right to exact military service whenever necessary and to impose fiscal levies as needed to repair and maintain roads, bridges, and Tokugawa castles. Moreover, the shoguns asserted the right to transfer daimyo to new holdings (doing so on 281 occasions between 1600 and 1650) or even to confiscate entire domains (213 daimyo lost all or a portion of their holdings during the first half of the seventeenth century; 172 warriors were promoted to daimyo status during the same period), and in 1615 Ieyasu instructed his officials to issue the "Regulations concerning Warrior Households," which established guidelines for the conduct of the regional lords. Finally, although daimyo theoretically could rule their domains as they saw fit, in fact they increasingly were expected to do so in a manner that was consistent with the shogun's practices on his own direct holdings.

The Vertical Component

In addition to extending their power outward over other elites, the Bourbons and Tokugawa initiated policies designed to penetrate downward into society, harnessing the resources of the realm for their own uses, bringing provincial areas under more direct central authority, and creating new bureaucracies to oversee taxation and administration. In some important ways the horizontal and vertical components of absolutism intersected: the Bourbon monarchy's quest to control taxation, for instance, was inseparable from its attempts to tame the aristocracy. The crown constantly needed new revenues, yet the high nobles, who wielded great influence in provinces where they held command or owned estates, and the judicial (robe) nobles, who enjoyed positions in the royal courts, were likely to balk at any attempt by the king to impose new kinds of indirect taxes or to raise the direct tax on the peasants to a level that might provoke rural unrest. None of these groups had a clear constitutional right to oppose the will of the monarch, but the courts could delay registering the laws or might entertain appeals for redress, royal officers could complain, bargain, or only halfheartedly execute unpopular laws, and peasants could rebel. Thus, when the Bourbons and their ministers (most notably cardinals Richelieu and Mazarin) doubled and tripled their fiscal demands in the early decades of the seventeenth century, the potential was great for alliances between various segments of the aristocracy, and if whole regions or aristocratic factions could join together, civil war loomed as a distinct possibility.

Such is exactly what happened in the 1640s. Mazarin, an unpopular foreigner acting on behalf of a child king, pressed the Parlement of Paris too far in an attempt to secure its seal of approval for increased taxes and subsequently set off a rebellion, first in Paris and then in the provinces. Named the Fronde after a slingshot employed by Parisian urchins, this uprising began as a resistance movement by royal officers against Mazarin's new financial demands, but ordinary people, too, soon entered the fray, advancing their own demands for lower taxes as economic conditions deteriorated. When officials of the crown admitted to "disorders and abuses" in financial administration in the autumn of 1648, Louis XIV fled his capital, and the young monarch suffered through a humiliating series of misfortunes until 1652, when the various rebellions, having failed to coalesce behind a coherent program of reform, gradually died away. Louis never forgot those frightening nights of his childhood, however, and when he assumed personal power in 1661, he made certain that the Parlement of Paris and its provincial counterparts were limited to remonstrating only *after* registering laws, and he took care that both military officers and aristocrats stayed out of his political affairs.

Louis XIV and his father also enhanced royal authority in the provinces. Louis XIII extended the effective reach of the monarchy by increasing to thirty-two the number of administrative districts known as *généralités*. The traditional provinces, of course, remained, but they were reduced somewhat in importance; here, as with many of the Bourbon reforms, new administrative structures were piled upon existing ones, with power squeezed into the new ones, which exercised authority on behalf of the center. Thus, over each of the new districts the Bourbon king placed an intendant, a revocable official loyal to the crown and capable of making its authority known locally. The Bourbons also attacked the autonomy of France's leading regional cities, and Louis XIV in particular advanced the centralization process by wearing down the resistance of local municipal elites who defended urban privileges. Finally, to oversee affairs nationally, the crown relied on its controller general to run a kind of superministry whose tentacles wrapped around everything pertaining to general administration, taxation, the economy, finance, and public works. By the end of the reign of Louis XIV, the administrative apparatus of absolutism was operating as effectively as it ever would: the *parlements* were cowed; in the districts, the crown appointed intendants, royal governors, military commanders, and even bishops; taxes flowed into royal coffers; and both the national bureaucracy and the standing army had reached unprecedented proportions, enforcing the royal will at home and expanding the influence of the dynasty abroad.

Since the daimyo held three-quarters of Japan on sufferance from the shogun, managing and taxing their territories in accordance with broad mandates laid down in Edo, Ieyasu and his successors focused their attention on administering and taxing their own holdings. Ultimately, the shogunal domain came to include the nation's major gold and silver mines, important commercial cities such as Osaka and Nagasaki, and about one-quarter of the entire agricultural base of Japan. The Tokugawa house government— the shogunate—administered the mines and cities directly, and the shogun retained a personal fief (the *tenryō*) that included nearly two-thirds of all the villages within his greater dominion. To oversee these villages the Tokugawa rulers appointed a network of intendants (*daikan*), who functioned under the supervision of the lord's closest advisers. From the villages the shogun claimed a share of the annual rice crop. The shogunate carefully honed its extractive mechanisms in order to maximize its tax revenues: officials conducted censuses, dispatched cadastral survey teams to measure the land and assess its output, and imposed increasingly uniform systems of taxation that put a third or more of the crop into the hands of the government.

The shogun distributed the balance of his rural holdings to vassals known as *hatamoto*, or bannermen. The conclusion of warfare and the beginning of the great Pax Tokugawa provided the shogun (and the regional daimyo as well) with an opportunity to convert their warrior corps into civilian administrators. Consequently, from the early seventeenth century, the slightly more than five thousand bannermen and their families lived in Edo, but they continued to hold title in fief to somewhat more than one-third of the shogun's dominion, over which they exercised administrative prerogatives, as defined by the higher levels of the shogunate to whom they reported. Each bannerman also drew from the shogun's granaries an annual income, an amount approximately equal to the tax receipts that the shogunate levied upon the villages within each warrior's fief, a stipend bestowed in exchange for loyalty and military-bureaucratic service.

In both East and West the transition toward absolutism was accompanied by new theories of ideological legitimacy. In Japan, the emperor, divinely descended from the gods, remained as he had been for a thousand years, the ultimate source of secular authority. But a newly evolving concept of *kōgi* articulated the idea that the powers the emperor delegated to the shogun were "public," meaning that authority was to be exercised not in the "private" interest of the shogun and warrior estate but rather in a manner that contributed to the well-being of all of the people of the realm. In France, philosophers broadened medieval concepts of personal fealty to one's lord to embrace a more generalized and abstract loyalty to the state. As a consequence, the Bourbon kings could lay bold claim to being the state incarnate: "L'Etat, c'est moi." Yet, for all the arrogance of that boast, the Bourbons realized that they were bound by the so-called fundamental laws of the realm and by the assumptions and procedures of existing society. Even Jacques Bossuet, an important theorist of Bourbon absolutism, admitted that it was one thing for a government to be absolute, another for it to be arbitrary. Laws and the "opportunity for redress," he argued, defined that difference. To act too dictatorially was to risk the charge of ruling tyrannically (in one's "private" interest) instead of absolutely (in a manner that brought a greater good to all). Consequently, as in Japan, a covenant of expectations increasingly undercut vainglorious posturings of absolutism. No less than the shogun, the king, at least by the time of Louis XIV, was to be a caring ruler. As God's representative on earth in the one case and as the delegate of a semidivine emperor alive on this earth in the other, the Bourbon monarchs and Tokugawa shoguns were to requite obedience from below with benevolence from above.

EDO AND PARIS: THE CAPITALS OF ABSOLUTISM

The Growth of Edo and Paris

Neither Edo nor Paris presented an attractive picture when Ieyasu and Henry marched onto the scene in the 1590s. Edo was a drab fishing village, and the fortifications that the medieval warrior Ōta Dōkan had constructed in 1457 lay in acute disrepair, their walls atumble and what remained of the roofs a patchwork of rustic farmhouse shingles and thatch. The people of Paris may or may not have greeted Henry with cries of "Vive le roi!" but they must have been happy to see him lift the siege. Paris, founded about six centuries earlier, long had been a great, imposing city, but the warfare of the early 1590s was extraordinarily destructive: commerce and artisan production had come to a virtual halt; streets were covered with garbage; hospital patients went without care at the great Hôtel-Dieu; the water supply was contaminated; the plague threatened everyone.

Fresh to the Kantō, Ieyasu spent his first decade in Edo constructing an elaborate military headquarters that he could defend against any foe. He replaced the old fort with several amply apportioned enceintes, had mammoth stone blocks shipped to Edo from as far away as the Izu peninsula to encircle the enclosures with massive walls, and enveloped all within a complex system of concentric moats. Concurrently, Ieyasu began to construct an infrastructure that would support his military presence. To ensure supplies of drinking water, his engineers dug waterways that linked the area around the castle with Inokashira and Tameike ponds; they cleared space along the bay to use as docks and lumberyards; and they even drove a canal all the way to the Bōsō peninsula to expedite the delivery of salt and other commodities to Edo. Also during the 1590s bridges went up across the Ara and Tama rivers so that construction materials and other supplies could flow into Ieyasu's military headquarters along the roadways that reached out to the north and south.

When Ieyasu was appointed as shogun in 1603, Edo's status changed as well. State power shifted to Edo, and what had been a simple (although increasingly large) military settlement became Japan's administrative capital. Ieyasu and his successors now turned their attention to creating an imposing metropolis, an urban center that would be unrivaled in scale and grandeur. As suited their new national importance, the Tokugawa shoguns expanded the castle and its grounds, ensuring the impregnability of the complex while dazzling everyone architectonically with Tokugawa power and wealth. A new five-tier donjon rose up for more than two hundred feet over the nearby moats and enormous stone walls stretched out for miles, dominating the streets and byways of the city. When Iemitsu enlarged the Second Enceinte in the 1630s he even brought the famed Kobori Enshū all the way from Kyoto to lay out a landscape garden that would add to the shogun's administrative center a touch of the grace and gentility of the old imperial capital.

Paris was as crucial to Henry's plans as Edo was to Ieyasu's, and the king immediately set to work rebuilding the city. Henry's dramatic appearance appealed to the people of the city, and the new monarch attempted to earn their loyalty by ordering streets repaved, bridges repaired, the filth cleaned up. Henry would live and have his chief agencies of power in Paris; and in this Paris—teeming, vibrant, proud—the new king could make his mark only by adding specific embellishments. Concerned no less than the shoguns with the monuments of power, Henry extended the Louvre palace along the Seine, making it the most tangible symbol of Bourbon power; and influenced by the Italian piazza, he undertook to build several magnificent public squares.

As the new Paris began to rise from the ground, nobles answered the beckoning call of the king. They mingled with the soldiers, stationed in Paris to protect a capital that lay dangerously close to the northern frontiers. Then, as Henry restored monarchical prestige and authority, carrying both to new heights, Paris became more than ever a town of administrators, officials, lawyers, and clerks. Nobles flocked to the capital, bringing with them valets, domestics, cooks, stable boys, and other servant personnel. The building projects sponsored by those elites gave employment to thousands of artisans and laborers, and helped to launch a surge of economic growth that drew a broadening flow of migrants to the city throughout the seventeenth century.

Paris easily weathered the departure of Louis XIV for his new château at Versailles in the aftermath of the Fronde. Although Paris became somewhat less a hub of royal authority than before, the city continued to serve as the preeminent center of French politics and administration. Moreover, Paris retained an enormous cultural and economic vitality. As in Japan, the fact that virtually all major roads led to the capital ensured the city's continued domination over the commercial life of the country. Edo was on the sea; the Seine linked Paris with the ocean, and other rivers opened up a rich hinterland to exploitation by the capital. Within Paris, the production of luxury crafts carved out for the city an important manufacturing role in France's economic life. Consequently, Paris's population continued to grow throughout the seventeenth century until it reached half a million persons, dwarfing other cities on the continent (see Table 1.1).

TABLE 1.1.

Estimated populations of Paris and Edo, 1550–1792

Date	Paris	Edo Total	Merchants and artisans
1550	250,000		
1590		7,000(?)	
1600	250,000		
1630		500,000	100,000+
1650	450,000		
1695		904,000	353,588
1700	510,000		
1731		1,076,000	525,000
1750	570,000	1,060,000	509,708
1790	660,000		
1792		1,032,000	481,669

Based on Philip Benedict, "French Cities from the Sixteenth Century to the Revolution, an Overview," in Benedict, ed., *Cities and Social Change in Early Modern France* (London: Unwin Hyman, 1989), p. 24; and Naitō Akira, *Edo to Edojō* (Kashima Kenkyūjo Shuppankai, 1979), pp. 141–43.

Even the ancient walls of the city eventually yielded to population growth. At first the Bourbons tried to halt the geographic spread of the city because of problems with public order in the faubourgs. Louis XIII even went so far as to place thirty-one markers around the circumference of the city, warning that anyone who built beyond that perimeter would have his house razed and be slapped with a stiff fine. But not even a king with absolutist ambitions could so define his capital, and Louis XIV finally surrendered to spontaneous population growth, ordering in 1670 that the walls of Paris be torn down, opening the city up to the principal faubourgs of Saint-Antoine, Saint-Denis, and Saint-Martin.

In Edo as in Paris, a sizable proportion of the population consisted of soldiers and officials (but not aristocrats, who remained in Kyoto). By the time Iemitsu became shogun in 1623, most of the area immediately to the north and west of Edo Castle was settled by his retainers, the bannermen and the more subordinate housemen (*gokenin*), whose skills increasingly were given over to running the new civil bureaucracy that governed both the shogun's direct holdings and all of Japan. Together with their families and attached servant personnel, these warriors-turned-administrators constituted a core urban population that probably numbered somewhat more than 250,000 persons, although that figure must be treated with caution because the shogunate never did conduct a census of the samurai population of Edo. In the 1630s and 1640s the shogunate institutionalized the practice of requiring all daimyo to spend alternate years in Edo and to leave in the city at all times a retinue that included the lord's principal wife and heir. This requirement added another quarter-million or more persons to the city, for a total warrior population of approximately 500,000 to 550,000 persons, a figure that remained relatively stable throughout most of the balance of the early-modern period.

By the early eighteenth century, an equally large number of merchants and artisans lived in Edo.[5] Commoners began to stream into the city during the 1590s, as Ieyasu promised his patronage to those who would help him construct his military headquarters and provision his warriors: armorers and smiths, lumber dealers and carpenters. Edo's emergence as shogunal capital after 1603 drew tens upon tens of thousands of other commoners, who migrated to the city to cater to the needs of the burgeoning samurai-administrator population. The heart of merchant Edo was the Nihonbashi area, much of which was created after 1603, when the shogun's engineers leveled the sizable Mount Kanda and filled in Hibiya Inlet. From that center merchant neighborhoods spread out, displacing the original farm villages in the valleys that twisted through the daimyo-dominated hillsides of the city. But wherever they lived, these commoners were as eager as Ieyasu to create what by the mid–eighteenth century they called with pride Great Edo (Ō-Edo), a city distinguished from others in the realm by its robust vitality and spirited lifestyle. No less than in Paris, the relentless energy of the people shaped the growth and history of the city, changing Edo during the seventeenth and eighteenth centuries from Ieyasu's town into the merchants' city.

Governing the Cities

The concept of rule by status (*mibun seido*) provided the nucleus around which the Tokugawa shoguns (and the daimyo on their domains) shaped their institutions of governance. Throughout the final decades of the sixteenth century and the early decades of the seventeenth, Japan's military lords divided society into status groups—samurai, peasant, merchant, and artisan—and then applied their authority through separate channels to the various groups. The shogun took an initial step toward divorcing the statuses geographically when he summoned his bannermen and housemen to Edo from the countryside and compelled them to live around his citadel. He then issued a distinct legal code for each estate: the "Regulations concerning Warrior Households" provided guidelines for the conduct of daimyo; a similar "Regulations concerning Vassals" pertained to the bannermen and housemen; compilations such as the "Edo machijū sadamegaki," issued in 1655, and the 1742 codification of penal codes and judicial procedures known as the *kujikata osadamegaki* applied to Edo's merchants and artisans; and still other sets of laws defined life for farmers. Sumptuary regulations complemented the legal codes. The samurai, for instance, had the right to

5. The shogunate did not begin to count merchants and artisans in any systematic fashion until the early eighteenth century, and even after that its censuses usually did not include priests, prostitutes, entertainers, outcasts, or people seeking seasonal employment. Similarly, the tallies in Paris did not enumerate those "sans domicile fixe," so that the population figures for both cities are general estimates, and they are apt to undercount the actual number of city residents; Edo's total population during the eighteenth century probably numbered in the range of 1.1–1.25 million persons.

bear arms and names (merchants took a shop name; peasants used only a personal name), and were permitted special foods and clothing materials (fancy silks, as opposed to ordinary silks and cotton for townspeople, cruder hemp and ramie for peasants).

The principle of rule by status was applied to governance within Edo, and it held profound implications for life in the city. Residence was segregated, with the daimyo, the shogun's bannermen and housemen, and the merchants and artisans living in clearly demarcated sections of the city. To each daimyo the shogun granted a residential estate (*hairyō yashiki*), whose acreage varied in accordance with the assessed productivity of the lord's domain, and he permitted the daimyo to construct lavish residences (and later secondary and supplementary estates as well). Bannermen and housemen received more modest plots of residential land from the shogun, but they were authorized to erect specified styles of entrance gates, a perquisite denied merchant and artisan families, who were forbidden as well such costly luxuries as lacquered furniture and interior decorations adorned with gold or silver leaf.

During the first half of the seventeenth century, and with particular vigor during the tenure of Iemitsu, from 1623 to 1651, the Tokugawa family designed an administrative structure for Edo that embodied the philosophy of rule by status. Like the physical appearance of the city itself, the jacket of government resembled a quilted fabric in which separate threads of authority ran from the shogun through the major offices of the shogunate and then spun themselves out in various directions to the samurai and to the merchants and artisans. But things were even more complicated than that, for slightly different institutional mechanisms were provided for those samurai who were retainers of the Tokugawa house and resided in Edo permanently and for those who served a particular daimyo and lived on his estate in accordance with the alternate-residence requirement. After some initial experimentation, Iemitsu assigned responsibility for overseeing the daimyo estates to the senior councilors (*rōjū*), his top advisers and policymakers, who also set standards of conduct for daimyo administration within their home domains. The bannermen and housemen, in contrast, came under the purview of the junior councilors (*wakadoshiyori*), a second important executive board. The shogun and the senior councilors sat at the apex of the administrative pyramid that governed the merchants and artisans, monopolizing executive and lawmaking responsibilities while delegating day-to-day management of the commoner neighborhoods to a variety of functionaries, the most important of whom were the city magistrates (*machi bugyō*) and city elders (*machidoshiyori*).

In Paris, a maze of overlapping zones of authority inherited from the centuries made for a political geography as fractured as that of Edo. Even in the late eighteenth century there were still within Paris nearly fifty semi-autonomous jurisdictions presided over by seigneurs, abbots, and other ecclesiastical officials, of which the Palais Royal and the abbey of Saint-Germain-des-Prés were just two of the most noteworthy. In addition, any number of officials and institutions claimed the right to levy some kind of tax or to administer justice to one group of Parisians or another. When Henry IV retook Paris, for instance, the major guilds of the city still possessed the right to select a provost of merchants (*prévôt des marchands*) and four officials known as *échevins*. Chosen by fellow bourgeois and ensconced at the Hôtel de Ville, those officials regulated river traffic and jealously guarded their prerogative to collect rents from market stalls, fees for monopoly concessions over particular commodities, and duties on goods brought into Paris. As representatives of the bourgeoisie, the provost and his assistants also bore responsibility for certain public services, such as providing water and cleaning the streets. The Parlement of Paris, for its part, intervened in military and police affairs, and the Châtelet, under the nominal control of the nobles in that august body, exercised control over the courts and prisons of the city. The *prévôt* of Paris, a royal appointee not to be confused with the provost of merchants, traditionally had rendered justice in the king's name and occasionally assessed special taxes for poor relief, although by 1600 many of his duties had been coopted by a civil lieutenant sitting in the Châtelet.

Indeed, it was difficult to find any sphere of urban life in Paris in 1600 where administrative imperatives did not overlap and where the Bourbon kings did not rely on a structure of indirect rule. Through intimidation, cajoling, and negotiation, Henry and his successors tried as best they could to cut through this confusion of powers and to assert royal prerogatives in their capital city. Henry managed to get his own man, Jean Séguier, appointed as civil lieutenant, thus extending the influence of the crown into the halls of the Châtelet. Moreover, he began to meddle in the selection of the officials of the Hôtel de Ville, and if by chance the guilds chose a provost of merchants who did not please him, he simply refused to swear that man into office. Henry's successors persisted with these tactics, and by the late eighteenth century the provost had become in effect a royal appointee.

Royal absolutism reached new heights in 1667, when Louis XIV created the office of lieutenant general of police, some three decades after Iemitsu presided over the elaboration of the instrumentalities of urban governance in Edo. Louis invested his first appointee, Nicolas La Reynie, with extensive authority over a broad range of policing activities, and though the lieutenants general never did entirely displace the Châtelet, they did come to constitute a pervasive presence in almost every aspect of public life. The jurisdiction of the lieutenants general included powers of arrest, suppression of prostitution and gambling, and surveillance over any suspect person. They also undertook many duties that were seen as part of the dynasty's administrative benevolence: gradually their duties were expanded to include responsibility for firefighting and for street cleaning and lighting, general administration of hospitals and prisons, and even provisioning the city, which gave the police the right to enforce market and guild regulations throughout France.

Despite the increasing centralization of power in the hands of the higher agencies of state control during the seventeenth century, the merchants and artisans of the residential quarters of both Edo and Paris enjoyed considerable license to act independently within their own neighborhoods, thus helping to shape the cities from the bottom up. The 500,000 merchants and artisans in Edo lived in more than 1,500 residential quarters known as *chō* (alternatively read as *machi*), from which derives the term *chōnin*, the people of the quarters. The shogunate instructed the landowners (and later their agents) to organize themselves into so-called five-family groups (*goningumi*). In this capacity, the landowners among the merchants and artisans were supposed to mediate local disputes, make certain that their family members and tenants obeyed all laws, tend to the welfare of the neighborhood, maintain custody of persons convicted of petty civil crimes, and oversee the repair of roads and bridges within the quarter. From among the members of the five-family groups the shogunate appointed neighborhood chiefs (*nanushi*), about 260 in all; one, typically, for each group of five to seven residential quarters. The chiefs stood at the point of articulation between state and neighborhood, communicating upward the wishes and demands of the commoners while at the same time assisting the superior city elders and magistrates and working with the five-family groups to make certain that they fulfilled their responsibilities.

The indirect nature of Tokugawa absolutism at the neighborhood level was echoed in the municipal system of Paris. Under the direction of the Hôtel de Ville, Paris was divided into 16 *quartiers*, 64 *cinquantaines*, and 256 *dizaines*, each a collection of adjoining streets looked after by an official appointed from above. As the superior agents in the neighborhood pyramid, the *quarteniers* administered the militia, and like the neighborhood chiefs of Edo, they apportioned municipal taxes, arranged care for the poor, inspected streets, and generally oversaw the activities of the quarter. Below that level, the 256 officials known as *dizainiers* helped local residents find jobs and even marriage partners, intervened to settle disputes, and provided emergency loans to the needy. In both Edo and Paris, family and neighborhood contributed to the growth of communal solidarities. As a consequence, the quarters existed and functioned as an integral part of the state, ultimately subject to the dictates of king and shogun; yet at the same time they retained an identity distinct from the larger state, forming enclaves of commoner values and lifestyles that higher government could not always control as it wished.

The emerging patterns of governance in Edo and Paris constitute the central concern of the first set of essays that follow. Katō Takashi (for Edo) and William Beik and Sharon Kettering (for Paris) describe the structure and functioning of the urban bureaucracies in the two capitals. What emerges collectively from the three essays is a picture of state power moving along a steadily ascending trajectory during the seventeenth century as the shogunate and representatives of the crown gathered more and more prerogatives unto themselves. But all three authors also direct our attention toward important questions about the limits of absolutism.

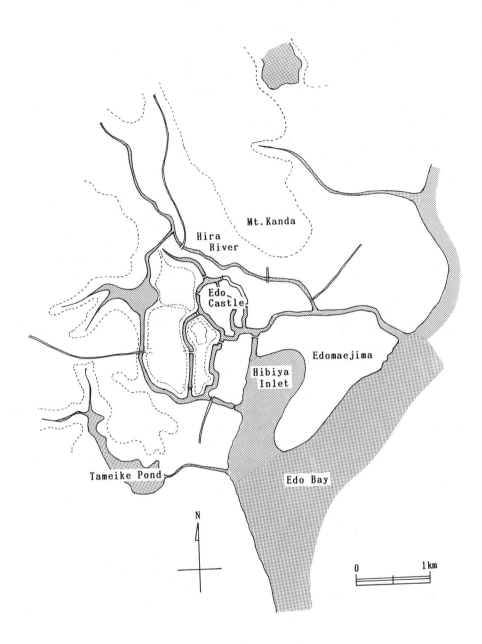

Edo at the end of the sixteenth century

Katō notes that the shogunate brought to Edo's governance the basic philosophy and institutions that it had designed originally with national purposes in mind, even if they did not always serve the shogun and his officials well in an urban setting. The daimyo, for instance, enjoyed considerable autonomy within their own regional domains and in many ways shogunal authority did not penetrate the walls that surrounded their estates in Edo. To rule the merchant quarters, Katō continues, the shogunate decreed, but often left it to neighborhood officials to implement those instructions, a style of indirect governance that permitted commoners great leeway in charting their own destinies. Both Beik and Kettering consider the relationship between throne and Paris within a broader national context of absolutism and urban growth. Each argues that the Bourbons had to confront various traditional elites and that they could extend royal influence within the city only by making concessions to entrenched interests. Beik details for us the nuances of how the king ruled by delegating authority, trading privileges and protection for compliance and loyalty, whereas Kettering focuses on identifying the "middlemen" (the police in Paris, provincial intendants in other towns) who could negotiate the complicated compromises that bound together the crown and powerful nobles. A common message emerges for Edo and Paris: shogun and king were supreme, but each remained so only by acquiescing in the realities of complexly structured urban societies.

Space

Absolutist rulers viewed the control of space as a necessary manifestation of their authority. Although the Tokugawa shoguns do not seem ever to have drawn up a master plan for the final design of Edo, their desire to settle the various status groups in discrete sectors of the city and to accord more prized sites to the elite warrior hierarchy did produce a distinctive, even if not entirely preconceived, layout that one scholar has characterized as the "Edo spiral."[6] Immediately to the east of the main gate to the castle, a location of enormous prestige, were the residences of the *fudai daimyō*, the

6. Naitō Akira, working with a plan of Edo in possession of one of the families of builders who supposedly laid out the city, was the first to identify this pattern (which he represents with the spiral-shaped *no* of the *kana* syllabary). More recently, other scholars have expressed doubts about the authenticity of that document, claiming that it was written after the fact. For these scholars, any spiral is more of a fortuitous accident than a premeditated design, and they see growth as taking place in a more spontaneous, ad hoc fashion. See Naitō Akira, "Edo no machi kōzō," in Nishiyama Matsunosuke and Yoshiwara Ken'ichirō, eds., *Edo jidai zushi* (Chikuma Shobō, 1975), pp. 32–54 (an abridged translation of this article appears as "Planning and Development of Early Edo," *Japan Echo* XIV: 5 (Special Issue, 1987), pp. 30–38); idem, *Edo no toshi to kenchiku*, supplementary volume to Suwa Haruo and Naitō Akira, eds., *Edozu byōbu* (Mainichi Shinbunsha, 1972), pp. 17–19; Suzuki Masao, *Edo no toshi keikaku* (Sanseidō, 1988); Jinnai Hidenobu, " 'Mizu no toshi' no hikaku toshi—Venezia to Edo·Tōkyō," in Ogi Shinzō, ed., *Edo to wa nani ka?*, vol. 5: *Edo—Tōkyōgaku*, special issue of *Gendai esupuri* (Shibundō, 1986), pp. 96–114; William H. Coaldrake, "Edo Architecture and Tokugawa Law," *Monumenta Nipponica* 36:3 (1981), pp. 235–84.

Shinobazu Pond

Koishikawa

Hongō

Yushima

Kanda River

Old Hira River

Kanda

Ban-chō

Hon-chō

Yotsuya

Edo Castle

Nihonbashi

Kōji-machi

Nakabashi

Hatchō-bori

Tameike Pond

Shinbashi

Edo Bay

N

Tōkaidō Highway

0   1 km

Edo circa 1630

"allied lords" who had been raised to daimyo status by the Tokugawa family and who during the early-modern period both ruled their own independent domains and staffed the most important posts within the shogun's growing administrative bureaucracy. The spacious grounds and homes of the *tozama daimyō*, the less-trusted "outside lords" who had achieved daimyo status independently or under the aegis of Nobunaga or Hideyoshi, occupied the next portion of the spiral. These outside lords did not hold office within the shogunate, but the shogun acknowledged their wealth and power by presenting them with choice land on the sunny sides of the verdant hillsides that rolled away to the south of Edo Castle. The shogun located his bannermen and housemen on the fanned-out portion of the spiral that wrapped around to the west and north of the castle. This area fronted the Musashi plain, a point of vulnerability in the defenses of Edo Castle, and it seems no accident that the Tokugawa family chose to station there its direct retainers, the families that could be counted upon to be the most loyal in the event of a military crisis.

As merchants and artisans arrived in increasing numbers in the early seventeenth century, they settled near Hon-chō and Nihonbashi, and when that commercial center filled up, they moved out along the highways and waterways of the city and into the valleys beneath the daimyo estates. This unplanned, organic growth imparted to Edo a geographic contouring that was at odds with the notion of an orderly spiral, and indeed, merchant culture itself can suggest a metaphor that reveals its spirit. No other entertainment came to typify Edo merchant culture so much as fireworks, whose displays over the rivers of downtown Edo became a part of every hot summer's night. People congregated from all over Edo to witness them; women of the licensed prostitution quarter and their patrons for the evening drifted down the rivers in pleasure craft to get a special, envied view; and some merchants were even known to plop down several months' worth of hard-earned profits just to provide a memorable spectacle for their guests.

Fireworks and Edo grew together, and fireworks symbolically represent that growth. Just as each display of fireworks erupted from a central explosion, so too did the Nihonbashi area pulsate with a vitality and energy that propelled commoners out across Edo's cityscape, to Asakusa and Ueno, and in time even as far as the former villages of Ikebukuro, Shinjuku, and Shibuya. Like a Toyoharu or Kunichika print, in which multicolored ribbons of soaring explosions ripped the night skies, the merchant sections sparked through the city of Edo, painting the landscape in the new hues of commoner business activities and cultural pursuits, more permanent by far than the fading tentacles of the fireworks.

In Paris, Henry's predecessors had already begun the process of imprinting royal power on the city. In the sixteenth century François I constructed a château in the nearby Bois de Boulogne and remodeled the dilapidated medieval fortress of the Louvre in the heart of Paris. The ability to manipulate space within the capital was equally important to the Bourbons, whose *places royales* were arguably the most revealing architectural works of

Fireworks over the Sumida River. Source: Shinpan ukie Edo ryōgokubashi nōryō no zu. Courtesy of Toritsu Chūō Toshokan.

seventeenth-century urbanism in Europe. Henry IV took the first initiative in 1603 (the same year that Ieyasu launched the great project to fill in part of Edo Bay and to construct the bridge at Nihonbashi) when he authorized the construction of the Place Royale (today's Place des Vosges) on the grounds of a former palace on the eastern edge of the capital where the *malheureux* Henry II had met death in a jousting accident. Even before that project was finished, the dashing Bourbon king ordered work to begin in 1607 on the Place Dauphine on the western tip of the Cité. For each of these projects Henry imagined a grandiose development filled with prosperous shops, bourgeois housing, and aristocratic mansions, and the Place Royale, at least, measured up to his expectations, providing a space where the fragmented groups of the social and political elite could meet on equal terms, joined in splendid togetherness like the uniform facades and arcades of the architectural triumph.

Despite Henry's best efforts to cajole nobles to take up residence within his grand projects, however, many of Paris's wealthy preferred life in the more elegant western quarters of the city, and Louis XIV's decision to leave Paris for Versailles accelerated the shift of Paris's center of gravity in that direction. The Sun King's love of Versailles, however, did not diminish his eagerness to make Paris undeniably his. "In the absence of impressive acts of war," intoned Jean Baptiste Colbert (1619–1683), royal adviser and zealous urban planner who envisaged Paris as a second Rome, "nothing marks the greatness of princes better than the buildings that compel the people to look on them with awe, and all posterity judges them by the superb palaces they have built during their lifetime."[7] Under the Sun King's patronage, Colbert demolished the old walls of Paris, encircled the city with tree-lined boulevards that became favorite places for Sunday-afternoon strolls, and installed new public fountains and street lanterns around the city. In 1670 he began work on the Invalides, a large military hospital with numerous courtyards, and he hired the architect André Le Nôtre (1613–1700) to design gardens for the Tuileries palace, which smartly faced the Invalides from the opposite bank of the Seine. Across the city, Colbert and his successors erected several monumental arches of triumph, such as the northern gates of Saint-Denis and Saint-Martin. Any number of royal statues went up. None, however, was more pretentious than a colossal likeness of Louis XIV, covered with 24-caret gold leaf and surrounded by bas-reliefs of four slaves representing defeated rival states, that was put up by a noble admirer, who then laid out the circular Place des Victoires to accommodate his creation.

The consequence of all of these building projects was a complex and constantly changing urban social geography. At the beginning of the seventeenth century, central Paris boasted important institutions such as the Hôtel de Ville and the Châtelet, and it attracted its share of lawyers, royal clerks, and well-to-do bourgeois. Nobles lived in nearly every quarter, and ordinary

---

7. Quoted in F. Roy Willis, *Western Civilization: An Urban Perspective*, vol. 1 (Lexington, Mass.: D. C. Heath, 1973), p. 486.

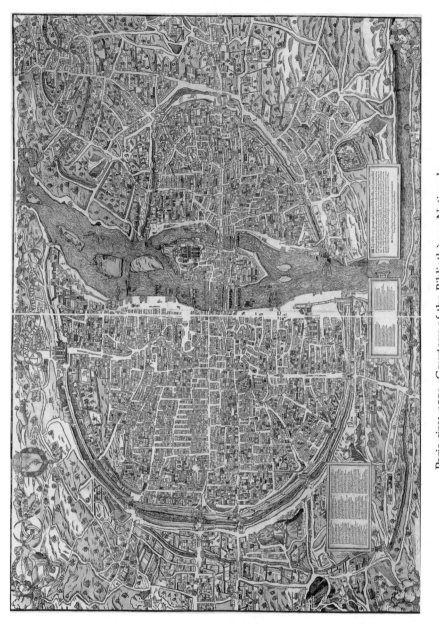

Paris circa 1551. Courtesy of the Bibliothèque Nationale.

LE PLAN DE LA VILLE CITE VNIVERSITÉ | FAVXBOVRGS DE PARIS AVEC LA DESCRIPTION DE SON ANTIQVITÉ

LA RIVIERE DE SEINE

Paris circa 1615. Courtesy of the Bibliothèque Nationale.

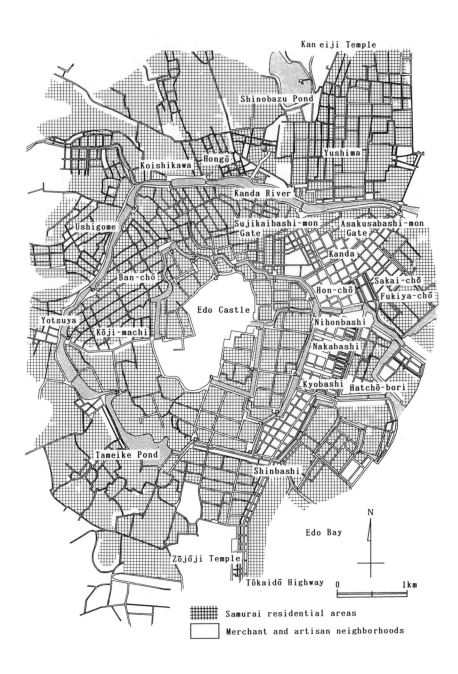

Kan eiji Temple

Shinobazu Pond

Koishikawa　Hongō　Yushima

Kanda River

Ushigome

Sujikaibashi-mon　Asakusabashi-mon
Gate　Gate

Kanda

Ban-chō　Hon-chō　Sakai-chō
Fukiya-chō

Yotsuya　Edo Castle　Nihonbashi

Kōji-machi　Nakabashi

Kyobashi　Hatchō-bori

Tameike Pond

Shinbashi

N

Edo Bay

Zōjōji Temple

Tōkaidō Highway　0　1km

|||||| Samurai residential areas

☐ Merchant and artisan neighborhoods

Edo circa 1670

Paris circa 1730. Courtesy of the Bibliothèque Nationale.

people were scattered throughout the city, with only a few artisans cluster-
ing together by virtue of their trades. Then, as aristocrats, ecclesiastics, and
financiers moved west during the seventeenth century, that quadrant became the center of wealth and power, while the east evolved into people's
Paris. Gradually the periphery of the capital became associated with illicit
activities and abject poverty (Saint-Marcel was commonly known as the
"sick faubourg" because by 1743 nearly two-thirds of its residents were so
destitute that they could not subsist without the assistance of charities).
Since outlying faubourgs (as well as a few islands of privilege within Paris
itself, such as Palais Royal) enjoyed partial immunity to royal power, they
attracted criminals, dissident workers, and entertainers normally banned
from the capital.[8] In Edo, too, poor people and sequestered activities could
be found on the periphery: prostitution quarters, execution grounds, outcast
communities, out-of-favor religious sects, and workhouses and charity hospitals were all situated at the city's edge, in such districts as Koishikawa,
Ishikawajima, Asakusa, and Shinagawa.

Three authors deal with the issue of power and space. James L. McClain
and Roger Chartier focus their attention on a single neighborhood and on an
entire city, respectively. In 1657 the shogunate ordered merchant families to
depart Edobashi, a flourishing commercial district in the center of merchant
Edo, so that it could be converted to a firebreak, and officials further instructed that the area was to remain permanently vacant. In the following
decades, however, wholesalers, shop owners, warehousers, and entertainers moved into Edobashi, transforming it once again into a thriving
merchant center. In his reconstruction of this neighborhood over a century
of time, McClain suggests that Edobashi's revival illustrates one aspect of
the commoners' appropriation of Edo and demonstrates the shogunate's
willingness to forgo the use of coercion in favor of negotiated settlements
with Edo's merchants. When Chartier casts his vision over the entire city of
Paris, he sees a similar thwarting of royal ambitions. A variety of powerful
spatial, juridical, and social constraints, he argues, stymied the crown's
efforts to reshape its capital; as in Edo, city planners ran headlong into
obstacles that denied them a free hand. What emerges from Chartier's study
is the picture of a Paris that grew "in related fragments," with the king,
nobles, ecclesiastical bodies, and private speculators all playing important
roles in determining the city's spatial growth.

William H. Coaldrake extends the discussion of monumental architecture into Edo with his chapter detailing the construction of Taitokuin mausoleum, built by Shogun Iemitsu in honor of his predecessor, Hidetada. On
the one hand, Coaldrake argues, this elaborate set of buildings represented
a powerful architectural statement about Tokugawa authority and demon-

---

8. Even in the fourteenth and fifteenth centuries the infamous, the miserable, and the
socially marginal—prostitutes, lepers, and beggars—could be found on the northern edge
of Paris. See Bronislaw Geremek, "Criminalité, vagabondage, paupérisme: La marginalité
à l'aube des temps modernes," *Revue d'histoire moderne et contemporaine* 21 (1974), p. 348;
idem, *Les marginaux parisiens aux XIVe et XVe siècles* (Paris: Flammarion, 1976).

strated, for all to see, the shogun's ability to mobilize manpower and materials. On the other hand, his analysis of the construction records also leads Coaldrake to conclude that the building of Taitokuin symbolized a dynamic intersection of the city from above with the city from below, as the builders became members of the city's social elite in a manner reminiscent of the Renaissance courts of Europe.

Provisioning the Capitals

The shoguns of Japan and the kings of France alike realized that adequate provisioning of their capitals was essential to the perpetuation of their power. Common sense, if nothing else, told them as much: Edo and Paris were the military and political centers of their rule; hegemony scarcely could be maintained if the cities were not well supplied. Image was a concern as well; power would not flourish in a tarnished setting. Ideology imparted the same message: provisioning was an expectation that the populations of Edo and Paris placed on benevolent kings and shoguns, an attribute of power in early-modern France and Japan. Fear, too, stirred the rulers' imaginations. If dearth were to render the social compact meaningless, disorder awaited. Even more acutely than the Tokugawa shoguns, who never experienced a Fronde, the Bourbon kings grasped the consequences they might suffer if the urban population were driven to violence because of threats to its subsistence. A poorly provisioned city could become ungovernable.

The attitudes of the king and shogun concerning the mechanics of actually moving goods and foodstuffs into their capitals also exhibited some intriguing parallels. In each instance, the regime was inclined to rely on the impersonal forces of the market, of supply and demand, to allocate resources and to ensure that food and finished goods reached the urban population in a timely fashion and at reasonable prices. Yet officials in France and Japan were never entirely comfortable with this position: too often, they believed, self-interest motivated merchants to line their own pockets at the expense of the rest of society. Too much freedom from government regulation, they feared, might breed a mercantile independence that would put social order at risk. In addition to the burden of natural suspicion, the shogunate placed on the shoulders of merchants the unkind distinction of being placed at the bottom of the neo-Confucian social hierarchy, and in France the aristocrats equally despised the humble tradesman. Thus ambivalence haunted policymakers in both royal circles and shogunal councils. Merchants were indispensable to commercial operations, but never could they be fully trusted: some degree of guidance, regulation, and supervision was essential.

Given these conceptions, it is not surprisingly that governments intervened in the economy in both Japan and France. In Japan, where both the polity and Edo were new, the problem was to encourage the growth of orderly marketing networks that would move food and finished goods into the city. There was some urgency to the task, because for the greater part of the seventeenth century the economically advanced areas around Kyoto and

Osaka remained the sole or primary sources of many important commodities, including silks, cotton cloth, saké, and soy sauce. One way the shogunate facilitated the flow of those goods into Edo was to promote the development of a transportation infrastructure. In the early decades of the seventeenth century, the government built or upgraded several major roadways that began at Nihonbashi and stretched out to all regions of Japan, with the celebrated Tōkaidō road linking Edo to Kyoto.

The forms of cartage that were available for overland transport were so rudimentary, however, that many merchants preferred to trust their goods to oceangoing barges and ships, and at mid-century the shogunate commissioned the entrepreneur Kawamura Zuiken (1618–1700) to develop shipping routes that would both remove some of the existing dangers to ocean craft and expand the number of regions from which Edo could draw sustenance. Kawamura charted coastal waters, erected beacons and lighthouses, and provided lifesaving and rescue facilities. Completed in 1670s, the "eastern sea circuit" (*higashi mawari*) connected the most distant parts of northern Japan directly with Edo, while the "western sea circuit" (*nishi mawari*) extended from the Japan Sea coast around the Straits of Shimonoseki and into the Inland Sea before continuing directly to Osaka and Edo.

The shogunate also privileged certain individuals important to the provisioning process. More than four hundred merchants and artisans were designated as *goyō tasshi*, purveyors to the lord. Among them were fishermen, drapers, armorers, carpenters, plasterers, and minters. In general, the shogunate bestowed upon these men an annual retainer, a residential site, and other perquisites (to some, the right to bear a sword), and in return it expected the best of their goods and services at favorable prices. In time the government extended special rights to organized groups of merchants as well, using them to regulate the marketplace. By the closing decades of the seventeenth century, many merchants in Edo were beginning to form closed, protective associations of families in the same line of business with the intent to stabilize prices, regularize business practices, and reduce intragroup competition. At first the shogunate was skeptical about such groups, fearing that their actions might stimulate inflationary pressures. But in 1694, after officials discovered that such monopolistic organizations could provide government with a means to monitor prices and control merchants' activities, the shogunate decided to coopt what it otherwise could control only imperfectly, and it authorized the so-called association of ten wholesale groups (*tokumidon'ya*), an umbrella organization for wholesalers who traded in cotton thread, cotton cloth, saké, kitchenwares, and other commodities shipped from Osaka to Edo.

The complementary impulses of privilege and regulation that characterized Tokugawa policy toward protective associations could be observed equally clearly in Bourbon attitudes toward the traditional corporate guilds of Paris, whose ancient charters provided them with a strong basis of independence. Merchant life was dominated by the "six corps"—the guilds of drapers, grocers, mercers, furriers, hatters, and silversmiths who, led by the provost of merchants and entrenched in the Hôtel de Ville, brought into Paris most of the commodities consumed in the urban center. Despite their apparent specializations, none of these merchants dealt exclusively in a particular commodity; the drapers and mercers, for instance, imported all kinds of luxury goods manufactured abroad. In conjunction with their trading activities, the major guilds functioned as banks: they issued letters of credit, lent money, and underwrote risky speculative ventures. Also important was their control over traffic along the Seine, which was dotted with ports on both sides and which remained the main artery for the transportation of most goods into and out of the city.

Although the Bourbons relied mainly on the traditional guild structure to bring manufactured goods into Paris, they also acted to supplement the efforts of private traders and to provide guidance that would improve the flow of goods into Paris. Thus, as Chartier observes, Henry IV supported royal manufactures by instructing that a large factory be added to the Place Royale to house his prized silkworkers, and by founding firms to produce exotic textiles, furniture, and jewelry for affluent Parisians (a move roundly opposed by the guilds, whose members prospered by importing such luxury goods from foreign sources). The main effort to reform the guild structure came in the 1660s, during Colbert's tenure as royal adviser. Claiming that change was necessary to improve the quality and quantity of goods in the markets of Paris, Colbert authorized the formation of some new guilds, reassigned certain monopoly privileges, and created new companies with exclusive rights to manufacture and export commodities such as cloth, tapestries, and mirrors.

Grain—rice in the case of Japan, wheat in France—provided a particularly sensitive barometer of state attitudes toward the operation of the market. As was the case with other commodities, the rulers of the island nation and the continental giant preferred in principle to leave the task of supplying grain to a quasi-independent market, while standing ready to act as the victualers of last resort in times of dearth. More often than the samurai who staffed the shogunate, French officials had to step into the role of quartermaster, intervening in the market to make certain that Parisians did not starve. Ironically enough, the great Bourbon capital was located relatively close to the most fertile lands in France, the Beauce, but throughout the seventeenth and eighteenth centuries the French state was beset by internal discord, foreign adventurism, and unpredictable weather, all of which took their periodic toll on harvests and visited the specter of privation upon the population of Paris.

Circumstances were different in Japan, where people enjoyed peace and steadily improving harvests throughout most of the seventeenth century. Moreover, because the shogun directly controlled nearly one-quarter of Japan's rice-producing lands, in normal years millions of bushels of rice, enough to feed what had become the world's largest city, flowed into Edo in the form of tax proceeds, stipends for retainers, and surpluses from hinterland villages. This bountiful providence changed in the eighteenth century, when poor weather and unanticipated bottlenecks in the distribution system caused food shortages in urban centers, compelling the shogunate to reexamine its traditional policies and to fashion new practices that would meet the needs of that city's residents for foodstuffs and other commodities.

Two chapters in this section investigate the provisioning of grain and state policy during times of crisis. Steven Laurence Kaplan chooses to look at the famine of 1738–1741, and he offers a detailed examination of the efforts to supply Paris as orchestrated by the lieutenant general of police, the provost of merchants, and Issac Thellusson, a special official appointed by the controller general to arrange for foreign purchases. Their combined efforts were Herculean. At one time Thellusson had more than two hundred ships at sea; the provost fined and imprisoned uncooperative port masters; and the lieutenant general commissioned purchases in the countryside, requisitioned stocks from hospitals and religious communities, and threatened to confiscate the property of any farmer who withheld grain from the market. In the end, Kaplan concludes, authorities gained control of the situation, but there they rested, unwilling or unable to commit the state to structural changes that would lessen the risk of future crises.

Hayashi Reiko's broad overview of shogunal policies regarding the supply of food and processed goods to Edo provides a context for her focus on the crisis of 1732–1733. In those two years a famine in western Japan drew supplies of rice away from Edo markets, causing serious shortages and increasing prices within the shogun's capital. Neighborhood chiefs in Edo submitted to higher officials numerous petitions that detailed the hardship suffered by the city's poorer merchants and artisans and appealed to the shogunate to release supplies from its granaries and to enact other policies that would bring down the price of rice. But the shogun's officials refused to act. The bannermen and housemen, the shogunate observed, were paid in stipends generated by the annual rice tax, and to dump more rice on the urban market would simply depress their incomes. Better, they counseled, to let samurai incomes stay high so that the benefits of their purchasing power could wash through the entire urban economy. Popular protest against this advice eventually prompted the government to reverse course and move rice into Edo, but its efforts were not decisive enough to prevent the first food riot in the city's history. The dramatic contrast between lordly responses to dearth in Edo and in Paris in the same decade illustrates how divergent social structures can influence government thinking and lead to different political priorities, even in two nations that can be considered absolutist states.

Another contrast between Paris and Edo emerges in the concluding chapter in the provisioning section, which takes up a commodity that is often ignored but that is as indispensable as food. According to Hatano Jun, the Tokugawa shogunate laid out six major water supply systems during the course of the seventeenth century. Each line drew its water from a source outside of the city, one of them as far as twenty-five miles away. The shogun's engineers constructed a network of canals and waterways to deliver the water to the city, where it circled the castle, fed daimyo estates, and supplied the residences of bannermen and housemen before traveling to the merchant quarters, often through underground pipes. It was, Hatano concludes, a network devised to give preference to the demands of the shogun and samurai, and the commoners got only what water remained after the warrior-administrators had satisfied their needs. It was a far cry from the public fountains that Chartier describes in his chapter on the spatial growth of Paris. In the City of Light, he argues, the crown and municipality built fountains in the seventeenth century as part of "an infinity of comforts" which, together with improved street lighting and cleaning, were intended to make Paris a safer, cleaner city.

Urban Culture

Considerations of power and political authority intersected with urban culture at several points. In each country authorities maintained a watchful eye over cultural activities, and both shogun and king endeavored to assert themselves as the cultural arbiters of their capital cities. The shoguns acted in concert with the dictates of rule by status, carving out for themselves and their warrior followers a cultural preserve that drew on arts and entertainments traditionally associated with the elite samurai of the medieval period. Thus the shogun at his castle and the daimyo on their estates built spacious landscape gardens set with rustic tea huts, where they could enact the rituals of the tea ceremony, and outdoor stages, where they could enjoy performances of noh drama. Inside their residences, these male leaders of Japan cultivated a taste for Zen-inspired painting and Confucian scholarship, the one to demonstrate their mastery of literati arts, the other to provide the knowledge to help them govern wisely. Outside of their estates, the samurai kept alive their martial spirit by riding horses on courses established at several places around the city, or by going on fishing expeditions and boar hunts in the hills and forests surrounding Edo.

It is common to posit a clear distinction between samurai and merchant cultures, but many affluent merchants shared an enthusiasm for tea and the recitation of noh texts (although attendance at performances of noh officially was denied them). Moreover, growing literacy opened up to elite merchant families the world of Confucian scholarship. Still, the hallmarks of entertainment for wealthy merchants, especially men, were the puppet and kabuki theaters and the licensed prostitution district at Yoshiwara, enclaves of relaxation and diversion officially off limits to samurai. Yoshiwara became the social setting for Edo's new elite merchant culture, giving rise to new genres of art (woodblock prints) and literature (fictional tales of the floating world) that exalted the courtesans and explored the nuances of this self-contained world of glorified eroticism. Political concerns met merchant culture on the kabuki stage. At the beginning of the seventeenth century, kabuki performances were little more than loosely arranged sets of skits and dances devised by prostitutes to promote their business. Although kabuki later evolved into a legitimate form of stage entertainment, many government officials never did approve of its presence in the shogun's capital, and they introduced restrictions by banning women and then young men from the stage, censoring material, and requiring every theater to be licensed.

The Bourbons and the nobles also drew around themselves the accoutrements of an elite culture. At the core of the noble's self-constructed image were the ideas of *noblesse* and *gentillesse*, the aristocrat as the epitome of integrity, honor, and personal courage. The social stage where the gentleman put these virtues on display in Paris was his *hôtel*, the elegant townhouse and garden complex designed to recreate the illusion of the rural château. In his urban garden the nobleman participated in the court tournaments, ballets, and jousts that were so popular in the first half of the seventeenth century. Inside, he decorated his rooms with paintings, sculptures, and tapestries that flattered aristocratic ideals, and he hosted lavish parties for the poets and scholars who fawned upon the *gentilhommes*.

Theater, too, was part of elite Parisian culture. Pierre Corneille dominated the stage in the 1630s, presenting dramas that idealized the world of the aristocrat no less than Japanese playwrights extolled the floating world of the prostitute and wealthy merchant. Later Louis XIV came to center stage, granting privileges to specialized theaters. In 1673 he extended to the Opéra, under the direction of Jean-Baptiste Lully, the exclusive right to perform works whose texts were sung. Several years later, in 1680, the Sun King authorized the establishment of the Comédie-Française. Throughout his life he maintained a paternal interest in this organization, bestowing upon it a monopoly over works in French verse and prose, personally selecting the troupe's performers, and patronizing the theater's playwrights.

Outside the walls of the townhouses and daimyo estates, a vibrant popular culture enlivened the two capitals. Roadside preachers and freelance prostitutes, storytellers and sword swallowers, puppeteers and jugglers and acrobats and tightrope walkers, hawkers offering up insults and witticisms to accompany a welcomed round of refreshments, human freaks and extraordinary mechanical devices, carnival barkers urging the curious to pay "just a small fee" for a peek at exotic animals—the clash of sights, sounds, and aromas that delighted commoners in Edo was equally familiar to the people of Paris. Performers wandered many of the streets within the merchant and artisan quarters of Edo, but they could be found in greatest profusion in the amusement centers known as *sakariba*, which became popular during the eighteenth century. Edobashi, the focus of McClain's chapter, had a minor reputation as an entertainment area, but more famous were the approaches to Ryōgoku Bridge, Asakusa Okuyama behind Sensōji Temple, and Shitaya Yamashita in the Ueno district, areas jammed with tens of thousands of persons on hot summer nights. In Paris, popular entertainments could be found at the fairs, the Bois de Boulogne, La Rapée, Les Porcherons, and the Pont-Neuf, and on several exterior boulevards.

The chapters by Jurgis Elisonas and Robert M. Isherwood take us to visit the street cultures of the two capitals. Elisonas focuses on descriptions of Edo's "notorious" places penned in the latter half of the seventeenth century by Asai Ryōi and other authors of travel narratives, introducing us to the male and female prostitutes of early kabuki, the puppet theater at Na-kabashi, the newly established prostitution district at Yoshiwara, and all kinds of rogues, mountebanks, and charlatans. Surprisingly, Elisonas shows, most early depictions of Edo's famous sites were largely fabrications, based on already existing guides to Kyoto and supplemented, at best, by casual observations of the Edo scene; only at the end of the seventeenth century did Edo writers begin to craft their own literary tradition based on the realities of life in the shogun's capital. Yet both the plagiarized accounts and the stunningly colorful descriptions of popular culture found in the later, firsthand narratives suggest that Edo's commoners had constructed for themselves a generic concept of the city and of urbanism that suited their preferences and that differed from the shogun's vision of his capital.

The image of a popular culture formed from below and at odds with an officially sanctioned view of the city emerges as well from Isherwood's de-scription of the quackery and foolery found on Parisian boulevards and from his vivid discussion of Les Grands Danseurs de Corde. Founded by Jean-Baptiste Nicolet in 1764, at a time when Edo's scandalously vibrant amuse-ment centers, its great *sakariba*, were coming into their own, this theater on the Boulevard du Temple presented plays enlivened by dance and song and popular *spectacles* of acrobats, funambulists, and other entertainers. Les Grands Danseurs achieved enormous popularity, drawing high and low alike onto the boulevards. Not surprisingly, Nicolet's theater aroused con-cern among many aristocrats (his dramas often mocked them), among the authorities (his plays' characters reveled in sexual innuendo and bawdy behavior, raising fears about public morality and social control), and among the owners of the established theaters of the elite (Nicolet poached on their privileges). Many nobles and the owners of the great theaters complained, but the authorities did little. The reason, Isherwood argues, is that the police lacked confidence in their ability to maintain public order in Paris, and they believed that popular entertainments provided a useful diversion for the working classes.

In a study of Edo's firefighters, William W. Kelly reminds us that culture not only is entertainment but includes the values and beliefs that infuse a particular style of life. Firefighting was a responsibility assumed by the shogunate and daimyo in early Edo, until the devastation of the Meireki fires in 1657 showed that warrior-staffed firefighting brigades were woefully unprepared to protect the city. After experimenting with various ways to coordinate efforts by commoners to combat fires in their own neighbor-hoods, the shogunate in 1720 divided Edo into forty-seven precincts and required each residential quarter to contribute a requisition of men who would turn out whenever a blaze threatened their section of the city. At first the commoners resisted this reform, objecting to the expenses that would devolve upon them. But the shogun persisted, and many quarters began hiring unskilled construction laborers to man their squads. In time the rough and unruly laborers-firemen became as celebrated for their fights,

acrobatics, and other antics as for their bravery. They captured Edo's imagination, and crowds turned out at fires to watch them battle each other as
well as the blaze. Fires, Kelly writes, were no longer tragic "incidents" but
well-attended public "events", and their incorporation into Edo street culture provides yet another measure of the transformation of Edo from
Ieyasu's town into the merchants' city.

The final chapter in this section takes us from the streets to the reading
salons and book-lending shops of Paris and Edo. In his study of the history
of the book in Edo and Paris, Henry D. Smith II addresses a wide range of
significant topics: the emergence and organization of the publishing industries in the two cities; the implications of different printing technologies
(woodblock versus movable type); and such matters as readership and reading habits. He notes that the state in both France and Japan feared the
printed word, the biggest threats being seen as attacks on the person of the
king or shogun and criticism of orthodox thought (neo-Confucianism and
the doctrines of the Catholic Counter-Reformation). Smith also observes that
in France (and perhaps in Japan to a lesser degree) print helped to create a
private sphere of existence where the individual might seek sanctuary from
state authority. Yet he also cautions that the political impact of print is ambiguous; it can serve either to advance state control or to mobilize opposition to
it. The former potential, he suggests, was more evident in Japan, the latter
more obvious in France.

Resisting the State

All of the chapters of this volume touch in some way on issues concerning
the acceptance of, acquiescence in, or rejection of state authority. The final
four contributions are distinguished by their focus on overt resistance, and
they direct our attention to the concluding decades of Bourbon and Tokugawa rule. Steven L. Kaplan and Takeuchi Makoto write about zones of
autonomy. Kaplan focuses on "false workers," the unlicensed workers who
did not join the official guilds authorized by the city and crown but fled to
the faubourg Saint-Antoine, outside the city walls, where they forged new
techniques and organizations of production. The guilds, finding their monopolies threatened, enlisted the support of state and city in their efforts to
impose sanctions on the illicit workers. The false workers, however, showed
great independence and ingenuity, and they successfully avoided being
brought to heel. As a consequence, Kaplan suggests, the *faubouriens* developed a sense of relative autonomy, a feeling of political distinctiveness vis-
à-vis state authority, and in 1789 the faubourg Saint-Antoine emerged as the
revolutionary quarter par excellence.

Takeuchi also chooses for his analysis an area on the periphery of the
city, Asakusa. Throughout the eighteenth century, Takeuchi notes, the shogunate gradually strengthened regulations against unlawful assembly and
collective protest. Yet at the same time it came to consider "fights" (*kenka*) as
private disputes nonadjudicable in shogunal courts, and generally it declined to discipline participants. This notion of disputes as private matters

that lie outside of the law provided an opportunity, Takeuchi suggests, for commoners in Asakusa to forge a zone of self-policing where they could take it upon themselves to punish persons who violated community norms and then claim that their actions were merely "fights," which stood "apart from the law." Like Kaplan, Takeuchi sees this sense of local autonomy as important for an understanding of the collapse of the regime: the popular determination to establish a zone of autonomy outside of the coercive control of the shogunate, he argues, gathered strength during the first half of the nineteenth century, permitting ordinary people to be important actors in the Meiji Restoration.

The final two chapters in this volume analyze collective violence in Edo and Paris. Anne Walthall examines documents pertaining to riots in Edo so as better to understand the commoners' perceptions of conflict and the relationship between their actions and weakening state power in the late eighteenth century and early nineteenth, a theme that complements the ideas advanced by Kaplan and Takeuchi. Eiko Ikegami and Charles Tilly explore how and why patterns of contention changed in Japan and in France during the course of the seventeenth and eighteenth centuries. They locate violence at the point where the growth of state power meets the emergence of cities, the repositories of concentrated commercial wealth. The different combinations of state coercion and merchant capital in the two countries, they argue, produced different rhythms and volumes of violence in Paris and Edo. Contention over royal taxation and the food supply loomed large in Paris. In Edo, protests in the first half of the Tokugawa period were directed against the aggrandizement of state authority, but later actions responded more strongly to the growth of a market-oriented economy, as Ieyasu's town became the merchants' city.

When Henry IV marched into Paris he knew nothing of Tokugawa Ieyasu or of Edo, and Ieyasu could scarcely have pretended to possess any serviceable knowledge about French kings and their capital, despite the presence in Japan of Western clerics, seafarers, and traders during the decades when the Tokugawa and Bourbon families rose to power. Yet in nations on opposite sides of the globe, in processes that drew no inspiration one from the other, king and shogun fashioned systems of governance that exhibited fascinating parallels, and they built capital cities that were the wonder of their countries and that stood as the largest on their respective continents. Today Paris and Edo (Tokyo) are still the capital cities of their respective countries, but despite the passage of four hundred years since Henry and Ieyasu laid claim to power and settled in those two communities, scholars are still but imperfectly aware of the significance of the comparative dimensions of the early-modern experience in France and Japan.

The chapters of this volume seek to formulate new ways of understanding the comparative dynamics of statemaking and urban growth in two countries, one Eastern, one Western. The multiple relationships between the expansion of state power and the emergence of great capital cities in

France and Japan are complex and diverse, relatively unfamiliar and still new to the touch. In order to be appreciated fully in their comparative dimension, they also must be understood within the rich subtleties of their own cultural and national traditions. For these reasons, an initial expedition into uncharted territory is best undertaken in the company of many specialists. Joint explorations have a special kind of value: they reveal paths that escape the attention of a single traveler and lead to vistas that might otherwise go unnoticed. Consequently, we have included in this exploration of Edo and Paris experts on both France and Japan, scholars whose individual interests range over the disciplines of anthropology, architecture, drama and the theater, economics, history, literature, and sociology.

The authors of these chapters put to rest any notion that occult cultural factors might serve as explanations for social and political development. In rejecting Orientalism, they strive to identify the similar social and political processes that were at work in two widely disparate societies. Consequently, the essays they offer are steeped individually in the factual specifics of the national cultures of France and Japan; in the aggregate, their findings and conclusions multiply our comparative viewpoints and enhance our understanding of the manner in which two societies separated by distance and by contrasting historical traditions were also joined by the similar experiences of the early-modern period. Some authors observe the city from above. They explore the multifaceted means by which king and shogun sought to accumulate power, and they investigate the numerous and fascinating ways in which the quest for absolutism affected the growth of Edo and Paris, as well as styles of life within the two capitals. Others call our attention to the city from below, leading us along pathways that reveal a different panorama, one which suggests that the relationship between absolutist states and capital cities was defined not just by the prerogatives of the rulers and their officials but also by the requirements and demands of the ordinary people. Some members of the expedition scout the terrain for similarities between the patterns of development in France and Japan; others are more captivated by the contrasts that help to clarify how important variations could exist within a more general construct of absolutist statemaking. Emerging from a journey that no single individual could have made alone, the chapters of this volume present a diversity of scholarly viewpoints that open up new ways of looking at the history of Edo and Paris, shoguns and kings, cities and power.

GOVERNANCE

都市支配

2

Governing Edo

KATŌ TAKASHI

Governing Edo was never a simple or an easy proposition. Because the city was home to the shogunate, it served as the seat of national government in Japan. Inexorably the problems of administering the single city of Edo became bound up in complicated ways with a philosophy and set of practices that originally had been created to rule an entire country. As the Tokugawa family's hegemony and capital city simultaneously grew and took shape over the course of the seventeenth century, the shogun and his top echelon of advisers and officials—the shogunate—labored long and hard to secure and amplify their authority nationally; only secondarily did they turn their attention toward designing the instrumentalities of governance on the more local, urban level. For better or worse, the various magistrates and commissioners who administered Edo largely were subsumed under the more elaborate structure of national government, and many institutions of Edo governance were hastily rerigged versions of bureaucratic devices initially conceived with national purposes in mind. Needless to say, what may have worked well enough nationally was not always equally effective within a different kind of setting, and officials were not always able to rule Edo's million-plus residents in a very direct or compelling manner.

Edo's role as the de facto secular capital of Japan imposed other burdens on the city's administrators as well. The city was a vast ceremonial stage for the shogunate. As William H. Coaldrake demonstrates in Chapter 7 of this volume, the cityscape was dotted with imposing architectural symbols of power, such as the shogun's castle and the expansive temple complexes at Zōjōji and Kan'eiji. The city, too, was host to important processions: some took place at irregular intervals, as when Korean embassies visited; others coursed through the streets more frequently, during annual festivals. These monuments and ceremonials at times tempted thousands of sightseers and celebrants into the streets of the city, posing problems of law and order of the sort that Takeuchi Makoto describes in Chapter 16. Outbursts of violence were of particular concern to those officials charged by the shogunate with administering the metropolitan area, if only because Edo was supposed to be a model of administrative efficiency where policing assumed special importance as a litmus test of the shogun's competence and legitimacy.

The mosaic of Edo governance evoked the political configuration of the entire country in another way as well. Under the Tokugawa shoguns, Japan was a status-divided society, and patterns of land use in Edo as well as shogunal institutions for urban control were similarly partitioned. Merchants and artisans lived in areas geographically separated from the samurai residences, and both of those groups were zoned off from shrine and temple precincts. Japan's nearly 280 daimyo were compelled to maintain extensive residential estates in Edo, known as *hairyō yashiki*. Generally a daimyo lived at his chief Edo residence in alternate years, and he left a sizable retinue there on a permanent basis. Each compound constituted a special administrative enclave, where the individual daimyo enjoyed a considerable measure of independent authority. The Buddhist and Shinto establishments nominally fell under the jurisdiction of one set of shogunal officials (although these institutions, too, retained a degree of autonomy over their internal affairs), whereas a different, more methodically structured assemblage of functionaries, appointed by and responsible to the highest echelon of ministers within the shogunate, administered the districts where the merchants and artisans, who made up approximately half of the city's population, had their homes and shops.

There is no question that the Tokugawa shogunate had a side that shaded into the coercive and despotic. There can be little doubt, either, that the shogun and his officials typically sought, and did not disavow, power. The natural universe, neo-Confucian scholars taught, was one of order and harmony, and the shogun would be judged by how well he could reproduce such conditions in this earthly realm. Better, then, to marshal power, strength, and authority in one's own hands than to leave it with others, who might use it unwisely or to perverse ends. But as William Beik and Sharon Kettering show in Chapters 3 and 4, France's monarchs—however grandiose their dreams of absolutism—had to face a world of reality, of limitations, and of competing interests. And what held true for the Bourbons held true as well for Ieyasu and his successors. Edo in the early seventeenth century surely was "Ieyasu's town," as McClain and Merriman point out in Chapter 1, but ultimately the city became more than Ieyasu's creation, and it was managed in ways that served the interests of the people who lived there.

THE BOUNDARIES OF EDO: DEFINING THE CITY

Some of the complications inherent in devising and implementing a rational plan of administration for this city of unprecedented size and complexity can be seen in the considerable effort that it took officialdom simply to figure out what Edo was geographically. In fact, there was not one spatial Edo, but many. The parameters of the city, which shogunal officials preferred to call the *gofunai*, or "the lord's city," were conceptualized in various ways, and the physical boundaries of Edo varied according to which ideation of Edo one advocated. Depending on the context, Edo, the *gofunai*, could transmute itself into a variety of shapes.[1]

In one very important and official sense, Edo was defined as the territory under the jurisdiction of the city magistrates (*machi bugyō*), officials appointed by the shogunate on a regular basis from the 1630s to administer the merchant and artisan residential quarters that had grown up around Edo Castle. As those neighborhoods multiplied and overflowed into agricultural areas, so too did the authority of the city magistrates expand. Perhaps the greatest single augmentation came after the Meireki fires of 1657, when a vast area from Shiba north to Asakusa was platted for merchant and artisan residential quarters. Yet ambiguity plagued even this simple definition of Edo. As the merchant and artisan population moved outward, what was rural and what was urban, which persons ought to fall under the authority of the city magistrates and which ought to remain under the control of the rural magistrates (*daikan*), were questions whose answers often remained troublesomely unclear.

Two other spatial versions of Edo were nearly conterminous. The commissioners of shrines and temples (*jisha bugyō*) authorized religious establishments to solicit funds within the city for the construction and repair of their buildings. The outer limits of this religious Edo followed the course of the Naka and Ara rivers to Itabashi, swung south around the village of Shibuya, and terminated at Minami Shinagawa. Yet another Edo fitted almost exactly into those same contours. This could be called the "public notice area" (*kōsatsuba*), because information concerning victims of accidental death and lost children discovered within its boundaries was posted on large notice boards located at Shibaguchi.

In still other circumstances, Edo was visualized as a place that could not be entered, or might not be left. The shogun's direct retainers, the bannermen (*hatamoto*) and the housemen (*gokenin*), were not permitted to venture outside of Edo without official permission. But the Edo of those warriors was not clearly demarcated, and throughout the seventeenth century and into the eighteenth they peppered the shogunate with questions about where they might proceed without written authorization. At the same time, persons convicted of crimes punishable by exile from the city were forbidden to reenter an Edo whose circumference was the narrowest of them all, running well inside the line of religious Edo.

Finally, nearly two hundred years after Ieyasu arrived in Edo, the government undertook to end the confusion about the city's boundaries. In 1791 shogunal officials defined "the lord's city" more certainly for Tokugawa retainers by declaring that their line of permission extended for a radius of four *ri* (approximately ten miles) around the outer walls of the castle. Then,

1. An account of the various spatial definitions of Edo can be found in Takami Yasujirō, *Edo no hattatsu* (Tōkyō-to, 1956).

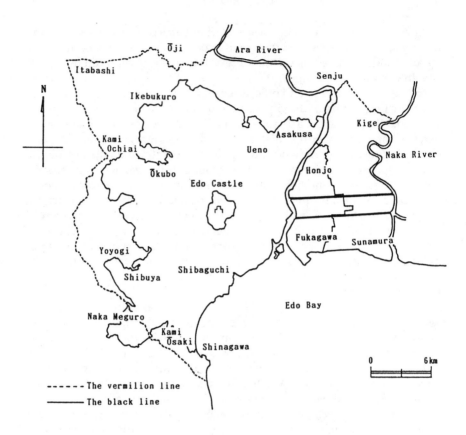

"The lord's city" in the early nineteenth century

in the Twelfth Month of Bunsei 1 (1818), the senior councilors, the shogunate's most important policy board, attempted to settle the matter of Edo's territorial extent once and for all, and for everyone, by boldly drawing two lines on a map of the city and its immediate hinterland. The first line, drawn in vermilion, circumscribed an area that began at Sunamura, a village near the mouth of the Naka River; traveled upstream to Kige village, where it turned west to Senju; ran up the Ara River to Ōji and swept out to Itabashi village; and then began a long bend south through the villages of Kami Ochiai, Yoyogi, and Kami Ōsaki before meeting the sea at Minami Shinagawa. The area so inscribed, the senior councilors declared, was henceforth to be the *gofunai*, the lord's city. Inside of this area they struck yet another line, in black. This arc began at the merchant quarters of Fukagawa and Honjo in the east; cut just north of Asakusa and Ueno; turned south at the village of Ikebukuro; skirted Ōkubo; jutted outside of the vermilion line just far enough to ensnare the newly commercialized section of Naka Meguro; and then ended at Shinagawa. This line, they said, delimited the jurisdiction of the city magistrates.

For all of the apparent decisiveness of the senior councilors, however, Edo's geographic identity remained malleable. For most people, and especially in the popular mind, Edo pretty much was understood to be the area administered by the city magistrates, the residential areas enclosed by the black line. Some shogunal offices also adopted this view of Edo; the "Notes on the Lord's City" (*Gofunai bikō*), a gazetteer compiled by the shogunate in the early nineteenth century, discusses only that region. Yet the inspectors general and the commissioners of shrines and temples had to be concerned with the broader *gofunai* described by the vermilion line; for there, outside of the black ring, were located many of the daimyo estates and religious establishments that fell within their dominion. Certain offices expanded even that definition. For instance, the "Maps and Writings on the Origins and Development of the Lord's City" (*Gofunai enkaku zusho*), compiled by the commissioners of engineering works (*fushin bugyō*) between 1807 and 1858, describes many districts that lie beyond the vermilion line.[2] To the end, "the lord's city" remained a concept of convenience, open to many interpretations.

The Instrumentalities of Shogunal Administration

Since there were many different spatial Edos, it is perhaps only natural that several agencies would be involved in ruling the people who lived within the various urban modules. Perhaps two of the most striking features of Edo governance were the physical separation of the various status groups and

2. The *Gofunai bikō* is located in the archives at the Tōkyō Kokuritsu Hakubutsukan (Tokyo National Museum); the *Gofunai enkaku zusho* has been published as Bakufu Fushin Bugyō, comp., *Edo jōka hensen ezushū*, ed. and rev. Asakura Haruhiko, 20 vols. (Hara Shobō, 1985–1987).

FIGURE 2.1.
The shogunate and the administration of Edo

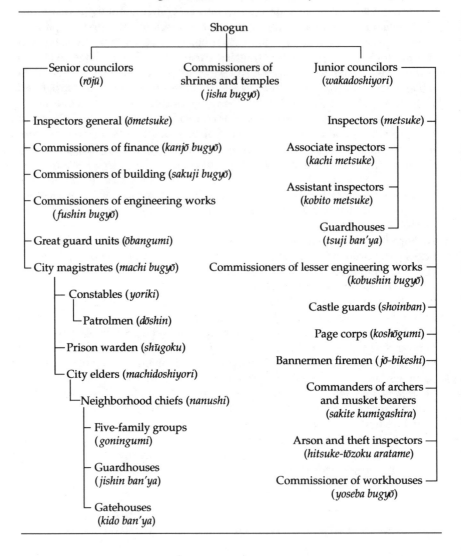

the apparent high degree of autonomy that these groups were permitted to exercise. The great daimyo estates, some of which sprawled over several acres, were in some sense islands, enclaves cut off from the rest of the city by high fences and elaborate gates. Within these private compounds the laws of individual domains prevailed; here each daimyo was the lord of his own small world, free to determine the incomes of his vassals, define crimes and mete out punishments, and manage the affairs of his wife, concubines, and children. The residential plots provided to the bannermen and housemen were more modestly proportioned than the daimyo estates, but these properties too were divorced from the rest of the city by gateways that demarcated the entry into a special realm where it was possible for these direct retainers of the shogun to supervise personally the lives of their family members and servant personnel. Persons who lived on lands granted to shrines and temples formed another urban zone. There, too, walls and imposing gateways imparted a visual reality to a distinct territory where the religious institutions in large part could administer themselves and the people in the surrounding residential neighborhoods who fell under their jurisdiction. Finally, wooden gates that could be closed at night defined the territorial extent of many of the residential quarters of artisans and merchants, who, as we shall see, were also intimately involved in creating the conditions under which they lived out their daily lives.[3]

For all the appearance of geographic autonomy, however, the shogunate was to some extent able to impose its will over the disparate parts of the city. One way in which it curbed the centrifugal forces that issued from the cardinal policy of status division was to bring bureaucratic order to Edo. As the shogunate fleshed out its own structure of national authority over the entirety of Japan during the seventeenth century, it assigned to some of its new offices jurisdiction over the various segments of Edo's population (see Figure 2.1). After the position of senior councilor (*rōjū*) was created in the 1620s, for example, this group of four to six officials constituted the highest policy-making board within the shogunate. On top of their other duties, in 1634 they were assigned the task of overseeing the affairs of the daimyo and their retinues in Edo, a duty that the councilors delegated on a day-to-day basis to inspectors general (*ōmetsuke*), first appointed in the 1630s. The three to five junior councilors (*wakadoshiyori*) composed a board second in importance only to that of the senior councilors after its establishment in 1633. Among their many obligations was supervision of the bannermen and housemen, a responsibility the junior councilors discharged through a group of subordinate inspectors (*metsuke*). It was also from the bureaucratically creative decade of the 1630s that commissioners of shrines and temples were appointed on a regular basis to oversee all of the shrines and temples of Japan, a chore that made them responsible as well for the merchants and artisans who lived within religious precincts in Edo.

3. On the matter of wooden gates and the residential areas of commoners, see Itō Yoshiichi, *Edo no machikado* (Heibonsha, 1987), pp. 124–65.

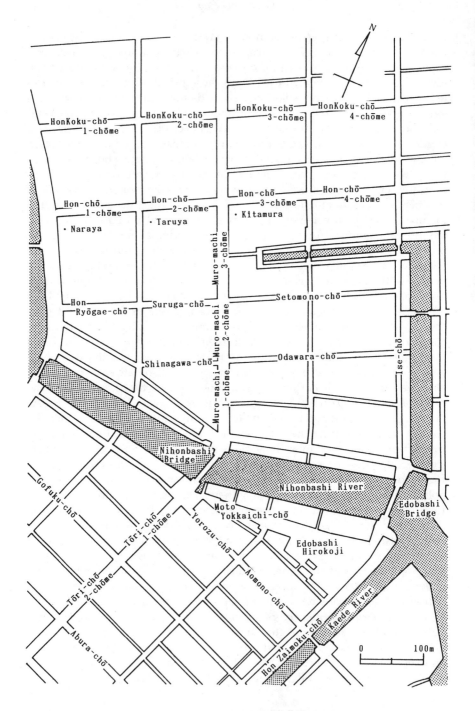

Nihonbashi in the late eighteenth century

Whereas the management of portions of Edo constituted only a part of the broader administrative mandates assigned to the councilors, inspectors, and commissioners, the city magistrates (who reported to the senior councilors) were concerned exclusively with the affairs of the merchants and artisans within the city. The residential blocks in which those commoners lived assumed a great variety of shapes and sizes, in accordance with the topography of Edo, but the ideal block measured roughly 120 meters by 120 meters. Residence-shops were situated around the perimeter of the blocks, and the vacant inner court contained communal facilities: a well, a toilet, and a garbage pit. The blocks were separated by streets that typically were some three to eighteen meters wide. It is important to note here that the official residential quarter, known in shogunal parlance as a *chō*, usually was not the block itself, but rather the two rows of houses that faced each other across a street. Naturally, the people within a block shared friendships and a set of common concerns, such as the cleaning and maintenance of the facilities that they all used, but as we shall see in some detail later, for administrative purposes the shogunate defined the quarters as the contiguous households lining a street.

The residents of those quarters were subdivided in a manner that reflected their rights to the land. Landlords (*jinushi*) and homeowners (*iemochi*) were men who enjoyed the prerogatives of landownership: the shogunate recognized their right to inhabit, rent, sell, and bequeath specific parcels of land (or the shop-residence that sat on the land) in exchange for the payment of annual imposts known as *kuyaku* and *kuniyaku*.[4] *Kuyaku* consisted of labor service (later converted to a cash payment) levied on merchants and calculated on the basis of the street frontage of the individual properties; *kuniyaku* was collected from artisans in the form of actual products or services (later converted to a cash payment as well). In addition, within each quarter there were usually a number of agents (known most frequently as *ienushi* and *yamori*) who acted as representatives for the landlords and homeowners. These agents collected rents and managed properties for the landowners; in exchange they received a salary and a house to live in. The renters, who typically made up the majority of residents of any particular quarter, consisted of those who leased land and built their own residence-shops (*jigari*) and those who rented land together with a residence-shop (*tanagari*).

Beginning early in the seventeenth century, the shogunate appointed city magistrates to oversee the affairs of these quarters (although until the 1630s the magistrates probably carried out duties in surrounding agricultural villages as well as).[5] The practice of appointing two magistrates, known

4. A convenient introduction to these terms and the other nomenclature in this paragraph can be found in Nishiyama Matsunosuke, ed., *Edogaku jiten* (Kōbundō, 1984), s.v. Yoshiwara Ken'ichirō, "Chōnin," pp. 198–99; and Hayashi Reiko, "Edodana," pp. 230–35.

5. The history of this office is treated in detail in Matsudaira Tarō, *Kōtei: Edo jidai seido no kenkyū*, ed. and rev. Shinji Yoshimoto (Kashiwa Shobō, 1978), pp. 482–535; and by Minami Kazuo in his *Edo no shakai kōzō* (Hanawa Shobō, 1973), pp. 11–62, and his "Machi

respectively as the "north magistrate" and the "south magistrate," was rou-
tinized in 1631. As was the case with the shogunal administrators who
oversaw the samurai and religious sections of Edo, the city magistrates were
appointed from the samurai estate. They lived in residence-office compounds granted to them by the shogunate and received annual stipends (set
at 3,000 *koku*, or nearly 15,000 bushels, of rice in 1723).

The chief duties of the city magistrates were to maintain law and order in
the commoner sections of Edo and to hear lawsuits and petitions brought by
merchants and artisans. To this end, the two appointees served on what
commonly was called a monthly rotation system (*tsukiban*). The "on-duty"
magistrate appeared at Edo Castle each morning to confer with his superiors
and after lunch returned to his residence-office, where he received new
petitions, accepted lawsuits, and presided over criminal cases. The "off-
duty" magistrate closed his gate to signal that he would not accept new
business, but he continued to work on the resolution of those matters that
had come his way during his month on-duty.

As the shogunate set in place the bureaucratic mechanisms for governing
Edo, so too it deployed legal codes to extend its authority over the residents
of the city.[6] Samurai throughout Edo increasingly were brought under a
uniform set of judicial procedures by the requirement that the daimyo's laws
(and the punishments meted out to their vassals) comply in general tenor
with those of the shogunate; by the issuance of sumptuary codes that regulated the dress and deportment of all warriors; and by the proclamation in
1632 (and its periodic revision thereafter) of the "Regulations concerning
Vassals" (*shoshi hatto*), which regulated the conduct of all bannermen and
housemen, their families, and servant personnel. Similar codes issued by
the commissioners of shrines and temples imposed a uniform body of law
over the persons living in those precincts. Laws for merchants and artisans,
known as *machibure*, were drawn up by the city magistrates on the basis of
instructions from the senior councilors, and the magistrates were responsible for making them known among the people of the city.

The enforcement of these various legal codes was entrusted to several
layers of lower appointees who reported to the councilors, inspectors, commissioners, and magistrates. From 1629, for instance, the castle guards
(*shoinban*) and page corps (*koshōgumi*) patrolled the grounds of Edo Castle,
while the *ōbangumi*, or "great guard units" that reported to the senior councilors, made their rounds through the samurai residential areas that circled
the citadel. In the Third Month of that year the shogunate, noting that
"since last year great numbers of persons have been cut down on the streets
of the city," ordered that guardhouses (*tsuji ban'ya*) be established in samurai
residential areas across the city.[7]

bugyō—Kyōhō-ki igo o chūshin to shite," in Nishiyama Matsunosuke, ed., *Edo chōnin no kenkyū*, 5 vols. (Yoshikawa Kōbunkan, 1972–1978), vol. 4, pp. 65–184.
    6. Katō Takashi, "Edo no chōhō," *Hikaku toshishi kenkyū* 11:1 (1992), pp. 27–56.
    7. Kokushi Taikei Henshūkai, ed., *Kokushi taikei*, vol. 39: Kuroita Katsumi, ed. *Tokugawa jikki*, vol. 2 (Yoshikawa Kōbunkan, 1964), p. 457.

By the end of the century, more than nine hundred such guardhouses had been set up in samurai neighborhoods. A very few of them were operated directly by the shogunate; slightly more than two hundred were financed and staffed by individual daimyo to provide security around their estates; and the great majority, nearly seven hundred, were managed by individual bannermen or by associations of bannerman families, with occasional daimyo participation. The guardhouses fell under the general supervision of the inspectors, and they were staffed by two to four watchmen called *bannin* during the day and by four to six men at night. These guards patrolled the neighborhood under their charge, and they were supposed to prevent violence, apprehend ruffians, and take into custody anyone acting in a "suspicious" manner. For these purposes, each guardhouse kept on hand a supply of lanterns, torchs, ropes, prods, and the two-pronged *sasumata*, a weapon whose devilish use can be grasped from the two characters used to write the word: "pierce" and "groin."[8]

The senior councilors delegated policing responsibilities for merchant and artisan neighborhoods to the city magistrates, who employed for this purpose about fifty constables (*yoriki*) and another two hundred or so patrolmen (*dōshin*). In theory each constable received an appointment for his lifetime only, but in fact many families served for generation after generation. The constabulary patrolled the city daily, kept an eye out for illegal activities, and reminded all merchants and artisans to be diligent and respectful of authority. Many of the constable's assistants, the patrolmen, also served on a hereditary basis. Their main function was not so much to apprehend criminals (although they did so when necessary) as it was to report on the "mood" of the city and to promote public morality so that crime would not occur in the first place.[9] Indeed, given the fact that Edo's police forces were so small—a consequence of inadequate funding by the shogunate— constables and patrolmen probably had little choice except to encourage voluntary compliance with the law and to rely on tactics of supervision and guidance.[10]

In addition, each merchant and artisan residential quarter was supposed to establish a guardhouse (*jishin ban'ya*) and a gatehouse (*kido ban'ya*). The *jishin ban'ya* were the functional equivalents of the guardhouses found in samurai districts; they were funded by the individual residential quarter and staffed by local residents. The guardhouses in large residential quarters usually were manned by five persons, those in smaller neighborhoods by three. The guards moved about the neighborhood, kept a sharp eye out for

8. At first only samurai served as guards, but later many neighborhoods hired commoners to staff the guardhouses. Further discussion of the *tsuji ban'ya* can be found in Ishii Ryōsuke, *Edo no machi bugyō*, Edo jidai manpitsu 1 (Akashi Shoten, 1989), pp. 47–48; and Itō, *Edo no machikado*, pp. 166–86.

9. Further details on the constables and patrolmen can be found in Matsudaira, *Edo jidai seido*, pp. 493–98; and Tokoro Rikio, "Machi bugyō—Shōtoku izen o chūshin to shite," in Nishiyama, *Edo chōnin*, vol. 4, pp. 47–57.

10. For additional information about the proliferation of offices subordinate to the constables and patrolmen and the lack of adequate financing, see Minami, *Edo no shakai kōzō*, pp. 22–43.

fire, and carried out any instructions received from the constables or patrolmen. They might also take suspicious persons into custody and hold them at the guardhouse until patrolmen arrived to carry out an investigation. Gatehouses were constructed next to the wooden gates that separated one neighborhood from the next and, like the guardhouses, were manned by household heads from the neighborhood. The gatehouse guards, known as *bannin*, or more colloquially as *bantarō*, closed the gates at night (or whenever patrolmen were in pursuit of a criminal), and each evening they made a circuit through the neighborhood banging together a pair of wooden clappers and calling out warnings against thieves and fires.

Although the separate policing systems for the various status groups could be charted out neatly on an organization table, in reality many problems cropped up during the seventeenth and early eighteenth centuries. One complication stemmed from the appointment of several additional policing agencies whose powers of surveillance and apprehension cut across existing jurisdictions. For instance, the inspectors supervised officials known as *kachi metsuke*, associate inspectors who toured the streets of Edo whenever the shogun made a journey outside of the castle, and *kobito metsuke*, assistants who helped to police construction sites, the prison, and the infirmary and convalescent center set up for commoners. In addition, the junior councilors from the 1660s frequently authorized the temporary appointment of theft investigators (*tōzoku aratame*) and, beginning in the 1680s, of arson investigators (*hitsuke aratame*) whenever those two particular problems became more troublesome than usual. Appointed from among the *sakite kumigashira*, the commanders of the companies of archers and musket bearers who guarded the entrance gates to Edo Castle, these ancillary police conducted patrols wherever necessary throughout Edo, pursued their investigations into every neighborhood of the city, and were empowered to arrest merchants and artisans. When such crimes proved impossible to stamp out, joint arson and theft investigators (*hitsuke-tōzoku aratame*) were appointed from the eighteenth century, and were assigned the additional task of suppressing gambling.[11]

Another complication concerned rights of adjudication over persons from one status jurisdiction who committed a crime in another area. No police official assigned to the office of the city magistrates, for instance, was empowered to enter a daimyo estate or bannerman residence to arrest a samurai who had committed a crime in a merchant neighborhood. Rather, the police had to rely on the inspectors general or inspectors to order the daimyo or bannerman to surrender the suspect. Moreover, since the authority of the city magistrates was bound geographically to the residential quarters of merchants and artisans, they did not even have the right to arrest a commoner who committed an offense within a samurai residential compound, where many went to gamble. In such cases the magistrates had to

11. Hiramatsu Yoshirō, *Kinsei keiji soshōhō no kenkyū* (Sōbunsha, 1960), pp. 427, 552, 620, 627, 809, 859, 891; Matsudaira, *Edo jidai seido*, pp. 569–74.

submit a report about the crime to the senior councilors, who could, if they so chose, empower the inspectors general or inspectors to make the actual arrest and then bind the prisoner over to the magistrates for trial. In addition, actors, sumo wrestlers, and other entertainers formally fell under the jurisdiction of the city magistrates, yet those persons typically performed on the grounds of religious institutions, space that was policed by the commissioners of shrines and temples. Consequently, any problems that occurred there had to be settled through negotiations between the magistrates and commissioners.[12]

The irritation of dealing with such administrative headaches prompted the shogunate to adopt certain expediencies, while still preserving a society and city that were structured along status lines. As a consequence, one can ascertain a gradual devolution of authority into the hands of the city magistrates. For one thing, the shogunate gave the magistrates a seat on its judicial council (*hyōjōsho*), which heard all nationally important legal cases, and it confirmed the right of the magistrates to investigate all crimes committed in merchant and artisan neighborhoods, including all but the most serious offenses involving samurai.[13] It also turned over to the magistrates some of the policing functions formerly assigned to officials under the junior councilors; in the early eighteenth century, for instance, the responsibility for patrolling the prisons and the convalescent center was delegated to the constables assigned to the magistrates. Then, in 1745, the merchants and artisans who lived in neighborhoods around religious institutions and who had been administered by the commissioners of shrines and temples were placed under the jurisdiction of the city magistrates in the hope that crime could be reduced. Despite these measures, policing Edo was never without its complexities, and the fragmentized geography of the city, the existence of a status-based society, and the lack of adequate funding required the city magistrates, like their subordinates, to develop skills of persuasion to complement the tools of coercion.

WITHIN THE RESIDENTIAL QUARTERS OF MERCHANTS AND ARTISANS

As the above discussion suggests, the veneer of administration over the commoner residential areas was thin: the population was great, the number of administrators and police relatively small. Consequently, to ensure that merchant and artisan quarters of the city ran in an orderly and peaceful fashion, the city magistrates delegated many important functions to the merchants and artisans themselves, and a rather elaborate set of supporting offices came into existence in Edo's commoner neighborhoods. The most

12. Chiyoda Kuyakusho, ed., *Chiyoda kushi*, vol. 1 (Chiyoda Kuyakusho, 1960), pp. 675–727.
13. For more on the emergence of the city magistrates as Edo's most important policing agency, see Hiramatsu, *Kinsei keiji soshōhō*, pp. 88–157, 422–23, 525, 617–27, 690, 988, 1018.

important of these functionaries were the city elders (*machidoshiyori*), the highest ranking nonsamurai involved in urban administration.

No extant documentation tells us exactly when this position was first established, but by the late 1610s three families—the Naraya, the Taruya, and the Kitamura—claimed the hereditary right to serve as city elders. The first two of these families descended from warriors who had served Ieyasu bravely on the battlefield but gave up samurai status when they moved to Edo. The Kitamura family hailed from Kanazawa, where they prospered as druggists and served the lord of their domain, the Maeda daimyo, as city elders. The head of the Kitamura family seems to have moved to Edo after Ieyasu explained to the Maeda lord his need to have an experienced, talented elder in Edo.[14]

The three city elders carried out a variety of significant duties:

1. To transmit laws, ordinances, decrees, and proclamations issued by the shogunate to the residential quarters of merchants and artisans.
2. To plat new residential wards on land reclaimed from Edo Bay or otherwise added to the city, and to transfer to individual merchants and artisan families properties within such newly created quarters.
3. To maintain copies of the census registers compiled for the individual neighborhoods and to update them twice annually.
4. To appoint and dismiss subordinate officials.
5. To safeguard membership registers and other important documents concerning the commercial activities of protective associations (*kabu nakama*).
6. To collect and submit to higher authorities the various corvée levies, business taxes, and licensing fees imposed on merchants and artisans.
7. To supervise investigations and inquiries in response to questions posed by the city magistrates.
8. To investigate the issues and verify the facts raised in petitions submitted by commoners, and to prepare commentaries for use by the city magistrates.
9. To arbitrate and settle all petitions and lawsuits involving merchants and artisans and to mediate nonviolent quarrels and disputes.[15]

For fulfilling these duties, the elders received a package of symbolic and material benefits. Like samurai, they were permitted to wear swords while performing their duties, and two families, the Kitamura and Taru[ya] (from 1790), were allowed to use surnames, the other well-known perquisite of the

14. For additional information on the Kitamura family, see James L. McClain, *Kanazawa: A Seventeenth-Century Japanese Castle Town* (New Haven: Yale University Press, 1982), pp. 61, 87–88.

15. The assemblage of duties took shape over time (the maintenance of census records began only in the early eighteenth century, for instance), and this list enumerates responsibilities assigned to the elders in the early eighteenth century. For additional details see Yoshiwara Ken'ichirō, "Machidoshiyori," in Nishiyama, *Edo chōnin*, vol. 4, pp. 185–332.

warrior class. The shogun received all three elders at Edo Castle on the third day of the festivities held annually to celebrate the New Year, and the men journeyed up to those exalted precincts to pay their respects each time a new shogun assumed office. Although not salaried, each elder did receive an extensive plot of land at Hon-chō, almost directly in front of the main entry gate to Edo Castle and very close to Nihonbashi, the heart of merchant Edo. Typically, each elder rented out a portion of this valuable land, and also leased to others several additional properties, scattered throughout the merchant and artisan districts, that he received from the shogun. In addition, the shogun occasionally bestowed extraordinary loans and grants upon the elders; each, for instance, received five hundred *ryō* of gold from the shogun in 1637.

Under the immediate supervision of the city elders were the neighborhood chiefs (*nanushi*), the officials who worked at the level that was closest to, and perhaps had the most immediate impact on, ordinary merchant and artisan families. Chiefs seem to have been named in a few neighborhoods during the early seventeenth century, but it was only in the middle of the century that the continuing expansion of the commoner population, and a predictable multiplication of problems over matters such as property ownership and inheritance rights, persuaded the city magistrates and elders to appoint chiefs for all neighborhoods. Consequently, by the early eighteenth century some 250 to 260 families served as neighborhood chiefs, generally on a heredity basis. Since Edo consisted of well over a thousand residential quarters at that time, few chiefs had the luxury of dealing with a single neighborhood; many were responsible for seven or eight quarters, and some even had jurisdiction over a dozen or more.[16]

The chiefs had a job assignment that was defined broadly:

1. To transmit to the merchant and artisan families within their jurisdiction all laws, ordinances, decrees, and proclamations announced by the city elders.
2. To maintain and to update twice annually a census register for each quarter.
3. To identify, as examples for the general population, persons who exhibited exceptional filial piety and benevolence.
4. To investigate the causes of fires.
5. To supervise firefighting squads at the scene of a blaze.
6. To conduct investigations as instructed by the city magistrates and city elders.
7. To verify the accuracy and procedural correctness of petitions, complaints, and reports drafted by merchants and artisans for submission to the city magistrates, attested to by the chief's personal seal affixed to the back of the document.
8. To investigate and verify, whenever a house or property was sold, the facts contained in the promissory note and the bill of sale (the *koken*, a

16. Additional information about the neighborhood chiefs can be found in Yoshiwara Ken'ichirō, *Edo no machi yakunin* (Yoshikawa Kōbunkan, 1980), pp. 63–91.

document that listed the sale price and other details), attested to by the chief's personal seal affixed to the back of the document.

9. To mediate and resolve neighborhood disputes.
10. To admonish ne'er-do-wells.
11. To audit the funds collected within each quarter to finance the operation of the guardhouse, gatehouse, and so forth.
12. To supervise festivals.

The elders and chiefs functioned at different levels of responsibility, but all relied on tactics of guidance, supervision, on-site inspection, and admonishment to carry out their tasks. That is, the actual day-to-day management of many activities within any one residential quarter was performed by members of the quarter themselves, organized into communal associations known as five-family groups, or *goningumi*, which were held accountable to the neighborhood chief. These groups, and there might be several within a single residential quarter, were composed of the homeowners, landlords, and their agents. The homeowners and landlords paid an assessment known as the *machi nyūyō* (also pronounced *machi iriyō*), which was based on the length of street frontage of their properties. The quarters then used the money collected through this assessment to organize and to pay for firefighting equipment and services, the expenses associated with holding festivals, the maintenance of fire towers, guardhouses, wooden gates and gatehouses, the repair and management of the canals and ditches that supplied drinking water to the quarter, and so forth.

To ensure that the system responded to the mandates laid down from above, the city magistrates in the latter half of the seventeenth century began to insist that each five-family group designate one of its members as a "group representative" (*gachigyōji*). The first documents referring to such representatives, who served on a rotating basis, date from the middle of the seventeenth century, and they suggest that the city magistrates wanted to have these men appointed so that they could be charged with ensuring that all taxes, fees, and levies due from merchant and artisan families were paid in a timely fashion. In time, however, the monthly representatives became yet another level of administration that the city magistrates could hold responsible for the performance of a variety of local obligations. By the early eighteenth century, the magistrates expected the monthly representatives to countersign, by affixing their own seals, all petitions originating from families within their group; to be present at all official investigations; to supervise firefighting squads under the direction of the neighborhood chiefs; to participate in the mediation of neighborhood quarrels; to care for abandoned children and travelers who fell ill; to maintain the streets of the neighborhood; to keep the gatehouses in good repair; and to circulate throughout the neighborhood nightly during the winter months, warning residents to observe care with their cooking and heating fires.[17]

17. Matsumoto Shirō, "Edo no machikata soshiki," in Toyoda Takeshi et al., eds., *Kōza: Nihon no hōken toshi*, vol. 2 (Bun'ichi Sōgō Shuppan, 1983), pp. 227–40.

The structure of authority and accountability that ran from city magistrates through the elders to the neighborhood chiefs and then to the monthly representatives of the five-family groups imparted a dual nature to governance within the merchant and artisan quarters of Edo. On the one hand, the system provided a mechanism for the shogun's government to make its will known on the neighborhood and even the family level. On the other hand, it also allowed the people of the quarters broad latitude in managing many significant aspects of urban life, and this is one reason that the shogunate was so intent on incorporating the representatives of the five-family groups into an integrated chain of authority and responsibility. The manner in which the shogunate disseminated its laws and cared for the poor of the city can illustrate these complementary dimensions of urban governance and the crucial role played by the people of the residential quarters.

The available evidence suggests that in the early and middle seventeenth century, the city magistrates periodically summoned the neighborhood chiefs and the monthly representatives of the five-family groups, apprised them of additions or changes to the laws, and then instructed them to make certain that the people of their neighborhoods were fully cognizant of the details contained in the legal codes.[18] As Edo grew, however, it became impractical to assemble all of the chiefs and representatives in one place, so the magistrates began to pass the laws along to the city elders, who then summoned the neighborhood chiefs to their offices. The chiefs next conveyed the edicts to the monthly representatives of five-family groups under their responsibility, who then communicated them to the homeowners and landlords (or their agents) who made up the groups. The members of the five-family groups shared responsibility for ensuring that their own families, as well as the families who lived on their properties, knew every law and comported themselves as expected, becoming in effect the last link in a long chain of disciplinary agents fashioned by the shogun.[19] The layers of responsibility were many, as if the shogunate hoped that with so many people involved, all would feel a heavier weight of accountability, all would take a hand in enforcing the laws of the realm and the city.

The shogunate's concern to regulate neighborhood life did not extend to direct involvement in poor relief (at least until the inception of the city savings association at the end of the eighteenth century). Instead, higher officialdom deferred to whatever goodwill the wealthier landowners of the quarters might possess to provide charity to renters who fell on temporary hard times and to the truly destitute within their own neighborhoods and in nearby unincorporated areas. Indeed, one reason that five-family groups

18. Katō Takashi, "Edo chōkan," *Minshūshi kenkyū* 24 (1983), pp. 43–72.

19. In 1722 the city magistrates divided Edo's 268 neighborhood chiefs into seventeen groups and inserted the head of each group as an intermediary between the city magistrates and the rest of the chiefs. Thus, in final form, the structure that was supposed to ensure that each family in Edo knew the legal codes ran from the magistrates to the elders, to the yearly heads of the chiefs' groups, to the chiefs, to the monthly representatives of the five-family groups, and finally to the landlords and agents who made up those groups. See Kōda Shigetomo, *Kōda Shigetomo chosakushū*, vol. 2 (Chūō Kōronsha, 1972), pp. 209–36; Matsudaira, *Edo jidai seido*, pp. 556–67.

were organized in the first place was to create a mechanism to provide such relief; yet this was a safety net with large holes, and it left especially vulnerable the poor who dwelled on the fringes of the city, where few well-to-do merchants or artisans lived, and who consequently had little hope for help in times of need.

Neighborhood chiefs often stepped forward to organize poor relief. In the second half of the seventeenth century, for instance, when famine struck and rice prices soared, many neighborhood chiefs successfully petitioned the city magistrates to have the shogunate lend relief rice from its granaries to the chiefs for distribution to people in need. Neighborhood chiefs also pressed the city magistrates in the early eighteenth century to devise specific policies that would reduce rice prices, and in another instance later that century, when they despaired of receiving a timely response from the magistrates concerning another petition to put into place policies that would lower prices, the chiefs simply pressured the well-to-do in their own quarters to make the necessary contributions.[20] Thus throughout the Tokugawa period the residential quarter remained an important institution in areas as widely separated as law enforcement and poor relief, and if in Edo there were a group identifiable as "middlemen" in the sense in which Sharon Kettering uses the term in Chapter 4, perhaps it was the neighborhood chiefs. These men did not arbitrate between elites, but they did stand at the point of articulation between the quarters and the outside world, presenting the demands of higher officialdom to their neighborhoods and mobilizing their constituencies to meet the demands of urban life.[21]

URBAN INSTITUTIONS

Neither the officials nor the samurai nor the commoners of Edo ever formulated a concept of "public services" as that term is used in its modern sense. Yet, for diverse reasons, including ambitions for greater social control, humanitarian impulses, and aspirations to improve the tenor of life, many persons within the city helped to bring into being what Japanese historians are inclined to refer to as *toshi shisetsu*, a term that can be rendered literally, although not felicitously, as "urban institutions." A brief examination of several of these facilities and institutions can help to amplify the themes set forth above concerning the governance of Edo.

The Prison and the Workhouses

Not far from Nihonbashi in Kodenma-chō, in an otherwise unexceptional neighborhood of druggists, confectioners, and artisans who made parapher-

20. Sasaki Junnosuke, ed., *Hyakushō ikki to uchikowashi*, Nihon minshū no rekishi 4 (Sanseido, 1974), pp. 285–313.

21. Examples of chiefs' mobilizing their wards on a variety of occasions are plentiful; see, for instance, Yoshioka Yuriko, "Kyōhō-ki Edo machikata ni okeru sogan undō no jittai—bōka seisaku o meguru chōningawa no taiō o chūshin to shite," in Chihōshi Kenkyū Kyōgikai, ed., *Toshi no chihōshi—seikatsu to bunka* (Yūzankaku, 1980), pp. 108–58.

nalia for use in wedding ceremonies, stood a walled compound, with moats six feet wide by eight feet deep flowing around both the inside and the outside of the walls. This barrier enclosed two acres of what Kawatake Mokuami, a Tokugawa period author of criminal fiction, called "hell on earth." This was the shogunate's prison and detention center, the feared *rōyashiki*. The walls and moats enclosed office-residences for the warden and his staff, several buildings where prisoners were housed (each itself surrounded by a pair of tall latticed fences), and an area where punishments were meted out.

The facility was financed by the shogunate, which delegated responsibility for running the prison to the city magistrates. The magistrates regularly dispatched special constables and patrolmen to observe and report on events at the institution, but day-to-day management was in the hands of the Ishide Tatewaki family, who served as wardens (*shūgoku*) on a hereditary basis throughout nearly the entire Tokugawa period. The Ishide received a small salary (300 *koku*) from the shogunate, and they used a subordinate corps of some fifty to seventy jailers (*rōya dōshin*) and a number of lesser guards to maintain control inside the prison compound. In addition, the Ishide traditionally appointed several "jail-yard bosses" (*rō nanushi*), prisoners who together with their own gangs of lackeys policed the inmate population and distributed to them the food, bedding, and clothing supplied by the warden's office.

Incarcerated at the prison were criminals apprehended all over Edo, whether by constables attached to the office of the city magistrates, by the arson and theft inspectors, or by subordinates of the commissioners of shrines and temples. In addition, certain samurai and persons convicted by the judicial council could be interned there. Among the 200 to 900 prisoners were some men and women who had been sentenced to lengthy terms, even lifetime confinement. But such prisoners were rare, for the facility was established chiefly to provide a detention center for persons who had been arrested but not yet brought to trial, and for persons who had been convicted and were awaiting the execution of their punishment. It was here too that many of those punishments were carried out: beatings, tattooings, and beheadings.

Prisoners were segregated according to status and gender. Buildings known as the *agari-zashiki*, a name that evokes an image of clean, spacious rooms furnished with tatami mats, housed relatively well-to-do samurai, most of whom hired prisoners of merchant or artisan status to look after their needs. Ordinary samurai, as well as Buddhist and Shinto priests, were interned in the *agariya* (the term is used in a different context to mean a rather well-appointed house of assignation). Men of merchant and artisan status lived with masterless samurai and samurai servant personnel in buildings whose names allude to crowded and primitive conditions: the "big lockup" (*tairō*) and the "four-mat cells" (*nikenrō*). The few unfortunate peasants who ended up in the prison were interned with the other commoners until 1755, when they got their own cells, and all women, regardless of social status, lived in a single building. Conditions were tolerable perhaps only for the more affluent samurai; for everyone else poor food and unsanitary conditions were the rule. Commoners and women especially were subject to abusive and exploitive behavior by the guards, particularly the jailyard bosses, and many died before ever coming to trial or before having to face the corporal punishments for which they had been incarcerated.[22]

Another institution in Edo connected with the maintenance of public order was a group of workhouses (*ninsoku yoseba*) constructed in 1790 on a vast tract (more than ten acres) of swampy, reclaimed land at Ishikawajima, close to where the Sumida River emptied into Edo Bay. The purpose of this facility was to provide housing and employment for the homeless and for persons who had been convicted of crimes and had received their punishments but did not enjoy the partonage of an established, gainfully employed merchant or artisan who would vouch for their future conduct. The regime had long been concerned with vagrants, and its apprehensions turned to alarm after the economically difficult 1780s, when the number of homeless coming into Edo increased dramatically. By placing vagrants in a supervised institution, Matsudaira Sadanobu, the senior councilor who ordered the establishment of the workhouses, intended to clear the streets of persons he considered to be threats to society, and by introducing such potential troublemakers to the discipline and rewards of work, he further hoped to reform them so that they would become productive members of society.[23]

Matsudaira placed the workshops under the jurisdiction of the junior councilors, who appointed a commissioner of workhouses (*yoseba bugyō*) to manage the facility. To assist this official, the inspectors dispatched a staff composed of associate and assistant inspectors, who resided permanently at the institution and handled the accounting and other supervisory and administrative tasks. The city magistrates also stationed at the workhouses several constables and patrolmen who carried out the disciplinary punishments ordered by the commissioner. The expenses of maintaining the workshops came from appropriations from the shogunate (typically 30 percent of the annual operating budget), from sales of commodities produced by the internees, and from rents collected on a neighboring tract of land, a former daimyo estate entrusted to the commissioner of the workshops in 1792.

In time the nature of the workhouses changed; from the 1820s they were used to house criminals who had been sentenced to exile from Edo and were awaiting transportation, usually to some offshore island. That is, in addition to preventing crime by vagrants and offering rehabilitation to them, the workhouses were used to detain convicts, just as the prison was. Conse-

22. Samurai who received annual stipends of 500 *koku* and above were not interned at the prison but were placed under a form of house arrest in the residence of a fellow samurai. See Ishii Ryōsuke, *Edo no keibatsu* (Chūō Kōronsha, 1964); Matsudaira, *Edo jidai seido*, pp. 535–40; Minami, "Machi bugyō."

23. Ninsoku Yoseba Kenshōkai, ed., *Ninsoku yosebashi—waga kuni jiyūkei, hoan shobun no genryū* (Sōbunsha, 1974); Minami, *Edo no shakai kōzō*, pp. 63–165; Tsukada Takashi, "Ninsoku yoseba shūyōsha ni tsuite," *Ronshū kinsei* 4 (1980), pp. 41–61.

quently, the population of the facility quickly jumped from the usual 140 to 150 internees to as many as 400 to 500, and at times it even topped 600 persons.

The inmates were lodged in several buildings, segregated according to gender, the reason for internment, and the talents they might possess. Everyone worked. The skilled did carpentry, made household furnishings, and produced lacquer ware. The less adroit pressed oil (whose annual sales amounted to some 800 *ryō* of gold, about 70 percent of all workhouse profits), polished rice, produced lime from roasted oyster shells, made charcoal, and so forth. A few—but only those who had never been convicted of a crime—worked on construction projects around the city. All inmates were paid for their labors, but the commissioners compelled them to deposit one-third of their wages in individual savings accounts maintained at the accounting office. Everyone attended thrice-monthly lectures on popular ethics and social behavior delivered by such prominent scholars as Nakazawa Dōni, Wakisaka Gidō, and Ōshima Yūrin. The combination of work, discipline, and moral training had the intended result on some inmates, who found sponsors to guarantee their conduct and started new lives with their savings. Others spent years in the workhouses. Poor food, unsanitary conditions, and abuse from officials prompted many of these people to try to escape; few succeeded, and all who failed returned to a beating and tattooing.

The Convalescent Center and the City Savings Association

In 1722 a doctor named Ogawa Shōsen submitted a petition to the city magistrates urging them to establish a facility that would provide free medical care for indigent commoners and a place for them to convalesce from serious illness.[24] The magistrates gave their approval, and in the Twelfth Month of that year a combination infirmary and convalescent center (*yōjōsho*) opened on the grounds of a spacious medicinal-herb garden at Koishikawa, in the northern part of the city. Persons wanting treatment applied directly to the facility and were admitted, space permitting, after the monthly representative of their five-person group and their neighborhood chief affixed their seals to the application. At first only the poor from the residential quarters under the jurisdiction of the city magistrates were welcomed into the facility, but from 1725 travelers who fell ill and commoners who resided in neighborhoods under the jurisdiction of the commissioners of shrines and temples were also eligible to apply for care, as long as they were not outcasts or "homeless." Treatment was provided by nine (later five) doctors, who were assisted by two constables and six patrolmen assigned by the city magistrates. Funds for the infirmary were taken from the budgets of the magistrates until the 1750s, when the shogunate provided an annual subsidy of 840 *ryō* of gold.

When the infirmary opened it had space for 40 patients; it later expanded

24. Minami, *Edo no shakai kōzō*, pp. 297–302.

to 117. The poor of the city used the facility to capacity during the early years of its existence, and the doctors enjoyed a measure of medical success. In 1726, for instance, the staff treated some 350 patients (316 males and 34 females), many of whom spent several months convalescing at the center, others of whom received care on an outpatient basis. Of this total, 134 made complete recoveries; 82 were deemed incurable and were told to return to their homes; 22 petitioned to return home before their course of treatment was finished; 12 died; and at the end of the year 100 persons were resident at the center (its capacity at the time). As late as 1785 the facility operated at or near capacity, but after that the number of patients gradually declined and by the 1830s and 1840s the center seldom was more than half full—a consequence, according to some reports, of negligence by the doctors, improprieties by the attendant constables and patrolmen, and a decline in the recovery rates.

The city savings association (*machi kaisho*) was an emergency savings institution established in 1792, in the wake of the riots by commoners that erupted in Edo and other cities during the 1780s, to provide relief for the poor.[25] As was the case with the convalescent center, the shogunate mandated and approved the establishment of this institution, but higher officials restricted their role to that of guidance and supervision, delegating the actual management of the association to representatives of the merchants and artisans.

The shogunate endowed the savings association with grants of 10,000 *ryō* of gold in 1793 and again in 1800, but the bulk of the funding came from Edo's merchants and artisans. After the savings association was organized, a portion of the money paid by landowners to fund guardhouses, gatehouses, and so forth within the residential quarters was diverted into endowment for the society. This capital fund was maintained both in cash and in grain, stored at some twelve warehouses managed by the association in the Asakusa area. Over time the endowment grew to a considerable size. In 1828, for instance, the society had reserves amounting to 462,400 *ryō* of gold and 171,109 *koku* of unhulled rice, and it carried on its books as assets the 280,200 *ryō* due it in outstanding loans. We can gain an appreciation of the rough purchasing power of the fund by recalling that one *koku* of hulled white rice sold for approximately 1.3 *ryō* of gold in Edo that spring and for about 1.7 *ryō* that autumn before the new harvest came in, and that a person of modest means spent roughly 3 to 5 *ryō* a year on food, shelter, and housing.

Mitani Sankurō and nine other wealthy merchants, who also advised the commissioners of finance about the shogunate's budgets, oversaw the uses of the association's funds. These men in turn appointed five neighborhood chiefs to serve annual terms on a board that actually managed the money. That board authorized expenditures, communicated with the neighborhood

25. Katō Takashi, "Edo machi kaisho to suteso hariso," *Minshūshi kenkyūkai kaihō* 17 (1981); Yoshida Nobuyuki, "Edo machi kaisho no seisaku to kinō ni tsuite—bakuhan taiseika ni okeru toshi kasōmin taisaku no kōzō to tokushitsu o kangaeru," pts. 1 and 2, *Shigaku zasshi* 82:7 and 8 (1973), pp. 56–72 and 76–88 respectively.

chiefs in the quarters, and arranged the collection of capital levies imposed on commoner neighborhoods, making certain that the wealthier quarters paid proportionately more than did the less well-to-do sections of the city.

The association became the principal source of charity in Edo, providing a direct grant to anyone who suffered a personal or business loss as a result of a fire, earthquake, famine, or one of the epidemics of cholera that occasionally struck the city. In addition, it furnished assistance to the poor even in ordinary times. The association also advanced low-interest loans (typically 5 percent) to commoners and to samurai who temporarily fell on hard times and who had property that they could pledge as collateral. Finally, the association attempted to help maintain stable rice prices in Edo by selling rice from its granaries when prices rose and by buying when prices fell. In time the association earned a reputation for using its funds wisely and for helping the poor and needy of Edo.[26]

Fire, Water, and Bridges

Indispensable to the lives of Edo townspeople were the organization of firefighting corps, the provisioning of drinking water, and the repair and maintenance of bridges. Firefighting and the water supply system are treated in detail elsewhere in this volume, but they are worth considering briefly here for the insights they provide about the nature of governance in Edo. In the opening decades of the seventeenth century there were no permanently organized firefighting units in Edo.[27] Daimyo were responsible for protecting their own estates, as were bannermen and housemen for their residences and the merchants and artisans for their quarters. Whenever a blaze threatened the castle, the great guard units, the corps of musket bearers, and other samurai would be ordered into action.

The inadequacy of such an ad hoc system was made evident by the great fires of 1657, which destroyed dozens of daimyo estates, burned through most of the castle, and left more than 100,000 dead in the city. In the wake of that disaster, the shogunate ordered some of its higher-ranking bannermen to captain permanent firefighting units, known as *jō-bikeshi*. At first there were two such brigades; later the number varied but ultimately settled at ten. These units fell under the jurisdiction of the junior councilors, who provided each unit leader with funding to maintain an office-firehouse (*hikeshi yashiki*) and to employ a crew of firefighters. These units answered calls for help from merchant and artisan quarters, but their principal obligation was to defend Edo Castle. Their ten firehouses were deployed in an arc around the northern and western quadrants of the castle, the directions from which the dry, dangerous winds of winter blew.

26. Matsumoto Shirō, *Nihon kinsei toshi-ron* (Tōkyō Daigaku Shuppankai, 1983), pp. 285–97; Yoshida Nobuyuki, "Edo machi kaishokin kashitsuke ni tsuite," pts. 1 and 2, *Shigaku zasshi* 86:1 and 2 (1977), pp. 33–59 and 33–54 respectively.

27. Material about firefighting is drawn from Uotani Masao, *Shōbō no rekishi yonhyakunen* (Zenkoku Kajohōrei Shuppan, 1965); Ikegami Akihiko, "Edo hikeshi seido no seiritsu to tenkai," in Nishiyama, *Edo chōnin*, vol. 5, pp. 91–169.

Even after the fires of 1657 daimyo still had to fight blazes on their own estates, but some were also ordered to form two types of standing units that would help to defend the shogun's properties. One such group was referred to as the "dispersed brigades" (*shosho-bikeshi*). At first these firefighters were responsible merely for safeguarding the Tokugawa mausolea at Kan'eiji, in Ueno; at Zōjōji, in Shiba; and at Momijiyama, inside Edo Castle. By the beginning of the eighteenth century, however, the councilors had instructed that many more such units be formed, and when fire threatened, these samurai moved out from their estates to guard additional shogunal properties across the city: Sannō Shrine; the rice granaries at Asakusa and Honjo; the lumber stockpiles at Honjo Sarue; the shogunal college at Yushima; and the Ryōgoku and Eitai bridges across the Sumida River. Five other units were assigned to the internal grounds at Edo Castle. In addition to the dispersed brigades, other daimyo contributed men to the "quarter squadrons" (*hōgaku-bikeshi*). That name springs from the fact that at one time there were four such units, each named after a cardinal direction; after 1716 there were just two "quarter units," and they were mobilized as necessary to guard the Ōte and Sakurada gates, the main entries into the castle.

The institutional structure of so-called *machi-bikeshi*, the commoner firefighter units organized in the merchant and artisan quarters of the city in the early eighteenth century, was complex and subject to frequent change, as William W. Kelly explains in Chapter 13. Moreover, although those units were originally formed to fight fires only in commoner areas, by the late eighteenth century they had proved themselves so superior to the samurai squads that they handled almost all firefighting duties outside the walls of Edo Castle. Throughout these changes, some general principles remained constant. Administrative authority over the units of commoner firefighters was vested in the city magistrates, who then delegated the actual management of the units to the neighborhood chiefs, who were assisted by the monthly representatives of the five-family groups. The expenses associated with firefighting efforts fell on the propertied families of the quarters.

Whereas the responsibility for firefighting was shouldered by samurai and merchants separately, and jurisdictional control was split among several bureaus within the shogunate, management of the water supply system represented a rare case of bureaucratic simplification and unity.[28] Clean lines of authority were not present at the beginning, however. In the early seventeenth century, as the network of pipes was being laid, the city magistrates administered the system. In 1666 a water supply commissioner (*jōsui bugyō*) was appointed, but he left the operation and maintenance of the extensive infrastructure of waterways and wells, which by then supplied fresh drinking water to nearly every samurai and commoner household in Edo, to the city elders. After the office of water supply commissioner was abolished in 1670, the elders hired contractors to operate the network. Later the road commissioner (*michi bugyō*) was granted a voice in running the system; the use of contractors was curtailed; the commissioners of engineering works

28. Itō Yoshiichi, "Edo no suidō seido," in Nishiyama, *Edo chōnin*, vol. 5, pp. 283–433.

and the commissioners of building were assigned certain responsibilities; the post of road commissioner was abolished; and finally in 1768 all responsibility for supervising the operation and maintenance of the system was lodged with the commissioners of engineering works. Out of sheer exhaustion if nothing else, bureaucratic accountability had come to rest in a single office.

Not unexpectedly, the commissioners of engineering works delegated a great deal of the actual responsibility for operating and maintaining the system to the people of Edo themselves. In the 1720s, neighborhood associations, known simply as *kumiai*, were created, one for each branch of pipeline. An individual association might be made up exclusively of merchant or artisan households, or it might include samurai residences and daimyo estates as well—whoever was served by that particular extension of the system. Each association was assessed a management fee, called "water money" (*mizugin*), and a maintenance fee (*fushinkin*), used to operate the system and to make necessary repairs to the waterways and wells that served the people in that association. The commissioners of engineering works supervised large-scale repairs that affected the entire system, and then billed each neighborhood association proportionally for the work, with payments stretched out over eight to ten years.

The pattern of jurisdictional cleavages and jumbled lines of authority and financing can be observed for a final time in regard to the construction and maintenance of Edo's nearly two hundred bridges. Things were fairly straightforward in the case of private bridges (*ittemochibashi*), which were built by a shrine or temple, a daimyo, or a wealthy merchant primarily for that person's or institution's own use, and in the case of so-called community bridges (*kumiaibashi*), which served the needs of a specific neighborhood and were constructed by local groups that, like the *kumiai* involved in the maintenance of the water supply system, were composed sometimes of both samurai and commoners. In each of these instances, the individual person, religious institution, or communal group put up the cost of construction and kept the bridge in good repair.

The story was different, however, when it came to "official bridges" (*gonyūyōbashi*), whose great spans arched far above major waterways (such as the Ryōgoku Bridge across the Sumida River) or carried major roadways over rivers, moats, and canals (such as the bridges at Nihonbashi and Kyōbashi, which were part of the great Tōkaidō highway). The shogunate financed almost all of these bridges, and the construction was carried out by the offices of building, engineering works, and lesser engineering works. Thus bridge building and river dredging were practically the only construction projects in the merchant quarters for which the shogunate appropriated funds from its own budget, preferring otherwise to spend construction money on the erection and repair of its own office buildings, the castle, and the system of protective moats.[29] Perhaps the reason that the shogunate was

29. Iijima Chiaki, "Bunkyū kaikaku-ki ni okeru bakufu zaisei jōkyō," *Tokugawa rinseishi kenkyūjo: Kenkyū kiyō* (1981), pp. 244–83; idem, "Genji-ki no bakufu zaisei," *Yokohama Shōdai*

willing to spend its own money on major spans is that such bridges were intimately intertwined with the defense of Edo Castle in the early seventeenth century, and with the economic prosperity of the entire city thereafter.

Once the major spans were in place, the shogunate supported the repair and reconstruction of some, while in other instances it assigned that financial burden to merchants and artisans who lived in the neighborhoods surrounding the bridges.[30] In all cases, however, several shogunal departments became involved: the offices of building, engineering works, and lesser engineering works all oversaw repair and reconstruction projects; the commissioners of finance, in their capacity as the watchdogs of the shogun's fisc, monitored expenditures; and the assistant inspectors (later the city magistrates) were supposed to ensure that no violent incidents or public disturbances interfered with work on the bridges. Sometimes the shogunate seemed to tire of it all. Exceptionally large spans such as the Ryōgoku Bridge were damaged frequently by the seasonally rapid currents and high waters of the rivers, and they proved very difficult to keep in good repair. In the mid–eighteenth century the shogunate threatened to pull the Ryōgoku and Eitai bridges down, but merchants near the spans complained that the loss of the bridges would hurt their businesses. The shogunate compromised by allowing the structures to stand, but it assigned the expense of repairing them to the neighborhoods surrounding them. The merchants at Eitai Bridge raised funds for this purpose by charging a small fee to each person who crossed the bridge, exempting only samurai, priests, and doctors.

CONCLUSIONS

Like the geography of Edo, the agencies of urban governance were split into zones that at various points touched, crossed, intertwined with one another, remained separate. Always the shogunate was supreme. But the shogunate itself was divided into many departments, and its instrumentalities of power did not always penetrate very far into Edo society. Nor did the agencies of the shogunate always express themselves in coercive ways. The various officials who made up the shogunate were most concerned with policing Edo; it is over that aspect of governance that the shadow of the shogunate loomed largest. The shogunate issued all legal codes, and it took care to see

ronshū 22:1 (1988), pp. 49–105; Ōno Mizuo, "Kyōhō kaikaku-ki no bakufu kanjōsho shiryō, Ōgōchi-ke kiroku," pts. 1–3, Shigaku zasshi 80:1–3 (1971), pp. 66–84, 42–64, and 39–64 respectively; idem, "Enkyō-ki no bakufu zaisei shiryō, Sakai-ke kiroku," pts. 1 and 2, Shigaku zasshi 89:6 and 7 (1980), pp. 65–89 and 64–83 respectively; Murakami Tadashi and Ōno Mizuo, "Bakumatsu ni okeru bakufu kanjōsho shiryō—Bunkyū sannen 'kin gin osame harai okanjōchō,' 'kome daizu osame harai okanjōchō' ni tsuite," Shigaku zasshi 81:4 (1972), pp. 47–70.
    30. See the examples cited in Tōkyō Shiyakusho, ed., Tōkyō shishikō: Kyōryō-hen, 2 vols. (Tōkyō Shiyakusho, 1936–1939).

that all who trespassed upon the law were brought to justice. It sent police officials out across the city, held local officials responsible for the conduct of their neighbors, and financed and managed a prison and workhouses where criminals and the potentially dangerous could be punished and perhaps even reformed.

In most other areas, however, the officials of the shogun contented themselves with laying down broad mandates, providing guidance and advice about their execution, and following up with inspections to ascertain that compliance met expected standards. As the officials with the greatest share of authority within the commoner sections of Edo, the city magistrates played a key role in carrying out decrees from above. Among other things, they were held responsible at least in an indirect way for organizing firefighting squads, overseeing the convalescent center, and regulating the savings association. But their authority was never complete. The magistrates never controlled the use of firefighting units that were made up of samurai personnel. Nor did have they have rights of direct management over the water supply and the bridges of the city.

In many important ways, the actual operation of urban institutions that most affected the lives of the ordinary residents of the city were left to the people themselves. The city elders and neighborhood chiefs supervised firefighting activities, managed the affairs of the savings association, helped keep bridges and water pipes and wells in good repair, collected taxes, and settled neighborhood disputes and quarrels. Indeed, the shogunate even relied on the elders, chiefs, and five-family groups to distribute its laws, to see that compliance was universal, and to help police their own quarters by maintaining guardhouses, wooden gates, and gate guards.

The patterns of governance evolved in this way because Edo was the administrative and commercial center of Japan. Samurai, merchants, and artisans gathered here, and under the dictates of the rule-by-status imperative, each group required its own set of laws, its own administrative structure. Here, too, were all of the important shogunal offices. Most of these officials exercised duties that were national in scope, yet their administrative obligations eventually involved most of them, in one way or another, with life in the city. In this sense, the governance of Edo must be appreciated in both of its dimensions: as a concept that spread from above but that was exercised in no small part from below.

3

Louis XIV and the Cities

William Beik

In the very heart of Tokyo sits the imperial palace, site of the former Edo Castle. Inside a colossal moat with ramparts that dwarf anything seen in Europe, vast open spaces enclose the last fragments of one of the world's most imposing seventeenth-century monuments. Across the globe in France, Louis XIV's palace and gardens of Versailles form a similar impression of artificial mastery of nature and society. Miles of formal gardens punctuated with fountains and statuary surround a palace known for its cold magnificence, with the entire ensemble of town, palace, and park orienting itself around a single, central focal point: the Sun King's bedroom. Each complex symbolizes a system of power. Edo evokes the Tokugawa rule by status, which decreed that the daimyo lords, who were themselves forced to spend alternate years in Edo away from their regional domains, lived administratively and spatially segregated from the various other categories of subjects, all ranged in a pattern of residential sectors spiraling around the castle. Versailles, in similar fashion, bespeaks the domestication of the French aristocracy in a "gilded cage," where they scrambled for favors while the Sun King undermined their authority and deprived them of their independence.

The similarities between the two cases are striking. Yet the castle at Edo lay in the very center of the system of domination, spatially and socially, whereas Versailles was built twelve miles outside the king's capital, reputedly as a way of evading dissidence on the part of groups in the city. The Tokugawa shoguns created their capital, building outward from their castle and using the city as a way to impress and control. The Sun King sidestepped his preexistent capital, creating an alternate focus for the aristocracy while trying to manipulate the other classes from a distance. Indeed, the comparison is more complex than it would appear at first glance. A closer look at the regime forged by Louis XIV can help us to explicate the relationship between power and urbanism in France, and it should suggest, as well, ways to understand that dynamic within a comparative setting. I will be arguing, first, that the development of French towns under Louis XIV was a logical expression of the nature of absolutism. Consequently, the cities have to be understood within the larger context of the nature of the Bourbon regime, and Paris within a broad environment that includes the other cities of France. Second, too much has been made of Louis XIV's centralizing, bureaucratic tendencies and not enough of his acquiescence in a traditional aristocratic society.

Despite historians' valiant efforts at redefinition, the Sun King's rule still is viewed all too frequently as an archaic personal despotism in which improved bureaucratic control facilitated increasingly arrogant assertions of state power, reducing the rest of society to obedience at the expense of the various liberties and privileges previously enjoyed. The standard view of the fate of cities is especially devastating. Louis was interested only in revenue and control. In 1683 he put the budgets and borrowing power of the municipalities under the tutelage of the intendants. In 1692 he created hereditary mayors (*maires*) with authority superior to that of elected city councils, and this was only the first round in a series of manipulations of municipal offices, election procedures, and governing councils. Descriptions of Paris sound even worse. Louis hated his capital. After the humiliating defeats of the Fronde, he constructed the court at Versailles as an alternative to living in Paris and visited the city only once or twice a year; after 1700 only four times in fifteen years.[1] To manage Paris he created in 1667 the lieutenant general of police (*lieutenant général de police*), an appointive supercommissioner who was soon operating like a modern police chief, complete with spies and powers to make arbitrary arrests. The resulting picture shows the cities as losers in a world of central direction and paternalistic manipulation. As Nora Temple put it in the most frequently cited article on the subject, Louis XIV brought about the "control and exploitation of French towns."[2]

These opinions derive from viewing the government too exclusively through the eyes of the ministers, whose archives give a misleading impression of centralization and standardization. They also reflect a failure to explore fully the implications of the phenomenon of "repression" exacting "obedience" and the hasty assumption that a group's loss of initiative meant its loss of importance.[3] Such approaches beg the question of the distribution of power socially and geographically. If Louis XIV's regime was successful, it

---

1. Leon Bernard, *The Emerging City: Paris in the Age of Louis XIV* (Durham: Duke University Press, 1970), p. 11.

2. Nora Temple, "The Control and Exploitation of French Towns during the Ancien Régime," *History* 51 (1966), pp. 16–34; reprinted in Raymond F. Kierstead, ed., *State and Society in Seventeenth-Century France* (New York: New Viewpoints, 1975), pp. 67–93.

3. Brilliant as it is, Pierre Goubert's *Louis XIV and Twenty Million Frenchmen*, trans. Anne Carter (New York: Pantheon, 1966), pp. 85–97, reproduces the traditional view of Louis repressing and controlling everything. More nuanced discussions are David Parker, *The Making of French Absolutism* (London: Edward Arnold, 1983), pp. 118–45; and Andrew Lossky, "The Absolutism of Louis XIV: Reality of Myth," *Canadian Journal of History* 19 (1984), pp. 1–15. An extreme revisionist is Roger Mettam, *Power and Faction in Louis XIV's France* (Oxford: Basil Blackwell, 1988).

was so because powerful groups in Paris and the provinces received valuable benefits even as they gave up earlier forms of autonomy, and the cities provide concrete evidence to this effect.

The key to understanding absolutism lies in the realization that French monarchs had to make peace with a preexisting society that they had increasingly infiltrated but never explicitly conquered.[4] In every province circles of powerful families were allied by lineage, clientage, or common interest. Most of these privileged notables based their influence on ownership of landed estates that gave them, in one form or another, access to much of the wealth France produced. These were no longer lords over serfs in the medieval sense and their control was checked by parallel royal institutions, but their powers over the peasantry remained considerable. They owned local law courts, dominated local political processes, and exerted economic influence by virtue of the fact that they were usually the largest renters-out of land, organizers of production, and accumulators of marketable goods. Some of these notables were traditional nobles with military pretensions. An increasing number were royal officers who had advanced socially by buying offices that conferred nobility. Such persons were doubly influential: they owned a share of royal power through their offices, and they claimed additional local influence through their estates. None of them were as powerful as the great magnates of earlier centuries, and all were dependent in one way or another on the crown for support. But organized into regional and corporate groupings, they could represent a formidable obstacle to policies that directly threatened their interests.

Through the centuries practical necessity had created procedures that became habits, then laws, stating that these people had special privileges. They were shielded from most taxes, treated differently before the law, and—often through groups—endowed with certain rights and procedures that caused them to be treated specially by the crown. These privileges were part of a long-evolving compromise between king and aristocracy. They were subject to interpretation by the crown and could be modified or abolished, but only selectively. Individuals could be punished but the king could not abrogate the *system* of privileges, nor would he have wanted to do so, because the idea of privilege was connected to the idea of a superior aptitude to rule, which constituted the theoretical justification for both king and aristocracy.

Though increasingly powerful, the monarch could not act in a truly despotic manner toward his more powerful subjects for at least three reasons. First, as indicated above, he was blocked by the system of privileges from indiscriminately tapping wealth or usurping the power to command. He could not simply rule through a bureaucracy because he had neither the resources nor the impartial bureaucrats to run it. Second, he drew part of his authority from the Catholic church, a vast network of interlocking organisms

4. Of course there had been military conquests of towns and provinces through the ages, but never a true subjection of the whole country like William the Conqueror's conquest of England, and for every area subdued another always received favors.

staffed with relatives of the same families that made up the rest of the elite, but tied to an organization that had international connections and a special moral authority, even over the king. Third, he never had enough armed force at his disposal to subjugate more than a few sections of the country at a time, largely because he constantly was involved in foreign wars as a consequence of France's extensive borders and the machinations of rival monarchs, who distracted the Sun King from internal affairs.

We must therefore think of the royal authority as reaching out to influence regional power centers through a triangular system of distinct, competing channels of influence; namely, the church, the royal courts, and the municipal governments.[5] Bishops, appointed for life by the crown and often resident at court, maintained complex ties with local cathedral chapters, religious houses, and ecclesiastical bureaucracies, and through them with the public. Royal courts, which interpreted and enforced the king's laws, were vehicles for both the dissemination of royal influence and the intervention of prestigious families of robe nobles. City governments, usually a committee of merchants or wealthy royal officers, served as intermediaries between crown and community through occupational associations (guilds) or local citizen militia companies. These three channels of influence—ecclesiastical, judicial, municipal—were cemented by client ties, common connections to the profitable tax-collecting mechanisms, and constant exchanges of loyalty and favors. The great originality of Louis XIV's regime was that for the first time royal institutions such as the system of ministers and intendants could coordinate on a higher, national level the overlapping, conflicting local interests—especially those that transcended the corporate concerns of single groups.

The cities, and above all Paris, were the arenas where most of this maneuvering took place. Given the rising power of Louis XIV and his incessant need for resources, it is not surprising that he exploited towns whenever he could. But the king's policies were pragmatic and had mixed effects. He certainly insisted on better cooperation from recalcitrant bodies. A rebellious *parlement*, a recalcitrant town council, a quarrelsome bishop might need to be disciplined, but he could usually resolve such problems by favoring rival authorities on the local level. When generation of tax revenues was the primary concern, the solution might be to encourage manufacturing by helping merchants evade the conservative oligarchies' stranglehold on municipal affairs. But it might just as well call for ruining the local economy by demanding large "gifts," or selling offices and privileges that *enhanced* the power of the very same oligarchs. The king also needed to establish and supply garrisons, fortresses, or naval stations in deliberately chosen cen-

5. This discussion is influenced by Emmanuel Le Roy Ladurie, "Réflexions sur l'essence et le fonctionnement de la monarchie classique (XVIe–XVIIIe siècles)," in Henry Méchoulan, ed., *L'état baroque: Regards sur la pensée politique de la France du premier XVIIe siècle* (Paris: Vrin, 1985), pp. ix–xxxv; and Denis Richet, *La France moderne: L'esprit des institutions* (Paris: Flammarion, 1973).

ters.[6] These measures could be expensive, but a garrison could make the fortune of the town where it was located and relieve the citizens of the more arbitrary lodgings of the past. In Besançon, annexed to France in 1674, royal conquest turned out to be an advantage because the city became the provincial capital at the expense of its perennial rival, Dôle, and obtained a *parlement*, a new *bailliage* court, a citadel and barracks, a seminary, a hospital, and an infusion of prosperous robe nobles into the community.[7] Another concern was public order. Seventeenth-century towns were organized around a precarious set of arrangements designed to keep the general population relatively quiescent. Here the king's intendants were particularly useful, and their new administrative expertise would serve the local elites as well as the royal need for obedience.

The way these objectives were pursued in any town depended on circumstances, always with as much regard as possible for hierarchy, privilege, and the interplay of private interests.[8] Cities that prospered did so largely because royal and aristocratic needs could be brought into a satisfactory balance; less important to urban growth than one might have expected were the expansion of production for the marketplace and the rise of a merchant bourgeoisie. We must remember that the seventeenth century was not an age of spectacular urban growth. Jan de Vries calls the 1650–1750 period one of urban restructuring, and Philip Benedict's figures show that in France a whole range of cities actually declined in population, while others stagnated.[9] Those that expanded were likely to be administrative centers such as the provincial capitals, which were growing because a new concentration of venal officeholders stimulated service industries while attracting auxiliary lawyers, notaries, and clerks. The Catholic revival was past its peak, but bishops and abbots participated fully in the construction of more elegant episcopal palaces and residence halls. All these people identified ever more closely with the monarch, whose power gave them the ability to participate in the monitoring and channeling of resources and the authority to dominate their communities. Regional capitals reflected the success of this inner circle of influential families. Townhouses became larger and more ostentatious,

6. André Corvisier, "Le pouvoir militaire et les villes," in Georges Livet and Bernard Vogler, eds., *Pouvoir, ville et société en Europe, 1650–1750* (Paris: Ophrys, 1983), pp. 11–20.

7. Maurice Gresset, "De la ville impériale à la capitale de la Franche-Comté: Besançon dans la seconde moitié du XVIIᵉ siècle," in Livet and Vogler, *Pouvoir*, pp. 591–98. Note also François Bluche, *Louis XIV* (Paris: Fayard, 1986), p. 195.

8. A good synthesis is Georges Duby, ed., *Histoire de la France urbaine*, vol. 3: Emmanuel Le Roy Ladurie, ed., *La ville classique de la Renaissance aux révolutions* (Paris: Seuil, 1981). See also the essays in Philip Benedict, ed., *Cities and Social Change in Early Modern France* (London: Unwin Hyman, 1989).

9. Jan de Vries, *European Urbanization, 1500–1800* (Cambridge: Harvard University Press, 1984), pp. 257–58. My summation owes much to Philip Benedict, "French Cities from the Sixteenth Century to the Revolution, an Overview," in his *Cities and Social Change*, pp. 7–68. Also helpful is Josef W. Konvitz, "Does the Century 1650–1750 Constitute a Period in Urban History? The French Evidence Reviewed," *Journal of Urban History* 14 (1988), pp. 419–54.

and elegant living reached new heights. Even country nobles began to frequent such urban *hôtels* in preference to rural châteaux, while robe and sword elites with increasingly similar lifestyles tended to buy up lands around such provincial capitals and to channel the resultant rural rents into urban consumption.

A good example is Dijon as described by James Farr; a community whose artisans grew prosperous serving *parlementaires* and regional grain suppliers just at the time when the more industrial weaving trades were declining.[10] A similar case was Toulouse, where the increasing interventions of the intendant and the crippling financial burden caused by the repeated sale of municipal offices between 1685 and 1722 hardly dampened the élan of the leading families as they collaborated in the planning of a public square to display the equestrian statue of the king and the construction of a new *capitole*, complete with a *salle des illustres* to celebrate their own fame. Meanwhile, they lent the city money at interest, providing themselves with a safe investment at public expense.[11] In Rouen industrial decline was overcome by the continuing importance of an oligarchy that maintained its hold over the town government and even scored gains against its rivals in the courts, thanks to a royal balancing act that was restricting the influence of the *parlement*. In Amiens, another industrial stronghold where cloth weaving was reviving, Colbert used the sale of municipal offices as a way of helping true merchant families undermine the power of the judicial oligarchs who had kept a stranglehold on economic progress for most of the century. In Nîmes, where Colbert's protectionist policies aided the takeoff of the silk fabric and hosiery industries that would generate an industrial boom in the eighteenth century, there was little aristocratic building in the historic center of town precisely because Nîmes lacked the ambitious officer class that lived by ostentation in such places as Toulouse and Rouen, and the principal new town embellishment was the palace of the bishop.[12]

In Lyon, which enjoyed a population increase of almost a third during the reign of Louis XIV as a result of the rapidly expanding silk-weaving industry, the municipal magistrates (*échevins*) had to manage a city with a large semiproletariat of silk weavers who represented potentially devastating social problems.[13] These officials were consequently very important per-

10. James R. Farr, *Hands of Honor: Artisans and Their World in Dijon, 1550–1650* (Ithaca: Cornell University Press, 1988); and his useful synthesis, "Consumers, Commerce, and the Craftsmen of Dijon: The Changing Social and Economic Structure of a Provincial Capital, 1450–1750," in Benedict, *Cities and Social Change*, pp. 134–73.

11. Robert A. Schneider, "Crown and Capitoulat: Municipal Government in Toulouse, 1500–1789," in Benedict, *Cities and Social Change*, pp. 195–220; and Philippe Wolff, *Histoire de Toulouse*, 2d ed. (Toulouse: Privat, 1961).

12. Jean-Pierre Bardet, *Rouen aux XVIIe et XVIIIe siècles: Les mutations d'un espace social* (Paris: SEDES, 1983), pp. 99–104; Pierre Deyon, *Amiens capitale provinciale: Etude sur la société urbaine au 17e siècle* (Paris: Mouton, 1967), pp. 430–32, 457–59; and Line Teisseyre-Sallmann, "Urbanisme et société: L'exemple de Nîmes aux XVIIe et XVIIIe siècles," *Annales E.S.C.* 35 (1980), pp. 965–66, 976.

13. André Latreille, ed., *Histoire de Lyon et du Lyonnais* (Toulouse: Privat, 1975), pp. 160–

sonages, all the more so in that they faced no rivalry from a *parlement* or a military garrison. By virtue of their office they acquired hereditary nobility and total exemption from local taxes. Since Henry IV their elections had been manipulated by agents of the king, but they were nevertheless powerful figures who succeeded in maintaining managerial control over the city by reconciling the interests of the merchants and artisanal consumers they represented with the fiscal demands of the crown. Their secret was an effective system of client relationships that linked them to the royal ministers in Paris. The municipality maintained a permanent "agent" there to lobby on behalf of the city and a "deputy" who traveled to Paris for specific negotiations whenever business required, accompanied on occasion by the provost (*prévôt*) or another *échevin*. Weekly letters between Paris and Lyon discussed court cases, political business, and lobbying efforts. Meanwhile the city was managed from Paris by an incredible dynasty, the Neuville-Villeroy family, which controlled the post of governor of Lyon and the Lyonnais from 1626 to 1789, the archbishopric from 1653 to 1693, and the office of military lieutenant general. Nicolas de Neuville, duc de Villeroy, was the young Louis XIV's personal governor and a commander in many of the king's battles; his son François, brother of the archbishop, became the personal governor of the young Louis XV and a major figure in the regency. They knew everyone of importance in Lyon, influenced the elections, and took the city agents under their wings; yet at the same time they remained loyal servants of the crown who were able to conciliate local, personal, and national interests. This system illustrates the centralization of influence through the personal ties of local elites with national aristocrats.

Finally, the port cities such as Bordeaux and Nantes were emerging as entrepôts for the colonial trade of the eighteenth century. The most interesting such place is Saint-Malo, Louis XIV's greatest boom town. Between 1650 and 1700 this Breton city increased its population by a third and its wealth many times over. It became France's busiest port in the 1680s, then enjoyed windfall profits during the war of 1689–1713, becoming momentarily what André Lespagnol calls a "true world port."[14] Saint-Malo's secret was that rarest of assets in early-modern France, a truly indigenous and dynamic merchant bourgeoisie, coupled—again—with special royal contacts. Throughout the period from 1500 to 1750 the same local families, reinforced by money and talent from other Breton towns, developed special expertise in the fisheries off Newfoundland and the Spanish Atlantic ports.

This success lay outside the context of Colbert's great merchant projects, and it took place in an unpromising urban environment. Politically Saint-Malo was a small fortified city, deprived of a municipal government and

---

61, 202, 235–36; Maurice Garden, "Formes de contrôle du pouvoir locale: Lyon en 1721," and Jean-Pierre Gutton, "Les députés de la ville de Lyon en cour," both in Livet and Vogler, *Pouvoir*, pp. 173–82 and 183–90 respectively.

14. André Lespagnol, ed., *Histoire de Saint-Malo et du pays malouin* (Toulouse: Privat, 1984), pp. 81–132.

dominated by the joint lordship of the bishop and the cathedral chapter. This lack of autonomy simply channeled energies toward the sea: "Saint-Malo has neither a présidial court nor any manufacturing. The city is populated with merchant bankers who have been raised in commerce from father to son," stated a memoir in 1701.[15] As elsewhere, Louis XIV's intendant established control over municipal finances, while the sale of offices milked the town of funds. Vauban himself drew up plans to refortify the city and a major urban renovation actually was carried out, mostly under the impetus of outsiders.

During the new boom of 1689 to 1717 fortunes were made from privateering, from trade with Peruvian ports reached via new sea routes around Cape Horn, and from the ability of local merchants to assume the defunct East India Company's rights to trade in the Indian Ocean. But these conquests were possible only because of close alliances between the merchant community in Saint-Malo and the authorities in Versailles. Colbert's nephew Desmarets became bishop of Saint-Malo in 1702, at the same time that the town was enjoying preferential treatment from the Pontchartrains, father and son, secretaries of the navy. The Pontchartrains facilitated the charters and financial contacts needed to fund the Peruvian expeditions and to win the monopoly in the East Indies. The importance of these relationships is underlined by the subsequent fate of the city. Trade with Peru was later banned by the king, privateering ended with the war, and the Pontchartrains' influence was eliminated by the regent, whose ally John Law took the East Indies trade away from Saint-Malo. In the eighteenth century the city fell back on its traditional resources, and its merchant oligarchs settled back to become rentier nobles allied with the provincial nobility.

A parallel story can be told about Marseille, which, paradoxically, also became the classic case of *louisquatorzian* repression. As a proud city, independent even of the province of Provence, Marseille established an unrivaled reputation for turbulence and insubordination in the first half of the seventeenth century. Dominated by groups of nobles loosely representing the landed interests of creditors on the one hand and maritime commercial interests on the other, local factions and their plebeian followers created "an ambiance of dictatorships, conspiracies, and revolutions in the Italian manner."[16] All of this changed in 1660, when Louis XIV arrived with an army and ended the city's long tradition of insubordination and rebellion. Military occupation, prosecution of the former leaders, symbolic destruction of the walls, construction of two fortresses dominating the harbor, and replacement of the consular regime were all measures symbolizing the end of an age of autonomy. This is the sort of takeover we expect from Louis XIV.

But the curious thing about this repression was that while it ended an era of colorful factional combat and began a period of heavier taxation and new

15. Ibid., p. 95.
16. Edouard Baratier, ed., *Histoire de Marseille* (Toulouse: Privat, 1973), pp. 163–66, 190–96; quotation, 230. See also René Pillorget, *Les mouvements insurrectionnels de Provence entre 1598 et 1715* (Paris: Pedone, 1975).

indebtedness, it also inaugurated a golden age of merchant prosperity. The king's reforms excluded the traditional noble families from office and enfranchised the commercial bourgeoisie. Taxes now spared commercial merchandise, and in 1669 the city was given a coveted duty-free status that virtually guaranteed it a monopoly on the Levant trade. Many of Colbert's special trading companies for the Levant failed, but the city nevertheless enjoyed moderate prosperity until the 1690s and then took off after 1700 in some of the same directions as Saint-Malo, but with more consistency. Once again, Louis XIV's policies cleared the way and provided opportunities for a city already experienced and well placed.

For the towns, progress meant association with one or more royal programs. Some remained dominated by medieval lords. Others saw the triumph of a sovereign court or a merchant oligarchy. What all had in common was a new validation of power associated with the crown and a lessening of the impact of alternative forces. The result was aristocratic construction, a flowering of Jesuit schools and church foundations, the opening of parklike extensions outside the old walls, and the triumph of an aristocratic form of finance tied to royal office, tax farms, and delegated advantage. There was a blossoming of the industries that supplied these activities, including handling of grain and basic foodstuffs, but not much innovation. Trade and commerce were secondary, but they also grew where royal policies left them some room. The towns became less independent, but the people who ruled them had a better hold over them. France's cities, taken collectively, were accurate reflections of the various aspects of a larger society built on adulation of superiority but grounded in familiar local agencies, provided those agencies continued to cooperate with one another.

Paris was a real metropolis of 500,000 people—the largest city in Europe, capital of the most powerful monarchy of its day, and thus in certain ways qualitatively different from a Rouen or a Marseilles.[17] Yet the capital plays remarkably little part in historians' perception of the reign, as if the propaganda from Versailles and the memoirs of a small circle of aristocrats could successfully obliterate the realities of half a million lives. Paris was, in fact, central to everything connected to Louis XIV.[18] The city was immense and expanding, especially to the west, as conscious policy and the interests of financier-investors dictated. The old walls to the north were torn down and replaced by boulevards in the 1670s, demilitarizing but opening up the city; and new fashionable quarters began spreading outward toward the west.

17. This account of Paris is based on Bernard, *Emerging City*; Orest Ranum, *Paris in the Age of Absolutism* (New York: Wiley, 1968); Roland Mousnier, *Paris capitale au temps de Richelieu et de Mazarin* (Paris: Pedone, 1978); Jacques Wilhelm, *La vie quotidienne des Parisiens au temps du Roi-Soleil, 1660–1715* (Paris: Hachette, 1977); Jacques Saint-Germain, *La Reynie et la police au grand siècle* (Paris: Hachette, 1962). On population and growth, see Daniel Roche, *The People of Paris: An Essay on Popular Culture in the 18th Century*, trans. Marie Evans (Berkeley: University of California Press, 1987), pp. 11–16, 19–21.

18. Many historians have pointed this out; for example, Wilhelm, *Vie quotidienne*, pp. 15–20; and François Bluche, *La vie quotidienne au temps de Louis XIV* (Paris: Hachette, 1984), pp. 79–118.

With the exception of the king's immediate councils, all the institutions of the various hierarchies of power were located in the heart of the capital. These included five sovereign courts, all the lesser courts, the university, at least thirteen abbeys and 200-odd religious orders, four "hospitals" enclosing at least 6,000 indigent persons, the royal academies, the royal manufactures (700 workers at the Gobelins tapestry works alone), and the Invalides, a magnificent new military hospital holding 7,000 disabled veterans, opened in 1677. All the royal ministers had *hôtels* in the city, and all the artists, architects, and writers who constructed the Sun King's cultural legacy lived there. Louis was not fond of Paris, to be sure, and he ceased to be resident there after 1671, but it was during his reign that triumphal perspectives and more ambitious uses of ordered space opened up the tight, walled city inherited from Louis XIII.[19] A number of familiar features were laid out: the ring of inner boulevards, the triumphal arches, the axis of the Champs Elysées intersecting the axis of the Invalides, the Pont Royal by the Tuileries, the Observatory, numerous fountains, the real estate developments to the west revolving around the Place des Victoires and the Place Louis-le-Grand (Vendôme), and the colonnade of the Louvre. Paris certainly reflected the grandeur of the Sun King more than any provincial city, and although there was no sharp break with the past, still it would be fair to say that the contours of the international capital that would dominate Europe until World War I were geographically and institutionally delineated during his reign.

In any event, it is immaterial how much effort the king personally spent on Paris; the issue, as always, was the effect of king *and* aristocracy, and here the influence was immense. The city was buzzing with notables who held offices in all the bodies mentioned above, and it was a basic pole of attraction even for families who frequented Versailles. It is remarkably easy to forget the aristocratic presence in Paris.[20] By 1715 it had 189 notable *hôtels*, a regular salon life involving several thousand people, seven royal academies, and a new theatrical tradition. The reconstituted companies of the Opéra and the Comédie-Française staged 800 representations per year, for which audiences paid a million livres for tickets. Twenty thousand carriages transported nobles and aspiring bourgeois back and forth from these places. As one historian put it, Parisian salons "represented so many smaller courts in the absence of the royal court, so many places for meetings between great lords, gentlemen, great bourgeois and men of letters who could not have met each other at Versailles."[21] Philippe d'Orléans, the king's brother and founder of the Orléans dynasty, took over the Palais Royal, a block from the Tuileries, redecorated it, and filled it with Gobelins tapestries and paintings by Van

19. On Louis XIV's relationship with Paris, see Orest Ranum, "The Court and the Capital of Louis XIV: Some Definitions and Reflections," in John C. Rule, ed., *Louis XIV and the Craft of Kingship* (Columbus: Ohio State University Press, 1969), pp. 265–85.

20. On the dual residency of aristocrats, see Emile Magne, *Images de Paris sous Louis XIV* (Paris: Calmann-Lévy, 1939), pp. 111–25.

21. Wilhelm, *Vie quotidienne*, p. 246.

Dyck, Titian, Tintoretto, Mignard, and Veronese. There he maintained a household of more than a thousand retainers and servants. This complex of buildings and gardens, whose master was often at odds with the king, became the hub of fashionable Paris. Even Saint-Simon reported that "there was always a crowd at the Palais Royal."[22] A new style of urban sociability was developing among the rich and well placed, involving enclosed vehicles, promenades on fashionable terraces, and reciprocal visits; Versailles was really only the pinnacle of attainment for a lucky few out of a much wider society of fashion.

In political terms Louis XIV is often presented as having taken over Paris by instituting the first modern system of police. This view is correct only if it is understood in the proper early-modern context. By the 1660s Paris was large enough to offer unprecedented problems of governance, and it had no coordinated way of dealing with them. Contemporaries blamed the rapid expansion of the city for all manner of evil: intense crowding, pollution, inadequate supplies of food and water, and an abundance of criminal elements. The traditional structure of overlapping, competing authorities was incapable of handling such a large agglomeration, and many of these authorities were under a cloud of suspicion for their activities during the Fronde.

But the young king of the 1660s was determined to seize control of the situation. In 1666 Colbert established a ministerial *conseil de police*, and by March 1667 the crown had created the post of lieutenant general of police, endowing the new agent with vast powers of regulation and surveillance. The first titular, Gabriel Nicolas de La Reynie (served 1667–1697), was a president from the présidial of Bordeaux. His successor, René Voyer de Paulmy d'Argenson (1697–1718), was from an eminent family of nobles and officers. Both proved to be geniuses at managing the city effectively and repressing disorder, with full support from the king and the royal council. Aided by the forty-eight commissioners of the Châtelet and a growing team of spies who reported on what was being said in cafés and taverns, they reorganized squads of patrolmen to provide security at night in the city, instituted a vast system of street lighting, arranged for better methods of waste disposal, experimented with firefighting patrols, and monitored street repairs. The amount of paved roadway probably doubled between 1662 and 1707. There were struggles with the Hôtel de Ville over funding, but the king did pay the new, higher salaries for the night patrolmen and for certain street-paving projects. In addition, the lieutenants general of police played a major role in the repression of scandalous behavior and unscrupulous schemes and in the regulation of markets and shops. Gradually the forty-eight commissioners were induced to keep archives, patrol their quarters, and send in regular reports about local disorders. Weekly meetings were held to draft police ordinances.[23]

22. Nancy Nichols Barker, *Brother to the Sun King: Philippe, Duke of Orléans* (Baltimore: Johns Hopkins University Press, 1989), pp. 81–84, 166–69; quotation, 168.

23. Philip F. Riley, "Hard Times, Police, and the Making of Public Policy in the Paris of Louis XIV," *Historical Reflections* 10 (1983), pp. 313–34.

As the reign progressed, social control and the enforcement of public morality were increasingly centralized. The reorganization of the Hôpital Général in 1657 had placed five hospitals under the control of a committee of laymen, which was soon taken over by the crown. By the end of the reign the king was administering "the largest social program for indigents attempted since Roman times," under which beggars and, increasingly, the sick and infirm were locked up in vast compounds.[24] In 1667 La Reynie marched several hundred armed men into the Cour des Miracles, traditional haven of an underworld of pickpockets and thieves, and cleaned them out. In 1684 the king ordered that prostitutes be locked up. In 1690 he reorganized the administration of all the hospitals that handled the sick under a committee called the Grand Bureau, headed by the archbishop of Paris, the first presidents of the sovereign courts, the provost of merchants (*prévôt des marchands*), and the lieutenant general of police. More and more information was collected and discussed concerning the monitoring and running of this great, sprawling mass of humanity, and much attention was given to the policing of morals: gambling dens, places of prostitution, family problems, even convents.

These measures, however, did not amount to a takeover of the city. Once again, as in the provinces, the issue of autonomy should not be allowed to obscure the issue of social control. We must remember, first, that Paris always had been a royal city and never had possessed an independent charter.[25] Its government historically was divided between the Hôtel de Ville and the Châtelet (or *prévôté*), a law court with regulatory powers representing the king's justice. The Hôtel de Ville was not a true city government, and it never had been. Its elections were a formality, for it was well known at least since the time of Henry II that the king customarily indicated in advance his choice for the provost of merchants (the equivalent of mayor), in much the same way that governors or intendants intervened in many provincial towns. The provost and *échevins* thus represented an institutional point of contact between the crown on the one hand and a circle of leading merchant families, especially those in the six most important guilds, on the other. The jurisdiction of the Hôtel de Ville had always been limited. The municipality had control over river traffic. It handled taxes levied on the city and loans guaranteed by the city (*rentes sur l'hôtel de ville*)—here again providing a collective entity to negotiate with and be used by the crown. It also commanded a network of unpaid *quarteniers* and *dizainiers*, the officers of the citizen militia traditionally found in each neighborhood. But these civic com-

24. Ranum, *Paris in the Age of Absolutism*, pp. 229–51; quotation, 247.
25. For additional historical background see Barbara B. Diefendorf, *Paris City Councillors in the Sixteenth Century: The Politics of Patrimony* (Princeton: Princeton University Press, 1983), pp. 3–29; and three illuminating essays by Robert Descimon: "L'échevinage parisien sous Henri IV (1594–1609)," in Neithard Bulst and Jean-Philippe Genet, eds., *La ville, la bourgeoisie et la genèse de l'état moderne (XIIᵉ–XVIIIᵉ siècles)* (Paris: CNRS, 1988), pp. 113–50; "Paris on the Eve of Saint Bartholomew: Taxation, Privileges, and Social Geography," in Benedict, *Cities and Social Change*, pp. 69–104; and (with Jean Nagle) "Les quartiers de Paris du moyen age au XVIIIᵉ siècle: Evolution d'un espace plurifonctionnel," *Annales E.S.C.* 34 (1979), pp. 956–83.

panies, once powerful neighborhood pressure groups, were now largely ceremonial, and their offices had been made venal under Louis XIII. In a sense they were superseded by the new administration of the lieutenant general of police and the commissioners, especially after the city and police *quartiers* were reorganized into more rational districts between 1680 and 1702. The commissioners provided better service at the expense of the participatory aspect that had characterized the traditional neighborhood organization. Thus the Hôtel de Ville was in no sense a representative body, even before Louis XIV reduced its influence. Nor was it intended to be. The king had always ruled Paris by negotiating with various corporate representatives, and he had always had the upper hand.

The rival of the Hôtel de Ville was the Châtelet, which was the equivalent of the royal *bailliage* court elsewhere and held much of the authority to regulate commerce and criminal activity on land, making for endless conflicts of jurisdiction with the *échevins*, the Parlement of Paris, and other special courts. In addition there were over fifty seigneurial enclaves in the city where private lords or corporate bodies held sway, including the archbishop and chapter of Notre-Dame, the Temple, the Louvre, the Palais Royal, the abbeys of Saint-Jean-de-Latran, Saint-Germain-des-Prés, and Sainte-Geneviève, the Bastille, the Parlement, and many more whose various owners held lucrative powers to authorize business enterprises, harbor fugitives, organize markets, manage construction permits, and fine or try people accused of infractions. Hundreds of Parisian streets "belonged" to various seigneurs, so that uniform justice was completely impossible.[26] In 1674 Louis XIV suppressed nineteen of the most important such jurisdictions, but the law could not be enforced and most of the major enclaves managed to regain most of their prerogatives.

When allowances are made for the greater size of Paris and its proximity to the royal person, its government does not look very different from those of the provincial cities. Jurisdiction here as elsewhere was shared by a municipal oligarchy in the Hôtel de Ville and several royal law courts. There were ecclesiastical complications and other special jurisdictions. To be sure, the king and his council, representing the source of the power of command, were close at hand. But the lieutenants of police, attached judicially to the Châtelet but with regulatory powers transcending those of all the other authorities, were nothing more than powerful coordinators. They were really the "intendants" of Paris, and like the rest of the intendants, they complained constantly about the magnitude of their responsibilities and the inadequacy of their resources. With a minimum of assistance, they were expected to see to sanitation, the control of disease, the water supply, building regulations, prices, fairs and markets, sumptuary laws, and the morals of a variety of individuals. Fortunately these regulatory matters called especially for information gathering and intelligent advising—the special talents

26. On seigneurial jurisdictions, see Alan Williams, "The Police and the Administration of Eighteenth-Century Paris," *Journal of Urban History* 4 (1978), pp. 157–82; Bernard, *Emerging City*, pp. 35–38, 46–47.

of such administrators. But when things had to get done, they had no choice but to collaborate with the other authorities, often through high-level committees sanctioned by the king.

A look at the voluminous correspondence between Argenson and the royal ministers in the later years of the reign conveys two overwhelming impressions about the crown's relationship with the capital. First is the regulatory impulse. Here, as in the provinces, the emphasis was not on taking over but on imposing authority to make things work smoothly, an impulse that could lead to repression but could also foster a conservative hesitancy to upset vested interests. Thus Argenson worked on locating and punishing the producers of contraband printed fabrics to protect the authorized manufacturers, and he tried to head off any measures that might cause the cost of basic commodities in the markets to rise. He supported the introduction of stocking frames by the master stocking makers—obviously a desirable technical advance—but at the same time he wanted to limit strictly the number of frames produced so that old-fashioned knitters who were very poor would not be put out of business, and he railed at the stocking makers of the faubourg Saint-Antoine who were not observing his limitations. He was constantly worrying that supplies would be inadequate, groups would cause disturbances, innovations would harm the public: if the number of peddlers was reduced, he warned, "it is to be feared that they might start complaining with that insolent tone that causes uprisings."[27]

A second impulse was the crown's desire to raise funds by selling exemptions and privileges, even though this practice often complicated Argenson's job: "I have noticed that those who exercise a trade by virtue of a privilege [special dispensation] are harder to discipline than those who do it by virtue of being a master [in a guild]." It was sometimes hard, the police lieutenant said on another occasion, "to reconcile the interests of finance with those of our police."[28] The issue was not whether to impose regulations but whom to favor. Choices were always being made between protecting a traditional organization and selling an exemption to its jurisdiction. The former facilitated policing by strengthening an existing corporate body, whereas the latter enhanced the mystique of proximity to the monarch by according new privileges to someone else. The government constantly was being besieged by courtiers acting as fronts for cartels of financiers peddling lucrative projects. Frequently there was tension between the royal power to create new privileges and the needs of traditional corporate bodies. Argenson was forever pointing out the detrimental effects of one special action or another, as when Madame la Maréchale de Coeuvres set up a lottery of merchandise in the enclave of Saint-Germain-des-Prés; her lottery, Argenson moaned, would ruin the regular merchants.[29]

27. A. M. de Boislisle, ed., *Correspondance des contrôleurs-généraux des finances avec les intendants des provinces*, 3 vols. (Paris: Imprimerie Nationale, 1874–1897), vol. 2, nos. 321, 641, 855, 326, 435, 1164, 1216, 1314; quotation, no. 435.

28. Ibid., nos. 333, 326.

29. Ibid., no. 889.

It is worth pointing out that all this regulation was designed to make Paris an aristocratic city par excellence. The English visitor Martin Lister marveled in 1698 that "all the houses of persons of distinction are built with *porte-cocheres*, that is, wide gates to drive in a coach, and consequently have courts within. . . . There are reckoned above 700 of these great gates," and he noted that "here the palaces and convents have eat up the peoples dwellings, and crowded them excessively together, and possessed themselves of far the greatest part of the ground; whereas in London the contrary may be observed that the people have destroyed the palaces. . . ."[30] The new urban projects were no longer enclosed squares punctuating the crowded streets, such as the Place Royale and the Place Dauphine of Henry IV's time, but vast, impersonal spaces framing a major monument such as the Invalides or providing alleys for promenades *en carosse*, in the manner of the parks of rural châteaux, which tended to reach outward from the center as if to conquer new territory. The two speculative real estate projects of the reign, the Place des Victoires and the Place Louis-le-Grand, were grandiose combinations of adulation of the Sun King with shrewd speculation by financiers, orchestrated at court. Both combined aristocratic initiative with royal grants, extracted subsidies from the Hôtel de Ville, and profited financiers tied to privileges from Versailles.[31]

The same aristocratic tone dominated other projects. Daniel Roche reminds us that under Louis XIV Paris daily had about two thousand cubic meters of running water provided by Henry IV's Arcueil aqueduct and by several pumps in the Seine, the upkeep of which was paid for by a tax on all consumers of wine. More than half of this water, however, went to supply the gardens of the Tuileries, the Louvre, the Luxembourg, and the properties of two hundred individuals who received from the king the privilege of siphoning it off from the public pipes. Of the water going to private parties, one-third went to religious and educational establishments, two-fifths to *parlementaires, échevins*, and other important individuals, and one-fourth to court aristocrats and royal ministers.[32] When a system of public coaches was inaugurated in 1662 on behalf of a group of noble investors, including the king's cupbearer and the governor of Poitou, soldiers, pages, lackeys, and artisans were forbidden to ride in them.[33] Depending on their station in life, persons who caused public scandal were variously sent to the Bastille (for aristocrats) or the Hôpital Général (for indigents).

The reign of Louis XIV brought a touch of grandeur to the cities of France as well as greater integration into a larger society. But if we look at the cities as places for the autonomous development of merchant capitalism or as

---

30. Martin Lister, *A Journey to Paris in the Year 1698*, ed. Raymond Phineas Stearns (Urbana: University of Illinois Press, 1967), pp. 9, 7.

31. Bernard, *Emerging City*, pp. 18–21.

32. Daniel Roche, "Le temps de l'eau rare: Du moyen âge à l'époque moderne," *Annales E.S.C.* 39 (1984), pp. 383–99.

33. Bernard, *Emerging City*, pp. 64–65.

seedbeds of political liberty, we are bound to be disappointed. Economic growth, if any, was slow and uncoordinated in this period. France had no unified national market. Unlike Edo (or London), Paris was not a major port and could not serve as the coordinating center of national economic life. France's busiest mercantile cities were located on the extremities of the territory, looking outward, and each region was semi-autonomous.[34] The clearest pattern therefore was growth related to the activity of the state through the creation of offices, the expansion of finance, and the reorganization of the military. This growth hardly ever coincided with the expansion of trade or manufacturing, although development did take place in such cities as Lyon and Nîmes, where the aristocratic element was less strong and the proper conditions presented themselves. Similarly port cities flourished where the necessary naval or tariff support happened to correspond to royal foreign policy goals.

It makes more sense to view France's cities as dispersed authority centers where groups of advantageously situated aristocrats interacted with a state that was beginning to coordinate their interests more effectively. French absolutism was distributive in the sense that whereas power emanated theoretically from the crown, it was exercised through regional centers where concentrations of powerful subjects competed for shares of authority. The king could rule only by delegating power to indigenous notables who had local pull; the notables could function only with royal support. Louis XIV's effect on the cities was hardly just "control and exploitation," because in every town a group of leading families was enjoying unprecedented security in the name of the king.[35]

Previously these individuals, whose power derived from various forms of locally based wealth and influence, had struggled to maintain their positions vis-à-vis each other, the populations below them, and the monarchy.[36] The absolute monarch helped them. His intendants became great coordinators of their relationships, as were the ministerial committees that so often attempted to conciliate competing vested interests. The Parisian *conseil de police* was a case in point, along with meetings concerning poor relief in Paris and certain consultations over financial reform. The *conseil de commerce*, established in 1700 to coordinate the interests of merchant oligarchies all over France, was a prime example too.[37] This was not consultation in the sense of representation but effective administration incorporating the opinions of the

34. On the national system, see Fernand Braudel, *The Perspective of the World*, trans. Siân Reynolds (New York: Harper & Row, 1986), pp. 315–35.

35. The logic of this situation is brilliantly explored for the eighteenth century in Gail Bossenga, "City and State: An Urban Perspective on the Origins of the French Revolution," in Keith Michael Baker, ed., *The Political Culture of the Old Regime* (Oxford: Oxford University Press, 1987), pp. 115–40.

36. William Beik, *Absolutism and Society in Seventeenth-Century France: State Power and Provincial Aristocracy in Languedoc* (Cambridge: Cambridge University Press, 1985), pp. 307–12.

37. Thomas J. Schaeper, *The French Council of Commerce, 1700–1715: A Study of Mercantilism after Colbert* (Columbus: Ohio State University Press, 1983).

elites concerned. To be sure, there were many losers in this contest, which was anything but democratic. Louis XIV narrowed participation, increased social distance, came down hard on dissidence, persecuted Jansenists and Huguenots, and massacred Camisard rebels in the south. By the end of the reign poverty and social discontent were rampant, and economic disruption resulting from excessive warfare and ruinous taxation had blackened the regime. But for the privileged elites a new ideological message was being transmitted. The king would protect the interests of the best-placed groups and individuals if they would let him have the power to define their privileges and monitor their activities. Instead of flailing at one another, the various groups were to learn a common frame of reference. In short, the reign of Louis XIV brought together the rudiments of the society we associate with the eighteenth century. The aristocratic style of the Enlightenment was a continuation of the Sun King's reign, not an aristocratic reaction against it.

This process raises interesting questions about state building and urbanism in Edo. In both France and Japan powerful rulers were attempting to centralize their control over a diverse and unruly society, but in France the king seems to have had to do much more accommodating. Louis XIV's relationship with Paris was symptomatic of the whole polity. The monarchy and the privileged groups had grown up together, mutually influencing one another. The size of the country as well as the distribution of national wealth had always required the king to transfer a share of power back to the persons he had just subdued. Paris was a gigantic organism, growing under its own momentum and containing all the social compromises that made up the absolute monarchy. There could be no building from scratch, no systematic reorganization of the city in the manner of the spiral layout at Edo.

Indeed, the French situation seems to have differed from the Japanese in several respects, although a full exploration of them must be left for further research. In the first place, the French kings never dominated France's systems of production, which were partly in the hands of privileged landowners and partly dominated by merchants in scattered regional capitals; unlike Edo, Paris was not the center of economic life. Second, the king's reputation was intimately tied to a principle of sacred authority that was beyond his ultimate control. In addition, Louis could not master the international balance of power, despite his repeated efforts to do so. The Japanese shogun might draw the curtain of national closure around his islands, making himself the undisputed lord of all he surveyed. But the French king was, after all, a monarch in a larger Europe, and his dynastic ambitions stretched well beyond the borders of what was then France. Every foreign adventure weakened the crown financially and subjected it to potential alliances between dissatisfied subjects within and enemies without. Moreover, although Louis XIV had access to the greatest and most regular tax revenues in Europe, he was nevertheless hindered by the privileges of the notables, towns, and regions whose special arrangements siphoned off significant parts of it and made collection inefficient. Tax farming and venality of office, neither of which existed in Japan, were clear evidence of this royal weakness. The end result was that the aristocracy in France, dependent though it was on the monarch for added glamour and reinforcement, always had distinct traditions. This phenomenon of aristocratic and ecclesiastical culture calls for further consideration. In France—and especially in Paris—it was a force so powerful that the king could hope only to deflect its strength, and then only by inventing an alternative—courtly culture at Versailles. The Tokugawa rulers in Japan, by contrast, isolated the traditional aristocratic culture of the imperial court in Kyoto, and they built a new culture in Edo directly around themselves. Thus conceptualizations of power and urbanism in Paris and Edo transcended the king's and shogun's relations with their cities, and we can understand the urban environment only within the broader context of early-modern cultures in France and Japan.

4

State Control and Municipal Authority in France

SHARON KETTERING

It is a commonplace of old regime history that the monarchy attempted to extend its control over self-governing French cities and towns from the seventeenth century to the Revolution, extinguishing traditional privileges of administrative autonomy as it did so, and that the governments of those cities consisted of small, self-perpetuating elites.[1] We can gain new insights into this process by looking at the crown's efforts to substitute venality for the traditional privilege of municipal elections. The intendants were the crown's principal agents in dealing with the cities and towns, and I propose to examine in detail their administrative role. The crown chose its relationship with the city of Paris as a model for the way it dealt with other French cities, so it is appropriate to begin with the Bourbon capital.

THE MONARCHY AND THE MUNICIPAL GOVERNMENT OF PARIS

As the medieval residence of the Capetian kings and the center around which they built their kingdom, Paris always had been politically significant, but the city never knew the independence from royal authority enjoyed by other French cities and towns. For example, Paris never possessed a written charter guaranteeing its municipal privileges, in contrast to such cities as Bordeaux, Angers, and the Provençal towns.[2] Instead, Paris had to petition each new king to reconfirm its customary unwritten privileges, which were renewable at royal pleasure. The monarchy was always careful to keep the

1. Alexis de Tocqueville, *The Old Regime and the French Revolution*, trans. Stuart Gilbert (New York: Doubleday, 1955), pp. 45, 47; François Furet, *Interpreting the French Revolution*, trans. Elborg Foster (Cambridge: Cambridge University Press, 1986), pp. 132–63.

2. Albert Babeau, *La ville sous l'Ancien Régime*, 2d ed. (New York: AMS Press, 1972), p. 11; Jacques Maillard, *Le pouvoir municipal à Angers de 1657 à 1789*, 2 vols. (Angers: Presses de l'Université d'Angers, 1984), vol. 1, p. 25; and Gustave Arnaud d'Agnel, *Politique des rois de France en Provence*, 2 vols. (Paris: A. Picard, 1914), vol. 2, pp. 61–64, 68–94, 126–30.

upper hand in its relationship with the Parisian municipal authorities, and the city's government necessarily functioned in close cooperation with the crown. The king remained, as he had always been, the dominant partner in the alliance, and he was not disposed to tolerate much resistance or independence from his capital city.

This attitude reflected the development of a new concept of loyalty. William Church has observed that French patriotism by Louis XIV's reign combined personal fidelity to the king as an individual, civic obedience to the king as the head of state, and national loyalty to the king as the embodiment of the French nation.[3] The king was the state incarnate. A combination of personal and abstract loyalties, therefore, characterized early-modern French patriotism.[4] Personal fealties had been primary under feudalism, but intellectuals during the sixteenth century began to broaden the medieval understanding of personal loyalty to include impersonal ties to the state and church.[5] The development of absolutism and the early-modern state during the seventeenth century accelerated this trend. The Bourbon absolute monarchy emphasized the unlimited obligations of its subjects to the state and refused to tolerate higher personal loyalties, which it subordinated to a king-centered patriotism. It insisted that unquestioning obedience to the king as the head of state should take precedence over other personal loyalties.[6]

Despite Bourbon pretensions, however, governing Paris was never easy or simple. Part of the problem was that the royal government was riddled with personal loyalties derived from kinship, clientage, friendship, regionalism, and venality.[7] Royal officeholders often gave priority to their personal allegiances over their administrative responsibilities and loyalty to the king as the head of state. The prevalence of personal loyalties in royal government, in fact, helped to generate the conflict and insubordination that were classic administrative problems of the old regime.

3. William Church, "France," in Orest Ranum, ed., *National Consciousness, History, and Political Cultural in Early Modern France* (Baltimore: Johns Hopkins University Press, 1975), pp. 43–66.

4. Herbert Rowen, "Louis XIV and Absolutism," in John Rule, ed., *Louis XIV and the Craft of Kingship* (Columbus: Ohio State University Press, 1969), pp. 303–4.

5. Donald Kelley, *The Beginning of Ideology* (Cambridge: Cambridge University Press, 1981); Julian Franklin, *Jean Bodin and the Rise of Absolutist Theory* (Cambridge: Cambridge University Press, 1973); William Church, *Constitutional Thought in Sixteenth-Century France* (Cambridge: Harvard University Press, 1941).

6. François Dumont, "French Kingship and Monarchy," in Ragnhild Hatton, ed., *Louis XIV and Absolutism* (Columbus: Ohio State University Press, 1976), pp. 56–57; Roland Mousnier, *The Institutions of France under the Absolute Monarchy, 1598–1789*, vol. 1: *State and Society*, trans. Brian Pearce (Chicago: University of Chicago Press, 1979), pp. 107–18, 645–80; William Beik, *Absolutism and Society in Seventeenth-Century France: State Power and Provincial Aristocracy in Languedoc* (Cambridge: Cambridge University Press, 1985), p. 197.

7. Mousnier, *Institutions of France*, vol. 2: *The Organs of State and Society*, trans. Arthur Goldhammer (Chicago: University of Chicago Press, 1984), pp. 148–52, 170–79, 211–14, 449–52; Yves Durand, *Les fermiers généraux au XVIIIᵉ siècle* (Paris: Presses Universitaires de France, 1971), pp. 60–97; Daniel Dessert, *Argent, pouvoir, et société au Grand Siècle* (Paris: Fayard, 1984), pp. 310–64; Daniel Dessert and Jean-Louis Journet, "Le lobby Colbert," *Annales: E.S.C.* 30:1 (1975), pp. 1303–36; Beik, *Absolutism*, pp. 223–44.

An additional handicap to royal efforts to rule Paris was the complicated set of administrative structures that came between the king and his municipal subjects. Paris, like other French cities, came under the jurisdiction of first the king and his ministers; then the controller general of finance, who was head of the national tax system; the city's royal governor; and finally the municipal government, which was divided between two institutions known for the buildings they occupied, the Châtelet and the Hôtel de Ville, or town hall. Medieval Paris had been governed by a provost (*prévôt*), who represented the king. But a royal edict in 1498 had made this office honorific, and its functions were transferred to two assistants, the civil and criminal lieutenants, who sat in the Châtelet. Louis XIV added a lieutenant general of police (*lieutenant général de police*), who became the head of a large municipal police force.[8]

The elected provost of merchants (*prévôt des marchands*) and four executive officials (*échevins*) met in the Paris town hall as the other important municipal authorities, and twenty-four elected councilors sat as members of the town council. The provost of merchants, the *échevins*, and the councilors served terms of two years, and every year half of each group was replaced. Elections were conducted annually in the town hall by a general assembly composed of the male bourgeoisie of Paris; that is, by property owners who had been resident in the city for at least a year and who paid taxes. Newly elected municipal officials were required to seek royal confirmation of the election results. Since the general assemblies took place only at the king's pleasure and he could reject the results, the assemblies took care to select candidates who they knew would be acceptable to the king.

The Bourbons used various tactics to control this complex administrative structure. Louis XIII, for instance, issued an ordinance making the office of councilor venal and hereditary, although the provost of merchants and *échevins* continued to be elected. Louis XIII and Louis XIV regularly intervened in municipal elections, naming their own candidates by royal letters and announcing them weeks before the elections actually took place. They intervened so often that electoral assemblies became a colorful sham and ceased to meet regularly during the eighteenth century. The provost of merchants became a royal appointee; the *échevins* were chosen from among the senior councilors; and the provost, *échevins*, and councilors ceased to play a significant role in the political life of Paris. The Hôtel de Ville was too financially convenient to suppress, however, so gradually its authority was shifted to the Châtelet, a trend that continued during the eighteenth century until the town hall had almost nothing to do. The single largest group of municipal

---

8. Alan Williams, *The Police of Paris, 1718–1789* (Baton Rouge: Louisiana State University Press, 1979); Steven Kaplan, *Bread, Politics, and Political Economy in the Reign of Louis XV*, 2 vols. (The Hague: Martinus Nijhoff, 1976), vol. 1, pp. 11–42; idem, *Provisioning Paris: Merchants and Millers in the Grain and Flour Trade during the Eighteenth Century* (Ithaca: Cornell University Press, 1984), pp. 33–40; idem, "Réflexions sur la police du monde du travail, 1700–1815," *Revue historique* 261 (1979), pp. 17–77; idem, "Note sur les commissaires de police," *Revue d'histoire moderne et contemporaine* 28 (1981), pp. 669–86.

officials in the seventeenth century had been magistrates from the royal courts of Paris. By Louis XVI's reign in the late eighteenth century, two-thirds were lawyers in these courts. Generally, judicial officials linked by kinship, friendship, and patron-client ties dominated municipal officehold-ing in eighteenth-century France, and they composed an important part of a municipal elite whose ranks also included nobles and merchants.[9]

Since administrative reforms never eliminated competing personalities, what ultimately permitted the Paris municipal government to operate effec-tively, and what allowed the king to exercise his authority, was the existence of middlemen—agents within this complex administrative system who rec-onciled authority from above with needs of the people from below. In Paris, the quintessential middlemen were the police. The biggest obstacle the lieu-tenants general of the Paris police faced in exercising their authority during the eighteenth century was clientage, the personal ties linking police agents to patrons elsewhere in royal government. In order to dismiss agents, the lieutenants general first had to undermine their protection by patrons. The last two heads of the Paris police, Lenoir and Crosne, struggled openly against the pervasiveness of personal ties that thwarted their authority, and they sought to establish the primacy of administrative ties.[10] Consider Jean Guillemain, who was named the commander of the Paris city guard in 1703 and enjoyed the patronage of the comte de Pontchartrain. Guillemain be-came a defendant in a criminal trial before the Parlement of Paris in 1714 on charges of bribery and police brutality, but his son inherited his office in the same year through Pontchartrain's protection, even though his father had been accused of serious abuses of authority.[11]

Only by acting as middlemen could the lieutenants general of police and their agents overcome the interference of personal loyalties. Alan Williams has noted, "Once each week, usually on Sunday or Monday, the lieutenant [general] of police journeyed to Versailles to confer with the king's ministers, and on occasion with the king himself. Once each week, on a day he found convenient, the same man opened the doors of his *hôtel* in Paris to throngs of aggrieved and powerless men, each seeking a form of aid or redress that he alone, they believed, was capable of granting them. The lieutenancy of police was a social and political nexus, a junction of the ancien régime, a point from which lines radiated in many directions, upward to the glitter and power of Versailles, downward to the dim retreats of Paris, to its room-

9. Mousnier, *Society and State*, pp. 574–90; Henri de Carsalade Du Pont, *La municipalité parisienne à l'époque d'Henri IV* (Paris: Cujas, 1971), pp. 33–169; Emile Magne, *Paris sous l'échevinage au XVIIe siècle* (Paris: Emile-Paul, 1960); Barbara Diefendorf, *Paris City Coun-cillors in the Sixteenth Century: The Politics of Patrimony* (Princeton: Princeton University Press, 1983); Orest Ranum, *Paris in the Age of Absolutism* (New York: Wiley, 1968), pp. 25–63; Leon Bernard, *The Emerging City: Paris in the Age of Louis XIV* (Durham: Duke University Press, 1970), pp. 29–55; Gérard Aubry, *La jurisprudence criminelle du Châtelet de Paris sous le règne de Louis XVI* (Paris: Librairie Générale de Droit et Jurisprudence, 1971); Maillard, *Pouvoir municipal*, vol. 1, p. 233.

10. Williams, *Police of Paris*, pp. 158–62.

11. Jean Chagniot, *Paris et l'armeé du XVIIIe siècle* (Paris: Economica, 1985), pp. 118–22.

ing houses, brothels, and cafés."[12] The lieutenant general's proximity to the king brought him not only personal power but also regular contact with chief figures in the government, including six royal ministers, which provided him with opportunities to influence policymaking. His extensive network of police agents permitted him to perform a variety of services for the royal family and other highly placed persons, and thereby to accumulate credit and goodwill. His role in filling several thousand positions in the Paris municipal government gave him considerable patronage power.[13]

The Paris police took an interest in every aspect of daily life, strengthening their control over provisioning, public morality, and the work force during the eighteenth century.[14] Soldiers and wetnurses, hawkers and street peddlers, coachmen, nightmen, and porters in the central market were all (in theory) registered and numbered by the police. Ordinances on a host of matters were codified and rationalized, and the apparatus for enforcement was enlarged and improved. Brothels and gambling houses were regulated, and political dissent received close attention. Street lighting was improved and extended, and the police took responsibility for collecting rubbish, maintaining the roads, and ensuring the safety of buildings. The police acted as middlemen between ordinary Parisians, the municipal government, the royal government, and the court at Versailles, a role that was compatible with the broad eighteenth-century understanding of policing.[15]

PROVINCIAL CITIES

Outside of Paris the monarchy faced a different set of problems. As was the case with Paris, however, the monarchy sought to assert its authority over provincial cities by using a variety of tactics. Every time a newly ascended king reconfirmed a community's traditional privileges, for example, he tried to restrict them in some way.[16] A prominent royal target was the traditional prerogative enjoyed by many communities of electing their own officials. Usually this was an indirect, two-step procedure in which delegates were elected to a general assembly, which then chose the town's officials. But municipal election results were always subject to the approval of the provincial intendants.[17]

There were three stages in the crown's efforts to assert greater control

12. Williams, *Police of Paris*, p. 17.

13. Ibid., pp. 39, 51, 54–55, 57.

14. David Garrioch, *Neighbourhood and Community in Paris, 1740–1790* (Cambridge: Cambridge University Press, 1986), pp. 209–11.

15. Robert Schwartz, *Policing the Poor in Eighteenth-Century France* (Chapel Hill: University of North Carolina Press, 1988), p. 6.

16. Maurice Garden, *Lyon et les lyonnais au XVIIIᵉ siècle* (Paris: Belles Lettres, 1970), p. 488; François-Georges Pariset, ed., *Bordeaux au XVIIIᵉ siècle* (Bordeaux: Fédération du Sud-Ouest, 1968), pp. 50–51.

17. Maurice Bordes, *Les institutions municipales d'Auch au XVIIIᵉ siècle* (Auch: Frédéric Cocharaux, 1964), pp. 7–11.

over municipal officeholding. During the first stage, the crown recognized the traditional privilege of municipal elections, but frequently intervened to suspend elections and to name its own candidates to office in royal letters delivered to the electing bodies by the provincial intendants or governors. The crown also changed election procedures and the structure of municipal governments in order to break elite monopolies on officeholding. Another problem was the constant feuding among local authorities. In such cases municipal elites remained firmly in control, but internal disputes between merchants and judicial officials and among noble factions weakened the community's ability to resist royal initiatives to reduce local autonomy. Of course, municipal elites protested monarchical encroachments on their privileges and power, usually to no avail, and ordinary inhabitants who were excluded from power futilely protested their exclusion.[18]

During the second stage, from 1692 to 1764, the crown no longer recognized the right of municipal elections, and it declared municipal offices to be venal and hereditary. A royal edict in 1692 announced the king's intention, first, to substitute for elected mayors more impartial ones who would buy their offices from the crown to hold in perpetuity; and, second, to replace elected mayors with venal mayors who would be irremovable. In reality, fiscal considerations had dictated the change in policy: Louis XIV needed money for his wars. The crown regularly announced sales of municipal offices, but cities were allowed to buy back venal offices and elect their holders, and many did so.

The rapidly escalating prices were always higher than the towns could afford, however, and many communities sank deeply into debt, agonizing over whether they should buy back an office or let it stay venal. The crown soon began to encounter difficulty in selling offices because it had overcharged and saturated the market. Cities and towns, already heavily in debt and facing endless new creations, refused to buy back the offices, while volume and price drove away individual purchasers, who considered them a bad investment. By 1733 both individuals and towns were refusing to buy the offices.

The crown at mid-century found itself with a huge backlog of unsold offices. The controller general of finance set a fixed price for all unsold municipal offices in a tax district, or *généralité*, and offered them for sale to the cities and towns in that district to reunite with their governments. To make reunion attractive and not simply another repurchase, the crown announced that municipal elections would be restored in those cities and towns that bought the offices, an implicit promise that there would be no more creations of venal offices. The results were mixed because not all municipalities availed themselves of the offer. But by the 1750s many French cities and towns were again electing their officials, and the elected officials

<hr />

18. Roger Chartier, "Oligarchies et absolutisme," in George Duby, ed., *L'histoire de la France urbaine*, vol. 3: Emmanuel Le Roy Ladurie, ed., *La ville classique de la Renaissance aux révolutions* (Paris: Seuil, 1981), p. 158.

existed side by side with venal officials who had bought their offices in perpetuity. Conflicts were frequent, disrupting municipal government.[19]

The third stage began in 1764 when Controller General Laverdy (L'Averdy) announced a general municipal reform in edicts issued in 1764 and 1765. His stated purpose was to restore order to municipal administration, now badly disrupted by venality, and to standardize administrative procedures throughout France. Laverdy's real purpose, however, was to take power away from municipal elites on behalf of newly created assemblies of notables and thereby to broaden elite participation at that level. In other words, the crown never intended to replace municipal elites with lesser social groups: the old regime state was always elitist. The crown sought only to replace those members of the elite holding municipal office with those who did not, thereby expanding elite participation.

But Laverdy's reforms ran into trouble almost immediately. Local resistance was strong; numerous towns protested to the crown; and as a result, the reforms were not applied everywhere. Paris, Lyon, and some other northern towns such as Beauvais were exempt—the king already controlled the municipal elections of Paris, and through the clientele of the dukes of Villeroy, who were royal governors of Lyon, he controlled the municipal elections of that city.[20] Laverdy's reforms were never introduced in the frontier provinces of Brittany, Alsace, Lorraine, Flanders, Burgundy, Provence, and Corsica, and they were applied only with modifications in Normandy, Artois, Gascogne, Guyenne, Béarn, Lower Navarre, Languedoc, Roussillon, and Dauphiné. Elsewhere they were introduced in accordance with the edicts. In other words, the reforms were put into effect as written in less than half of France, and most of those regions were in the north.

Laverdy found himself politically isolated, the object of much opposition at court as well as in the provinces, and he was removed as controller general in October 1768. A year later the abbé Terray, who had opposed the reforms because they reduced the power of the central government, was named controller general, and on his advice in November 1771 the crown revoked the Laverdy edicts and reestablished venal municipal offices. Predictably, the new offices found no purchasers: they were too expensive, and the indebted towns refused to buy them. The edict of 1771 merely increased municipal disorder throughout France.

Many historians believe that a turning point was reached in the mid–eighteenth century, and that after 1750 the crown was unable to accomplish real administrative reform in France. The old regime state had become the prisoner of its privileged classes, such as the municipal elites, who were interested only in maintaining the status quo and defending their own privileges. They resisted the idea of change and forced the crown to abandon its attempts at reform after 1750. Royal initiatives were too limited, too ad hoc,

19. Maurice Bordes, *L'administration provinciale et municipale en France au XVIIIᵉ siècle* (Paris: Société d'Editions d'Enseignment, 1972), pp. 231–53; Olwen Hufton, *Bayeau in the Late Eighteenth Century* (Oxford: Oxford University Press, 1967), pp. 117–45.

20. Garden, *Lyon*, p. 491.

and too dominated by the need for money to be truly effective. A revolution was needed to break the impasse.

There was complete confusion in municipal administration by 1789. Royal letters had settled the form of government in a few fortunate communities such as Angers, governed by elected officials.[21] More common were towns that had purchased the new offices to merge them with their old form of municipal government, now restored. Even more numerous were communities that had neither purchased the new offices nor had their old offices restored. The crown appointed their officials on the intendants' advice, in reality on the recommendation of the intendants' agents, the subdelegates. There can be little doubt that Laverdy's reform had disastrous consequences for municipal administration.[22] By the end of the old regime, the need for a thorough reform of municipal administration was widely recognized and urged upon the monarchy from all sides.[23]

Venality was an obvious administrative failure. It reinforced the monopoly of elites over municipal officeholding and intensified their resistance to royal reforms by increasing their investment in officeholding. Elites already enjoyed social and political advantages from officeholding, and now they acquired economic interests as well, personal financial investments that they sought to protect. The intendants discovered that venal municipal officials were more difficult to control than elected officials because none of the tactics available in stage one could be used, and although venality eliminated election disputes, it increased feuding among municipal officials so that urban government continued to be disrupted by factional strife.

The intendants were the crown's chief agents in the provinces, responsible for establishing municipal venality. They were appointed royal commissioners, serving at royal pleasure, and their offices were not venal or hereditary. Their regulatory authority was defined in royal letters of commission. They were first sent as surveillance agents into the provinces in the 1630s and 1640s, and their functions included supervising municipal finances and verifying municipal election results.[24] The crown's use of the intendants to establish municipal venality, however, brought unexpected administrative problems.

21. Maillard, *Pouvoir municipal*, vol. 1, p. 33.

22. Michel Vovelle, *The Fall of the French Monarchy*, trans. Susan Burke (Cambridge: Cambridge University Press, 1984), pp. 36–37; François Furet and Denis Richet, *French Revolution* (London: Weidenfeld & Nicolson, 1970), pp. 13, 15, 42–44; Mousnier, *Organs of State and Society*, p. 551; Bordes, *Administration provinciale*, pp. 143–47, 343–45; William Doyle, *The Origins of the French Revolution* (Oxford: Oxford University Press, 1980), pp. 53–65.

23. Maurice Bordes, *La réforme municipale du contrôleur-général Laverdy* (Toulouse: Association des Publications de l'Université de Toulouse, 1968); idem, *Administration provinciale*, pp. 254–327; idem, "La réforme municipale de 1764–1765," *Annales du Midi* 75:1 (1963), pp. 49–76; Mousnier, *Society and State*, pp. 598–604; Hufton, *Bayeux*, pp. 122–30.

24. Richard Bonney, *Political Change in France under Richelieu and Mazarin* (Oxford: Oxford University Press, 1978); Nora Temple, "The Control and Exploitation of French Towns during the Ancien Régime," *History* 51 (1966), pp. 16–34; François-Xavier Emmanuelli, *Un mythe de l'absolutisme bourbonien: L'intendance* (Paris: Publications Université d'Aix-en-Provence, 1981), pp. 73–115, 175.

At first the intendants were regularly rotated in service throughout the provinces. But their tours of duty became considerably longer under Colbert, who is usually credited with failing to establish permanently the tradition of rotation, and they became even more lengthy during the eighteenth century. The intendants had averaged about three years in office between 1653 and 1666, and five years between 1666 and 1716.[25] Roland Mousnier notes that by Louis XVI's reign in the late eighteenth century, however, the intendants remained in office for long periods: of the "intendants in office, 29 . . . had held the same post for more than ten years; 24 . . . had served for more than twenty years; 13 for more than twenty-five years; 7 for more than thirty years; and 2 more than forty years."[26]

The intendants also began to use subdelegates extensively, even though Colbert had opposed the practice. The subdelegates' authority was derived from letters of commission issued by the intendants in the name of the crown, and they came from all walks of life, although the majority were former officials who brought with them their local interests, sympathies, and ties. The intendants passed along reliable subdelegates to their successors, who discovered that they already had agents in place when they arrived in a province. Because the new intendants were usually strangers to a province, they relied on their subdelegates to provide information on local affairs and to give them advice; for instance, to recommend potential purchasers for the new venal municipal offices.[27] As members of the local elite, the subdelegates usually recommended as purchasers men who were also members of the local elite. Instead of destroying municipal oligarchies, therefore, the intendants and their subdelegates tended to reinforce them.[28] The same families monopolized municipal officeholding whether their offices had been acquired by election or purchase, and these families had often held office for more than a century.[29]

Expected to act in a dual capacity as officials of royal and municipal

25. Bonney, *Political Change in France*, p. 205.

26. Mousnier, *Organs of State and Society*, p. 555.

27. Ibid., pp. 523–24, 529–32, 547; Julien Ricommard, "L'édit d'avril 1704," *Revue historique* 195 (1945), pp. 123–39; idem, "Les subdélégués en titre d'office en Provence (1704–1715)," *Provence historique* 14 (1964), pp. 243–71, 336–78; idem, "Les subdélégués des intendants aux XVIIe et XVIIIe siècles," *L'information historique* 24: 4 and 5 (1962), pp. 139–48 and 190–95 respectively; idem, "Les subdélégués des intendants," *Revue d'histoire modern* 12:4 (1937), pp. 338–407; Michel Antoine, *Le dur métier du roi* (Paris: Presses Universitaires de France, 1986), pp. 125–79; Maurice Bordes, "Le subdélégué général Jean de Sallenave (1710–1781)," *Annales du Midi* 61 (1949), pp. 422–37; Henri Fréville, *L'intendance de Bretagne (1689–1790)*, 3 vols. (Rennes: Plihon, 1953), vol. 1, pp. 82–84, 112–13; idem, "Notes sur les subdélégués," *Revue d'histoire moderne* 12 (1937), pp. 408–48; Joseph Marchand, *Un intendant sous Louis XIV: Lebret en Provence, 1687–1704* (Paris: Hachette, 1889), pp. 55–60.

28. Nora Temple, "Municipal Elections and Municipal Oligarchies in Eighteenth-Century France," in John F. Boster, ed., *French Government and Society* (London: Athlone, 1973), pp. 70–91.

29. Maillard, *Pouvoir municipal*, p. 234; Garden, *Lyon*, pp. 499–506; Lynn Hunt, *Revolution and Urban Politics in Provincial France, 1786–1790* (Stanford: Stanford University Press, 1978), pp. 22–26, 37–38.

government without a clear allocation of duties, the intendants tended to develop dual loyalties, especially during the eighteenth century, when they began serving long tours of duty and employing large numbers of subdelegates. It became almost impossible for the intendants to avoid some form of local entanglement since they awarded contracts for public works projects and for naval and army supply, supervised the sale of municipal offices, appointed local officials, approved tax exemptions, and tended to accept sizable cash gifts and enjoy lavish hospitality from the provincial estates and the municipalities.[30] The pressure of such local ties and interests, according to Paul Ardascheff, created dual loyalties that impaired the intendants' administrative performance as royal agents. Concerned for provincial welfare, the intendants sought to improve the appearance of cities and the condition of roads and waterways, raise the level of culture and education, expand commerce, develop agriculture, and increase economic prosperity. In pursuit of these goals, Ardascheff contends, they became representatives of the provinces vis-à-vis the central government; that is, the intendants became "men of the province" instead of serving, as they had done under Louis XIV, as agents of the central government in the provinces, or "men of the king."[31]

But the question is not whether the intendants were men of the province or men of the king. Such a formulation is simplistic, arbitrary, and inherently *centraliste*, a mere rephrasing of a problem from the vantage point of the central government. The administrative documents of the Bourbon monarchy encourage a centralist view, emphasizing the obedience and loyalty of subjects to their king, and a portrayal of the Bourbon monarchy as a tentacled, absolutist government reaching into the far corners of France to extinguish provincial and municipal liberties. Recent studies have suggested, however, that the old regime state depended more than we have realized on local cooperation in governing.[32] In consequence, the question of the intendants' loyalty needs to be rethought to include the subtleties posed by the dual nature of their responsibilities.

Attention must be paid to the ways in which the intendants' administrative role changed during the eighteenth century, including a shift in empha-

---

30. Paul Ardascheff, *Les intendants de la province au XVIIIe siècle* (Paris: Félix Alcan, 1909), pp. 447–54.

31. Ibid., pp. 119–20; Michel Lhéritier, *Tourny, 1695–1760* (Paris: Félix Alcan, 1920), pp. 768–69; Mousnier, *Organs of State and Society*, pp. 549–62; Maurice Bordes, "Les intendants de Louis XV," *Revue historique* 223 (1960), pp. 45–62; idem, *D'Etigny et l'administration de l'intendance d'Auch (1751–1761)*, 2 vols. (Auch: Frédéric Cocharaux, 1957); idem, "Les intendants éclairés," *Annales du Midi* 74:1 (1962), pp. 177–94; Fréville, *Intendance de Bretagne*, vol. 3, pp. 164–65; Emmanuelli, *Un mythe de l'absolutisme bourbonien*, pp. 1–33.

32. Alain Guéry, "Les finances de la monarchie française sous l'Ancien Régime," *Annales: E.S.C.* 33:2 (1978), pp. 216–39; James Collins, *Fiscal Limits of Absolutism* (Berkeley: University of California Press, 1988), pp. 214–22; Beik, *Absolutism*, pp. 279–339; Sharon Kettering, *Patrons, Brokers, and Clients in Seventeenth-Century France* (Oxford: Oxford University Press, 1986), pp. 232–37; Daniel Hickey, *The Coming of French Absolutism* (Toronto: Toronto University Press, 1986), pp. 179–91; Hilton Root, *Peasants and King in Burgundy* (Berkeley: University of California Press, 1987), pp. 205–14.

sis from coercive to legitimate authority. Increasingly, the intendants in the provinces began to act as intermediaries between local authorities and the central government at Paris and as middlemen in efforts to integrate local needs with national demands.[33] As a result, the intendants extended and diversified their regulatory functions to include persuasion, conciliation, and negotiation. They translated and transmitted the views of different political environments, mediated conflicts between local authorities and with the central government, established royal reforms, sought national assistance for local needs and local cooperation with national demands.[34]

The change in the intendants' administrative role had its roots during Louis XIV's reign. William Beik has observed about the intendancy of Languedoc during the late seventeenth century: "In its growing function of mediating between a monarchy wanting various things done in the province and a collection of (local) rulers wanting various measures enacted by the monarchy, it was probably not unlike the intendancies in other provinces."[35] The intendants' legitimacy as royal officials, challenged during the seventeenth century, was widely accepted by the early eighteenth century. Their new legitimacy allowed them to expand their functions to include the role of middleman.[36] In addition, provincial conditions were less turbulent during the eighteenth century, and the intendants less often had to use direct coercion to accomplish the crown's goals. Moreover, the intendants' diversification of function may have been necessary if absolutism was dependent on local cooperation, and if the central government became weaker during the eighteenth century.

The intendants, as middlemen, explained the municipal viewpoint to the royal government at Paris. The intendant at Caen wrote Controller General Terray and Secretary of State Bertin in May 1772 that venal municipal offices created in the previous year were not selling in Normandy because the communities were deeply in debt, and no one wanted to assume control of a town facing bankruptcy. He advised the crown to consider helping the towns out of their financial difficulties if it wanted to sell the offices.[37] The intendants also explained royal demands to local officials. Charles Boucher, intendant at Bordeaux in 1737, assembled all officials of the three tax districts in Guyenne to answer their questions on the levy of a new royal tax, giving

33. Middlemen by definition belonged to the formal administrative hierarchy, represented legitimate authority, and were salaried officials. They could also act as brokers, arranging exchanges of resources such as patronage, for which they received a commission. Brokers were not necessarily salaried officials, representatives of legitimate authority, or members of the bureaucracy. Brokers could perform middleman functions, but they were not middlemen because they belonged to an unofficial patronage system separate from the bureaucracy. On brokers, see Kettering, *Patrons*, pp. 40–67, 98–140.

34. Marc Swartz, *Local-Level Politics* (Chicago: Aldine, 1968), pp. 199–271; Dennis Wrong, *Power, Its Forms, Bases, and Uses* (Chicago: University of Chicago Press, 1988), pp. 32–34, 71–75, 86, 91–92, 97–98.

35. Beik, *Absolutism*, p. 116.

36. Wrong, *Power*, pp. 84–123

37. Hufton, *Bayeux*, pp. 125–26.

them copies of the crown's instructions and asking them to report on their experiences in levying the tax.[38]

The intendants, as middlemen, mediated conflicts among local authorities, including disputes over municipal elections. In 1723 Intendant Boucher settled quarrels between the royal tax court of the Cour des Aides and the Bordeaux city government, and between members of the city government.[39] In the Languedocian town of Clermont-de-Lodève, to take another example, there were bitter election disputes in the 1720s between newly enriched clothiers and an entrenched elite, and the intendant had to intervene on several occasions.[40] Intendant d'Etigny regularly supervised the recruitment and election of consuls in the intendancy of Auch. For instance, he obtained royal letters in 1753 prohibiting Consul Pascal Avezac of Torbes from entering the town hall, and conducted the elections to replace him. When the sieur de Fornets was elected, the intendant maintained him in office by royal letters from 1754 to 1760, and he did the same thing for consuls at Serenc, Mont-de-Marsan, Bagnères-de-Bigorres, and Saliès-de-Béarn.[41]

In their capacity as representatives of the monarchy, the intendants were responsible for enforcing royal reforms, the classic example being their unsuccessful attempt to implement Laverdy's program. But the intendants also sought to secure royal assistance for local needs. Intendant Esmangart, for instance, appealed to Secretary of State Bertin for help in 1776 when the municipal government of Bayeux came to a standstill. Whenever the question of electing new officials arose, half of the town demanded that the elections take place according to the reform of 1766, and the other half insisted that this method had been nullified by the edict of 1771 and that retiring officials should choose new officials according to the pre-1766 method. Bertin sent Esmangart a copy of a ruling he had made for the towns of Champagne, directing the intendant to name municipal officials after consulting with a town's principal inhabitants, and Esmangart enforced this procedure in Normandy.[42]

As middlemen, the intendants were expected to secure local cooperation with royal demands, although this was not always an easy task. The political reality was meticulous regulation at the top of the system and widespread disobedience at the bottom.[43] The intendants used patronage to secure the cooperation of local elites, and their use of patronage created local ties of loyalty. For example, they proposed candidates for the purchase of judicial offices.[44] They suggested potential purchasers of venal municipal

38. Pariset, *Bordeaux*, pp. 16–17, 21.

39. Ibid., pp. 21, 51.

40. J. K. J. Thomson, *Clermont-de-Lodève, 1633–1789* (Cambridge: Cambridge University Press, 1982), p. 294.

41. Bordes, *D'Etigny*, vol. 1, pp. 315–19; idem, *Institutions municipales d'Auch*, p. 21.

42. Hufton, *Bayeux*, p. 127.

43. Furet, *Interpreting the French Revolution*, p. 143; Beik, *Absolutism*, pp. 179–97.

44. Pierre Dubuc, *L'intendance de Soissons sous Louis XIV* (Paris: Albert Fontemoing, 1902), pp. 155–56; Marchard, *Un intendant sous Louis XIV*, pp. 263–66.

offices, and they named new mayors, *échevins*, consuls, and councilors by royal letters.[45] The intendant in Brittany considered the incumbent mayor of Vannes so unreliable that he bought the office himself and awarded it to Le Menez de Kerdelleau, an outsider from Quimper with a large family and modest means who had proved his loyalty to the crown during the Estates of 1778.[46] Fernand de Villemin, intendant in Brittany, enlarged provincial postal routes and named the new postmasters in 1715. Intendants in Provence forwarded names of candidates to serve as royal provosts; recommended commoners for ennoblement; suggested nonnobles who should be allowed to buy fiefs; and recommended that young nobles be admitted to military academies.[47]

The intendants also did favors for friends, patrons, and influential members of local elites. Public projects for urban renewal, road and bridge building, and port expansion gave intendants opportunities to award lucrative contracts, and these could be used to put money into the hands of families belonging to local elites. In addition, public land continually entered private hands discreetly and illegally during the eighteenth century as cities expanded—for instance, when their walls were torn down and not rebuilt—and the intendants usually turned a blind eye to these transfers. They also exempted the lands of colleagues from troop billeting, reduced their tax assessments, or forgave their tax obligations entirely, and they frequently requested the same favors for themselves.[48]

Finally, the intendants enjoyed extensive personal patronage powers. For example, they allowed local seigneurs who had traditionally named municipal officials to continue doing so, a privilege reconfirmed by royal edicts in 1766 and 1787.[49] They chose their own secretaries and subdelegates, often numbering a dozen or so. Intendant Tourny at Bordeaux, for example, employed 9 secretaries and 17 subdelegates. The number of subdelegates ranged from highs of 90 in Brittany in 1730 and 61 in Provence in 1790, the two most independent provinces, to lows of 7 at Lille, 8 at Strasbourg, 15 at Amiens, and 12 at Tours, all provincial capitals in the north near Paris.[50]

45. Pariset, *Bordeaux*, p. 56.

46. Timothy Le Goff, *Vannes and Its Region* (Oxford: Oxford University Press, 1987), p. 126.

47. Fréville, *Intendance de Bretagne*, vol. 1, pp. 130–32; Dubuc, *Intendance de Soissons*, pp. 35–38; M. J. Bry, *Les viguéries de Provence* (Paris: A. Picard, 1910), pp. 221–35; François-Xavier Emmanuelli, *Pouvoir royal et vie régionale en Provence*, 2 vols. (Lille: Université de Lille, 1974), vol. 1, pp. 277–82.

48. Kettering, *Patrons*, pp. 199–202; Ardascheff, *Intendants de la province*, pp. 449, 452–54; Jean-Claude Perrot, *Caen au XVIIIe siècle*, 2 vols. (Paris: Université de Paris, 1970), vol. 2, pp. 571–80; idem, "Conflits administratifs," *Annales de Normandie* 13:2 (1963), pp. 131–38.

49. Georges Frèche, *Toulouse et la région Midi-Pyrénées* (Paris: Cujas, 1974), pp. 399–403; Nicole Castan, *Les criminels de Languedoc* (Toulouse: Association des Publications de l'Université de Toulouse, 1980), pp. 116–26, 133–35, 140–57, 256–57; Bordes, *D'Etigny*, pp. 310–11, 319–21.

50. Antoine, *Dur métier*, pp. 158–63; Emmanuelli, *Un mythe de l'absolutisme bourbonien*, pp. 51–52; Temple, "Municipal Elections," pp. 70–91; Castan, *Criminels de Languedoc*, p. 251.

MIDDLEMEN AND EARLY MODERN GOVERNMENTS

For what purposes did the police of Paris and the provincial intendants use their patronage powers? Did the local ties of loyalty thus created influence their judgment and impair their ability to carry out the royal will? For the most part, the lieutenant generals of police and the provincial intendants used their patronage powers on behalf of the crown to obtain local coopera- tion with royal demands, thereby facilitating their administrative perfor- mance. In doing so, they acted as middlemen, even if the crown did not always recognize their administrative role. Middleman functions precluded blind loyalty to either side. To be successful, middlemen needed to have local sympathies and interests, as the police and intendants did.

There is no evidence that the police or the intendants used their patron- age powers to their own advantage at the expense of the crown's interests or those of the municipalities. Almost no intendant made a personal fortune while in office (unlike the subdelegates).[51] The intendants did not have family ties in the provinces where they served; the great majority were Parisian in origin. They married into other Parisian administrative families, not into the local nobility, and their advancement depended on their Paris connections rather than their local ties. Their family property was located elsewhere in France, not in the provinces where they served.[52] Ardascheff notes that some intendants were accused of abuses of authority and were criticized for exempting themselves and others from taxation or for accept- ing financial assistance and extravagant hospitality from the municipalities and provinces.[53] Contemporaries, however, regarded these favors not as abuses of authority but as perquisites of office. The early-modern attitude toward corruption was different from our own.[54] Evidence of abuses, in fact, consisted mostly of acts committed by the subdelegates, although the doc- trine of *respondeat superior* applies. The evidence for abuse of authority by the intendants is so sparse that their occasional lapses could not have been serious or frequent enough to have impaired their administrative perfor- mance.

I would also argue that the view of dual loyalties as detrimental to ad- ministrative performance is essentially a modern, bureaucratic notion with limited applicability to early-modern government. What is at issue is the nature of political loyalty during the old regime. The prevalent, widely tolerated problem of competing loyalties calls into question Ardascheff's argument that the intendants were "men of the province" (a notion that makes the lieutenants general of police into "men of the city") because they represented local interests vis-à-vis the central government. Acting as middlemen did not affect their performance in the eyes of their contempor-

51. Ardascheff, *Intendants de la province*, p. 451; Bordes, "Jean de Sallenave," pp. 428– 37.

52. Vivian Gruder, *The Royal Province Intendants in Eighteenth-Century France* (Ithaca: Cornell University Press, 1968); Fréville, *Intendance de Bretagne*; Lhéritier, *Tourny*.

53. Ardascheff, *Intendants de la province*, pp. 452–54.

54. Kettering, *Patrons*, pp. 192–206.

aries; in fact, their local ties and interests probably facilitated their performance.

We have been discussing state power and municipal administration in one of the first European bureaucracies. The Bourbon monarchy chose its relationship with the city of Paris as the model for its relationship with other French cities, thereby ignoring political reality in the rest of France and overlooking the uniqueness of Paris as the national capital. Paris was very much like Edo in this respect. As the administrative capital of Tokugawa Japan, Edo was the seat of the shogun's government, and it also had its own municipal government. Edo was the largest, most important Japanese city, although it was newer than Paris and had a smaller police force. The shogunate was an early-modern bureaucracy that had developed after a lengthy period of feudal warfare, and may, in fact, have been more centralized than the French state. The Edo municipal government was dominated by the shogun, at least in theory, in much the same way that the Paris municipal government was dominated by the king.

There were, however, some important differences between early-modern French and Japanese municipal administrations. Japanese municipal governments were not venal and did not struggle to keep elected offices from becoming venal, and they came under the control of higher authority to a greater extent than their French counterparts. The relationship of most Japanese cities to the regional lords, the daimyo, was much the same as that of Edo to the shogunate. There was a reason for this.

Medieval French cities and towns had grown rapidly during the commercial expansion of the twelfth and thirteenth centuries. The cities used their newfound ability to generate tax money to obtain self-governing privileges from the monarchy and the feudal lords, whom they played off against each other.[55] The monarchy later used the preservation of these privileges as a form of indirect municipal taxation. In contrast, Japanese cities had usually originated as administrative centers of the daimyo and shoguns and then had become commercial centers.[56] Japanese cities underwent commercial expansion during the Tokugawa period without obtaining privileges of self-government because the daimyo were firmly under the control of the shogun. As a result, the cities were unable to manipulate the daimyo to gain their independence. In a downward delegation of authority, the shogun demanded that the daimyo preserve law and order in the provinces, and the

55. Henri Pirenne, *Economic and Social History of Medieval Europe*, trans. I. E. Clegg (London: Kegan Paul, 1936); Duby, ed., *Histoire de la France urbaine*, vol. 2: André Chédeville, Jacques Le Goff, and Jacques Rossiaud, eds., *La ville médiévale des Carolingiens à la Renaissance* (Paris: Seuil, 1980).

56. James L. McClain, *Kanazawa: A Seventeenth-Century Japanese Castle Town* (New Haven: Yale University Press, 1982), pp. 15–31, 68–117; Nakai Nobuhiko and James L. McClain, "Commercial Change and Urban Growth in Early Modern Japan," in John W. Hall et al., eds., *The Cambridge History of Japan*, vol. 4: John W. Hall, with McClain, ed., *Early Modern Japan* (Cambridge: Cambridge University Press, 1991), pp. 519–95; Katō Takashi, "Governing Edo," chap. 2 of this volume.

shogun and daimyo alike taxed the cities and people under their jurisdiction.

Did middlemen exist in the municipal governments of Tokugawa Japan? There was a need for middlemen because the Tokugawa shogunate developed a system of rule by status in which higher authority was applied in separate parallel structures to social groups within the cities. An official policy of divide and rule made it difficult for Japanese cities to achieve the unity needed to assert independent self-government. The shoguns exercised direct authority over their own retainers and landholdings and the city of Edo, their feudal seat and administrative capital. Through the inspectors general and inspectors, the shoguns also exercised direct authority over the daimyo, who governed their own cities and lands through samurai councils of advisers and city magistrates. Side by side with the samurai city magistrates were the governing officials drawn from the merchant and artisan statuses—the city elders, neighborhood chiefs, and five-family groups. Middlemen were needed to link these different levels of government. Did the Tokugawa inspectors general and inspectors act as middlemen similar to the French intendants and their subdelegates and to the lieutenants general of police and their agents? Or, as Katō Takashi suggests in Chapter 2, were the neighborhood chiefs in a better position to perform middleman functions? Were these functions generic by office or individual by personality, and how formal or informal were they? How much legitimacy did a middleman need? Were such officials linked by personal ties of loyalty?

Middlemen played a more important administrative role in early-modern bureaucracies than historians have recognized. What pressures did middlemen experience in representing the demands of the lower levels of society? What strategies did they develop to function effectively? What impact did they have on policy-making? We have already discussed some of the administrative problems created by personal ties of loyalty, which were still important in the government of a Tokugawa Japan recently emerged from a long feudal period. What political role did these ties play in Japanese municipal government? Did they contribute to centralization or were they detrimental to administrative performance? I have asked more questions here than I can answer in the hope that historians of early-modern Japan may turn to them in the future.

SPACE

都市空間

5

Edobashi

Power, Space, and Popular Culture in Edo

JAMES L. McCLAIN

The first fire began early on the eighteenth afternoon of the new year of Meireki 3, 1657, at Honmyōji, a small, inconsequential temple located in Hongō, on the northern rim of the city. Edo was dry—it had not rained for nearly three months—and a strong wind, gathering force as it howled across the great Kantō plain, drove the fire into the heart of the shogun's capital. By late afternoon flames had burned through Hongō, charred Yushima. Carried by flying sparks, the blaze jumped across moats and canals, wiped out dozens of daimyo estates clustered to the north of the castle, made short work of hundreds of bannerman compounds, scorched merchant housing in the thickly settled districts that lined the Kanda River. In the early evening the treacherous winds shifted and hurried the flames into the merchant quarters along the banks of the Sumida River. By the time the fire burned itself out early on the morning of the nineteenth, little but ashes and rubble remained in a broad arc that swept from Hongō to Reiganjima.

Several hours later a carelessly tended cooking fire in a samurai residence in Koishikawa ignited a second day of terror. The wind, still fierce, quickly fanned the flames into another major conflagration. First lost were several large daimyo estates, and then the blaze leaped into Edo Castle, consuming large portions of the central residential keeps and swallowing up the great donjon, towering symbol of the shogun's wealth and power. In the afternoon the wind carried sparks from the castle into merchant and artisan quarters. Spared the previous day, people living between Nakabashi and Kyōbashi, in the very heart of merchant Edo, now had to flee for their lives. Asai Ryōi described the scene in his *Musashi abumi*:

> People poured out of the residential quarters, hoping to escape the rapidly spreading fire. Discarded family chests clogged street crossings. . . .
> Tongues of raging flames shot into the crowds of jostling people, pushing and shoving against one another. All around, from Nakabashi to Kyō-

bashi, bridges fell, reduced to ashes. Hemmed in by flames, the crowd first surged to the south, then came back to the north. Struggling helplessly, they tried the east, the west. They cried out together in fearful anguish. When the fire drew upon them, burning up completely all that was near at hand, some people could no longer bear the heat and they formed themselves into a human shield to try to ward off the fire, but they were choked by the billowing smoke. Others were consumed by the fire, their limbs burned to ashes.[1]

Asai estimated that some 26,000 persons died in the Nakabashi area alone. Not all of this commentator's observations are to be accepted on mere faith, as Jurgis Elisonas reminds us in Chapter 11 of this volume, but Asai's depiction of the fires of 1657 cannot be far from the mark. Official sources confirm that nearly three-quarters of Edo smoldered in ruin. Totally destroyed were the major living quarters within the castle; 160 daimyo estates; nearly 350 shrines and temples; more than 750 residential compounds of bannermen and housemen; close to 50,000 merchant and artisan homes. An estimated 108,000 people died, perhaps as many as one in every seven or eight persons who resided in the city. Most perished in the flames; some were crushed to death on overcrowded bridges; thousands drowned when they jumped into rivers and the ocean; others succumbed to exposure during a siege of frigid temperatures and snowstorms, whose first flakes began to fall just as the last of the fires was extinguished on the morning of the twentieth. The scribes could consult the ancient records, but never before, not in the entire recorded history of their country, had the Japanese suffered through a natural disaster such as this.[2]

The shogunate quickly mobilized its resources to deal with the tragedy. In the days and weeks after the fire, it set up kitchens around Edo to feed survivors; dug mass graves to bury the dead; constructed a new temple to minister to the needs of their tormented souls; conferred money upon merchant quarters to help rebuild the city.[3] With a long-range view toward

1. Asai Ryōi, *Musashi abumi* (Edo: Yamamoto Kyūzaemon and Nishinomiya Shinroku, 1772), fasc. 2, fol. 3. A more accessible version, based on the original 1661 edition as published in Kyoto, is available in Nihon Zuihitsu Taisei Henshūbu, ed., *Nihon zuihitsu taisei*, ser. 3, vol. 6 (Yoshikawa Kōbunkan, 1977), p. 394. For a cautionary note about the authorship of this work see pp. 5–6 of the introduction to that volume.

2. Documents concerning the fire are brought together in Tōkyō-to, ed., *Tōkyō shishikō: Sangyō-hen*, 35 vols. (Tōkyō-to, 1929–1991) (hereafter cited as *TS:S*), vol. 5, pp. 252–87. See also Kinsei Shiryō Kenkyūkai, ed., *Shōhō jiroku*, 3 vols. (Nihon Gakujutsu Shinkōkai, 1964– 1966) (hereafter cited as *Shōhō jiroku*), vol. 1, docs. 148 and 149, p. 49. A great mythology surrounds the origins of the fire on the eighteenth (almost surely accidental); Kuroki Takashi discusses the origins and path of the fire in great detail in his *Meireki no taika*, Gendai shinsho 390 (Kōdansha, 1977).

3. *Shōhō jiroku*, vol. 1, doc. 165, p. 49. In his *Bukō nenpyō*, Saitō Gesshin, another of Edo's great chroniclers, states that a total of 10,000 *kanme* of silver, equivalent to 160,000 *ryō* of gold, was distributed to merchant and artisan homeowners according to a formula based on the street frontage of their properties. Saitō completed in 1848 the first eight volumes of his journal-like work, covering the years 1590–1848, and by his death in 1878

preventing future catastrophes, the shogun's officials reorganized the city geographically. One reason that the Meireki fires had spread so quickly was that buildings were packed close together, especially in the areas to the north and east of the castle. To relieve this congestion, the shogunate ordered nearly all shrines and temples out of the city center, relocating most of them on the northern outskirts of Edo. To encourage the dispersal of the merchant and artisan population, the shogunate transferred to the jurisdiction of the city magistrates (*machi bugyō*) extensive territory between Shiba and Asakusa, which was then subdivided into new residential quarters, and it opened up Honjo and Fukagawa to settlement (and built the great Ryōgoku Bridge to encourage migration across the Sumida River).

The shogunate also decided to create firebreaks, generically called *hiyokechi* (literally, "fire-prevention land") and *hirokōji* ("widened streets"), at key locations across the Edo cityscape. Officials had in mind several purposes: to open up before important buildings and crowded neighborhoods broad spaces that flying embers could not easily overfly; to provide unobstructed access to important bridges that served as escape routes in times of emergency; and to afford a place of temporary refuge to the victims of fire. Consequently, the shogunate banished merchant shops and housing from nearly twenty newly designated firebreaks—along the approaches to the Ryōgoku and Eitai bridges and in districts such as Asakusa, Shitaya (Ueno), Atago Shita, and Akabane in Shiba.[4] Edicts made very clear what the shogunate expected: land designated as a firebreak was to remain vacant; under no circumstances were shops or residences to intrude into space so defined.[5]

Whatever the shogun's intentions, however, few of the newly cleared spaces remained empty for long. Open land was an extremely valuable commodity in Edo, especially tracts such as the firebreaks, which tended to be situated adjacent to major commercial areas, along heavily traveled roadways, and near shrines and temples frequented by sightseers and Edoites out for a day's excursion. Rather quickly, merchants slipped in and opened up shops; wholesalers imagined the barren sites filled with warehouses and storage facilities; and entertainers sang and danced along their streets and pathways. More often than they wished, the shogun's senior officials, intent on preserving the firebreaks as links in Edo's defenses against fire, found themselves locked in uncomfortable negotiation with a variety of mer-

---

he had finished another four volumes, carrying events forward to 1873. The entire work is available in Kaneko Mitsuharu, ed., *Zōtei: Bukō nenpyō*, 2 vols., Tōyō bunko 116 and 118 (Heibonsha, 1988). The relief measures are described in vol. 1, pp. 59–60. For information about the complex history of this text and revisions made to it, see Kaneko's essay in vol. 1, pp. 225–37.

4. A listing of firebreaks can be found in Nishiyama Matsunosuke, ed., *Edogaku jiten* (Kōbundō, 1984), s.v. Yoshiwara Ken'ichirō, "Hirokōji," pp. 19–21; Ogi Shinzō et al., eds., *Edo Tōkyō jiten* (Sanseidō, 1987), s.v. Tamai Tetsuo, "Hiyokechi," p. 88, and "Hirokōji," pp. 174–75.

5. For an informed discussion about the shogunate's concept of vacant land and its determination that firebreaks remain open, see Itō Yoshiichi, *Edo no machikado* (Heibonsha, 1987), pp. 37–43.

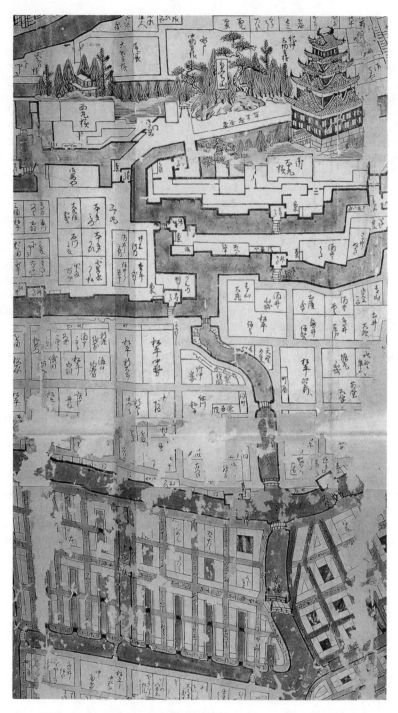

Edobashi circa 1630. Source: Bushū Toshima-gōri Edo shōzu.
Courtesy of Kokuritsu Kokkai Toshokan.

chants, artisans, entertainers, and even their own subordinates, all of whom had quite different visions of how those spaces ought to be used. Conceived of as voids in the urban landscape, the firebreaks filled up with contention. Disputes over the firebreaks demanded settlement. Their resolution draws our attention to the complex subtleties embedded in the transmutation of "Ieyasu's town" (to quote Chapter 1 of this volume) into the merchants' city, and what happened in the firebreaks suggests, as well, some new ways of understanding the exercise of political authority in Tokugawa Japan.

EDOBASHI: FROM MERCHANT QUARTER TO FIREBREAK

Of all the neighborhoods to be designated as firebreaks in 1657, none was more prominent than Edobashi. By the time of the Meireki fires this area had, quite literally, risen from the depths of Edo Bay to become part of the capital's most prosperous merchant district. On the day that Ieyasu marched into the village of Edo in 1590 the area was under water, submerged in the bay just to the east of the island known as Edomaejima. It stayed that way until 1603, when Ieyasu, newly appointed as shogun, decided to create more space for his castle and for Edo's expanding merchant community by leveling Mount Kanda and filling in Hibiya Inlet and the shallows on the eastern flank of Edomaejima. As part of this enormous landfill project, Ieyasu's engineers extended eastward a section of the moat known as Dō-sanbori. The Nihonbashi Bridge was put up across this extension, which then was renamed the Nihonbashi River. The new tributary emptied into the bay at its intersection with the Sumida River, but before it did so, engineers drove a branch southward to supplement the castle's already extensive web of defensive moats. This offshoot became known as the Kaede River, and the wedge of land extending for three hundred yards from the intersection of the Nihonbashi and Kaede rivers to the approach to Nihonbashi Bridge is what became known colloquially as Edobashi (see the maps on pp. 18, 20, and 48). The people who constructed houses and shops on the point of new land did not immediately call it that, however, for the "Edo Bridge," genesis of the common appellation for the district, would not span the Nihonbashi River for another thirty years.[6]

Ieyasu's officials platted four residential quarters on this portion of the landfill. Zaimoku-chō, the "Lumber Merchants Quarter," stretched along the Kaede River. There, where they could easily offload and store cargoes arriving by ocean barge, Ieyasu settled lumber dealers from Suruga and Ōmi

6. For a discussion of the complexities of determining the exact year in which Edobashi Bridge was constructed, see Tōkyō-shi Nihonbashi Kuyakusho, ed., *Shinshū: Nihonbashi kushi*, vol. 1 (Tōkyō-shi Nihonbashi Kuyakusho, 1927) (hereafter cited as *Nihonbashi kushi*), pp. 142–43; Tōkyō Shiyakusho, ed., *Nihonbashi*, Tōkyō shishi gaihen 6 (Tōkyō Shiyakusho, 1932) (hereafter cited as *Nihonbashi*), pp. 30–37; Hatano Jun, "Edobashi hirokōji no hensen to fukugen," *Kokuritsu Rekishi Minzoku Hakubutsukan kenkyū hōkoku* 14 (1987), pp. 26–30.

Edobashi before the Meireki fires. Source: Edozu byōbu. Courtesy of Kokuritsu Rekishi Minzoku Hakubutsukan.

whom he earlier had invited to come to Edo so that they might supply him with building materials. The names of the other neighborhoods on the new point of land reveal as well the occupations of their residents. Aomono-chō and Yorozu-chō, which ran perpendicular to Zaimoku-chō, became home to families who marketed vegetables and handled general merchandise such as tea, umbrellas, soy sauce, and incense. In both cases, the merchant families had moved to Edo from Odawara at the end of the sixteenth century and had lived close to the shogun's castle before relocating to the new quarters. Others from Odawara also settled Yokkaichi-chō, which bordered the Nihonbashi River: they managed wharfs, operated inns for mariners, and organized great outdoor markets four times a year.[7]

The new neighborhoods flourished as an integral part of the commercial center of Edo that ran from Hon-chō through Nihonbashi south to Nakabashi and Kyōbashi. The four quarters were fortuitously located, adjacent to Nihonbashi Bridge, terminus for the great Tōkaidō highway. But even more important, as the research of Jinnai Hidenobu has shown, people and commodities moved on water in early Edo.[8] The Nihonbashi and Kaede rivers constituted key links in an extensive network of waterways that tied the city together, and it is small wonder that the wharfs of Yokkaichi-chō and Zaimoku-chō became busy transshipment points for goods arriving by sea or that flourishing rice and fish markets could be found on the northern bank of the Nihonbashi River. Two screen paintings thought to depict the area in the early 1630s show the quarters throbbing with economic vitality; crowding the riverbanks are mountainous bales of rice and great stockpiles of lumber—rough timbers, squared-off framing members, and smooth-cut planks.[9] Miura Jōshin, Edo's first chronicler, wrote about the area a decade or so after its founding in his *Keichō kenmonshū*:

7. For the early history of the Edobashi area, see Tōkyō Shiyasho, ed., *Tōkyō shishikō: Kyōryō-hen*, vol. 1 (Tōkyō Shiyakusho, 1936), pp. 69–74; *Nihonbashi kushi*, pp. 137–44, 192–93; *Nihonbashi*, pp. 62–74, 187–258; Tōkyō-to Chūō Kuyakusho, ed., *Chūō kushi*, vol. 1 (Tōkyō-to Chūō Kuyakusho, 1958), pp. 169–70; Kitahara Susumu and Yamamoto Sumiyoshi, *Chūō-ku no rekishi* (Meicho Shuppan, 1979), pp. 40–47.

8. Jinnai Hidenobu, " 'Mizu no toshi' no hikaku toshi—Venezia to Edo·Tōkyō," in Ogi Shinzō, ed., *Edo to wa nani ka?*, vol. 5: *Edo—Tōkyōgaku*, special issue of *Gendai no esupuri* (Shibundō, 1986), pp. 96–114; idem, "The Spatial Structure of Edo," trans. J. Victor Koschmann, in Chie Nakane and Shinzaburō Ōishi, eds., *Tokugawa Japan: The Social and Economic Antecedents of Modern Japan*, translation edited by Conrad Totman (Tokyo: Tokyo University Press, 1990), pp. 124–46.

9. The screens are the *Edo meishozu byōbu* at the Idemitsu Bijutsukan (Idemitsu Museum of Art) and the *Edozu byōbu* at the Kokuritsu Rekishi Minzoku Hakubutsukan (National Museum of Japanese History). Reproductions are available in Suwa Haruo and Naitō Akira, eds., *Edozu byōbu* (Mainichi Shinbunsha, 1972) (see esp. pls. 1 and 13–16); and in Suzuki Susumu, comp., *Edozu byōbu* (Heibonsha, 1971) (see the foldout of the entire *Edozu byōbu* and pls. 6 and 7). Controversy surrounds the date when the screens were executed and the historical era that they are thought to depict, but scholarly opinion seems to be settling on the notion that the *Edo meishozu byōbu* represents Edo in the early Kan'ei period, perhaps the late 1620s, and the *Edozu byōbu* portrays Edo a few years later. For a discussion of the issues involved, see Suwa's essay "Edozu byōbu no gaisetsu," in Suwa and Naitō, *Edozu byōbu*, n.p.; Murai Masao, "Edozu byōbu no rekishiteki haikei," in Suzuki, *Edozu byōbu*, pp. 22–46; Suitō Makoto, " 'Edozu byōbu' seisaku no shūhen—sono sakusha·seisaku

Waterways crisscross Edo in all directions; north, south, east, and west; and there are bridges, too, in numbers beyond knowing. One great river joins the current of the moat in front of Ōte Gate and then flows through the city, southward to the ocean. Nihonbashi Bridge is just one of the spans crossing this river, and it is used by people going back and forth through the city. . . . When one looks at Nihonbashi, one sees long lines of people morning and night. Just as the city prospers, one hears the feet of people and horses beating like thunder upon the bridge.[10]

The fires of 1657 reduced the merchant quarters at Edobashi to ashes, and that summer government officials decided to turn the triangle of land into a firebreak. To open up vacant space, the shogunate expropriated portions of Yokkaichi-chō and Zaimoku-chō, granting those residents who had survived the holocaust new land on Reiganjima, and it declared the cleared tract to be *goyōchi hiyokechi*, land reserved for official use as a firebreak. The government also rebuilt Edobashi Bridge (an important evacuation route), and within the new firebreak it constructed a tall embankment, designed to block the passage of flames and flying sparks driven by northern winds. Maps and screens from the late seventeenth century show four sections of the embankment stretched out along the southern bank of the Nihonbashi River and a fifth on the western bank of the Kaede.[11] Some reports describe these embankments as towering nearly twenty-four feet high, and one screen shows them topped with plantings of a type of fire-resistant pine tree.[12]

The shogunate assigned the responsibility for looking after the bridge and the firebreak to the residents of Aomono-chō and the remaining portion of Zaimoku-chō (now referred to as Hon Zaimoku-chō). In practical terms, this task required the two residential quarters to maintain the bridge in good repair, keep the firebreak clean of debris and litter, arrange care for abandoned children, construct a wooden palisade around the firebreak (with passage gates on the roadways running west to Nihonbashi and south along the Kaede River), build and maintain several guardhouses, and appoint

nendai·seisaku no ito nado no mosaku," *Kokuritsu Rekishi Minzoku Hakubutsukan kenkyū hōkoku* 18 (1991), pp. 27–43.

10. Miura Jōshin, *Keichō kenmonshū*, in Edo Sōsho Kankōkai, ed., *Edo sōsho*, vol. 2 (Seishinsha, 1980), p. 116.

11. The screen titled *Kanbun Edo ezu byōbu* is reproduced on a foldout following p. 80 of *Nihonbashi kushi*; typical cartographic depictions include the *Genroku Edo ōezu* and the *Edo ōezu: Genroku jūyonnen shōgatsu* in the Kanō Bunko at Tōhoku Daigaku Fuzoku Toshokan (Tōhoku University Library).

12. Foldout following p. 80 of *Nihonbashi kushi*; the reports are contained in the manuscript collection "Edobashi hirokōji narabi ni moyori kyūki" (hereafter cited as "Edobashi"), Aki, doc. 49, original at the Kokuritsu Kokkai Toshokan (National Diet Library), microfilm reproduction available at the Kanō Bunko, Tōhoku Daigaku Fuzoku Toshokan; and in *TS:S*, vol. 21, pp. 545–49, and vol. 22, pp. 59–65. Saitō describes the embankments, but he seems to rely on Asai's earlier work; see the entry for Meireki 3 in Kaneko, *Zōtei: Bukō nenpyō*, vol. 1, p. 60, and Asai's comments in his *Musashi abumi*.

gatemen and "bridge guards" (*hashi bannin*) to patrol "day and night." In addition, the shogunate nominated a resident of Aomono-chō, a man named Magobei, to serve as its own guard man (*tsuji bannin*). Magobei, and his descendants after him, received a stipend and an "oil subsidy" of thirteen *ryō* of gold a year, for which they were supposed to assist the quarters and to ensure peace and order in the firebreak, seeing to it that no one used it as an arena to settle "fights and quarrels."[13] The most important responsibility assigned to Magobei and to the residents of the two quarters, however, was simply to make certain that Edobashi retain its function as a firebreak, for a shogunal decree of 1658 directed all persons living between Nihonbashi and Nakabashi to gather there whenever a fire threatened from the north.[14]

The First Intrusion: Quais and Commerce, Warehouses and Wagon Yards

The oversight responsibilities assigned to Aomono-chō and Hon Zaimoku-chō imposed heavy financial obligations on the two quarters, which the leaders of the neighborhoods sought to lighten by leasing out space within the firebreak to seasonal merchants. The first to breech the sanctity of Edobashi, in the very summer of 1657 if the documentation is reliable, were seasonal merchants who rented a small plot on the Kaede River, just south of the bridge, and from summer through autumn sold vegetables, herbs, and plants. The following winter the cheerful orange of the tangerine-like *mikan* brightened the still ashen firebreak as shipping agents from the Kii peninsula occupied the same landing used by the vegetable dealers in the summer.[15] Within another year or so, men from Bōsō peninsula began to rent space from the twentieth day of the year's final lunar month. They harvested pine branches and bamboo cuttings favored for New Year's decorations and sent them on barges across Edo Bay for sale at Edobashi. Sometime in the 1660s, wholesalers of "Western melons" (*suika*), a variety of watermelon introduced to Japan in the 1570s from Africa, staked out a claim in the firebreak as well. Year after year until the end of the Tokugawa period, the same groups of vegetable, fruit, and pine-bough dealers appeared in turn at Edobashi, marking the cycle of the seasons.

13. As Katō explains in chap. 2 of this volume, *tsuji ban'ya* guardhouses were established in samurai neighborhoods. Edobashi merited one because it was shogunal land (*goyōchi*), and as was common practice when such land was located in commoner neighborhoods, the shogunate employed a merchant to manage the facility. See "Edobashi," Aki, doc. 49; *TS:S*, vol. 21, pp. 545–49.

14. Takayanagi Shinzō and Ishii Ryōsuke, eds., *Gofuregaki Kanhō shūsei* (Iwanami Shoten, 1934), doc. 1437, pp. 764–65.

15. It seems likely that the vegetable and tangerine merchants were reopening seasonal businesses that had flourished at Edobashi before the great fires. The history of the various markets can be found in "Edobashi," Haru, doc. 6; *TS:S*, vol. 20, pp. 652–69, and vol. 22, pp. 365–70.

While the seasonal merchants came and went along the periphery of the firebreak, more permanent establishments began to put down roots near the bridge approach and along the roadway that ran to Nihonbashi. In a quest for still more revenues Aomono-chō and Hon Zaimoku-chō began to lease space to men who wished to put up shops and who, throughout all the months of the year, purveyed *komamono*, told fortunes, managed teahouses known as *niurijaya*, dealt in used books, and sold firewood.[16] The last two occupations need no explanation; the first involved persons who stocked specialized categories of merchandise that included face powders and rouges, fragrances and soaps, hair lotions and decorations (ribbons and spangles, combs and ornamental hairpins fashioned from a variety of woods and shells), false sideburns and toupees, pouches of all sorts (for eyeglasses, fans, smoking accessories), socks and underclothing, and love potions, sexual gadgetry, and how-to manuals.[17] Some fortunetellers (those known as *toshiura*) peered into the minds of the gods in order to fathom the course of the customer's future or to predict a specific event, such as the outcome of a sumo match; others (the *zenchō*) studied omens (dreams, the behavior of foxes, unusual weather patterns) and prescribed taboos and incantations for clients who faced possible misfortune. The teahouses offered passers-by tired from shopping and divination a cup of tea and side dishes of vegetables and fish stewed in a house recipe of soy sauce, sugar, salt, and spices.

Although the documentation is clear about the kinds of shops that opened their shutters at Edobashi, the chronology of their appearance is less certain. Some digests submitted by the neighborhood chiefs (*nanushi*) of Aomono-chō and Hon Zaimoku-chō to the city magistrates claim that more than one hundred businesses opened "during the office tenure of Kamio Bizen no Kami and Murakoshi Nagato no Kami."[18] Since Kamio served as city magistrate from Kan'ei 16 (1639).5.18 until Kanbun 1 (1661).3.8 and Murakoshi from Manji 2 (1659).2.9 to Kanbun 7 (1667).12.16, the shops would have begun operations sometime between the Second Month of 1659 and the Third Month of 1661. The authors of these memoranda also claim, in somewhat affected self-righteousness, that all the merchants concerned had faithfully secured permission from the shogunate before hanging out their shop signs.

Perhaps, but later submissions to higher officials amended that story and set forth what ultimately became the officially accepted history of the enterprises. According to this version, the two quarters concluded lease agreements with fifty-two shops between 1657 and the spring of 1661.[19] Moreover, it seems that neither the officials of the quarters nor the merchants sought prior approval for the leases, almost surely because of apprehensions

16. *TS:S*, vol. 23, pp. 243–45.
17. Ema Tsutomu, *Sōshin to keshō*, Ema Tsutomu chosakushū 4 (Chūō Kōronsha, 1976), pp. 283–343.
18. "Edobashi," Haru, doc. 11; *TS:S*, vol. 22, pp. 307–9.
19. "Edobashi," Haru, docs. 27, 39, 40; *TS:S*, vol. 23, pp. 243–45; vol. 27, pp. 374–76; vol. 32, pp. 379–85.

that such requests would be refused. When the shogunate later discovered what had happened, it demanded an explanation and conducted an investigation. In later negotiations, the neighborhood chiefs stressed their need for revenues sufficient to permit them to discharge their responsibility to look after the firebreak, and in the end the shogunate permitted the shops to stay open. But it also imposed several conditions, by which it hoped both to demonstrate its authority and to maintain Edobashi as a firebreak, even if in somewhat mutated form. The most important of these conditions required that all shops be "stalls" (*tokomise*). That is, each structure was to contain a shop only; there were to be no combination shop-residences, as in ordinary merchant neighborhoods. No one would be allowed to live within the firebreak. Moreover, the stalls were to be constructed in a simple manner so that they could be pulled down quickly and carted away if a fire did break out (or if the shogun, as was sometimes his wont, decided to journey to the hunting grounds north of Edo by barge, up the Nihonbashi and Sumida rivers).

Renting space to fifty-two stalls did not bring in enough revenue for Aomono-chō and Hon Zaimoku-chō, however, and the two quarters continued to lease out additional commercial space within the firebreak, so that by the opening of the eighteenth century customers at Edobashi could choose from the wares and services of more than one hundred stalls. When in 1707 the leaders of the two residential quarters seemed to be on the verge of signing still another round of leases, the owners of the existing stalls objected in a strongly worded petition requesting that the shogunate limit the number of businesses permitted at Edobashi.[20] The subsequent negotiations were intricate, involving as they did a three-way reconciliation of conflicting interests. Set against the obvious desires of Aomono-chō and Hon Zaimoku-chō to exploit the commercial potential of the area were the wishes of the established stall owners to limit further competition and the preference of the shogunate to retain the integrity of the firebreak.[21]

Caught in a swirl of tides that pulled in opposing directions, the city magistrates referred the issue to the senior councilors (*rōjū*), the top echelon of officials within the shogunate. After careful deliberation, a compromise was struck. The shogunate respected the claims of Aomono-chō and Hon Zaimoku-chō for additional lease income by authorizing all existing shops to remain open, while at the same time reminding the leaders of the two quarters about the duties incumbent upon their neighborhoods.[22] The stall owners were pleased with the decision to limit the number of businesses to 107 in perpetuity. (Of these stall operators, 71 specialized in one sort or

20. *TS:S*, vol. 27, pp. 374–76, and vol. 32, pp. 379–80.

21. See, for instance, the government's earlier prohibitions against the establishment of "general merchandise shops" (*yorozu akinai*), as well as "little theaters and public toilets" (*koya setchin*), in all firebreaks: *Shōhō jiroku*, vol. 1, doc. 287, pp. 96–97, and doc. 551, p. 191.

22. The shogunate did not hesitate to compel the neighborhoods to honor their obligations; see, for example, documentation concerning extensive repair work required on Edobashi Bridge in *TS:S*, vol. 27, pp. 83–87.

another of *komamono*, 15 told fortunes, 11 managed teahouses, 7 featured used books, and 3 sold bundles of kindling and firewood.) But in exchange for this concession, the shogunate reaffirmed the principle that the businesses were to be run out of stalls, not combination shop-residences, and it insisted that the stall owners share the burden of firefighting duties around Edobashi and assume responsibility for the stipend and allowances paid to the shogunate's guard man.[23] In addition, officials soon required stall owners to sign a written oath "to obey all laws"; "to refrain from quarrels and arguments"; "to forgo wooden clogs [*geta*]"; and never to be "rude" or "to stand around idly, hands tucked into one's sleeves."[24]

As the seventeenth century gave way to the eighteenth, still more merchants found ways to justify acquisition of space within the firebreak, and Edobashi reemerged as an important transshipment center. In 1674, for instance, a group of fish wholesalers received permission from the shogunate to offload cargoes at a wharf on the Kaeda River just downstream from the boundaries of the firebreak, and for this privilege they agreed to supply fresh fish to the shogun's household at reduced prices. The Kaede River, however, tended to silt up frequently near the landing, so in 1710 the group sought permission to construct a new wharf upstream, inside the firebreak proper. The city magistrates conducted an investigation and sent a recommendation to the senior councilors, who approved the use of a site some fifty feet square just south of the bridge for the offloading and sale of fish.[25]

In 1693, even before the fish wholesalers arrived, a group of shipping agents from Kisarazu, on the Bōsō peninsula, sought permission to construct a wharf for offloading cargoes on the south bank of the Nihonbashi River, just to the west of Edobashi Bridge. For some time these men had rented a similar facility on the opposite shore (so prosperous that it commonly was called the "Kisarazu riverbank"), but a disagreement had arisen with officials of that neighborhood, and the Kisarazu shippers now wished to transfer their business operations to a new site. The city magistrates carried out an investigation and, after conferring with their superiors, granted the request to relocate, provided that all agree that only boats from Kisarazu use the new landing.[26]

As commodities began to move through Edobashi, some men sought to profit by opening warehouse facilities. The first to do so were the city elders (*machidoshiyori*) Kitamura Hikoemon and Naraya Ichiemon, men whose official positions supposedly obligated them to safeguard the government's

23. Ibid., vol. 22, pp. 307–9, and vol. 32, pp. 219–20, 379–85.
24. Ibid., vol. 20, pp. 658–60.
25. "Edobashi," Natsu, doc. 83; *TS:S*, vol. 22, pp. 63–64. In 1792 this group of wholesalers received permission to construct offices to the west of the wharf; Ōkuma Yoshikuni, *Edo kenchiku sōwa* (Tōe Shuppansha, 1947), pp. 63–64.
26. *TS:S*, vol. 22, p. 64. One cannot be certain about the volume of cargoes offloaded at these new wharfs, but by the end of the eighteenth century the Kisarazu wholesalers annually shipped more than 200,000 *koku* of rice alone through that facility: Yoshiwara Ken'ichirō, "Edobashi hirokōji no keisei to kōzō," *Rekishichiri gakkai kaihō* 101 (1979), p. 29.

interests. As Katō Takashi points out in Chapter 2 of this volume, the city elders performed a wide range of administrative services within the merchant and artisan quarters on behalf of the shogunate, but received no salaries. Rather, the shogunate granted to the three families who held the office on a hereditary basis the right to use various plots of land, which the elders then rented out in order to acquire income for both personal and often burdensome office expenses. In the Kanbun period (1661–1672), Kitamura petitioned the shogunate for usage rights to two portions of the embankment at Edobashi. He intended, he said, to erect warehouses, in response to requests from merchants in the neighborhood who, he claimed, wished to have a place to store their valuables in case another major conflagration broke out.[27] In 1694, Naraya deployed similar arguments when he successfully petitioned to convert the three remaining sections of the embankment to warehouses.[28] According to Hatano Jun, who has inspected several screens that depict the new storehouses, it seems likely that Kitamura and Naraya actually tore down the earthen embankment and replaced it with five warehouses constructed of stone walls and roofed with a sod thatch.[29]

In the early eighteenth century, the neighborhood chiefs (*nanushi*) of Aomono-chō and Hon Zaimoku-chō decided to ask the city magistrates to permit them to build commercial storehouses. Their arguments played on two themes. For one thing, there was a shortage of adequate warehouse space, and whenever fire threatened, residents of the area ("commoner and samurai alike") dragged their goods and belongings into the firebreak, increasing the danger that flying embers would spread the blaze. In addition, the leaders of the two quarters touched a shogunal nerve that always had proved sensitive in the past: the shouldering of obligations ought to be reciprocated with special perquisites. In the decades since Edobashi had been designated as "fire-prevention land" in 1657, they declared, the residents of Aomono-chō and Hon Zaimoku-chō faithfully had done all that was required of them: they had paid the expenses of guardhouses and bridge guards; erected and maintained the wooden fence and entry gates into the firebreak; kept the bridge and its southern approach clean and in good repair; looked after abandoned children and discarded property; and maintained the public peace with patrols "day and night." On top of that, every time the shogun made an outing by river barge, the neighborhood chiefs were kept extremely busy—"from the preceding day," they complained—making certain that all was in order and that nothing illegal or offensive caught the hegemon's eye.[30]

27. Minami Kazuo, ed., *Kyōhō sen'yō ruishū*, vol. 2, Kyū-bakufu hikitsugisho eiin sōkan 2 (Nogami Shuppan, 1985), docs. 14, pp. 184–85, and 62, pp. 239–41.

28. *TS:S*, vol. 22, p. 628.

29. For Hatano's report on the screens in the collection at Tōkyō Toritsu Chūō Toshokan (Tokyo Metropolitan Central Library), see his "Edobashi hirokōji," pp. 35.

30. "Edobashi," Haru, doc. 17; *TS:S*, vol. 22, pp. 60–61, and vol. 23, pp. 221–22; Tōkyō Daigaku Shiryō Hensanjo, ed., *DaiNihon kinsei shiryū: Shichū torishime ruishū*, vol. 10 (Tōkyō Daigaku Shuppankai, 1972) (hereafter cited as *Shichū*), doc. 217, p. 197.

The petition from the two neighborhood chiefs went to the city magistrate, Nakayama Izumo no Kami, who conducted an investigation, solicited the opinions of the surrounding neighborhoods that would be affected by the request, and sent his report to the senior councilors. The shogun's top echelon of officials responded positively, as they nearly always had done, to the notion that responsibility and accountability were tied in a Gordian knot with privilege, and in the Seventh Month of 1720 they signified their approval of the project. However, the senior councilors also instructed the two quarters to erect and maintain within the firebreak a large, roofed signboard (*kōsatsu*) where official notices and proclamations could be posted. Moreover, officials specified, no wood could be used to construct the warehouses. All walls, eaves, and fittings had to be molded from fire-resistant mud-plaster, and the buildings had to be situated along an east-west sewer line that separated the Edobashi firebreak from commercial neighborhoods to the south, thus adding another line of defense against fires driven by winds from the north. Finally, as part of the reforms in firefighting preparations that William W. Kelly discusses in Chapter 13, the two quarters were required to share with several other neighborhoods the costs of building, maintaining, and repairing a fire tower, whose silhouette came to dominate the immediate skyline.[31]

The increased pace of commercial traffic also brought oxen and transportation wagons into Edobashi. One group of teamsters traditionally kept their beasts and equipment in the Shiba area but did most of their business along the wharfs at Edobashi. The daily commute took considerable time, and in 1707 they asked to rent space within the firebreak. The neighborhood chief of Hon Zaimoku-chō submitted the petition to the city elders on behalf of the teamsters. As part of proper bureaucratic procedure, the elders passed it to their superiors, who quickly signaled their approval. From then until the Meiji period, the oxcart drivers leased a plot of land some thirty yards square in the southern portion of the firebreak, where they stabled their animals and parked their wagons.[32]

To some extent, the shogunate could permit these commercial activities and still persuade itself that Edobashi retained its integrity as a firebreak. After all, the wharfs were situated along the periphery of the tract; the warehouses were constructed of fire-resistant materials (and those managed by the elders Kitamura and Naraya functioned very much like an embankment); the stalls could be collapsed and removed; and the sheds in the wagon yard presented the minimum of combustibles. But clearly the wind was shifting to a new quarter, and as was so often the case, the commoners of the city were the first to sense it. In 1657 the shogunate had instructed that two different types of firebreaks be created: *hiyokechi*, "fire-prevention

31. *TS:S*, vol. 31, pp. 933–43, and vol. 23, pp. 221–23.
32. "Edobashi," Aki, doc. 59; *TS:S*, vol. 22, pp. 63–64. From 1712 to 1717 the teamsters had to cede their space to Nezu Shrine to use as a *tabisho*, the resting site for the shrine's sacred palanquin (*mikoshi*) during the annual summer festival. See *TS:S*, vol. 22, pp. 318–20.

land," which officials imagined would remain permanently vacant (and often encircled with a fence); and *hirokōji*, "widened streets," which could be lined with commercial establishments as long as those structures did not intrude into the open space that was designed as a sanctuary or escape route in case of fire. Thus *hirokōji* included the broad approaches to Ryōgoku and Eitai bridges, famous for tiny theaters that featured oddities and grotesqueries, as well as such places as Atago Shita and Shiba Akabane, near the great Zōjōji temple, whose spacious streets were edged with shops catering to crowds of pilgrims and sightseers.

Originally Edobashi was designated as *hiyokechi*, and according to the research of Hatano Jun, that term was applied to the area consistently throughout the seventeenth century. But from the early eighteenth century, people began to speak of the "Edobashi *hirokōji*."[33] The evolution in contemporary parlance was eloquent; it measured Edobashi's decline as a firebreak, bespoke its emergence as a commercial center. Even more than that, the new phraseology legitimated still further incursions into the firebreak, changes that would transform Edobashi's character irrevocably and negate forever its utility as any kind of firebreak, whether *hiyokechi* or *hirokōji*.

THE SECOND INTRUSION: BURGHERS, GODS, AND ENTERTAINERS

As had been the case earlier, city officials drawn from the merchant status group helped to drive in the wedges of the new incursions. In 1732 the city elders Kitamura and Naraya petitioned their superiors, the city magistrates Ōoka Echizen no Kami and Inō Shimotsuke no Kami, for permission to convert two of their five storehouses to "residential warehouses" where "cooking and heating fires would be freely permitted."[34] As part of their request, the current heads of the Kitamura and Naraya families complained that they could not attract sufficient numbers of customers to keep their warehouses full. The facilities themselves were to blame: the stone walls were clammy, interiors damp; the roofs leaked, clumps of sod fell onto the goods below. The two elders scarcely needed to harp on the obvious: rent collections were meager, but their own office expenses continued to mount.

Moreover, the two men asserted, precedent was in their corner. The shogunate, they were happy to point out, already had been party to a similar metamorphose of a firebreak at Hon Shiragane-chō, in the Kanda

33. Hatano, "Edobashi hirokōji," pp. 42–43. The first reference to Edobashi as a *hirokōji* appears in an entry for Shōtoku 2 (1712) in Saitō's *Bukō nenpyō*. The eighteenth-century documents in "Edobashi" and *TS:S* consistently employ the term *hirokōji* when they refer to Edobashi in the eighteenth century and use both *hirokōji* and *hiyokechi* (*goyō hiyokechi*) when they discuss the early history of the firebreak.

34. *TS:S*, vol. 22, pp. 628–30, and vol. 25, pp. 115–16; Minami, *Kyōhō sen'yō ruishū*, vol. 2, doc. 20, pp. 192–94; "Edobashi kurayashiki sono hoka moyori kyūki," original at the Kokuritsu Kokkai Toshokan, microfilm reproduction available at the Kanō Bunko, Tōhoku Daigaku Fuzoku Toshokan, entry for Tenmei 5 (1885); Hatano, "Edobashi hirokōji," p. 36.

area. There, too, the shogun's engineers had erected a set of embankments after the Meireki fires, and the senior councilors had authorized their conversion to warehouses in 1713 and then to merchant housing just a few years later. Ōoka and Inō carried out the obligatory investigation, and then lent their support to the petition, provided that all new residents be formed into five-family groups (*goningumi*) and placed under the authority of local neighborhood officials. By the autumn of 1732 Kitamura and Naraya had demolished two warehouses, one each at the eastern- and westernmost ends of the firebreak, and put up rental housing for merchants.[35] Kitamura and Naraya referred to the dwellings as "warehouse residences" (perhaps in order to continue the conceit that Edobashi essentially remained a firebreak), but the new buildings in fact were done in the so-called *nuriyazukuri* style, the most common type of construction for merchant housing, with tiles on the roofs and clapboard-like planks for the exterior walls (except for the painted, mud-plaster upper facades of two-story houses).

In 1767 the head of the Naraya family returned with another petition.[36] One of his remaining warehouses had been damaged badly in a fire in the Fourth Month of that year. He could rebuild it, he explained, but that might not be a wise business decision, for he still had trouble attracting customers. The family had ripped off the sod-thatch roofs in 1738, replacing them with the new lightweight terra-cotta tile that had won favor with Edo builders, but, Naraya complained, the same old stone blocks supported the new tiles. The interiors were still exceedingly damp. Moreover, he had resorted to leasing space in one facility to merchants who dealt in fish preserved in salt, and the "offensive" odor of the fish "defamed" his reputation. After a quick investigation, the city magistrates concluded that the facts were as Naraya stated them; his warehousing operations were in financial difficulty.

The city magistrates sent a memorandum to the senior councilors supporting Naraya's request, but things did not go smoothly for the city elder. Edobashi's integrity as a firebreak may well have been compromised in the past, but officially it was still a *hirokōji*, and the current senior councilors did not seem inclined to denigrate appearance or function further. Consequently, they instructed the commissioners of engineering works (*fushin bugyō*) to conduct another investigation; raised questions about what sorts of buildings Naraya intended to construct; asked how Edobashi could function as a firebreak if more housing crowded in; surveyed the residents of nearby neighborhoods about their reactions to Naraya's proposal; and generally dragged their bureaucratic feet. Naraya renewed his application in 1772. Again he argued that warehousing could not be profitable, drew attention to the existing need for more merchant housing, recalled the past precedents in Hon Shiragane-chō, and alluded to the taxes that the renters would contribute annually to the shogunal treasury. Finally Naraya won out. In

35. See the Kyōhō-period map reproduced in Bakufu Fushin Bugyō, comp., *Edo jōka hensen ezushū*, ed. and rev. Asakura Haruhiko, vol. 6 (Hara Shobō, 1985), p. 143.

36. *TS:S*, vol. 25, pp. 109–19.

1775 he received permission to build merchant housing on the warehouse plot adjacent to Edobashi Bridge; the rents, he was reminded, must be used to cover the expenses he was obligated to shoulder as a city elder.[37]

As people took up permanent residence within the firebreak, they constructed an Inari Shrine, a place of worship for the tutelary god of Edobashi. Indeed, such a shrine probably had existed before the great fires of 1657; the tangerine dealers, it is said, carried the deity with them from the Kii peninsula in the 1630s or 1640s to protect their cargoes on the high seas, and the residents of Edobashi then adopted him as their guardian deity.[38] What happened to that shrine right after the fire is a mystery; it is not until the 1760s that it reappears in the documents and maps of the Edobashi area, to the west of the grounds where the oxcarts were kept.[39]

Like all Inari shrines, the Edobashi shrine was linked, however indirectly, to the great Inari Taisha in Fushimi, and the local deity was considered to be a manifestation of the principal fox divinity, worshiped at countless shrines in rural Japan as a harvest god. Whenever Inari was enshrined in an urban center, however, merchants and artisans usually attached an additional name to their fox and sought his divine favor to help them overcome the problems of daily life, especially those posed by fire and ill health.[40] The Edobashi deity was known as the Okina Inari, and he reputedly had great powers to cure toothaches and gum disease. "Old and young alike," the documents claim, came to Edobashi "from all over the city" to offer prayers and incantations for relief from the pain and distress of dental problems.[41]

Other changes also were transforming Edobashi, detracting from its value as a firebreak and making it increasingly akin to other merchant neighborhoods around the city. In 1720, for instance, at the same time that Aomono-chō and Hon Zaimoku-chō solicited approval to enter the warehousing business, fifty-two stall owners won consent to rebuild their stalls in the *nuriyazukuri* style typical of ordinary shops.[42] Then, in the 1730s, Aomono-chō and Hon Zaimoku-chō complained that the orientation of their warehouses left them vulnerable to the ravages of wind and rain, and leaders of the two quarters received permission to relocate their operations.[43] It is perhaps true that the old structures had suffered repeated damage, but

37. Bakufu Fushin Bugyō, *Edo jōka hensen ezushū*, vol. 6, p. 144.

38. *Shichū*, doc. 215, pp. 189–91.

39. Ibid., doc. 209, pp. 174–77; *TS:S*, vol. 23, p. 222.

40. Miyata Noboru, "Edo chōnin no shinkō," in Nishiyama Matsunosuke, ed., *Edo chōnin no kenkyū*, vol. 2 (Yoshikawa Kōbunkan, 1973), pp. 249–71.

41. *Shichū*, doc. 209, pp. 174–77; *Nihonbashi kushi*, pp. 929–30.

42. Hatano, "Edobashi hirokōji," p. 38; *TS:S*, vol. 22, pp. 252–53. It is a matter of conjecture whether the stall owners actually built new shop-residences or merely reconstructed their stalls with the materials used in residential construction, but later descriptions refer to shops that were indistinguishable in style from ordinary establishments; see the early nineteenth-century depiction of the residences at Edobashi in Kitagawa Morisada, *Morisada mankō*, ed. Asakura Haruhiko, vol. 1 (Tōkyōdō, 1973), p. 72.

43. *TS:S*, vol. 22, pp. 59–63, and vol. 23, pp. 221–23.

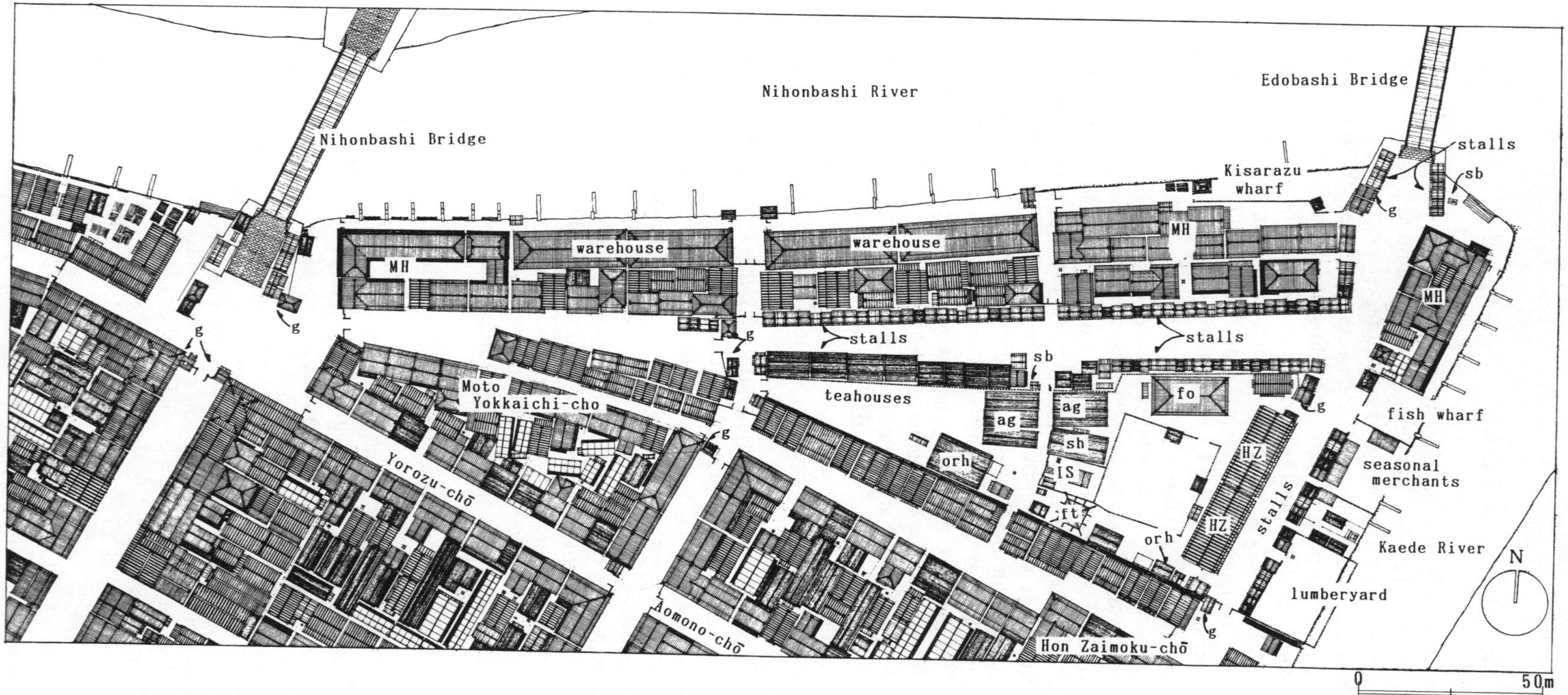

Edobashi in the late eighteenth century

ag=archery galleries
ft=fire tower
HZ=Hon Zaimoku-chō warehouse
MH=merchant housing
sb=signboard

fo=fishery offce
g=guardhouse or gatehouse
IS=Inari Shrine
orh=outcast rooming house
sh=storytellers hall

Edobashi Bridge

Kisarazu wharf

Nihonbashi River

Nihonbashi Bridge

fish wharf

seasonal merchants

Kaede River

lumberyard

Hon Zaimoku-chō

Aomono-chō

Yorozu-chō

Moto Yokkaichi-chō

teahouses

warehouse

warehouse

warehouse

stalls

stalls

stalls

stalls

stalls

N

50m

0

the new buildings reopened on sites that offered enhanced commercial advantages and that were well away from the sewer, where the warehouses had formed a secondary line of defense against fire from the north. Aomono-chō rebuilt its facility close to the roadway that ran to Nihonbashi Bridge, and Hon Zaimoku-chō relocated its warehouse on the busy north-south street that paralleled the Kaede River and linked Edobashi with Nakabashi and Kyōbashi. For this advantage the quarters agreed to construct and keep in good repair a new quai next to the bridge.

The entertainers arrived in the 1760s. They added a final dimension of play and amusement to Edobashi's evolving character, but not before their appearance on the scene pitted neighbor against neighbor and called the wrath of the shogunate down upon one of the leaders of Aomono-chō. As was perhaps appropriate for Edobashi, a fire kindled the incident. The leaders of Aomono-chō lost their warehouse in the same blaze that put Naraya out of business in 1767. Like the city elder, the leaders of the residential quarter calculated that it would not be profitable to rebuild their structure, so they began to rent out the vacant space to teahouses and archery galleries, street performers and storytellers, an action they kept secret from higher officials even while petitioning (unsuccessfully) to put up rental housing.

Some of the entertainers offered innocent, enjoyable amusement to residents and visitors to Edobashi. Tucked away on a lane just behind the teamsters' stables was a hall where masters of the *kōdan* genre of storytelling held forth. This form of entertainment reached its peak of popularity in the late eighteenth century, when little theaters could be found in nearly every amusement center in the downtown sections of Edo.[44] Admissions were scaled to the pocketbooks of commoners, not much more than a bowl of noodles (half price for children), and the storytellers appeared in turn for several hours in the late afternoon and then again after the dinner hour. The men performed solo, and they cribbed their material from traditional warrior epics, from contemporary scandals involving merchants and their amorous escapades with women from the prostitution quarters, and from the dramas acted out on the city's much more expensive kabuki and puppet stages. Individual storytellers became famous for their embellishments: audiences crowded into the little theaters to hear them conjure up dreadful villains, concoct new and potentially fatal ordeals for well-known heroes and heroines, and contrive bizarre twists of plot that transformed familiar and long-cherished stories into fresh and exciting adventures.

Just a few steps away from the storytellers' hall was a *hiningoya*, a rooming house for a hereditary category of outcasts that included former convicts and families that had fallen into poverty and lost their shop-residences. The shogunate prohibited these persons from engaging in commerce, artisanal enterprises, or even manual labor.[45] The outcasts were permitted to beg,

44. Sekine Mokuan, *Kōdan rakugo konjakutan*, in Abe Kazue and Sugita Kenji, eds., *Kōdan rakugokō* (Yūzankaku, 1967).

45. For additional information on outcasts, see Minami Kazuo, *Bakumatsu Edo shakai no kenkyū* (Yoshikawa Kōbunkan, 1978), pp. 325–96; Ishii Ryōsuke, *Edo no senmin* (Akashi Shoten, 1991).

however, and they moved around the city, renting lodgings by the day at any of several hundred outcast rooming houses in Edo. An "outcast headman" (*hiningashira*) presided over each lodge, and for a fee (commonly a portion of a day's take) he assigned "begging space" within his bailiwick to outcasts who rented rooms from him. Each headman was held accountable for making certain that his tenants obeyed all laws. In a complicated chain of command that ran to the top echelons of the shogunate, the headman of each lodge reported to one or another of four higher regional headmen, who in turn received their directions from "Danzaemon," the name taken by successive heads of a family whom the shogunate entrusted with regulating the activities of all outcasts in Edo.[46]

Like their fellow outcasts, the persons who stayed at the two rooming houses in Edobashi (a second, smaller lodging stood near the Kaede River) seldom simply begged, preferring instead to amuse people with street performances and then to accept offerings from the crowds they attracted.[47] The outcasts displayed remarkable creative energies, mastering and helping to shape a range of entertainments that included *shikatanō*, abbreviated renditions of classical noh dramas; *kadosaimon*, in which the performer set up an altar in front of a person's house or on a street corner and offered prayers and songs to bring forth blessings from Buddhist and Shinto deities; *toriai*, in which outcast women dressed in special clothing and solicited offerings for playing the samisen; and *kowairo*, imitations of scenes made popular by famous kabuki actors or chanters for puppet performances.

More risqué entertainments also were available at Edobashi. Next to the storytelling hall stood several archery galleries. Patrons paid a small fee and received a willow bow nearly three feet long and a supply of arrows, which they winged at targets set up some forty or fifty feet away. But many would-be sharpshooters, both at Edobashi and at similar shooting galleries in more famous amusement centers such as the one at Ryōgoku Bridge, were really aiming at the so-called *yatorime*, the "arrow-pulling maidens." If contemporary accounts are to be accepted, these young women were to the very last one beautiful, with ne'er an exception, and their customers inevitably became infatuated with them.[48] Most of the young ladies were also trollops, their arrow-fetching duties little more than an opportunity to advertise their other talents (and fees).[49]

Clustered together along the roadway that connected Edobashi with Nihonbashi were a number of "water teahouses," *mizujaya*. These establish-

46. Shiomi Sen'ichirō, *Danzaemon to sono jidai* (Hihyōsha, 1991).

47. Miyao Shigeo and Kimura Senshū, *Edo shomin gaigei fūzokushi* (Tenbōsha, 1970); Takayanagi Kaneyoshi, *Edo no daidōgei* (Kashiwa Shobō, 1982); Asakura Kamezō (pseud. Asakura Musei), *Autorō no geinō—misemono, daidōgei* (Gakugei Shorin, 1969).

48. See the early nineteenth-century accounts in the entries "Atago" and "Kinryūsan Sensōji," in Terakado Seiken, *Edo hanjōki*, ed. Asakura Haruhiko and Andō Kikuji, Tōyō bunko 259 and 276 (Heibonsha, 1989), vol. 1, pp. 63–77, and vol. 2, pp. 228–43.

49. Nishiyama Matsunosuke, ed., *Yūjo*, Nihon kohyakka 9 (Kondō Shuppan, 1988), p. 249.

ments differed from the stalls that for decades had served tea and light refreshments to tired shoppers. The new water teahouses, which began to proliferate in Edo during the 1740s and reached the height of their popularity at the end of the century, were much more exuberant places of entertainment. Like the shooting galleries, the teahouses employed women. Young "signboard girls" (*kanban musume*) stood outside on the roadway, where they displayed advertisements, implored passers-by to venture in for a cup of tea, and sometimes even physically dragged potential customers into the shops.[50] "Tea-ladling women" (*chakumi onna*) served the patrons. Some of these women (O-Sode of the Sakaiya in Asakusa and O-Hisa of the Takashimaya at Ryōgoku, among others) became famous throughout Edo for their grace and beauty, and they were celebrated in the woodblock prints of Harunobu and Utamaro, although such an honor does not seem to have touched any of the women who worked at Edobashi.[51]

At first most teahouses in Edo were done in "hanging reed screen" construction (*yoshizu hari*). That is, posts and beams supported the roof and lateral trusses, from which reed screens could be lowered to keep out the elements, or internally to provide a suggestion of privacy. Generally a fire was kept going under a large cauldron in front of the shop, where the tea-ladling women presided over the service of customers. Increasingly teahouses of this rustic style gave way to more elaborate structures that boasted fixed walls and tatami floors. Generally these later shops contained private rooms that clients rented for social gatherings or business discussions, and neighborhood shops catered foods and other provisions to supplement the complementary tea. Not uncommonly a room or two in the rear were reserved for use by prostitutes or by lovers for their romantic assignations. By the 1790s, most of the teahouses at Edobashi were of this latter variety.[52]

Surely the entertainers injected a new vitality into Edobashi in the 1760s, and just as surely the street performers and storytellers, prostitutes and tea ladies did well enough economically, attracting customers throughout the 1770s. But they were not welcomed by all; many residents of Edobashi believed that the entertainers threatened the quality of life in their neighborhood. For some time those persons held their tongues, but an opportunity to protest came in 1784, when the city elders heard a rumor that Kozaemon, neighborhood chief of Aomono-chō, had built rental housing on the site of the quarter's former warehouse, despite the the shogunate's earlier rejection of a petition to construct such residences. Called to account, Kozaemon tried

50. Satō Kanando, *Ehon mizujaya fūzokukō* (Yūkō Shoten, 1977).

51. For an Utamaro print featuring O-Hisa, see Hashimoto Sumiko and Takahashi Masao, eds., *Ukiyoe ni miru Edo no kurashi* (Kawade Shobō Shinsha, 1988), p. 103.

52. The first teahouses at Edobashi were of "hanging reed screen" construction, and a report submitted by local officials to the city magistrates in 1788 listed fifteen such teahouses. However, a document prepared just three years later, following an on-site inspection by shogunal officials, referred to ten teahouses, all of permanent plank-and-clapboard construction. See *TS:S*, vol. 27, p. 227, and vol. 32, pp. 379–85; Yoshiwara, "Edobashi hirokōji," p. 29.

as best he could to skirt the most troublesome aspects of the issue. He finally admitted, however, that because the fire had deprived Aomono-chō of its traditional warehousing income, the quarter had been renting a single house to Tamagaki Gakunosuke, an elder of the sumo profession, to use as a training center for his stable of Goliaths. But, Kozaemon declared, no one actually "resided" there and the wrestlers "did not use cooking or heating fires."[53]

That revelation touched off an intense inquiry that spread out over several months.[54] The shogunate ordered an on-site inspection; collected affidavits from Kozaemon and Tamagaki; heard out the opinions of the leaders of surrounding residential quarters; held discussions with virtually everyone touched by the incident. The investigation accepted mixed evidence about whether Kozaemon had constructed rental housing on an extensive scale, but it did establish beyond any doubt that the neighborhood chief and his wife had built their own large, two-story residence, lived in it for some time, and then rented it to Tamagaki and his wrestlers, who used it not just as a training center but also as a "standard residence." Kozaemon's transgressions were serious: he had openly defied an official injunction and the shogunate stood prepared to order stiff penalties.

The inquiry also presented an opportunity for the representatives of neighboring quarters to submit documentation that retraced the chronology of privileges within the firebreak. They took care to specify very precisely just what prerogatives had been authorized in the past, to identify the recipients of those considerations, and to review the responsibilities that accompanied the privileges. Quite clearly, all of the local officials were irked by the manner in which Kozaemon had managed Aomono-chō's holdings at Edobashi, and they supplied information to the city magistrates that spelled out for the first time exactly what entertainers now made Edobashi home. Representatives of several quarters joined in declaring Kozaemon's behavior "inappropriate" for a person "who held the office of neighborhood chief," and they concurred that his excesses had to be dealt with harshly. In the end, the shogunate ruled that the sumo giants had to go. ("Their house is to be demolished immediately.") So, too, did Kozaemon. By official decree, he was removed from office, stripped of his property, deprived of his status as a merchant, and, on the ninth day of the Fifth Month of 1785, "at the seventh hour of the evening, he was accompanied to Tokiwabashi Gate and exiled from Edo," condemned to live out his days as an outcast.

Eventually calm returned to Edobashi. The shogunate transferred oversight responsibilities from Aomono-chō to Moto Yokkaichi-chō.[55] Interestingly enough, with more responsible local leadership in place, the shogunate permitted the entertainers to stay on; after all, even they could make some claim on precedent, having been in business by that time for nearly

53. "Edobashi," Haru, doc. 30; *TS:S*, vol. 29, pp. 401–3.
54. "Edobashi," Haru, doc. 31; *TS:S*, vol. 29, pp. 586–612.
55. *TS:S*, vol. 32, pp. 214–22.

two decades. (But the government rejected out of hand a request from the famous Nezu Shrine to introduce more performers into Edobashi, following objections from the chiefs of Hon Zaimoku-chō and Moto Yokkaichi-chō.)[56] Four years after Kozaemon was exiled, the shogunate decided to requisition some land at Edobashi for its own needs, claiming a portion of the Kaede riverbank as a storage area for lumber to be used to maintain the water supply system.[57] That the government itself would store combustibles and tolerate entertainers at Edobashi made visible what was already in everyone's mind: a century of change had transformed the once barren triangle into an important center of commerce, transportation, residence, religion, and play. Saitō Gesshin included a description and illustration of the Edobashi neighborhoods in his famous multi-volume guide to Edo, the *Edo meisho zue*, published in the early nineteenth century. Tellingly, he referred to the area simply as "Yokkaichi," and while Saitō described its commercial establishments in some detail, he alluded to its past as a firebreak only briefly.[58]

POWER AND SPACE AT EDOBASHI

Not all of the changes that occurred at Edobashi were replicated in exact detail at other firebreaks created in the aftermath of the Meireki fires. A few, such as the approaches to Ryōgoku Bridge, became known as great centers of entertainment, famous throughout the land. Several (the *hirokōji* at Eitai Bridge comes to mind) combined commerce with amusements; others (Nagasaki-chō in Honjo) emerged as ordinary residential neighborhoods. But regardless of what particular garb change might don, it visited virtually every firebreak by the end of the Tokugawa period.[59] The transformations within these spaces can be viewed as part of what might be termed the "chōninization" of Edo: the appropriation of the space, institutions, and cultural motifs of the city by its merchants and artisans at the expense of the government and the ruling samurai status group.

For some scholars who have examined Edobashi and other firebreaks, one important manifestation of the assertion of commoners' interests was

56. "Edobashi," Haru, doc. 37; *TS:S*, vol. 32, pp. 323–26.

57. Ōkuma, *Edo kenchiku*, pp. 62–63.

58. Gesshin's grandfather and father compiled over several decades a great amount of the material that appeared when Gesshin finally published the guide in 1834–1835, with illustrations by Hasegawa Settan. The volumes have been reprinted several times; the reference to Yokkaichi in the original edition (Kanō Bunko, Tōhoku Daigaku Fuzoku Toshokan) appears in fasc. 2, fols. 55–59. The accompanying illustration of Yokkaichi-chō is thought to portray the Edobashi area in the Bunka period (1804–1818).

59. Several additional *hirokōji* were established during the Kyōhō reforms of the early eighteenth century, and none of them seems to have survived the Edo period as a pure firebreak either; see Yoshioka Yuriko, "Kyōhō-ki Edo machikata ni okeru sogan undō no jittai—bōka seisaku o meguru chōningawa no taiō o chūshin to shite," in Chihōshi Kenkyū Kyōgikai, ed., *Toshi no chihōshi—seikatsu to bunka* (Yūzankaku Shuppan, 1980), pp. 108–58.

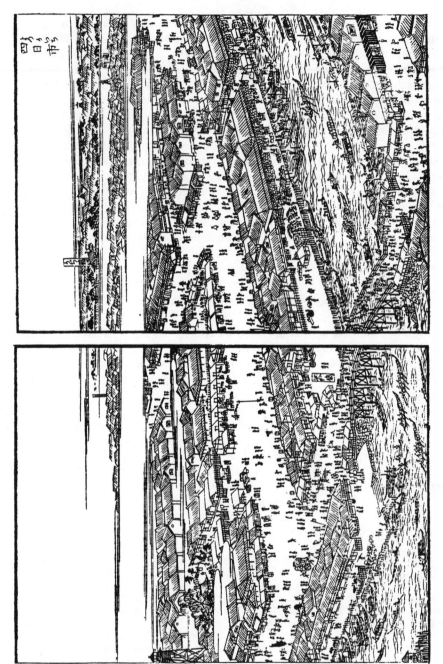

Edobashi in the early nineteenth century. Source: Edo meisho zue. Courtesy of Kokuritsu Kokkai Toshokan.

the mutation of many *hirokōji* into so-called *sakariba*: amusement centers brought to life by the vivid personalities and establishments that defined the world of popular entertainments—the teahouses and storytelling halls, street performers and prostitutes.[60] Other commentators have preferred to focus on the more mundane manner in which merchants advanced their rights to land use. At Edobashi, the conversion of the embankments to warehouses; the compromise of 1707, which conferred a monopoly over certain commercial activities upon the managers of 107 stalls; the construction of commercial warehouses by Aomono-chō and Hon Zaimoku-chō in 1720; and the replacement of three of the embankment warehouses with rental housing stand out as pivotal moments when commoners extended their claims to use space within the firebreak for their own purposes.[61]

Moreover, the agreements that the merchants negotiated with the shogunate proved to be durable and enforceable. The government protected the stall owners' monopoly by refusing permission to open new businesses to several merchants in the 1770s and to Nezu Shrine in 1788. Other examples are plentiful: the teamsters fended off an attempt by textile dyers to use land next to the stables as a drying ground; merchants' objections prompted the shogunate to deny a daimyo permission to build a residential estate at Edobashi; and similar refusals awaited artisans who wished to open workshops there.[62]

If, in the long run, the shogunate did surrender ground to the various pressures from below, suffering the transformation of Edobashi from an officially designated firebreak into a merchant neighborhood, it undertook at the same time to protect its own most vital interests. Perhaps most important, the shogunate bestowed privileges on various people in exchange for their continued and repeated recognition of its legitimacy as the paramount political authority in the land. In no instance was a permanent change in the use of space permitted at Edobashi without the consent of government officials. If some individuals circumvented the purview of officialdom, violated the negotiated agreements, then the shogunate either required them ex post facto to obtain approval for their actions (as the original stall owners did) or subjected them to punishment (as Kozaemon learned to his chagrin). The shogunate would condone change; it would strike compromises with merchants' interests. But in turn the people had to honor its judgments, pay deference to its legitimacy.

In further calculation of its advantage, the shogunate seldom dispensed a privilege without extracting a specific concession in return. Thus, when the government complied with the request of the 107 stall owners to prohibit

60. See, for instance, Nishiyama Matsunosuke, *Edo bunkashi* (Iwanami Shoten, 1989), pp. 53–70, 119–59; Jinnai Hidenobu, *Tōkyō no kūkan jinruigaku* (Chikuma Shobō, 1985), pp. 116–20, 132–34; Kawasaki Fusagorō, *Edo—sono seiji to shakai* (Kōfūsha Shuppan, 1987), pp. 226–31.
61. This point is pursued in Yoshiwara, "Edobashi hirokōji no keisei to kōzō"; and Hatano, "Edobashi hirokōji no hensen to fukugen."
62. *TS:S*, vol. 22, pp. 672–85; vol. 23, pp. 37–39; vol. 29, pp. 375–81.

new competition, it also compelled them to assume new financial burdens; when officials permitted Aomono-chō and Hon Zaimoku-chō to construct warehouses, they required the leaders of those quarters to erect a signboard where the shogunate's ordinances and proclamations would be posted for all to see; and when the senior councilors authorized Naraya and Kitamura to convert warehouses to merchant housing, they ordered the two elders to organize five-family groups and to appoint neighborhood chiefs so that all of the new residents would be incorporated into the government's administrative structure. More examples could be summoned, but the lesson would remain the same—the government bartered privileges and concessions in order to make its authority visible and tangible at Edobashi; to demonstrate its right to place claims upon the people and their resources; and to make certain that everyone who lived and worked at Edobashi was held accountable to higher officialdom.

One additional perspective needs to be stressed. The "people" were scarcely monolithic, or even united around a common set of aspirations and goals. Some community leaders wished to exploit to the maximum the commercial advantages of Edobashi's location; but many established merchants endeavored to restrict certain aspects of economic expansion. Some residents and visitors to Edobashi thoroughly enjoyed the entertainments offered by the storytellers and the maidens at the archery galleries; others considered them to be a plague on the neighborhood. As often as not, Edobashi's changing appearance reflected a contest between complicated commoner interests; the dynamics of historical change ran along lateral as well as perpendicular lines of stress. Yet even contention among commoners might be turned to the government's advantage, for the shogunate could step in and demonstrate anew its authority by negotiating a settlement, reconciling conflicting interests, bringing peace to the realm.

The notion of reciprocal and entangled relationships leads to a final point about the nature of political authority as exercised by the Tokugawa shogunate. The shogunate enjoyed enormous powers of coercion; it was an autocracy that monopolized ultimate legislative, policing, and executive powers; and it may well have exercised its prerogatives even more fully than did the Bourbon kings of France. But like the French monarchy, the shogunate was not all-powerful, and as events at Edobashi show, its officials valued conciliation and persuasion. The reasons they did so are complicated. To some extent, their preferences were pragmatic. The people were many, as Katō points out, officials relatively few. In large part, the shogunate's inclinations were philosophical. Tenets drawn from an imported neo-Confucianism wound around strains of nativist thought to produce in the early-modern period the concept of *kōgi*. Usually rendered as "public authority," *kōgi* embraced the twin notions that the shogun and his officials exercised power in the interests of all of the people of the realm, rather than for their own private benefit, and that their claims to legitimacy rested on their ability to demonstrate such to the satisfaction of all concerned.

This perception of political legitimacy steered the shogunate toward a particular style of governance that relied more on persuasion than on coercion; one that might be called a "negotiated autocracy." The shogunate insisted on the right to act as the ultimate source of legitimacy, the final decision maker in the bureaucratic-political process. In arriving at its judgments, it might make decisions that protected its own interests, but it very seldom did so without reference to what those rulings implied for the populations of Edo and the rest of Japan. The shogunate created mechanisms that allowed voices from below to be heard, and the transformations witnessed at Edobashi demonstrate how it took such opinions into account when it formulated policy. Before arriving at any important decision at Edobashi, the shogun's officials conducted investigations, received reports, heard out competing interests. It is this willingness to enter into negotiation, to build a consensus with the people whom it ruled, to give in exchange for getting, that lent the Tokugawa shogunate such great vitality in the seventeenth and eighteenth centuries. It also permitted the people to play a role in shaping the cultural life, economic institutions, and political environment of the country and its urban centers. Consequently, Edo was not brought into being solely by the shogunate or by the people. It arose from the ashes of its fires because of creative contributions both from above and from below, and for that reason Edo could remain the shogun's town even as it became the merchants' city.

6

Power, Space, and Investments in Paris

ROGER CHARTIER

I spend all day locked in a small, overheated room where I have the leisure to be sustained by my thoughts. Among these, one of the first that I have had the occasion to consider is that one cannot find in works composed of several pieces, and made by the hand of several masters, the same perfection as in those undertaken by a single master. Thus one sees that buildings which a single architect has planned and constructed are customarily more elegant and better executed than those which several builders have attempted to improve, using old walls that were erected for other uses. Thus in contrast to those well-ordered places that an engineer draws from his fantasy upon a plane, the old settlements which were in the beginning only little more than market towns and which became in turn great cities are ordinarily very badly laid out; yet, considering their buildings separately, one finds more often as much or more art in them than in others. Still, to see how they are arranged, with a large one here and a small one there, making streets winding and ill proportioned, one would say that it is due to chance rather more than to the will of the several men who, using their intelligence, laid them out.[1]

In thus legitimizing his self-appointed task—to reform anew his own way of thinking, in opposition to the "science of books" and the accumulated knowledge of the ages—Descartes expressed an idea common to his time: the ideal city would have to be the work of a single man, and not of history; it should follow the dictates of reason, not of chance. For Descartes as for the theorists of the Renaissance, the perfect city could not possibly result from the remodeling of cities already in existence. It could only spring

---

This chapter elaborates on ideas and material in my "La ville-chantier," in Georges Duby, ed., *Histoire de la France urbaine*, vol. 3: Emmanuel Le Roy Ladurie, ed., *La ville classique de la Renaissance aux révolutions* (Paris: Seuil, 1981), pp. 109–55.

1. René Descartes, *Discours de la méthode*, in *Oeuvres et lettres*, ed. André Bridoux, Editions Gallimard (Paris: Pléiade, 1953), pp. 132–33.

up from nothing, requiring a regular design that permitted an exact correspondence between space and function (whether military, commercial, artisanal, residential, or political). Regulated, ordered, harmonious, the ideal town supposed a virgin space ("a plain") upon which, without constraints or obstacles, it would inscribe its geometric shape. It thus could come into being only apart from old towns on which history had imposed the disorder of spaces and the confusion of functions.

In sixteenth- and seventeenth-century France, several attempts were made to transform the dream of a perfect town into reality by the creation of new communities where only nature had been: fortified settlements (the eight fortress towns designed by the brilliant military engineer Sébastien Vauban between 1679 and 1698), ports (Le Havre under François I; Brest, Lorient, Rochefort, and Sète under Louis XIV), and residential towns (Richelieu, undertaken at the instigation of the cardinal after 1631, and Versailles, built in several stages after 1661). New cities, which permit experimentation with architectural forms entirely as reason dictates, can be created only in exceptional circumstances and on the peripheries of existing communities. Perhaps Tokugawa Ieyasu had this sort of extraordinary chance in Japan, but in Europe the great cities of ancient foundation, "ordinarily very badly laid out," presented the most massive urban reality. Human interventions in the texture of these cities are always subject to powerful constraints—spatial, juridical, and social. This can be seen in Paris, where, from François I to Louis XIV, a multiplicity of initiatives, sumptuary and speculative, monarchical and private, refashioned the urban landscape.

Constraints on Urban Expansion

If we are to understand the impulses behind urban innovations, we must first measure the heritages that constrain them. The first impediment can be discerned in the way dictionaries defined *city* at the end of the seventeenth century. They always referred to the existence of walls that distinguished the city visibly and juridically: "A place full of houses, and enclosed by terraces and ditches, or walls or moats," according to Richelet, writing in 1679.[2] The very sign of urbanity, the walls were at the same time a great obstacle to free urban extension. In Paris, it was only in the 1670s that the wall of Charles V (r. 1364–1380) on the right bank was demolished and replaced by a continuous mall from the Bastille to the terraces of the Tuileries. Until then the fortified walls constituted a major servitude imposed on the town. Certainly the urban habitat sometimes leaped over them, permitting some faubourgs beyond the walls to undergo a veritable urbanization that led to their incorporation into the city. The very existence of the walls, however, invested with a strong symbolic meaning in that they constituted

2. Quoted in Bernard Lepetit, *Les villes dans la France moderne (1740–1840)* (Paris: Albin Michel, 1988), pp. 52–69.

and differentiated the town from the outside, restricted urban growth to the interior of a defined perimeter, thus imprisoning the city in its traditional space.

A second constraint on urban expansion was the seigneurial appropriation of urban soil. Indeed, much of Paris was divided among three great landowners. The property of the king stretched along the right bank of the Seine River, with additional parcels on the opposite shore; the archbishop claimed extensive and scattered holdings in the north of town and on the Ile de la Cité; and the estates of the Abbey of Saint-Germain sprawled along the left bank. A considerable part of the Parisian soil was the seigneurial property of yet other ecclesiastical institutions: such abbeys as Saint-Victor, Sainte-Geneviève, and Saint-Martin-des-Champs, and religious chapters such as Sainte-Opportune and Saint-Benoît.

This particular mode of appropriation was manifested above all in the right of the seigneurial property owner to levy transfer taxes, the so-called *lods et ventes*, on the sale of each parcel or building belonging to his domain. Fixed by the Custom of Paris at a twelfth of the purchase cost, this transfer tax was paid by the buyer, who in some circumstances could obtain a reduction, normally a fifth to a quarter of the amount due. In fact, the transfer taxes were well below the customary level during much of the seventeenth century; generally 5 percent of the purchase price at the end of the sixteenth century, they fell to 4 percent toward 1630, then to 3 percent at mid-century before rising again in the 1690s. This decline prompted many sellers to lower their price, provided that the buyer agree to an official fiction that the transaction constituted a mere "exchange of buildings," which the Custom of Paris exempted from all transfer taxes. Despite such subterfuges, the *lods et ventes* constituted an undeniable brake on the vitality of the real estate market while markedly increasing the cost of both land and houses.[3]

The last obstacle to the transformation of the capital was a decline during the latter half of the sixteenth century in the practice of parcelization; that is, the division of larger properties into several smaller building lots so as to facilitate the sale of raw land. An increase of the Parisian population during the sixteenth century, from between 200,000 and 250,000 persons at its beginning to about 300,000 in 1565, led to the division of property.[4] But by century's end the parceling of land within built-up and densely settled quarters ground to a halt, and it did not revive until the Revolution. A survey undertaken in the quarter of the Halles suggests why.[5] The very nucleus of urban life, according to this document, had become "the portion of land upon which a house is built (as one or several main buildings) and belong-

3. Jean Nagle, "Un aspect de la propriété seigneuriale à Paris aux XVIIe et XVIIIe siècles: Les lods et ventes," *Revue d'histoire moderne et contemporaine*, 1977, pp. 570–81.
4. Jean Jacquart, "Le poids démographique de Paris et de l'Ile-de-France au XVIe siècle," *Annales de démographie historique: La démographie avant les démographes (1500–1670)*, 1980, pp. 87–96.
5. Françoise Boudon et al., *Système de l'architecture urbaine: Le quartier des Halles à Paris* (Paris: CNRS, 1977).

ing to a single property owner." This description attests not to the timeless and unchanging nature of land parcelization but rather to its freezing after the sixteenth century.

The layout of parcels of land within the capital added another kind of restraint. At the level of the residential quarter, two types of property distribution coexisted, one tight and homogeneous, the other loose and free. The first, generally characteristic of lots that fronted a major street, imposed an urban logic by which the division of the land into small rectangular units was regular so that the morphology of the properties could be conserved even when the number of units was large. This pattern, typical of streets with a dominant commercial function, introduced limits on the malleability of the urban texture, both by immobilizing spatial patterns and by resisting consolidation of single lots into larger units of property. The latter pattern, in contrast, presented a great variety of forms and a certain flexibility. Associated with large residences and the presence of aristocratic townhouses (*hôtels*), the large units constituted a point of weakness in the urban fabric, a tear where property could be subdivided and new streets opened. It was thus within these limits that transformations could take place in the sixteenth and seventeenth centuries.

Within the walls that defined its circumference, Paris constituted a space that could be modified only with great difficulty, because the number, form, and distribution of the parcels of land that formed its texture hardly changed after the sixteenth century. Consequently, Parisians could transform their city in only three ways: by leaping over or pushing out walls so as to extend the city's surface; by developing land situated within large estates or ensembles of properties and within the less rigidly defined parts of the urban fabric; and, finally, by increasing the height of houses standing on lots that were small and tightly packed together, as if frozen in time.

REDESIGNING PARIS

In Paris, building took the form of large-scale speculative projects, the work of the king, convents, and entrepreneurs. We can distinguish three periods in the redesigning of Paris, differentiated by the sources of such initiatives and by the significance of the real estate transactions.[6] The first phase occurred even before the Bourbon monarchy. It can be dated to the decades between 1540 and 1560, when the Valois kings began the practice of developing property by dividing up the royal domain situated in the eastern part of town. In 1543, property that included the *hôtels* of Saint-Paul, Bourgogne, Artois, Flandre, Etampes, Petit-Bourbon, and Tancarville was broken into thirteen lots and auctioned to the public; in 1548 the Hôtel de Beautreillis was sold; and in 1564 the property of the Hôtel des Tournelles was divided "to build houses as uniform and similar as possible" (but several pieces of

6. Maurice Dumolin, *Etudes de topographie parisienne*, 3 vols. (Paris, 1929–1931).

The Place Royale. Courtesy of the Bibliothèque Nationale.

land not having found takers, the Place Royale one day would be established here). The first subdivisions were the corollary of the improvements at the Louvre, which, after 1527, left the old townhouses of eastern Paris deserted in favor of the new palace. These subdivisions denoted no particular impulse of urban planning: intended to bolster the royal treasury and to encourage the development of the city in the context of its monarchial character, they reflected no ordered plan or architectural program.

The king was not the only one to parcel and sell off land in the middle of the sixteenth century as demonstrated by the ventures undertaken by the canons of Sainte-Catherine in 1545 and 1549. On the lands held in trust from the abbey of Saint-Victor and the priory of Saint-Catherine, until then occupied by gardens and tiltyards for equestrian jousts, the canons put together a new parcel of land, formed into an octagonal grid that determined the direction of the new streets. In 1545 these 33,000 square meters were platted and sold. The purchasers included minor officials and master artisans (barrel makers, plasterers, joiners, locksmiths, goldsmiths) who acquired just one or two parcels as well as the "grands robins," the councilors or presidents of Parlement, who bought four or five lots at a time in order to form a large unit or to enhance their existing residences. Extremely successful in this first endeavor, the clergy of Sainte-Catherine repeated the venture in 1549 by developing the lands on the western and northern sides of their enclosure. The lots were rapidly laid out; already in 1561 Corrozet noted in his *Antiquités de Paris* that one could now find there "handsome streets and sumptuous houses."

The second period of the story began with the reign of the first Bourbon monarch, Henry IV, when the politics of land development changed significantly. The crown had a double goal: to clear away the ruins of the siege of 1589–1594 and to bring a measure of order to the city, where the texture of urban life permitted it, by giving squares and promenades a monumental character while restoring equilibrium to the distribution of functions and population. The increase in building that resulted from these subdivision projects thus cannot be separated from a more grand royal design that considered the capital in its entirety. Three schemes were launched in succession, each linked to the opening of a square: the Place Royale (now the Place des Vosges), the Place Dauphine, and the Place de France (never completed).

The creation of the Place Royale on the site of the old Hôtel des Tournelles, occupied by a horse market in the recent past and now divided into multiple building lots, was the first scheme to unfold.[7] By 1603 Sully, who owned part of the property and who was in charge of maintaining the city as *grand voyer de France* and *voyer de Paris*, decided that the project should include the creation of a square and a spinning mill to produce silk cloth. In

7. Jean-Pierre Babelon, "Les origines de la place des Vosges," in *Annuaire 1975–76* (Paris: Ecole Pratique des Hautes Etudes, IVᵉ Section, 1976), pp. 695–713; Michel Le Möel, "Aux origines de la place Royale," in *Colloque international sur l'urbanisme parisien et l'Europe au XVIIᵉ siècle* (Paris, 1966), pp. 111–15.

1605 the realization of the project began with the sale of the lots that formed the sides of the square (a number of the purchasers were among Sully's entourage and clientele) and by the concession of royal *lettres patentes*, authorizations that committed the purchasers of the parcels to a certain number of obligations. Some were juridical; for example, the residences might not be subdivided at the time of inheritance. Others were architectural: the height of facades was fixed at eight *toises* (about sixteen meters); their appearance was to be identical (four arcades on the ground floor and four windows on the remaining two floors); and the materials used were to be similar (brick for the walls, stone for the arcades).

In 1607 the king ordered the demolition of the spinning mill in order to complete the fourth side of the square, which he reserved for residences for money changers and bankers, although in fact the latter preferred to live in the Palais de Justice and on the Pont-aux-Changeurs. This development gave the new Place Royale a function that was at the same time residential, with the construction of surrounding aristocratic residences, and festive, in that its sandy central square, flanked by rows of trees, could provide space for manly jousts and for genteel amusements such as carousels. The creation of the Place Royale thus marked a major stage in the redesign of Paris— aristocratic residences graced a zone that hitherto had not been built up; the capital could take pleasure in its first geometric and closed square, on the model of Nancy, Pont-à-Mousson, and Metz in Lorraine; and the city could boast of its first ensemble of planned constructions (if one excepts the sixty-eight uniformly gabled and painted houses constructed on the bridge of Notre-Dame between 1507 and 1512, replacing identical ones built in 1421).

The second development project in the Paris of Henry IV concerned the Pont-Neuf. Originally begun in 1578, the construction of the Pont-Neuf was delayed for several years until Henry revived the project, using the original plan, which excluded the presence of buildings or houses on the new bridge itself (an innovation that would not be extended to bridges subsequently constructed). The Pont-Neuf, which came to rest on the point of the Cité, was completed in 1607 and led immediately to another project: the establishment of a triangular *place*, allocated to operations of money changing, banking, and commerce, which would take the name of the Place Dauphine. For this purpose the crown in 1607 ceded land to the first president of Parlement, Achille du Harlay, who then sold it in separate lots, which were purchased mostly by the councilors of the sovereign court and by silversmiths. A program of uniform construction was imposed on the builders, but the obligations were less burdensome than those at the Place Royale, since the houses constructed at the Place Dauphine were destined for commercial activities. The created ensemble was brought to conclusion in three steps: by completion of the rue Dauphine on the left bank in 1609 (it was a dozen meters wide but the intended uniformity of construction was virtually ignored); by the laying out of quais on the point of the Cité; and by erection in 1614 of an equestrian statue of Henry IV on a piece of land adjoining the Pont-Neuf.

The last project initiated by Henry was the construction, on lands belonging to the Coutures du Temple, of the semicircular Place de France. Designed to be set against the ramparts in a fashion that would permit the intersection of six streets laid out in a semi-star shape, the project never was completed. But one here finds the salient traits of the king's policy toward Paris—the desire to see the open spaces within the city walls filled in so as to halt the proliferation of constructions in the faubourgs; the attribution of a dominant function (here administrative) to the new ensembles of buildings; the recourse to intermediaries for the actual subdivision and sale of property (in the case of the Place de France, it was the financier Claude Charlot, who exercised a monopoly on the collection of royal taxes); and finally the priority given to the geometric organization of urban space and to planned construction.

Closely dependent during the reign of Henry IV on monarchical planning and controls, real estate development projects subsequently freed themselves from royal tutelage to become purely speculative operations, detached from all preoccupations with urban planning and undertaken simply to enrich (or sometimes to ruin) the investors. The mechanisms of this third phase of the subdivision of property in Paris can be seen where they had the greatest effect: the Ile-Saint Louis, the Pré-aux-Clercs, and the "Quartier Richelieu."

First in date came the subdivision of the Ile Saint-Louis, which demonstrated the difficulties of such undertakings. In April 1614 the representatives of the king signed a contract with three entrepreneurs, Christophe Marie, "general entrepreneur of the bridges of France"; Lugles Poulletier, commissioner of war; and François Le Regrattier, treasurer of the Swiss Regiment. The partners agreed to construct a bridge made entirely of stone between the Quai des Ormes and the Quai de la Tournelle on opposite banks of the Seine and to pave the streets opened on the new island that would be formed by the joining of two small uninhabited islets (Notre-Dame and the Ile des Vaches). In return, the three associates would receive title to the lands on the new island (which the king agreed to buy from the chapter), the rights to the quitrents (*cens*) and the *lods et ventes* transfer taxes for a period of sixty years, and the revenues from river tolls. In execution of the contract, work began in 1615, as did the sale of parcels of land. By 1622, all of the eastern half of the island had been sold; the pattern of land use was fixed by the tracing of two transverse streets set off against another thoroughfare, named the rue Saint-Louis in 1624, that formed the great axis of the island.

This contact engendered multiple conflicts. The first pitted the chapter of Notre-Dame against the king and centered on the purchase price of the land (which the canons considered too low); on seigneurial rights, quitrents, and the transfer taxes (which the chapter now decided that it did not want to give up); and on the risks inherent in constructing the new bridge (which depended on an inadequately reinforced extremity of the Ile de la Cité, known as the Terrain, that required bolstering with rocks). The conflict played itself out over a decade: from 1634, when the king, in consideration for a promised payment from the chapter of 50,000 livres, recognized its seigneurial rights and confirmed that the entrepreneurs would receive the rents and taxes only for a period of sixty years before they reverted to the chapter; until 1643, when the holders of parcels of land finally paid the 50,000 livres and agreed to finish the work on the so-called Terrain and in return began to collect the rents and taxes previously granted to the entrepreneurs.

A second conflict pitted rival financial groups against one another. Indeed, in 1623 a consortium of six financiers, represented by Jean de La Grange, titular secretary to the king and a collector of royal taxes, took over the obligations and rights that the three associates had agreed to in 1614. Obliged to reimburse Marie for the work already completed and anxious about opposition from the chapter of Notre-Dame, the La Grange group pulled out in 1627, after having built the bridge of Saint-Landry between the Ile Saint-Louis and the Ile de la Cité. From this move followed difficulties with Marie, Poulletier, and Le Regrattier, who, by a second contract, took the enterprise in hand again, only to find themselves obliged to pay back the La Grange group and to submit to the financial oversight of two representatives of the king, a "master of accounts" (*maître des comptes*) and a municipal magistrate (*échevin*).

After 1627, it was the turn of the original associates to confront one another. Marie and Le Regrattier quarreled with Poulletier over the portion that each should receive from the projects, argued about the price of the building lots, and contested the choice of master masons employed to construct the bridge and lay out the streets. The master masons in turn entered into conflict with the entrepreneurs, who were late in paying them and who, unable to reimburse the La Grange group as agreed, ceded lots to displeased creditors. The multiplicity and interlocking nature of these conflicts explains the slow pace of the work, which was completed only in 1645 with the opening of the Pont de la Tournelle on the largest branch of the Seine.

On the Ile Saint-Louis, the real estate market was fluid and changes in ownership were frequent. The cadastral survey of 1643 (undertaken at the moment when the king wanted to tax the holders of parcels of land in order to pay back the canons of Notre-Dame) allows us to establish the distribution of property in the new neighborhood twenty-five years after the beginning of the subdivision of the property. Of the seventy-seven property owners whose social origins can be identified, the world of offices clearly dominated, with forty-seven property owners. Very significantly, the most numerous group was composed of financial officials, who generally were also tax farmers, army suppliers, and creditors of the king.[8] At their side the island welcomed all the hierarchy of the robe, from legal clerks to the president of Parlement. Another important group, with nineteen new property

8. Françoise Bayard, *Le monde des financiers au XVIIe siècle* (Paris: Flammarion, 1988), pp. 367–71.

owners, consisted of master artisans, mostly from the building trades. Some, such as the master masons, had received several parcels of land in payment for their work on the bridge, while others purchased their land. All used their lots to construct their own personal residences, which were thus situated near the aristocratic townhouses of their clientele, as well as other homes that they put up for rent. As with the Place Royale, the creation of a new subdivision on the Ile Saint-Louis bestowed upon Paris a residential habitat where the newly rich lived side by side with master artisans whose work depended directly up the patronage of aristocratic neighbors.

The second extension of building in Paris during the opening decades of the seventeenth century could be found outside the walls, on the emplacement of the old *hôtel* of Queen Marguerite, built on the Pré-aux-Clercs in the faubourg Saint-Germain. Put up for sale to pay back the queen's creditors, the palace and its garden and park were purchased in 1622 by a consortium of five financiers, officeholders who were closely linked to the state. Jacques de Garsanlan, for instance, was comptroller of the domain of Navarre, treasurer and financial steward of the house of Monsieur, and master of the *chambre aux deniers* (which oversaw household expenses of the king). Jacques de Vassan was *conseiller d'état, commissaire général des vivres, munitions et magasins de France* (and thus an army supplier), and someone quite familiar with leases and agreements. Jacques Potier was a financier, Joachim de Sandras a commissioner of artillery, Louis Le Barbier an investor whose wide-ranging activities included tax farming, real estate transactions, and public works projects. These men were also bound together by family ties. Potier was brother-in-law both to Le Barbier, who married Potier's sister, and to Sandras, the half-brother of Potier's wife. The group would later add Guillaume Moynerie and Etienne Briois. Both were employees of the crown and on several occasions had been associates in tax farming.

The consortium of developers destroyed the old palace and drew up a plan to subdivide the property, with building lots organized along two longitudinal avenues and six cross streets. The sale, first of collective parcels of land, went very slowly, and in 1629 the terrain was apportioned among the members of the consortium, who kept some lots for themselves. Three types of operations followed and coexisted: the construction, at common expense, of a market at the center of the project; the sale of vacant parcels of land by Potier, Sandras, and the heirs of Vassan and Garsanlan; and the multiplication of constructions by Le Barbier, who built *hôtels* because the profit from the sale of such townhouses could be much greater than that earned from the sale of raw land. The example spread outside the walls. The Petits-Augustins, the Université, and the abbey of Saint-German-des-Prés subdivided their properties, a process that completely overwhelmed the old market town of Saint-Germain, which became an aristocratic faubourg.

The final example of speculative activity in the Paris of Louis XIII was the formation of the "Quartier Richelieu," the famous Palais Royal. Its origins may be found in Richelieu's purchase in 1624 of the Hôtel d'Argennes. From that point, the mechanism put into motion was completely comparable to that seen in the case of the subdivision of the Ile Saint-Louis. The king conferred an initial contract upon Pierre Pidou in 1631, then concluded a second agreement with Charles Froger in 1633 (both were royal secretaries and Pidou on seven occasions had been a signatory to financial agreements with the king). The two men agreed to demolish the old ramparts, to build new gates, and to construct new walls between the Porte Saint-Honoré and the Porte Saint-Denis in order to bring the faubourgs Saint-Honoré, Montmartre, and Ville-Neuve into the city. In return the entrepreneurs received the land on which the old walls stood, lots within the new fortifications, and the right to develop property and to construct markets and market halls. But both Pidou and Froger were only figureheads acting on behalf of Le Barbier, who was already the principal speculator. Thus were undertaken at the same time the erection of a new wall (built a kilometer outside of the wall of Charles V) and the laying out of the cardinal's residence and garden, the Palais Cardinal (with Richelieu retaining a band eighteen meters wide on three of its sides; the forty-five lots laid out on this land were sold to Le Barbier, who constructed identical residences, destined to be sold). The design of the Palais Cardinal determined the direction of the new streets, both those parallel to it and those cutting across its terrain. As in the cases of the Place Royale and the Ile Saint-Louis, the new quarter attracted members of the legal profession and the newly rich, men of office and finance who were the faithful and obligated clients of the cardinal.

Since these projects required an enormous allocation of funds, and thus necessitated heavy borrowing (the associates involved in the Ile Saint-Louis project estimated that they fell more than 50,000 livres in debt between the beginning of the operation and 1640), the developments did not always enrich their promoters. At his death Le Barbier was in bankruptcy and his belongings were up for sale. Two years later, the situation of Christophe Marie and Lugles Poulletier (François Le Regrattier having died the preceding year) was not any better. In 1643 they were dispossessed of their property rights on the Ile Saint-Louis; those rights were awarded to one Dublet, who took it upon himself to finish the work. Investment in real estate, if it could bring handsome profits, was also a high-risk activity in a system based on multiple—and therefore fragile—chains of credit and dependent on the initiative of individuals in possession of royal favor and privileges.

Risky for the entrepreneurs, the creation of subdivisions and the sale of individual parcels of land nonetheless markedly transformed Paris by extending the surface of built-up land. In the sixteenth and seventeenth centuries, such land development obeyed a double principle. First, it avoided the old urban center, where the division of plots had been common earlier, the seigneurial appropriation of land was virtually complete, the distribution of urban functions long since established, and land costly. Neither the king nor promoters had the power to remodel that space, already built up. The development of property thus occurred on the edge of the old urban core, on the virgin lands, the open lots, where urban functions were not yet fixed. However—and this was the second principle—all of the great victories of building in the first half of the seventeenth century took place inside the walls, the old or new ones, with the single exception of the growth of the faubourg Saint-Germain.

The battle between the crown, determined to prohibit construction outside the city walls, and entrepreneurs and a burgeoning urban population who desired more space was continuous. At times the monarchy prevailed: the construction of the Place Royale and the Place Dauphine should not be separated from the edict of 1609, by which the king obliged the owners of vacant lots or houses standing in ruin inside of the walls to build within six months or risk having their land auctioned off. But the completion of elite housing developments could not satisfy the needs generated by population growth within the walls—Paris's population reached 510,000 inhabitants in 1700, nearly double what it had been in 1565.[9] In response, in 1638 the king attempted to fix the city limits permanently. In Edo the senior councilors defined the city by striking lines on a map; in Paris the crown erected thirty-one markers, placed somewhat outside of the old ramparts, beyond which all construction was forbidden. Yet even this measure, rooted in anxieties about defense, provisioning, epidemics, and acts of sedition and stimulated by the desire to limit urban financial exemptions, hardly prevented the town from advancing toward the suburban villages.

In the old heart of the city, where the possibility of initiating new subdivision projects was quite limited, people built up rather than out. The survey of the quarter of the Halles indeed demonstrates an increase in the height of buildings between the second half of the sixteenth century and the late seventeenth. Each reconstruction of a building led to the addition of one or two new floors, at least according to the somewhat exaggerated reports of some contemporaries. In his *Notice pour le plan de Gomboust* in 1652, Pierre Petit asserted: "The houses are so high that it seems that two or three towns are piled on top of one another," and he noted "a number of houses of six and seven stories." In reality, the information provided by the depictions and notarial records suggests that houses of more than five stories were rare in seventeenth-century Paris. Nevertheless, the increase in the height of buildings was certain, and it was a consequence of escalating land prices, as Nicolas Delamare suggested in 1722 in his *Traité de la police*: "There are indeed many properties that sell for more than it costs to build houses on them; the high cost of both mean that most people dream only of rental income, thus no one ever thinks that their houses are too high." The increased height of houses was in direct relation to the specifics of property development; the smaller the lot, the higher the house. Thus the buildings of the central quarters were higher than those on the periphery, where greater possibilities for the subdivision of land permitted wider facades.

9. Philip Benedict, "French Cities from the Sixteenth Century to the Revolution: An Overview," in Benedict, ed., *Cities and Social Change in Early Modern France* (London: Unwin Hyman, 1989), pp. 6–68 and esp. Table 1.2, pp. 24–25.

BUILDING PRACTICES

In the course of the sixteenth and seventeenth centuries, the construction of buildings in the capital underwent two transformations. The first, of regulatory origin, aimed at the alignment of facades. The medieval habitat considerably encroached upon the space of the street, both at ground level, where parts of structures jutted out beyond official property boundaries, and in the air above, where half-timbered stories overhung passers-by at various heights. Legislation, by the king, the Parlement, and the city, tried to impose order on this chaos. On the one hand, all new streets, whether cutting through the old fabric of urban life or in zones recently developed, were to be precisely aligned with facades constructed neatly in a row. On the other hand, along old streets, parts of houses that projected too far into the thoroughfare were to be hacked off, the most irregular fragments straightened. An edict in 1554 directed property owners to "knock down and carry away the projections of old houses that hang over the street," and this order was reaffirmed in decrees announced in 1564, 1645, 1666, and 1683. In an attempt to force compliance, an edict in 1607 imposed the obligation on the commissioner of building (*voyer de Paris*) to "ensure that the streets be embellished and widened as much as possible and to oversee the alignments and the straightening of walls with bends and recesses and to prevent any projections and overhangs." Despite the authority of the *voyer de Paris* over each construction or reconstruction project in the city, the efforts to obtain the alignment of houses clashed with the inertia or ruses of the property owners, who held to architectural freedom and were strongly attached to their own spatial appropriations. The decisions to impose order thus often remained a dead letter, and in any case obtained only very approximate conformity along the streets of the traditional quarters.[10]

The second change in Parisian building was more significant: the transformation of the town of wood into a city of stone.[11] The "common laws of Paris" (*coutume de Paris*) had for a long time prohibited houses of wood, but it was only after the edict of 1607 (which forbade timber framing on the street) and still more the ordinance of 1667, proclaimed several months after the great London fire, that the proscription became reality. It allowed wooden construction only on bridges (for considerations of weight) and for dwellings inside courtyards. Quickly stone emerged victorious, enjoying increasing vogue as a substitute for wood for both framing and the facades of houses. In the structure of buildings as a whole, blocks of freestone provided vertical reinforcement for lintels and roofing members. Between these uprights, the skin of the house was sometimes brick (as in medieval houses) and, more often, less costly ashlar, which was covered on the outside with plaster, limestone, or a rough cast of river sand.

10. Bernard Rouleau, *Le tracé des rues de Paris: Formation, typologie, fonctions* (Paris: CNRS, 1965).
11. Jean-Pierre Babelon, *Demeures parisiennes sous Henri IV et Louis XIII* (Paris: Le Temps, 1965)

The Parisian house permitted speculative activity that brought handsome profits. In the first half of the seventeenth century, the construction or renovation of buildings for rent multiplied. Alongside the newly rich financiers and the men of the robe were many bourgeois, merchants, and master artisans who invested their money in the construction of one or several rental houses. Despite the marked increase in the price of land, the construction of a house remained an attractive place to put one's money, even for someone of modest fortune; rents were more certain than the return paid by the state and a fruitful hedge for the future, since their value rose by 300 percent between the beginning of the seventeenth century and the Fronde.[12]

In the new houses of the sixteenth and seventeenth centuries, traditional models enjoyed continued popularity.[13] The most widely used prototype remained the single extended dwelling, with a very narrow lateral passage leading to a spiral staircase that was always located at the rear of the property, either in a wing on the courtyard or incorporated into the main building itself. When the size of the property permitted, a small building stood at the back, on the opposite side of the courtyard. Until the mid–seventeenth century, this was most often a low edifice, serving as a kitchen or stable. Later this structure took on a residential function, often rising to several stories and linked to the main building on the street by a single staircase that served the entire complex. It was only at the beginning of the eighteenth century (about 1715–1730 in the quarter of the Halles) that this arrangement gave way to another design, in which the house had a central courtyard flanked by one or two lateral staircases.

Inside the house, lodgings were arrayed on several levels.[14] Seldom was one apartment located on a single floor. The property owner (or principal renter) generally lived on the ground floor, where the kitchen and main room were located, and used one or more additional rooms on each floor. The other renters divided the remaining rooms (uniformly called *chambres*) into apartments that spread across two or three floors. Examples of such arrangements abound. In 1686 a royal prosecutor on the rue Jean-de-l'Epine had a lodging divided among four levels (a large room and a kitchen on the ground floor, a room and an office on the second floor, an additional room and office on the third, and an attic on the fourth floor); in 1694 the apartment of a master barrel maker on the rue des Billettes was divided among three floors (a kitchen on the ground floor and a single room each on the second and third floors); and in 1702 a grocer on the rue Saint-Antoine owned rooms on six levels (a shop on the street, a room each on the second and third floors, two more rooms on the fourth, a kitchen and two rooms on

12. Emmanuel Le Roy Ladurie and Pierre Couperie, "Le mouvement des loyers parisiens de la fin du Moyen Age au XVIIIe siècle," *Annales E.S.C.*, 1970, pp. 1002–23.

13. Annik Pardailhé-Galabrun, *La naissance de l'intime: 3,000 foyers parisiens, XVIIe–XVIIIe siècles* (Paris: Presses Universitaires de France, 1988), pp. 211–34.

14. Michelle Jurgens and Pierre Couperie, "Le logement à Paris aux XVIe et XVIIe siècles: Une source, les inventaires après décès," *Annales E.S.C.*, 1962, pp. 488–500.

the fifth, and a room and storage area on the sixth floor).[15] We should recall that in the Palais Royal, Molière occupied four rooms: two were on the second floor and two on the third, and to go between them he had to cross through the apartments of the other renters. It was only at the beginning of the eighteenth century that the practice of renting apartments situated entirely on a single floor became customary.

In the second half of the seventeenth century, another type of investment became popular (not that it was unknown before that). Here the purpose was not to construct a house that was destined to remain in the family patrimony but rather to buy and then to sell, after ten or twenty years' possession, one or several buildings that were already standing. Such an operation promised a double profit. On the one hand, it generated a regular income, provided by rent; on the other, if all went well it permitted a certain return beyond cost at the time the house was resold. Such investments, based on the temporary ownership of rental property, may have represented an adaptation to the stagnation of rents (the nominal value of which remained stable between 1660 and 1710). This turn of events did not encourage construction, but rather accelerated the circulation of capital invested in the game of purchases and sales.

THE CHURCH, ARISTOCRATS, AND PARIS

The church, too, changed the face of Paris. The Catholic Reformation had its architectural concomitant in the construction and renovation of churches and the erection of new conventual buildings. The flowering of convents reached its heyday in the first half of the seventeenth century, particularly in the 1630s.[16] At least seventy-seven new religious houses, fifty of them for women, appeared in the capital before 1670. The chronology of the appearance of these new institutions in the city and its surroundings was as follows: five arrived in the first decade of the 1600s, nine in the 1610s, fourteen in the 1620s, twenty in the 1630s, fourteen in the 1640s, ten in the 1650s, and five in the 1660s. Monasteries tended to be placed, for the most part, outside the walls, whether in a distant suburb (Charonne, Belleville, Chaillot, Picpus) or in a more nearby faubourg. Two faubourgs in particular attracted the conventual establishments of the Catholic Reformation: Saint-Jacques, which saw the first Parisian implantation of the new congregations (the Carmelites in 1605, the Ursulines in 1611, the Capuchins in 1613, and the Visitation in 1623), and Saint-Germain, which possessed the richest cluster

15. Pardailhé-Galabrun, *Naissance de l'intime,* pp. 247–50, provides the cited examples. A sample of estate inventories compiled upon the deaths of individuals indicates the composition of 1,570 lodgings of at least two rooms for the period 1600–1789; 45 percent of the apartments consisted of rooms dispersed over more than one floor.

16. Marcel Poëte, *Une vie de cité: Paris de sa naissance à nos jours,* vol. 2: *La cité de la Renaissance;* and vol. 3: *La spiritualité de la cité classique: Les origines de la cité moderne* (Paris: Picard, 1927, 1931).

of religious establishments with thirteen houses belonging to female congregations and seven to the masculine orders, all of which arrived between 1600 and 1670. Inside the walls, the Marais was the zone with the greatest density of convents.

As Du Breuil attested in his *Théâtre des antiquités de Paris* (1630), and as Gomboust's map of 1652 verifies, the arrival of new congregations in Paris stimulated considerable architectural activity. Indeed, even when a religious community received a building as a gift, the traditions of conventual life required it to be reconstructed. This custom led to the multiplication in the city, and especially in the faubourgs, of enclosures where the buildings were laid out in an ordered manner and where most of the ground was taken up by courtyards and gardens. From this impulse also came the construction of new churches, which dotted the urban landscape. Among them were the church of Val-de-Grâce, begun before 1645 at the convent of the Benedictines, and two Jesuit churches, one linked to the teaching house on the rue Saint-Antoine and the other, inspired by the Gesù in Rome and built by Père Martellange, connected to the novitiate in the faubourg Saint-Germain.

The establishment of a convent often was accompanied by the construction of rental houses in the surrounding neighborhood. Fearing that the religious orders would remove excessive amounts of land from the real estate market, both the Parlement and the king enacted restrictive measures. In 1626 Parlement decided that no new monastery could be founded, "given the great number there now are"; in 1629 the monarch made any new establishment contingent on obtaining royal letters of patent. In 1659 it was decided that all religious houses that had been founded in the past ten years without authorization would be dissolved. But these measures, late as they were, could hardly prevent the continual proliferation of convents, already considerable by 1630.

In the old heart of the city, the construction of a religious edifice had several consequences. First of all, it entailed the destruction of a built-up space and the radical transformation of a parcel of land. The construction of the church of Saint-Eustache (between 1532 and 1632) and that of the Oratoire (beginning in 1621) in the quarter of the Halles demonstrated the slowness with which the land destined to belong to the new church was actually transferred to the canons. Construction invariably was under way before all of the necessary land had been obtained. Moreover, the alteration in built-up space that resulted from the consolidation of several plots into a single unit of land entailed the demolition of a considerable number of houses.[17] Church and convent obliterated the preexisting divisions of property; at the same time they annexed land that could otherwise be used for residences. Sometimes, however, their lay neighbors were able to exact a measure of revenge; the layout of their lots sometimes limited the extension of the church or encircled it with haphazard constructions.

The construction of a new church could bring about two-pronged archi-

17. Boudon et al., *Système de l'architecture urbaine*, pp. 247–303.

tectural activity. In wiping out the old property divisions, each religious building set off around itself a wave of new constructions, bourgeois or aristocratic, which benefited from the destruction of the old habitat. On the other hand, the evolution of religious architecture, with its opulent cupolas and turrets, made the existence of squares and open views desirable. In Paris, the Place de la Sorbonne provides a good example of this aesthetic impetus. Richelieu wrote in 1642 to the marquis de Noyers: "I am very glad that you are demolishing the houses that block the view of the chapel of the Sorbonne." The square, constituted after the purchase of land and the destruction of the houses in front of the church, thus came into existence only because of the view it opened up in front of the Sorbonne's chapel. In this way, religious construction, much of it dating from the period between 1600 and 1650, not only modified the city's profile, it also upset the division of property (a fact that, as one knows, is rare enough in the old center of cities) and transformed the use of land on nearby properties.

Aristocratic construction transformed the division and use of property infinitely less than did religious building. With some exceptions, the great townhouses of nobles occupied plots of land that were already sizable and considered to be habitats of prestige.[18] It was only to aggrandize or impose uniformity that certain small neighboring parcels were taken and added to an aristocratic ensemble. In the heart of the city, the aristocratic townhouse appeared closely subservient to the preexisting layout of lots and their functions. That is without doubt why the subdivision of land, which took place away from the central and historical core, held so much attraction for the wealthy, who found there property that could be used more flexibly.

In addition, the townhouses wove themselves into the fabric of the urban life that surrounded them. No building was detached from its immediate neighbor—it either faced the street or was connected to the street by a passage or a courtyard. Thus noble townhouses fundamentally were indistinguishable from the neighboring domestic architecture. For some time it was the quality of construction material—stone in a city where the houses were of wood—that constituted the only distinctive originality (aside from sheer size) claimed by the aristocratic residence. In the seventeenth century, a double change took place, although it affected only a minority of noble residences. First, following the model of seigneurial architecture of the countryside and of the Italian palace, the *hôtel* sought to differentiate itself from neighboring buildings in order to be visible to passers-by. Second, when it remained locked in a small parcel of land within a predominantly bourgeois habitat, the aristocratic residence abandoned the street for the isolation of an enclosing wall with a gate through which one could discover the buildings distributed around an interior courtyard. The *hôtel* thus interrupted the continuous ribbon of facades and made itself conspicuous not by its physical constitution but by its segregation from the surrounding neighborhood.

18. Ibid., pp. 181–246.

Urban Improvements

In the sixteenth and seventeenth centuries, a triple intervention—that of city, church, and private builders—modified the urban texture of the capital. But none, not even that of the municipality, heralded the cycles of urban planning seen in the eighteenth century, when regional changes intertwined with urban transformations to bring about different projects in the interior of the city.[19] In earlier centuries, the transformation of towns was fragmented, each initiative disjointed from the other, and the orientation remained focused on the goals of immediate convenience or decoration. But during the eighteenth century, the fundamental cultural perceptions about city planning (still not concerned with functionalism) underwent a basic change.

Whereas in Edo the construction of bridges and quais was left largely to the initiative of individual neighborhoods, in Paris this was a municipal task. Between 1500 and 1700, nine bridges were constructed or renovated in Paris: Pont Notre-Dame, Pont Saint-Michel (twice), Pont-Neuf, Pont Saint-Landry, Pont-Marie, Pont de la Tournelle, Pont-au-Change, Pont de l'Hôtel-Dieu (also called Pont-Double), and Pont de Bois des Tuileries (or Pont-Rouge, reconstructed in stone in 1695 under the name of Pont-Royal). In addition, the quais of the Hôtel de Ville, Saint-Bernard, Saint-Michel, and Saint-Landry, rectilinear constructions of cut stone, were laid out on the branches of the Seine in the sixteenth century. In the next century were built the Quai des Augustins, the Quai de Gevres between the Pont Notre-Dame and the Pont-au-Change, the Quai Malaquais, the Quai Le Pelletier, and finally the Quai de la Grenouillière (which became the Quai d'Orsay in 1707).

The opening of so-called public squares, the *places*, in the old urban fabric added a major embellishment to the canons of classic town planning. With the reign of Louis XIV, the prototypes put to the test under Henry IV at the Place Royale and at the Place Dauphine were bent to give birth to a new architectural model. The Parisian squares of Henry IV had three fundamental characteristics. First, each was closed, only tentatively linked to the urban routes that bordered it, whether the rue Saint-Antoine or the Pont-Neuf. Second, the squares were tied to the development of property and were dedicated to a public function (aristocratic residence and monarchical festivity, money changing and commerce). Finally, they were embellished with a royal statue only after the fact: in 1614 the Place Dauphine was overlooked by a statue of Henry IV, assassinated four years earlier (and, indeed, the statue was erected away from the square, on the Pont-Neuf), and from 1639 a statue of Louis XIII graced the Place Royale.

Beginning with the squares constructed by Jules Hardouin-Mansart in the 1680s, the order was reversed. The statue of the glorious king came first, and the public *place* was created after that. Several changes stemmed from initiatives to honor the king, both by groups and by individuals (including

19. Jean-Claude Perrot, *Genèse d'une ville moderne: Caen au XVIIIe siècle*, vol. 2 (Paris: Mouton, 1975), pp. 643–56.

that of the duc de la Feuillade on the Place des Victoires). Designs shunned square and rectangular shapes in favor of the circular (the Place des Victoires) and the octagonal (Place Louis-le-Grand, today the Place Vendôme), layouts that permitted the royal statue to be viewed from the same distance on all sides of the *place*. Finally, the construction of these public "squares" was not tied to a more grand development scheme. On the Place Louis-le-Grand, for example, the first improvement was the construction of administrative buildings, although just the facades were put up, and it was only after great financial difficulty that the operation was transformed into a subdivision project between 1690 and 1701, as the residences of men of finance were placed around the square. From the earlier model only one element remained: the establishment of public squares on property situated away from the great axes of urban circulation.

As was the case with Edo, the problem of providing water preoccupied the municipality of Paris. And as in Edo, the size of the urban population and the technological complexities of provisioning made it particularly difficult to maintain a certain supply of pure drinking water. In the shogun's capital, as Hatano Jun points out in Chapter 10, the government assumed major responsibility for creating a system of reservoirs and delivery canals, and the crown played a role in provisioning Paris with water as well. Some Parisians drew water from private wells dug in courtyards or even inside the buildings, and others purchased it from commercial carriers. But increasingly, people of the city came to rely on public fountains. Fed by the sources that surrounded the city (in Belleville, Pré-Saint-Gervais, and Rungis) and by the waters of the Seine (after the installation of pumps at the Pont-Neuf, the Pont des Tuileries, and the Pont Notre-Dame), the fountains constituted improvements that combined utility with embellishment. The town counted about twenty of them by the mid-1600s, and that number doubled during the last quarter of that century.

But if the Tokugawa shoguns and the Bourbon kings both had their hands in constructing bridges and creating water-supply systems, their thinking diverged on the matter of other urban improvements. "Urbis securitas et nitor" read the inscription on the medal struck by the Académie des Inscriptions et Belles-lettres to celebrate the lighting and the cleanliness brought to the streets of Paris by the royal ordinance of 1667. It expressed well a monitory ideal that was not always apparent in Edo. Above all, it implied, Paris should be a place where "an infinity of comforts," as Descartes put it, could be found. From this concern stemmed the attention given by municipal officials and by the monarchy to proposals that could make the city safer and more sanitary. The struggle for clean streets was an old one, and its chronology was marked by a series of measures that were more or less effective—often less rather than more. From the sixteenth century, the major texts are those of 1506, which for the first time established a tax to pay for street cleaning (and thus broke with the medieval principle by which the inhabitants had to maintain the cleanliness of the length of street that ran past their houses); and of 1539, in which the king ordered the inhabitants to pave the street in front of their houses, to provide drainage ditches, and to put their rubbish into baskets, which would then be picked up by wagons and dumped in specified locations outside the city walls.

Confronted with the meager success of these measures, Henry IV adopted another policy by contracting for the cleaning of the streets and by making arrangements in 1604 for the maintenance of the street network. Here, too, success was limited. The decisive steps were taken only by Louis XIV, who provided a subvention of approximately 50,000 livres a year for street paving and then made each residential quarter responsible for the cleanliness of its thoroughfares. Contracts, financed by a tax on the removal of mud and on lighting, were signed by neighborhood officials with various wagon drivers. The creation of the office of lieutenant general of police and the increased role of the commissioners of the Châtelet explain why these measures for street cleanliness had a greater impact than preceding ones. In any case, it proved difficult to uproot old habits, such as emptying chamber pots into the street, depositing garbage at night in the street, and even worse. The will to clean the streets, which came both from medical concerns (dirty streets polluted the air) and from a desire for convenience and amenity, was a break with the ancient familiarity with impurities and waste products. Consequently, it required the imposition of new standards of civility and decorum on the entire urban population, and was accomplished only with difficulty.

The lighting of streets was a second result of the monitory impulse. The first edict dated from 1504 (inhabitants were obligated to place lanterns in their windows), another from 1558 (one or more lanterns had to be placed in each street and lighted between 10 P.M. and 4 A.M.). Neither decree had much effect, nor did an ordinance dated 1594 which established a tax to pay for the production and installation of new lanterns. As in the case of cleaning, only the new authority of La Reynie, the lieutenant general of police, could get the streets lit. In 1667 an ordinance provided for more than five thousand lanterns to be lighted until 2 A.M. each night between October 20 and March 31. Observed and effective, the ordinance of 1667 constituted an innovation of considerable psychological importance. The lighting of streets both reassured and enchanted, and it enhanced security in the city by discouraging thieves and robbers.

The first urban improvements, intended to bring order and comfort to the old city, reflected the royal and municipal desire to organize the city's growth, balance its functions, and embellish and order the urban fabric. But in Paris more than elsewhere, history had imposed its own heritages. The parcelization of land, construction practices, custom, and administrative policy had left traces so deep in the accumulated past that they were impossible to efface. That is why the operations that transformed the capital— whether they were of royal, ecclesiastical, or private origin; whether they aimed to embellish a capital marked by the embodiment of power or sought maximum profits through wise investments—preferred the circumference to the heart, the peripheries and the empty spaces to the fully occupied spaces of the old urban core. This is why, also, changes that altered urban countenances and functions took place in related fragments and not as part of a coordinated transformation of the urban texture that was inspired by attention to utility. For the city to be thought of no longer as a garden of connected flower beds but as an organism of dependent functions would require the planning of the Enlightenment.

7

Building a New Establishment

Tokugawa Iemitsu's Consolidation of Power and the Taitokuin Mausoleum

WILLIAM H. COALDRAKE

The importance of architecture for investigation of the past has been recognized in Western scholarship since the nineteenth century. John Ruskin, that elegant exponent of Victorian ideas and language, wrote in 1849: "There are but two strong conquerors of the forgetfulness of men, Poetry and Architecture, and the latter in some sort includes the former and is mightier in its reality; it is well to have, not only what men have thought and felt, but what their hands have handled, and their strength wrought, and their eyes beheld all the days of their life."[1] Ruskin's language may be dated but his message is timely for the discipline of history; architecture can help us rebuild the past. Buildings find a central place in the history of the institutions that are housed within their physical frame. These buildings may serve as articulate statements of political power and furnish convincing evidence of the contemporary perception of government, its authority and its all-encompassing inevitability. Monumental architecture not only symbolizes authority; it may also act as the carefully contrived setting or stage for the performance of solemn rites such as the investiture of rulers, for acts of obeisance by their subordinates, and for extravagant public pageants that reinforce power.

Buildings are also significant to historians for the insights they bring to the processes of organization in a society. The creation of monumental buildings is an eloquent demonstration of the effectiveness of a governing elite. The capacity to mobilize labor and materials for construction on a colossal scale has been a hallmark of power from Mesopotamia and Egypt to China and Japan. As they do with written texts, scholars can look to the great structures of the past to advance their understanding about the workings of state and about the technological and human infrastructures of their day.

1. John Ruskin, *The Seven Lamps of Architecture*, Everyman's Library (London: J. M. Dent; New York: E. P. Dutton, 1907), p. 182.

The first half of the seventeenth century in Japan was one of the great epochs in world history for urban and architectural development. The period offers an ideal opportunity to examine architecture as a source material for throwing light on the relationship between the workings of the Tokugawa government and the process of monumental building construction, for the extensive resources of the Tokugawa state were mobilized to build from the ground up a physical establishment to house and to make manifest a new political order. The Tokugawa regime set out to solidify a fluid political situation by pouring society into a newly fashioned mold. During the primary phase of consolidation of the shogunate, from 1603 to 1651, the first three Tokugawa shoguns were extremely effective in translating their political ambitions into physical forms, sharing a universal ambition of rulers through the ages to create palpable manifestations of authority. The state became a work of art and art became a work of state, to borrow Jakob Burckhardt's classic characterization of the Italian Renaissance.[2]

Within just a few decades Edo grew from the marshes of the Kantō plain to become a swarming metropolis, almost surely the world's most populous city by the early eighteenth century. It was, as well, the national headquarters of the shogunate, and the construction of this enormous city constituted the most extensive physical achievement of the entire period of Tokugawa hegemony. At the same time as the early shoguns built Edo, they also sponsored the construction of castles, temples, and palaces throughout the nation. These projects included the castle-palace complexes at Fushimi, Sunpu, Nagoya, Osaka, and Nijō Castle in Kyoto, as well as reconstruction of the Imperial Palace at Kyoto and of major temples such as Chion'in, Nanzenji, Kiyomizudera, and Myōshinji in the same city. The shogunate even sponsored the rebuilding of Izumo Taisha, the great Shinto shrine in western Japan, thereby usurping the patronage of the Mōri daimyo over the most important religious center in their domain. In overall effect the architectural largesse of the Tokugawa line of shoguns promoted their political legitimacy by building tangible associations with long-established religious institutions, the imperial court, and important regional daimyo, and by this process the country's new rulers appropriated the traditional prerogative of patronage of great architectural monuments.

Historians consistently underestimate the role played by official building projects in the institutional consolidation of Tokugawa power, partly because institutional historians seldom have scrutinized architecture as a source for understanding political processes and partly because few buildings of the period have survived to the present day. However, architectural research, with the aid of written, pictorial, and architectural sources, is now reaching a more complete understanding of the destroyed buildings of the period, and it is important to consider the implications of these findings for the theme of state intervention in the architectural sphere.

2. Jakob Burckhardt, *The Civilization of the Renaissance in Italy*, vol. 1 (New York: Harper and Row, 1958).

Of particular importance in this process was the Taitokuin mausoleum (*reibyō*), a spectacular complex of buildings dedicated to the second shogun, Hidetada, and built by his successor, Iemitsu, in 1632 at Shiba, in the southwest of Edo. It was the direct predecessor both chronologically and stylistically of the Nikkō Tōshōgū, Ieyasu's mausoleum as rebuilt by Iemitsu in 1634–1636. Today the Tōshōgū occupies center stage, capturing in its polychromed and gilded snare the attention of historians and architects along with the thronging hordes of tourists. The dazzling brilliance of its Yōmei Gate now blinds us to any less insistent evidence of the aspirations and architectural activity of the same era in which it was created. Yet it is on the Tōshōgu's predecessor, now all but forgotten, that scholarly attention must be focused, for it was the Taitokuin mausoleum that inaugurated the era of Iemitsu's personal power with its bold architectural statement of authority and which set the pattern for the architectural design at Nikkō.

The Taitokuin mausoleum has slipped almost unnoticed from postwar historical awareness, largely because its main buildings were totally destroyed by bombing in 1945. Several of the gateways that guarded the approaches to this sacred shogunal precinct survive, but in locations so far removed in space and spirit from their original positions that assessment of their historical importance becomes difficult. Despite the damage that time has wrought, however, it is possible to reconstruct a detailed picture both of the architectural style of the Taitokuin and of its state-directed construction process by means of prewar photographs, a set of folding screens known as the *Edozu byōbu* in the collection of the National Museum of Japanese History (Kokuritsu Rekishi Minzoku Hakubutsukan), and official records compiled at the time of construction. These sources enable us to reestablish the architectural characteristics of the Taitokuin mausoleum, and thus to understand in a new way the character of Iemitsu's rule in Edo.

PRIMARY SOURCES FOR THE ARCHITECTURAL FORM OF THE TAITOKUIN MAUSOLEUM

Like his father before him and his successors after him, Hidetada was known in death by a Buddhist name, suggesting that he had achieved spiritual enlightenment. Hidetada's mausoleum took his religious name, Taitokuin, and was built on the southeastern side of the precincts of Zōjōji, the Tokugawa family temple at Shiba. In the early Edo period Shiba had a refreshing and pleasing air; it lay on the southwestern fringe of the city, a site pleasantly proximate to the coast.

The main part of the Taitokuin construction project was completed within six months, an extremely short period for a project of such size and detail. The *Edozu byōbu* provides a comprehensive overview of the site as it must have existed in the early Edo period. The left screen shows the Taitokuin complex in a great panoply of splendor lying to the immediate left of the principal buildings of the Zōjōji. The main Taitokuin structure consists of

Taitokuin mausoleum. Source: *Edozu byōbu*. Courtesy of Kokuritsu Rekishi Minzoku Hakubutsukan.

three separate but physically integrated buildings: the Worship Hall (*haiden*) at the front, linked to the Main Hall (*honden*) at the rear by an enclosed chamber known as the Ainoma (the "in-between room"), also referred to as the Ishinoma because of the stone flagging originally used for the floor. This complicated building mode is known as *gongen-zukuri*, a term wished upon us long after the creation of the architectural form to which it refers.[3] Architecturally, *gongen-zukuri* was based on the style of Buddhist temple halls, with strong timber framing and multiple-arm cantilevered bracket sets supporting the eaves, but theologically it was associated with religious centers where Buddhist and Shinto rites were conducted. The *gongen* style owed much to the Hachiman shrine form, which originated in the eighth century, during the Nara period.[4] Buildings such as the Usa Hachimangū in Kyushu, an Edo-period rebuilding of a Nara-period shrine, show its features clearly, with the Main Hall and the Worship Hall set parallel to each other. The Worship Hall was used for performance of the various ceremonies connected with religious observances at the shrine. The space between the buildings covered by the roof was gradually incorporated into the ritual space of the interior. The composite structure thereby created was eventually appropriated as a mausoleum.

The Taitokuin as shown in the *Edozu byōbu* displays unmistakably the characteristics of this style. The Main Hall is a two-roofed structure which towers over the Worship Hall at the front with elaborately intersecting roof planes; each of the two halls is covered by a hip-gable roof abutting a simple gable roof over the Ishinoma. A small "lean-to" roof (*kōhai*) is set above the steps at the front of the Worship Hall to protect visitors making simple oblations. The line of the eaves is accentuated by a gracefully flowing cusped gable (*kara hafu*). The walls and gables are bedecked with gold and there is a profusion of polychrome sculptural ornament beneath the upper-level eaves of the Main Hall. From the depiction in the *Edozu byōbu* it is clear that these were buildings of size and splendor, rivaled in Edo only by the castle keep and by the most important daimyo palace-residential compounds (*hairyō yashiki*) at the center of the city.

Walls and gates set the Taitokuin precincts apart from the city to the south and the Zōjōji on its eastern side. The main southern approach is

3. *Gongen-zukuri* was derived from Ieyasu's posthumous title of Tōshō Daigongen ("August Illuminator of the East, Buddha Incarnate"), but the first recorded use of *gongen* to indicate a style of mausoleum architecture rather than the spirit of Ieyasu occurs in the "Sharui tatechiwari," a 1739 compendium on the siting of Shinto shrines. In this document the term *gongen gosha*, or "the shogun's gongen shrine," is used; see Adachi Kō, "Gongen-zukuri to ishima-zukuri," *Kenchikushi* 3 (1941), pp. 393–97. The appellation *zukuri*, as a contraction of *tsukurikata*, or "way of building," was applied to architectural styles during the later Edo period in popular building compendia such as the *Kaoku zakkō*, published in 1842; see Sawada Natari, *Kaoku zakko*, in Zōtei Kojitsu Sōsho Henshūbu, ed., *Zōtei: Kojitsu sōsho*, vol. 15 (Yoshikawa Kōbunkan, 1928), pp. 234, 300; Inoue Mitsuo, "Zukuri ni tsuite," *Kenchikushi kenkyū* 23 (1956), pp. 20–23.

4. Kondō Yutaka, *Kokenchiku saibu goi*, rev. ed. (Taiga Shuppan, 1972), pp. 156–57; Ōta Hirotarō, *Nihon kenchikushi josetsu*, rev. ed. (Shōkokusha, 1969), pp. 75–76.

The Main Hall and inner gateways at Taitokuin. Source: Edozu byōbu.
Courtesy of Kokuritsu Rekishi Minzoku Hakubutsukan.

shown guarded by a moat and a high wall. A second wall of wooden palings and a protective roof subdivides the grounds into two courtyards, while a delicately latticed wall with a cypress-bark roof protects the inner sanctum. Gateways, individually distinct in character, stand watch at both of these walls. The gateway in the outer wall has a tiled roof, and a cusped gable is set into its front eaves to greet the visitor and warn the intruder. The next gateway, providing entry through the paling wall, has a cypress-shingle roof, indicating a more private mood, but is crowned by a ridgepole decorated with gold-inlaid lacquer to heighten the sense of impending majesty evoked by the Okuin, the Inner Precinct, where Hidetada's remains are interred. The third and most inner gateway, set into the latticed wall before the steps to the Worship Hall, is decorated by cusped gables at both front and sides, a virtuoso technical performance by carpenters and roof shinglers which provides an unprecedented rhetorical flourish to the entry to the Inner Precinct. Only at the Tōshōgū of Nikkō may be found a gateway of similar curvilinear exuberance.

It is clear from the disposition of walls and gateways in the painting that access to the Taitokuin mausoleum was restricted to a privileged few. Outside the main entrance sit the servants and dignitaries accompanying some esteemed visitor. The mausoleum grounds are virtually deserted, except for some dozen figures in distinguished garb, surely high-ranking shogunal retainers, seated before the Inner Precinct, and four white-clad figures, presumably priestly acolytes, in attendance beside the steps of the Worship Hall. All of the mausoleum that would have been visible to the humble populace of Edo was the outer wall and gateway and the upper story of the Main Hall, which probably explains the rhetorical crescendo it reaches in the decoration of its elevated eaves and ridge. This sight would have been sufficient, however, to excite the imagination and sharpen the sense of status separation between shogun and commoner.

On the rising ground to the left of the main complex is an octagonal two-story hall with gateways and a subsidiary building in front. A five-story pagoda is located farther to the left. Minor buildings are also shown in the main part of the complex, and another mausoleum, similar in style but smaller in scale, is situated immediately adjacent to the east boundary wall. Altogether, the Taitokuin mausoleum is strikingly similar to its counterpart at Nikkō, from the general organization of the various precincts to the architectural character of the elaborately decorated *gongen-zukuri* buildings, including details such as the multiple cusped gables on the inner gateway.

The *Edozu byōbu* thus contains a wealth of detail about the architecture of the destroyed mausoleum, but it is essential to corroborate this information with evidence from other primary sources. Although the screens seem to depict Edo before the great Meireki fires of 1657, which destroyed the castle keep and many of the temples and daimyo residences in its vicinity, the architectural content of the screens is internally inconsistent, as Naitō Akira has noted, with buildings dating to different eras coexisting in one great urban scene.[5] The sumptuous materials and excellent condition of the screens suggest that they were executed after the 1657 fires, although not later than the end of the seventeenth century. Assisted by his artistic imagination, the artist must have recreated the appearance of the pre-1657 city from a collage of earlier drawings, paintings, and maps.

The most reliable source for evaluating the accuracy of the depiction of the Taitokuin buildings in the *Edozu byōbu* is a report published in 1934 by the Tokyo Municipal Government. This document was compiled under the supervision of Tanabe Yasushi, then an associate professor at Waseda University, who conducted a comprehensive survey of the mausoleum complex as it stood at Shiba a decade before its destruction during World War II.[6] The survey includes extensive technical descriptions, photographs, site plans, and measured elevations of the Main Hall. The detailed site plan clearly identifies by name the buildings shown in the *Edozu byōbu*. The gates are labeled as the Sōmon or main outer gateway, the Chokugakumon or second gateway, and the Chūmon or inner gateway. These main entry gateways are aligned axially and orientated eastward. Two sacred ablution pavilions (*suibansha*) flank the approach between the second and inner gates. Tanabe's plan does not include a scale but, judging by the dimensions of the main building supplied in the report, the distance between the outer Sōmon and the inner Chūmon gateways was approximately one hundred meters.

The group of buildings to the south of the main complex forms the Inner Precinct, Hidetada's final resting place. It comprises a reliquary hall (*hōtō*), with a Chūmon-style gateway and a worship hall situated in front. Tanabe's report reveals that the nearby pagoda belonged to Zōjōji and was constructed prior to the Taitokuin mausoleum. Access to the Inner Precinct was by a path leading from the left of the open court area in the vicinity of the sacred ablution pavilions. The Onari Gate, reserved for official visits by the shogun, provided the ceremonial entrance. The plan shows that the Sōgen'in mausoleum was situated immediately adjacent to the Taitokuin complex on the opposite or north side. This mausoleum was dedicated to Hidetada's wife and constructed at a later date. Access was via another gateway, the Chōji Gate, set into the northeast corner of the Taitokuin site.

In general Tanabe's plan and the *Edozu byōbu* agree on the arrangement of buildings. In the painting the appearance of physical distance has been abbreviated by the tilted picture plane so that the outer and inner gateways

5. Naitō Akira, *Edozu byōbu bekkan: Edo no toshi to kenchiku*, suppl. to Suwa Haruo and Naitō, eds., *Edozu byōbu* (Mainichi Shinbunsha, 1972).

6. Tanabe's report is contained in Tōkyō-fu, ed., *Tōkyō-fu shiseki hozonbutsu chōsa hōkokusho*, vol. 11: *Shiba-Ueno reibyō* (Chūgai Insatsu, 1934) (hereafter cited as Tanabe report). Tanabe later published the material in this report together with additional photographs of the extant buildings and a discussion of other Tokugawa mausolea at Shiba and Ueno under the title *Tokugawa-ke reibyō* (Shōkokusha, 1942). Information in Tanabe's original report was collated with other government records by Itō Nobuo in a Cultural Affairs Agency publication on registered cultural properties destroyed during the war; see Bunkachō, ed., *Sensai ni yoru shōshitsu bunkazai: Kenzōbutsu-hen* (Kyoto: Benridō, 1965) (hereafter cited as CAA report).

seem only a few meters apart. The buildings of the Inner Precinct appear out of alignment because the Reliquary Hall is shown frontally, whereas the Worship Hall and Chūmon gateway are aligned with the dominant receding orthogonal of the entire composition. Tanabe's plan of the site and the *Edozu byōbu* differ only in one major respect. The painting shows the path to the Inner Precinct as running directly from the main compound via a steep stairway crowned by the Onari Gate. Tanabe's plan also shows this path, but the Onari Gate has been moved to a second path that branches off near the ablution pavilions.

The plan and elevation of the main *gongen-zukuri* building in Tanabe's report have a total length, including the masonry base, of approximately forty meters, and the Main Hall rises to a height of some sixteen meters. The Worship Hall is five bays wide by three bays deep and is surmounted by a hip-gable roof covered with *dōbuki-ita*, or copper-sheet tiling. The Ishinoma is one bay wide and five deep with a simple gable roof also of copper-sheet tiling. The Main Hall is square in plan, five bays wide and deep. Although the exterior has the appearance of a two-story structure because of its double roofs, the photographs in the Tanabe report reveal that the interior consisted of a large, soaring space with a corbeled roof in the standard form found in most Buddha worship halls (*butsuden*). Also typical of that style is the division of the interior on the horizontal plane into an inner sanctuary (*naijin*), with an altar (*shumidan*) set against the rear wall, and an outer sanctuary (*gejin*).

This prewar record, together with other photographs held by the Cultural Affairs Agency (CAA), confirms the accuracy of the general representation of the main buildings as shown in the *Edozu byōbu*, with two important exceptions. First, in reality a *chidori hafu*, or decorative triangular gable, was set into the front of the roof of the Worship Hall. Combined with the cusped gables on the lean-to roof over the steps, it gave the building much stronger frontal emphasis than the painting indicates. Even more significant, the artist of the *Edozu byōbu* has managed to paint the Main Hall sideways, with the ridge aligned with the Ishinoma, instead of at right angles, as the Tanabe survey shows it.

The prewar Tanabe report also offers more detailed stylistic information than does the Edo-period painting. Important stylistic differences may be discerned in the photographs and elevations between the Worship Hall and the Ishinoma on the one hand and the Main Hall on the other. The Main Hall is built in the curvilinear style of China's Sung dynasty, known in Japan after its introduction in the Kamakura period (1185–1333) as *Zenshūyō* (because of its association with Zen rites). It has strongly curved tie beams, chamfered pillar heads, and multiple-arm bracket sets tightly clustered under the eaves. By contrast, the Ishinoma and Worship Hall are in form predominantly *Wayō*, the older, more nativist, and more rectilinear style characteristic of Nara-period temple buildings. The wall frames are braced laterally by external, nonpenetrating ties known as *nageshi*, and the bracket sets are located directly above the pillars with the intercolumnar support provided by *kaerumata*, or frog-leg-shaped wooden fascias. In contrast, the bracket sets on the Main Hall have the tighter *Zenshūyō* profile, and the corner sets are penetrated diagonally by double *odaruki*, cantilever arms that greatly enhance their load-carrying capacity. Intercolumnar support is given by additional bracket sets in the typical *Zenshūyō* manner. The Main Hall has other *Zenshūyō* features such as cusped windows (*katōmado*) and paneled doors that swing open (*sankarado*). By contrast, the Worship Hall is equipped with the typical *Wayō* horizontally placed shutters (*shitomido*) and with sliding doors that feature tightly grouped horizontal battens (*mairado*).

The *Edozu byōbu* is not sufficiently detailed to permit close comparisons of architectural details with the information provided by the Tanabe report and prewar photographs, but it does serve to establish the visual impact of the decoration, particularly the color scheme, which is not, of course, clear from the black-and-white photographs. The pillars of the Worship Hall are black with gold detailing, those of the Main Hall red. The bracket sets throughout the building are shown as green, red, gold, and black. The ridge courses are a glossy black with gold detailing, which would have dazzled all who witnessed the buildings from afar on a sunny day.

The photographs in both the Tanabe and CAA reports provide much of the information about the sculpture, which is not discernible in the *Edozu byōbu*. These photographs make it clear that the buildings were alive with an impressive profusion of applied ornament. Chinese lions (*kara jishi*) are set above the pillars, and unidentifiable creatures thrust forward as carved nosings on the cantilever arms of the multiple bracket sets of the *Zenshūyō* system of the Main Hall. Dragons frolic along the outer eave purlins that carry the rafters, their mouths open and tongues outstretched. The rafters are in two horizontal tiers and are splayed in the standard *Zenshūyō* radial style.

Thus the precise architectural form and decorative details of the destroyed main buildings of the Taitokuin mausoleum may be established from careful collation of the Edo-period visual source and the prewar architectural survey of the extant structures. This comparison permits the following conclusions about the character of the architecture to be drawn. First, *Zenshūyō* was the style favored for the most important building projects, an indication of a new preference for exuberantly curvilinear forms by the shogunate under Iemitsu. Second, there was a wealth of applied ornament, identical in subject matter and style to the decorative programs used on palaces and mansions of Edo, and for the later Nikkō mausoleum.

EXTANT TAITOKUIN BUILDINGS

Three of the four gateways that guarded the various precincts of the mausoleum survived the war years, thanks largely to their physical separation from the conflagration that followed the bombing of the main buildings in 1945. These are the two outer gateways on the main approach, the Sōmon and the Chokugakumon, and the Onari Gate, which protected the Inner Precinct on the hill behind. The Chōji Gate, added as the entry to the neighboring Sōgen'in mausoleum when that edifice was rebuilt in 1646–1647, is also extant. With the redevelopment of the Shiba area after the war, however, all were removed from their original locations and any assessment must be based on their siting and function as revealed in the *Edozu byōbu* and the Tanabe report, not on the present state of the site.

The Sōmon gateway of the Taitokuin has been moved farther east from its original site within the Zōjōji precincts, and the other two great entry portals, together with the Sōgen'in Gate, were dismantled in 1960 to allow for development plans to be implemented at Shiba Park. All of these gateways have been relocated at Fudōji, near the UNESCO Village in Saitama prefecture, but no detailed records are available concerning the extent of repair and replacement of deteriorated parts, which was doubtless necessary at that time.

Despite these concerns regarding the lack of information about recent restoration work, the extant gateways conform closely with their depiction in the *Edozu byōbu*. They display the same dramatic visual impact the Taitokuin must have had in the Edo period, combining as they do energetically curved structural and roofing effects with exuberantly polychromed sculpture in the round. They reveal not only the subtle domination of *Zenshūyō* features but also close similarities with the host of magnificent ceremonial gateways that bejeweled the outer walls of shogunal and daimyo palaces in Edo.

When the various buildings are considered in their original setting as Tanabe's plan and prewar photographs reveal them, it is clear that they did not exist in isolation but were planned as a concert of desired effects, with contrasts in style, size, and location carefully plotted to achieve a total impact that would far exceed the impression conveyed by the simple sum of the parts. Other than these gateways, only a handful of buildings survive from the city of Edo before the devastating fires of 1657.[7] It is necessary to turn to Kyoto, Nikkō, and elsewhere to find further evidence of the type of buildings constructed in Edo during this early period. For this reason alone the Taitokuin gateways provide priceless evidence for establishing the physical identity of early Edo architecture.

THE BUILDERS OF THE TAITOKUIN MAUSOLEUM

Many students of architecture in Japan believe that tradition is anonymous and that the individual is subsumed within a group identity. Building forms are therefore interpreted in broad categories of style such as *Wayō* and *Zenshūyō*, or they are identified with a specific building mode such as *gongen-*

---

7. These structures include the Sangedatsu Gate of Zōjōji, the Honbō Gate and five-story pagoda of Kan'eiji, the Asakusadera Niten gateway, the Ueno Tōshōgū, and the Shimizu and Tayasu gatehouses of Edo Castle.

zukuri. Such terms are useful only to the extent that they indicate collections of characteristics commonly found together and are the names accepted in the field. They are as much historical afterthoughts, however, as "Classical," "Romanesque," and "Gothic" in the West, where in recent years it has proved more useful to examine the contributions of architects as individuals or, in the case of customary building traditions, to identify the characteristic building techniques employed by families of master artisans.

The distinctive design details that become clear from analysis of the Taitokuin mausoleum records and extant gateways reflect the skills and artistic preferences of the particular persons chosen by the shogunate to build the mausoleum. If we are to understand the Taitokuin architecture, we must put faces on those persons.

In 1934, when Tanabe compiled his report on the Taitokuin mausoleum, a stone stele was discovered under the floor of the Main Hall. On it were inscribed the names and titles of sixty-nine principal participants in the building project, ranging from the chief commissioner of construction (*zōei sōbugyō*) to the master craftsmen who represented all of the major building trades, from carpenters to stone masons, artists to lacquer specialists.[8] This stele is a historical landmark, one of the most detailed sets of attributions in the entire history of Japanese architecture. It is therefore of inestimable importance to examine it carefully for what it reveals about the overall organization of the building project and about the contributions of individual master craftsmen.

According to the stele, the major participants were the chief commissioner of construction and the *shimo tōryō*, or subordinate master carpenters. The chief commissioner of construction was the official charged with overall responsibility for the administration of the project by the shogunate; the stele identifies this person as "Sakura Jijū Fujiwara Tokitomi Toshikatsu." This was Doi Toshikatsu (1573–1644), daimyo of Sakura domain in Shimōsa until 1633; thus the first part of the title inscribed on the stele. The *Kansei chōshū shokafu*, a compendium of genealogies of daimyo and the shogun's direct retainers completed in 1801, records that Doi was "appointed supervisor [*bugyō*] of the construction of the mausoleum for Taitokuin at Zōjōji" in the Second Month of 1632, confirming the information given on the stele.[9] Doi was one of the most important daimyo to hold an official position in the shogunate. He served as an elder (*toshiyori*) during Hidetada's lifetime and became a senior councilor (*rōjū*) when that position was given a permanent place in the shogunal bureaucracy during Iemitsu's reforms of the 1630s. The management of the Taitokuin construction by so important a daimyo is an immediate indication of the significance Iemitsu attached to this project.

The *shimo tōryō* were the master carpenters who worked under the official direction of the so-called supervising builders (*onhikan daiku*). In reality

8. Quoted in full in Tanabe report, pp. 22–25.
9. Hayashi Jussai, comp., *Kansei chōshū shokafu*, 8 vols. (Eishinsha, 1917–1918), vol. 5, p. 249.

the master carpenters were the actual builders of the Taitokuin mausoleum, their central role disguised by the complexity of shogunal titles and hierarchy. The stele identifies the master carpenters as: Kōra Bungo no Kami Munehiro, Heinouchi Echizen no Kami Masanobu, Kōra Saemon no Jō Munetsugu, Kōbō Osakabe Shōho Nobukichi, and Tenma Izumi no Kami Munetsugu. Little is known for certain about either Kōbō or Tenma, except that Kōbō was a member of the Tsuru family workshop and was probably a relative of Osakabe Saemon Kunitsugu, noted for his work for the Date family of daimyo in Sendai, in northern Japan. Naitō suggests that Tenma may have been from the Osaka area of the same name and therefore a member of a collateral branch of the Heinouchi, master builders who had served the Toyotomi family when Hideyoshi had underwritten so many large-scale construction projects in the Osaka-Kyoto region.[10]

The involvement of the first three men listed as master carpenters in the Taitokuin building project—Kōra Munehiro, Kōra Munetsugu, and Heinouchi Masanobu—is of utmost significance in the context of the Edo architectural establishment. In 1641 the same three master carpenters were jointly responsible for rebuilding, after a fire, the principal Edo palace of the Owari daimyo family, a collateral branch of the Tokugawa, whereas Kōra Munehiro alone is credited in the records of his family with two earlier Edo commissions for important "outside lords" (*tozama daimyō*). The first of those jobs was the construction of a palatial residence, including a remarkable Onari gate, for the Gamō family when they ruled the great domain of Aizu-Wakamatsu. The second commission was for an enormous tiger-and-bamboo sculpture on a service building (*daidokoro*) for Katō Kiyomasa at his elaborate residential complex in Edo.[11] The Taitokuin stele establishes that the same three members of the Kōra and Heinouchi families were the principal on-site master builders of the Taitokuin mausoleum, indicating that by 1632 they and their family workshops had become the major force in Edo architecture, relegating the earlier master builders brought by the Tokugawa to Edo in the 1590s to administrative and supervisory positions. With the Taitokuin project, the Kōra and Heinouchi had moved from the periphery of official building practice, from executing commissions for daimyo such as Gamō and Katō, to the center of shogunal building practice in Edo, working on mausolea for the Tokugawa and urban mansions for the Owari family, blood relatives of the shogun.

It is possible to analyze knowledge of the architectural style and decoration of the Taitokuin buildings gained from the pictorial and written sources in terms of the building practices of the Kōra and Heinouchi. The Kōra were *Zenshūyō* specialists whereas the Heinouchi, together with the Tsuru, worked in the *Wayō* mode. The following specific correlation between architectural features and workshop practices becomes clear for the first time:

10. Naitō, *Edozu byōbu bekkan*, p. 98.
11. Details recorded in the "Kōra oboegaki," edited in the early eighteenth century on the basis of earlier written records and quoted in full in Ōta Hirotarō et al., eds., *Nihon kenchikushi kiso shiryō shūsei*, vol. 17 (Chūō Kōron Bijutsu Shuppan, 1974), pp. 7–8.

1. The Worship Hall and Ishinoma of the main building, together with the Sōmon gateway, are *Wayō* in style, suggesting that the Heinouchi and Tsuru, practitioners of this mode, were responsible for their construction.[12] The Sōmon follows closely the style of that same name, as prescribed by the Heinouchi in *Shōmei*, the definitive design manual of their family tradition.[13]

2. The *Zenshūyō* features of the Main Hall indicate strongly that it was built by the Kōra. The presence of the Kōra in the Taitokuin project also accounts for the notable divergence in the plan of the Main Hall from the bay pattern observed at the Toyotomi-related structures associated with the Heinouchi, such as the Kitano Tenmangū in Kyoto. The Taitokuin Main Hall is square, five by five bays, and thus is significantly different in concept from the rectilinear five-by-four-bay plan used for similar halls of mausolea belonging to the Toyotomi tradition. It has also been shown that the Main Hall was built directly on the pattern of a *Zenshūyō*-style Buddhist hall. The Kōra clearly adopted the standard *Zenshūyō* hall type from their existing family tradition, thereby injecting a new element into the *gongen-zukuri* form. It is interesting to note that the Worship Hall and Ishinoma also departed from the standard Toyotomi mausoleum plan, the Worship Hall narrower and the Ishinoma more elongated. Moreover, the consummate mastery of the *Zenshūyō* idiom evident in the design of the Chokugaku and Ōnari gates suggests Kōra authorship, as does the decorative sculpture under their eaves. The figures of celestial beings (*tennin*) on the outer gable of the Onari Gate in particular have that sureness of delicate detail, that grandeur of conception, of the master sculptor. In view of Munehiro's reputation as a sculptor, evidenced by the gable tiger in bamboo executed for Katō Kiyomasa, it may be concluded that this masterpiece is also the product of his hand.

12. It is difficult to distinguish between the Heinouchi and Tsuru contributions without a broader understanding of the Tsuru tradition. One avenue of exploration would be the Sendai projects of Date Masamune, with whom the Tsuru were associated before coming to Edo. However, the position of the Tsuru on the list of *shimo tōryō*, lower than the Kōra and Heinouchi, suggests a subsidiary rather than principal role in the Taitokuin project.

13. Ōta Hirotarō and Itō Yōtarō, eds. *Shōmei*, 2 vols. (Kajima Shuppankai, 1971), vol. 1, pp. 54–56; vol. 2, pp. 98–99. Both the Shiba and Shōmei gateways are so-called *yatsuashimon* executed in the *Wayō* mode with *mitsumune-zukuri* ceilings. There is also a suggestive correlation between specific details of the two gateways, such as the three-level bracket sets and the distribution of rafters over the central bay. Rafter arrangement is a key indication of proportions used in building design and amounts to the artistic signature of a workshop when it acts as a module for determining the dimensions of the rest of the building. The *Shōmei* specifies, and the Shiba Sōmon gateway uses, eighteen rafters set above the entrance bay. Such precise correlation is more than coincidence. It should be noted, however, that the *sue hafu*, the pointed gables with cusped flair set into the roof planes of the Sōmon, are not part of the Heinouchi design in *Shōmei* and must be attributed to another source, possibly the Kihara family, who were supervisors of the overall project and designed similar gables for the worship halls of the Iga Hachiman (1636) and Iga Gosho (1641) shrines.

These conclusions are based on correlation of formal features of the Taitokuin buildings with knowledge of the technical and stylistic practices of the carpenters identified by the stele inscription as having been engaged in the construction project. Written evidence from the Kōra family records confirms their accuracy: "In Kan'ei 9 [1632] Kase Saemon was ordered to be the chief builder of a Buddha worship hall for Hidetada [Taitokuin-sama] at Zōjōji. Heinouchi Ōsumi was in charge of the mausoleum and Bungo Munehiro was ordered to do all the carvings."[14] "Kase Saemon" was Kōra Munetsugu, son of Munehiro, whose name appears on the Taitokuin stele as "Kōra Saemon no Jō Munetsugu."[15] The "Buddha worship hall" that the shogunate ordered Munetsugu to construct was the Taitokuin Main Hall, which took the standard form of such a structure.

The Kōra document also attributes the building of a "mausoleum" to Heinouchi Ōsumi. "Osumi no Kami" was the honorific title for Masanobu, head of the Heinouchi family, whom the Taitokuin stele refers to as "Echizen no Kami." The title was granted Masanobu later in his career, probably in recognition of his services at the Taitokuin project.

The "mausoleum" referred to in the document is indubitably the tabernacle containing Hidetada's remains. The prewar photographs of the Inner Precinct show that the Reliquary Hall was built in *Zenshūyō* style and was virtually identical to the Main Hall, constructed by Kōra Munetsugu. It seems likely, therefore, that Munetsugu was also responsible for the Inner Precinct and that Heinouchi made only the bronze tabernacle housed within. In fact, one of the volumes of the Heinouchi design manual, *Shōmei*, is devoted exclusively to pagoda design and includes specifications for a reliquary pagoda that is identical in style to that shown in the photograph of the interior of the Taitokuin Reliquary Hall.[16] Both structures have a cylindrical body set on a lotus-petal stand and are capped by a pyramidal roof with nine rings on top.

The final attribution in the document to "all the carvings" to be done by Bungo—that is, Kōra—Munehiro is consistent with our knowledge of his remarkable career as an architectural sculptor. It also accords with the conclusion that the carving of celestial beings, the dominant feature of the Onari Gate, was the creation of a master sculptor, now demonstrated in all likelihood to have been Munehiro himself, and establishes the general importance of the decorative programs of the extant Taitokuin gateways as representing Munehiro's style.

Munehiro's primary concern with sculpture at Taitokuin goes a long way

14. "Kōra-ke shiryō," as quoted in CAA report, p. 14.
15. *Kase* may also be read *segare*, "son."
16. Ōta and Itō, *Shōmei*, vol. 1, pp. 162–64; vol. 2, figs. 15–23. The description of the reliquary pagoda concludes by noting that the example given was built by Heinouchi Yoshimasa for the interior of the great hall of Buddhist worship at Hōkōji in Kyoto, constructed for the Toyotomi family at the beginning of the Keichō era (1596–1615). The *Shōmei* also includes detailed descriptions of the system of proportions used in the design of the nine rings on top of the roof; see vol. 1, pp. 165–72.

toward explaining the major role played by his son in architectural work at the project. Munetsugu was the building specialist directly responsible, under the general supervision of his father, for the architectural execution of the family commissions. Munehiro, freed from tedious on-site building responsibilities, took charge of the elaborate decorative programs that charged these buildings with such declaratory power. On the basis of existing evidence it is thus possible to reach firm conclusions about the authorship of the three extant gateways as well as the destroyed building complex of the Taitokuin mausoleum, thus greatly increasing our knowledge of official architecture in the city of Edo.

Significance of the Taitokuin Project

The architectural and documentary evidence greatly enhances our understanding of the relationship between the political priorities of Tokugawa government and the internal processes of building projects. Three separate but closely related aspects of the architectural institutionalization of the Tokugawa shogunate demand further examination.

The Taitokuin Mausoleum and Iemitsu's Personal Consolidation of Power

The mausoleum was conceived as a fundamental physical statement of Tokugawa authority at a critical juncture in the establishment of the personal authority of the third shogun, Iemitsu, after 1632. Although Iemitsu had become shogun in 1623 upon Hidetada's nominal retirement, he was not able to exercise significant prerogatives in government until Hidetada's death, nearly a decade later. Ordering the construction of the Taitokuin mausoleum was one of Iemitsu's first direct acts in government. The occasion offered him far more than an opportunity to demonstrate filial piety to his immediate predecessor. It provided a suitable and immediate chance to create an impressive architectural monument of his own initiation in the shogunal capital. The siting, size, and magnificence of the buildings speak more of vaunting ambition than they do of filial piety.

The project was to set the tone for Iemitsu's rule and his consolidation of the institutional apparatus of the Tokugawa state through landmark measures. In a remarkable career, the third Tokugawa shogun further centralized his own personal authority within the shogunate (by institutionalizing the post of senior councilor and by defining more fully the role of the junior councilors); acquired greater authority over his direct retainers, the bannermen (by issuing codes regulating their conduct in 1632 and 1635); imposed a fuller measure of control over the daimyo (by appointing inspectors general from 1632, reworking the "Regulations concerning Warrior Households" in 1635, and dramatically increasing the incidence of daimyo transfer and attainder); proscribed Christianity; and fashioned a policy of national seclusion in a series of measures taken between 1633 and 1639.

Architecturally, the Taitokuin project inaugurated a series of state building projects that were assertively shogunal and self-consciously Edocentric. The preceding decade had seen considerable architectural activity, but many of the most spectacular projects had been concentrated in the Kansai region, where the shogunate rebuilt Osaka Castle, the Ninomaru Palace within Nijō Castle, and the Imperial Palace in order to balance the equation between imperial and shogunal authority in Kyoto and Osaka. Iemitsu's focus, in sharp contrast, was more strictly concentrated on Edo projects. In the short space of seven years, starting with the Taitokuin mausoleum in 1632, the shogun rebuilt the main structures of Zōjōji in 1634–1635, repaired the soaring keep and principal enceintes of Edo Castle in 1637–1638, and reconstructed the keep in 1638. Even the reconstruction of the Tōshōgū in the mountains at Nikkō, commenced in 1634 and built with the same techniques as the monuments physically sited in Edo, such as the Tokugawa mausolea, was a direct extension of the Edocentric architectural policy.

The 1630s and 1640s were, therefore, an era of frenetic architectural activity, undertaken not only by the shogun Iemitsu directly but also at his behest. For instance, the renewed vigor of official visits by the shogun obliged the daimyo to build impressive new gateways and chambers to receive him at their principal residential compounds in Edo. The great monuments created by the well-oiled machinery of state building and the harder-pressed workshops of the daimyo exceeded in scale and spectacle the architectural achievements of the founding Tokugawa shogun, and even of Toyotomi Hideyoshi a generation earlier, at the height of the extravagant Azuchi-Momoyama epoch (1568–1600). Iemitsu's architectural preoccupations offer an interesting parallel to Henry IV's concern, just a historical moment earlier, with creating the Place Royale and the Place Dauphine in Paris as a reflection of his own authority.

A further dimension to the relationship between Edo architecture and Iemitsu's building program, his aspirations and their architectural expression, may be found in the reasons for the choice of the distinctive style of building and decoration revealed by the Taitokuin mausoleum. An important question should be asked: What were their origin and their ultimate meaning in the context of shogunal power relations?

Ieyasu's first mausoleum at Nikkō certainly provided the immediate precedent for the Taitokuin project, but the practice of building spectacular mausolea to deceased warrior leaders had been established earlier by the Toyotomi family. After Hideyoshi's death in 1598, the Toyotomi family constructed the lavish Hōkōku Daimyōjin in the southeast of Kyoto to enshrine his deified spirit. Hideyoshi's successors also were responsible for rebuilding the Kitano Tenmangū in Kyoto in 1607. This shrine, dedicated to Sugawara no Michizane, that paragon of Heian courtly nobility, was an act of piety by the Toyotomi designed to pay handsome political dividends in the uncertain years that followed the Tokugawa ascendency at Sekigahara.

The general language of architectural authority was thus well defined by the time Ieyasu became shogun in 1603, but the specific stylistic vocabulary changed under Tokugawa patronage of shogunal mausolea. The main structures at Taitokuin correspond in general terms with the *gongen*-style buildings associated with the Toyotomi line, but they diverge markedly in the detailed organization of pillars and bays, in overall proportions (particularly of the Ishinoma), and in the shift in emphasis away from *Wayō* aesthetics. The growing importance of *Zenshūyō* as the architectural style of the Tokugawa establishment must be attributed to the ascendancy of the Kōra family of master carpenters.

The Taitokuin Mausoleum and the Shogun's Building Administration

The construction of the Taitokuin mausoleum was undertaken as a state project with great expedition. The principal phase of construction was completed within six months, a remarkably short period for a project of this stylistic complexity. Careful documentation of the organization of the project reveals to the modern researcher in highly specific terms the administrative structure of an important facet of shogunal government in the 1630s.

Moreover, as a consequence of the experience of the Taitokuin project, the shogunate tightened its upper-level administrative control over the hitherto ad hoc array of builders in diverse trades brought into government service at Edo. Centralization of control was achieved by the appointment of three shogunal officials to the newly regularized post of commissioner of building (*sakuji bugyō*) less than four months after the main construction activities at Shiba had been completed. The "Kan'ei nikki," a record of daily events compiled by shogunal officials, remarks that Sakuma Naokatsu (Masakatsu), Kamio Motokatsu, and Sakai Katsuhisa were appointed commissioners of building by the shogun on the third day of the Tenth Month of 1632. All three were Tokugawa household retainers, and all held important posts; indeed, at one time Sakai served as *shoinban*, a position that made him responsible for maintaining the defenses of Edo Castle.[17] The new commissioners of building ranked with the city magistrates, commissioners of finance, and other key officials in the shogunal government (see Figure 2.1). The day the three commissioners were appointed, the "Kan'ei nikki" also notes, master builders and craftsmen in "all the [building] trades were instructed that it was the shogun's will that they follow the orders of the commissioners of building."[18] The effect of this measure was to place under the control of a single office the multitude of workshops of carpenters and sawyers, shinglers and tilers, lacquer specialists and sculptors, smiths and toolmakers needed as contractors and subcontractors for the shogunate's building projects.[19]

17. Hayashi, *Kansei chōshū shokafu*, vol. 2, p. 60; vol. 6, pp. 218–19; vol. 8, p. 106.

18. Quoted in full in Tanabe Yasushi, "Edo bakufu sakujikata shokusei no tsuite," *Kenchiku zasshi* 598 (1935), p. 28; summarized in Kokushi Taikei Kankōkai, ed., *Kokushi taikei*, vol. 39: Kuroita Katsumi, ed., *Tokugawa jikki*, vol. 2 (Yoshikawa Kōbunkan, 1930), p. 568.

19. On the specialist nature of building trades and professions during the early Edo period, see William H. Coaldrake, *The Way of the Carpenter: Tools and Japanese Architecture* (Weatherhill, 1990), pp. 13–18, 137–48.

This measure was particularly significant because hitherto no senior official in government service had been charged with ongoing administrative responsibility for architectural projects of state. Until the 1630s officials appointed on an ad hoc basis and given the temporary title of commissioner for engineering works (*fushin bugyō*) had been responsible for land reclamation, for the excavation of moats and canals, and for the collection of stone and the erection of castle walls. As a result of the experience of castle construction during the Azuchi-Momoyama and early Edo periods, architectural construction in the opening decades of the Tokugawa period was seen as subordinate to the massive task of wall engineering, which, after all, guaranteed the security of a castle headquarters in uncertain times. What was viewed as the ancillary task of erecting timber-frame superstructures on these walls and residential compounds within their compass usually was delegated to lesser functionaries under the overall control of the hard-pressed commissioners of engineering works.

Creation under Iemitsu of the new office of commissioner of building, its incumbent to be equal in rank to other key officials, including the commissioner of engineering works (a permanent part of the bureaucracy from 1652), and with direct responsibility to the senior councilors under Iemitsu's reorganization, is evidence of a shift in political emphasis in state-sponsored construction in Edo that put architecture on the same basis as engineering. It is also a signal to historians that Iemitsu was readying his government for even more grandiose building projects than the Taitokuin mausoleum, and it indicates the determination of the shogun to exercise personal direction of this new phase of architectural formation. All three of the commissioners of building had rendered loyal service to either Ieyasu or Hidetada from a young age, and they were to be entrusted collectively with the administrative responsibility for the Edo Castle projects of the late 1630s.[20] From the broader historical viewpoint, the determined and large-scale reorganization of state-administered construction under Iemitsu paralleled the high priority given to the organization of building agencies in Nara in the eighth century under Emperor Shōmu, and it encapsulated the bureaucratic ordering of construction that has been a common preoccupation of rulers from antiquity to the present.

Arbitrary Will, Technical Necessity, and the Architecture of Authority

Primary sources, particularly the stone stele discovered in 1934 that recorded the names of the major participants, support the analysis of the formal features of the buildings and establish the identity of the master builders responsible for the Taitokuin mausoleum. These findings are of singular significance not only for architectural but also for social and political history. Until recently there has been little cognizance of the contribution of individual artisans and artists to the creation of Japanese architecture, com-

---

20. Sakuma was rewarded handsomely in 1640 for the speed with which he rebuilt the main enceinte and the keep of Edo Castle; see Hayashi, *Kansei chōshū shokafu*, vol. 8, p. 106.

mentators conceiving of buildings only in stylistic terms. In the absence of effective argument to the contrary, it has been acceptable to subscribe to the theory of the "anonymous artisan." The Taitokuin project permits the attribution of buildings to individual builders, sculpture to particular sculptors—in other words, it is now possible to identify artistic personality in the architecture of early Tokugawa Japan, a giant step forward. The Promethean artistic character of Kōra Munehiro now distinguishes him as the leading architect and master sculptor working for the Tokugawa government. On this point it is instructive to recall that it is only the scholarly research of the last century that has led to the attribution of the architectural masterpieces of the Renaissance to the hands of Alberti, Bramante, and Michelangelo.

The Taitokuin project raises the significant issue of the relationship between how a building is made and how a patron believed it should look. Intrinsic to state organization of building projects, such as Iemitsu's tightened control through the appointment of commissioners of building on a permanent and regular basis, is the tension between bureaucrat and builder. This is a case of the intersection of a sphere of arbitrary will, that of Iemitsu's shogunate, and technical necessity, in this case the internal dictates of the hereditary building traditions of the Kōra family of master builders. How did the Tokugawa doctrinaire concern with image accommodate the equally dogmatic traditions of the *Zenshūyō*, of which the Kōra were exponents?

This situation may be interpreted as a dynamic intersection of the city above and the city below, although the master builders became members of the elite in a manner reminiscent of the leading artists and architects of the Renaissance courts. The appointment of Kōra Munehiro as the chief master builder in charge of the rebuilding of Ieyasu's mausoleum at Nikkō constituted official recognition of the supremacy of the Kōra school and its style of architectural design after the dramatic success of the portions of the Taitokuin project for which the Kōra were directly responsible, particularly the Main Hall and the Onari Gate, at the entrance to the Inner Precinct, where Hidetada's remains were interred. Although *Wayō* elements are still in evidence at Nikkō, the project was carried out under Munehiro's direct technical supervision and reflects closely his family tradition of *Zenshūyō* as well as his personal taste and sculptural talents. There was some artistic accommodation with the *Wayō* style by the addition of external horizontal ties to the timber frames of the main Tōshōgū buildings at Nikkō, but the overall conception and control of the project and the dominant stylistic characteristics are Kōra. In the shogunate's official building projects thereafter, the hereditary exponents of the more restrained *Wayō* mode remained active or enjoyed high rank as officials, but the commitment of the shogun's government to a single master builder and his workshop from 1634 indicates that the desires of the lord and architect-builder had reached a state of harmonious correspondence.

PROVISIONING

物資補給

8

Provisioning Paris

The Crisis of 1738–1741

STEVEN LAURENCE KAPLAN

The relation between the capital and the state in matters of provisioning is perhaps best symbolized by the march of the women of Paris upon Versailles in October 1789 to force the royal family to return home with them. Triumphantly the women brought back to Paris "the baker, the baker's wife, and the baker's boy." Hungry, anxious, and politically mobilized, these women—the conventional agents of legitimate subsistence insurgency—reproached the king for failing to fulfill the social contract by which the people agreed to submit to taxation, military service, and "subjectly" fealty in return for the promise that the mythic nourishing prince, embodied in the state, would spare them from starvation.[1] Though it was never inscribed in the fundamental laws of the realm, the commitment to subsistence became, in the vernacular, a responsibility and an attribute of kingship. It was not merely something the monarch-father did for his subject-children; it was something he was expected and in some sense required to do.[2] Doctrinaire of absolutism and divine monarchy, Jacques Bossuet asserted that the king's obligation to ensure subsistence was the "foundation" of all his claims on his people. Despite Montesquieu's very different conception of political legitimacy, his belief that the state owed its citizens "an assured subsistence" expressed the same notion. The paramount human right to exist which such radical social critics as Gabriel Mably and Simon Linguet contended the monarch was bound to guarantee had more in common with the old vision of the providential and liturgical vocation of kingship than with the new Enlightenment conception of the rights of man. During the dire subsistence troubles of the 1770s a petitioner lectured the ministry that "if by divine right the people owe a tribute to their Sovereign, there is one [tribute] perhaps equally indispensable due them . . . a guarantee against dearth." Instru-

---

1. On the role of women in food riots, see Steven L. Kaplan, *Bread, Politics, and Political Economy in the Reign of Louis XV*, 2 vols. (The Hague: Martinus Nijhoff, 1976), vol. 1, pp. 90–92.
2. For a fuller development of this argument, see ibid., pp. 1–8.

mentally, Jacques Necker, the banker-philosopher who became minister at the end of that decade, held very much the same view, though it was predicated on a less sentimental theory of reciprocity: "The subsistence of the people is the most essential object that must occupy the government."[3]

The state had many reasons to be keenly interested in the management of the food supply. Its growth depended on its ability to create and then expropriate part of an agricultural surplus. To finance its ambitions and its apparatus, the state taxed; direct taxation fostered the commercialization of agriculture, forced peasants into the market, and helped make grain supply accessible. The state endeavored to eliminate feudal excrescences and obsolete fiscal privileges that hindered circulation and exchange. It wrenched from the countryside supplies for its armies. Decisions about floating population and public assistance issues were always made with reference to the subsistence question. Provisioning policy was at the core of the tension between agricultural and industrial strategies, the latter requiring low prices to ensure international competitiveness and the former demanding higher prices to obtain investment and keep pace with population. The state had to mediate among rival claimants to food resources: institutions, territorial jurisdictions, its own *missi dominici*. By the beginning of the sixteenth century the state was already deeply enmeshed in the regulation of production, distribution, and consumption. But its preoccupation with provisioning was above all the result of its intense concern for social stability.

SOCIAL CONTRACT AND SOCIAL CONTROL

The policy of provisioning as a means of social control had been practiced, in one form or another, since the beginning of urban civilization. It was premised on the assumption that the failure to ensure an adequate food supply could imperil the political and social structure of the kingdom. Ancien régime officials and observers were profoundly impressed by the historical linkage between subsistence difficulties and "revolutions" that they discovered in Rome, Constantinople, China, and their own national past.[4] Though popular disorder had many sources, none was so permanent or so pervasive a prod to disruption, none caused such profound disaffection toward state and society, and none excited the people to such fury as a threat to subsis-

3. Jacques St.-Germain, *La vie quotidienne en France à la fin du grand siècle* (Paris: Hachette, 1965), p. 191; J. Hecht, "Trois précurseurs de la sécurité sociale au dix-huitième siècle," *Population* 14 (1959), p. 73; Montesquieu, *De l'esprit des lois*, as quoted in André-Lichtenberger, *Le socialisme au dix-huitième siècle* (Paris: F. Alcan, 1895), p. 91; Simon-Nicolas-Henri Linguet, *Du pain et du bled*, in *Oeuvres*, vol. 6 (London, 1774), p. 67; idem, *Annales politiques, civiles et littéraires du dix-huitième siècle* 7, pp. 203–4; anon., "Essay sur le moyen d'établir des greniers d'abondance" (30 May 1771), Archives Nationales (hereafter cited as AN), F[11] 265; and Necker to Sartine, 14 February 1778, AN, F[11]* 1, fol. 238

4. Nicolas Delamare, *Traité de la police*, vol. 2 (Amsterdam, 1729), p. 566; *Journal de l'agriculture, du commerce, des arts et des finances*, 1772, p. 48; and Jacques Necker, *Sur la législation et le commerce des grains* (Paris: Pissot, 1775).

tence. As an eighteenth-century intendant put it, the "prerequisite" for order was "to provide the subsistence of the people, without which there is neither law nor force that can contain them."[5] Of course one could not govern by bread alone. Public policy had its own imperatives beyond social control and compassion for suffering. Yet the combined exigencies of social control and social contract entailed significant constraints on the freedom of the state to elect certain strategies for its own growth and for the development of the economy and the society.

Theoretically king and state were committed to defend the interests of all consumers. In practice, however, they systematically favored Paris because its immense size, its large concentration of laboring poor and floating population, and its perceived combustibility worried them most. Voltaire joked that Paris needed only "bread and circuses" to prosper, but the police commissioner and codifier Nicolas Delamare took the Roman lesson seriously: the police felt confidence in their ability to maintain peace in the capital only so long as they could keep the markets supplied. Its mammoth scale made the provisioning of Paris logistically difficult as well as politically imperative. Without the special administrative advantages that the capital enjoyed, remarked the author of a dictionary of police, "one would have trouble imagining that there are sources capable of meeting the needs of this vast pit." Finally, authorities felt that it was important for there to be "a secret and invisible hand"—the police, not self-interest!—in the provisioning of the capital because Paris served as a regulator market, setting a price standard that had an impact, like Parisian fashion and Parisian revolt, far beyond the limits of the city.[6]

One of the great and enduring themes of French history, the tension between Paris and the provinces, was sharply exacerbated by the provisioning differential. Portrayed as "blood-sucking Babylon" and "plundering Rome," Paris was denounced for the "odious violence" it exercised on the rest of the kingdom. The "sacrifices" that the central government imposed on France in favor of Paris, wrote the physiocrat Pierre-Samuel Du Pont, "are the object of the jealousy of the whole realm."[7] The philosopher-social critic

5. Bertier de Sauvigny, "Observations sur le commerce des grains," Bibliothèque Nationale (hereafter cited as BN), manuscrits français (hereafter cited as ms. fr.) 11347, fol. 228.

6. Voltaire to François de Chennevières, 22 October 1760, in Theodore Besterman, ed., *Voltaire's Correspondance* (Geneva: Institut et Musée Voltaire, 1953–1965), vol. 37, p. 156; Voltaire to S. Necker, 6 February 1770, ibid., vol. 74, p. 81; Delamare, *Traité de la police*, p. 600; Nicolas-T.-L. Des Essarts, *Dictionnaire universel de police*, vol. 1 (Paris: Moutard, 1786), p. 329; Daguesseau fils to controller general, 24 February 1709, in Arthur de Boislisle, ed., *Correspondance des contrôleurs généraux des finances avec les intendants des provinces* (Paris: Imprimerie Nationale, 1874–1897), vol. 3, p. 102; and A. de Gazier, "La police de Paris en 1770, mémoire inédit composé par ordre de G. de Sartine sur la demande de Marie-Thérèse," *Mémoires de la société de l'histoire de Paris et de l'Ile-de-France* 5 (1878), p. 116.

7. Gabriel-François Coyer, *Essai sur la prédication* (Paris: Veuve Duchesne, 1781), p. 15; Paul-Jacques Malouin, *Description des arts du meunier, du vermicellier et du boulanger*, ed. Jean-Elie Bertrand (Neufchâtel: Société Typographique, 1771), p. 429; Simon-Nicolas-Henri Lin-

Louis-Sébasatien Mercier's wry "supposition" must have struck a sympathetic chord (and probably still does):

> If all the orders of the state assembled, having recognized after a mature examination that the capital exhausts the kingdom, depopulates the countryside, retains far from it the great proprietors, ruins agriculture, hides a multitude of bandits and useless artisans, corrupts morals little by little, postpones the epoch of a government more formidable abroad, freer and happier; if all the orders of the state, I say, everything considered and reviewed, ordered the whole city to be burned after having previously given the inhabitants a year's warning, what would be the result of this great sacrifice made for the fatherland and for future generations? *Would it in fact be a service rendered to the provinces and the kingdom?* I leave it to you, reader, to study and decide this interesting problem.[8]

But to privilege Paris did not mean to provision it, at least not directly. The women of Paris who marched on Versailles regarded the king as the victualer of *last resort*. Ordinarily the state was expected not to supply the city on a day-to-day basis but to make sure that it was supplied with sufficient quantities of good-quality merchandise at reasonable prices. The state was not equipped to undertake the primary food trade. Its lively sense of its own limitations, reinforced by a desire not to deter those persons whose profession and social function it was to trade in flour and grain, induced the government not only to eschew ordinary provisioning operations but also to refrain from instituting organizations of "abundance" in imitation of Joseph's Egypt, sixteenth-century Venice, or eighteenth-century Geneva. "Most nations," lamented the farmer-general Claude Dupin,

> have placed themselves on guard against the disastrous events of dearth and of inordinate abundance by means of storehouses that absorb grain when there is too much and disgorge it when it is lacking. . . . We who have the glory to possess the wisest rules in the universe on other matters have remained far behind our neighbors on this one, which is nevertheless the most important, since the wealth or poverty and even the life of all the Subjects depend upon it.[9]

For all its anguish over food supply, the state never elaborated a master plan for lean years or fat. Directly on the supply side the government intervened as most French people lived, *au jour le jour*, sometimes massively, sometimes

---

guet as cited in André Morellet, *Théorie du paradoxe* (Amsterdam, 1775), pp. 99–100; Du Vaucelles, "Mémoire," AN, F[10] 215–16; and Pierre-Samuel Du Pont de Nemours, *Analyse historique de la législation des grains* (Paris: Petit, 1789), p, 182.

8. Louis-Sébastien Mercier, *Tableau de Paris* (Amsterdam, 1782–1788), vol. 4, pp. 309–10.

9. Claude Dupin, "Mémoire sur les bleds" (1748), BN, ms. nouvelles acquisitions françaises (hereafter cited as n.a.) 22777, fols. 155, 167.

selectively, and always reluctantly. Parisian authorities established a modest, decentralized emergency granary network lodged in religious communities, *collèges*, and hospitals in the wake of the subsistence crisis of 1725–1726. Not until the 1760s did the state attempt to maintain a tactical reserve on its own initiative.[10]

Regulation was the characteristic expression of government intervention in provisioning. Authorities nervously stalked grain from the time it was planted until consumers put it on their tables. They followed each stage of transformation, and they tracked the behavior of the agents who shipped, milled, stored, sold, bought, and so forth. The actual task of provisioning was to be consigned to commerce. But the authorities feared that if it were left strictly to commerce, without vigilance and tutelage, society would live in relentless jeopardy. The police attitude toward commerce and toward merchants was deeply ambivalent. On the one hand, liberty was the acknowledged "soul of commerce," and only a vigorous commerce could feed the capital. On the other hand, merchants were naturally given to "cupidity" and "manipulation," and liberty quickly degenerated into license and into the antisocial crime of monopoly, an omnibus rubric that meant causing artificial dearths by hoarding, buying futures, recklessly overbidding, disseminating disinformation, and so forth. Since society depended on the provisioning trade for survival, the police conceived of it as a sort of public service, and imposed restrictions on it that other forms of commerce escaped. To enable or compel commerce to perform its victualing service, the police relied on an array of regulations that I have associated with the marketplace as physical site and as *idée-force*. The single most important rule concerning provisioning trade was the requirement that all transactions occur in the marketplace. This was the surest guarantee of honesty and efficiency, in the view of consumers as well as the authorities. Even the (constantly) revocable derogation accorded to registered Paris merchants allowing them to operate outside the marketplaces of the supply zone was construed as part of a larger marketplace design that aimed at giving the edge to metropolitan merchants over their local rivals (even as it permitted Parisian jurisdiction to supersede local jurisdiction) and at guaranteeing the hegemony of the central or final marketplace of the capital over the subordinate collector marketplaces. Other regulations, such as those dealing with permits for dealers and passports for grain and flour, derived from the marketplace even if they were meant to govern the space outside it.[11]

10. On the Paris emergency network, see Steven L. Kaplan, "Lean Years, Fat Years: The Community Granary Sytem and the Search for Abundance in Eighteenth-Century Paris," *French Historical Studies* 10 (1977), pp. 197–230. On the state-sponsored reserve, see Kaplan, *Bread*, vol. 1, pp. 344–90, and vol. 2, pp. 614–58.

11. On the notion of the marketplace and the market principle, see Steven L. Kaplan, *Provisioning Paris: Merchants and Millers in the Grain and Flour Trade during the Eighteenth Century* (Ithaca: Cornell University Press, 1984), pp. 23–29. On the regulations, see Kaplan, *Bread*, vol. 1, pp. 63–72.

The Police of Provisioning

The art (contemporaries called it a "science") of the police of provisioning was finding the proper balance: navigating between the Scylla of (over-)regulation and the Charybdis of (excessive) liberty. In theory the police never deviated from their marketplace engagement; in practice they were often moderate, indulgent, and supple. Delamare endorsed a differential police of provisioning: extreme rigor for famine, firmness for flagrant dearth, tolerance for abundance. Guillaume-François Joly de Fleury, procurator general of the Parlement of Paris, never tired of reminding officials that the controls "are not strictly executed in times when there is no dearth to fear." When the circumstances did not absolutely warrant zealous intervention, the highest authorities in the realm repeatedly exhorted their subordinates "to shut their eyes" to abuses.[12] Physiocratic propaganda to the contrary notwithstanding, the police of provisioning was not inexorably iron-fisted and diabolical. Still, it was a police regime: a regime of prohibitions and constraints, of permissions rather than permissiveness. Less rigid and oppressive than it was often portrayed, it was still meddlesome and forbidding. If the authorities frequently overlooked the rules in easy times, in periods of stress they tended to enforce them vengefully, as if to atone for their laxity. If the critics of the police system exaggerated its tyranny by emphasizing the extraordinary episodes of police intervention, they were after all not so being unreasonable because the dearth experience was the ultimate test, and it left the deepest mark on the minds of merchants, officials, and consumers.

The king exercised the supreme police power in the realm. Royal legislation, framed in ministerial committee or royal council, devised or reaffirmed the general rules forged to govern the provisioning trade. The king's chief deputy for matters of provisioning was the controller general, who presided over a sort of superministry that encompassed virtually everything pertaining to the economy, finances, public works, and public order. Organized in specialized bureaus, including one known as the grain or subsistence department, his staff collected detailed data throughout the kingdom that helped him to anticipate deficits and surpluses, stimulate circulation, and diffuse useful information to rectify imbalances. Familiar with every aspect of the provisioning trade, the controller general became actively involved only in times of emergency. The intendants operated in the field directly under his aegis. Endowed with an extremely wide range of authority, they toiled to reconcile the demands of the periphery with the injunctions of the

12. Delamare, *Traité de la police*, p. 794; BN, Collection Joly de Fleury (hereafter cited as Joly) 1130, fols. 156–57; 2418, fol. 177; 1107, fols. 6–9; Bertin, "Mémoire à consulter sur la liberté du commerce des grains," 1761, C. 69, Archives Départementales (hereafter cited as AD) Ille-et-Vilaine and C. 2420, AD Bouches-du-Rhône; Levignen to Bertin, August 1761, C. 89, AD Orne; subdelegate of Verneuil and subdelegate of Falaise to Levignen, 14 August 1761, C. 89, AD Orne; intendant of Soissons to Bertin, 19 August 1761, AN, K 908; intendant of Brittany to Terray, May–June 1774, C. 1653, AD Ille-et-Vilaine; and Parlement of Aix to Louis XV, 21 November 1768, B. 3677, AD Bouches-du-Rhône.

center. The authority of the intendant of Paris was eclipsed by the lieutenant general of police of Paris, royal judge and administrator, whose responsibilities impinged on every aspect of city life and whose jurisdictional appetite expanded ravenously after the creation of the post in 1667. Another victim of the lieutenant general's irredentism was the provost of merchants (*prévôt des marchands*), who proved unable to arrest the continuing decline in the influence of the venerable municipal government, erstwhile rampart against monarchical excesses. The lieutenant general and the provost of merchants negotiated some of their differences in the informal assembly of police, convened as often as once a week by the first president and the procurator general of the Parlement of Paris to discuss the administration of the capital. Aside from its frankly political and its more narrowly juridical responsibilities, the Parlement exercised a sort of parallel grand police vis-à-vis the royal administration, sometimes complementing it, sometimes supplanting or challenging it. Embracing almost a third of the kingdom in its competence, the Paris court issued quasi-legislative acts called *arrêts de règlement* in addition to interpreting and executing royal law; and it controlled a sprawling juridico-administrative network of local officials of justice and police who reported directly to the procurator general of Parlement, making him one of the most powerful and best-informed leaders in the realm.

THE DEARTH OF 1738–1741

Virtually all the facets of the police of provisioning were illustrated in the grave dearth that buffeted much of the kingdom in the years 1738–1741. In 1737 an extremely uneven harvest in the Paris supply zones—"mediocre," "scarce," "half a normal year"—engendered hardship in some places and anxiety throughout the region. Alternately high and low water levels and prolonged winter ice compounded the problem. Reports converged on a widening and deepening "misery" during the first quarter of 1739. A clement spring excited false hopes, for a series of hailstorms ruined a considerable part of the 1739 crop. As a result of cold and wet weather in the late spring and summer, the following year endured an even greater shortfall— at best between a third and a half of a "common" yield.[13] Officials through-

13. Odile to procurator general (hereafter cited as PG), 19 October 1738, BN, Joly 1119, fol. 108; Joly 1119, fols. 83–86 (October 1738–January 1739); deliberations, bureau de l'hôtel de ville (hereafter cited as BV), 19 December 1738, AN, H* 1358, fols. 63–64; deliberations, assemblée de police (hereafter cited as AP), 3 July, 25 August, and 5 December 1738, BN, ms. fr. 11356, fols. 345, 365, 370; Baussau to controller general (hereafter cited as CG), 26 November 1738, Bibliothèque de l'Arsenal (hereafter cited as Arsenal), ms. de la Bastille (hereafter cited as ms. B.) 10275; AP, 22 January 1739, BN, ms. fr. 11356, fol. 379; BV, 3 February 1739, AN, H 1939¹; AP, 8 January 1739, BN, ms. fr. 11356, fol. 376; BN, Joly 1120, fols. 82 and 162 (16 May and 5 July 1739); Simon-Henri Dubuisson, *Lettres du commissaire Dubuisson au marquis de Caumont, 1735–1741*, ed. A. Rouxel (Paris: Arnould, 1882), p. 550 (6 May 1739); BN, Joly 1120, fols. 144–45; Jean-Michel Desbordes, ed., *La chronique villageoise de Vareddes: Un document sur la vie rurale des XVIIᵉ et XVIIIᵉ siècles* (Paris: Editions de l'Ecole,

out the northern part of the kingdom deplored "extraordinary suffering." Terror-riven women in the faubourg Saint-Marcel talked of dying of hunger as the loaf surpassed twice its standard price. Misery provoked demographic disarray. Thousands of poor people took to the roads, hoping to find relief in the cities. Beggars engulfed the capital. Parish priests complained that their resources were stretched to the limit. It was but a short step from mendicancy to crime. The case of a harvest worker, one Dubois, from the outskirts of Versailles, was symptomatic. He stole "for the first time in his life . . . because of extreme necessity, seeing his family lacked bread." Faced with "famine," the "populace was ready to revolt," according to police warnings from hinterland towns. "Common sicknesses" ostensibly caused by "bad food" accelerated the influx into the Hôtel Dieu hospital that had begun in 1739. Writing in November 1740, before the effects of one of the century's harshest winters could be felt, the marquis d'Argenson reported that "more people had died of misery during the previous two years than had been killed in all the wars of Louis XIV."[14]

Winter floods in 1740–1741 interrupted transport on roads and waterways, destroyed or disrupted mills, disgorged sewers, corrupted drinking water, and inundated buildings in the capital. Bakers rowed to market at the Place Maubert. The subsistence crisis swelled quickly into a general economic crisis as consumers shifted virtually all of their declining revenue to the

---

n.d.), p. 25; BV, 30 August 1740, AN, H 1859, fol. 10; AP, 30 June 1740, BN, ms. fr. 11356, fols. 420–24; Pierre de Narbonne, *Journal des règnes de Louis XIV et de Louis XV de l'année 1701 à l'année 1744 par Pierre Narbonne, premier commissaire de police de la ville de Versailles*, ed. Joseph-Adrien Le Roi (Versailles: Bernard, 1866), pp. 477, 483; Edmond Jean-François Barbier, *Chronique de la régence et du règne de Louis XV (1718–1763), ou journal de Barbier*, 8 vols. (Paris: Charpentier, 1857–1858) (hereafter cited as Barbier, *Journal*), vol. 2, pp. 206 (May 1740), 214 (August 1740); Foucaud to PG, 18 September 1740, BN, Joly 1121, fol. 265; Odile, 5 November 1740, 4B 1140, AD Seine-et-Oise; and letter of local officials, November 1740, AN, F^{11} 222. For a study of the evolving crisis in the hinterland of the capital and in the provinces of the distended jurisdiction of the Parlement of Paris, see Michel Bricourt, Marcel Lachiver, and Julien Quéruel, "La crise de subsistances des années 1740 dans le ressort du parlement de Paris (d'après le Fonds Joly de Fleury de la Bibliothèque Nationale de Paris)," *Annales de démographie historique*, 1974, pp. 281–333.
14. Guillaume to PG, 4 September 1740, BN, Joly 1123, fol. 166; procurator fiscal, Corbeil, 22 August 1740, ibid., fol. 261; (?) to Marville, 13 September 1740, Arsenal, ms. B. 10027; Gazetins, 19/20 September 1740, ms. B. 10167, fol. 137; curé, St. Jacques de la Boucherie, to lieutenant general of police (hereafter cited as LG), 18 May 1739, Joly 1120, fol. 28; Thomassin to Marville, 18 May 1739, and Breteuil to Marville, 29 July 1739, Arsenal, ms. B. 10321; Joly 1308, fols. 49–50 (30 June 1740); AN, Y 18617, 17 October 1740; anon. to Marville, 23 September 1740 (Dourdan), ms. B. 10027, p. 389; Poix to PG, 24 May 1740, Joly 1123, fol. 276 (Crécy-en-Brie); Guillen to PG, 19 October 1740, Joly 1123, fol. 112 (Châlons); BV, 6 May 1739, AN, H 1939^1; deliberations, bureau of Hôtel-Dieu, Archives de l'Assistance Publique (hereafter cited as AAP), 14 December 1768, no. 137, and 7 October 1740, no. 109; René-Louis de Voyer d'Argenson, *Mémoires et journal inédit du marquis d'Argenson*, ed. marquis d'Argenson, 5 vols. (Paris: P. Jannet, 1857–1858), vol. 2, p. 34 (November 1740). Cf. Marcel Couturier, *Recherches sur les structures sociales de Châteaudun, 1525–1789* (Paris: SEVPEN, 1969), pp. 102–6; Louis Henry and Claude Lévy, "Quelques données sur la région autour de Paris au XVIIIe siècle," *Population* 17 (April–June 1762), p. 306.

purchase of food and as employers in the city, emulating those in the countryside, cut back drastically on production in response to stagnant demand. ("The merchant sells nothing and thus he cannot give occupation to the worker.") Countless observers, officials as well as ordinary citizens, regarded 1740 as worse than 1709, the benchmark year for disaster in the collective memory of the eighteenth century and the last real famine, in the judgment of many modern historians.[15]

The authorities responsible for Parisian supply reacted to the first signs of dearth with characteristic ambivalence, oscillating between a paralysis of discretion ("Let us not act for fear of broadcasting alarm among the public, which will only make matters worse") and a panicky urge to move quickly ("We face the prospect of a universal disaster if we fail to take immediate precautions"). A survey of the secondary and tertiary supply zones led the assembly of police to request an immediate halt to exportation abroad. Even before the harvest outcome was known, the provost of merchants—Turgot's father—proposed the laying up of a large stock in England which could be rapidly shipped to Paris in case of a disastrous shortfall, or resold locally. Despite the municipality's willingness to absorb losses of up to a half-million livres, the plan was not implemented. The assembly decided to curb "maneuvers" of merchants and bakers by circumscribing freedom to bid up prices. The logic was somewhat tortured, and revealing of police malaise about an overly aggressive policy of control: "If it was dangerous during a time of marked dearth to intervene to contain prices, it was necessary when there was not [yet] such a dearth to hold the line and not succumb to excesses."[16]

But the entrepôt markets were increasingly deserted as owners hoarded and transactions took place in barns and inns. Though authorities remained

15. BV, 21 January 1741, AN, H 1939²; Orry to Jomarron, 28 December 1740, AN, G⁷ 57; Maurepas to Marville, 29 December 1740, Archives de la Seine et de la Ville de Paris, 3 AZ 10² pièce 3; "Inondation de 1740," BN, ms. fr. 5682, fol. 194; livre de la Conciergerie, Archives de la Préfecture de Police, AB/l64; Gazetins, 15 January 1741, Bibliothèque Historique de la Ville de Paris (hereafter cited as BHVP), ms. 620, fol. 51; deliberations, Hôtel-Dieu, 23 November 1740, no. 109, AAP; ordinance of police, 28 January 1741, AN, Y 9499; *Mémoires du duc de Luynes sur la cour de Louis XV*, ed. Louis-Etienne Dussieux and Eudore Soulié, 12 vols. (Paris: Firmin-Didot, 1860–1865), vol. 11, p. 87 (21 March 1754); Orry to PG, 18 May 1739, BN, Joly 1120, fol. 27; Missy to PG, 5 December 1740, Joly 1307, fols. 77–78; anon. to Marville, 1740, Arsenal, ms. B. 10027, fols. 391–92; Orry to PG, 19 September 1740, Joly 1121, fol. 83; Joly 1120, 23 and 31 May 1739, fols. 188–89, 201–3; conseil secret, 27 October 1740, AN, X¹ᴬ 8468, fol. 161; "Le journal d'un bourgeois de Corbeil," *Bulletin de la société historique et archéologique de Corbeil, d'Etampes et du Hurepoix*, 4th year (1898), p. 36. Cf. the influence of 1740 on 1709: St-Simon composed his description of the latter during the former. See Arthur de Boislisle, "Le grand hiver et la disette de 1709," *Revue des questions historiques* 73 (1903), pp. 447–48.

16. Equally revealing of official thinking in a kindred domain was the indecision about whether to publish an edict to disabuse the public of the conviction that the government was about to manipulate the value of the currency, a situation that discouraged grain holders from selling: but "these sorts of declarations often appearing suspect to the public, [they] are often rather capable of causing [the public] to believe the opposite of what they proclaim." AP, 28 August 1738, BN, ms. fr. 11356, fol. 366.

loath to sound the alarm and accelerate dearth behavior by publishing an emergency regulatory decree, it became impossible to sustain the fiction that a crisis was not in the making. Deeply dejected, the assembly implored the controller general and Cardinal André-Hercule de Fleury, the de facto prime minister, to provide 12,000 muids of foreign grain—about 13 percent of annual consumption—as soon as possible. At the same time the assembly asked the procurator general to refuse authorization to local police in the hinterland to requisition supplies or to require holders to make public declarations of their stocks.[17] Yet who could doubt the gravity of the situation when the lieutenant general of police began to call upon the monasteries, convents, *collèges*, and hospitals to release to the markets of Paris small portions of the emergency reserve they were required to store for the capital's extraordinary needs? Foreign and military-provisioning grain began to arrive in modest doses in December, but some of it was of poor quality, and the authorities did not dare risk provoking public wrath by offering it as a famine ersatz.[18]

For the next two years, crisis management focused on three major sectors. First, the task of purchasing and distributing foreign and surplus domestic grain assumed titanic proportions. The controller general took direct responsibility for this enterprise, though the Parisian authorities also sponsored provisioning campaigns, sometimes in competition with the ministry. The organizational demands were complex and Herculean: to marshal supplies from all over the Western world; to find transport and ensure conservation (or rehabilitation); to set priorities and targets; to devise timetables and communications linkages; to sell the merchandise at strategically useful prices that would not cripple the capacity of the market system to function on its own, but that would reasonably satisfy consumer expectations without burdening the government with exorbitant losses; and to hold accountable factors and agents, public and private, across the entire chain. The second task was to mobilize indigenous supply in the context of the regulation of the grain and flour trade. The crisis induced changes not in regulatory theory but in its interpretation and implementation, and prophylaxis continued to be at least as important as repression. The lieutenant general of police aggressively asserted his claim to a general stewardship over provisioning, including the behavior of hinterland markets, the functioning of the entire land-based trade, pricemaking, and the practices of millers and bakers. The provost of merchants governed his traditional bailiwick, river-borne commerce, once the predominant source of Paris supply, now seriously

17. The next July, even as the crisis deepened, the assembly denounced the initiatives of certain subdelegates and local magistrates "to visit granaries and force deliveries to market" because "these sorts of visits generate much alarm, and this alarm increases the number of buyers and decreases the number of sellers," thus aggravating the dearth: AP, 14 July 1740, BN, ms. fr. 11356, fol. 425.

18. Ibid., fols. 349–5l (26 June 1740), 354–55 (3 July 1740), 360 (31 July 1740), 365–66 (28 August 1740), 369 (27 November 1740), 370–71 (4 December 1740); PG to CG, 5 December 1738, BN, Joly 1119, fol. 24.

challenged by the traffic drained to the Halle, the central market of Paris. The third concern was relations with consumers, which ranged from the fairly straightforward business of mediating between bakers and the public to the more prickly task of dealing with attitudes incubated by the dearth experience. It ought to be emphasized that, by and large, the government intervened with reluctance rather than with relish. Even after the early denial phase, which highlighted their agony, the authorities moved with prudence. To be sure, officials close to the grass roots were more directly constrained to act than those at the central apex; and some administrators were tempted to use the crisis for self-aggrandizement, to encroach on rival jurisdictions, or to settle scores. But at every level of administration, officials were aware of the political, commercial, and psychological as well as the financial costs of intervention.

CENTRAL CRISIS MANAGEMENT: THE CONTROLLER GENERAL

It is said that Philibert Orry, the controller general, was so obsessed with fiscal concerns that he responded very slowly to the burgeoning crisis. (The duc d'Orléans is alleged to have brandished a horrid famine bread made of fern to capture his attention at a council meeting in the late summer of 1739.)[19] The evidence suggests that he moved very cautiously, waiting for requests for help rather than anticipating them, endorsing import proposals rather than initiating them (and indeed, expressing repeated doubts about the availability of grain on the international markets), recommending recourse to rice rather than grain, as if the need would be short-lived and despite notorious resistance to ersatz foods.[20] It was not until the third consecutive shortfall in 1740 that he launched a vast campaign of royal provisioning—the direct purchase of "king's grain" supplemented by the commissioning of private deals—primarily for the capital, but also for other stricken regions. Once he acknowledged in September 1740 that the dearth was "more real today than [it had been] in 1709 and 1725," subsistence became his paramount preoccupation for the next year or more.[21]

Orry moved first to take control of the disparate supply undertakings that were either in operation already (the massive importation by the Genevan banker Isaac Thellusson) or in gestation. Schemes he had scoffed at earlier—a merchant's plan to buy grain in the Saumur region; a project promoted by the comte de Maurepas, the minister of state, to import grain

19. Louis-Etienne-Alphonse Jobez, *La France sous Louis XV, 1715–1774*, 6 vols. (Paris: Didier, 1864–1873), vol. 3, p. 164.

20. On the controller general's cautious early measures, see PG to CG, 5 December 1738, BN, Joly 1119, fol. 34; Hérault to CG, 16 November 1738, Arsenal, ms. B. 10275; AP, 10 December 1738, BN, ms. fr. 11356, fol. 373; Thellusson to Hérault, 15 November 1738 and 14 March 1739, ms. B. 10275, 10270; CG to PG, 5 May 1739, Joly 1120, fol. 14.

21. CG to PG, 25 September 1740, BN, Joly 1121, fol. 102. But like modern-day politicians, Orry avoided calling the crisis a crisis. He referred euphemistically to "the present conjuncture." To Dodart, 13 October 1740, AN, KK 1005F.

from "Abbanie"—he now adopted.[22] Orry tried to make sure that rival institutional buyers working on behalf of the army, the municipality, the hospitals, and other corporate entities did not bid up prices and damage one another. Even as he urged police to crack down on dealer abuses, he blandished merchants with a system of bonuses.[23] He vowed to reach "everywhere," at home as well as abroad. To facilitate the movement of grain toward the capital from southern France, where it was quite abundant, and from Italy, Sicily, North Africa, and the Levant, the controller general organized a reception and relay system that linked Arles with Lyon, Roanne, and the Briare canal. He named an agent at each entrepôt, either a merchant or an administrator, whose work he monitored with intrusive attention. To this infrastructure he added correspondents, again drawn from both private and public sectors (the terms are of course anachronistic, given the structural overlapping and confusion), for the purpose of buying grain, reporting on market conditions, marshaling transport (especially boats and carts), and spying on other members of the team.[24]

The handful of key players in Orry's enterprise enjoyed no more than his contingent confidence, which was wholly dependent on their performance. The banker was Pierre Babaud de La Chaussade, son of a government contractor, who purchased a post of secretary to the king, converted to Catholicism, and went on to become one of France's richest industrialists. Using his own network and the circuitry of the controller general, Babaud advanced funds for purchase and received the proceeds from sales. The principal buying coordinator for Paris was Jacques Masson, Babaud's father-in-law, former business partner of Babaud's father, former high official in the government of Lorraine, and former Protestant. Masson's death in June 1741 jolted Orry, and induced him to become even more closely involved with the behavior and the accounts of the buying agents.[25] An old friend of Orry, the

22. PG to CG, 20 September 1740, and reply, BN, Joly 1121, fols. 91–93; CG to PG, 27 September 1740, ibid., fol. 106. For other provisioning propositions, see Joly 1121, fol. 113 (September 1740); Noailles to PG, 28 January 1741, Joly 1109, fols. 92–93; CG to La Bourdonnaye, 3 and 11 February 1741, AN, KK 1005F; report from "Dantzick," 11 November 1740, Archives des Affaires Etrangères, B¹ 476. Cf. Barbier's evocation of a private company with a plan for northern and Mediterranean imports: Barbier, *Journal*, vol. 3, pp. 236–37 (November 1740).

23. CG to PG,19, 23 September 1740, BN, Joly 1121, fols. 83–84, 100. On how Provost of Merchants Turgot earned Orry's disfavor through his efforts to organize purchases, see Luynes, *Mémoires*, vol. 4, p. 223 (September 1742).

24. See the patronage and financial rewards Orry later accorded the subdelegates, local magistrates, constables, etc. for their contributions to his provisioning campaign: CG to Charart, 24 January 1742, and to Breteuil, 10 May 1742, AN, G⁷ 59; CG to Jomarron, 1 May 1744, G⁷ 61. For an example of the surveillance of agents by other agents, see the efforts of the subdelegate at Roanne to check on the honesty and efficiency of Jars and Prost: CG to Prue, 8 January 1743, G⁷ 60.

25. Paul W. Bamford, "Entrepreneurship in 17th and 18th Century France: Some General Conditions and a Case History," *Explorations in Entrepreneurial History* 9 (1957), pp. 204–13; Herbert Luethy, *La banque protestante en France de le révocation de l'édit de Nantes à la Révolution*, 2 vols. (Paris: SEVPEN, 1959–1961), vol. 2, pp. 12–13; AN, T 308; AN, Minutuer

comte de Buron, who held the title of lieutenant general of the Ile-de-France, supervised the field operations from the Briare canal. He oversaw purchases in the Loire area, managed the transport system, vetted Paris-bound grain for quality, and served as liaison with Claude-Henri Feydeau de Marville, the lieutenant general of police in the capital, who determined the rhythm of deliveries.[26] A Lyonnais merchant named Michel Henry shared buying responsibilities in Burgundy, Franche Comté, Dauphiné, and Provence with Gabriel Jars, another wholesale trader based in Lyon, who was seconded by the international trading firm of Jars and Prost, located in Roanne. Artaud, a merchant who had also served in the royal administration, was the general receiver of all foreign grain of Mediterranean provenance and of all Provençal grain as well. Stationed at Arles, he was responsible for keeping the pipeline full of Paris-bound merchandise. Despite his intensely felt concern for local and regional needs, Pallu, the intendant of the Lyonnais, found himself charged with a mission of general supervision, serving as bridge between Versailles and the Rhone valley.[27]

Orry was keenly aware that buying and removing grain were extremely delicate operations, especially since subsistence apprehension was beginning to spread everywhere. He exhorted his agents to buy with extreme discretion and to ship with dispatch. They had to avoid the temptation to buy heavily at one time and place, yet they could not afford to protract their purchases and thus communicate alarm through an entire region. They were to buy only the prescribed amount no matter how attractive opportunities appeared. They were to respect the "current" price: any speculative overbidding would result in their immediate revocation. The professional merchants were expected to hire hometown buying commissioners, locally well known. Orry worried about the several subdelegates who were purchasing agents because they probably lacked commercial experience and their activities could readily be misinterpreted by wary inhabitants. A buying visit to Sancerre orchestrated by Buron provoked a riot when an inhabitant, terrified at the prospect of seeing his town stripped of its sustenance, "beat the drum to rally the citizenry." Much to Orry's ire, the subdelegate here clearly sympathized with the crowd and failed to arrange for "exemplary punishment." In this high-stakes business, Orry was prudent but not risk-averse. He encouraged the subdelegate general of the Dauphiné to keep

Central , XCI-887, 3 September 1752, and VI-694, 29 March 1742; CG to Buron, 5 June and 17 and 23 July 1741, AN, G⁷ 58; CG to Buron, 7 July 1741, AN, KK 1005F; CG to G. Jars, 15 June 1741, G⁷ 58; CG to La Porte, 12 May 1742, G⁷ 59; CG to Marville, 16 April 1742, G⁷ 59; CG to Babaud, 15 June 1741, G⁷ 58, and 18 January 1742, G⁷ 59.

26. CG to Buron, 13 January 1742, AN, G⁷ 59; *Almanach royal, 1741,* p. 96; CG to Buron, 31 October and 11 December 1740, AN, KK 1005F, and 23 July 1741, G⁷ 58.

27. CG to M. Henry, 31 March 1742, AN, G⁷ 59, and 27 April 1743, G⁷ 60; CG to Babaud, 15 June 1741, G⁷ 58; CG to G. Jars, 15 June 1741, G⁷ 58, and 2 November 1740, AN, KK 1005F; CG to Jars (Roanne), 15 June 1741, G⁷ 58; Pierre Dardel, *Navires et marchandises dans les ports de Rouen et du Havre au XVIIIᵉ siècle* (Paris: SEVPEN, 1963), p. 503; CG to La Tour, 26 May 1741, KK 1005F; CG to Gerins, 11 February 1741, KK 1005F; CG to Pallu, 1 November 1740, KK 1005F.

alert for the biggest stocks of grain during his tax-assessing visits through the province and to pressure the holders to sell to government buyers.[28]

The controller general counted upon the intendants to facilitate the purchases by orienting the agents to the appropriate markets, arranging for priority access to transport, and ensuring order. Guaranteeing them against losses, he empowered them to contract for purchases on their own. In fact, despite the intense pressure from the center, the intendants frequently resisted the buying incursions. At various moments the intendants of Tours, Soissons, Moulins, and Dauphiné, along with military officers from Franche Comté and the town fathers of Marseille, blocked the removal of grain specifically destined for Paris—the administrative analogue to the most common form of grain riot. The pretext was almost always the apprehension of popular uprisings locally, predicated on the fear that further depletion of stocks would be objectively catastrophic. Orry responded in a variety of voices, depending on the circumstances and the interlocutor. On some occasions he flourished the banner of liberalism, arguing that only wholly untrammeled circulation could serve the interests of growers, merchants, and consumers. But his appeal had a hollow and even hypocritical ring, given his own authoritarian methods, the hegemonic regulatory ethos, and the privileged Parisian objectives that this liberty was designed to serve. Sometimes he negotiated. He promised the Lyonnais and Provence compensation in foreign grain for what they sacrificed immediately in favor of the capital. He allowed the intendant of Moulins to requisition a fourth of the king's grain that was to leave his region. He asked the intendant of Auvergne for 2,000 *muids* but settled for 800. The intendant of Burgundy received a similar offer: a reduced quota in return for immediate cooperation. The controller general was prepared to deal behind the backs of his chief deputies in the field. He listened to his subdelegate from the generality of La Rochelle, who volunteered to supply Paris with 380 *muids* on condition of absolute secrecy because "he does not want to be compromised with his intendant, who might accuse him of starving his own province." More rarely, when Orry's will was provocatively thwarted, he fulminated and threatened the renitent administrators not merely with punishment but with community reprisals.[29]

28. G. Jars to CG, 30 May 1739, Arsenal, ms. B. 10277; CG to Vanolles, 3 November 1740, AN, KK 1005F; CG to La Porte, 12 May 1742, AN, G⁷ 59; CG to Buron, 5 June 1741, G⁷ 58; CG to G. Jars, 2 November 1740, KK 1005F; CG to Nizon, 11 and 23 October 1740, KK 1005F; CG to Jomarron, 1 November 1740, KK 1005F.

29. BN, Joly 1122, fols. 141–42, 183 (September 1740); Joly 1120, fol. 29; CG to Fleuriau, 29 December 1740 and 23 January 1741, AN, KK 1005F; CG to Bertier, 23 and 31 October 1740, KK 1005F; CG to Jomarron, 11 and 13 December 1740, KK 1005F; CG to Pallu, 15 December 1740, KK 1005F; CG to Buron, 31 October 1740, KK 1005F; CG to La Tour, 17 October, 2 November 1740, KK 1005F; CG to Rossignol, 13 October 1740, KK 1005F; CG to Vanolles, 29 October 1740, KK 1005F; CG to St-Contest, 17 October and 6 November 1740, KK 1005F; Tastevin to LG, 20 July 1740, Arsenal, ms. B. 10277; CG to PG, 19 September 1740 (2d letter), Joly, 1121, fols. 83–84. On the fury of the people against those who "remove their bread" and on the ruses for such removals, see René Louis de Voyer d'Argenson, *Journal et mémoires*, ed. E.-J.-B. Rathery, 9 vols. (Paris: J. Renouard, 1859–1867), vol. 3, p. 223 (14 November 1740).

The King's Grain

Orry did not give away the king's grain, even in places where consumers lacked the wherewithal to buy. He provided subsidies for public workshops and for parish charities, and he made rice available for token sums, but grain was another matter. The controller general's aim was economic rather than social: to repair rather than relieve, to make the market system work again by prodding it more or less gently rather than deepening its dislocation through "spectacular but artificial gestures." His policy was endorsed by the assembly of police, which articulated it this way: "We conclude that every time the king furnishes grain, it must never be sold by more than five or ten sous below the market price, lest the merchants stop their shipments and the bakers buy up everything in sight; with all our resources thus dissipated, grain would quickly soar again in price, and the merchants would profit from these disasters." Orry tirelessly preached this injunction to his entire distributional network: "Sell at the current price or just below it." He devised a somewhat harsh test for local needs that officials as well as consumers deeply resented. If the king's grain did not sell promptly at the going price or just below it, "this was proof that the need was not great," or that grain was beginning to come out of hiding in local granaries. Short of instant gratification, consumers could take solace in the visible plenitude of supplies. Officials who defied the controller general on the price issue faced stringent reprimand and a cutoff in future deliveries. Orry's desire to lose as little as possible on this huge provisioning operation reinforced this policy, but it surely was not his cardinal motive, despite the charges of fiscalism, insensitivity, and venality that contemporary critics leveled.[30]

In the same breath in which Orry was denounced as a miser he was taxed for prodigality and mismanagement. Waste and inefficiency were unavoidable in an undertaking of such colossal proportions—probably involving between 40 and 80 million livres' worth of purchases.[31] Yet in many ways frugality and rigor were the hallmarks of the enterprise. The controller general zealously pressed for economy in matters large and small. Merchants tapped as distributor-factors had to be "plainly solvent persons" so that the government could recover funds in case of discord or debacle. Buying agents should purchase hay along with grain to use as a bargaining tool with teamsters and bargemen in an effort to obtain lower transport costs. After a "reasonable moratorium"—generally six months—Orry re-

---

30. AP, 22 January 1739 and 19 May 1740, ms. fr. 11356, fols. 413–14; CG to Buron, 5, 10, and 30 June 1741, AN, G^7 58; CG to Belamy, 4 May 1740, G^7 58; LG to PG, 19 September 1740, BN, Joly 1122, fols. 25–26; CG to PG, 17 September 1740, Joly 1121, fol. 76; Argenson, *Journal et mémoires*, vol. 3, pp. 215–16 (6 November 1740); Narbonne, *Journal*, pp. 484–85; Barbier, *Journal*, vol. 3, p. 276 (April 1741).

31. Du Pont claimed that Orry spent 80 millions: *Analyse*, p. 33. The *Mercure suisse*, October 1740, p. 107, put the figure at 40 millions, but just through the early fall of 1740. Police Inspector Poussot estimated over 25 millions, but he did not specify the period covered. See Arsenal, ms. B. 10141, fol. 480 (13 May 1760). Cf. Argenson on Orry's incapacity, negligence, opacity, obduracy, cruelty, etc. in *Journal et mémoires*, vol. 3, pp. 178 (27 September 1740), 206–7 (29 October 1740).

lentlessly pressed institutional recipients of the king's grain to pay their bills. He calculated mean percentages of waste or loss incurred in transit and in storage, and even conducted trials to simulate conditions in order to ferret out "infidelities and malversations." Orry even insisted on a precise reckoning of the worth of errant grain that he learned had slipped beneath the planks of a granary floor, and he demanded that another granary be dismantled so that part of its cost could be recovered from the sale of used building materials. Three years after the fact Orry ordered restitution of the value of 2,800 new grain sacks that he had loaned to Lyon and an audit on wages that the municipality had paid to grain day workers.[32]

For political and psychological reasons it was imperative to furnish Paris only with the highest-quality grain and flour. But Orry also regarded this as a matter of economy. While Paris received "only the prettiest and healthiest" merchandise, the damaged goods had to be resold as quickly as possible in the provinces (where their flaws were unlikely to produce serious disorder) or else be subjected to vigorous reconditioning in order to reclaim their value. Once he calculated cost and benefit, the controller general did not hesitate to salvage the grain of a sunken ship for rehabilitation and local sale.[33] Orry's greatest frustration occurred toward the end of the crisis when he had to manage a huge, deteriorating stock that he could not market without incurring losses he viewed as mortifying. He pressed hospitals and army suppliers to buy some of it, he offered special passports for the reexport of large portions, he accorded favorable terms to wholesalers, and he instructed his agents to dump as much as possible locally provided the price was "not too low," a requirement that he had to abandon by the summer of 1743 after a second successive good harvest.[34]

In order to keep full control of the operation and to guarantee its efficacy and integrity, Orry demanded a ceaseless flow of documentation: quantitative data on the merchandise and its circulation and disposition; reports on methods of transaction and on field conditions; budgets and balance sheets; and so on. This vast correspondence permitted him to see the big picture and make the big decisions, to survey supply and demand, to follow prices, and to monitor public disorder. At the same time it revealed weaknesses,

32. CG to Buron, 26 May 1741, AN, KK 1005F; CG to Pallu, 26 June 1741, AN, G⁷ 58; CG to La Porte, 9 July 1743, G⁷ 60; CG to Chappen, 21 April 1743, G⁷ 60; CG to Henry, 17 April 1742, G⁷ 59; CG to Le Pautre, 20 April 1744, G⁷ 61; CG to Pallu, 20 October 1742, G⁷ 60; CG to Fleuriau, 12 January and 17 April 1744, G⁷ 61.

33. CG to Pallu, 22 June 1741, AN, G⁷ 58; CG to G. Jars, 25 June 1741, G⁷ 58; CG to Buron, 10 January 1741, AN, KK 1005F; CG to Buron, 23 July 1741, G⁷ 58; CG to Artaud, 19 April 1741, KK 1005F; CG to Artaud, 13 July 1741, G⁷ 58.

34. CG to Buron, 23 April and 12 May 1742, AN, G⁷ 59; CG to Lemaistre, 9 July 1742, G⁷ 59; CG to Delure, 9 June 1743, G⁷ 60; CG to Thellusson, 9 April 1743, G⁷ 60; CG to Argenson, 9 April 1743, G⁷ 60; CG to Chappen, 1 February, 15 April, and 23 August 1743, G⁷ 60, and 14 January 1744, G⁷ 61. Chamousset and Lemercier, both harsh critics of royal provisioning operations, claimed that Orry was unable to sell 13 million livres' worth of grain, much of which simply rotted. See Chamousset, "Observations sur la liberté," *Journal de commerce*, September 1740, p. 109; and Pierre-Paul-François-Joachim-Henri Lemercier de La Rivière, *L'intérêt général de l'état* (Amsterdam: Desaint, 1770), p. 269.

contradictions, untruths. From it Orry learned that one subdelegate was probably skimming grain from the Briare shipments while another was using his official function to mask personal speculation. The controller general learned about the nature and timing of Babaud's banking transactions, the arrears of the sales brokers, the successes and failures of the purchasing agents. Punctilious and stern, he demanded a precise accounting from everyone in his orbit. Despreaux, an agent of the lieutenant general of police in Paris, failed to record the revenue from the sale of Briare barges and boats. The intendant Pallu forgot to allow for the cost of cleaning grain. The receiver Artaud counted certain transshipments between Arles and its port twice. Orry refused to discharge a subdelegate who had served him diligently for three years for lack of substantiation concerning a freight bill of 300 livres. The only nasty confrontation involved the Jars of Lyon and Roanne, whom the controller general had praised effusively and promised rewards in November 1740. Less than a year later they were badly lagging on reports on purchases, transport, stockage, and so forth. Orry came to suspect them of inflating costs, delaying shipments, diverting merchandise, and engaging in private deals. He cut off payments to them and threatened to seize G. Jars's property and arrest him if he failed to restitute 120,000 livres.[35]

THE GENEVAN DEUS EX MACHINA

Though Orry himself arranged for some foreign purchases through diplomatic and merchant channels, he confided the primary responsibility for imports to Isaac Thellusson. Born in Geneva but long established in Paris, Thellusson was a member of the Protestant banking international, with two brothers running a bank in Amsterdam and closely linked correspondents in the other major European cities. The government turned to him in 1738 as it had to another influential Protestant banker, Samuel Bernard, during the dearth of 1725–1726. Given the structural fragility and fragmentation of the Paris grain trade, the government appealed to powerful outsiders in times of crisis, typically to cosmopolitan bankers with tentacular reach. Like Bernard, Thellusson was an international business virtuoso, intimately acquainted with currency conversions, weight and measure equivalencies, regulatory practices, and commercial protocols in all the leading grain centers. Like his predecessor, the Genevan was supremely self-confident, vain, and avid to monopolize the title of savior of Paris. The government had already employed him in the 1720s and mid-1730s to supply the army with grain and to

35. CG to Buron, 5 May 1742, AN, G⁷ 59; CG to LG, 19 January 1742, G⁷ 59; CG to Artaud, 19 April 1741, AN, KK 1005F; CG to Pallu, 9 April 1741, KK 1005F; CG to Henry, 11 July 1742, G⁷ 58; CG to Veytard, 13 June and 9 July 1743, G⁷ 60; CG to G. Jars, 21 June and 7, 13, and 25 July 1741, G⁷ 58; CG to Pallu, 22 June and l July 1741, G⁷ 58, and 5 May 1742, G⁷ 59; CG to Babaud, 11 July 1742, G⁷ 59; CG to Jars and Prost, 11 July 1742, G⁷ 42; CG to G. Jars, 20 April 1743, G⁷ 60; CG to Pallu, 20 October 1743, G⁷ 60.

transfer funds to Italy.[36] Solicited first by the lieutenant general of police in the summer of 1738 to procure grain on his own account and then by the municipality to furnish rice, Thellusson rapidly went to work "in the king's name." In November he and two associates, including his banking partner François Tronchin, another Genevan later celebrated for his ties to Voltaire, formed a *société* to which the government pledged a 2 percent commission on all operations (buying, selling, shipping, etc.) plus a 1 percent fee in compensation for capital advances (a key part of a banker's allure to the ministry), losses on exchange, and miscellaneous expenses.[37]

Thellusson's first shipment of king's grain reached Paris in early December 1738. Before Christmas he had twenty vessels ready for unloading at Le Havre. Hundreds of thousands of pounds of English flour were also quickly en route. He continued to supply the capital until the fine harvest of 1741, which left him with substantial inventories that Orry had to assume. It is impossible to determine how much grain and flour he imported in all. In monetary terms, it was certainly over 20 million livres, perhaps even double that amount—gigantic sums. In a period of nine months, from October 1740 to June 1741, Thellusson accounted for 33,000 *muids* (85 percent in wheat), which represented about a third of total annual Parisian consumption. At one point in this period he had more than two hundred ships at sea, of whose stormy impetuousness he wrote with awe and trepidation. That sea claimed at least a dozen bottoms over the entire campaign. He lost as many craft to flood and ice on the rivers of France, where the shortage of transport slowed him down and tried his patience. Orry's network conveyed his Mediterranean purchases, while he organized his own domestic freighting for northern wheat, rye, and barley via Le Havre and Rouen. Long-distance

36. Luethy, *Banque protestante*, vol. 1, pp. 89–90, 391–411, and vol. 2, p. 205; Herbert Luethy, " Une diplomatie ornée de glaces: La représentation de Genève à la cour de France au XVIIIe siècle," *Bulletin de la société d'histoire et d'archéologie de Genève*, 1960, pp. 16–24; André Corbaz, "Genève et la politique du cardinal Fleury," *Bulletin de la société d'histoire moderne*, 1921–1924, pp. 389–400; Thellusson to intendant of Paris, 16 January 1725, AN, G7 444; Thellusson, "Mémoire pour servir de réponse au deuxième mémoire imprimé de Claude Courtin," August 1726, G7 675; "Mémoire," 18 July 1723, G7 1660–65; Léon Cahen, "Le pacte de famine et les spéculations sur les blés," *Revue historique* 152 (1926), pp. 39–40. On the Paris grain trade, see Kaplan, *Provisioning Paris*, pp. 80–220. On S. Bernard, see Steven L. Kaplan, "The Famine Plot Persuasion in Eighteenth-Century France," *Transactions of the American Philosophical Society* 72 , pt. 3 (1982), pp. 8–11, 14, 19, 21–24, 40–42.

37. Thellusson to LG, 15 November and 25 December 1738, Arsenal, ms. B. 10276, 10275; Thellusson to Turgot, 21 January 1739, ms. B. 10276; Thellusson to PG, 20 September 1740, BN, Joly 1109, fol. 22; Luethy, *Banque protestante*, vol. 2, pp. 194–98. The first provision came from three ships that Thellusson located and purchased at Le Havre, laden with grain bound for Portugal. Orry was later severely criticized by Parisian authorities and other commentators for granting too many export licenses. The rumor of orchestrated exports fed suspicions of the existence of a "famine plot." See Hérault to CG, 16 November 1938, Arsenal, ms. B. 10275; AP, 3 July and 9 November 1738, BN, ms. fr. 11356, fols. 345, 367; Dubuisson, *Lettres*, p. 550 (6 May 1739); Gazetins, 23 September 1740, 18 and 19 October 1740, ms. B. 10167, fols. 140, 161; Argenson, *Journal et mémoires*, vol. 3, pp. 84 (28 May 1740), 95 (2 June 1740), 183 (29 September 1740); Jules Michelet, *Histoire de France*, vol. 16 (Paris: Flammarion, 1897), p. 196.

sea transit caused serious problems of deterioration. It is not clear how Thellusson dealt with conservation issues. He was constantly seeking warehouses for storage or conditioning. (In Paris, which had no public granaries, he usurped awkward space in hospitals, convents, and the Invalides.) He insisted—perhaps too emphatically—that the merchandise he delivered to the capital was always of "Parisian quality," that is, the very best. Rotten or damaged grain was sold to the Normands.[38]

Thellusson drew his grain from all corners of the Western world: rice from Carolina, wheat and flour from Philadelphia, various grains from Archangel, Riga, Koenigsberg, Hamburg, Danzig, Amsterdam, London, Livorno, Genoa, Sicily, Marseille, the Levant. As war (the conflict over the Austrian succession), politics, and subsistence crises shut down one source, Thellusson easily shifted to another. He wrote about local customs and constraints in far-off markets with astonishing familiarity. He shared Orry's quasi-military conception of how to organize purchasing. He recommended buying "not only the same day but if possible at the same hour" in as many places as possible, but in places large enough to sustain the removals without grave aftershocks. He was less meticulous and exacting in relations with his agents, perhaps because he had more confidence in them. (Yet he refused to execute the procurator general's written order—confirming an inadmissible oral one—for the purchase of 200,000 pounds of rice because that magistrate had omitted his signature.) Thellusson submitted his bills regularly for certification to the office of the lieutenant general of police, but the staff had conceptual and cultural difficulties in decoding them. They erred on conversion of Dutch, English, and Italian weights and measures, and they conflated French and English money expressed in pounds. ("The sum you calculate," the banker gently scolded them, "is twenty-three times greater than you think.") Like Orry, Thellusson made a fetish of economy ("I require more thrift in your affairs than I have ever applied to my own"), though it is hard to distinguish real practice from self-regarding puffery. Still, time after time he boasted, and claimed to demonstrate, that he earned for the king on a particular operation more than he spent. He involved himself on the marketing side, though sales were strictly in the hands of the lieutenancy, under Orry's aegis. He cautioned repeatedly against undue haste and argued over the wisdom of accelerating deliveries when sales stagnated. Like Orry, no matter how dire things were today, he always looked beyond the short term. Along with the controller general, he fretted

38. Thellusson to Hérault, 25 December 1738, Arsenal, ms. B. 10275; CG to Buron, 22 July 1741, AN, G⁷ 58; Thellusson to PG, 1 July 1741, BN, Joly 1109, fol. 125; Thellusson report, 27 December 1738, ms. B. 10275; Thellusson to Turgot, 21 January 1739, ms. B. 10277; *états* Thellusson, ms. B. 10276, 10277; Joly 1109, fols. 56, 67, 104–8; Thellusson to PG, 1 April 1741, Joly 1109, fol. 113; Thellusson to LG, 30 May and 2 and 7 September 1739, ms. B. 10277, and 21 March and 18 April 1739, ms. B. 10276; Thellusson note, 7 March 1739, ms. B. 10277; CG to La Bourdonnaye, 3 and 11 February 1741, AN, KK 1005F; CG to Pallu, 29 December 1740, KK 1005F; "Blés étrangers," ms. B. 10276 (10 January and 27 March 1739); Thellusson to PG, 15 January 1741, Joly 1109, fol. 88; *état*, Joly 1109, fol. 128 (July 1741).

about the eventual outbreak of good times, and what a conjuncture of abundance would mean for his operations.[39]

Psychological insight as well as technocratic skill informed Thellusson's action. Always lucid, he drafted best- and worst-case scenarios for his Parisian interlocutors. For 1741, for instance, if spring proved as auspicious as the fall planting season, then the hoarders would be flushed out and current supplies would suffice. But a poor crop would mean that Paris would have to feed 1.5 million rather than 800,000 people, "and we will need to call upon Divine Providence"—and Isaac Thellusson! But when the situation was really bleak and the authorities themselves were near panic, he showed remarkable sangfroid. "Count on me," he exuded in one calamitous moment; "you will no longer lack anything," he reassured in another. The "minister of the republic of Geneva in the court of France"—his official title—knew how to practice therapy and diplomacy at once. In one of the darkest hours, he invited the "provisioning council," more or less coterminous with the assembly of police, to share "a beautiful Genevan trout" that had just arrived by courier. He urged Parisian officials not to flee from such arduous tasks as persuading the people to eat bread made partly of rye ("we know how painful it is for Parisians"), and to use the rice that was offered to them fruitfully (instead of selling it or preparing it improperly and then rejecting it out of hand).[40]

Perhaps the most surprising aspect of Thellusson's undertaking was its relatively tranquil denouement. The Genevan was one of the rare victualers called upon by the government to rescue the capital and other parts of the realm who was not ritually lynched after the crisis eased. Virtually every other campaign, including Bernard's, stirred suspicions and provoked scandals concerning motives, methods, disposition of funds, quality of merchandise, and the like. In an effort to purge the body politic of toxic wastes (and to placate the remarkably convergent streams of public opinion emanating from widely diverse sociocultural and professional milieux), the postcrisis ministry habitually investigated, censured, and sometimes punished its quondam provisioning heroes. Thellusson not only escaped this obloquy but emerged with great prestige. Though his records were somewhat sloppy and probably incomplete, Orry does not appear to have made any reproaches. Police informants and other commentators marveled at the positive light in which the public regarded him—unlike, say, Bernard, whose every gesture seemed tarnished with self-aggrandizement. Thellusson

39. Thellusson to PG, 26 and 30 September, 16, 23, and 28 October, 1 and 5 December 1740, 1 May and 1 July 1741, BN, Joly 1109, fols. 27, 37, 46–47, 52, 66, 69–71, 116, 124–26; Joly 1109, fols. 109, 128; CG to Thellusson, 30 December 1740, AN, KK 1005F; Thellusson to Duval, 3 February 1739, Arsenal, ms. B. 10276; Thellusson to Duval, 10 July 1739, ms. B. 10277; Thellusson to LG, 13 June and 25 July 1739, ms. B. 10277.

40. Thellusson to PG, 18 August and 5 December 1740, 23 January and 1 July 1741, BN, Joly 1109, fols. 18, 69–71, 91, 124–26; Thellusson to LG, 28 February 1739, Arsenal, ms. B. 10276; PG to CG, 15 September 1740, Joly 1121, fols. 71–72; BV, 26 May and 18 December 1739, AN, H 1939¹, and 30 August 1740, H* 1859, fol. 16.

helped his own case considerably by renouncing, in the name of a breathless altruism, his commission and even his percentage for expenses in September 1740, just as his operations began to swell dramatically. He had ample opportunity to make money along the way, in currency transactions and private speculations financed by the king, and he probably found ways to build his expenses into the reported costs of purchases. Still, his gesture of abnegation seems consonant with his temperament. He craved "honor"— by which he meant public recognition—more than lucre. He was deeply gratified to receive formal praise from the municipality in its register and an elegant snuffbox from the beholden hand of the king. There was an ugly postscript to the campaign: a bitter, protracted legal struggle between Thellusson and each of his original associates. (A severe Calvinist, Thellusson accused Tronchin of writing verse, despite his promise to abjure this conceit, while Paris languished in hunger and inquietude.) These confrontations do not appear, however, to have had any bearing on Thellusson's public image.[41]

PARISIAN CRISIS MANAGEMENT: THE LIEUTENANT GENERAL OF POLICE

For the most part administrators shared a common view of the provisioning world, marked by a deep investment in the marketplace as a governing vehicle and a concomitantly acute suspicion of the market principle. But they often disagreed over strategy, on the proper tension to set between marketplace (regulation) and market principle (laissez-faire). It was never a simple matter of easing up in good times and squeezing hard in trying moments, at least not for an arena of the scale and complexity of Paris. Timing, transition, dosage, methods, manner, discourse—all these variables mattered greatly. It is no surprise that the police response to the developing crisis of 1738–1741 was not reflexive, save perhaps at some of the grass-roots stations. In the assembly of police and in their correspondence, the leading administrators worried and argued about the wisdom of rival policies and tactics. Nothing illustrates the harrowing nature of the debate better that the draft recommendations that Joly de Fleury, the veteran pro-

41. Thellusson to PG, 19 September 1740 and 27 June 1741, BN, Joly 1109, fols. 16, 121–22; BV, 18 December 1739, AN, H* 1858, fols. 340–41; Gazetins, 3 and 4 November 1740, Arsenal, ms. B. 10167, fol. 170; Luethy, *Banque protestante*, vol. 2, pp. 200–201; *Times* (London), 26 November 1968. The royal council named an elite commission to review all the accounts of grain and flour purchased for Paris and to judge all contestations arising from these operations. Thellusson does not appear to have been troubled by its scrutiny. See *Arrêts du conseil*, 21 May 1741 and 23 October 1742, in *Lettres de M. de Marville, lieutenant général de police, au ministre Maurepas (1742–1747)*, ed. Arthur Michel de Boislisle, 6 vols. (Paris: H. Champion, 1896–1905), vol. 1, pp. 215, 220. One wonders why Marville, a member of that commission and lieutenant general of police during the most difficult moments of the crisis, intervened personally in 1755 to confiscate the papers and accounts of one Lebrun concerning the king's grain in 1739–1741. See ms. B. 11904, 19 August 1755.

curator general, prepared for Orry. As prices rise and misery spreads, he noted, "everyone" sees draconian measures such as the forced opening of granaries and mandatory provisioning of markets as "the necessary and efficient remedies."

> I shared the same prejudice for a long time. But I learned through forty years of experience that one must almost never rely on speculative princi-ples in the absence of practice. One's reasoning founders at the point of execution. Nothing is more dangerous than implementing these [coer-cive] means when there is still cause for discreet action and for hope, because the alarm produced by the channels of constraint, far from re-sulting in the cure, aggravates the disease.

Less is sometimes more: this is the standard "enlightened" police line. Joly's application of its logic to the unfolding crisis was strained and uncertain. When alarm was widespread and irreversible, recourse to constraint could be fruitful, as it was in 1709. But since such dire conditions today afflicted only parts of the kingdom, there was still a chance of salvaging calm in the Parisian supply zones. Yet he was admittedly in a quandary, for circum-stances varied sharply and brusquely from place to place, and the sharpness of social distress seemed incommensurate with the objective situation that spawned it. Because "general rules are dangerous," one could deal only "in particular cases." So far, however, even on a case-by-case basis, he had not yet taken a firm leadership position vis-à-vis the more brutal initiatives of local authorities: "I have neither condemned nor approved: only time will tell us the right path."[42]

For the men who occupied the post of lieutenant general of police—René Hérault till December 1728, then his son-in-law Marville—the capital had no time to spare. They endorsed the procurator general's philosophical re-straint, but they saw no merit in his battlefield equivocation. They were not eager to wield the bludgeon, but they doubted that they could get the job done entirely "without uproar." They deployed a cost-benefit calculus akin to Orry's. In response to Joly's reluctance to ratify a plan to impose weekly market quotas on all identifiable grainholders in the intendancy of Paris, the controller general wrote: "We must try all the different ways to provide for the provisioning of Paris; let us compare the disadvantages of the execution of the quota regulation with those that would result from a [sustained] bread shortage."[43] Hérault and Marville envisioned a vigorous albeit "discerning and judicious" action on several fronts at once. Even as they tapped "ex-traordinary" sources, they had to reestablish "ordinary" channels of supply by reviving the official market system and by purging the provisioning trade of the "abuses" that dearth engendered with such startling speed. The coun-tryside and the provinces had to be reminded of the absolute primacy of

42. BN, Joly 1120, fols. 119–20 (8 May 1739).
43. CG to PG, 19 September 1740, BN, Joly 1121, fol. 83.

Parisian needs. To preempt resistance from official as well as popular quarters, Parisian extraterritorial authority had to be extended far into the supply regions. Everyone, from the *laboureur* (the farmer who sold his surplus grain on the market) to the intendant, had to pay a tribute to the capital. Meanwhile, the lieutenant general of police had to work on the demand side in order to reassure consumers and reduce consumption. Finally, he had to keep the bakers in line, without, however, jeopardizing their commercial survival. In all of these tasks there was no fundamental discontinuity between the approaches of Hérault and Marville.

The lieutenant general of police supervised the reception and sale of all extraordinary supplies and on several occasions personally commissioned purchases in the provinces and abroad. At critical junctures, to create the fiction of abundance for a market day or two, he requisitioned stocks from the very modest reserve maintained for his use by the hospitals, *collèges*, and religious communities of the capital and its environs.[44] But he focused his attention on the now derelict regular provisioning system. To restore order meant above all to reassert the dominion of the marketplace—the authorized site where all transactions (with one critical exception) had to take place in the open. Grain growers, collectors, and diverse owners had to be made to return to the market, where their conduct could be monitored and their supply concentrated and made visible. Agents of the lieutenant general of police undertook frequent "censuses"—really rough estimations—of grain holdings throughout the supply zone. (They also spread the news of the impending arrival of massive doses of king's grain in order to lure hoarders out of hiding while prices still favored them.) In 1738 Hérault used the threat of quotas as an inducement to draw the *laboureurs* to resume regular shipments, even as Marville two years later sent agents to press seigneurs as well as peasants under the menace of requisition. The recalcitrant *laboureurs* learned quickly that the authorities were serious. Argenson, the intendant of Paris, fixed weekly quotas, and fined delinquent contributors up to 300 livres, payable on pain of immediate imprisonment and confiscation of property.[45] *Laboureurs* who boycotted the Beaumont market in favor of clandestine rendezvous with buyers in the fall of 1740 risked even

---

44. LG to PG, 15 September and 12 October 1740, BN, Joly 1121, fols. 74, 205; CG to Artaud, 25 July 1741, AN, G⁷ 58; Arsenal, ms. B. 11495, 10277; AP, 27 November 1738 and 30 June 1740, ms. fr. 11356, fols. 368, 419.

45. Foucaud to LG, 22 November 1739, Arsenal, ms. B. 10275, and 30 May 1739, ms. B. 10276; *état des greniers et des magasins*, ms. B. 10277; BN, Joly 1121, fols. 261–62; ms. B. 10276, 20 January 1739 (Labenardière); Marion (Brie) to LG, 19 January 1739, ms. B. 10276; anon. to LG, 1740, ms. B. 10895, fol. 392; AN, O¹ 383, pp. 239 (22 August 1738), 260 (29 September 1738); LG to PG, 15 September 1740, BN, Joly 1121, fol. 173; CG to PG and PG to CG, 19 September 1740, Joly 1121, fols. 83, 87–88; ms. B. 10141, fol. 261 (16 October 1759); Gazetins, 21 September and 8 November 1740, ms. B. 10167, fols. 138, 174; Joly 1121, fols. 155–56. Cf. the repeated charge that *laboureurs* were forbidden to go to market because of the "abundance of rotten king's grain that had to be sold off." This claim gave credence to famine plot rumors. See anon. to LG, 1740, ms. B. 10027, fols. 391–92; Barbier, *Journal*, vol. 3, p. 224 (October 1740).

harsher punishment, as did *laboureurs* in the Dourdan area in the autumn of 1738 who engaged in "monopoly," buying instead of selling with a view toward speculative gains from the patiently awaited price rise.[46]

Many *laboureurs* stayed home, or never reached the market, because buyers visited their farms or intercepted them on the road. Only licensed merchants working exclusively "for the provisioning of Paris" (as their *qualité* stipulated) could buy outside the market. This is the exception evoked above, the double standard that infuriated the local police authorities in the supply zones, who were instructed to tolerate market desertion as long as the capital profited from this galling derogation. Thus Hérault complained bitterly when authorities at Melun inhibited suppliers in Paris from buying in its hinterland, but Marville scoffed at protests from a fiscal procurator at Bray against "hoards" being amassed in the countryside for shipment to the capital. Three merchants from Orléans who "burned over" the Beauce in 1740 were not Paris benefactors. In 1738 and again in 1740 the lieutenant general of police set traps to catch the dealers who "ran the farms" around Dourdan. The police went after merchants from Bray who paid *laboureurs* to hold their purchases on the farms and dealers from Nogent and Montlhéry who transacted business in inns. Off-market transactions characteristically took place "on sample" rather than on the physical examination of the entire stock, favoring speed and secrecy and rendering detection extremely difficult. A number of market officials made exposure even less likely by selling blank passports to "cover" illicit exchanges. The practice of regrate became rampant: traders bought in one market to resell in another, or sometimes in the same one, without regard for metropolitan or local subsistence needs.[47] The proliferation of new faces in the grain trade further complicated the police task. Smitten with "speculative fever" or driven by "a violent appetite," scores of newcomers plunged into business without authorization and without concern for or even knowledge of the rules. The police at Châlons reported five hundred instead of fifty dealers; at Etampes, wigmakers, gardeners, and blacksmiths dabbled in grain. The first to "poison" the provisioning trade were sometimes the police themselves. Magistrates at Etampes, Dourdan, and Nogent were among many officials denounced for illicit grain dealings, corruption, and conflict of interest.[48]

46. Picque to PG, October 1740, BN, Joly 1123, fol. 52; Odile to PG, 19 October 1738, Joly 1119, fol. 108.

47. Anon. to LG, 23 September 1740, Arsenal, ms. B. 10027; Odile to PG, 19 October 1740, BN, Joly 1119, fol. 108; Barlé to PG, 17 September and 26 October 1740, Joly 1123, fols. 88, 90; Gurand to PG, Joly 1119, fol. 158; AN, Y 9440, 21 August and 11 December 1739; Balize to LG, 22 November 1738, ms. B. 10275; Y 11227, 27 September 1740; AP, 30 June 1740, ms. fr. 11356 BN, fol. 420; Theumay to CG, 22 November 1738, ms. B. 10275; ms. fr. 21635, fol. 170 (22 May 1739); Y 9440, 21 August 1739; Y 9441, 8 July 1740; Joly 1123, fol. 47 (30 May 1740).

48. BN, Joly 1126, fol. 44; Therbaud to PG, July 1739, Joly 1120, fol. 33; Joly 1119, fols. 4–7; Foucaud to LG, 30 September 1739, Arsenal, ms. B. 10277; Foucaud to PG, 18 January 1739, Joly 1119, fol. 28; Guillemin to PG, 8 November 1740, Joly 1123, fol. 194; Le Roy to LG, 30 October 1738, ms. B. 10275; substitut at Dourdan to Marville, 23 September 1740, ms. B. 10027; Joly 1125, fols. 43, 45.

The Paris police enjoyed a flexible *droit de suite* that enabled them to extend their authority into the supply regions practically at will—as long as the Parlement approved. Convinced that Etampes, a collector market to the south of Paris, was "utterly without police," Hérault dispatched his own staff to do the work of cleaning up. Defacq, a Paris police commissioner, accompanied by a technical adviser, the grain trader Gibert, and several enforcement agents, set up surveillance in the market. They issued summonses against farmers who bought large amounts, against dealers who bargained on sample, and against regraters. Enraged at this "encroachment upon our jurisdiction," the local magistrates warned that the crackdown would "ruin" the town, a quarter of whose population depended for their livelihoods directly on the grain business. The suppliers, they fretted, would flee to such rival markets as Auneau, Dourdan, and Pithiviers, where there was a comparable regulatory lethargy. In the name of equity, the elders of Etampes demanded that the "execution of the rules be general and uniform so that we are not the only ones to suffer." Hérault not only promised to suppress "libertinage"—the moral charge of the term is revealing—throughout the zone but also eased up on enforcement of entry rules at Etampes, probably in response to pressure from the prince de Conti, who owned market rights there. At the same time Hérault assigned a town crier and his trumpeters to spy on the Arpajon market, where they discovered hoarding, sales on samples, and police involvement in the grain trade. Marville dispatched similar missions of inspection to Etampes, Montlhéry, Gonesse, and other market towns where abuses were rife and the local police could not be trusted.[49] When espionage did not reveal the whole truth, the authorities turned to a sort of psychocultural blackmail. In 1738 they instituted *monitoire*, a solemn procedure in which the parish priests called upon the faithful in three successive weekly injunctions from the pulpit to denounce any misdeeds of which they were aware upon penalty of excommunication.[50]

PARIS VERSUS FRANCE

Parisian authorities did not labor to reimpose order and discipline for their own sake. Their single-minded goal was the provisioning of the capital. That the producing area might be hurt did not deter them. Paris disdained what a parlementary commission called "this ancient principle [which 'the people bear in their heart'] that grain is first reserved for the province where it was born." The textbook expert in Parisian colonialism, Commissioner Delamare, acknowledged that "natural equity" spoke strongly in favor of

49. AP, 21 October 1738, BN, Joly 1119, fols. 18–20; Arsenal, ms. B. 10275; Joly 1119, fols. 104–18; AN, Y 11225, 25 October 1738; ms. B. 10275, October 1738; Y 9499, 19 July 1740; LG to PG, 23 May 1740, Joly 1123, fol. 46; Y 9442, 11 August 1741.

50. Odile to PG, 29 November 1738, BN, Joly 1119, fol. 110. On the *monitoire* used for similar purposes in 1694, see BN, ms. fr. 21643, fol. 36, and 21634, fol. 280; André Cochut, "Le pain à Paris," *Revue des deux mondes* 46 (1863), p. 976.

local claims, but equity had to be weighed against other, more compelling demands. Over the years the Paris provisioning machine had become a juggernaut, extending its poaching grounds in all directions and encroaching on areas customarily allotted to Rouen, Orléans, Reims, Troyes, Bourges, Dijon, and other cities at an even greater remove. Once Paris staked out a region as its turf, it shut out competitors. Yet to ensure its access to areas that it could not wholly subordinate, the capital opportunistically espoused the cause of free internal circulation. Throughout the ancien régime (and afterward) there were tensions of the sort that developed at Châlons-sur-Marne in 1740. The news that officially commissioned buyers for Paris would soon descend upon the town "to strip it bare" cast "alarm in the mind of everyone." "I don't know of any remedy," wrote a magistrate, "to contain a population of ten to eleven thousand who have no bread at all and who will watch [Parisians] take away [supplies] on which they seem to have the right to rely." Paris has many alternative sources: if it siphons grain this year from the Champagne, "it is to put the knife to the throat of all the people of this area."[51]

Like the controller general on the national scale, the lieutenant general encountered local resistance from both officials and ordinary inhabitants. The authorities of Calais, Nogent, and Provins blocked grain departures for Paris. The people of Soissons enforced their intendant's ban on outflow to the Paris feeder markets of Pontoise and Beaumont by massing with sticks and pitchforks to prevent removals. To protect the provisioning of Paris, the lieutenant general of police did not hesitate to usurp local jurisdiction. "Declaring that all the grain must remain in this country," the procurator of Lagny, an important market town on the Marne, forbade Louis Paschot, a Paris flour merchant, to buy there. Determined to prevent Paschot's defection, "for his substantial trade was of great succor to us," Marville had the Lagny official rebuked and his anti-Paris policy repudiated. Prodded by "the people," the police of Crécy-en-Brie confiscated the grain purchased by the Parisians J.-B. Jauvin the younger and Denis Bocquet, port merchants protected by the provost of merchants, who rushed to their defense by obtaining a ruling from the procurator general forbidding "any obstacles to the purchase and shipment of grain to Paris." In 1739 three hundred demonstrators at Dreux, mostly women, violently opposed the departure of grain for the capital; in July 1740 a crowd in a hamlet near Gonesse halted a wagonload of bread that was believed headed for the capital.[52]

Even the royal city of Versailles was subject to Paris in provisioning matters. When more than a hundred Paris bakers bought up over a thou-

51. Chambre des Enquêtes, "Mémoire," BN, Joly 1111, fol. 145; Delamare, *Traité de la police*, p. 823; Guillemin to PG, 4 October 1740, Joly 1123, fols. 177–78.

52. LG to PG, 22 August 1740, BN, Joly 1124, fol. 213; Joly 1123, fol. 135; CG to PG, 21 September 1740, Joly 1121, fol. 97; Theumay to LG, 22 November 1738, Arsenal, ms. B. 10275; AP, 14 July 1740, BN, ms. fr. 11356, fol. 424; Argenson, *Journal et mémoires*, vol. 3, p. 223 (14 November 1740); Joly, 1123, fols. 281–87, 290–91, 302; AN, Y 15047, 13 July 1740; Joly 1126, fols. 71–72 (12 July 1740).

sand sacks of flour, frightened local consumers rose up to prevent their departure in late August 1740. Between two and four thousand rioters, depicted as women in the great majority, overturned several carts, pillaged a few sacks of flour, assaulted a number of bakers, and shouted, "Kill these Paris baker bastards!" Outnumbered, the local police were also divided in their reaction. One official wanted to placate the crowd by requiring the bakers to allocate half their purchases to the Versaillais, while another insisted on the danger of "giving in to the threats of the little people." Even as the women warned the bakers that they would be "strangled if they returned," Marville took over the investigation and arrested seven women and a man in an effort to make sure that his bakers would not be frightened away.[53]

BAKERS AND BREAD

As grain and flour suppliers, as the makers and sellers of bread, and as the most highly exposed players in the provisioning chain, the bakers preoccupied the lieutenant general of police. Once largely confined to making purchases at the Paris ports and the Halle, the bakers expanded their country buying prodigiously between 1730 and 1760. The Paris police viewed this development with two minds. On the one hand, they were alarmed about the loss of control it implied, and they fretted about trading abuses (hoarding, regrating, monopoly, off-market acquisitions, and purchases in the unauthorized markets located within the decommercialized zone that covered a forty-five kilometer radius around the capital). On the other hand, country buying palpably increased the capital's total provision, especially of precious flour, and it multiplied the lines of supply. From 1738 to 1741 the authorities gave the bakers considerable latitude in the field, provided what they bought went directly into their baked goods. In early October 1740 three constabulary raids on Montlhéry, a taboo market situated just within the decommercialized zone, resulted in summonses for nine bakers, all of which were dismissed by Marville at his weekly audience. But there was no such indulgence for a baker who bought and resold flour speculatively or for another who masked illicit farm purchases with false certificates obtained from a corrupt market official at Meaux.[54]

Given the gravity of the crisis and the unnerved and suspicious feelings of consumers, the police had to worry about the hundreds of points of combustion represented by the bakeshops every day and by the twelve official bread markets on Wednesdays and Saturdays. From the spring of 1740 troops as well as police agents patrolled each market. They helped quell a disturbance in September 1740 when frustrated women at the Halle called

53. AN, Y 11227, 26 August and 23 October 1740; Luynes, *Mémoires*, vol. 3, pp. 243–44 (August 1740); *Mercure suisse*, September 1740, p. 74; Narbonne, *Journal*, pp. 459–67.

54. AN, Y 11227, 3 October 1740, and Y 9441, 12 February and 14 October 1740; Lepoupet to LG, 12 November 1739, Arsenal, ms. B. 10277.

for an attack on the bakers. They also intervened to admonish bakers to obey price guidelines, or to sell at rebate in the late afternoon. They prevented bakers from taking bread home after market and from concealing bread in the city.[55]

To contain the public, the police had to contain the price of bread. Unlike many other cities of the ancien régime, Paris had no formal *taxation*, or price schedule, calibrated to the *mercuriale*, or grain price register. But in ordinary times prices were incredibly sticky and the standard of 2 sous per pound for the basic white wheaten loaf remained the norm for much of the eighteenth century. In crisis, however, the authorities intervened to slow the price rise as much as possible and to make sure it reflected real changes in cost, availability, and quality of the raw materials. In 1739 and 1740 the lieutenant general of police organized a series of trials in which wheats of different provenance and quality—local, king's, reconditioned, and so on—were transformed into bread of various sorts. The purpose was to establish guidelines and to test bakers' (and millers') claims of productivity, costs, and profit margin.[56] Bakers were forbidden to sell above what was variously called the current or common price. Beginning in the spring of 1739, this price was checked by a maximum set by the police, called "the fixation" or "the tax." Hérault and then Marville frequently convoked the leaders of the bakers' guild, sometimes to cajole them in the hope that they would exercise voluntary restraint in face of the growing calamity, sometimes to castigate them for lack of civic "reasonableness." Though the police assisted them with the loan of horses for transport and arranged for oven-sharing to increase capacity, there is no evidence that they offered subsidies to compensate them for losses, as they were to do in the last three decades of the ancien régime. Nor do bakers seem to have discontinued baking and furnishing in significant numbers, as they had done in 1725–1726.[57]

Bakers' infractions came to light as a result of both complaints by consumers and police rounds of shops and markets. Upon the complaint of a woman who lived near the Halle, Commissioner de Courcy issued a summons to a market baker from the outskirts who not only sold above the currently prevailing price but also had sixty-six loaves of short weight, all of

55. AN, Y 9441, 24 August 1740, and Y 13747, 21 May 1740; Barbier, *Journal*, vol. 3, pp. 218 (September 1740) and 251 (January 1741); LG to PG, 28 September 1740, Joly 1121, fol. 112; Gazetins, 21 and 26 October, 29 November, 1 and 3 December 1740, Arsenal, ms. B. 10167, fols. 166–67, 187, 195. The line between order and disorder was often indistinct in ancien régime Paris. Peacemaker at the market, a soldier savagely beat the wife of a master baker with his rifle in her shop because he believed (correctly) that she overcharged him for a half pound of bread. See Y 12583, 18 October 1740.

56. Courcy to PG, 29 January 1739, BN, Joly 1119, fols. 41–42; Joly 1143, fol. 107; Joly 1120, fol. 4; Joly 1121, fol. 118; Joly 1122, fol. 65. Cf. the elaborate table that the procurator general "amused himself" by drafting: PG to LG, 29 September 1740, Arsenal, ms. B. 10277.

57. AN, Y 9619, 29 May 1739; AP, 30 April 1739, BN, ms. fr. 11356, fol. 396; Gazetins, 26 May and 14 September 1740, Arsenal, ms. B. 10167, fols. 118 and 130, and 15 April 1741, ms. B. 10168, fol. 167; ms. B. 10027, fol. 392 (1740).

which were confiscated. The baker was fined 100 livres. Indicted twice in two months, Amart, who as an official of the guild was expected to set the right example, was stripped of his leadership post and fined 300 livres. During 1740, while the price at one juncture climbed to just under 5 sous a pound, scores of bakers endured fines of up to 400 livres, payable immediately and conveying liens on property, for price violations. They defended themselves most commonly on the grounds that the rising price of wheat required them to adjust their prices. A few shifted the blame to consumers, who failed to bargain, a practice that was expected of them at the market stalls but not at the shops. Generally the contravening bakers surpassed the maximum by an increment of 3 deniers a pound. Staunch but realistic, Marville held the line only as long as conditions permitted. Between the harvest and Christmas, the maximum changed at least a dozen times. To economize on supplies by eliminating the making of the whitest loaves, which put a given measure of wheat to least productive use, the Parlement published a decree in September that enjoined bakers to make only two sorts of bread, mid-white (*bis-blanc*) and dark (*bis*). This measure also broadcast a social message contrived to project a credo of subsistence justice—not yet the "equality bread" of the Revolution but a step in the direction of crisis solidarity. Bakers apprehended for selling white loaves faced fines of 400 livres with the threat of having their shops walled in the event of further contravention.[58]

At the beginning of 1741, public frustration thickened as prices remained high despite the return of (relative) abundance to the markets. Mid-white sold for up to 4.5 sous a pound. In January a rumor circulated that Marville planned to sell bread made in specially constructed "royal ovens" as cheaply as 2 sous a pound as a way of helping the poor and pressuring the bakers to show more elasticity.[59] As winter receded, the authorities simultaneously relaxed and toughened their stand. Beginning in late March they allowed bakers to produce white bread and luxury ("fantasy") loaves. But for the first time those who violated the ceiling were thrown in jail. The standard fine swelled to 500 livres. Indeed, the less tense the supply situation became, the more stringently the police behaved. In early 1742, no longer worried about

58. AN, Y 9440, 5 May 1739; Y 9441, 14 May, 24 August, and 2 September 1740; Y 9619, 20 May 1740; Y 9489, 2 Septemer 1740; BN, ms. fr. 21640, fol. 186 (6 March and 29 May 1739); Gazetins, 21 September 1740, Arsenal ms. B. 10167, fol. 139 (21 September 1740). Cf. Y 12141, 4 March 1739; Y 9619, 29 May 1739.

59. AN, Y 9441, 14 October and 18 November 1740; AN, AD XI 23ᴬ (25 November 1740); Gazetins, 31 January, 24 February, and 27 September 1741, Arsenal, ms. B. 10168, fols. 47, 52, 332; Gazetins, 20 January 1741, BHVP, ms. 620, fol. 67; Gazetins, 11 and 12 October and 17 and 18 November 1740, ms. B. 10167, fols. 156 and 175, and 16 and 19 January 1741, ms. B. 10168, fols. 6 and 10. In one version, the rumor spoke of using eight bakers from Marseille to rehabilitate wheat and rye capable of "causing disease." Municipal-royal bakeries, constructed in the Louvre, served the indigent population in the crisis of 1693. See Pierre Clément, *Portraits historiques* (Paris: Didier, 1885), pp. 192–95. Cf. Paul Bondois, "La misère sous Louis XIV: La disette de 1662," *Revue économique et sociale* 12 (1924), p. 93.

the subsistence cost of driving a baker into failure and more inclined to make didactic examples, Marville fined one baker 1,000 livres and another 3,000 livres for price and weight offenses.[60]

The effort to reduce consumption was not confined to the prohibition of white bread. The Parlement prohibited starchmakers to use flour and past-rycooks to produce festive king's cakes. Marville halfheartedly attempted to curtail beer production pursuant to another parliamentary decree. He applied himself more vigorously though perhaps no more successfully to the task of expelling the swarm of beggars who had taken refuge in the capital. He asked the parish priests to help inventory the floating population, but he lacked the means to subsidize the floaters' return home. Through the priests, the authorities distributed substantial portions of beans and rice, but there is reason to suspect that not all of it was effectively used.[61] The least prudent measure to dampen consumption was the reduction of the daily bread ration in the prisons by between a half and a third, a decision that Marville laid squarely at the feet of the procurator general. It provoked a "furious rising" of the vagrants, paupers, and petty criminals interned at Bicêtre ("They want to kill us by starvation"), which resulted in as many as thirty deaths.[62]

THE PROVOST OF MERCHANTS AND THE PORT

Far more restricted in his regulatory range than the lieutenant general of police, the provost of merchants presided over the river system that chan-neled merchandise to the capital, in particular grain to the port called the Grève. Even before the crisis of 1738–1741 the port had been losing ground to the Halle, just as the lieutenant eclipsed the provost and flour gradually became more important than grain in the provisioning nexus. The crisis

60. Arsenal, ms. B. 10136, fol. 78 (8 and 9 March and 2 April 1741); ms. B. 10140, fol. 252 (16 March 1741); Gazetins, 26 March and 11 and 12 April 1741, ms. B. 10168, fols. 126, 159; AN, Y 9442, 14 April 1741, Y 9443, 19 January and 13 April 1742, Y 9499, 14 and 28 April 1741, and Y 9619, 28 April 1741; LG to Maurepas, 8 Febuary 1742, *Lettres de M. de Marville*, vol. 1, p. 9.

61. AN, Y 9499, 9 December 1740; arrêt, 31 December 1740, *Lettres de M. de Marville*, vol. 1, p. 214, and BHVP, ms. 620, fol. 6 (6 January 1740); conseil secret, 9 July 1740, X[1A] 8467, fols. 477–81; BHVP, ms. 621, 30 May 1741; curés to LG, 18 and 20 May 1740, Arsenal, ms. B. 10276; Breteuil to LG, 29 July 1740, ms. B. 10276; Barbier, *Journal*, vol. 3, p. 249 (December 1740); BV, 26 May 1739, AN, H 1939[1]; *Mercure suisse*, May 1739, pp. 147–48; AP, 23 April 1739 and 18 Febuary 1740, BN, ms. fr. 11356, fols. 393, 409.

62. BN, Joly 1111, fols. 73–74; LG to PG, 22 September and 10 October 1740, Joly 1121, fol. 53; Gazetins, 23 and 26 September 1740, Arsenal, ms. B. 10167, fols. 140, 145; *Mercure historique et politique* 109 (October 1740), p. 476; Narbonne, *Journal*, p. 469 (20 September 1740); Luynes, *Mémoires*, vol. 3, p. 255 (September 1740); Argenson, *Journal et mémoires*, vol. 3, p. 173 (24 September 1740); Barbier, *Journal*, vol. 3, p. 219 (September 1740). Riots at Bicêtre recurred later in the century. See Hardy's Journal, BN, ms. fr. 6680, l Febuary 1771; Sartine to Guyot, 8 May 1773, AN, Y 13551; Emile Richard, *Histoire de l'hôpital de Bicêtre* (Paris: G. Steinheil, 1889), p. 93.

further weakened the port's influence, as its merchants proved to be unable or unwilling to fulfill the government's expectations. As early as January 1738 the assembly of police expressed sharp dissatisfaction with a portentous decline in port supply, which it attributed to "maneuvers" on the part of the merchants, "evil intentions" later confirmed by the municipal officials dispatched to investigate buying and stocking practices in the field.

"With almost no grain on the ports," in January 1739 Provost of Merchants Turgot took the stringent step of levying a fine of 10,000 livres on "all the merchants of the ports"—that is, on the twenty-six traders who really counted—"for not having kept the ports of this city sufficiently furnished as they are obliged to do." What the police interpreted as a broken contract and a breach of the public trust the merchants attributed to excessive infringement on their commercial freedom (too much government interference), insufficient municipal "protection and encouragement" (too little government interference), disastrous weather, and unrealistically inflated expectations. "Shamed" and "dishonored" in the public eye and damaged in their capacity to do business, the merchants collectively threatened to resign in the midst of the crisis.[63] Buoyed by the arrival of Thellusson's king's grain, the assembly demanded the "submission" of the merchants and a commitment to a fixed weekly provision. The merchants called the assembly's bluff: "They continued to bring no grain at all." Félix Aubery de Vatan, who replaced Turgot in August 1740, finally struck the much-delayed exemplary blow: he arrested Jean Delu, the richest member of the port clan, and kept him in prison until he paid the entire 10,000-livre fine.

After unnerving the merchants, Vatan sought to mollify them by reducing the magnitude of the weekly quotas that the assembly had proposed the year before, and by offering substantial bonuses for each *muid* delivered above the weekly obligation. The merchants appear to have reacted positively, despite or perhaps because of the scourging of Delu. Ten traders, nine of whom had been among the twenty-six stigmatized in 1739, received almost 4,000 livres in rewards in the six weeks that followed Delu's incarceration. Vatan kept the merchants and their commissioners in the hinterland under surveillance by his resident subdelegates and his itinerant agents. He assisted them materially by ensuring them priority for transport and politically by interceding with local police, frequently in conjunction with Joly de Fleury and Marville, so as to guarantee their freedom to buy and ship on and off the markets.[64]

63. AP, 30 January 1738 and 22 and 29 January 1739, BN, ms. fr. 11356, fols. 343, 380–82, 385; BV, 18 December 1738, AN, H* 1358, fols. 63–64; "La cherté du pain" (1738), AN, F11 264; AN, K 1026 (3 January 1739, 25 October 1740); F11 264 (16 January 1739); BN, ms. fr. 8089, fols. 521–22 (16 January 1739); BN, Joly 1120, fols. 34–40.

64. AP, 1 September 1740, BN, ms. fr. 11356, fols. 425–27; BV, 17 September 1740, AN, H 1859, fols. 20–22; AN, F11 264; AN, K 1056 (4 October 1740); Barlé to PG, 26 October 1740, BN, Joly 1123, fols. 90–91; Guillen to PG, 26 October 1740, Joly 1123, fol. 109; BN, ms. n.a. 1032, fol. 93; BV, 3 March 1739 and 11 November 1740, AN, H 1939¹; Bocquet petition, Joly 1123, fol. 291; Kaplan, *Bread*, vol. 1, pp. 28–41.

Public Opinion: The Famine Plot Persuasion

The public rarely spared the government blame for grave subsistence crises. The dearth crystallized a set of deeply held assumptions about nature and culture, about the kingdom's underlying carrying capacity and the administration of the commonweal, about reality and contrivance, about fidelity and betrayal. In the bruising climate of dearth, the world no longer seemed to work as it was supposed to. Anomalies, contradictions, and misrepresentations gave credence to a conspiratorial view of things. The evidence that surged to their attention convinced a wide range of observers—officials, seigneurs, writers, and businessmen as well as the putatively more susceptible "little people"—that the crisis was not authentic. Too many signs pointed to some sort of heinous plot geared to profit an insatiable and unfeeling state, or a treacherous and venal clique of highly placed individuals, or both. Every gesture the government made or from which it abstained seemed to corroborate suspicions. Aware that the wave of incriminating rumors significantly damaged its reputation and incidentally amplified the disorganizing impact of the crisis, the government nevertheless considered it politically unpalatable to accept the notion that it owed an account of its conduct to the public. Elsewhere I have closely scrutinized the structure and functioning as well as the periodic manifestations of this famine plot persuasion.[65] Here I will merely sketch the salient features during 1738–1741.

Numerous reports of abundant crops and copious granaries seemed to prove that the dearth was "artificial," that it was due to "the malice of men" rather than the wrath of God or nature. News of grain dumped in rivers and of *laboureurs* repeatedly prohibited from selling their grain in the marketplaces reinforced this conclusion. Suspect grain removals by intendants and the discovery of large caches of grain confirmed it. Upon inspection, the foreign grain imported in the king's name appeared to be French grain that had been hidden or temporarily exported. It was notorious that the controller general had allowed large amounts of grain to leave the kingdom in the mid- and even late 1730s: numerous observers believe that Orry and his brother Orry de Fulvy, who held a major appointment under the controller general, sold permits for the departure of grain shipments. The Company of the Indies, veteran scapegoat of the crisis of 1725–1726, was widely identified as the principal illicit conveyor of grain in and out of the realm. A hydralike monster reaching into virtually every sphere of economic life and involving some of the richest men in the kingdom, the company was under the direct supervision of Orry de Fulvy, whose enormous gambling losses were allegedly covered by one of the company's directors and whose profligate wife was dubbed "Madame Flour." Operating in the king's name, the company's agents "pillaged" the markets, plotted with the bakers, kept away needed supplies, and "sustained the dizzying level of prices."

Without the cunning direction of the "barbarous" controller general,

65. Kaplan, "Famine Plot."

however, the "monopoly and duty on bread" could not have been contrived. Two images of Orry circulated, sharply different in emphasis but not mutually exclusive. One depicted a rapacious man who forged a gargantuan family fortune at the expense of the people. The other portrayed a minister consumed with "public avarice" who speculated on popular misery in order to replenish the coffers of the treasury. The incongruous persistence of very elevated prices even after the highly publicized arrival of bountiful quantities of foreign grain further tainted Orry. Perhaps the most surprising aspect of the famine plot persuasion in 1738–1741 is the failure to implicate Thellusson, who, as banker, foreigner, and Protestant had all the qualities that elicited suspicion.[66]

It was generally believed that the controller general could not have masterminded this plot without the complicity of the chief minister, Cardinal Fleury. As Cardinal Richelieu had bled the realm and Cardinal Mazarin had purged it, so Fleury "put it on a diet," according to a macabre crisis vignette. Fleury's perfidy was ironic as well as odious, for it was he who had effected the disgrace of the duc de Bourbon in 1726 precisely because he and his mistress and their banker friends were alleged to have speculated in the grain trade to create and nourish a scarcity. Like Orry, Fleury projected multiple visages: "sordid and self-aggrandizing"; "greedy for the state"; or merely confused and helpless. One leitmotif was that the cardinal misled the king.

In the most common representation of royal behavior, the king preserved his innocence at the price of his competence and his moral authority. At best, he was misinformed (he was told the loaf sold at 2 sous 6 deniers when it was really 4 sous 6 deniers). At worst, he was indifferent (engrossed in philandering and hunting). Very rarely was he denounced for the conscious crime of *lèse-peuple*. That was the substance of one of the Orléanist renditions, in which the duke tried to awaken the monarch to the duties of kingship, warning him "that the public of Paris is saying aloud that His Very Majesty is mixed up in the grain trade." Louis XV was shocked to hear "Misery! Hunger! Bread!" instead of "Long live the king!" when he traversed the outskirts of the capital in September 1740. It is a measure of his absolutism to recall that his advisers cautioned him "to avoid Paris because of the bread crisis." Fleury received a rowdy reception from women crying "Misery!" and "Bread!" at the Place Maubert about the same time. Wall posters threatened to burn Orry's house and the Indies offices. Observers predicted that Paris would explode. "The people are starting to say openly,"

66. Gazetins, 10 January, 16, 17, 23, and 28 September, 16 and 18 October, 3 and 8 November, 11 December 1740, Arsenal, ms. B. 10167, fols. 7, 132, 134, 140, 144, 147, 159, 161, 170, 174, 193; Gazetins, 28 April and 2 May 1741, ms. B. 10168, fols. 181, 218; anon. to LG, ms. B. 10027, p. 39l ; *état* Thellusson, March 1741, BN, Joly 1109, fol. 109; Dubuisson, *Lettres*, pp. 399–400 (20 November 1737), 535 (5 April 1739); Argenson, *Journal et mémoires*, vol. 2, p. 84 (25 February 1739) and vol. 3, pp. 84 (28 May 1740), 170 (23 September 1740), 183 (29 September 1740); Barbier, *Journal*, vol. 3, p. 159; Charles Collé, *Journal et mémoires de Charles Collé*, ed. Honoré Bonhomme, vol. 1 (Paris: Firmin-Didot, 1868), p. 314.

noted one police spy, "that they have only one life to lose, but before dying they will cause others to perish."[67]

Certain plot accusations were true and cast an aura of verisimilitude around the rest. Rotten grain was thrown in rivers; Orry de Fulvy gambled recklessly and was closely tied with the Indies directors; the company did some importing, as it had earlier done some exporting; the *ferme générale* lent its administration to provisioning operations; there were major storage depots along the Briare-Orléans canal system; king's grain was sold at surprisingly high prices in some places; in others, inhabitants became ill from eating bread made of king's grain. But the representation ultimately was more significant than its referents. Dearth was bad enough for the luster of the government. The extensive belief in a plot further alienated substantial sectors of opinion. Orry fully understood that "the spectacle of the [king's] trade in grain can upset the people and the magistrates." But, beyond preaching discretion, his government did nothing to educate or court or disabuse public opinion. In many eyes the government got all the credit for causing the crisis and none for ending it.[68]

SHORT TERM, LONG TERM

In Braudelian terms, there is a sharp contrast between the conjunctural energy and resolve of the state and its structural insouciance and passivity. After some tergiversation, the state intervened vigorously and in multifarious ways to try to cope with the subsistence crisis of 1738–1741. Through an uneven mix of negotiation, regulation, repression, and large-scale victualing, the authorities gradually gained control of the situation. From their point of view, they had averted the worst. Despite acute economic disarray, widespread and often devastating misery, and repeated predictions of imminent and universal social explosion, there was remarkably little collective mutiny or violence during the prolonged siege of troubles. "Public tranquility" was the crude bottom line of crisis management for the ancien

67. Gazetins, 14 , 17, 19, 20, 21, 25, 26, 28 September, 1, 14, 16, 18, 21, 26 October, 23 November, 13 December 1740, Arsenal, ms. B. 10167, fols. 130, 134, 136, 137, 139, 141, 145, 147, 148, 151, 158–60, 165–67, 179, 195; Gazetins, 1 April 1741, ms. B. 10168, fol. 155; Fleury to PG, 19 September 1740, BN, Joly 1121, fol. 81; LG to PG, 28 September 1740, Joly 1121, fol. 110; ms. B. 10277 ("Meur de fint," October 1740); Barbier, *Journal*, vol. 3, pp. 219–20, 240; Argenson, *Journal et mémoires*, vol. 3, pp. 171, 222, 224; Argenson, *Mémoires et journal*, vol. 2, pp. 34, 181; Louis de Rouvroy, duc de St-Simon, *Mémoires de St-Simon*, ed. A. de Boislisle (Paris: Hachette, 1879–1928), vol. 17, pp. 209–11; vol. 20, p. 203; vol. 34, p. 314; Narbonne, *Journal*, pp. 468, 485; Luynes, *Mémoires*, vol. 3, p. 255; Emile Raunié, *Chansonnier historique du XVIIIe siècle*, 10 vols. (Paris: A. Quantin, 1879–1884), vol. 6, p. 263.

68. BN, Joly 1109, fol. 109 (March 1741); Gazetins, 19 September and 11 December 1740, Arsenal ms. B. 10167, fols. 137, 193; ms. B. 12405; ms. B. 12423, p. 55; CG to L. de Betz, 14 February 1741, AN, KK 1005F; CG to Pallu, 5 October 1740, KK 1005F; J. Letaconnoux, *Les subsistances et le commerce des grains en Bretagne au XVIIIe siècle* (Rennes: Oberthur, 1909), p. 167.

régime—not mortality, morbidity, mendicancy, morale, unemployment, or business failures. It was a reductive but decisive litmus test. Nor did near misses count: the fact that tension ran unbearably high for well over a year had no impact on the final balance sheet.

The crisis revealed no egregious new weaknesses in the regime's short-term capacity to react. Paris suffered and its equilibrium was strained. But it was the object of prodigal compensations in the guise of remedy, exacted at considerable cost to many other parts of the realm. Overcoming his dilatory start, the controller general performed effectively and even imaginatively, but to a large extent by improvisation, outside or rather beyond the confines of his own bureaucracy. The Parlement played a constructive role, flexing its dense administrative muscles in favor of the capital and eschewing any temptation to score partisan points in the name of its own paternalistic pretensions. The lieutenant general of police reinforced his authority at the expense of the municipality and the royal provincial administration. In the provisioning theater, Marville anticipated the quasi-ministerial status that his successors Antoine-Raymond-Jean-Gualbert de Sartine and Jean-Charles-Pierre Lenoir would enjoy in the 1760s and 1770s.

There was no coherent police posture, however, at any level or at any moment of operation. Conflicts erupted between hard-liners and (grain) liberals, between civic and merchant logics, between center and periphery, between competing collector markets, between pro- and antimetropolitan forces, between institutional rivals in the same place. Neither the controller general nor the lieutenant general of police was indifferent to commercial imperatives. Both worked to build a postcrisis market system that could tolerate more stress. The crisis accelerated the reorganization of the provisioning trade that privileged flour over grain, businessmen-bakers and commercial millers over the old-style merchants, and the central market, the Halle, over the river port, the Grève. It impelled the subsistence specialists of the Paris police to launch a patient and far-reaching campaign of centralization and rationalization that improved market efficiency from their vantage point without stultifying off-market ambitions or precluding commercial initiatives. Save for two fleeting alarms in the late 1740s and the late 1750s, the capital experienced a quarter century of provisioning calm, thanks in some small measure to the adjustments elicited by the crisis of 1738–1741.

Still, the state's lack of long-term preparation is striking. France lived tremulously under the tyranny of grain, and its huge urban agglomeration stood at chronic risk. Failures of production and distribution were hardly uncommon. A gaping incongruity looms between the embrace of the consumer interest dictated by royal paternalism and *raison d'état* and the means that the state put into play to prevent disaster or attenuate its ravages pre-emptively. This ostensible heedlessness was partly an avowal of helplessness. The cost of arming the capital against dearth was prohibitive. Financially exorbitant, it was also politically parlous, given the profound popular suspicion of any form of hoarding, sanctioned or not. Storage posed equally dissuasive technological and logistical problems on the scale that Paris would require.[69] A certain kind of Malthusian fatalism may also have shaped policy formation. Leaders realized that they could not master the physical environment, acknowledged that Paris had been allowed to become far too big (despite persistent monarchical efforts to set strict growth limits), and resigned themselves to the idea that periodic catastrophes were ineluctable and in some sense even necessary. The state's only recourse was to attempt to allocate the impact in a politic manner. The countervailing but complementary belief was that France was the breadbasket of the world, and thus required no special reserve organization as a buffer against scarcity. Since crises were rarely general, an alert and aggressive central government could always find surpluses in some areas to eradicate deficits in others. According to this view, harvests were characteristically overabundant, so most dearths issued from market distortions rather than natural shortfalls, and thus could be administratively rectified. But officials increasingly questioned this thesis's sanguine assumptions about production and regulation and its pessimistic assumptions about the workings of unfettered commerce. When we allow for all these problems, doubts, and debates, however, it still seems astonishing that there was such a paucity of institutional memory, such an aversion to contingency planning, and such an absence of infrastructure for coping with crisis. Subsistence Gallicanism did not spare the putatively absolute state from chastening dependence, in the last analysis, on the intercession of miraculous saints and heretical dei ex machina.[70]

69. On the many granary schemes proposed to the government, ranging from tax collection and storage in kind to civil-military provisioning linkages, see Kaplan, "Lean Years, Fat Years."

70. The best guide to dependence on the Protestant dei ex machina is still Luethy's masterful *Banque protestante*. On the recurrent appeal to the patron saint of Paris, renowned for having saved the capital countless times from subsistence disasters, see Steven L. Kaplan, "Religion, Subsistence, and Social Control: The Uses of Saint Genevieve," *Eighteenth-Century Studies* 13 (1979–1980), pp. 142–68.

9

Provisioning Edo in the Early Eighteenth Century

The Pricing Policies of the Shogunate and the Crisis of 1733

Hayashi Reiko

Sardines and bonito; eels, octopus, and squid; rice and barley; tangerines and persimmons; burdock, turnips, and lotus root; fine silks and cotton textiles; hair decorations and all manner of personal accessories—even a cursory glance through the illustrations that accompany the *Edo meisho zue*, Saitō Gesshin's famous guide to Edo, reveals the abundance of the city's markets. But where did all of those commodities and finished goods come from, and how did they end up in Edo? As we shall see, public authority in Japan, as in France, assumed an obligation to keep supplies of agricultural products and finished goods flowing into the nation's most populous city. But the Tokugawa shoguns were no more equipped than the Bourbon kings to actually provision their political capital: that task fell to commerce. In accordance with neo-Confucian functionalism, peasants and artisans were to produce; merchants were to bring goods to market; and the responsibility of government, as discharged by its samurai officials, was to monitor and regulate so that the production and distribution systems worked toward their designed ends. As Steven L. Kaplan has written in a statement that suits Japan as well as it does France, the government did not have to feed the people, but it was obligated to make sure that they were fed.[1]

Most of the time a mix of quasi-institutional and quasi-independent market arrangements supplied Edo reasonably well, but not always. Bad weather or infestations of insects might destroy crops, just as poor human judgment or self-interested greed might induce artificial dearth, throwing out of balance the calculus of provisioning. In such instances the shogunate intervened in the economy more openly and more forcefully. But its actions sometimes took a direction that could scarcely have been imagined in France. Between Japan and France were crucial variations in social structure, in the composition of the urban population, and in power configurations

1. Steven L. Kaplan, *Provisioning Paris: Merchants and Millers in the Grain and Flour Trade during the Eighteenth Century* (Ithaca: Cornell University Press, 1984), pp. 23–27.

The fish market at Edobashi. Source: Edo meisho zue. Courtesy of Kokuritsu Kokkai Toshokan.

within government. In times of crisis, such as the dearth of 1732–1733, those differences provoked from the shogun's officials policies that stood in stark contrast to those pursued later in the same decade by their absolutist counterparts on the opposite side of the globe.

EDO AND THE NATIONAL MARKETING SYSTEM

In broad terms, the provisioning of Edo included two categories of goods, rendered in the contemporary vernacular as *kudari* and *jimawari* commodities. The former, as the name suggests, were agricultural products and finished goods that flowed "down," into Edo, from the "higher" *kamigata*, the region surrounding the two great Kinai metropolises of Kyoto, the ancient imperial capital and locus of traditional craft production, and Osaka, the newer center of manufacture and commercial exchange. *Jimawari* commodities, by way of contrast, were foodstuffs grown in Edo's immediate hinterland in eastern Japan.

Kudari Commerce

Edo remained highly dependent on western Japan for a variety of commodities throughout the seventeenth century and well into the eighteenth. Many of them came from Kyoto, which owed its prominent position in the structure of national exchange to the elegant crafts produced by its artisans. The weavers in the Nishijin section of that city, for instance, enjoyed a technological advantage over other producers—the sophisticated *takabata* loom, whose construction and method of operation they managed to keep secret until the middle of the eighteenth century. That loom permitted the operator to remain seated, leaving the hands and even the feet free to manipulate thread so that the Nishijin weavers could fashion more complex patterns than were possible with the *izari*, a hand loom used elsewhere and capable of producing only a plain-weave fabric. Kyoto was a major center of production for pottery, household furnishings, and military supplies as well. Its artisans also were renowned for their *komamono*, the combs, wigs, pouches, and other personal accessories sold across Edo in shops and outlets such as the stalls that McClain describes at Edobashi. The shogun, daimyo, and affluent bannermen in Edo surrounded themselves with goods produced in Kyoto, and even commoners in the eastern metropolis were able to experience the pleasure of owning Kyoto-made merchandise such as folding fans, cutlery, and *santome* cloth, woven in imitation of originals from India.

Edo drew on the regions along the Inland Sea for agricultural products and salt, and the residents of the capital prized highly the saké brewed in such places as Itami and Nishinomiya. Similarly, Edo's residents came to rely greatly on what they called "ten-province salt," the name given to the food seasoning and preservative produced in the former imperial provinces that stretched along the coast of the Inland Sea from modern-day Kōbe to Hiroshima. In the early seventeenth century, salt was produced on flats along Edo Bay, but the city's burgeoning population soon grew beyond the capacity of those sources, and as early as the 1620s villages in western Japan turned to making salt commercially. Most of this salt was shipped directly from these provinces to Edo's markets; in the early 1650s nearly 300 shiploads, a total of 500,000 bags, arrived in the shogun's capital.[2]

Although salt may have been packed in bags and shipped directly to Edo, many other raw materials and semifinished goods from western Japan went first to Osaka for further processing, and by the middle of the seventeenth century that city had emerged as a significant transshipment node in the Kinai region, as well as a major center for the manufacture of metal products, processed foods, pharmaceuticals, and a wide variety of other goods. Wholesalers also hung out their signs in Osaka. As early as the 1610s agents who shipped lamp oil to Edo were prospering, and by century's end approximately three hundred wholesale houses had become involved in some aspect or another of the oil trade alone, while several hundred other wholesalers and distributors handled other products bound for Edo and eastern Japan.[3]

There is no reliable statistical evidence that would permit us to know the exact dimensions of Edo's reliance on western Japan in the seventeenth century, but we can gauge its proportions by looking at the economic institutions that grew up to serve commodity exchange. Among the first of those organizations were the *higaki* shippers (*higaki kaisen*). In 1619 a merchant from Sakai leased a coastal cargo ship with a capacity of 250 *koku* (about 24 gross tons) from a trader at the port of Tomida, on the Kii peninsula, and started to ship everyday goods to Edo. Inspired by his success, others soon began to do the same. Some of these shipping agents owned their own ships, others leased one whenever they contracted for a cargo, but all seemed to prosper by sending to Edo shiploads of cotton, oil, saké, vinegar, soy sauce, paper, lacquer, tatami-mat facing, and so forth. As another sign that commerce was booming, the cargo capacity of the ships grew, first to 500 *koku* and then to 1,000. In the 1660s, as Edo became Japan's largest consumption center, another group of shippers organized themselves as the *taru* shipping agents (*taru kaisen*). At first they, too, loaded mixed cargoes, but as their name suggests, they came to specialize in shipments of casks, and from the 1730s they handled practically all the saké shipped to Edo from brewers in such famous areas as Nada and Itami.[4]

Also important in provisioning Edo were individual entrepreneurial merchandisers. Many of these men heralded from villages or small towns in Ise and Ōmi, where they purchased agricultural products such as tea or fin-

2. The standard capacity of a "bag" (*hyō*) is often given as four *to*, or the equivalent of approximately 72 liters, but this measure fluctuated greatly by region, date, and commodity. See Tsurumoto Shigemi, *Nihon shokuen hanbaishi* (Zenkoku Shio Urisabakunin Kumiai Rengokai, 1939), pp. 81–122.

3. Nakai Nobuhiko, "Kinsei toshi no hatten," in Iwanami Shoten, ed., *Iwanami kōza Nihon rekishi*, vol. 11, *Kinsei* 3 (Iwanami Shoten, 1963), pp. 80–83.

4. Yunoki Manabu, *Kinsei kaiunshi no kenkyū* (Hōsei Daigaku Shuppankyoku, 1979).

ished goods such as paper, mosquito netting, tatami-mat facing, and cotton cloth. They transported these items to Edo and sold them at their own retail outlets, referred to generically as Edo branches (*Edodana*). Also prominent in the provisioning of the shogun's capital were wholesaler-retailers known as *Edodanamochi Kyōakindo*, or merchants who maintained their headquarters and main purchasing shops in Kyoto but did most of their retail business in Edo.

Perhaps the most famous of the Kyoto-based merchandisers were the Mitsui family, who in 1673 rented a building at Hon-chō in Edo and opened a retail outlet they named the Echigoya, the forerunner of today's Mitsukoshi chain of department stores. At first this was a small operation, specializing in fine textiles and employing about ten clerks, who took samples to the homes of potential customers, negotiated a price that varied with the depth of the customer's purse, and accepted orders on credit. The Echigoya, however, soon revolutionized retailing practices in the textile business by encouraging customers to come to the shop, where they paid cash for goods whose prices were fixed and openly advertised. Sales volume grew dramatically and in 1683 the Mitsui family purchased a piece of land at Suruga-chō, just a few paces north of Nihonbashi Bridge. In 1691 the shogunate nominated the Mitsui family as one of several agents entrusted with transmitting to Edo receipts from the sale of its tax rice in Osaka, a responsibility that involved the Mitsui in the complicated business of money changing, converting the silver coins of varying purity that circulated in Japan. Despite this expansion of its Edo business, however, the Mitsui family kept its headquarters and purchasing offices in Kyoto. There a family-dominated council set policy, made hiring decisions, and enforced house rules.[5]

Another Kyoto-based merchandiser was Ōmura Hikotarō. Raised in the village of Nagahama in Ōmi, Ōmura in his youth moved to Kyoto, the city of his birth in 1636, took Shirokiya as his commercial name, and ventured into the lumber business. In 1662 Shirokiya opened a retail outlet at Tōri-chō in Edo, on the main street that ran to Nihonbashi Bridge, where his clerks sold personal accessories produced in the old imperial capital. Soon Shirokiya expanded into high-quality silks and other fine textiles, which he preferred (like the Mitsui family) to ship to Edo by courier service along the great Tōkaidō highway, since the textiles could not tolerate well the dampness of a sea journey.[6] Shirokiya's store prospered (the Nihonbashi store employed 46 clerks in 1711 and 150 by 1749) and he opened three additional stores in Edo, but the headquarters remained in Kyoto.[7]

Wholesalers, distributors, and purchasing and consignment agents ap-

5. Hayashi Reiko, *Edo ton'ya nakama no kenkyū*, rev. ed. (Ochanomizu Shobō, 1978), pp. 49–50.
6. Kodama Kōta, *Hikyaku kankei shiryō*, Kinsei kōtsū shiryōshū 7 (Yoshikawa Kōbunkan, 1974).
7. Hayashi, *Edo ton'ya*, pp. 44–49; idem, *Edodana hankachō*, [Edo] sensho 8 (Yoshikawa Kōbunkan, 1982), pp. 10–20.

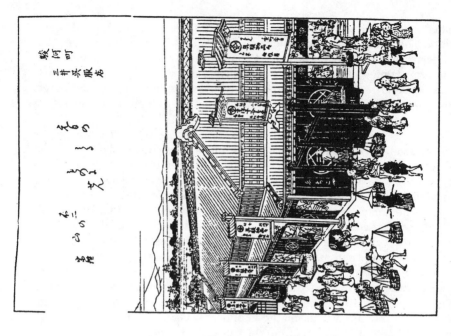

The Echigoya. Source: Edo meisho zue. Courtesy of Kokuritsu Kokkai Toshokan.

peared in Edo in increasing numbers during the course of the seventeenth century, and ultimately many organized themselves into closed protective associations (*nakama* and *kabunakama*) so that they might better control markets, reduce intragroup competition, and maximize profits. In general, such associations issued a license, or *kabu*, to each member, and the membership as a whole then set prices, maintained standards of quality, and controlled the distribution and sales of its commodities. An important turning point in this process came late in the seventeenth century, when wholesalers in Edo and major merchandisers such as the Echigoya reached the end of their patience with the coastal shipping agents. The captains were proving to be unreliable even in the best of times, and many had developed the nasty habit of selling cargoes on the sly and then claiming that bad weather and rough seas had forced them to toss the merchandise overboard. In response, ten groups of Edo merchants in 1694 formed themselves into the "organization of ten associations of wholesalers" (*tokumidoiya*). Somewhat later, merchant houses in Osaka that served as purchasing agents for the Edo wholesalers also formed an alliance (the *nijūshikumidoiya*, or "organization of twenty-four associations of wholesale agencies").[8] Tolerated by the shogunate for their usefulness, the two groups together were able to compel better performance from the shipping agencies.

During the first half of the eighteenth century these associations also came to monopolize, with the blessings of the shogunate, nearly all aspects of commodity trade between Osaka and Edo. Collectively they oversaw the purchase, shipment, and distribution within Edo of silk, cotton cloth, oil, nails, tatami, lacquerware, face powder, *funori* (a seaweed used to make paste), kelp, wooden footwear (geta), umbrellas, paints and pigments, kitchenware, personal accessories (*komamono*), wicker baskets, bamboo flutes, crockery, pharmaceuticals, unprocessed bamboo straw, dried foodstuffs, paper, hardware, iron, copper, zōri sandals, hibachi charcoal braziers, whetstones, tobacco, fertilizers, dried marine products, dried bonito, and so forth.[9]

Jimawari Commerce

Throughout the seventeenth century, Edo depended on its immediate hinterland for a variety of foods and raw materials, known as *jimawari* commodities. Charcoal and firewood arrived in the city daily, as did many perishables—fish, vegetables, and local fruits, taken from Edo Bay and villages on the Kantō plain. Significant amounts of rice came from local sources, and villages on the Bōsō peninsula, across Edo Bay, supplied the city with much of its rice bran.[10] Indeed, many villagers designed their agricultural cropping patterns to meet the needs of the urban markets. When the construction of irrigation canals that drew water from the Tama

8. Hayashi, *Edo ton'ya*, pp. 56–64.
9. Ibid., pp. 64–71.
10. Itō Yoshiichi, *Edo jimawari keizai no tenkai* (Kashiwa Shobō, 1966).

River made agriculture possible in formerly desolate areas to the west of Edo at mid-century, for instance, settlers there grew barley, wheat, mullet, buckwheat, *daikon* radishes, and so forth for sale in Edo.[11]

During the late seventeenth century and into the eighteenth, some producers in the Kantō region began to challenge the dominance of the value-added *kudari* goods, such as textiles, from western Japan. Edo's commoners prized cotton for its warmth—clothes made from that material were better suited to chilly days than garments woven from hemp and ramie—and for its relatively low price in comparison with most silks. In response to growing urban demand, villagers in the Kantō region started to plant cotton and to engage in spinning and weaving as forms of by-employment, and within a century this *jimawari* cotton cloth had grabbed a visible share of the Edo market. About the same time, the *takabata* loom and knowledge about the superior weaving and dying technology of Kyoto's Nishijin artisans also crept into the Kantō region, and weavers began to proliferate in Edo's hinterland. By the middle of the eighteenth century, the fifty-four villages that made up Kiryū, a portion of the shogunate's holdings located just a two-day trip to the north of Edo, had emerged as an important center of silk production, and Edo merchandisers such as the Echigoya were purchasing textiles in bulk from its weavers.[12]

In the 1730s the shogunate undertook an extensive survey of eleven items that it considered essential to the daily life of the residents of Edo. Information derived from the documents that remain from that survey are summarized in Tables 9.1 and 9.2, which reveal several interesting details about *kudari* and *jimawari* commerce. In the first place, the distribution network for some commodities, such as rice, was elastic and capable of making rapid adjustments to conditions of supply and demand. The volume of rice grown in Japan varied radically from year to year, and the amount shipped to Edo from Osaka depended on price differentials between the two cities, which in turn moved in accordance with the effects of weather and other factors on particular local growing areas. In 1726, for instance, an almost unbelievably minuscule amount of rice was sent to Edo markets from Osaka, but three years later somewhere in the vicinity of 8 to 10 percent of Edo's rice moved through Osaka.

Despite such fluctuations, however, it is also readily apparent that Edo in the 1720s continued to rely overwhelmingly on western Japan for oil and soy sauce, with three-quarters of all Edo imports still coming from Osaka suppliers. Rape and cotton, whose seeds were squeezed, pressed, and ground into "water oil" and "white oil," respectively, were grown extensively throughout the Kinai region, and production of lamp oil (and soy sauce) in the Kantō region was still several decades in the future. Moreover, we can suppose from the records of the shipping agencies that western Japan sup-

11. Kodaira Machiyakuba, ed., *Kodaira chōshi* (Kodaira Machiyakuba, 1959).
12. Ichikawa Kōsei, "Kiryū no orimono," in Chihōshi Kenkyūkai, ed., *Nihon sangyōshi taikei*, vol. 4: *Kantō chihō-hen* (Tōkyō Daigaku Shuppankai, 1959), pp. 287–310.

TABLE 9.1.
Shipments of commodities from Osaka to Edo, 1724–1730

Commodity	1724	1725	1726	1727	1728	1729	1730
Ginned cotton (bales)	103,530	69,012	98,119	134,381	78,696	102,398	84,025
Cotton cloth (bolts)	10,471	8,180	12,171	20,179	13,926	12,893	13,947
Oil (casks)	73,651	62,802	69,172	49,744	57,301	48,639	77,022
Saké (casks)	265,395	236,066	177,687	211,443	189,828	221,846	235,997
Soy sauce (casks)	112,196	136,247	101,457	131,817	158,088	153,469	162,411
Rice (bales)	13,278	450	3	3,870	37,201	74,946	4,780
Charcoal (bags)	251	30	764	1,053	565	300	168
Fish oil (casks)	296	22	—	77	—	—	23
Salt (bags)	6,780	—	248	400	—	—	2,400
Firewood (bundles)	—	—	—	—	—	—	—
Miso (casks)	—	—	—	—	—	—	—

Adapted from Hayashi Reiko, "Kinsei chūkōki no shōgyō," in Toyoda Takeshi and Kodama Kōta, eds., *Ryūtsūshi*, vol. 1, Taikei Nihonshi sōsho 13 (Yamakawa Shuppansha, 1969), pp. 191–92.

plied Edo customers with more significant amounts of saké, salt, and cotton cloth than the survey indicates. Most saké and salt was loaded onto cargo vessels at the production site and shipped straight to Edo, bypassing Osaka, so those amounts were not counted in the survey. Similarly, by the early eighteenth century cotton cloth manufactured in Mikawa, Owari, Ise, and other locales between Edo and Osaka was transported directly to the sho-

TABLE 9.2.
Imports of commodities into Edo, 1726

Commodity	(A) Amount shipped into Edo from all sources	(B) Amount shipped into Edo from Osaka	(C) Percent of Edo imports from Osaka (B/A)
Ginned cotton (bales)	82,019[a]	98,119[a]	119.6%[a]
Cotton cloth (bolts)	36,135	12,171	33.7
Oil (casks)	90,811	69,172	76.2
Saké (casks)	795,856	177,687	22.3
Soy sauce (casks)	132,829	101,457	76.4
Rice (bales)	861,893	3	0.0
Charcoal (bags)	809,790	764	0.1
Fish oil (casks)	50,501	—	0.0
Salt (bags)	1,670,880	248	0.0
Firewood (bundles)	18,209,687	—	0.0
Miso (casks)	2,898	—	0.0

Adapted from Hayashi Reiko, "Kinsei chūkōki no shōgyō," in Toyoda Takeshi and Kodama Kōta, eds., *Ryūtsūshi*, vol. 1, Taikei Nihonshi sōsho 13 (Yamakawa Shuppansha, 1969) pp. 191–92.
[a]The impossibility apparent in these figures is probably related to the transshipment of ginned cotton from Edo to villages where it was processed into thread and cloth.

gun's capital, giving *kudari* cotton cloth a larger market share than the survey suggests.

Almost no charcoal or firewood was shipped from Osaka to Edo. These were *jimawari* commodities, and wholesalers and distributors routed them overland or sent them by river barge from villages in Edo's hinterland directly to the city's markets. Fish oil was produced in many fishing villages and ports along the Pacific coast, as at Kujūkuri Beach on the Bōsō peninsula, and local records indicate this oil came to Edo together with pressed fish-oil cakes (*shimekasu*). Only minor amounts of miso, however, were shipped into Edo from any source. Miso was made from commonly available ingredients—soybeans and salt—so everyone who could buy or otherwise acquire the malted rice starter (*kōji*) necessary to ferment the beans could make this soup base at home. Many people, samurai and townspeople as well as farm households, made miso for their own use, so there was little need to import large amounts of it either from Osaka or from the villages in Edo's hinterland.

One of the more startling points to emerge from Table 9.2 is that the volume of ginned cotton shipped into Edo from Osaka alone in 1726 appears to be greater than the total volume of ginned cotton imported into Edo from all sources. Quite obviously, that cannot be. The explanation for this impossibility must have something to do with Edo's role as a transshipment point. The manufacture of cotton thread and cloth was not done in Edo, but such processing did take place in villages in the Kantō and Tōhoku regions. Consequently, although it is probable that most of the cotton consumed in Edo came from Osaka, it also is likely that the total amount of ginned cotton shipped into Edo from Osaka and all other sources combined amounted to considerably more than 98,119 bales.

THE SHOGUNATE'S PRICING POLICIES

The shogunate aspired to implement policies so that goods and commodities would flow smoothly into Edo and so that commodity prices would remain stable. In the early seventeenth century, however, most commodities became so expensive in relation to rice that the shogunate undertook its first large-scale program of political and economic reform. Known as the Kyōhō reforms, these measures included calls for austerity in government; the issuance of detailed sumptuary regulations designed to encourage frugality in private life; the promulgation of moral injunctions exhorting the samurai to revive their martial spirit; the implementation of a new rice-tax system designed to increase rice-tax collections; and a return to hard currency.[13]

Perhaps the most significant action undertaken as part of the reforms

13. For a discussion of the Kyōhō reforms, see Nakai Nobuhiko and James L. McClain, "Commercial Change and Urban Growth in Early Modern Japan," in John W. Hall et al., eds., *The Cambridge History of Japan*, vol. 4: John W. Hall with McClain, ed., *Early Modern Japan* (Cambridge: Cambridge University Press, 1991), pp. 570–79.

was the widescale licensing of merchant protective associations. Indeed, between 1721 and 1726 the authorities instructed virtually every merchant in Edo to join such an organization. The officials of the shogunate hoped through this measure to reap a harvest of benefits. But their grandest ambition was to sharpen their surveillance of market activities and thus to gain some control over commodity prices. The survey of the Edo-Osaka trade was one step in this direction. This policy affected Edo's residents in a variety of ways, as a look at oil and rice pricing policies and the riot of 1733 reveals.

Oil Pricing Policies

In the medieval period, lamp oil was pressed chiefly from castor beans, but during the seventeenth century producers began to use rape- and cotton-seeds, which produced a cleaner, longer-lasting flame. There were advancements as well in processing equipment as "standing timber" presses and waterwheels came into more general use. The most advanced production area was Kinai, and as Table 9.2 shows, three-quarters of all lamp oil entering Edo came from Osaka. Since lamp oil was used by everyone in the city, from the shogun and daimyo down to the most humble artisan family, the shogunate aspired to stabilize prices at a level that was as affordable as possible. During the 1720s and 1730s, authorities sought to achieve this goal by regulating the activities of wholesalers and retailers.

The shogunate began to work toward a defined pricing policy in 1717, when officials became concerned that hoarding was causing unduly high oil prices. In that year they ordered a site inspection of the warehouses of wholesalers and tallied the number of casks of oil in storage. This measure had little effect, however, so in the First Month of 1724 the shogunate established an official maximum price that dealers might charge for oil.[14] Two months later the shogunate freed prices, but shortly thereafter authorities publicly accused some oil wholesalers of making excessive profits and attempted to curb their greed by imposing a correctional fine on them. Increasingly disgruntled with the merchants, the shogunate later the same year designated Yamatoya Shichirōzaemon of Nakabashi in Edo as a "buying agent" and entrusted him with a monopoly right to purchase rapeseed. Four years later, in 1728, two merchants who owned shops in Asakusa (and who identified themselves only by their given names, Kihei and Sakuemon) petitioned the city elders for the exclusive right to sell castor-bean seeds to farmers in the Kantō provinces, to purchase the crop, and to press the mature seeds into oil. The elders passed the request to their superiors, who signified approval in the hope that the merchants' energy, ingenuity, and monopolistic privileges would increase production and lower commodity prices.[15]

14. Tsuda Hideo, *Hōken keizai seisaku to shijō kōzō*, rev. ed. (Ochanomizu Shobō, 1977), pp. 19–39.
15. Kinsei Shiryō Kenkyūkai, ed., *Shōhō jiroku*, 3 vols. (Nihon Gakujutsu Kankōkai, 1965) (hereafter cited as *SJ*), vol. 2, doc. 2113, p. 389.

As part of the Kyōhō reforms during the late 1720s, the shogunate gave its formal recognition to associations of wholesalers and distributors of oil, and in 1741 officials turned to those groups to help correct what the authorities saw as continuing problems in the distribution system that kept the cost of rapeseed oil at objectionably high levels in urban centers. Shogunal leaders led off by ordering the city magistrates to conduct a survey. That investigation disclosed that shipments of rapeseed into Osaka had declined in late 1740 as a consequence of a poor harvest in western Japan, thus driving up the wholesale price. Those high prices, however, attracted to market the rapeseed that many farmers had carefully stockpiled, and the price of oil edged downward in Osaka. Nevertheless, prices did not budge in Edo. The reason, the investigators suggested, was that "outsiders" had been going to Osaka and buying up so much oil that the distributors and Edo-based wholesalers belonging to the officially recognized protective association could not acquire sufficient supplies. Naturally, the investigators concluded, prices rose in accordance with the dictates of the marketplace.[16] When the shogunate received that information, it sent the following statement to Edo's city officials:

> Unauthorized distributors and outsiders have been going to Osaka and paying money to oil merchants and receiving shipments of oil. Thus the amount of oil available for purchase by officially authorized wholesalers has decreased. Moreover, the unauthorized distributors and outsiders hide their oil off-market and so the amount of oil that reaches [the Edo] market through the official distribution system is not sufficient to meet the demand. Certainly this increases the likelihood of high prices. Henceforth, all trade that is being carried on outside of the officially authorized system must cease. Only properly designated authorized wholesalers are to handle all oil. All supplies must be shipped from Osaka to Edo, and none may be secreted off-market. You must report to us the names of any transgressors who carry on hidden trade or who refuse to sell their oil through official wholesalers. You must also investigate why oil prices have been high recently. Prices must come down.[17]

Two years later, in the Second Month of 1743, the shogunate encouraged farmers to increase the production of rapeseed in various provinces in the hope of curtailing prices in Osaka. Moreover, officials reminded everyone that oil from production centers between Edo and Osaka (that is, from Ōmi, Owari, Ise, Mikawa, Suruga, Izu, and Sagami) was to be shipped into Edo, just as it had been in the past, whereas raw seeds and oil pressed in Settsu and points west were to be transported into Osaka, where they would pass into the hands of authorized distributors and wholesalers. Just two days later, the shogunate announced that commodity prices recently had risen

16. Tsuda, *Hōken keizai seisaku*, pp. 25–39.
17. *SJ*, vol. 3, doc. 2601, p. 86.

steeply "without any reason." Retail prices, it complained, were especially high in relation to wholesale levels, and therefore merchants were to lower prices "immediately."[18]

The shogunate's tactics varied with the occasion during the early decades of the seventeenth century, but the authorities hewed to a consistent "Edo first" policy objective: to bring all oil to market through the authorized distribution system so as to ensure sufficient supplies for Edo's consumers. In addition, the shogunate wanted to maintain stable prices at the lowest possible level. This pricing policy in regard to oil stood in sharp contrast to the shogunate's pricing policy for rice. Officials wanted to maintain a stable price for rice, too, but they preferred that price to be as high as possible, higher sometimes in fact than market conditions justified.

Rice Pricing Policies

The eighth shogun, Tokugawa Yoshimune, was called "the rice shogun," an allusion to the vigor with which his administration pursued new policies concerning rice. As part of his Kyōhō reforms, Yoshimune and his officials tried to encourage the development of new paddy, and they increased the level of the annual rice taxes imposed on villagers. Many daimyo followed suit within their own domains, and as a consequence tax collections nation-wide reached new heights in the early decades of the eighteenth century. Since daimyo and the shogunate sold significant amounts of tax rice in the markets of Edo and Osaka in order to raise cash to buy necessary goods and to operate their governments, the two great cities of eastern and western Japan were awash with grain. Shogunal authorities decried the resulting state of affairs as "cheap rice, expensive commodities." Ironically, the very success of the Kyōhō reforms threatened the financial underpinnings of the shogunate, the daimyo, and the entire samurai class, all of whom received rice as their principal form of income. In the minds of the shogunate's officials, action was called for, and in the Second Month of 1724, the shogun-ate instructed the city elders to distribute the following proclamation throughout the merchant and artisan quarters of Edo:

> The price of rice has declined since last year. Yet the prices of other commodities have stayed high. This has caused hardship for everyone. Needless to say, the value of saké, vinegar, soy sauce, miso, and goods made from rice ought to rise and fall with the price of rice. Moreover, the worth of bamboo, charcoal, firewood, salt, oil, textiles, and even com-modities produced by artisans—although not made directly from rice— ought to bear a relationship to the cost of rice, as should even the wages of the craftsmen. Producers have an ethical obligation to sell at a low cost. . . . People should not make excessive profits. From now on, prices must be lowered. We will conduct an investigation of prices, to be com-pleted by the first day of the Third Month. Everyone must obey our

18. Ibid., doc. 2632, pp. 114–15.

FIGURE 9.1.
The Edo rice distribution network

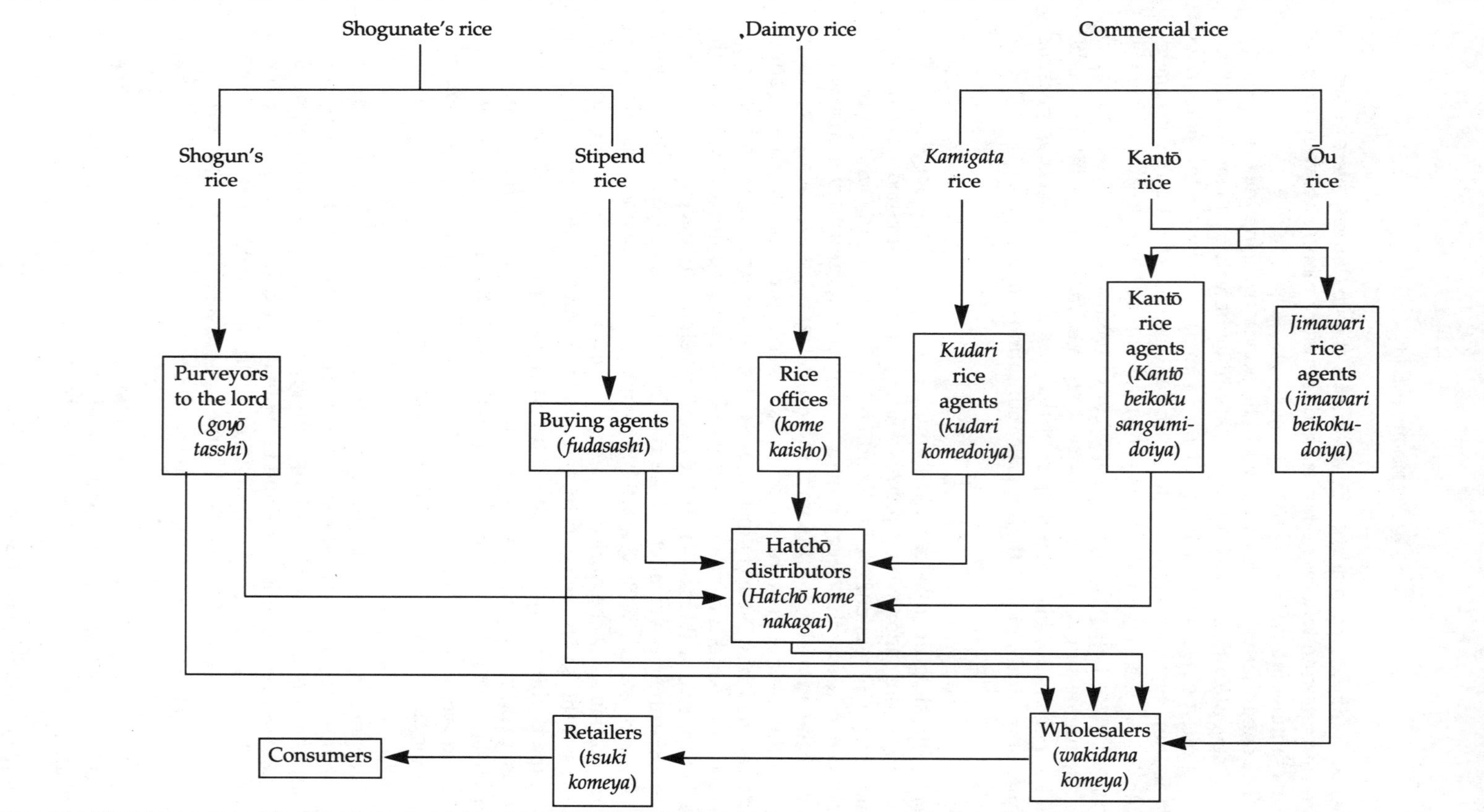

Adapted from Dohi Doritaka, *Edo no komeya*, [Edo] sensho 7 (Yoshikawa Kobunkan, 1981), p. 53.

instructions. All the details are to be announced in every province, in every place; and if prices are not reduced at the place of production, complaints should be brought against the producers.[19]

Very obviously, shogunal officials were disturbed that the costs of wages, rice, and other essential commodities no longer oscillated in a harmonious amplitude, and they launched a two-pronged attack. On the one hand, as the proclamation reveals, they sought ways to bring down the prices of commodities other than rice. In the Sixth Month of 1724, for instance, government officials instructed neighborhood chiefs in Edo to monitor prices and to admonish merchants thought to be making unwarranted profits.[20] In addition, that same year the shogunate ordered protective associations of wholesalers and shippers to draw up and submit lists of goods that they handled, so that the authorities could better monitor the channels of distribution, the volume of goods traded, and the nature of price fluctuations.[21] Two years later, in the Twelfth Month of 1726, the wholesale prices of such goods as saké, paper, charcoal, firewood, and used clothing had fallen slightly as a result of these measures, but retail prices had changed hardly at all. The shogunate then targeted specific commodities, as when it ordered a reduction in the retail price of tofu in Edo in the Fifth Month of 1730.[22]

At the same time that officials pursued policies designed to tame high commodity prices, they intervened in the marketplace in order to push up the price of rice. The points of intervention that the shogunate might choose from were many, for the system of rice distribution in Edo had grown up in an ad hoc manner and was extremely complex. Figure 9.1 depicts the channels by which rice flowed into the city in the 1730s and 1740s.

As can be seen, rice sold in Edo could be divided roughly into three categories: the shogunate's rice, daimyo rice, and commercial rice. The shogunate's rice was further subdivided into tax rice collected on the lord's direct holdings (*tenryō*) and used to finance the shogunate and to maintain the shogun's household, and tax rice collected from the enfeoffments of retainers and disbursed to them as annual stipends (one-half after the harvest and the remainder in equal installments in spring and summer). The sale of the shogun's rice was handled by special merchants, "purveyors to the lord," who sold a portion of the hulled rice to the thirty or so Hatchō distributors (*Hatchō kome nakagai*), whose appellation derived from their place of residence in eight quarters along or near the banks of the Nihonbashi River, opposite Edobashi. The balance of the lord's rice (as well as that marketed through the Hatchō distributors) passed to wholesalers known as the *wakidana komeya*.[23] About two hundred of these men operated shops at

19. Ibid., vol. 2, doc. 1938, p. 275.
20. Ibid., doc. 1959, p. 284.
21. Hayashi, *Edo ton'ya*, pp. 73–87.
22. *SJ*, vol. 2, doc. 2046, p. 349; 2180, p. 423.
23. The association of *wakidana komeya* was divided into eight groups, each of which took the name of a specific residential quarter or section of Edo: Kamakura-chō, Moto Iida-

various locations across the city, and they serviced the city's approximately two thousand retail outlets, known generically as *tsuki komeya*. There the rice was polished and sold to the final consumers. The bannermen and housemen, by way of contrast, entrusted their allotments to one or another of the approximately one hundred buying agents known as *fudasashi*, who arranged deals with Hatchō distributors and the wholesalers.

Many daimyo also marketed some of their rice in Edo. Most of it was tax rice, but occasionally daimyo in northern Japan followed the lead of the Date family of Sendai in compelling farmers to sell a portion of their crop (in addition to the tax assessment) to domain agents, who then could market it at a profit in Edo. Each daimyo who wished to sell rice in Edo established his own office (*kome kaisho*), which usually accepted sealed offers from the distributors, who moved the rice into the wholesaler-retailer-consumer chain.

Commercial rice—grain that farmers or independent purchasers in local towns wished to market in Edo—followed yet another route. According to regulations issued by the shogunate, Kantō rice and Ōu rice, which together comprised the crop harvested in the nineteen provinces along the Pacific seaboard from Shima and Ise east through the Kantō and then north into Dewa and Mutsu, had to be handled by the Kantō rice agents (*Kantō beikoku sangumidoiya*) or the *jimawari* rice agents (*jimawari beikokudoiya*). The former of these two groups sold to the distributors, whereas the latter dealt directly with the *wakidana* wholesalers. Rice from the rest of Japan was known as *kamigata* rice, and the shogunate mandated that it enter Edo's distribution network through the association of *kudari* rice agents (*kudari komedoiya*), who then sold it to the Hatchō distributors.

One stratagem that the shogunate used to support rice prices was to decrease the supply of grain available for purchase by Edo's consumers. In the Eleventh Month of 1725, for example, just as the new crop was making its way into the urban centers, the shogunate instructed three Edo merchants (Kinokuniya Genbei, Ōsakaya Riemon, and Nomuraya Jinbei) to use their own funds to make purchases from distributors and wholesalers in Edo and Osaka. The men were authorized to store the rice so acquired at the shogunate's granaries in Asakusa, and to sell the stocks "at their own discretion," presumably after the price had risen. At the same time, the shogunate inflated the price of rice artificially by announcing that any dealer who successfully bid on rice being sold by daimyo from northern or western Japan had to pay a surcharge, to be divided equally between the association of Hatchō distributors and the three merchants, who, of course, could use the money as capital to make their purchases.[24]

Four years after officials tapped the three men to act as temporary acquisition agents, the shogunate itself entered the market to make purchases of

---

chō, Sakuma-chō Kandagawa, Sanjikkenbori, Shibaguchi-chō, Teppōzu, Tsukiji, and Yushima. Thus the organization was also known as the *waki hakkasho komeya*, or the wholesalers of the eight locales.

24. *SJ*, vol. 2, doc. 2001, pp. 313–14.

rice in order to stabilize prices. In the Twelfth Month of 1729, officials declared that "the world was suffering" because of low rice prices, and they announced that they would buy rice. People who wished to sell were instructed to come to the shogunate's granary at Asakusa "at the fourth hour of the twenty-fifth day" to submit a sealed offering that specified how much rice they wished to sell and at what price. That price, officials proclaimed, "must accord with the price in the city market." Those submitting offers were told to return on the twentieth-six to learn which bids had been accepted. The shogunate instructed that this notice be posted throughout the city.[25]

In the Seventh Month of the next year, 1730, the shogunate decided not to ship into Edo 600,000 *koku* of tax rice from its own direct holdings, but to hold it off-market in storage facilities in the villages. At the same time, officials bemoaned the fact that "samurai and rice dealers are suffering great financial losses because of low rice prices," and they announced that they would purchase the stipend rice paid to bannermen and housemen so that the sales of rice by those families would not cause a glut and further depress prices. In this instance, the sales would not be conducted by sealed offerings. Rather, retainers who wanted to sell grain were told to submit samples, graded "superior," "middle," and "poor," and bearing a tag with a suggested price.[26] The shogunate made additional purchases that fall in the Osaka market as well, realizing that it had to act in order to keep daimyo tax rice from inundating the market and causing prices to drop sharply.

In addition to keeping its own rice off the market, the shogunate occasionally limited the amount of rice that daimyo, peasants, and local merchants were permitted to ship into Osaka and Edo. In 1725, for instance, the shogunate instructed various daimyo to stockpile their rice.[27] A few years later, in the Second Month of 1732, the shogunate announced that it would suspend shipments of tax rice to Edo from its holdings in the provinces of Suruga, Tōtōmi, Mikawa, Owari, and Ise. Moreover, it declared, no daimyo rice or commercial rice from those areas would be permitted into Edo either.[28]

The shogunate also imposed many controls over distributors, wholesalers, and retailers. In the Fourth Month of 1729, the shogunate announced that since recent harvests had been abundant, rice dealers were encouraged to buy up stocks of rice for indefinite storage. Soon the shogunate received petitions from rice dealers asking for permission to delay repayment of money that they had borrowed from fellow merchants so that they could purchase as much rice as possible.[29] A decade earlier, in 1719, when the city magistrates and other shogunal officials had been besieged with similar petitions, the shogunate had issued a decree underscoring the legal obliga-

25. Ibid., doc. 2148, p. 410.
26. Ibid., docs. 2183–84, pp. 424–25.
27. Dohi Noritaka, *Kinsei beikoku kin'yūshi no kenkyū* (Kashiwa Shobō, 1974), pp. 255–61.
28. *SJ*, vol. 2, doc. 2275, p. 486.
29. Ibid., doc. 2121, p. 392.

tion of persons to settle their debts in timely fashion. Now, however, the authorities decided to permit exemptions, a sign that they were encouraging the availability of capital to be used to purchase rice.

In the Ninth Month of the following year, 1730, officials concluded that shipments of grain from western Japan into Edo by unauthorized distributors and wholesalers was "interfering" with the price of rice. To tighten control over the distribution system, officials decided to limit to eight the number of *kudari* rice agents, the dealers who arranged the shipment of commercial rice from western Japan to Edo's distributors. Prominent among these agents were Takama Denbei and other merchants from the quarters along the northern banks of the Nihonbashi River. The new arrangement, the official announcement concluded, "is to be proclaimed throughout the city, to every quarter without exception."[30]

THE PROVISIONING CRISIS OF 1733

The Violence of 1733

Even as the shogunate continued to experiment with ways to keep rice prices high enough to ensure the well-being of its retainers and allied daimyo, the dearth of 1732–1733 touched off a crisis of provisioning that drove rice prices to exceptionally high levels and posed a dilemma for the shogunate: to tolerate expensive grain for the sake of the samurai or to lower prices in order to help Edo's commoners.

In 1732 an infestation of locusts caused severe damage to the rice crop in western Japan, especially on the island of Kyūshū, bringing on widespread misery and starvation. In response, the shogunate quickly purchased large amounts of rice in Osaka and Edo for shipment to the famine area. As a consequence rice prices in those urban centers, low until the previous year, surged rapidly. Edo's poor were especially vulnerable, and many neighborhood chiefs jointly petitioned the shogunate to institute relief measures. But the response by the leaders of the shogunate was dilatory. Finally, on the twenty-first day of the Twelfth Month, one of the city elders delivered the government's response to the neighborhood chiefs, assembled at his residence-office:

> Yesterday several neighborhood chiefs presented a petition to Inō Shimotsuke no Kami [the city magistrate] claiming that high rice prices have caused great suffering and asking him to lower the price of rice. That petition has not been accepted. Low rice prices would cause hardship for the samurai. Moreover, if rice prices remain high, the financial situation

30. Ibid., doc. 2191, p. 427. This document also says that the shogunate had "in the previous Year of the Chicken"—that is, in 1729—issued a proclamation prohibiting the activities of unauthorized wholesalers, but this document is not extant. Similar proclamations were reissued in the Eleventh Month of 1736, the Fourth Month of 1747, and the Second Month of 1755, an indication of the necessity for constant monitoring.

of the samurai will improve. In our opinion, commerce and merchants will benefit from their purchases, and no one will be distressed.[31]

Moreover, in their petition the neighborhood chiefs had requested that the shogunate cease buying up rice for shipment to western Japan, complaining that such purchases merely caused prices to rise in Edo and brought "great suffering" to the people. But officials of the shogunate were skeptical. "Undertake a survey of how many people are distressed," the city elder commanded, "and report the results to me." Quite clearly, the shogunate was more concerned with the samurai's finances than with the privation of Edo's commoners.

The chiefs conducted their survey as instructed, and they submitted report after report about the sad plight of people in their neighborhoods: even some of the "fine shops on the main streets" had fallen into "financial ruin"; families that lived in "the small shops on the back streets" had been "reduced to begging"; it was just a matter "of days" before people began to starve to death. Unimpressed, the city magistrates replied that it was "insolent" for merchants and artisans to send in so many petitions; admonished commoners to channel any appeals through the chiefs; and transmitted the following message to the chiefs of each residential quarter: "You have sent us several pleas complaining that we have not promptly implemented any policies to lower rice prices and claiming that people in the residential quarters are suffering. We encourage everyone to continue to be frugal. You are to explain this to each shopkeeper."[32] Clearly, the city magistrates had not constructed any policy to deal with the crisis, and they refused even to consider halting shipments of Edo rice to western Japan.[33]

As pressures from below mounted in the days after the new year, and as the neighborhood chiefs submitted more memoranda repeating their fears that "the people are on the verge of starvation," the shogunate finally responded by lifting its embargo, in place since the previous year, on the shipment of daimyo and commercial rice into Edo from the provinces just to the south and west of the city. Moreover, the authorities announced that they would distribute relief rice.[34] But these measures were not enough to satisfy Edo's commoners, and the neighborhood chiefs pressed for further action. Among other things, the chiefs asked the shogunate to make certain that rice dealers did not hoard rice; to open shogunal granaries to public inspection; to authorize ships with rice from daimyo in the Hokuriku area to dock at Edo and unload their cargoes; and to abolish monopoly rights within the rice trade. The political authorities brusquely turned the petition aside.

On the twenty-third day of the First Month of 1733 officials released five thousand bales of relief rice for distribution to the needy: two *gō* per day for males, half that for females. Three days later, merchants and artisans sub-

31. Ibid., doc. 2259, pp. 465–67.
32. Ibid.
33. Ibid., doc. 2260, p. 467.
34. Ibid., docs. 2275, p. 486; 2268, pp. 474–75.

mitted petitions repeating their earlier requests for increased shipments of
daimyo rice, the abolition of merchant monopolies in the grain trade, and a
public inspection of granaries.[35] The crisis had sharpened commoners'
views about the rice marketing system: they now wanted a complete reform,
and they were unlikely to be quieted by a temporary "benevolent gift" of
relief rice.

But the shogunate answered the petitions with silence, and on the
twenty-sixth occurred the first riot in Edo's history, an attack on the shop of
Takama Denbei, who had become one of the city's wealthiest rice dealers
after he was designated a *kudari* rice agent in 1730. In response to this action,
the shogunate on the twenty-ninth instructed retailers to sell their stocks
immediately. At the same time, the government ordered the various agents
who normally dealt only with the Hatchō distributors to begin selling directly to consumers, vowed to confiscate rice from anyone found guilty of
hoarding, and promised to sell its own stockpiles of tax rice (while at the
same time encouraging rice dealers to report anyone who tried to "extort"
money or who made "unreasonable" demands when buying rice). The shogunate followed up with additional measures, allowing the rice merchants
to sell stocks of daimyo tax rice from the Second Month and then, in the
Fifth Month, discontinuing the practice of encouraging dealers to stockpile
rice.[36]

Reverting to High Prices

Despite its efforts to deflate rice prices during the crisis of 1733, the shogunate soon reverted to its customary practice of maintaining rice prices at the
highest possible level. In 1735, just two years after the riot, officials reaffirmed the monopoly rights of the Hatchō distributors. Moreover, they approved plans for representatives of those distributors to make a daily inspection tour of the city to ascertain that no one was violating their privileges,
and the authorities even promised the support of patrolmen assigned to the
city magistrates' office. The shogunate also agreed to erect inspection stations at each point of entry into Edo.[37]

In the Tenth Month of 1735, policymakers ventured into new territory:
because low rice prices were causing "suffering among samurai and peasants alike," officials decided to set minimum prices for rice bought by agents
and distributors. Furthermore, the authorities decreed, if a rice dealer
bought rice for less than the floor price, the shogunate would impose on that
merchant a levy of ten *monme* of silver for each *koku* of illicit rice. Moreover,
in the future rice merchants would be required to submit monthly reports to
the city magistrates detailing how much grain each dealer bought and sold
that month, and any levies assessed for buying below the minimum price
would have to be paid within a month after the submission of the report. In
addition, the shogunate encouraged samurai and peasants to report to the

35. Ibid., docs. 2269–70, pp. 475–82.
36. Ibid., docs. 2271, p. 482; 2275, p. 486; 2282, p. 489.
37. Ibid., docs. 2363, pp. 545–46; 2366, p. 547.

TABLE 9.3.
Minimum amount of rice to be sold for one ryō *of gold, 1735–1736*

| Year | Month | Grade | | |
		Superior	Middle	Poor
1735	Tenth	1.40	—	—
	Twelfth	1.35	—	—
1736	First	1.25	1.35	—
	Third	1.20	1.50	1.75

city magistrates the names of any agents who refused to buy rice. A month later, officials bared their teeth once again by declaring that they would establish minimum retail prices as well.[38]

Still, for all the shogunate's efforts, some merchants found ways to buy below the floor price; others used rice in barter transactions as a way of trading at less than the official price; and some rice shops simply reduced the volume of rice they handled, so that in the end the price of rice did not go up. Consequently, on the fifth day of the Twelfth Month the shogunate issued another proclamation, this time raising the minimum price for superior-grade rice to 1 *koku* 3 *to* 5 *shō* per *ryō* of gold. On the fourth day of the new year, officials again boosted prices, and they pegged the minimum price for middle-grade rice at 1 *koku* 3 *to* 5 *shō* per *ryō*. On the twelfth day of the Third Month, authorities shoved up the price of superior-grade rice yet again, so that it sold for 14 percent more than it had the previous fall.[39]

In the 1740s the shogunate returned to the practice of ordering merchants to buy up rice in order to prop up prices. More than one hundred wealthy Edo merchants—rice dealers, money changers, and textile houses—were saddled with this responsibility in 1744, and some did not fare well. The great merchandiser Shirokiya, for instance, received in a sealed envelope his instructions about how much rice he had to acquire. Later, as he purchased the rice and arranged to store it in rented warehouses, officials inspected the amounts in storage and required Shirokiya to present documents bearing the seals of himself, his neighborhood chief, and his five-family group certifying that the specified amounts of rice were in fact in storage. Shirokiya began to make his purchases late in the Ninth Month, and by the beginning of the Eleventh Month he had acquired nearly 2,350 *koku* of grain at a cost of approximately 2,550 *ryō* of gold. On the eighteenth day of the Eleventh Month, he received from the shogunate a message relieving him of the need to make further purchases, but by the time he liquidated his existing stocks he had suffered a loss of more than 743 *ryō* of gold.[40]

In the Eleventh Month of 1744, the shogunate acted to cut off rice that

38. Ibid., docs. 2355, pp. 542–53; 2366, p. 547.
39. Ibid., docs. 2367, pp. 547–48; 2369, p. 549; 2376, p. 551.
40. Hayashi Reiko, "Enkyō gannen Edo kaimairei shiryō—Shirokiya monjo ni yoru," *Ryūtsū Keizai Daigaku ronshū* 16:3 (1984), pp. 23–48.

was moving into Edo through unauthorized conduits. To this end, it reorganized the association of retail rice shops; declared that only the Hatchō distributors could handle rice destined for its granaries; and specified that all commercial rice from nearby villages be handled by members of the distributors' association or by the *jimawari* agents. A month later the shogunate established the Rice Surveillance Office (*kome ginmisho*) in order to impose further controls of rice sales. Representatives of the wholesalers' association and the buying agents who managed the warehousing and sale of rice for samurai were instructed to appear at this office to be informed about the regulations governing the distribution and sale of rice in Edo.[41]

CONCLUDING OBSERVATIONS

Just a few years after Edo's crisis of 1733, the people of Paris would suffer a period of dearth. There government officials responded with extraordinary measures designed to increase grain supplies and to lower prices paid by consumers in the nation's capital: they appointed special agents, put hundreds of ships to sea, and scoured the Western world for grain. In Japan, the government was reluctant even to open its own granaries to provide relief for Edo's commoners. One fundamental difference between France and Japan was that rice was both Japan's most important food and a unit of commercial exchange, and this double function could complicate the formulation of policy. At times the shogunate had to confront an unpleasant choice: to preserve the commercial value of rice or to drive down the grain's price in order to promote its availability as a foodstuff. In such instances, the shogunate acted instinctively to protect the incomes of its retainers and the integrity of its own financial base by emphasizing the commercial role of rice and keeping prices high. In doing so, the government risked violence from below and accepted threats and challenges that the Bourbon regime abhorred.

Yet, for all the favoritism shown to the samurai, rice policy was an exception. In other respects the shogunate advanced an Edo-first policy that sought to move raw materials and finished goods into Edo in quantities that would provide sufficient supplies and reasonable prices for all of the city's residents. As McClain and Merriman point out in Chapter 1, it made sense for officials to do so, and policies directed toward this end included development of transportation and communication facilities, formal licensing of merchant associations, and advancement of a pricing policy for commodities such as lamp oil. In times of crisis, the shogunate first took care of its retainers; naturally so, perhaps, since the samurai were the military and police arm of government. But that predilection existed within a broader set of Edo-first policies. The measures designed to provision Edo worked reasonably well in the first half of the Tokugawa period. In the late eighteenth

41. *SJ*, vol. 3, docs. 2694, pp. 176–77; 2697, pp. 177–78; 2700, pp. 178–79.

century, as Takeuchi Makoto notes in Chapter 16, new problems would lead officials to reconsider their commercial policies. But until that time, goods and foodstuffs flowed into Edo from its hinterland and from all over Japan through the quasi-institutional, quasi-independent market arrangements devised by the shogunate and the merchants of Japan.

10

Edo's Water Supply

HATANO JUN

One of the defining characteristics of early-modern cities—what made Edo Edo and Paris Paris—was the way in which governments increasingly provided what Japanese historians call "urban facilities" (and what Roger Chartier in Chapter 6 terms "urban improvements"). In the case of Japan, such facilities, or improvements, included roads and bridges, water supply networks and sewer systems, the wooden gates and guardhouses that stood at entry points into residential quarters, and the fire and bell towers that punctuated the urban landscape. Perhaps even neighborhood graveyards should be considered among such facilities. The collection of garbage and human waste and the organization of firefighting brigades were, strictly speaking, services rather than facilities, but they also supported human life in urban centers.

The characteristics of urban areas emerge very clearly when we compare the roles assigned to public facilities in urban areas with those in rural areas. It was possible to construct facilities that serviced a small village or a limited geographical area. Farm families drew water for drinking and household use from nearby rivers or even from wells sunk down in their own yards, and they usually put their garbage and human waste to use on croplands. In cities, by contrast, people drank water that was delivered to them from the upper reaches of rivers, far distant from the urban center. They also had to rely on farmers from the surrounding hinterland to journey into the city to buy human waste for use as fertilizer, and they had to bury their dead in communal graveyards. To be blunt, people in cities were entirely dependent on others for everything from the food they ate to the water they drank, and even to the disposal of the consequent garbage and waste. In this sense, cities can be seen as settlements that lacked the most fundamental essentials necessary to support human habitation. Still, one should not think of early-modern cities just in a negative sense. Rather, the fact that city residents could rely on others for the basics of existence permitted them the freedom to create a wide variety of business enterprises, to establish a high level of handicraft technology, and to fashion an enduring legacy of artistic accomplishments.

Beyond setting the city in contrast to the village, the way urban facilities were brought into existence during the seventeenth century illuminates important dimensions of the political philosophy embraced by the governing authorities. Such was certainly the case when it came to providing drinking water for the people who lived in Japan's early-modern cities. Urban planning in Edo and the castle towns was based firmly on the feudalistic notion of rule by status. Consequently, the shogun in Edo and the daimyo lords in their regional cities established geographically distinct neighborhoods for warriors, merchants, and artisans. Typically, samurai residences clustered together around the castle, which was usually located at the strategic heart of the community. In the samurai portion of the city, each warrior family was assigned a residential plot whose dimensions and location depended on its standing within the samurai hierarchy and on the amount of its stipend or fief. The homes and shops of the more prosperous merchants lined the major thoroughfares that radiated like spokes from the castle center, while less affluent merchants and artisans lived on the back streets.[1]

Across Japan, daimyo laid out water supply systems that both respected and reinforced the basic referents of status and power. So did the shogun in Edo. Yet in the end, the shogun's water would come to belong to the people. In the eighteenth century, the Edokko—those proud, cocky plebeians of the downtown area—were extremely proud of Edo's supply of fresh water, and they boasted of it in earthy expressions that became clichés, such as "I was bathed in this water at the moment of my birth." But we can best understand the development of Edo's water supply system, and the ironic hollowness of the Edokko's bravado, by beginning with an overview of the castle towns.

THE CASTLE TOWNS

Open and Enclosed Systems

The organization of the water networks that flowed through castle towns can be divided roughly into two broad categories: open systems, in which canals, moats, trenches, and flumes carried the water exposed, on the surface of the earth; and enclosed systems, which employed stone-covered waterways, pipes, troughs, and culverts to deliver water to the urban popu-

1. Residential organization varied among cities, in accordance with the size of the community, topography, antecedent communities, and so forth. Still, not a few communities made the transition into the modern period from this basic pattern. Yamori Kazuhiko has mapped many castle towns in his *Toshizu no rekishi* (Kōdansha, 1974), and those communities are examined in depth in Ono Hitoshi, *Kinsei jōkamachi no kenkyū* (Shibundō, 1928); Nakabe Yoshiko, *Jōkamachi* (Yanagihara Shoten, 1978); and Toyoda Takeshi, *Nihon no hōken toshi* (Iwanami Shoten, 1952).

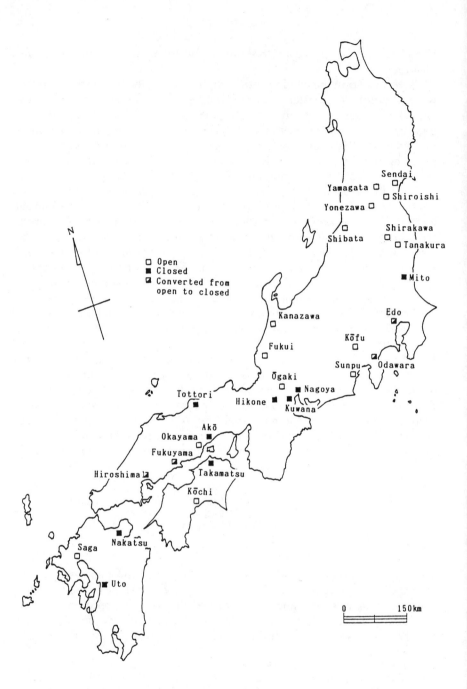

Distribution of open and closed water supply systems

lation.[2] The overwhelming majority of castle towns in eastern Japan relied on open networks, in contrast to western Japan, where nearly all daimyo built enclosed systems. Moreover, almost all of the castle towns in eastern Japan that employed open-type systems were located some distance inland from the ocean on fan-shaped alluvial cones and elevated plains, whereas virtually all of the castle towns in western Japan that used an enclosed system had grown up on deltas and flood plains adjacent to the sea. Thus cities in eastern Japan that constructed closed-type systems—such as Edo, Mito, and Kōfu—were exceptions to the general pattern.

Historians have long been aware that most daimyo at the end of the sixteenth and beginning of the seventeenth centuries built their castles on sites that permitted them to control transportation routes and thus to dominate economic activity in the surrounding region. In western Japan, lords of domains that fronted the Seto Inland Sea attached particular importance to exerting their authority over ocean shipping, so at the beginning of the early-modern period they tended to erect fortifications on the coast, where they could develop harbors. In eastern Japan, most daimyo favored building larger, more magnificent castles where cruder, rudimentary fortifications and small trading communities had existed since the medieval period. Many of those sites were inland from the ocean, but the lords were able to extend their control over river ports and to use river transportation to their own benefit.

Differences between eastern and western Japan can be seen as well in the manner in which topography influenced the placement of residential wards within the cities. In the late-medieval period, daimyo commonly chose the highest piece of ground available for their redoubt, and the altitude of the samurai and merchant housing areas in relation to the castle expressed the difference in status between the two groups, with samurai residential areas being physically above those of the merchants and artisans. This principle was clearly followed in many castle towns in eastern Japan which grew up on the sites of medieval settlements. Along the coast of the Seto Inland Sea, by contrast, it was common for daimyo to erect castles whose walls and ramparts actually sat on rock formations or on spits of land that jutted out into the ocean. These lords usually instructed their samurai followers to live near the castle, virtually at sea level. Consequently, the principle of associating eminent social status with a lofty geographical location was nullified, and it was the merchants that resided at higher elevations.

Differences of this sort between east and west had an influence on the planning of water supply networks. The open type of water supply system was prevalent in eastern Japan, where many castle-town lords put to use

2. For additional details see Hatano Jun, "Kaikyo no jōsui no kensetsu-ki to jōkamachi sekkei ni hatashita yakuwari—toshi shisetsu to shite no jōsui o tōshite mita jōkamachi sekkei hōhō no kenkyū 1," *Nihon kenchiku gakkai keikakukei ronbun hōkokushū* 397 (1989), pp. 100–111; and "Ankyo no jōsui no kensetsu-ki to jōkamachi seibi ni hatashita yakuwari—toshi shisetsu to shite no jōsui o tōshite mita jōkamachi sekkei hōhō no kenkyū 2," *Nihon kenchiku gakkai keikakukei ronbun hōkokushū* 400 (1989), pp. 105–14.

whatever facilities remained from earlier medieval settlements. Also, since most of those cities were located well above sea level on fan-shaped alluvial cones and elevated plains, they were assured of plentiful and dependable reserves of fresh water. Moreover, the chief source of that water usually was the runoff from nearby mountains, and there probably was little danger of contamination of the water supply even though the waterways were left uncovered. In the castle towns of western Japan, by way of contrast, the lord's engineering corps often laid clay pipes and wooden troughs underground, probably because those western cities were located on flat deltas. Thus the flow of water through these areas was sluggish, and there was a constant danger that ocean salt would pollute underground reservoirs of fresh water.

Castle Towns and the Provisioning of Water

Most of Japan's great early-modern castle towns came into being between the beginning of the 1580s and the end of the 1650s. Planning for the provisioning of water began at the same time, and most urban water supply systems were completed by the end of the seventeenth century.[3] When they designed the layout of their fortified enceintes, most daimyo thought of water as useful to their defenses. Thus many opted for open-type systems that would assure them of plentiful amounts of water to fill their castle moats. Of course, many daimyo also acted to furnish drinking water to the castle and to the residences of their samurai, but few concerned themselves at first about the needs of ordinary residents of the community. By the middle decades of the seventeenth century, however, most daimyo had come to realize the utility of drawing water from their interlocking system of rivers, canals, and moats to provision the merchant and artisan quarters of their cities. Their new consciousness may have been inspired in part by the concept of public authority, or *kōgi*, which compelled them to act benevolently toward their subjects; in part it surely derived from a fuller appreciation of the contributions that merchants and artisans made to the prosperity of their lord's domain. In any event, many daimyo in the middle and late seventeenth century extended their open-type water supply networks into the commoner sections of the castle towns.

There were some exceptions to this general chronological pattern, particularly in castle towns that were founded in the latter half of the Keichō period; that is, between roughly 1605 and 1615. In some locales there were insufficient supplies of water below ground which merchant or artisan families could reach easily by boring wells (as was the case at Yonezawa), and in those communities the ruling lords sometimes decided to include the merchant quarters within the coverage of the open, above-ground network of canals at the time of their construction. In other cases (Kōfu is an example), the daimyo was particularly anxious to attract to his city merchants and artisans who could provide him with essential goods and services, so

3. Hatano, "Kaikyo no jōsui" and "Ankyo no jōsui."

he tried to create a hospitable living environment for them at an early date.

In contrast to the open networks, the enclosed, underground systems had no military utility; their sole purpose was to provide water, indispensable to the daily lives of the city's residents. In some castle towns that were constructed at a comparatively late date, in the 1620s and even thereafter, the daimyo went to considerable expense to lay out an enclosed system at the same time that the castle town came into being. (Akō and Nakatsu are examples). In the 1610s and early 1620s, however, most enclosed systems generally were designed to supply water only to the castle complex, and their extension into the merchant and artisan neighborhoods had to await the middle decades of the seventeenth century.

From the 1620s enclosed systems were figuring more prominently in the water supply networks of many cities, even in the castle towns with the longest pedigrees. In many cases, daimyo extended existing enclosed systems as a way of encouraging settlement of low-lying areas (Mito, Nagoya). In other instances, daimyo converted open systems to the enclosed variety as they extended the water supply network into the commoner sections of their cities. Conversion generally took place where the open waterways interfered with transportation (at Fukuyama), or where water supplies had become contaminated as the population expanded. Only in a very few communities, however, were the extended enclosed systems actually capable of supplying the entire needs of the residents. Most enclosed systems were fairly simple and rudimentary, and peddlers continued to sell water from door to door (as at Kuwana), or the daimyo's engineers diverted additional water from nearby rivers (at Tottori), or individual families drew their water from wells that served a neighborhood or even an entire community (Takamatsu). This conversion of open to enclosed systems and their expansion into merchant neighborhoods marked a matched pair of turning points in the history of Japan's early-modern cities—the transition of castle towns first from military headquarters to residential communities that centered on the samurai and then finally into diverse and complexly structured centers of urban living that included increasingly significant merchant and artisan populations.

Water Supply Systems and Rule by Status

If we reconstruct the water supply networks found in castle towns throughout Japan and then examine them in relation to the layout of residential wards, whose spatial contours evolved in accordance with the dictates of the system of rule by status, three classifications become evident (see Figure 10.1).[4]

4. Hatano Jun, "Kaikyo no jōsui no haichi keikaku to jōkamachi no jūku settei—toshi shisetsu to shite no jōsui o tōshite mita jōkamachi sekkei hōhō no kenkyū 3," *Nihon kenchiku gakkai keikakukei ronbun hōkokushū* 408 (1990), pp. 17–29; and "Ankyo no jōsui no haichi keikaku to jōkamachi no jūku settei—toshi shisetsu to shite no jōsui o tōshite mita jōkamachi sekkei hōhō no kenkyū 4," *Nihon kenchiku gakkai keikakukei ronbun hōkokushū* 416 (1990), pp. 8–14.

FIGURE 10.1.
Water supply systems in three castle towns

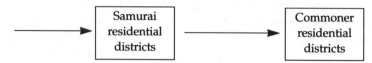

Kōfu
(Priority given to samurai households)

Yonezawa
(Distinct subsystems for samurai
and commoner residential districts)

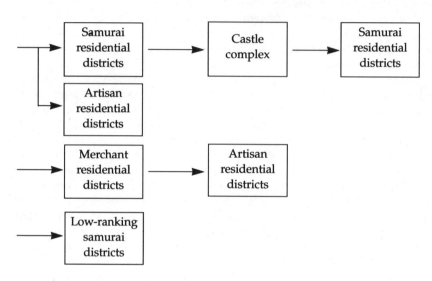

Fukui
(A combination of the two above types)

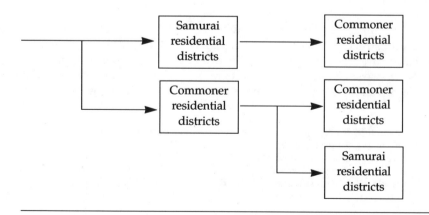

Type 1: A single water supply network served the entire city, but the samurai residential quarters were given priority in use of the water, and whatever water remained then was directed into the merchant and artisan neighborhoods. Among such cities were Sunpu (modern-day Shizuoka) and Fukui, which used open systems, and Kōfu, which changed from an open to an enclosed system during the early-modern era.

Type 2: Water was drawn from a single source but the supply network was divided into two or more distinct subsystems, one to serve samurai residential areas and another for merchant and artisan neighborhoods. The network might split either at the source itself or at the point where water from the source entered the castle town. Such cities include Yonezawa and Shirakawa, which employed open systems; Nakatsu and Takamatsu, which had enclosed systems; and Fukuyama, which converted from an open to an enclosed system.

Type 3: A single, integrated system served samurai and commoner neighborhoods equally, with neither having priority. Such cities include Sendai, Yamagata, and Saga (open systems) and Mito and Akō (enclosed).

Factors that influenced the design of any particular system included the topography of the city, the purpose for which the water was being used, and the chronology of the system's construction. Topological features were especially important. As we noted earlier, in those castle towns in eastern Japan which had existed as settlements from the medieval period and which had inherited the traditions of that earlier time, the lords were able to place the homes of persons of distinction at a higher altitude, thus ordering their early-modern cities in accordance with the concept of rule by status. In those cities, residential areas for samurai and commoners were clearly delineated, and it was possible to design a water supply network that served samurai homes first, and to direct the water supply into merchant and artisan neighborhoods (type 1) only after the samurai's needs had been satisfied. It was not physically possible to engineer this sort of system in the castle towns along the Seto Inland Sea, and there the relationships between elevation and status were reversed.

The period when any particular water supply system was constructed also had a lot to do with its design. A great many of the water supply systems that were laid out during the final decades of the sixteenth century or in the early seventeenth century were constructed principally to provide water to the moats that surrounded the castle or to the canals that functioned both as defensive moats and as sources of drinking water. Many of these cities designed systems to give priority to samurai households, as in type 1. Later, when lords became more concerned with providing drinking water to their communities rather than with constructing elaborate systems of defensive moats, the second type of system, with separate subsystems for samurai and merchant residential areas, became more prevalent.

Founding Edo: Eastern Tradition, Western Technology

As we have seen, the site selection for castles and the planning for water supply systems answered to very different principles in eastern and western

Japan. An anomaly, Edo confounded the general rules in several ways. The shogun's city was located in the east, of course, but it was situated on the ocean, and it was thus constructed on a site typical of the west. Moreover, in contrast to the lords of the other cities of the east, who depended on open-style water supply networks, Ieyasu favored enclosed waterways, just as did the daimyo of the west, whose castle towns, like Edo, were also located on low ground near the sea.

When Toyotomi Hideyoshi awarded the Tokugawa family a domain in the Kantō region in 1590, it would not have been surprising if Ieyasu had chosen one of two existing cities, Odawara or Kamakura, as the site for his new castle and town. Odawara had some advantages: it was the most prosperous city in eastern Japan, and it had been designed and built up as a sophisticated military bastion. Kamakura's allure derived from its historical prestige as the home of an earlier warrior shogunate from 1192 to 1333. Yet, in the end, Ieyasu forswore both of those possibilities in favor of Edo, and the reason was that he could build secure port facilities at the innermost reaches of Edo Bay.

When Tokugawa Ieyasu made his entry into Edo in 1590, eastern Japan economically and culturally still lagged far behind those regions in the west that surrounded the older cities of Kyoto and Osaka. Thus it is easy to speculate that what Ieyasu wished to do was to create for himself in eastern Japan a thriving economic realm similar to those in western Japan with which he was familiar. In Chapter 9 Hayashi Reiko details how the Tokugawa shoguns enacted various policies designed to make Edo the center of a national system of economic distribution. Many of those measures involved great expense and remarkable feats of engineering, as when the shogun's engineers diverted the Tone River, which originally emptied into Edo Bay, so that it flowed from the Ara River to the Pacific Ocean at Chōshi. This change permitted raw materials and goods from northeastern Japan to be sent more directly to Edo, without having to be shipped around the dangerous outer reaches of Bōsō peninsula.

But even if Ieyasu chose Edo as the site of his castle town in accordance with his notions of urbanism in western Japan, the ultimate spatial organization of Edo was influenced by the medieval traditions of eastern Japan. In the medieval period, military lords in the east often built their headquarters at that point on a conical, alluvial plain where a river emptied out from a mountain valley onto the tableland, or where the mountains swept down onto the tip of a tongue-shaped plateau that intruded between mountain and ocean and that constituted prime agricultural land. The basic reason for the lords' choices is straightforward: at such places they could erect military strongholds that overlooked and dominated the people and the agricultural resources of their domains.

This was not the sole reason, however, for those locations also permitted the lords to control water. By commanding the key topographical points on the landscape, the medieval lords were able to construct waterways that directed the flow of cold water down the steep slopes of nearby mountains into the moats that encircled their fortifications. Then, after the water had warmed and its volume had reached sufficient proportions, the lords released it for use in rice paddies in the villages surrounding their cities. Thus the moats were not just part of an encirclement of military defenses; they also constituted reservoirs of agricultural water, and by controlling the distribution of this crucial resource, the daimyo tightened domination over their domains.

These considerations weighed on Tokugawa Ieyasu as he pondered the location of his castle and the organization of his city. He erected his citadel on the tip of the plateau where the Musashi plain, which spread out to the west, dropped off toward Edo Bay to the east. Thus from his headquarters Ieyasu was able to control water and the rice-growing villages on the rich Kantō plain. He answered defense concerns by stationing his direct retainers, the bannermen (*hatamoto*) and the housemen (*gokenin*), in an arc around that portion of the perimeter of the city which fronted the plain. He instructed the daimyo to build their mansions to the east and south of the castle, and beyond those estates, again to the east and south, Ieyasu reclaimed land to use for roads and merchant quarters. In other words, in laying out Edo, he preserved in a comparatively full sense the relationships between place of residence, elevation, and the requirements of the status-based feudal order.

THE EDO WATER SUPPLY SYSTEM

In early Edo, much of the water used for daily needs came from the many small rivers and streams that emptied into Edo Bay and from the numerous natural springs and fountains that bubbled up out of the ground and provided good-quality drinking water. As the city's population continued to grow, however, such sources became inadequate, and the shogunate turned to designing a supply network that drew water from the major rivers that traversed the Kantō plain and entered Edo Bay. Although the documentary evidence is not conclusive, it seems likely that by the 1630s the so-called Koishikawa system of canals and ditches fed water to some neighborhoods in the northern section of the city, and a second rudimentary system, referred to as "Edo's water supply system" in contemporary documents, took its water from the Akasaka Tameike Pond.[5]

By mid-century the institutionalization of the system of alternate residence, which brought the daimyo and their retinues to the shogun's capital, together with the continued expansion of Edo's commoner population, necessitated more sophisticated means for provisioning water. This water was intended not only for drinking but for firefighting and craft production, and

5. This document is in the manuscript collection of the Tokyo Metropolitan Central Library (Tōkyō Toritsu Chūō Toshokan); it probably dates to the 1630s. Printed documentation concerning Edo's water supply can be found in Tōkyō-shi, ed., *Tōkyō shishikō: Jōsui-hen*, vol. 1 (Tōkyō Shiyakusho, 1919).

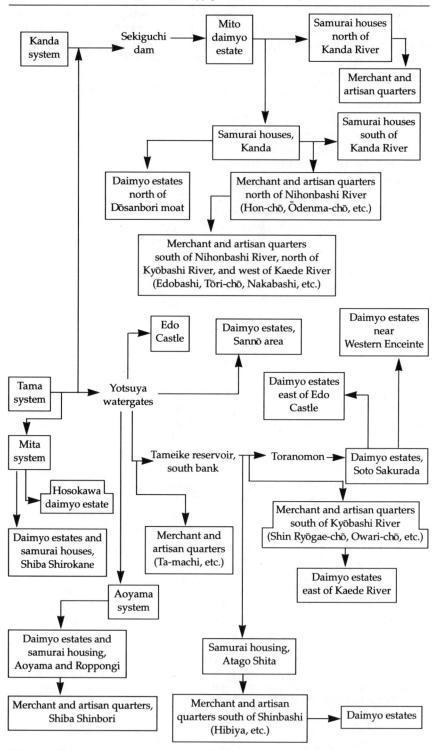

FIGURE 10.2.
Edo's water supply network circa 1690

to fill the ponds and streams that fed the gardens that adorned the shogun's castle and major daimyo estates. The shogun put his engineering corps to work, and by the end of the seventeenth century they had completed two major and four supplementary systems that carried water to every part of Edo.

Much of northern Edo received its water from the Kanda system. This was probably the first of the systems to come into operation, although we cannot be certain about the exact date. One document, the "Tenshō nikki" (Events of the Tenshō Period), bestows upon Ieyasu the foresight of appointing, even before he arrived in Edo, a certain Ōkubo (Monto) Tadayuki to construct a system of waterways that the overlord envisaged, but historians have long harbored doubts about the reliability of this source.[6] It seems more likely, when we take a closer look at the features of the Kanda system, that it constituted an expansion of the earlier Koishikawa system and was completed sometime during the middle decades of the seventeenth century. This judgment is made more certain by the appearance of the Kanda system on the first map to depict reliably Edo's complete water supply network, the "Jōkyō jōsuizu," a source that probably dates to the late 1660s (despite the inclusion in its title of the era name Jōkyō, 1684–1688).[7]

The Kanda system took its water from Inokashira Pond, some ten miles to the west of the city, and it ran aboveground until huge flumes downstream from a dam erected at Sekiguchi, on the northern fringe of Edo, diverted the water underground. Construction workers recently came across a section of these flumes as they excavated ground for the foundation of a new office building, and their gigantic proportions testify to the expense that the shogunate assumed in order to complete this urban improvement. The bottom of each section of the flume was made of wood into which grooves had been cut and then packed with hardened sand and clay to make a bottom as durable and impervious as armor. The sides consisted of large stones, hewed into rectangles and piled one on top of the other, and wide slabs of stone were placed across the top to complete the enclosure, which was so large that a person could easily walk upright inside it.[8] Only the main trunk line was this elaborate, however; the secondary branches were fashioned of hollowed-out logs or of planks joined together, while bamboo commonly was used for the small feeder tubes that led to the individual wells from which people pulled up buckets of water.

The Kanda system also embodied two features that would characterize each of Edo's water supply systems: it was laid out in a planned, methodical manner and it gave priority to the needs of the shogun and samurai, with the provisioning of merchant and artisan neighborhoods being only a secondary concern (see Figure 10.2). Thus, after disappearing underground downstream of the dam at Sekiguchi, the flumes, sluices, and troughs that made up the Kanda system directed water first to the extensive residential compound at Kōrakuen that belonged of the lord of Mito domain, a collat-

6. Itō Tasaburō, "Tenshō nikki to kana seiri," *Nihon rekishi* 196 (1964), pp. 2–13.
7. See the illustrations in Tōkyō-shi, *Tōkyō shishikō*.
8. Bunkyō-ku Kanda Jōsui Iseki Chōsadan, ed., *Kanda jōsui* (Bunkyō-ku, 1988).

eral line of the main Tokugawa family. From there the water ran into Edo
Castle and through daimyo neighborhoods. Only after the shogun and the
vast retinue who lived within the castle complex had taken their fill could
merchant and artisan families in northern Edo (along the Kanda River and
from Ryōgoku Bridge south to Kyōbashi) receive water from the pipes and
culverts that ran beneath their quarters.

The Tama system was even more extensive. The date of its completion is
no more certain than that of the Kanda network, but an interlacing set of
rivers and canals carried water from the Tama River as far as Toranomon by
1654, and the entire maze of waterways probably came into operation not
long thereafter. In its final form, the system began upstream on the Tama
River nearly twenty-five miles from Edo Castle. Secondary rivers and open
canals brought the water as far as Yotsuya, where it entered a complexly
structured set of underground passageways. Two main branches directed
water into the castle and to daimyo estates in the Sannō area, to the southwest of the castle. Another branch carried water through Toranomon and
then to numerous daimyo estates on the eastern flank of the castle walls, as
well as to the residences of bannermen and housemen at Atago Shita. Sub-
branches supplied the needs of the many densely populated merchant and
artisan neighborhoods south of Kyōbashi.

Two other systems, the Mita and Aoyama, took their water from the
Tama trunkline, and like the Kanda and Tama networks, they were inten-
tionally designed to give priority to the needs of the shogun and of Edo's
samurai residents. Commissioned in 1660, the Aoyama underground lines
began at the great watergates at Yotsuya and served daimyo estates and
samurai housing in Aoyama and Roppongi before traversing merchant and
artisan quarters at Shiba Shinbori. From 1664 the Mita system tapped into
the Tama network at the village of Shimo Kitazawa and flowed in parallel
channels, one leading to the estate of the eminent Hosokawa daimyo family,
which hailed from Higo in Kyūshū, the other to daimyo estates and samurai
households around Shiba Shirokane. Two additional systems had rather
short life spans. The Kameari system was established in 1659 to supply
water from Kawarazone Pond on the Ara River to the Honjo area, where the
shogunate was encouraging merchant and artisan families to settle in the
wake of the disastrous fires of 1657. But the Kameari system was plagued by
trouble from the very beginning: the quality of the water was extremely
poor; shortages were common in the dry seasons; and even slightly higher
than normal tides carried salt water into the lower portions of the system.
As a consequence, the shogunate stopped using the line as a source of
drinking water in 1683 and decommissioned the system in 1722. The Sen
River system, another offshoot of the Tama network, supplied water to
Hongō, Yushima, and Asakusa, in northern Edo, between 1696 and 1722.

WATER AND EDO'S COMMONERS

As long as the shogun and daimyo enjoyed priority in use of the water
delivered by the various systems that crisscrossed Edo, they also shouldered

the main responsibility for managing and maintaining the system. When the Tama system came on line, for instance, the shogunate appointed a "general commissioner" (*sōbugyō*), who supervised two men, Shōemon and Seiemon (identified in some documents as peasants, in others as merchants), who actually oversaw the day-to-day operation of the system. For their services Shōemon and Seiemon received salaries and the privilege of using the surname Tamagawa. Assisting these two men were patrols dispatched by the shogunate to make certain that farmers did not bathe in the waterways or let their draft animals get into the rivers and canals. Salaries, office expenses, and the cost of repairing the system came from levies imposed on the samurai and merchant households served by the Tama network, with the samurai bearing a disproportionately heavy burden.

This situation changed during the eighteenth century. Increasingly dissatisfied with the quality of water drawn from the Tama and Kanda systems, many daimyo and samurai families began to bore wells for fresh water, as did the shogunate itself. One after another the shogunate and many other heavy users disconnected themselves from the established network, and the water carried in the maze of waterways increasingly served just the needs of the ordinary people of Edo. Responding to this transition, the shogunate shifted administrative authority over the water system to the city elders in 1670 and then to the city magistrates in 1693. Perhaps a more sensitive barometer of change was the reallocation of the main burden of maintaining the systems away from the samurai and onto the merchant and artisan neighborhoods. Commoner property owners had to dig deeper into their own pockets to pay the salaries of the functionaries, such as Tamagawa Shōemon and Tamagawa Seiemon, who continued to oversee matters that affected the various systems as a whole, and merchants and artisans also had to maintain the branch and feeder lines that extended into their own neighborhoods. This was an onerous duty, requiring hundreds of days of labor each year to dredge the lines, which silted up easily and frequently became clogged with dead fish and other debris. At first neighborhoods organized their own work crews, but many people quickly tired of this unpleasant task and instead increased the levies collected for local needs (*machi nyūyō*) so that they could employ day laborers.

Many commoners resented the imposition of the extra duties and expenses, just as they reacted negatively to the delegation of new firefighting responsibilities in the early eighteenth century, as William W. Kelly explains in Chapter 13. But just as merchants and artisans came to incorporate the horrors, adventure, excitement, and rituals of firefighting into their own Edokko culture, making an honored virtue of what had been an unwelcomed burden, those same families become extremely proud of their water system, no matter how muddy or fouled it might became.

Probably the reason for this about-face was that the provisioning of water became complexly interwoven with the social life of the commoner neighborhoods. It is helpful to recall that two-story merchant houses lined the main streets of all those neighborhoods. The lots on which they sat were narrow but rather long. Behind the merchants' houses were rows of back-

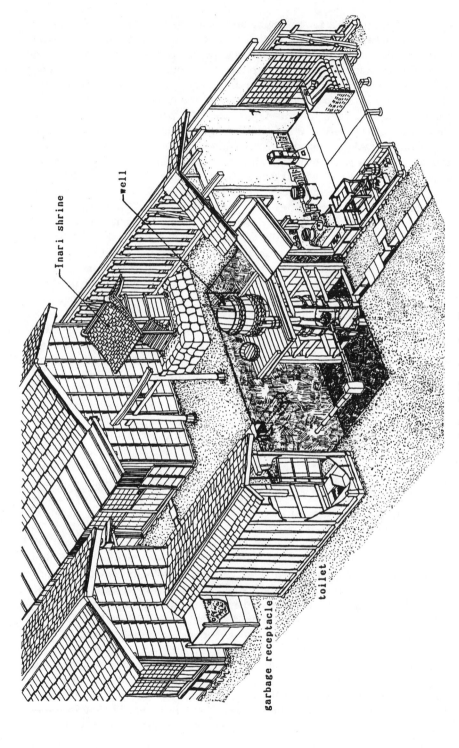

Inari shrine

well

garbage receptacle

toilet

A neighborhood well

court tenement houses, divided into tiny apartment-style accommodations, where the poorer artisans and day laborers lived. Most such apartments were entered through an unfloored kitchen area equipped with an earthen oven. Beyond lay a single room: "2 by 3s," they were called, since they typically accommodated 6 tatami mats (each approximately 3 feet wide by 6 feet long), although 4.5-mat-sized rooms were not uncommon. A communal latrine was located in a common area outside, together with a well for drawing drinking water from the water supply system and an area to dispose of garbage. This well constituted an important "community center" for the women of the row houses, who traded news and gossip as they fetched drinking water or washed clothes together.

The water supply system helped to shape social customs in other ways as well. The periodic drying out and cleaning of the well was a particularly important event, and all of the people who used the well would come together to carry out this task. It is easy to imagine that the same sort of communal spirit that historians have noted among persons who "ate rice out of the same pot" probably also joined together those who drank water from the same well. Thus the water supply fostered a spirit of communal responsibility, a sense of what historians in other contexts have termed *Gemeinschaft*. And the commoners of Edo came to celebrate their water supply network in pithy sayings ("I was bathed in this water at the moment of my birth") and in poetry:

Kane mo waku Edo e tennyo no mizu ga kuru,
Hanjōsa masu de hakatta mizu o nomu
Tamagawa o kakedoi ni tsukau hana no Edo.

Into Edo, where money too gushes forth, flows the water of the celestial maidens;
Oh, what a luxury! Drinking this water, measured out in serving boxes,
Carried along the flumes of the Tama River, a flower of Edo.

Concluding Remarks

Heretofore historians have supposed that the water supply networks constructed in the various castle towns across Japan were based on the design of the system that provisioned Edo. However, nearly the opposite seems to have been the case: the shogunate modeled its water supply network on daimyo precedents. It was quite common for a castle town's original water supply system to serve two purposes—to provide drinking water and to form a network of interlocking moats and canals for defensive purposes. In such a case open waterways were employed and water might be supplied only to samurai households. Later the system would be extended into merchant and artisan neighborhoods, and culverts would replace ditches. This change reflected a broader set of transformations that were coursing throughout all of society as castle towns evolved from military bastions into settlements where samurai could set up households and then into complex urban centers that welcomed merchants and artisans and became important points of economic consumption and commercial production.

In a similar pattern, the shogunate first designed and laid out a water supply system for Edo that gave priority to the needs of the shogun, the daimyo, and other samurai families. Only later, when the warrior estate could rely on water drawn from its own wells, was the great network converted into a facility that served the needs of Edo's commoners. As this development took place, the various systems could be managed and maintained successfully only if a communal consciousness emerged among the residents of the city. Contributing to the growth of that community spirit was the particular composition of commoner neighborhoods, as well as the ironic, almost perverse delight that the Edokko took in boasting about something that was in many ways repulsive. Yet, as untasty as that water may have been, it had become the water of the commoners, and its passage through the city carried in its flow another suggestion of Edo's transformation into a city of merchants and artisans. There is, of course, a very great difference between the early-modern period and today, when we drink water out of faucets with few worries about its purity. City folk may well be losing the old sense of communal solidarity as bureaucracies expand and become so impersonal that we are not even aware of them as we go about our daily affairs.

CULTURE

都市文化

11

Notorious Places

A Brief Excursion into the Narrative Topography of Early Edo

JURGIS ELISONAS

Sometime in the course of the year 1659, a certain scapegrace suddenly got religion (for the sake of worldly gain, it seems, not of otherworldly deliverance), took the name Rakuamida Butsu, and embarked on a mendicant pilgrimage that would eventually take him by way of Kumano to Edo. Because he was not a paying passenger, he was not given his choice of a landing place there but was unceremoniously put off the ship at Teppōzu. Down but not out, this "polished swindler" here turned himself into a holy man collecting funds toward the upkeep of the pigeons of the Kumano Shrines and headed for the places where those of his feather flocked together. It was to the entertainment quarters of the big city that his homing instinct unfailingly brought Rakuami. From Teppōzu he went straight to Kobiki-chō, "where Kidayū puts on his *jōruri* plays and where all sorts of other illusions and freaks are on show—is *that* for real?" Then, with no stops in between, he followed the crowd to Sakai-chō, that other grand concourse of lovers of the theater, admirers of young actors, and all the rest of that sort who are only too ready to be gulled by one means or another.

That is the entry to Edo chosen for his readers by Asai Ryōi (c. 1612?–1691) in his "Account of Famous Places along the Tōkaidō Highway," *Tōkaidō meishoki*.[1] Ryōi is the representative author of the *kanazōshi* genre, which comprehends most of the popular prose produced in Japan in the seventeenth century's first eight decades, and *Tōkaidō meishoki* (a book that was probably completed in 1660 and first published in 1661) is a good example of this vast if amorphous literary category, which is the basic matrix for a survey of the narrative topography of the early Tokugawa period's city. But these are not the only reasons why the passages that deal with the fake pilgrim's progress to the entertainment quarters of Edo will also serve as the

---

1. Asai Ryōi, *Tōkaidō meishoki*, ed. Asakura Haruhiko, 2 vols., Tōyō bunko 346 and 361 (Heibonsha, 1979), vol. 1, pp. 6–10.

introduction to this study. Those passages deserve to be traced with some
care. They lead to some curious discoveries.

How does Ryōi represent Edo's theatrical scene? He draws what certainly looks like a true-to-life picture of Sakai-chō, where "Ōzatsuma and
Kozatsuma have set up their mousetraps [nezumido] and are drumming up a
crowd" for their puppet shows and the "famous clown Kanzaburō" packs
them into the boxes of his "extravagant" playhouse to watch "female imper-
sonators [onnagata], as I think they're called . . . perform à la kabuki." The
author's observant eye notes that theatergoers must hunch, "with their
backs arched like a cat's," as they enter the "mousetrap," the purposely
small wicket where tickets to the performance are collected. Some of the
crowd are there for amusement; others are out looking for trouble, such as
the "lean fellow with a chin that juts out like a spear." Other details of
physiognomies, attitudes, and apparel complete this brief but vivid sketch
of a rough but exciting milieu, which is followed by a somewhat more
elaborate account of kabuki's character.[2]

Kabuki originated, we are told, in a type of dance performed by yūjo—
that is, female prostitutes—which eventually proved so popular that it engendered profligacy and contentiousness among the public; hence the authorities "put an end to this 'women's dance,' adjudged to be injurious to
the realm and ruinous to the people." From the standpoint of the defenders
of public morals, the next development of this protean genre was surely not
much better: kabuki reemerged in the form of a mime played by wakashu—in
other words, male prostitutes, for that, according to Asai Ryōi, is in essence
what these actors were.

Ryōi's view of wakashu is stern. Too many men, he says, "have had their
souls stolen . . . by the beautiful boys" and have even crippled their bodies
out of infatuation with these seductive youths. Particularly blameworthy are
Buddhist priests who raid "the offerings box for change to buy mousetrap
tickets" and dip into the building fund for bigger sums "to reward the
coquetry" of the boy actors. Eventually, having pawned their vestments and
the very furnishings of their altars to finance their folly, they are forced to
flee their temples and come to a sad end, destined to wander in delusion
through the next world as they did through this one. Examples of pederasty,
Ryōi does not neglect to point out, can be found among the most respectable
people: in China, one might cite the philosopher Ch'eng I-ch'uan or the poet
Su Shih, in Japan the prelate Shinga Sōjō, who addressed amatory verse to
no less a lover than Ariwara no Narihira. On the whole, however, the
practice cannot be said to foster exemplary behavior. Hence the authorities
determined to trim away kabuki's main attraction by "having the forelocks of
the wakashu lopped off, which gave them a most disagreeable appearance."
But the youths found ways to hide their bald spot, and so their popularity,
onstage and off, remained undiminished. Who could blame Rakuami, too,
for becoming infatuated? Rather than dally in Sakai-chō, however, he left it

2. Sakai-chō: ibid., pp. 10–16 (illus., pp. 12–14).

at the recitation of a verse that proclaimed "kabuki's lovely female imper-
sonators" to be "central to the universe," and kept going; there were sure to
be more sights to be seen on the town.

Rakuami's route to his next destination, Asakusa, is unclear. He could
not have gone from Sakai-chō (if that is what Ryōi means by *sore yori*, "from
there") to Reiganjima—the next place that is mentioned—without considerable backtracking; and the vague mentions of Ushijima Shinden, the Eitaijima Hachiman Shrine, and Fukagawa that follow are accompanied by no
intimation as to the complicated way thither.[3] To be sure, he was back on
solid ground soon enough in Asakusa, famous for its temple to Kannon. He
lingered a while on the banks of the Sumidagawa, an obligatory stop in
guidebooks to Edo because the river's associations with classical literature
distinguish it as a rare if not unique "poetic site" (*utamakura*) in that city. And
then he headed toward—where else?—a place where "the sound of the
samisen could be heard faintly. 'What place is that?' he asked someone, who
said: 'It is called San'ya. The courtesans' quarter [*keisei-machi*] known all
along as Yoshiwara was moved here in the Fifth Month of the year Meireki 3
[1657].' Fool that he was, Rakuami went to have a look around there."[4]

As was the case with Sakai-chō, Ryōi first sketches the contours of the
place in a few short but vivid sentences and then goes into the history of the
trade plied there. An exegesis of the term for courtesan—*keisei*, literally
"wrecker of castles"—with reference to Chinese poetry is accompanied by a
brief account of other names given the practitioners of that trade as it developed in various Japanese way stations and watering places. The reader is
then taken to the approaches of Yoshiwara proper, where "there are those
who cross the Bridge of Recklessness and those who turn back at the Bridge
of Reconsideration, saying, 'Oh, no. *That*'s not for me!' Within San'ya, however, there are twenty-nine *grandes dames* [i.e., prostitutes of the highest
class, *tayū*], and the ones of particular renown among them are, I believe,
called Takao, Karasaki, and Chitose." These are haughty beauties; others,
lower in rank but not necessarily in seductiveness, are more approachable;
there would appear to be a variety to suit all. The appeal of these enchant-
resses is described in lofty terms, but the cost is also reckoned high.

Sex, if Asai Ryōi can be believed, is an addiction. They who "fall prey to
this disease," which is transmitted by prostitutes, will stop at nothing, not
even robbing their parents, to feed their habit. Ryōi delivers a fearsome
broadside at these profligates: "In the end, such a one has earned the name
of Disloyal, Unfilial, Immoral. Having squandered all his patrimony, he has
nothing to call his own except one paper kimono and one hempen robe, and
is left all by his lonesome, disowned by his parents and separated from his
wife and his children. For a moment's passing pleasure, he has earned an
eternity of grief." The grim effect of this tirade is tempered by the reap-
pearance of Rakuami and the revelation that the rascal is lily-livered—he

3. Ibid., p. 27.
4. Yoshiwara: ibid., pp. 30–33 (illus., p. 32).

flees the scene of temptation, but not before delivering his own scattershot discharge in the form of a vulgar poem (*kyōka*):

keisei ni	lustful excess with
kuruisugureba	prostitutes will first cause your
ginkyo shite	silver to dry up;
hate wa hijini no	then you'll starve, if your spleen and
wazurai to naru	if your kidneys don't go first

What follows such a dramatic discussion of the thrills and dangers of visiting Yoshiwara can only be an anticlimax. Indeed, the rest of the tour of Edo offered by *Tōkaidō meishoki* appears perfunctory and trivial in comparison.

From Yoshiwara, Ryōi conducts his readers past Shinowazu Pond and its Benzaiten chapel to the great temple of the Tendai sect, Tōeizan Kan'eiji, noting its associations with Hieizan, which guards the "Devilgate" to the northeast of Kyoto. The tour continues to the Yushima Tenjin Shrine, reminiscent of the Kitano Tenmangū on Kyoto's northern outskirts, and goes on to the Kanda Myōjin Shrine. After a hurried visit to Edo Castle and a short introduction to its history, we are then rushed past the Sannō Gongen Shrine and Tameike Pond to Atagosan, yet another place that evokes rich associations with Kyoto. Then there remain only the Nishi Kubo Hachiman Shrine, the Jōdo sect's temple Zōjōji with the Tokugawa shogunal family's mausolea on the hillside behind it, and the Shiba Shinmei Shrine before we are at the Shibaguchi exit and "that's it for our tour of Edo."[5] Was there really nothing else to be seen or noted in that great city?

In order to get from the puppet and freak shows of Kobiki-chō to the Sakai-chō theater district, Rakuami—unless he purposely went out of his way—would have first had to go to Kyōbashi. He could have approached this intermediate destination along the east side of the canal known as Sanjikkenbori, crossing the canal by the Kinokuni Bridge; from there, Kyōbashi was only two or three blocks away. More probably, however, he would have crossed by the bridge known as Sanjikkenbashi or Kobikibashi, which was located close to the theaters. Then he would have walked through Owari-chō and Shin Ryōgae-chō, proceeding along the city's central artery to Kyōbashi and farther northward along the same main street to Nihonbashi. A turn east from this center of mercantile activity would have brought him shortly to the "Bridge of Reconsideration," Shianbashi, from which Sakai-chō was but another few blocks away. To be sure, had Rakuami deliberately chosen to use side streets, he might have avoided the axial avenue called Nihonbashi-dōri by some scholars and Chūō-dōri on maps of present-day Tokyo; indeed, he could have spurned Nihonbashi in favor of its near neighbor Edobashi, another popular concourse. One way or another, however, he would have traversed the commercial heart of Edo on his

5. "Edo no meguri wa kaku no gotoshi," p. 57; Shinowazu Pond-Kanda Myōjin, pp. 41–43 (illus., Tōshō Gongen Shrine in the precincts of Tōeizan, p. 42); Edo Castle-Shibaguchi, pp. 47–50 (illus., castle, pp. 48–49), all ibid.

way to Sakai-chō. Surely this sharper was acute enough to take in the great variety of activities that anyone but the most unobservant of visitors must have witnessed along these busy streets. About the manifold occupations and pursuits to be seen there, however, Asai Ryōi has not a word to say.[6]

If Rakuami went from Sakai-chō to Asakusa by land, then his most logical route was the other main street of the seventeenth-century city, often called Honchō-dōri. He would have passed many tradesmen's establishments on his way along that route through Tōri Hatago-chō, Tōri Abura-chō, and Yokoyama-chō to Asakusabashi; beyond that bridge, he would have continued along the extension of that same Honchō-dōri to Sensōji, the temple of Kannon in Asakusa. As noted above, how Rakuami got or was conveyed to that destination is unclear, and it may therefore be improper to criticize Ryōi for failing to mention the prosperous commercial quarters in that part of Edo. The fact remains, however, that were it not for one or two banal phrases which situate "shopkeepers' shelves" and "artisans' houses" in the general bustle of the city in the most cursory way[7]—the author complains in the same breath about the choking dust of the streets—one would be justified in concluding on the basis of *Tōkaidō meishoki* that contemporary Edo was a truly unique metropolis, one in which no commerce, save for prostitution and show business, was conducted.

Yoshiwara takes up fully a quarter of the account of the "famous places" of Edo that Asai Ryōi gives in this book before he calls an end to his tour around town. The theaters claim even more space than the brothels in his layout of the city: Sakai-chō by itself occupies almost a third of the total, and the sum becomes fully that when the paragraph dealing with Kobiki-chō is added. There are, in short, two centers of overwhelming attraction in the magnetic field that draws the author's attention. Little wonder that his representation of its appearance is distorted. What, at first sight, looks like a true-to-life picture fails to pass a closer inspection.

What sort of picture of Sakai-chō do we actually get in *Tōkaidō meishoki*? Except for the fact that Ōzatsuma, Kozatsuma, and Kanzaburō, the heads of troupes that were performing there at the time in question, are briefly mentioned by name, nothing at all is said here that is specific to Edo. Indeed, the

6. The sketches of the immediate area provided by Asakura Haruhiko in *Tōkaidō meishoki*, vol. 2, pp. 303 and 305, are based on a map of Edo first published in 1657.1 (just before the great Meireki fires) by the printing establishment of Taroemon in Nihonbashi. A reproduction of the entire map may be seen in Iida Ryūichi and Tawara Motoaki, *Edozu no rekishi* (Tsukiji Shokan, 1988), pl. 6. For a more comprehensive picture of the Edo traversed by Rakuami, also see the survey map produced in 1658 (directly after the Meireki fires) on the orders of the Tokugawa shogunate, ibid., pl. 7; and cf. the so-called Kanbun five-sheet map, prepared by Ochikochi Dōin and published in five installments between 1671 and 1673 by Kyōjiya Kahei in Nihonbashi, ibid., pl. 8. A nicely illustrated introduction to the notions of Nihonbashi-dōri and Honchō-dōri is found in Tamai Tetsuo, *Edo: Ushinawareta toshi kūkan o yomu*, Imēji riideingu sōsho (Heibonsha, 1986), pt. 1, pp. 15–76; the maps in pl. 3 and on pp. 21, 25, 30–31, 43, 59, 166, and 167 are of great help in efforts to understand the routes available to Rakuami through downtown Edo.

7. Asai, *Tōkaidō meishoki*, vol. 1, p. 57.

258   Jurgis Elisonas

scene presented before us could be played in the entertainment districts of
any big city—let us say Osaka or Kyoto. The author is obviously more
interested in being clever than in being accurate. Moreover, his aim is to
instruct rather than to inform; he is nothing if not censorious. Didacticism
may be endemic to the genus *kanazōshi*; even so, can a taxonomic imperative
excuse self-indulgence to the point of inaccuracy in a guidebook to "famous
places"? So eager is Ryōi to preach a sermon on the evil effects of prostitution that he appears to forget the way to the place where his "castle-
wrecking" hetaerae dwell. Or is there another reason why the reader, who is
first told that "the courtesans' quarter known all along as Yoshiwara" was
moved from another, unspecified location to San'ya some time previously,
must then be misdirected to Wazakurebashi and Shianbashi, the toponymic
"Bridge of Recklessness" and "Bridge of Reconsideration"—that is, to landmarks still remaining near that old, abandoned, and distant location in the
Nihonbashi district?[8] The answer is that Ryōi's account is a sham: his
Yoshiwara is just as counterfeit as his Sakai-chō is artificial. As far as the
prostitute quarter, too, is concerned, practically nothing in *Tōkaidō meishoki* is
specific to Edo. But if Ryōi's description of these "famous places" does not
really represent any part of Edo, then what is represented here?

The underlying image is that of Kyoto. The description is modeled on
Kyō warabe (A Child of Kyoto; 1658) by the physician and poet Nakagawa
Kiun (1636?–1705), the book that established the "account of famous places"
or *meishoki* as a distinct category within *kanazōshi*.[9] But this is not a simple
case of admiring emulation. A more questionable kind of imitative zeal
moved Asai Ryōi. In a word, he plagiarized.

The passages dealing with Sakai-chō are taken from *Kyō warabe*'s section
on Shijō Kawara, Kyoto's theater district. Not only is the general concept of
those passages clearly derived from Kiun, whose sequence of thought Ryōi
follows; as much as a third of their language is copied almost exactly. The
plagiarism is not so blatant in the passages dealing with Yoshiwara; less has
been borrowed verbatim. Still, it is obvious that what Ryōi purports to be a
picture of the "courtesans' quarter" of Edo is actually reproduced from a
design, drawn by Kiun, which depicts Shimabara, the *keisei-machi* of Kyoto.
The mention of three of Yoshiwara's *grandes dames* by name is the kind of
original touch that merely points up the copyist's pretense.

For anyone captivated by Ryōi's facile rhetoric, it will be a special disap-

8. There is some confusion regarding the identity of these bridges, as the one named
as Shianbashi in the map of 1657 was later called Aramehashi, and the one identified as
Wazakurebashi in the same map subsequently became known as Shianbashi; see the
detailed sketch ibid., vol. 2, p. 305. See also *Tōkyō shishikō: Kyōryō-hen*, vol. 1 (Kyoto: Rinsen
Shoten, 1973; rpt. of 1936 volume edited and published by Tōkyō Shiyakusho), pp. 119–23.
Cf. *Tōkaidō meishoki*, vol. 1, p. 33.

9. Nakagawa Kiun, *Kyō warabe* (Kyoto: Yamamori Rokubei, Meireki 4 [1658]), "Shijō
Kawara," fasc. 1, fols. 15–20 (illus., kabuki, fols. 20v–21); and "Keisei-machi," ibid., fasc.
2, fols. 23–26 (illus., Shimabara, fols. 26v–27). More accessible modern editions include the
one in Takemura Toshinori, ed., *Nihon meisho fūzoku zue*, vol. 7: *Kyōto no maki*, vol. 1
(Kadokawa Shoten, 1979), pp. 11–13 and 26–28 respectively.

pointment to discover that many if not most of his wittiest observations and nicest turns of phrase have been neatly lifted from Nakagawa Kiun. The theatergoer who arched his back in catlike fashion as he entered the "mousetrap" in Edo's Sakai-chō came straight from Shijō Kawara in Kyoto, as did the fellow with the chin that protruded like a spear. The priests of Edo were apparently no different from those of Kyoto, raiding the offerings box and dipping into the building fund with the same licentious abandon. Only the authorities who banned "women's kabuki" (for practically identical reasons, to be sure—it was adjudged "injurious to the realm and unhealthful for its subjects") were evidently not the same; in any event, Ryōi made sure that Kiun's reference to a prohibition issued by the *shoshidai*, an official specific to Kyoto, was kept from reappearing in the context of Edo, a city not under his jurisdiction. There is no need to multiply examples. Suffice it to say that even Ryōi's lament that too many men "have had their souls stolen" by the boy actors of Sakai-chō was purloined from the "Child of Kyoto."

Perhaps one also should reiterate that Ryōi's *femmes fatales* are on display in a milieu, supposedly Yoshiwara, which readers of *Kyō warabe* will find déjà vu. The bottom line of Ryōi's sermon on sexual addiction—"for a moment's passing pleasure, . . . an eternity of grief"—is carried over directly from the balance sheet drawn up by Kiun for Shimabara—"for a moment of bliss, a lifetime of sighs." Where Kiun concludes that "though a viper will disintegrate when charred black and pulverized," amatory vice cannot be made to vanish,[10] Ryōi observes that the addiction cannot be fully shaken until the afflicted person dies and his body is "burnt to white ash." The reader may well be justified in taking such verbal twists as evidence not of originality but rather of the reverse on Ryōi's part.

These passages of *Tōkaidō meishoki* are, however, not the most flagrant examples of a lack of originality in this author's treatment of Edo. Let us take a look at the chapter on Yoshiwara in *Edo meishoki*, the elaborate "Account of Famous Places in Edo" that Ryōi published in 1662. The reader who values verisimilitude in the description of the historical city but knows Asai Ryōi is apt to be more dismayed than surprised to discover that at least a third of this chapter has been pilfered word for word from *Naniwa monogatari* (1655), an early example of that warped literary species, the pornocritique (*yūjo hyōbanki*). That booklet has nothing to do with Edo or, for that matter, with Osaka, the city suggested by its title. Rather, it deals with Shimabara, the "pleasure quarter" of Kyoto.[11] The borrowed materials, needless to say, are

10. "Tatoi kuroyaki ni shitareba tote gohassō wa kiyuru tomo," in *Kyō warabe*, fasc. 2, fol. 26; *Nihon meisho fūzoku*, p. 28. There is more sting in Kiun's observation than may appear at first glance. *Gohassō* (written with the characters for "five," "eight," and "grass") was the name of a contemporary patent medicine, prepared from pulverized sun-dried viper, which was used to cure buboes. *Gohachi* ("five-eight"), however, is another name for "prostitute," possibly referring to a price of 40 *monme* for services rendered. Powdered viper (*mamushi no kuroyaki*) is still reputed to be an aphrodisiac.

11. See Asai Ryōi, *Edo meishoki*, ed. Asakura Haruhiko (Meicho Shuppan, 1976), pt. 7, no. 9, pp. 237–44 (illustration, pp. 242–43), on Yoshiwara. The portion from the middle of

adjusted by Ryōi to suit the framework of his account; but the stuff is merely trimmed, not transformed, and the "famous place" that he puts on view is amorphous, even if he calls it Yoshiwara. After the first few perfunctory sentences, which give minimal directions to the place and roughly sketch its layout, nothing that is specific to Edo will be found in this chapter. The author's purpose is to sermonize, and his subject is prostitution in general, not Yoshiwara in particular. The location of the dens of iniquity that he damns with his familiar arguments could be anywhere.

Edo meishoki is the oldest comprehensive guidebook devoted entirely to Edo, even if it was written by a Kyoto priest and published in Kyoto; the chapter on Yoshiwara has pride of place in the book as its concluding section. Hence Ryōi's unashamed borrowing from another work—and one, moreover, set in a different locale—raises some important issues. No doubt the standards of authorial honesty in seventeenth-century Japan were less stringent than today's (indeed, they were scarcely an issue at all, as many writers considered imitation the sincerest form of flattery), but there is no need to expatiate on that. Of far greater interest are the following two questions. If important segments could be transplanted at will and almost unchanged from the account of one city to the description of another, then what sort of image of the city prevailed in general? And what did the apparent interchangeability of the vital parts of cities mean for the literary image of seventeenth-century Edo in particular?

If the basis for judgment is to be *Kyō warabe* and works that follow the pattern it established, prominently including *Edo meishoki*, then it would appear that there existed at best an inchoate concept of conurbation in seventeenth-century Japan. The city was viewed in essence as a mosaic produced by a more or less accidental arrangement of "famous places" (*meisho*), with only the loosest connecting links between them. The definition of a place as "famous" and its inclusion in a catalogue of *meisho* depended on its political prominence, ritual status, or historical, poetical, and prurient associations. More mundane criteria, such as commercial importance, scarcely applied. Beauty did not by itself make a site noteworthy.

At its best, as in the case of *Kyō warabe*, the topographical *kanazōshi* comes close to achieving the kind of completeness that one might expect of a modern-day *Guide Michelin*: while being overtly instructional, it manages to entertain; the facts it chattily presents to the reader are intermingled with a lot of pleasant fiction; often wrong in the historical description of the places

---

p. 238 to the middle of p. 240 is cobbled together from three passages of *Naniwa monogatari* (n.p., Meireki 1 [1655]); cf. Ono Susumu, *Kinsei shoki: Yūjo hyōbanki-shū*, vol. 1: *Honbun-hen*, Kinsei bungei shiryō 9 (Koten Bunko, 1965), pp. 128–29, 132–34. Note that *yūjo hyōbanki* do not merely serve as guides to the "courtesans' quarter" but also offer critiques of good or bad performance on the prostitutes' part; these critiques are sometimes exceedingly nasty. It is not to the city of Naniwa—that is, Osaka—but rather to this critical element that the title *Naniwa monogatari* refers, alluding to the proverbial reeds (*ashi*, a homonym for "bad") of Naniwa Bay, which sometimes go under the name of bulrushes (*yoshi*, a homophone for "good").

one "must see," it is nonetheless a welcome companion to the foot-weary as also to those who merely visit the famous sites in spirit. In the case of the *kanazōshi*, there is the bonus of poetic diversion, as the account of each *meisho* typically includes the citation of "elegant" verse (*waka*) that may have been written by classical poets about the site and concludes with "inelegant" or "vulgar" verse (*kyōka*) composed by the author to encapsulate its most salient features. It is obvious that the author of any such guidebook to Edo started with a severe handicap vis-à-vis the writer about Kyoto: whereas the majority of the "famous places" that were the attributes of the old imperial city were in fact famous, many of them hallowed by centuries of poetic tradition, the new shogunal capital's *meisho* were largely spurious, most of them validated by no tradition whatever. As already noted, the Sumidagawa was Edo's only genuine "poetic site." (To be sure, the legend of Umewaka, a child carried away by slavers and buried on the bank of that river, also made "famous places" of Myōkisan and a few other sites supposedly associated with his and his mother's tragedy.)[12]

Nonetheless, *Edo meishoki* aims at the same sketchy sort of completeness that characterizes *Kyō warabe*. It begins by locating Edo in the province of Musashi and then starts the tour of the city with a view of the shogunal residence, Edo Castle (as *Kyō warabe* had begun with the imperial palace in Kyoto). The first part of the tour progresses past Nihonbashi to Tōeizan Kan'eiji in Ueno, continues to the Yushima and Myōjin shrines in Kanda, and then carries on via Yanaka, where the Shimizu Inari Shrine and three Buddhist temples are visited, to the shrine of Nanaomote no Myōjin in Nippori. Six other parts and a long catalogue of other Buddhist temples and Shinto shrines follow on the tour, but Asai Ryōi is drawn as though by an irresistible force to two places, on which he lavishes a disproportionate amount of attention. These are the theater district, evidently still a fatal attraction for the "ridiculous fools" who "have had their souls stolen . . . by the beautiful boys" of kabuki (the author seems to be as enamored of this phrase as those he chastises are of the *wakashu*),[13] and the prostitute quarter, where his "Account of Famous Places in Edo" concludes. There are eighty entries in all, each accompanied by an illustration. Only thirteen of these entries do not deal with places of worship. The rest are rehearsals of the foundation legends of religious shrines; some of these traditional stories are more authentic and less tedious than others. Throughout, the premise appears to be that description alone suffices and that there is no need to give directions. In short, the "famous places" are treated as individual sites and not as parts of an integrated urban complex. Often no logical progression from one to the next is apparent. The concluding Part Seven, in particular, is chaotic.

12. The Sumida River was established as an *utamakura* by its mention in the early tenth-century classic *Ise monogatari*, 9. The legend of Umewaka was made famous by the noh play *Sumidagawa*.

13. "Negi-chō jōruri," in *Edo meishoki*, pt. 4, no. 4, pp. 140–41 (illus., pp. 142–43); and "Negi-chō kabuki," ibid., no. 5, pp. 141, 144–47 (illus., pp. 148–49); quotation from p. 144.

As was the case with Ryōi's *Tōkaidō meishoki*, this account of Edo disappoints because the author neither shows a genuine interest in the life of the city he pretends to describe nor indicates an actual experience of its vital processes. The disappointment is all the greater because the coverage is so much wider than the previous book's. For all the seeming thoroughness and comprehensiveness of this *catalogue raisonné* of "famous places," however, it is clear that Ryōi could have written *Edo meishoki* without visiting a single one of them.[14]

Just how shallow *Edo meishoki* is at bottom is shown by its treatment of the city's theater district, located in Negi-chō. After noting that *jōruri*, kabuki, and various other arts and entertainments have been on show there "from way back," Ryōi allots almost half of the first of his two chapters on Negi-chō to a stock scene, depicting the hubbub on the street outside the theaters, where "rude types [*yakko*] out looking for trouble, dressed outlandishly and behaving idiotically . . . terrify the honest townsman, who blanches from fear; women and children burst into tears and flee." An equal amount of attention is given to the origins of the term *jōruri* in a legend associated with the medieval hero Minamoto no Yoshitsune. Then, after the bare mention of Ōzatsuma, Kozatsuma, and Tango no Jō, who are alleged to have "set up their mousetraps" and to be "drumming up a crowd" in Negi-chō, a pious *kyōka* concludes what was meant to be (or so one had been led to believe by the title, "Negi-chō jōruri") a discourse on puppet theaters in Edo.

The second chapter, titled "Negi-chō kabuki," is just as uninformative regarding its supposed topic. Ryōi begins by pointing out that he has already discussed the essential character of kabuki in *Tōkaidō meishoki* and that he knows it would be "idle prating" for him to rehearse what he said there; but, he admits, he cannot resist doing just that. Then he proceeds to rehash his account of kabuki's hoary origins and pours out again his tirade against beautiful boy actors, profligate priests, and the frightening price of pederasty. The reader is finally informed that as a consequence of a crash in the kabuki world of Kyoto, the celebrated Sennojō and several other actors are "going down," that is, heading east; and then the obligatory vulgar verse concludes a chapter in which not a word has been said about Negi-chō or about Edo.[15]

That the famous *onnagata* Tamagawa Sennojō did in fact "go down" from Kyoto to Edo, where he joined the troupe of Nakamura Kanzaburō sometime about the end of 1661 or early 1662, is known from the diary of Ma-

14. To be fair, one must point out that there is only one instance in *Edo meishoki* (pt. 3, no. 4, p. 97) where Ryōi claims or at least implies that he has visited one of the "famous places" he describes: the custodian of the Enmadō in Asakusa is criticized for his rudeness in failing to respond to a direct question.

15. The closest the narrative gets to Edo is Kamakura, where Minamoto no Yoshitsune's mistress, Shizuka Gozen, described by Ryōi as one of the original kabuki performers, is said to have danced and sung before Yoshitsune's implacable brother, the future shogun Yoritomo: ibid., pt. 4, no. 5, p. 144.

tsudaira Naonori, a daimyo who was a great aficionado of the stage, as well as from other sources.[16] But the theater district no longer was in Negi-chō when *Edo meishoki* was written. It was located in Sakai-chō, as any reader of *Tōkaidō meishoki*, the earlier of his two guidebooks by at least a year, could have reminded Asai Ryōi.

This slip of the pen on the part of an author considered authoritative by many has obviously done nothing to reduce the mists of uncertainty that cover extensive portions of the history of show business in seventeenth-century Edo, a field made difficult to work by the paucity of reliable source materials and the overabundance of myths. A good example of the latter is the old story that assigns the role of the founding father of kabuki in Edo to Nakamura Kanzaburō, said to have established his company of actors at Nakabashi in 1624; the fact that countless textbooks and reference works accept this legend does not authenticate it. The roots of kabuki go deeper than that in Edo. The Tokugawa shogunate in its early days used festive entertainments as displays of the regime's magnificence and as invocations of prosperity for the young city that was its capital. According to *Tōdaiki*—a chronicle that, to be sure, is not an unimpeachable source—the mother of all kabuki players, Okuni herself, put on a public show in Edo Castle in 1607.[17] Less than a decade later, in all likelihood, kabuki was being staged in Yoshiwara by prostitutes as a draw to Edo's newly founded "pleasure quarter" and an ancillary to its central industry.[18] Apparently little time passed before the authorities decided that while they could tolerate (or, rather, license and thereby legitimate) indulgence in one vice in a specified place, they were unprepared to countenance the coexistence of two in the identical location. Hence they banned kabuki from Yoshiwara, but their segregation policy had only a mixed success.

By 1617, Tokunaga Tanehisa's travel account tells us, *kyōgen odori* (dance pantomime interspersed with dialogue: that is, kabuki by another name)

16. Matsudaira Naonori notes under Manji 4.12.11 (30 January 1662) that "the famous *onnagata* Tamagawa Sennosuke [*sic*]," whom he describes as "so beautiful that the pen cannot express it," has "come down from the *kamigata*" and is among those actors who have joined forces with Kanzaburō: *Matsudaira Yamato no Kami nikki*, ed. Asakura Haruhiko, in Geinōshi Kenkyūkai, ed., *Nihon shomin bunka shiryō shūsei*, vol. 12 (San'ichi Shobō, 1977), p. 53. There is no doubt that Sennojō is meant.

17. "Kuni, the kabuki woman," is said to have done her famous dance in Edo on Keichō 12.2.20, at a location used the previous week for noh performances; that is, "between the Main and Western enceintes" of Edo Castle: *Tōdaiki*, in Hayakawa Junzaburō, ed., *Shiseki zassan*, vol. 2 (Kokusho Kankōkai, 1911), pp. 99–100.

18. On *yūjo* or "women's" kabuki in Yoshiwara circa 1615–1616, see Ogasawara Kyōko, "Edo shibai-machi no keisei," pt. 1: "Sōsōki no kōgyōchi," *Musashi Daigaku jinbun gakkai zasshi* 12:2 (1980), pp. 208–10. Ogasawara casts serious doubt on Yoshiwara's traditional foundation date, 1617, pointing out quite rightly that Tokunaga Tanehisa, who wrote his account of his travels from Kyūshū that very year, would scarcely have remarked that Yoshiwara had prospered "even more than it did before" (*Yoshiwara no machi koso nao mo sakaekere*) if it had been a brand-new establishment; see *Tokunaga Tanehisa kikō*, in Iwamoto Sashichi (pseud. Darumaya Kattōshi), *Zoku Enseki jisshu*, vol. 1, ed. Ichishima Kenkichi (Kokusho Kankōkai, 1908), p. 480.

Show business at Nakabashi. Source: Edo meishozu byōbu.
Courtesy of Idemitsu Bijutsukan.

and *jōruri* were flourishing in Nakabashi.[19] Reliable literary evidence regarding this entertainment district is next to nonexistent, but a remarkable pictorial representation partially fills in this lacuna in the sources: one of a magnificent pair of folding screens that depict the "famous places" of Edo about the year 1633 (*Edo meishozu byōbu*; now in the collection of the Idemitsu Museum of Art, Tokyo) shows that Nakabashi was then the haunt of a sizable and varied demimonde.[20]

The waterfront that extended to the south and west of the bridge called Nakabashi toward Shinbashi, Utagawabashi, and Shibaura—an area that corresponds roughly with what is now Yaesu, Kyōbashi, and the Ginza—stretches in all its tinsel glory across five of the screen's eight panels, commanding the viewer's fascinated attention. Flanked on the Shinbashi side by two public baths of anything but unimpeachable character and on the Nakabashi side by a complex of teahouses at least as dubious as the bagnios, this is a veritable "game center," jam-packed with amusements that range from target shooting and *nenbutsu odori*, a salvationist dance performed by mendicants of Rakuami's stamp, to such damnable pastimes as dallying with *wakashu*. At the center of the activities on this island of pleasures is a row of four theaters. The first from the right is presenting what is unquestionably "women's dance," otherwise known as *yūjo kabuki*; the second is a puppet theater; in the third, another performance of kabuki is taking place; and the fourth offers an acrobatic show.[21] Those who had a chance to take in Asai Ryōi's repeated sermons on the soul-captivating attraction exerted on Buddhist priests by boy actors will no doubt have noted that a teahouse attached to the second of the two kabuki theaters is crowded with priests, who apparently are waiting for the public spectacle to end so that terms for private diversion can be negotiated. To assume on that basis that *wakashu kabuki* is the attraction in this theater would, however, be to follow a false scent. That women players are on display here is clear from the presence of several young girls on the runway leading to the stage and in the dressing room. These children are *kamuro*, apprentices in training for the (world's oldest) profession.

The Idemitsu Screen projects a brilliant evocation of one of the major features of the early-modern metropolis, the presence of a permanent, public theatrical establishment. What is on view here is show business in the true sense, as opposed to that unsettled trade, a vocation adrift in a floating world, the medieval performing arts. To be sure, there also are plenty of

19. *Tokunaga Tanehisa kikō*, p. 480.

20. Excellent reproductions of this pair of eight-panel screens can be found in Suwa Haruo and Naitō Akira, eds., *Edozu byōbu* (Mainichi Shinbunsha, 1972), pls. 1-a (right screen), 1-b (left screen), 2–28 (details). Readers of the companion volume (*bekkan*) by Naitō, *Edo no toshi to kenchiku*, pp. 146–47, will be startled by his conclusion that the *terminus ad quem* of this work of art (Kan'ei 8 [1631].4.2, if one is to believe Naitō) antedates the *terminus a quo* (Kan'ei 10 [1633].1.24)!

21. See *Edozu byōbu*, pls. 24–25 (bagnios; left screen, panels 5–6), 18 (teahouses; panel 2), 20 (*yūjo kabuki*; panel 3), 21 (puppet theater; panel 4), 22 (second "women's kabuki" performance and acrobatic show; panels 4–5).

itinerant performers and street artists to be seen, not only on the fringes of Nakabashi but throughout the variegated public and festive space—streets, bridgeheads, shrines, and temples—that is illustrated in this work of art; but its focus is on that specific place where resident troupes perform.[22] The character of those troupes is of considerable interest: if we assume that the screen was not painted before 1633 (when the five-story pagoda of the Zōjōji, an edifice that dominates its leftmost panel, was built),[23] then the fact that it shows *yūjo* occupying the stage of two theaters in Edo's main entertainment district must surely call into question another commonly accepted story. If the shogunate had really prohibited *onna kabuki* and other theatrical performances by women in 1629—as is often asserted, even if no documentary evidence is extant—then, more than three years later, that interdiction was being ignored either blatantly by the *artistes* or indolently by the authorities. Indeed, women were appearing on the public stage in Edo as late as 1646, ten years or so after the entertainment district had been moved from Nakabashi to Negi-chō.[24]

When exactly that move occurred is not clear. Possibly it took place as late as 1641, in the train of a fire that devastated the Oke-chō quarter, immediately to the south of the bridge known as Nakabashi. More likely it was brought about by the completion of a project to expand the outer works of Edo Castle in 1635: having come thereby into too close proximity with that citadel of order and propriety, the raucous, thoroughly disreputable recreation center had to be cleared of its riffraff to make room for more honest folk, even if the new occupants were for the most part tradesmen. In any event, by 1642 not Nakabashi but another part of town was the place to go for high jinks and low comedy, as we learn from *Azuma monogatari*, a guide to the diversions available in Edo which was published (in Kyoto) that year. It was to Negi-chō that the "tunes of popular song, the samisen, and the flute" lured the anonymous narrator of this "Tale of the Eastland." His "heart stirred," he said, at the "sounds of the lute, the zither, and the drum" heard throughout the booming quarter, where the "grand kabuki of Mu-

22. On the various performance types that appear in the "Idemitsu Screen," see "Hakkyoku issō Edo meishozu byōbu ni miru Kan'ei shoki no shogeinō," the unpaginated chap. ii in the back matter of *Edozu byōbu*. On the entertainment quarter as one of the defining features of the early-modern city, see Hattori Yukio, "Toshi no naka no shibaimachi," *Ōi naru koya: Kinsei toshi no shukusai kūkan*, Sōsho: Engeki to misemono no bunkashi (Heibonsha, 1986), pp. 29–56.
23. *Edozu byōbu*, pl. 27 (left screen, panel 8).
24. The source of the commonly accepted date 1629 appears to be the early Meiji-period work by Sekine Shisei, *Gijō nenpyō*; see the edition by Kikuchi Akira and Hayashi Kyōhei, in Geinōshi Kenkyūkai, ed., *Nihon shomin bunka shiryō shūsei, bekkan* (San'ichi Shobō, 1978), p. 342. But the same work, p. 344, also cites a city magistrate's directive, dated Shōhō 2 (1645).10.23, which prohibits the employment of women dancers and the mixing of the sexes on the stage; the year after this directive, we are told ibid., a theater manager was arrested for defying the ban with productions that continued to use a mixed male-female cast. On these questions as well as on the date of the move from Nakabashi to Negi-chō, see Ogasawara Kyōko, "Negi-chō jidai no kōgyōkai," in *Engeki to sono shūhen*, special issue of *Kokugakuin zasshi* 85:11 (1984), pp. 125–27.

rayama Sakon, the puppets of Satsuma Takumi . . . and countless other amusements" competed for his custom.[25] Having given the theater district the once-over, he could then proceed to his true objective, which was nearby, and went on to probe the erogenous zone of Yoshiwara, the other one of the two *akusho*—"bad places"—where the action was in the big city.

A similar progress is seen in the following year's venture by the same Kyoto publisher, *Shikionron* (Debate on Color and Sound). This poetic travelogue (*michiyuki*), which traverses Edo in seven- and five-syllable meter (*shichigochō*), first trips lightly through Negi-chō—where "Sakon's kabuki troupe is / Dancing up a storm"—and then segues naturally into Yoshiwara.[26] What, in the meantime, had become of Nakabashi? If we can believe the nameless author of *Shikionron*, it had been transformed from an amusement to a shopping arcade, one where everything from fans and mirrors of the finest artisanship to medicines from South Barbary was on sale. (It would be wise, however, to take him with a grain of salt. Wordplay being the obvious guiding principle of the "exhaustive catalogue" he has compiled, his list of the trades pursued in Nakabashi is apt to be largely imaginary).[27]

The talent that congregated in Negi-chō after having been driven from Nakabashi would, however, not be vouchsafed a durable nesting place there. Instead, the fine-feathered flock of theatrical entrepreneurs, their troupes of *wakashu*, and their ménages of "kept children" (*kakae no kodomo*) were all chased off to Sakai-chō. Apparently, the eviction was ordered in the summer of 1651, shortly after Shogun Iemitsu's death.[28] If the event can indeed be referred to that year and season, the timing of the purge was surely no coincidence. The fact that the shogun was partial to young actors (even during his final illness, he repeatedly summoned Kanzaburō's and Hikosaku's troupes to entertain him in Edo Castle)[29] had no doubt discouraged his officialdom from taking concrete measures against *wakashu kabuki* until his demise. All the same, the theater and the boy players' entire extended milieu remained suspect in the shogunate's councils, being identi-

25. *Azuma monogatari*, in Asakura Haruhiko, ed., *Kanazōshi shūsei*, vol. 1 (Tōkyōdō, 1980), p. 337.

26. *Shikionron*, in Hanawa Hokiichi, ed., *Zoku gunsho ruijū*, vol. 33B, rev. Ōta Tōshirō (Zoku Gunsho Ruijū Kanseikai, 1928), *kan* 989, pp. 226–27. Note that this work is also known as *Azuma meguri*.

27. Ibid., p. 224. The fixed epithets that overload this "exhaustive catalogue" (*monozukushi*, a time-honored Japanese literary category) also strain one's credence in the author, whose fan shops are conventionally "auspicious" (*medetaki ōgiya*), mirror shops "unclouded" (*kumori kakaranu kagamiya*), dyed goods shops "fast fading" or "inconstant" (*utsuroiyasuki somemonoya*), and so forth.

28. Sekine, *Gijō nenpyō*, p. 345. The likelihood of a connection between Shogun Iemitsu's death, the move of the theaters from Negi-chō to Sakai-chō, and the crackdown on *wakashu* is discussed by Ogasawara in "Negi-chō jidai no kōgyōkai," p. 132.

29. Iemitsu was taken ill on Keian 4 (1651).1.6. Between that date and 4.20, when he died, he enjoyed kabuki performances on at least nine occasions. See Kokushi Taikei Kankōkai, ed., *Shintei zōho: Kokushi taikei*, vol. 40: Kuroita Katsumi, ed., *Tokugawa jikki*, vol. 3 (Yoshikawa Kōbunkan, 1964), pp. 681–88.

fied as a seedbed of profligacy or worse. When Iemitsu died, the *wakashu* lost
their all-powerful protector and a crackdown followed. First Negi-chō was
cleared of the theatrical crowd. Next the shogunate took a slash at *wakashu*
kabuki as such.

   Tokugawa jikki, the "Veritable Record" of the Tokugawa regime, notes
under the date Jōō 1 (1652).6.20 that the city magistrates had issued orders
for the "*kabu*[*ki*] boys of Sakai-chō to have their forelocks shaved off completely." Similar orders, it states, had been transmitted to Kyoto and Osaka.[30] With a stroke, the actors would be deprived of their beauty. The regime's official chronicle justifies this measure by the patent need to control
the social excesses that were being committed by daimyo and bannermen
"besotted" with the handsome youths. This verdict meant the end of
wakashu—"boys'"—kabuki; more significant, it brought on the beginning of
yarō—"men's"—kabuki, a critical stage in the maturation of kabuki as a
theatrical art.

   The shogunate's attempt to rob the actors of their attractiveness evidently did not cut to the bone, as indeed we have already learned from Asai
Ryōi. Their deformity, if a bald pate can be called that, did not prove to be
fatal; they found clever ways to disguise it. If truth be told, their side careers
as male prostitutes did not suffer. But it is also true that the kabuki theater
ceased being primarily a platform for the exhibition of their sexual allure.
Forced by the shogunate's decree to abandon its reliance on physical beauty,
the theater became more sophisticated. New forms of dramatic expression
were generated, and the complex typology of acting skills and specializations that was to characterize kabuki until the very recent past began to
develop.

   In short, the move to Sakai-chō marked an epoch in the history of the
kabuki theater. A decade after that move, as Ryōi's *Edo meishoki* was being
prepared for publication, Sakai-chō had evolved into the center of a variety
of theatrical entertainments, where at least two or even three kabuki troupes
as well as several *jōruri* and *sekkyō* theaters were packing them in.[31] Why,
then, did *Edo meishoki* nevertheless locate the theater district in Negi-chō?
Surely this was reprehensible carelessness on the part of Asai Ryōi. Was he
not sending his trusting readers on a fool's errand?

   While the guidebook's author certainly was inaccurate, the theater-loving
public did not run much risk of being misguided. In this case, Ryōi may be
absolved of gross culpability: as it happens, the two quarters, Negi-chō and

   30. Ibid., vol. 41: *Tokugawa jikki*, vol. 4 (1976), p. 53. It should be kept in mind, however,
that an entry in *Tokugawa jikki* is not proof positive of the authenticity of a date, or indeed of
the actuality of an event: "veritable" though it may be, it is not a contemporary record but a
chronicle compiled between 1809 and 1849.
   31. Two kabuki troupes were active in Sakai-chō from about 1660 to the autumn of
1661, when they were joined by a third; the number went back down to two in 1664; see
Ogasawara, "Edo shibai-machi no keisei," pt. 3: "Kanbun nenkan ni okeru Sakai-chō no
shoza," *Musashi Daigaku jinbun gakkai zasshi* 17:1 (1985), p. 20. A good picture of the variety
of entertainments on show there in the 1660s may be derived from *Matsudaira Yamato no*
Kami nikki; see p. 52 for the autumn of 1661.

Sakai-chō, were only one city block apart. Possibly Negi-chō was so closely identified in the popular mind with the notion of an entertainment center that its name continued to signify the theater district of Edo long after it had ceased to be one in actuality; after all, when we say "Broadway," we do not necessarily mean it as a strict reference to the street in New York which bears that name. In any event, the confusion continued well after Ryōi committed his mistake in *Edo meishoki*. "Sakai-chō, also called Negi-chō," is how the entertainment center is labeled in another work with a reputation for reliability, *Edo suzume* (The Edoite Sparrow), which appeared in 1677.[32]

Edo suzume is a genuine landmark in the narrative topography of the shogunal capital because it was the first guide to the city to be published in Edo itself. As one is invariably reminded by modern commentators, it was meant to be a "practical (*jitsuyōteki*)" vade mecum. Its preface points out, accurately enough, that the order maintained by the shogunate facilitated travel, which used to be hazardous; part of the peace dividend bestowed on the country by the Tokugawa shoguns, we are told, was that natives of the most distant province could come to see the sights of Edo as easily as stepping around the corner. The author, once a greenhorn himself, has acquired street wisdom by his more than ten years' experience of the city; he is willing to share that expertise, he declares, and to provide the visitor (who will, of course, at first lack a sense of direction; the streets are not straight, after all, but run in twists and turns) with a reliable guide to patrician residences and plebeian wards—*buke yashiki* and *minka no machi*—alike. In addition, the preface promises to include descriptions of the "temples, shrines, famous places, and historical sites" of Edo.[33]

In its own fashion, *Edo suzume* delivers what it promises. It is a comprehensive guide to the city, or rather, put more precisely, it gives a minute account of the urban agglomeration of Edo. Its predecessors, *kanazōshi* of the *meishoki* category, dealt in a more or less random sequence and a stereotypical fashion with a select group of "famous places" that remained isolated from one another. What makes *Edo suzume* a new kind of guidebook is that it covers the city's amalgam of neighborhoods in exhaustive detail and in a logical order. Hence this gazetteer is still as "practical" today for the historian who wants to get about the alleys of the seventeenth-century city as it must have been then for deliverymen, country samurai, and others who needed directions to the antechambers of the great or to the shop fronts of commoners. The detailed enumeration of the place names of Edo along with the names of at least the most aristocratic occupants of those places is one of the book's great virtues (the other is the splendid set of thirty-three illustrations by Hishikawa Moronobu). To be sure, the urge to enumerate everything is also one of the "Edoite Sparrow's" major weaknesses.

---

32. *Edo suzume* (Edo: Tsuruya Kiemon, Enpō 5 [1677]), fasc. 3, fol. 4. More accessible modern editions include the one in Nihon Zuihitsu Taisei Henshūbu, ed., *Nihon zuihitsu taisei*, 2d ser., vol. 10 (Yoshikawa Kōbunkan, 1974), p. 98.

33. *Edo suzume*, fasc. 1, fols. [1–2v]; and *Nihon zuihitsu taisei*, pp. 47–48.

Edo suzume begins with a brief summary of the city's location in Musashi
province and proceeds to Edo Castle, on which the author wastes little time,
summarizing its history in a few sentences and then listing the principal
events on the schedule of its recurrent yearly rituals. After that, he rushes
on at a breakneck pace through twelve volumes, which comprise (again,
"enumerate" would be the *mot juste*) some 520 daimyo residences, 2,870
residences of lesser lords, 850 Buddhist temples, 120 Shinto shrines, more
than 900 residential quarters of commoners, and 270 bridges, as we are told
at the end of the journey—"the distance of the route described herein being
above 2,880 *chō* or, since 36 *chō* make one *ri*, in excess of 80 *ri*"; that is, a bit
less than 200 miles or somewhat more than 300 kilometers.[34]

The reader is expected to follow along in a sequence of chapters that bear
such titles as "Inside the Area from Sakurada Gomon past Hibiya Gomon,
Yamashita Gomon, Onari Gomon to Tora no Gomon" and have a descriptive
content which is made up in the main of lists of daimyo residences, drawn
up in a truly desiccative style—"On the left are the outbuildings of Lord
Uesugi Kiheiji, as well as Lord Itakura Oki and Lord Hijikata Kawachi no
Kami; on the right side are Lord Nagai Ichi no Kami, Lord Honda Tsushima
no Kami, and Lord Matsudaira Aki no Kami,"[35] and so forth, until the
shogunate's *nomenklatura* (whose name was legion) has been itemized in
full. This sort of preoccupation with detail no doubt makes for a good
reference work, but not in the long run—more than 300 kilometers!—for a
discourse on the character of a city. Only the truly committed are likely to
persevere in such a marathon. Those who are not fully inured to the rigors
of scholarly inquiry must surely tire of all those lordly titles and designa-
tions, those distances, and those directions long before completing even one
of the twelve stages of the course. In no time at all, even the most dedicated
seeker after minutiae develops a thirst for digressive passages, as if they
were verdant oases in some vast and rock-strewn labyrinth, a dreary monot-
ony of street names, bridge names, daimyo names through which one is
condemned to trudge until he drops from weariness.

To attempt exhaustiveness is to risk exhaustion; enumeration is not the
same as description; detail may possibly delight the historian but is sure to
lose the ordinary reader; and mass does not necessarily equal energy in the
composition of a book—these are some of the lessons taught us by *Edo
suzume*. In some reference works, the book's unknown author is called Chikayuki Tōmichi.[36] If this was indeed his pseudonym, he bore it appro-

34. *Edo suzume*, fasc. 12, fol. 9rv; and *Nihon zuihitsu taisei*, p. 283.

35. *Edo suzume*, fasc. 1, fol. 13v; and *Nihon zuihitsu taisei*, p. 65.

36. The entries under "Edo suzume" in *Kokusho sōmokuroku*, vol. 1 (Iwanami Shoten,
1963), p. 473, and in *Kokushi daijiten*, vol. 2 (Yoshikawa Kōbunkan, 1980), p. 323, both
attribute authorship to Chikayuki Tōmichi. Nevertheless, the name and the identity of the
author of this book remain mysteries. In his classic bibliography of the early Edo period's
narrative topography, first published in 1916 and again in a revised edition in 1933, Wada
Mankichi ascribed both the illustrations and the text to Hishikawa Moronobu. In the
"newly revised and expanded" edition of that bibliography, Asakura Haruhiko states that

priately, although its meaning is ambiguous. Should it be translated as "Shortcuts to a Long Road" or "Detours to a Short Trip"? The latter will no doubt be the choice of many of the readers whom this author takes on a circular journey through a maze, making them wonder if there is no end, no focus, and no pattern to the urban mosaic he attempts to circumscribe. This book is so crowded with patrician residences and plebeian wards that it has no room for the question "What is a city?"

Should an answer nevertheless be expected from the author of *Edo suzume*? For all his encyclopedic coverage of Edo, it is apparent that Chikayuki Tōmichi was no *encyclopédiste* of the well-known genus whose *métier* was just definitions. He lacked the sensibility of, for instance, the chevalier de Jaucourt, who viewed the city as a construct that ideally conforms to a rational order and possesses an aesthetic function as well as a public character.[37] To be sure, it may be unfair to blame a seventeenth-century Japanese topographer for failing to share the ideals of the *gens de lettres* of eighteenth-century France, Edo for failing to be Paris, or (for that matter) the reality of seventeenth- and eighteenth-century cities for failing to reflect the utopian vision of Louis, the chevalier de Jaucourt. Still, one wishes that Chikayuki Tōmichi had taken the time to contemplate what he was observing and recording. Insofar as he was concerned, what in the final analysis was the city? An indeterminate multiplicity, nothing more.

The sought-after narrative oases do, of course, exist amidst all the enumeration in *Edo suzume*. The "Edoite Sparrow" dutifully if all too briefly stops at the conventional "famous" places, such as the theater district of the time. In the chapter titled "Negi-chō: On Jōruri as Well as Kabuki,"[38] visitors to Sakai-chō—"also called Negi-chō"—are presented with a compendious disquisition on the origins of *jōruri*, the character of kabuki, the connections between the world of the theater and the demimonde of prostitution, and the reasons why the authorities had to step in. What value one attributes to such expository passages, however, depends on the sequence in which one has read *Edo suzume* and other guides to Edo. The fact is that the oases, too, are arid. To lead us to them, Chikayuki took a shortcut. He followed none other than Asai Ryōi.

---

a variant copy of the first (1677) printing of *Edo suzume* specifies Chikayuki Tōmichi as the author; Asakura notes, however, that he has not seen that copy, which is attributed to the Kaen Bunko collection. See Wada Mankichi, supp. Asakura Haruhiko, *Shintei zōho: Kohan chishi kaidai* (Kokusho Kankōkai, 1974), p. 178 and supp. p. 15, respectively. Only the illustrator, Hishikawa Kichibei (Moronobu), is identified in the Kyoto University Library copy that I used.

37. Louis, chevalier de Jaucourt, "Ville," in *Encyclopédie, ou Dictionnaire raisonné des sciences, des arts et des métiers, par une société des gens de lettres*, vol. 17 (Neufchatel: Samuel Faulche, 1765), p. 277. Jaucourt gives exact prescriptions "pour qu'une ville soit belle," and invokes the classical authority of Vitruvius to make the point that in laying out a city, one should pay due regard "à l'utilité & à la commodité du public."

38. *Edo suzume*, fasc. 3, fols. 4–6v (illus., fols. 4v–5); and *Nihon zuihitsu taisei*, pp. 98–100 (illus., pp. 96–97). Though the supertitle of the narrative refers to Negi-chō, the accompanying illustration is clearly labeled "Sakai-chō."

What the "Edoite Sparrow" has to say about the origins of *jōruri*, which it traces back to the liaison between a lady of that name and Minamoto no Yoshitsune, is a barely disguised copy of Ryōi's treatment of the same topic in *Edo meishoki*; the most that can be said in the author's defense here is that he has brought the list of the master performers of *jōruri* and *sekkyō* in Sakai-chō up to date. Much the same is true of *Edo suzume*'s account of kabuki. Apart from the news that Ichimura Takenojō had established himself alongside Nakamura Kanzaburō as the leading kabuki impresario in this theater district, everything has been borrowed freely from Ryōi and trimmed to suit the inclinations of Chikayuki—everything, down to the phrase about the benighted whose "souls were stolen" by the young actors.

One who progresses thus through the narrative oases of *Edo suzume* after having traversed Ryōi's "Famous Places in Edo" does so with a growing sense of familiarity, as the major landmarks reappear one after another in an easily recognizable form, even if their contours have been reshaped or reduced. It becomes increasingly difficult to avoid the conclusion that in Chikayuki Tōmichi's Edo, every descriptive passage from Meguro Fudō to Mejiro Fudō has been recycled from Asai Ryōi's city.[39] Indeed, Chikayuki was indebted to Ryōi not only for his narrative fuel but in an even more fundamental way: the general concept of his city directory and, for that matter, the very title of his book were derived from *Kyō suzume* (The Kyotoite Sparrow), that prototype of the Edo period's "practical" gazetteers which Ryōi published in 1665.[40] In view of Asai Ryōi's own penchant for unacknowledged borrowing from other authors, would it be too harsh to call *Edo suzume* the secondary stage of plagiarism in the narrative topography of Edo? And should one perhaps look elsewhere for yet another, a more advanced stage?

Let us try "A Chat about Edo with One Who'd Settled There but Is Going Home" (*Kokyōgaeri no Edo-banashi*), a guidebook by an anonymous author that appeared in the summer of 1687. A quick check of the theater district reveals that the place is haunted by the usual suspects, men who "have had their souls stolen" by the "beautiful boys" of kabuki. Prominent among them are high ecclesiastical dignitaries—which is a shame, because their infatuation with the actors is an obvious impediment to their "observance of the service for each day and to Zen meditation," but perhaps not unnatural, because consorting with female prostitutes "makes one conspicuous," so

39. There are just enough substantially different treatments of the same topics to make it impossible to allege that *every one* of the descriptions of "temples, shrines, famous places, and historical sites" promised in the preface to *Edo suzume* has been copied. Examples to the contrary are Atagosan (*Edo meishoki*, pt. 7, no. 8, pp. 235–37; *Edo suzume*, fasc. 4, fol. 9r–v [illus., fol. 10]; *Nihon zuihitsu taisei*, pp. 122–24), and Kanda no Myōjin (*Edo meishoki*, pt. 1, no. 10, pp. 33–37; *Edo suzume*, fasc. 9, fols. 5v–6 [illus., f. 3]; *Nihon zuihitsu taisei*, pp. 203–5).

40. Asai Ryōi, *Kyō suzume*, in Hayakawa Junzaburō, ed., *Kinsei bungei sōsho*, vol. 1 (Kokusho Kankōkai, 1910), pp. 399–483. Though this book is not chatty in the manner of guidebooks of the *kanazōshi* variety, sticking fairly close to the ground rather than striving for airy belletristic effects, its general character is nevertheless far more literary than *Edo suzume*'s.

"sex with women is not a Way that priests ought to pursue." In any event, "the love of beautiful boys" has had a long history in India, China, and Japan; the most distinguished personages, including Mañjuśrī, Ch'eng I-ch'uan, Su Shih, Shinga Sōjō, and Ariwara no Narihira, have been among its devotees. Hence the practice will no doubt continue, even if its price is high and its result at times disastrous: it's but an easy step from prelate to mendicant (*gannin bōzu*) for those who dip into the poor box to cover their excesses.[41]

These are the telltale signals of a travesty. It is a purloined tale that the returnee is spinning to the neighbors who have gathered to bid him farewell on the eve of his departure from Edo. They might just as well be listening to Asai Ryōi preach one of his threadbare sermons. Even so, the account of the theater district is one of the more original parts of *Edo-banashi*. The chapter on *jōruri*, in particular, contains much of interest, although two-thirds of its substance are made up of legendary material that has nothing to do with Edo (the bulky centerpiece is a scene set at the court of Toyotomi Hideyoshi, which would locate it either in Osaka or in Kyoto, or possibly Fushimi). The author shows himself to be au courant with the state of the puppet theater in Sakai-chō, commenting on the contemporary rage for the bravura plays of the "Kinpira jōruri" cycle and reporting such recent intelligence as the news of the demise of their creator, the playwright Oka Seibyōe, if only for the sake of a truly lamentable pun on the manner of his passing—death from disease, "Oka Seibyōshi shite."[42]

The account of Yoshiwara, too, reflects some of the latest knowledge, in pornotypology if nothing else: the *sancha*, a new, low grade of prostitute, is introduced here to the reading public, and there are some other touches that would appear to be more appropriate to a *yūjo hyōbanki* than to the more upright kind of *kanazōshi*. (What some of the more prurient-minded might savor as the pièce de résistance of this chapter is a perfectly filthy bit of chinoiserie on one of the physical attributes of the lovely Yoshino—a prostitute of Kyoto, not of Edo, it will be noted.) As a whole, however, this vicarious tour of the brothels proves quite insipid; too much warmed-over fare is dished up by the author. In fact, the pith of his discourse on the fatal allure of prostitution is a light paraphrase of Asai Ryōi's lecture on the same topic in *Edo meishoki*. Since the essential part of that lecture had in turn been pilfered from another writer's critique of the "pleasure quarter" of Kyoto, as

41. See *Kokyōgaeri no Edo-banashi* (facsimile of the original published in Jōkyō 4 [1687] by Yamashita Hikohei, Sumidoriya Jinbei, and Kagiya Heiemon in Edo), in Yokoyama Shigeru, gen. ed., *Kinsei bungaku shiryō ruijū: Koban chishi-hen*, vol. 10 (Benseisha, 1980), pt. 6A, no. 3 ("Kyōgen-zukushi"), pp. 316, 318–26 (illus., pp. 308–9); or the same text in *Zōho Edo-banashi*, a variant edition published in Genroku 7 (1694), in Hayakawa, *Kinsei bungei sōsho*, vol. 1, pp. 275–78. Cf. Asai Ryōi, *Edo meishoki*, pt. 4, no. 5 ("Negi-chō kabuki"), pp. 141–47. Approximately one-quarter of the wording is identical; to be sure, the tone is quite different, as Ryōi is far more censorious than the anonymous author of *Edo-banashi*. Also cf. Ryōi's *Tōkaidō meishoki*, vol. 1, pp. 11 and 15, on the history of pederasty.

42. "Sakai-chō jōruri no hajimari, narabi ni Hōraiji," *Kokyōgaeri*, pt. 6A, no. 2, pp. 305–7, 310–17; *Zōho Edo-banashi*, pp. 271–75.

we have seen, what measure of originality was left in this portion of "A Chat about Edo"?[43] If the degree of creative imagination is to be the standard of judgment, then the returnee certainly had reason not only to pull up stakes but also to choose anonymity. On first sight, his tale appears doubly derivative. A detailed inspection reveals something even more curious.

Kokyōgaeri no Edo-banashi is divided into six parts (originally published in eight fascicles) and a total of one hundred chapters; there are thirty-eight illustrations. Part One begins inauspiciously: Chapter 1, "The Antiquity of Musashi Province," incorporates two-thirds of the corresponding item in *Edo meishoki* almost verbatim. Chapter 2 enumerates 472 residences of daimyo and lesser lords grouped about Edo Castle. (These establishments are merely listed according to the names of their occupants; to look for any sort of comment regarding the significance of the use of this central urban space for the mansions of the ruling class would be far too much to expect of the author.) Chapter 3 is a brief account of the historical background of Edo Castle; one half is copied from its equivalent in *Edo meishoki*. The following entry, a list of the gates in the castle's main enclosure and its outer works, is new.

The book's only substantial claim to originality rests, however, on the next four chapters of Part One, which run through the merchant quarters "North of Nihonbashi," "To the South of Nihonbashi, as far as Kyōbashi,"[44] "From Kyōbashi to Shinbashi," and "South of Shinbashi to Shinagawa." The course, metered in *shichigochō*, is not at all uninteresting, and the author pursues it with a good deal of ingenuity, stopping here and there to comment on a trade that is plied or a special product that is found in a particular part of town. But the seven-and-five beat arouses the same doubt that it awakened in the case of *Shikionron*: is this the description of a real place, or is the author merely doing his best to be clever? At times his doggerel is mildly amusing, if a bit simple, as in "Got too used to the good life / On Easy Street" (*Sumiyoshi-chō ni / suminarete*), or even "What a great joy to couple / On Defloration Street" (*musubu mo ureshi / Mizuage-chō*).[45] At other times the effect is labored. Whatever its literary merit, such onomastic wordplay clearly was not the most felicitous technique to use in the definition of an urban landscape. On seeing a place described stereotypically as "A bit of a climb is / Mountain Fastness Street" (*noboru mo takaki / Yamashiro-chō*), the reader must surely wonder whether any slope to speak of was to be found there at all.[46]

After Part One, all goes downhill for the author of *Edo-banashi*, as the

43. "Yoshiwara Keisei-machi," *Kokyōgaeri*, pt. 6A, no. 1, pp. 295–305; *Zōho Edo-banashi*, pp. 268–71. For the pilfered passage, see pp. 301–3 and 270–71, respectively; and cf. *Edo meishoki*, pt. 7, no. 9, pp. 238–40. The more distant provenance is *Naniwa monogatari*; see n. 11 above.

44. This title is something of a misnomer, as the contents include an account of distances to various places on the periphery of Edo along roads that radiate from Nihonbashi in all directions: *Kokyōgaeri*, pt. 1, no. 6, pp. 36–39; *Zōho Edo-banashi*, pp. 190–91.

45. Quotations from *Kokyōgaeri*, pt. 1, no. 5, p. 36, and no. 7, p. 40; *Zōho Edo-banashi*, pp. 190, 191.

46. *Kokyōgaeri*, pt. 1, no. 7, p. 40; *Zōho Edo-banashi*, p. 192.

fleeting impulse to try being original deserts him and he starts copying wholesale. Any attempt to demonstrate his larcenous tendencies comprehensively is apt to founder immediately upon launching because of the overly great weight of the evidence. Hence only a few exhibits, selected at random, will be introduced.

The first is the narrative description of a group of "famous places" located in the Yanaka district, which are approached in Part Two of *Edo-banashi* via the closest possible reading of Asai Ryōi.[47] The tour of the district begins at the Shimizu Inari Shrine, expediently described in *Edo meishoki* with references to a legend that associates the Buddhist patriarch Kōbō Daishi (a Heian-period figure) with its foundation and to a verse from the *Senzaishū* (a twelfth-century poetic collection) that apotheosizes Mount Inari, on the outskirts of Kyoto. This treatment is remote from the subject, yet it is not only reproduced in *Edo-banashi* almost exactly but also amplified with a gloss on the deity Inari Daimyōjin that links the shrine's identity even more closely with Kyoto. Contrastingly, *Edo-banashi* abbreviates Ryōi's text in the case of the Nichirenist temple Hōonji, dropping some of his Buddhist jargon from what would otherwise be a faithful copy of *Edo meishoki*. The account that Ryōi gives of the Yanaka nunnery Zenkōji is the legend of a far better-known temple with the identical name, Zenkōji in the distant province of Shinano; he explicitly disclaims any knowledge of when or why the Yanaka convent was founded. *Edo-banashi* repeats that account (complete with the disclaimer), adding some embellishments. The final stop on the tour of Yanaka is Kan'ōji. Ryōi's discussion of this temple consists in the main of an exegesis of the Buddhist term *kan'ō*, "response evoked by faith," and *Edo-banashi* copies his text almost exactly, merely tacking on a list of the various halls of the temple.

One of the two segments of Part Five of *Edo-banashi*, which surveys the "famous places" in the Asakusa area, is the next exhibit.[48] The first item, "Asakusa no Enmadō," is a precise copy of one-third of the corresponding piece in *Edo meishoki*; as if to make up for the truncation, a list of various Buddhas and kings of the underworld associated with this temple is appended. The account of the Dairokuten Shrine is an abbreviated but very close copy of *Edo meishoki*, as is that of Saifukuji, a temple of the Pure Land sect. The first paragraph of *Edo meishoki*'s chapter on Monjuin is retained practically intact, the rest is dropped. The account of Komakatadō is subjected to cutting and pasting. The chapter on Asakusa's central concourse,

47. *Kokyōgaeri*, pt. 2, nos. 9–12, pp. 80–88, 90–91; *Zōho Edo-banashi*, pp. 205–8. Cf. *Edo meishoki*, pt. 1, nos. 11–14 (identical sequence), pp. 37–46.

48. *Kokyōgaeri*, pt. 5A, pp. 221–60 (I treat all the entries in this segment, nos. 1–12, seriatim); *Zōho Edo-banashi*, pp. 247–59. Cf. *Edo meishoki*: "Enmadō tsuketari Jūō," pt. 3, no. 4, pp. 96–99; "Dairokuten," pt. 3, no. 3, pp. 94–96; "Saifukuji," pt. 3, no. 2, pp. 92–94; "Monjuin," pt. 3, no. 6, pp. 102–5; "Komakatadō," pt. 3, no. 5, pp. 100–102; "Asakusa no Kannon," pt. 2, no. 4, pp. 56–60; "Myōōin tsuketari Ubagafuchi," pt. 2, no. 5, pp. 60–63; "Kinryōsan tsuketari Matsuchiyama," pt. 2, no. 7, pp. 66–68; "Sōsenji tsuketari Myō-kisan," pt. 2, no. 6, pp. 63–66; "Sumidagawa," pt. 3, no. 7, pp. 105–9; "Narihira no Tsuka," pt. 3, no. 11, pp. 116–18. Also see "Sensōji Kannondō no koto" and "Ubagaike no koto," *Edo suzume*, fasc. 10, fols. 2v–6; *Nihon zuihitsu taisei*, pp. 227–33.

the temple of Kannon formally called Sensōji (and alternatively known as Asakusadera), is a different case, as it has been copied not from *Edo meishoki* but from *Edo suzume*. In its account of the temple's origins, *Edo-banashi* sticks close to that source; consequently, only two-fifths of that account are identical with Asai Ryōi's wording, as the balance of *Edo suzume*'s text derives from a variant hagiology. *Edo-banashi*'s version of the Ubagaike legend is also copied faithfully from *Edo suzume*; but the paternity in this incident of plagiary should nevertheless be fixed on Ryōi, because the "Edoite Sparrow" did little more than paraphrase and puff up his language in its own treatment of this material.

While it incorporates most of what Ryōi had to say about Kinryōsan (also known as Matsuchiyama), *Edo-banashi* treats that popular stop for wayfarers to Yoshiwara at far greater length than its predecessor, as the returnee from Edo shows how well informed he is by adding a disquisition on *yone manjū*, a type of pasty that was a "famous product" of this *meisho*.[49] The chapter on Sōsenji and Myōkisan is a close copy of the one in *Edo meishoki*, although the passage dealing with Sōsenji has been abbreviated and the treatment of Myōkisan expanded. The chapter on the Sumidagawa is also a fairly close copy, even if much of Ryōi's extensive poetic quotation has been cut and the account of Mokuboji, a temple built on the legendary site of Umewaka's tomb, has been brought up to date. "Ushi Gozen" is new, as *Edo meishoki* does not discuss this shrine. The final entry in this fascicle of *Edo-banashi*, "Narihira Tenjin," is a slightly reshuffled copy, one that is longer than its model because it quotes more poetry associated with Ariwara no Narihira than Asai Ryōi considered necessary.

The purloined texts, however, are but a part of the serious problem of falsification that infects *Edo-banashi*. One need not be a connoisseur of the Japanese print to find fault with the pictorial illustrations of the "Chat about Edo." Even the most desultory browser will notice how clumsily most of them have been put together. Viewing one of those illustrations for the first time, readers who are familiar with *Edo meishoki* and *Edo suzume* are apt to be overcome with the disconcerting feeling that they have already experienced the situation they see. A close, comparative look at the three books will bring the needed reassurance: the initial feeling was not an illusion.

A witless eclecticism is the integral characteristic of these pictures. Again, only a few examples need be given; the Yanaka Hōonji would be a good place to start.[50] As has just been noted, the text of *Edo-banashi*'s chapter

49. That Kinryōsan was a ritual stop on that Way of All Flesh, the road to Yoshiwara, is also apparent from contemporary guides to the "pleasure quarter," such as *Yoshiwara koi no michibiki*, illus. Hishikawa Moronobu (Edo: Hondon'ya, Enpō 6 [1678]); see the facsimile published by Suzuki Jūzō in *Kinsei Nihon fūzoku ehon shūsei*, vol. 5 (Kyoto: Rinsen Shoten, 1979), fols. 6v–8v. According to the dictionary of libertines' argot compiled by Sasama Yoshihiko, *Kōshoku engo jiten* (Yūzankaku, 1989), p. 465, the term *yone manjū* was Edo-period jargon for the female pudenda, a usage perhaps derived from an association with the shape of the "famous" pasties.

50. See *Kokyōgaeri*, pt. 2, no. 10 ("Hōonji"), p. 83. Cf. *Edo meishoki*, pt. 1, no. 12 ("Yanaka Hōonji"), p. 40; ibid., pt. 5, no. 3 ("Shiba no Kanasugimura Saiōji"), p. 165; and *Edo suzume*, 4:6 ("Hibiya Shinmei"). Saiōji is not illustrated in *Edo-banashi*.

on this temple of the Nichiren sect has been copied from *Edo meishoki*. The illustrations, too, are remarkably similar, but that merely disappoints; it is their failure to be identical that discomposes. The building and its surroundings clearly are the same, and the same priest inhabits the precincts. Some sort of reverse mechanism seems, however, to have interrupted his stately progress toward an exit at stage left, which he had already approached in *Edo meishoki*, only to be pulled back now to the other side of the temple. Conversely, a visitor previously observed drawing near the temple's gate has been propelled forward into its grounds, but has in the process been deprived of his servant; that the pattern of his kimono has been changed may no doubt be considered an additional creative touch. Two other male visitors, prominent in *Edo meishoki*, are out of the picture in *Edo-banashi*. They have been replaced by an elderly lady who supports herself on a cane as she shuffles along through the temple grounds. A search of the rogues' gallery will reveal that she was last seen on the other side of town, in Shiba, where the illustrator of *Edo meishoki* captured her as she was attending services at the Amidist temple Saiōji.[51] What is truly perplexing, however, is the sight of the samurai and his footman striding purposefully past Hōonji in *Edo-banashi*. They have strolled into this picture straight from the Hibiya Shinmei Shrine, where Hishikawa Moronobu had fixed their presence in *Edo suzume*. In other words, the perpetrator of this bizarre pastiche was not contented with clipping one source but snipped away at two.

And how does the Hibiya Shinmei Shrine appear in *Edo-banashi*? The narrative description is a close copy of the equivalent entry in *Edo meishoki*. The picture of the shrine buildings has been taken from *Edo suzume*'s depiction of the same place practically unchanged (but the two pine trees shown at the right side of the sanctuary by Moronobu have been transplanted to the left). The four people on the scene are not habitués of Moronobu's Hibiya, but none seems a stranger; one is annoyed at not being able to place them immediately. What are their antecedents? A rudimentary inquiry will soon enough discover three of them installed at a trader's stand by the torii of the Hakusan Gongen Shrine in *Edo suzume*. The fourth is a trifle more difficult to trace, perhaps because his previous situation was so different: he was last seen, in the company of a lady, walking the plank at the Fukagawa ferry landing in *Edo suzume*.[52]

It goes without saying that such illustrations are in essence depersonalized. Sometimes that is literally the case, as a scene is simply purged of a

---

51. The old ladies who worshiped at Saiōji that day were evidently in serious jeopardy of being abducted: another one was carried off from that temple's congregation as *Edo meishoki* portrays it and delivered to what *Edo-banashi* represents as Zōjōji; at least (unlike her fellow victim) she did not have very far to go, as both of these temples were in Shiba, and was not coopted into a different religious persuasion, as both belonged to the Jōdo sect. See *Edo meishoki*, pt. 5, no. 3, p. 165; and cf. *Kokyōgaeri*, pt. 4, no. 11 ("San'enzan Zōjōji"), p. 203.

52. See *Kokyōgaeri*, pt. 4, no. 10 ("Hibiya-mura Shinmeigū"), pp. 192–98 (illus., p. 193). Cf. *Edo meishoki*, pt. 7, no. 6 ("Hibiya Shinmei"), pp. 229–33; and *Edo suzume*, fasc. 4, fol. 6 ("Hibiya Shinmei"), fasc. 8, fol. 7v ("Hakusan Gongen"), fasc. 12, fol. 5v ("Fukagawa no Ōwatashi").

Hōonji in *Kokyōgaeri no Edo-banashi*. Source: Kokyōgaeri no Edo-banashi. Courtesy of Kokuritsu Kokkai Toshokan.

Hōonji in *Edo meishoki*. Source: Edo meishoki. Courtesy of Kokuritsu Kokkai Toshokan.

Saiōji in *Edo meishoki*. Source: Edo meishoki. Courtesy of Kokuritsu Kokkai Toshokan.

Hibiya Shinmei in *Edo suzume*. Source: Edo suzume. Courtesy of Kokuritsu Kokkai Toshokan.

part of its human contents. The picture of Hōmyōji, for example, has been copied from *Edo meishoki* (as has the text), but seven of its ten human occupants have been removed in the process; much the same is the case with Higashi Honganji, a temple that *Edo-banashi* depicts within the same framework as *Edo meishoki* but depopulates in the clumsiest manner—there are no people left praying!—as though shifting a few figures in or out of a pictorial frame would somehow make the presentation original.[53] The manipulations are on occasion so startling in their arbitrariness that they manage to amuse, as when a man known from *Edo meishoki* to be the Asakusa Kannon temple's sweeper is whisked off to the Ekōin, where he is forced to do double duty in *Edo-banashi*.[54] At other times they are so slipshod that they can only annoy, as when the beautiful portrayal of a kabuki performance that Hishikawa Moronobu contributed to *Edo suzume* is butchered by the crudest of transplant procedures.[55]

Here is what happens. First, the balance of the composition is wrecked by the removal of two intent spectators from their position just below stage center. Awkward adjustments then destroy the verisimilitude of the portrayal. For instance, the hands of the sedge-hatted man watching the action from below stage left remain positioned as though he were holding onto something, but they are empty—the sword he was grasping in *Edo suzume* has been taken away. When last seen and admired, the samurai enjoying the action from his box seat at stage right was elegantly leaning on the balustrade, where Hishikawa Moronobu had positioned him. He is reincarnated in *Edo-banashi* with a new head but the same posture; since he has been shifted slightly away from the railing, however, his elbow now is depended in midair and his arm appears painfully stiff. Two female attendants have been removed from the box; instead, the samurai and his page have been joined by a group of four male figures previously observed amusing themselves at two distinct spots elsewhere—two of them at a picnic under the blossoms of the "famous" cherry tree, Emonzakura, and the two others watching a fireworks display from boats by the Ryōgoku Bridge. Jammed as they are into a highly limited space in *Edo-banashi*, these four are made to appear as pygmies or children, so out of scale are they with the rest of the composition. But the fate of the samisen players is perhaps most symbolic of the folly of all such manipulations: they were perfectly attuned to each other in *Edo suzume*, but their mutual harmony has been destroyed. While their postures remain the same, their positions on the music stand

53. See *Kokyōgaeri*, pt. 3, no. 6 ("Sōshigae Hōmyōji"), pp. 115–18, and pt. 5B, no. 14 ("Higashi Honganji"), p. 268; and cf. *Edo meishoki*, pt. 6, no. 7, pp. 205–7, and pt. 2, no. 9, p. 71.

54. See *Kokyōgaeri*, pt. 6B, no. 4, p. 339 (illus., "Shoshūzan Muenji"); and cf. *Edo meishoki*, pt. 2, no. 4, p. 59 (illus. to "Asakusa no Kannon").

55. See *Kokyōgaeri*, pt. 6A, pp. 308–9 (illus. to no. 3, "Kyōgen-zukushi"); and cf. *Edo suzume*, fasc. 3, fols. 4v-5 ("Sakai-chō"), fasc. 7, fol. 5v ("Emonzakura"), and fasc. 11, fol. 2 ("Ryōgokubashi"). Not satisfied with abusing the Emonzakura group once, the compiler of *Edo-banashi* impressed them into service again in illustrating the Takada Ana Hachiman Shrine; see *Kokyōgaeri*, pt. 3, no. 7, p. 125.

have been reversed. Faces turned away, they are no longer part of the same ensemble. It is clear that they have nothing to do with each other.

How could the compiler of *Edo-banashi* have conceived of the "famous places" he pretended to describe with the help of such illustrations? Surely—to come back to a previous example—the view of Hakusan Gongen could not have been so easily superimposed on the representation of Hibiya Shinmei unless the stencil image of a generic shrine underlay that conception. The readers of his guidebook were, in effect, being told, "Once you've seen one *meisho*, you've seen them all." It might be alleged in his vindication that he merely manipulates people, who may be freely dispensed with as long as no violence is done to the sanctuaries themselves; after all, people—unlike buildings—are mobile. If so, then what is the Ikegami Honmonji's bell tower doing in the precincts of Meguro Fudō?[56] No one was sacred, and no place.

Are there any redeeming features in this book, apart from the few gestures toward originality that have already been mentioned? Is there anything new in its contents? The *kyōka* poems are new. Two dozen new *meisho* are introduced, as the city has grown in the twenty years since *Edo meishoki* was published. This increase in the list of "famous places" does not mean, however, that the concept of the city expands with *Edo-banashi*. One might make a virtue of the fact that its compiler views Edo as a real, continuous space to be trod rather than a disjointed amalgam of "famous places" to be admired vicariously in the vaporous context of the legends of their origin (to be sure, he cannot do without those legends in his narrative). At least he links the *meisho* with directions on how to get from one to another, something Asai Ryōi neglected to do in *Edo meishoki*; moreover, he himself appears and reappears frequently on location throughout his extended tale in the role of a guide to a country cousin who has come to summon him home from Edo. These personal intrusions are more than welcome. They make *Edo-banashi* less arid than *Edo suzume* and less artificial than *Edo meishoki*. But does all that suffice to make the "Chat about Edo" any more complete or vivid a representation of the city than its predecessors? That its compiler had a contempt for his sources is clear, and that contempt may even have been justified. Was he a cynic without a conscience or one with a grotesque sense of humor? In either case, his was the tertiary stage of plagiarism, and it was fatal.

With *Kokyōgaeri no Edo-banashi*, the shallow well shared by Asai Ryōi and his epigones ran dry. They lacked the inspiration to create a real city. To put it another way, the image of Edo they constructed was no more real than the phantom evoked in a well-known *kanazōshi*: Mokuami, a down-and-outer of the most ragged sort (*surikiri*), decides to turn his back on a miserable existence in Kyoto and to try his luck in the East. Having made his *kyōka*-strewn

---

56. See *Kokyōgaeri*, pt. 3, no. 20, p. 149 ("Meguro Fudō"); and cf. *Edo suzume*, fasc. 5, fol. 5v ("Ikegami Honmonji"). Significantly, neither *Edo suzume* (fasc. 5, fol. 10) nor *Edo meishoki* (pt. 6, no. 1, pp. 188–89) shows a bell tower on the grounds of Meguro Fudō.

way down the Tōkaidō, he arrives in Edo, where his first stop is the kabuki wonderland, Sakai-chō. On his way back from the theater to a friend's house, passing Edobashi, Mokuami takes a tumble over a large leather bag that turns out to be cram-full of gold. He invests his newly found fortune in a visit to Yoshiwara, where he beds that most desirable of all the goddesses of love who dwell there, Takao—and at the critical moment awakes from his dream in his familiar Kyoto shack, the "Same Old Mokuami" (*Moto no Mokuami*; c. 1675).[57] The soi-disant expert guides to Edo, too, were the victims and at the same time the agents of a delusion. Down to the anonymous author of *Edo-banashi*, they followed a pattern derived from the same old Kyoto model.

Edo kanoko, which was published in Edo five months after *Edo-banashi*, is cast in a different mold. For once, one cannot complain about an author's slighting the trades in his description of a city. Indeed, no fewer than 185 categories are included under the heading "Master Craftsmen and Merchants" in Part Six of this book, not to speak of the 42 entries under "The Professions and the Arts" and the 20 kinds of wholesalers.[58] Upon consulting this index, one could then look up the recommended specialist he or she needed, whether it be a saddler, a wigmaker, or a seller of face powder; a pediatrician, a poet, or a Shinto priest; an express courier to Kyoto or a hotel that catered to foreigners (*Tōjin-yado*; there was only one, the Nagasakiya). In other words, the view of the city as a center of diversified manufacture, craftsmanship, and commerce emerges at length with the appearance of *Edo kanoko*. Unfortunately, that view is not presented in an articulate manner in this work, which is essentially a book of lists. It is a treasure lode of raw information, but its literary value is negligible; as a narrative work, it is worth even less than its flawed predecessor in the "practical" genre of guide-books, *Edo suzume*. Hence it would be difficult to justify lingering at *Edo kanoko* in a brief excursion into the narrative topography of the seventeenth-century city. The author, Fujita Rihei (dates unknown), was aware of the problems he faced. In attempting to describe Edo, he states in the preface, he knew that he was taking on a huge topic, one that was difficult to treat faithfully. A rough outline would be the best that he could manage, a work daubed here and there with speckles—hence he would call his book *Edo kanoko*.[59] In view of these words of the preface, the title should not be

57. *Moto no Mokuami* (comp. c. Enpō 2–3 [1674–1675]; first published Edo: Kashiwaya Yoichi, Enpō 8 [1680]), ed. Kishi Tokuzō, in Jinbō Kazuya et al., eds., *Kanazōshi-shū, ukiyozōshi-shū*, Nihon koten bungaku zenshū 37 (Shōgakukan, 1989), pp. 283–318.

58. *Edo kanoko*, comp. Fujita Rihei, was first published in Edo by Kobayashi Tarobei in Jōkyō 4.11; that is, between 5 December 1687 and 2 January 1688. See the facsimile edition, *Edo kanoko*, in Asakura Haruhiko, gen. ed., *Koban chishi sōsho*, vol. 8 (Sumiya Shobō, 1970), pt. 6, pp. 245–95; or the more accessible modern edition, *Edo kanoko*, in Tōkyō-to, ed., *Tōkyō shishikō: Sangyō-hen*, vol. 7 (Tōkyō-to, 1970), pp. 1362–420. *Zōho Edo sō-kanoko meisho taizen*, the variant issued in 1690 with illustrations by Hishikawa Moronobu, is available in Edo Sōsho Kankōkai, ed., *Edo sōsho*, vols. 3 and 4 (Meicho Kankōkai, 1964); for pt. 6, see vol. 4, pp. 81–131.

59. *Edo kanoko*, p. 3; *Tōkyō shishikō*, p. 1175.

translated with the dictionary term for *kanoko*, "dappled cloth," but rendered "The Spotty Fabric of Edo." Almost a hundred years had passed since Tokugawa Ieyasu made it his capital, but Edo was still without a literary identity.

The exception that proves this rule is *Murasaki no hitomoto* (A Sprig of Purple), a book completed by 1683 but not published for another two centuries.[60] Its author, Toda Mosui (1629–1706), came from the family of a high-ranking Sunpu samurai who lost his status in the wake of his lord Tokugawa Tadanaga's disgrace in 1631. In political terms, Mosui never recovered from this eclipse of his family's fortunes, and his career in service to lordly households can at best be described as unremarkable. That may, however, have been a blessing in disguise: his connections were extensive and his relatives well off, permitting Mosui to live a life of leisure and literature in Edo; his choice of the pseudonym Iitsu—the first word of a classical maxim meaning "discarded but not resentful"—would appear to be a true indication of his feelings. Indeed, one would expect nothing less of this advocate of genuine emotion in art. Mosui, who is better known for his contributions to poetry than as a writer of prose, was a vehement critic of the hidebound traditions that dominated *waka* poetics in his day; not niggling rules but the pristine values of *makoto* and *nasake*—truth and sentiment—were of the essence in composing Japanese verse, he maintained. No doubt this radical doctrine startled the Kyoto aristocrats, self-appointed guardians of "secret transmissions," and other mystifiers who constituted the fogydom of *waka* in Mosui's day; more to the point, however, this breaker of poetic conventions was also an iconoclast in at least one category of prose. He shattered the form established for composing accounts of "famous places."

Asai Ryōi and his followers merely described what their interchangeable *meisho* were; worse, they could not rid themselves of the habit of diffusing attention on the historical backgrounds of those sites. Their history was all too often merely legend; their city is a sterile landscape. Toda Mosui, in contrast, defined his sites in terms of what went on there, focusing on the human activities in their foreground. Much of what he says in *Murasaki no hitomoto* is anecdotal or overtly fictional, yet one senses the substance of truth in his portrayal of Edo. Mosui makes it obvious that he knew the city inside out, down to its most intimate corners. He succeeds in evoking the atmosphere of a rich variety of urban locales, each with its own specific character. He makes seventeenth-century Edo come alive. Paradoxically, his

60. The body of *Murasaki no hitomoto* concludes with the date Tenwa 2.12.– (that is, in the month beginning 29 December 1682), but there is a postface dated Tenwa 3 [1683].5.–. The first published version, in Nakane Kiyoshi, ed., *Hyakumantō* (Kinkōdō, 1881), has been bowdlerized and should not be used. The only usable edition remains the one in *Toda Mosui zenshū* (Kokusho Kankōkai, 1915; rpt. 1969), pp. 213–305. The title is an allusion to the anonymous poem "Murasaki no hitomoto yue ni," *Kokinshū* 867. The *murasaki* (*Lithospermum erythrorhizon*) is a Japanese plant whose root yields a purple dye. The English name for plants of the genus *Lithospermum* is the less-than-elegant "gromwell," and the indulgent reader is therefore asked to excuse the metonymy in my translation of the book's title.

representation of the city is all the more powerful in its effect because the organization of "A Sprig of Purple," contrary to precedent, is not topographical but topical. After the initial section on Edo Castle, the table of contents of Part One reads as follows: "Hills," "Slopes," "Valleys" (1), "Hollows," "Valleys" (2), "Rivers," "Islands," "Moats," and "Ponds." Part Two comprises "Wells," "Bridges," "Ferry Crossings," "Ships," "Fields," "Alleys," "Tombs," "Riding Grounds," "Blossoms," "Cuckoos," "The Moon," "Maple Leaves," "Snow," "Festivals," and "Bells That Strike the Hour." (Part One of *Edo kanoko* has a similar organization, surely not by accident.) Notable by their absence are "Temples" and "Shrines."

Whimsy, not orderly method, dictated the selection of what to discuss, but the book is much more comprehensive than the initial look at its table of contents might indicate. The chapter titled "Hills," for instance, turns out to be a disquisition on whatever is notable about places that have the character for "hill" or "mountain" in their names. Thus the great ecclesiastical complex in Ueno is included in this chapter, not because it is located on high ground but because its formal temple name is Tōeizan Kan'eiji; Aoyama, too, is classified under this label, but the author notes that this quarter is called so not because it is hilly but because the residence of the Aoyama family is located there.[61] Those who have an interest in the world of kabuki should look up "The Moon." They will find there an elegant nocturne on the theme of a poetic session in Kobiki-chō: Mosui and three or four friends are the participants, and their extraordinarily charming host turns out to be Dekishima Kozarashi, the celebrated *onnagata*.[62] Those curious about the state of Japanese poetry in Mosui's day may be directed to "Moats." This chapter includes an account of a visit to the hermitage of a poetically gifted nun in Hatchōbori, a pretext for Mosui to borrow an entire collection of *waka*, which he then smuggles into *Murasaki no hitomoto*.[63]

Those with a taste for the lurid will find much to delight them in this book, but the most rewarding episode, from their standpoint, may well be the tragic melodrama included in the entry on Kagamigaike under "Ponds." Contrary to expectation, this is not the old story of Umewaka's mother (although there is a reminder that she "is said to have leaped into this pond and expired") but rather the contemporary tale of Uneme, "the number one prostitute of Edo." Uneme's misfortune was to have a priest become infatuated with her. The brothel keeper would not permit such an unlikely client entry into his house; but the priest's attachment to the object of his fantasies was "as sticky as the *yone manjū* of Kinryōsan," and he refused to go away. Or, rather, he kept coming back, like some latter-day Fukakusa no Shōshō,

61. *Murasaki no hitomoto*, in *Toda Mosui zenshū*, pp. 219–20 ("Tōeizan") and p. 222 ("Aoyama"). Tōeizan is also treated under "Blossoms," pp. 284–86, and Mosui's eloquent account makes it clear that Ueno was as popular—and, indeed, as crowded—a site for the annual cherry-blossom hunt then as it is now.

62. Ibid., pp. 291–92. Kozarashi, said to be particularly good at love scenes (*nuregoto*), was one of the most admired actors of "young female" roles; cf. *Moto no Mokuami*, p. 298.

63. *Murasaki no hitomoto*, in *Toda Mosui zenshū*, pp. 244–59.

to admire Uneme from the other side of the lattice where she was on display—until one day he "slit his whistle and gave up the ghost" right there. Uneme, needless to say, did the only honorable thing under the circumstances: she followed her unrequited lover unto death. After a brief, solitary *michiyuki* through the surroundings of Yoshiwara, "She sank into the waters / Of the Mirror Pond" (*Kagamigaike ni zo / shizumikeri*).[64]

The skeptically inclined should by all means refer to the first entry under "Islands," Eitaijima. Readers of Asai Ryōi and his followers may remember it as a holy place, the site of a Hachiman shrine where "divine grace was so amply manifest that people thronged the island, their throats parched for solace and their eyes directed heavenward." Mosui provides an excellent antidote to this pious pap. He points out that Eitaijima was distant from Edo and the shrine out of the way; hence visitors were rare and the place had no prospects of ever coming to life until the authorities "took mercy and tempered the stringency of the law" against unlicensed prostitution. Now that the approaches to the shrine are occupied entirely by teahouses, each of which employs "ten women of remarkable beauty" prepared to "comfort the pilgrims," prosperity has come to Eitaijima—that is, to Fukagawa, as this extramural prostitute quarter (*okabasho*) would come to be known. The comfort women reputed to be "tops" are listed by name.[65]

The difference between these two accounts of Eitaijima is startling. Toda Mosui enters the actualities of the scene. The writers of the Asai school take a view so remote as to be unreal. The contrast is even more stark in the way Sensōji, the temple of Kannon in Asakusa, is treated. To Ryōi it is a sacred place where worshipers are certain to find themselves inundated with "boundless blessings, an ocean of longevity and good fortune." Immersing himself in what he thinks is history, he begins his story with an account of the temple's origins in 628, when brothers fishing in the bay off the mouth of the Miyakogawa pulled up a wonder-working statue of Kannon in their nets; proceeds to 645, when the statue was declared sacrosanct and hidden from the view of ordinary mortals; takes up the story again in 942, when Taira no Kinmasa, grateful to Kannon for helping him to obtain high official appointments, rebuilt the main hall and surrounded it with a grand assemblage of religious edifices; and then concludes with a brief mention of Minamoto no Yoritomo and Ashikaga Takauji, who endowed Sensōji with landed properties. Typically, Ryōi's interest stops there, in the dim medieval past.[66] Fortunately, *Kokyōgaeri no Edo-banashi* updates the list of the temple's benefactors to include Tokugawa Ieyasu and includes an anecdote about one

---

64. Ibid., pp. 260–62.

65. Ibid., p. 241. Cf. *Edo meishoki*, pt. 4, no. 3, pp. 136–39; *Edo suzume*, fasc. 12, fols. 4–5 (the illustration, fol. 8, shows some suspicious teahouses at the entry to the shrine but the text, a slightly abbreviated copy of Asai Ryōi, does not allude to them); *Nihon zuihitsu taisei*, pp. 275–77; *Kokyōgaeri*, pt. 6B, no. 8, pp. 346–51; *Zōho Edo-banashi*, pp. 284–86.

66. *Edo meishoki*, pt. 2, no. 4, pp. 56–60. Note that three brothers are named as responsible for fishing up the statue in this account; in *Tōkaidō meishoki*, vol. 1, p. 27, Ryōi subscribed to the theory that there were two.

of its treasures, the miraculously lifelike votive painting of a horse attributed to Kano Eitoku (1543–1590)[67]—otherwise nothing more recent than the fourteenth century would be learned from the standard guidebooks about one of the most famous of all of Edo's *meisho*.

Could this be the same Asakusa that is described by Mosui under "Blossoms"?[68] All the way from the vicinity of Komakatadō onward, he says, the crowds of people streaming to the Kannon Hall for the flower viewing were "pressed sleeve against sleeve," presenting an even more memorable spectacle than the cherry blossoms themselves. Evidently, one who took the avenue called Namiki no Chaya had to run the gauntlet of young women offering various services; his soul, Mosui confesses, "melted away as the spring snows" at the sight of one of these temptresses (her sash "wrapped casually about the crest of her buttocks") opening the sliding door to the words "Enter, friend!" He decided to press on, but it was impossible to make any progress along the usual route; "there were people on top of people." Throngs sought to get inside the Kaminari Gate, colliding with other crowds that tried to exit. Oldsters were pushed into the dirt, falling in a faint; women and children wept and screamed; mountain ascetics (*yamabushi*) sought to clear their way by swinging their staffs and yelling; pedlars shouted the names of their wares at the tops of their voices; artful dodgers picked pockets. Realizing that it was fruitless to persevere in the attempt to catch a glimpse of the flowers, Mosui decided to go have a drink. He was in the right neighborhood, judging from the number of public houses he lists, and he chose the best known and most auspicious-looking of the lot. This was the Fukuya, where he was served a truly stupendous meal. Merely reading the menu of the "famed local products" Mosui was fed would satiate any glutton.

In short, something will be found to please all tastes in the pages of *Murasaki no hitomoto*. This book fascinates with its wealth of informative detail about the genre scene; it persuades because its author does not preach; it has integrity because it is the product not of a scrivener's but of a critic's mind; and it succeeds because Toda Mosui is an imaginative comic writer. Much of the time, the butts of his humor are the two companions—the "shrunken gentleman" Yōyōsai and the "half-baked recluse" Iitsu (that is, Mosui himself under his pseudonym)—whom he has wander about town as they please, making observations that are often dispensed poetically (true to form, Iitsu considers himself an expert at *waka*; Yōyōsai prefers Chinese verse).[69] Some of the escapades of these two consist of pure buffoonery. A good example is the scrape in which they find themselves involved at the

67. *Kokyōgaeri*, pt. 5A, no. 6, pp. 232–39; *Zōho Edo-banashi*, pp. 249–52.
68. *Murasaki no hitomoto*, in *Toda Mosui zenshū*, pp. 286–88. The account of the carnival atmosphere that prevailed on the waterfront of the Sumida from 1677, "when a rage for the dance called *Ise odori* broke out," is another extraordinarily well-managed crowd scene: ibid., "Ships," p. 273.
69. Ibid., p. 214. The name Yōyōsai is written with characters that may also be read "Tōtōsai."

well called Horikane no I. Iitsu expects to turn whiter than white after washing himself in this well's water of legendary efficacy; no matter how hard he scrubs, however, he stays the same dark-colored and shriveled slug he has been from birth. Instead of water, Yōyōsai tells him to try fire—perhaps, after dying and being cremated, he will be reborn as clean as the famed amianthus (a cloth made of mouse fur that is washed in flames to burn off dirt). Infuriated, Iitsu grabs the bamboo used for lowering the bucket into the well and breaks it over Yōyōsai's back. The keeper of the well, enraged, threatens to give Iitsu a hip fracture with another stick. The "half-baked recluse" has to buy himself free by improvising a poem.[70]

One hesitates to call this a *kyōgen*-like situation and leave it at that. Something more modern is in evidence here: about Toda Mosui's scaramouch pair there can be detected a whiff of Jippensha Ikku's two jackanapes, the immortal Yaji and Kita. To be sure, Mosui manages to keep his heroes' frivolity within the bounds of good taste, something Ikku never worried about. After all, Iitsu and Yōyōsai, no matter how shrunken and shriveled, are literary gentlemen, not common fools like the other twosome; and Mosui, when all is said and done, still represents the relatively restrained seventeenth century, not the vulgar nineteenth. He is, however, no medieval storyteller but quite a with-it raconteur. His fine sense of timing, adroit imagination, and light touch are on display throughout *Murasaki no hitomoto*, but perhaps nowhere more strikingly than in the episode dealing with Jigokudani, the "Valley of Hell."[71] In depicting this place, Mosui appears hell-bent on doing justice to its name, which reflects (he says) a grisly past: the corpses of derelicts and executed criminals used to be dumped there, and the valley remains littered with skeletons. Before we know it, we are lured into a twilight zone and beguiled into accepting Mosui's tale as an event that took place on the level of the fantastic; that is, as a ghost story. It is only the comic ending that brings on second thoughts, as it dawns on us that so preposterous an incident could only be mundane.

It was a dark and stormy night as Iitsu and Yōyōsai, on their way home from an evening service at Zenkokuji, found themselves in Jigokudani. The sermon having been on death, bad karma, and reincarnation, with emphasis on how desires and attachments cause the spirits of the dead to wander about this world, it is no wonder that the two pluckless heroes need to keep encouraging each other to stay manful but tread carefully in their passage across the Valley of Hell. As they reach a footbridge across some particularly nasty drainage, their progress is arrested by a wailing voice. "A ghost!" they conclude, and themselves prepare to die.

The "thing" that now appears out of the gloom looks like a woman of twenty but is dressed in a bizarre white costume and waves a branch of star anise, a shrub commonly planted in graveyards. Iitsu and Yōyōsai shiver

70. Ibid., "Wells," pp. 264–65.
71. Ibid., pp. 229–32. Jigokudani is identified as the low area leading from Kōjimachi 2-chōme to Niban-chō.

with terror. The apparition seeks to put them at ease, and assures them that she is "neither a demon nor a monster" but rather the properly brought-up daughter of a shopkeeper in Ichigaya. At seventeen (so goes her story) she was married to a man in Kawara-chō, Asakusa, with whom she enjoyed a life of perfect nuptial bliss:

> Legs intertwined on the damask quilts, face to face on the satin pillows, breasts pounding; stroking somewhere that shall remain nameless and then gulping it into a place by my loins; hands clasping each other's back, with not a chink left between our interlocked bodies; biting and then kissing, relaxing only to cleave to each other again—when one comes together like this a thousand times and more (breathless, eyes closed tight; then before long the pulse eases, but the ears stay hot down to their roots, and the body is drenched with sweat), it is difficult to part.

She may have felt so, but her husband evidently did not feel the same; in any event, he "redeemed" a prostitute by the name of Takahashi, with whom he has now set up a separate ménage. Naturally, a woman scorned wants revenge. Indeed, the reason this fury is wandering about in the dead of night is that she wants to go to the Sannō Shrine to put a whammy on her husband. Too eager to reach the witching ground by the proper hour, she has lost her way in the dark.[72] "Please show me how to get there!" she asks Iitsu and Yōyōsai.

A more sensible pair would no doubt realize that this overexcited lady's weird getup is just the proper attire for the occasion (she has, after all, told them that she is about to perform an imprecation) and would take her for what she claims to be. Mosui's easily daunted duo are all the more convinced, however, that they are in the presence of a ghost. Iitsu promises to make her evaporate, boasting of his own great thaumaturgic powers. Yōyōsai stretches on tiptoe, vaunting his prowess as a samurai descended from Emperor Seiwa through the Minamoto clan, and threatens to pulverize her. She, however, bids them to do their worst, as she would rather die than live plagued by her memories. As she advances toward them, they flee.

Jigokudani is made unforgettable by this appeal to fancy. In his account of Yoshiwara (likewise found under "Valleys," because San'ya, the prostitute quarter's alternate name, contains the character for "valley") Mosui then goes on to show that a whimsical touch can fix an image in the reader's memory more firmly than heavy-handed insistence on a moral.[73] First he gives directions to the place, along with a list of its principal denizens and a

72. The proper witching hour is *ushi no toki* (the hour of the ox), from one to three in the morning; hence this hoodoo is called *ushi no toki-mairi*, ox-hour devotions. The malediction must have no witnesses, or else it will not work.

73. *Murasaki no hitomoto*, in *Toda Mosui zenshū*, pp. 233–35. Note that the phrase *shitamachi no Genzaemon* ("Genzaemon from downtown") contains one of the earliest known instances of the use of the term *shitamachi* in the sense of the low-lying area of town that was the classical home ground of Edo's commoners.

brief outline of its internal layout; he takes care to name not only the *grandes dames* currently in residence but also the *filles* of the next lower price category, called *kōshi*, who are known to be willing to "break their bones" for a customer. So far, his approach to the topic seems straightforward and ordinary; what follows, however, is neither a pedestrian account of a "famous place" nor the edifying discourse on prostitution that we would expect from an Asai Ryōi. Instead, Mosui regales us with a farce about misadventures in a brothel.

We are introduced to the Fujiya, a *maison de rendezvous* that enjoyed the reputation of a haunted house and as a result "prospered exceedingly, because young swaggerers went there in the hope of seeing the monster." This bogey, however, was not necessarily such stuff as dreams are made on— that much a gentleman called Genzaemon "from downtown" and his lady of the evening, Seishū, found out to their regret in the course of a coitus interruptus, as a "huge baldhead with a mug that was three feet long for sure" turned up by the bedside lamp, "his eyes mere slits but his long tongue thrust out as if ready to make short work of them both." The terrified Genzaemon "throws off Seishū" and "leaps stark naked" for the door; a screen falls on the lamp, the light goes out, someone yells, "A fight! A fight!" and a free-for-all results in the dark; not only the Fujiya but also the neighboring houses of assignation are all in an uproar.

There is a certain "practical" aspect to this narrative, because Mosui, putting on a straight face, pays a good deal of attention to brothel etiquette in setting the scene of his story, pedantically insists on identifying the female members of the cast by their past and present noms de guerre ("Iwa, the present Tanshū," and so forth) throughout, and manages to squeeze the names of no fewer than nine Yoshiwara establishments into his riotous postlude. But the author's deadpan attitude also makes this episode surreal in the Marxian (that is, Groucho Marxian) sense. It is a burlesque, but it is certainly no misrepresentation. Mosui evokes the atmosphere of the "pleasure quarter" as directly and—one would like to think—as accurately as do the "funny pictures" (*warai-e*) that may be considered the most peculiar product of Edo art.

If a specter haunts these scenes, it is the specter of *gesaku*, the quintessential literary spirit of Edo: immature and indistinct though it may be as yet, it hovers about the "Sprig of Purple." Mosui's portrayal of the city represents a great step forward from the *kanazōshi* tradition. The narrative topography of Edo entered the early-modern era with *Murasaki no hitomoto*. That this book circulated only in manuscript during the Tokugawa period is a pity. The places depicted so vividly by Toda Mosui deserved a greater notoriety.

12

The Festivity of the Parisian Boulevards

ROBERT M. ISHERWOOD

On the eve of the Revolution, Thomas Rousseau characterized the Parisian boulevards as odious, infected thoroughfares of sin frequented by impudent libertines, nymphs of the chorus, spangled scoundrels, and corrupt recruiting sergeants, where people were pushed, tripped, battered, and thrust into orgiastic dissipation, where innocent girls learned prostitution and young men lost all sense of decency, reason, and propriety, and ended up contracting "*le mal Amériquain.*"[1] Others, however, believed that these beautiful lanes lined with sparkling cafés and sprightly *spectacles* displayed the magnificence of the capital city.[2] Certainly they were the greatest show in prerevolutionary Paris, the center of a renaissance of marketplace culture.

The boulevards were formed in the sixteenth century when François I extended the wall on the northern side of the Temple and had a trench dug to create ramparts that extended from the door of the Temple to the Porte Saint-Antoine, on the eastern edge of the city.[3] In 1668 the first trees were

Excerpted from *Farce and Fantasy: Popular Entertainment in Eighteenth-Century Paris* by Robert M. Isherwood. Copyright © 1986 by Oxford University Press, Inc. Reprinted by permission. This chapter also draws on my article "Entertainment on the Parisian Boulevards in the Eighteenth Century," *Proceedings of the Western Society for French History* 11 (1984).

1. Thomas Rousseau, *Lettre à M . . . sur les spectacles des boulevards* (Paris: 1781), pp. 12–32.

2. See, for example, Pierre-Thomas-Nicolas Hurtaut, *Le dictionnaire historique de la ville de Paris et de ses environs*, 4 vols. (Paris: Moutard, 1779), vol. 1, p. 659.

3. Information on the boulevards can be found in the following works: Jacques-Antoine Dulaure, *Nouvelle description des curiosités de Paris* (Paris: Lejay, 1785), pp. 70–72; *Le provincial à Paris, ou État actuel de Paris*, 4 vols. (Paris: Watin, 1787), vol. 3, pp. 33–34; *Almanach parisien, en faveur des étrangers et des personnes curieuses*, 1765, p. 156; Edmond-Jean-François Barbier, *Journal historique et anecdotique du règne de Louis XV*, 4 vols. (Paris: Charpentier, 1847), vol. 3, p. 475; Hurtaut, *Dictionnaire historique*, vol. 1, p. 660; François-Marie Mayeur de Saint-Paul, *Le désoeuvré, ou L'espion du boulevard du Temple* (London, 1781); Henri Sauval, *Histoire et recherches des antiquités de la ville de Paris*, 3 vols. (Paris: C. Moette, 1724), vol. 1, pp. 671–72; Michel Marescot, *La folie du jour, ou La promenade des boulevards*

planted adjacent to the trenches, and in 1670 the Council of State ordered the demolition of the wall of Philippe Auguste and the extension of the boulevard westward from the rue du Temple to the Porte Saint-Martin. By 1705 the boulevards comprised an extended avenue one hundred feet wide flanked by three rows of trees on the outer side, forming smaller lanes, and by two rows on the inner side. Houses sprang up along the ramparts, and the gardens of the stately townhouses of the Marais bordered the boulevards on the inner side. Beyond the ramparts lay fields of lettuce, sorrel, mushrooms, and artichokes, and to the north the windmills of Montmartre.

By the eighteenth century the boulevards had become a real thoroughfare linking one side of Paris to the other and an increasingly popular place to promenade. Working to make them attractive and clean, the provost of merchants had the pedestrian lanes sanded and the main avenue watered every day in summer. In the 1780s the bastions and counterscarps were destroyed, the trenches were filled, the land was leveled, and the central thoroughfare was paved. The city began installing street lamps in 1781, and the side lanes were outfitted with stone benches and chairs.[4]

The boulevards offered a variegated spectacle. There was glamour: diamond-clad courtesans and countesses, indistinguishable to onlookers, wended their way under the trees in decorous coaches. There was filth: the clogged lanes were often turned into miniature dust bowls or muddy ravines, and the unwary stroller was sopped with urine and feces hurled from upper-story windows. There was music: an unremitting blare of chanting, drumming, and tooting. The bells and cymbals of the clowns fought for the ear's attention against the squalls of merchants selling cocoa, apple turnovers, and barley sugar. Insults streaked the air like summer lightning. There was thievery, brawling, prostitution: the police regularly rounded up prostitutes in the cafés, at brothels in the area, and in front of the boulevard

---

(Paris, 1754); Luc-Vincent Thiéry, *Almanach du voyageur à Paris* (Paris, 1783), p. 145; Théodore Faucheur, *Histoire du boulevard du Temple depuis son origine jusqu'à sa démolition* (Paris: E. Dentu, 1863); Nicolas Brazier, *Chroniques des petits théâtres de Paris*, 2 vols., 3d ed. (Paris: Rouveyre et Bond, 1883), vol. 1, pp. 165–78; Georges Cain, *Anciens théâtres de Paris* (Paris: Charpentier et Fasquelle, 1906), pp. 1–4, 37; Jacques Hillairet, *Dictionnaire historique des rues de Paris*, 2 vols. (Paris: Minuit, 1963), vol. 2, pp. 541–49; Victor Fournel, *Le vieux Paris, fêtes, jeux et spectacles* (Tours: A. Mame, 1887), pp. 111–33; Eise Carel Van Bellen, *Les origines du mélodrame* (Utrecht: Kemink, 1927), pp. 65–66; Germain Brice, *Nouvelle description de la ville de Paris et tout ce qu'elle contient de plus remarquable*, 4 vols., 8th rev. ed. (Paris: J. M. Gandovin, 1725), vol. 2, pp. 69–75. When *boulevard* is used in the singular, the reference is to the Boulevard du Temple, which in the early-modern period bent farther to the north in the area of the present Place de la République than it does today. The name comes from the Templars, a religious order of knights founded in the eleventh century who at one time were installed in a fortress beyond the walls to the north of the city. After their suppression in 1307, Philippe le Bel gave the Temple to the knights of Saint-Jean de Jérusalem. In 1389 Charles VI built the Porte du Temple on the northern side of the fortress. It was protected by a large trench and a bastion located on the present Place de la République.

4. *Le Courier d'Avignon*, 19 October 1781, p. 348; and *Journal de Paris*, 62 2 March 1788, pp. 277–78.

A Parisian boulevard. Courtesy of the Bibliothèque Nationale.

theaters. They were whisked to the Châtelet, where their heads were shaved, and then taken to Salpetrière.[5]

People gathered on the boulevards ostensibly to promenade or to attend the "little spectacles," but really to ogle each other, shout at the grimacers and stuntmen on the outdoor scaffolding, get drunk, and feel the physical press of unsegregated human flesh, as on the Paris métro at rush hour. For some, the shoving and elbowing were disagreeable. A young law student from Leiden wrote in disgust:

> At the end of two hours we felt harassed, black and blue, and choked by the dust we had swallowed. We deplored the empire of fashion, which swept away reason and comfort, and we promised each other never to return to breathe the suffocating air charged with pestilential fumes. The noise of the charlatans had made us deaf and dried out the palate: our sense of smell was swollen by the suffocating vapors, and of all our senses the only free one remaining was touch.[6]

Everyone came to what Benjamin Franklin called the club of the Quatre Nations.[7] Bejeweled ladies mingled with ragged street urchins. Fops showed off their mistresses and luxurious carriages.[8] Enticed by the pungent smell of new wine, swishing skirts, and bare bosoms, artisans, merchants, and coachmen flocked to the cafés, where they drank eau-de-vie, ratafia, and scalded beer, played cards or billiards, and listened to the Savoyard girls play their hurdy-gurdies.[9] Even a penniless person could sit in a café listening to the music. "His ear will enjoy more than his stomach," Louis-Sébastien Mercier wrote, "and the symphony will take the place of supper."[10] Old men sat on the benches along the shady lanes telling strollers the latest gossip about the boulevard entertainers or engaging them in games of chess, dominoes, or peg-top.[11] Hester Thrale, visiting from England, was struck by the numerous shopkeepers who brought their families to the boulevards. The shopkeeper, she declared, belies the traditional image of "the fawning Parisian, the supple Gaul. . . . He lives as well as he wishes, he goes to the Boulevards every Night, treats his Wife with Lem-

---

5. See, for example, Archives Nationales (hereafter cited as AN) MS Y 13962, pièces dated 5 July 1769 and 16 May 1769; Y 13970, pièce dated 4 July 1771; and François Métra, *Correspondance secrète, politique et littéraire, ou Mémoires pour servir à l'histoire des cours, des sociétés et de la littérature en France depuis la mort de Louis XV*, 18 vols. (London: Adamson, 1787–1790), vol. 7, pp. 228–29.

6. Jean-Henri Marchand and J. A. Desboulmiers, *L'esprit et la chose* (Paris, 1767), p. 62. A provincial visitor also complained about the odor of stale tobacco smoke, the mud and filth in the streets, and the terrible smell of horse manure: *Lettre d'un provincial à un ami sur la promenade des boulevards* (Paris, 1760), p. 5

7. Cited in Fournel, *Vieux Paris*, p. 133.

8. Dulaure, *Nouvelle description*, p. 72

9. Mayeur, *Désoeuvré*, pp. 38–41; Fournel, *Vieux Paris*, pp. 126–28.

10. Louis-Sébastien Mercier, *Tableau de Paris*, 12 vols., 2d ed. (Amsterdam, 1782–1788), vol. 6, pp. 19–20.

11. Mayeur, *Désoeuvré*, p. 11.

onade, and holds up his Babies by Turns to see Harlequin or hear the Jokes of Merry Andrew."[12] Marquis and lackeys, young pages and financiers, attorneys and tramps, all were engaged by the giddy gallimaufry of sights, sounds, and aromas. Mercier spoke of the boulevards as the place "most open to every estate."[13] Society was not polarized on these lanes of leisure. The complete social integration of this marketplace was evoked vividly by Pierre-Jean-Baptiste Nougaret:

> Do you hear the sharp little voice of the impatient marquise blending with the awful swearing of a porter addressing Hell and Paradise? See in the glass carriage the ugly woman of title with her rouge, her diamonds, the paste shining on her face; whereas the ordinary girl just to the side in a simple dress is brilliantly fresh and plump. Look at this wealthy canon sunken into his cushions dreaming of nothing, while the old magistrate in his antique carriage reads some petition.[14]

Aside from the cafés, gambling dens, brothels, and the parade of humanity, people of all social ranks were attracted to the boulevards by acrobatic buffoons performing on open-air scaffolding, carnival barkers displaying curious animals, giants, and mechanical devices, *farceurs* who regaled the crowd from balconies with lewd slapstick, and the colorful array of hucksters such as the herb-tea peddler wearing his heron-feathered cap, carrying a tin fountain on his back with two silver goblets chained to his belt, and shouting, "À la fraiche, qui veut boire?"[15] His clients were bemused by the witticisms, roulades, and popular rebuses that flowed from his lips as steadily as the liquid from his fountain.

The principal attractions on the boulevards, however, were the little theaters that sprang up in the 1760s and 1770s. Prices for tickets to such *spectacles* as the Ambique-Comique and the Théâtre des Associées were fixed by the police in a range from 6 to 26 sous so that the general public could afford to attend, thus preventing "the dangerous consequences of idleness" and, many hoped, in order to discouraging "*la bonne compagnie*" from going

12. Hester Lynch Salusbury Thrale Piozzi, *The French Journals of Mrs. Thrale and Doctor Johnson*, ed. Moses Tyson and Henry Guppy (Manchester: Manchester University Press, 1932), pp. 199–200.

13. Mercier, *Tableau de Paris*, vol. 1, p. 168.

14. Pierre-Jean-Baptiste Nougaret, *Les historiettes du jour, ou Paris tel qu'il est*, 2 vols. (Paris: Duchesne, 1787), vol. 2, pp. 18–19. See also *Lettre d'un provincial*, p. 13; Nougaret, *Les astuces de Paris* (Paris: Cailleau, 1775), p. 99; François Cognel, *La vie parisienne sous Louis XVI* (Paris: Levy, 1882), p. 21. The latter account by a magistrate from Nancy was written in 1787. Additional discussion of boulevard crowds can be found in Alexandre-Jacques Du Coudray, *Nouveaux essais historiques sur Paris pour servir de suite et de supplément à ceux de M. de Saintfoix*, 3 vols. (Paris: Berlin, 1781–1786), vol. 1, p. 115; Jèze, *Journal du citoyen* (The Hague, 1754), p. 192; Merescot, *Folie du jour*, pp. 1–7; Jean-Joseph Vadé, *Le boulevard*, in *Nouveau théâtre de la foire*, 5 vols. (Paris: Duchesne, 1763), vol. 2; and Charles Favart, *La soirée des boulevards*, in *Théâtre de M. Favart, ou Recueil des comédies, parodies et opéras-comiques donnés jusqu' à ce jour, avec les airs, rondes et vaudevilles notés dans chaque pièce*, 8 vols. (Paris: Duchesne, 1763), vol. 4.

15. Mercier, *Tableau de Paris*, vol. 5, pp. 310–14.

to a "cheap" show.[16] The earliest of these theaters, Les Grands Danseurs de Corde, exemplifies the nature of popular entertainment on the boulevards. An analysis of its repertoire may help to clarify the character of Parisian popular culture and to distinguish it from the street life of Edo, as McClain and Elisonas describe it in their contributions to this volume.

Founded by Jean-Baptiste Nicolet (1726–1796), who had taken over his father's marionette show in 1759, Les Grands Danseurs were a troupe of acrobats, dancers, actors, and musicians who performed in a wooden theater built in 1764 on the Boulevard du Temple.[17] Many of Nicolet's performers, especially the acrobats, became stars of the Parisian entertainment world. Le Petit Diable, a funambulist, became an overnight sensation when he executed a dance with eggs tied to his feet. He also did balancing acts on planks and chairs, and walked an inclined tightrope while wearing wooden shoes.[18] He attracted the attention of the comte d'Artois, who hired the Diable to teach him the art of funambulism, establishing a vogue at court.[19] Le Beau Dupuis, a funambulist who later fell to his death, was celebrated for his somersaults over a burning plank, leaps over a racing horse, and springboard vaults over a pyramid of twelve men.[20] An abandoned child like many of the popular entertainers, Dupuis won the court's approbation after a performance at Choisy-le-Roi in 1772. The king was so impressed by Nicolet's troupe at Choisy that he authorized the title of Spectacle des Grands Danseurs et Sauteurs du Roi. Popular entertainment found an easy passage from the marketplace to the court.

Alexandre-Placide Bussart, who wrote pantomimes with acrobatic choreography for Nicolet, was often featured in the advertisements of the Grands Danseurs, which called attention to his "leap over a ribbon strung six feet in the air, flips from one side of the theater to the other, and a rope dance swinging a flag bearing the arms of France."[21] A Polish acrobat did a balanc-

16. *Almanach forain, ou Les différens spectacles des boulevards et des foires de Paris,* 1776, p. 41, and 1778, pp. 87–88. See also Arthur Pougin, *Dictionnaire historique et pittoresque du théâtre et des arts qui s'y rattachent* (Paris: Firmon-Didot, 1885), pp. 34, 42, 113. Accounts of the theaters can be found in Ernest Lunel, *Le théâtre et la Révolution* (Paris: H. Daragon, n.d.), pp. 12–22; Arthur Pougin, *Acteurs et actrices d'autrefois* (Paris: F. Juvenet, n.d.), pp. 33–38; Brazier, *Chroniques des petits thèâtres,* vol. 1, pp. 3–24; Emile Campardon, *Les spectacles de la foire,* 2 vols. (Paris: Berger-Levrault, 1877), vol. 2, pp. 149–64; Henri Beaulieu, *Les théâtres du boulevard du crime* (Paris: Daragon, 1905), pp. 11–101; Charles Rabou, *Les Grands Danseurs du Roi* (Brussels: Meline, 1846).

17. Max Aghion, *Le théâtre à Paris au XVIIIᵉ siècle* (Paris, 1926), p. 261. Hillairet (*Dictionnaire historique,* vol. 2, p. 542) places his theater at the angle of the present boulevards du Temple and Voltaire.

18. *Journal de Paris,* 12 February 1779, p. 172, 7 February 1782, p. 152; *Les affiches, annonces et avis divers,* 5 March 1779, p. 512.

19. Louis Petit de Bachaumont, *Mémoires secrets pour servir à l'histoire de la république de lettres en France depuis 1762 jusqu' à nos jours, ou Journal d'un observateur,* 31 vols. (London: J. Adamson, 1779–1789), vol. 13, pp. 383–84 30 March 1779.

20. Fournel, *Vieux Paris,* p. 346.

21. *Journal de Paris,* 1 September 1777, p. 4; 7 February 1782, p. 152; 8 February 1782, p. 156.

Nicolet's theater. Courtesy of the Bibliothèque Nationale.

ing act on a chariot rolling along an iron wire.[22] The illustrious equilibrist Joseph Brunn pushed a child in a wheelbarrow balanced on an iron wire.[23] Mr. and Mrs. Storkinfeld danced the Hungarian Onion in high boots and spurs.[24] Nicolet's eight Spanish tumblers and dancers performed carrying wooden batons two feet long and wearing sonorous buckles strapped to their wrists.[25] During the quadrilles, they unleashed a shower of baton blows, twisting their arms in every direction. The dance was executed in such a way that the batons struck the wrist buckles in perfect cadence and without injuring the dancers.

In an age bathed in an ocean of criticism, Nicolet's performers and his shows had their share of shrill detractors. François-Marie Mayeur de Saint-Paul found his players to be as unbridled on the streets as the rest of the boisterous boulevard crowd:

> If one did not know these people to be Nicolet's *danseurs de corde*, one would think he was in the woods in the midst of assassins when one encounters them on the boulevards. Pantaloons, long frock coats, a large cloak, uneven hat, curled-up hair in a braid, a fat, knotty stick in hand, that is the attire of these gentlemen; to insult everyone, to injure whomever they must, to create an uproar at the places of all the wine merchants of the rampart, to get drunk with scoundrels, that is their conduct.[26]

Nicolas-Edme Rétif de La Bretonne was the most abrasive critic of Nicolet's show and his audience. He called the *spectacle* "a monstrous heap of things that astonish, . . . a chaos that the spirit cannot unravel and that is appropriate only to divert this species of spectators who see only mechanically and who understand nothing."[27] Contending that since Nicolet's gross farces were "appropriate to a certain class of citizens," Rétif believed that they spared the Opéra and the Comédie-Française from bothersome competition. Nonetheless, he was concerned that Nicolet was making too great an impression on artisans. Rétif was joined by Alexandre Du Coudray, who accused Nicolet of perpetuating "bad taste, the obscene genre. . . and shameful morals," and by Louis Gachet, who objected to dances by "men disguised as women who execute some roulades and turns," which "have offended urban spectators."[28] But the critics could not stifle the mounting popularity of the boulevard shows. Louis Petit de Bachaumont, who claimed

22. Ibid., 25 June 1779, p. 720.

23. Fournel, *Vieux Paris*, p. 348.

24. *Journal de Paris*, 28 August 1786, p. 992.

25. Métra, *Correspondance*, vol. 2, pp. 113–15 (12 August 1775).

26. Mayeur, *Désoeuvré*, p. 76.

27. Nicolas-Edme Rétif de La Bretonne, *Les Contemporaines par gradation, ou Avantures des jolies femmes de l'âge actuel, suivant la gradation des principaux états de la société*, 42 vols. (Paris: Duchesne, 1783–1785), vol. 42, p. 351.

28. Alexandre-Jacques Du Coudray, *Il est temps de parler et il est temps de se taire* (Paris: Ruault, 1779), p. 11; Lous Gachet, *Observations sur les spectacles en général, et en particulier sur la Colisée* (Paris: Le Prieur, 1772), p. 20.

Nicolet had earned over 100,000 écus by 1769, wrote of the "public ardor" for Nicolet. "Women of the greatest distinction," he declared, "are infatuated with his indecent *parades*."[29] The increased coverage given in the newspapers and almanacs of the time to the Grands Danseurs and other boulevard *spectacles* is also evidence of the public's increasing enthusiasm for these shows.

How accurate were the perceptions of Rétif de La Bretonne and others that Nicolet's *spectacles* were obscene and immoral? Thirty-eight of the pieces, selected at random from the years 1763 to 1789, give us a picture of Nicolet's repertoire. Twenty-eight of the plays in this sample exist only in manuscript, and twenty-seven are anonymous. Although the genres indicated for thirty-two productions are labeled in fourteen ways, Nicolet's repertoire does not appear to have varied much over the years. The Grands Danseurs relied heavily on visual communication through slapstick, stunts, gesture, and dance, but most productions had dialogue and song as well. Rustic places and enchanted isles were the favored settings (thirteen pieces); others included boutiques, cafés, shops, châteaux, and the streets.

Efforts to sort out the characters with special attention to the occupations and professions that they depicted on Nicolet's stage encounter many problems. In several instances the character's socioeconomic status is not indicated and is impossible to guess. Nor is it always possible to distinguish artisans from businessmen or apprentices from employers. A separate category of people with service jobs could be established to differentiate them from other types of workers, though the former greatly outnumber the latter. Traditional Opéra-Comique characters such as Arlequin, Colombine, Gilles, Colin, and Isabelle, who appeared in more plays (fourteen) than any other type of character, are presented sometimes just as themselves, while in other productions they have designated occupational roles. It is necessary to establish a miscellaneous category that includes characters who appear frequently as well as ones that grace the stage only once or twice. This diverse group includes coquettes, foreigners, slaves, corsairs, virgins, lechers, and thieves.

Of all the characters in Nicolet's plays, nobles constituted the largest category; they appeared in fourteen of the thirty-eight productions examined. Sometimes they were lampooned, especially when they were identified as Gascons or when they used their wealth and rank to press an unwilling girl into marriage. More often, however, they were treated sympathetically, often acting as beneficent arbiters in village imbroglios. Artisans, including millers, forgers, wigmakers, tailors, cobblers, and pastry chefs, figured in twelve of the thirty-eight pieces. The same number of plays depicted people in the arts and letters and professionals such as doctors, judges, and teachers. Twelve productions also featured workers— woodcutters, washerwomen, chimney sweeps, fishwives, stable keepers, café waiters, gardeners, and peasants. Along with nobles, characters from

29. Bachaumont, *Mémoires*, vol. 3, p. 303 (1 January 1768).

these three categories were thus the ones most frequently used by the play-wrights whom Nicolet employed.

In descending order of frequency, servants (including lackeys and valets) appeared in eleven plays. Three character types were each presented in nine pieces: officials (bailiffs, commissaries, tax assessors and collectors, and process servers); merchants (florists, perfume sellers, café proprietors, and ribbon sellers); and gods, demons, ogres, fairies, and magicians. Soldiers and clerks were each depicted in five plays, and abbés and apprentices each in two. Several plays included many characters of the same type, such as servants and merchants.

What observations can be drawn from these data? First, the characters familiar to fair audiences in the early part of the century reappeared on stage at the Grands Danseurs. They had simply migrated from the old Opéra-Comique of the fairs to the boulevards. Second, while the folk of the Parisian streets, the village bumpkins, the garçons and coquettes, and the Arlequins were as numerous as ever, there was a noticeable decline in the frequency of superhuman creatures from the early fair shows to the boulevard *spectacles*. Some plays were still set in exotic, utopian lands, and magic still played a role in boulevard theater, but fewer productions involved these elements than in the early years of marketplace theater. Third, although nobles figured in more of Nicolet's pieces than any other character type, when workers, apprentices, clerks, and servants are grouped together, *le bas peuple* emerge as the preponderant group on Nicolet's stage. Artisans and petty merchants swell the lower ranks further. Moreover, workers, artisans, merchants, clerks, and servants were always treated sympathetically, if humorously, while mockery and derision were usually reserved for officials and professionals. Boulevard theater still pitted the cultural world of ordinary people against an establishment of wealth and power. But did the thematic material of these plays also reveal the celebration of the common people and of marketplace culture?

More than half (twenty) of the plays examined revolved around ridicule of established society and of a range of recognizable social types, forming the largest thematic category.[30] A procurator is the principal victim of derision in *La bourbonnaise* (1769).[31] Two plays titled *L'avant-souper* (1770 and 1774) mocked the lifestyle of the urban aristocrat, especially the cheeky, fast-living sons of robe and sword aristocrats, who, roving from loge to loge, made a spectacle of themselves in the theaters.[32] A lecherous tutor is the object of scorn in *Le bal masqué* (1775), and a fat, boorish Gascon marquis in *Arlequin amant et valet* (n.d.), both favorite boulevard characters.[33] *L'apo-*

30. For a different kind of thematic analysis with conclusions that contrast to mine, see Michele Root-Bernstein, *Boulevard Theater and Revolution in Eighteenth-Century Paris* (Ann Arbor: UMI Research Press, 1984).

31. Bibliothèque Nationale (hereafter BN), Nouv. acq. 2877, fols. 244–72.

32. Ibid., 2869, fols. 361–87.

33. Bibliothèque de l'Arsenal (hereafter BA), Rondel Collection, MS 321; BN, MS fr. 9720, fols., 312–43.

ticaire, ou La nopce grivoise (1768) mocks a master apothecary called Anodin, who must suffer canings by a coal merchant, a wigmaker, a young girl, and a bourgeoise for prescribing drugs that have killed members of their families.[34] *Arlequin aux fêtes flamandes* (1767) pits a seigneur, his friend Valère, and his valet, Arlequin, against a vindictive bailiff who has forbidden dancing to the boys and girls of a village because a peasant woman refuses to let her daughter marry the bailiff.[35]

In *L'avantageux puni* (1786) the target is a penniless city-dwelling marquis who seeks to marry a baron's daughter for her money.[36] His plan is to get her dowry, then leave her to her parents and return to Paris. A simple villager, Dinval, who loves Julie, argues his moral beliefs with the marquis, who calls honor a chimera, reason a foolish mask, virtue a meaningless label, and fidelity a useless word used by our parents. The play also depicts the contrast between the marquis, who turns the baron's grounds into an English garden and makes love to his wife, and the coarse but kindly baron who rises at sunup, protects his peasants, treats women honorably, cultivates the earth, and gives assistance to the unfortunate. Enraged by the marquis's attitude toward women, Dinval reasons that if rich aristocrats did not seduce women with gifts and promises, all, regardless of class, would be honorable. Dinval, of course, wins Julie, a victory of the nobility of virtuous character over urban aristocratic pretension, hypocrisy, and vice.

These sketches of pieces in Nicolet's repertoire reveal that characters drawn from the upper social ranks—the urban aristocracy, professional people, and especially officials—were all fair targets for the derisive mockery of the boulevard theater. So were merchants and artisans, who often are difficult to tell apart. Poets and musicians were usually depicted as ridiculous and pretentious, fawning over their aristocratic patrons. Intellectuals were always either pedants or charlatans. A distinction was made between the hardworking, well-meaning country seigneur and the dissipated, immoral dandies of the city. Officials of the crown were never portrayed, but the boulevard writers showed no mercy toward tax men, procurators, and bailiffs. They were corrupt, unjust, mercenary, and lecherous. It was evident what kinds of people, behavior, and values boulevard audiences wanted to see lampooned. Behind the stereotypes lay the people of the real world with whom the people of the streets had to cope. The distinctions of rank on the boulevard stage were real. On the stage, however, the villains always lost. Nicolet's theater was piled high with duped nobles and imprisoned officials, providing the fantasy of victory for the virtuous little people.

Who were the heroes? *L'avantageux puni* points to a second thematic category that identifies the heroes and that usually can be found as an accompaniment to ridicule: the idea that distinctions of rank are artificial, that true nobility arises from virtuous behavior, and that happiness stems

34. BN, Nouv. acq. 2864, fols. 13–25.
35. Ibid., fols. 250–70.
36. Ibid., fols. 341–55.

from ordinary domestic existence, hard work, honesty, and fidelity. Sixteen of the thirty-eight plays examined, of which two examples will suffice, involve that theme.

In *Arlequin récompense, ou La justice des dieux* (n.d.) a sharp contrast is drawn between a wealthy seigneur, Damelas, and an impoverished shepherd, Arlequin, who is denied the hand of Damelas's daughter.[37] Seeking to verify the humanity of men, Jupiter and Mercury descend to earth dressed as indigents. Requesting shelter at Damelas's residence, they are turned away by his servant Pierrot because his master does not "receive people of their kind." After Damelas slams the door on the disguised gods, the generous Arlequin welcomes them at his humble cabin, where they sleep on an earthen floor. That night Damelas recognizes his mistake when the gods appear to him in luminous garb in a dream, but it is too late: Jupiter and Mercury destroy Damelas's house with a thunderclap and transform Arlequin's hut into a palace. Arlequin's generous nature has not changed, however, as he tosses the palace keys to Damelas, taking as his sole prize the seigneur's daughter.

The nobility of work and the simple life is graphically set forth in *Arlequin fendeur* (1777).[38] Robert, a farmer, ties Arlequin, a servant, to a tree to be eaten by wild animals because he has dared to woo Colombine, whom Robert has promised to Pierrot, a miller. Woodcutters rescue Arlequin, however, and take him to their camp, where his potential as a woodsman is tested by the master and his cousins. *Cousin hermite* instructs Arlequin in the code of the workers: they help each other and the less fortunate. They subsist on black bread and water. "Drink this cup of water; it is the drink given us by nature. He who will be content with this nourishment will be the richest and happiest of men because he will never know poverty." After teaching Arlequin how to cut wood, the hermit initiates him into the fraternity of cutters, whose motto is "Work and humanity." In the final act Arlequin and the woodsmen save Robert from thieves, and Arlequin disdainfully refuses Robert's money as a reward.

Sexuality in various forms constitutes the third major type of thematic material in Nicolet's plays. Eighteen of his productions deal with adultery, promiscuity, seduction, abduction, loss of virginity, prostitution, debauchery, or lechery. Usually these matters form part of a satire on the morality and frivolous amusements of the aristocracy. In *Les aventures du Gascon aux boulevards* (n.d.), for example, the chevalier de Rapigac recounts his adventures among effeminate fops and amorous abbés in the salons and *spectacles* to Blaisac, a renter of chairs.[39] Realizing that rich married women who do not have lovers are "*du mauvais ton*," the penniless marquis takes up with a lady named Lucinde de Montfardée, who, feigning great wealth, accompanies him to the boulevards. He soon learns, however, that she is a cob-

37. Ibid., 2866, fols. 208–15.
38. Ibid., 2865, fols. 190–205.
39. Ibid., 2870, fols. 153–72.

bler's daughter and that she has gone off to a house of ill repute with two horsemen.

La bourbonnaise (1769) concerns an abbé's abduction of an innkeeper's daughter from Vichy to Paris and her instruction in the art of coquetry by a prostitute named Mademoiselle Des Usages.[40] In *La colique* (n.d.) a lecherous old teacher named Cassandre tries to trick his young pupil into marrying him by convincing her that marriage is the only cure for her vapors.[41] Feigning colic, Isabelle dupes Cassandre into summoning the village surgeon, with whom she elopes. *L'Hymen et le dieu jaune* (1782) treats Hymen's attempt to seduce three virgins.[42] When he attempts to rape one of them, the god Jaune intervenes and sends him into exile on the banks of Cythère. Finally, in *Colinette, ou La vigne d'amour*, Amour gives Colin a magic vine that will enable him to seduce Colinette: "If the first arrow with which love is aroused causes a few tears, pleasure will soon dry them." Rosette assures Colinette, who fears that the vine will be bitter, that the second taste is delicious. Colinette's mother, Simone, warns her that if she tastes a single grain of the vine, she will lose her "basket" (*panier*) and will not be able to face the villagers. Encouraged by Amour, Colinette cuts the vine with Colin's pruning knife and enjoys the "innocent pleasures" of love.

Only ten of the plays in manuscript in this sample show any evidence of the censor's pen, and none of the material eliminated changes the plays in a substantive way. The lieutenant general of police or the censor selected from the Comédie-Française or the Comédie-Italienne cut two kinds of passages: sexually suggestive words or expressions, such as *beszée* (*Le bal de Passy*, 1767), and pejorative references to royalty or to high-ranking nobles, officials, and authors. There was no consistency in the first type of censorship. The plays abound in sexual innuendo, most of which the censor passed. In addition, the actors were probably quite explicit in their visual posturing. Nor was much consistency maintained in the second type of censorship. Nobles and officials were mocked and ridiculed with great regularity in Nicolet's productions. It seems likely that the censors recognized specific individuals in the few instances in which they eliminated passages.

No doubt censorship was lax because the police had no desire to stifle a form of entertainment that kept the public diverted. Furthermore, the censors from the great theaters were primarily interested in preventing the boulevard troupes from presenting or imitating the classical repertoire. They wanted Nicolet's offerings to be episodic and vulgar on the mistaken assumption that *le monde* would stay away from such shows. Finally, the dramatists who wrote for the Grands Danseurs were quite aware of the kinds of material the censors objected to. It seems evident, therefore, that they exercised self-censorship.

Used to perpetuate a distinction between the classical theaters and the

40. Ibid., 2877, fols. 244–72.

41. Ibid., 2888, fols. 183–207.

42. Alexandre-Louis-Bertrand Robineau Beaunoir, *L'Hymen et le dieu jaune* (Paris: Cailleau, 1782), pp. 18–25.

popular ones, censorship was a major weapon in the struggle of privileged theaters to maintain the divide between popular and elite culture. The censors, Mercier declared, ensure that "the people are condemned to hear only expressions of licentiousness and foolishness." They make themselves the arbiters of public morality, denying moral standards to the very people "who have the greatest need to receive some salutary instruction."[43] The great theaters also got the police to keep ticket prices low at the boulevard theaters as a means of segregating taste publics. Moreover, the privileged theaters flooded the Council of State, the Parlement of Paris, the Châtelet, and the First Gentlemen of the Chamber with demands that their theatrical monopolies be enforced.

The three privileged theaters of Paris—the Opéra, the Comédie-Française, and the Comédie-Italienne—had held these monopolies since the reign of Louis XIV. The Opéra enjoyed the exclusive right to present, for the court and for the public, works whose texts were sung, unless Jean-Baptiste Lully and his successors chose to grant or sell that right to someone else. In one attempt to invoke its privileges at the turn of the century, the Opéra proposed to collect fees from players at the Parisian fairs who used music and dance, and, debt-ridden after Lully's time, the Opéra pursued a policy of taxing the Opéra-Comique for the right to sing and dance. The Comédie-Française procured a similar monopoly, first granted by the crown in 1680, over works in French verse and prose. To the fury of the classical troupe, the fair players concocted various stratagems to skirt this privilege. The resultant struggle between the elite and the popular theaters entailed police actions and court cases throughout the century. These confrontations resumed when the popular entertainers migrated to the boulevards.

The aim of the privileged theaters and the authorities, officially at least, was to keep cultural worlds separate and unequal and, it was hoped, taste publics as well. Determined to restrict the Grands Danseurs to pantomime, the Comédie-Italienne (which had taken over the Opéra-Comique in 1762) remonstrated angrily to the police and to the First Gentlemen of the King's Chamber, who supervised the Italians and the Comédie-Française. The complaint lodged by the Comédie-Italienne was straightforward: Nicolet was doing pieces in verse, prose, and song for which the Italian players were obliged to pay the Opéra 20,000 livres annually.[44] The troupe's campaign prompted this remark by Friedrich Melchior Grimm: "If one did not know our passion for exclusive privileges, one would have difficulty believing that the three *spectacles* of Paris. . . have united against a miserable player of farces of the boulevard called Nicolet to prevent him from performing spoken pieces and to reduce him to pantomime."[45] In response to the com-

43. Mercier, *Tableau de Paris*, vol. 3, p. 41; vol. 8, p. 60.
44. Emile Campardon, *Les comédiens du roi et la troupe italienne pendant les deux derniers siècles*, 2 vols. (Paris: Berger-Levrault, 1880), vol. 2, pp. 285–89, 301–27. See also Du Coudray, *Nouveaux essais historiques*, vol. 1, pp. 117–18.
45. Frédéric Melchior Grimm, *Correspondance littéraire, philosophique et critique*, 16 vols. (Paris: Garnier, 1877–1882), vol. 6, p. 100 (November 1764).

plaints, the police ordered Nicolet to present nothing resembling the fare of the privileged theaters. Vaudevilles and dialogue were forbidden; the orchestra was limited to six violins; and a ceiling of 24 sous was placed on tickets out of the conviction that inexpensive tickets would discourage the elite from attending.

In 1771 the directors of the three elite theaters petitioned the Council of State to limit the orchestra of the Ambigue-Comique, one of the boulevard shows, to four musicians, to outlaw song and dance, and to officially rank the Ambigue a *spectacle* of the last class.[46] One observer declared: "It is believed that the minister of Paris will strip these *spectacles* of everything that can interest people of taste in order to leave only those things that would satisfy the *menu peuple*."[47] It is interesting that on this occasion the authorities did not act.

The Comédie-Française also registered complaints with the Council of State. In 1778 it charged that the Opéra was intruding on its privilege because its productions of *Iphigénie* and *Andromaque* were nothing more than Racine's plays set to music, and it demanded that the Parlement of Paris prevent Nicolet and Audinot from presenting "continuous pieces, embellished with brilliant decorations and machines."[48] The Comédie also requested that, as the boulevard theaters existed for the people, they be limited to a maximum of 12 sous a ticket. In its lengthy report to the Parlement, the Comédie-Française reviewed all the rulings of the seventeenth and eighteenth centuries which defined its privileges and limited the original fair players to simple *parades*, rope dancing, and pantomime, a clear effort to prove that the original assumption behind the privileges—that theatrical competition weakens theater by dividing its resources—was still valid.[49] The Comédie-Française argued that its traditional rights had steadily eroded since the early 1760s with Nicolet's move to the boulevards, the Ambigue's switch from marionettes to child actors, the boulevard directors' disregard for the prohibitions against song and speech, the expansion of their troupes, and Nicolet's performance of genuine comedies and grand *spectacles*. These developments, the French comedians concluded, had led to a loss of taste, the prostitution of talent, and the public's desertion of the classical theater.

The directors of the boulevard theaters responded that Louis XIV's action in 1680 was not intended to be a permanent theatrical policy; that the Opéra had legally authorized the establishment of popular theaters; and that theatrical competition was healthy and stimulated progress in the arts. Throughout the century, the course of action followed by the Opéra differed from that of the other two privileged troupes. Rather than attempt restrictions or censorship, as it had done in the days of the fairs, the Opéra chose to tax the boulevard shows for the right to have music. The policy paid off. In 1784

46. E. Deligny, *Histoire de l'Ambigue-Comique* (Paris: Lacombe, 1841), p. 31; Bachaumont, *Mémoires*, vol. 6, p. 59 (2 December 1771).
47. *Le Courier d'Avignon*, 24 December 1776, p. 122.
48. Ibid., 26 June 1778, p. 404.
49. Bachaumont, *Mémoires*, vol. 29, pp. 110–15.

the crown gave the Opéra proprietary control over all the little *spectacles* of the city.[50] The little theaters were safe, though everyone now had to pay tribute. Monsieur Albini paid one livre a year to display his crocodile, and Monsieur Marigny was assessed 2 sous a day for his dwarf exhibition.

Another means of keeping popular and elite cultures separate was to make clear distinctions among the theaters in the press. In the early 1770s Parisian journals listed the programs of the privileged theaters. In its first year (1777) the *Journal de Paris* provided résumés of plots, commentaries on productions, and letters to the editor. Popular *spectacles* were categorized separately under the rubric "Boulevard," and in 1777 only Nicolet's show was listed, without commentary.[51] Even after 1779, when other shows began to appear in the press, they were carefully distinguished from the prominently featured grand *spectacles* by means of a heavy bar, a space, or a distinctive rubric.

Thus censorship, ticket pricing, assertions of monopolistic privilege, and journalistic reporting were the principal means by which theatrical cultures were distinguished. Nevertheless, the walls of cultural separation were crumbling. Keeping ticket prices low did not discourage *le monde* from going to the boulevards. All the accounts of Parisian life stress the gathering of high- and lowborn on the boulevards, the social mixture of theater audiences, and the enormous popularity and success of the Grands Danseurs and other shows. The little theaters may have been aimed at *le bas peuple*, but everyone came. Moreover, the trend in the press by the 1780s was toward increased coverage of boulevard entertainments and elimination of the traditional separation of theater listings. By the 1780s the *Journal de Paris* provided the programs for all the principal boulevard attractions. A similar trend was evident in the *Almanach des muses*, which in 1779 began a column titled "Pièces des Boulevards," listing the programs of the Grands Danseurs. The number of pieces mentioned grew from two in 1782 to twenty-one in 1784. Moreover, in 1785 both the *Journal de Paris* and the *Affiches, annonces et avis divers* lifted the "Variétés-Amusantes" out of its subordinate place and listed it just below the three grand *spectacles*, thus creating a tripartite division of theaters. The *Affiches* later completed the obliteration of the old hierarchical separation by deleting the lines between theater programs.

As for the invocation of privilege by the great theaters, most of the government's rulings were in their favor. The only problem was that they were not enforced. Although Nicolet made a specialty of pantomime *spectacles*, he and other directors used speech, dance, and song, despite the police ordinances and the complaints of the privileged theaters. It is apparent that Nicolet knew he had little to fear from the authorities. The police were justifiably concerned about maintaining public order in a city with a large, growing, and restless working-class population. Popular entertainments

50. Louis-Henry Lecomte, *Les variétés amusantes, 1778–89* (Paris, 1908), p. 103. See also Campardon, *Spectacles*, vol. 1, pp. 354–57; *Almanach forain*, 1786, pp. 93–97; AN, H² 2158, doss. 2.

51. See, for example, *Journal de Paris*, 19 June 1777, p. 4.

were useful in diverting the population, more useful than enforcing the theatrical monopolies of the past.[52] An anonymous observer declared: "Make a nation laugh, put before it some diversions of its own taste, and you will never have to fear its discontent."[53] The comte de Saint-Florentin, secretary of state in charge of Paris, echoed the official attitude best when he declared that "spectacles for the people are necessary, the system of Louis XIV has changed."[54]

Changes in censorship in the 1780s provide the best window into the approaching end of distinctions between theatrical cultures. Whereas offensive phrases or passages were struck from the early boulevard farces, the censors of the two comedies began appropriating entire plays from the boulevard theaters for their own stages. From the Variétés-Amusantes the Comédie-Française took Dorvigny's *Noces houzardes* and the Comédie-Italienne copped Beaunoir's *Fanfan et Colas*, a work that Grimm characterized as morally instructive.[55] It was apparent to the censors that such plays as *L'avantageux puni* (1786) at Nicolet's theater were elevated in tone. The boulevard theaters did not abandon farce, but in the mid-1780s they began to replace bawdy buffoonery with more serious plays containing moral lessons and celebrating the dignity of labor, fidelity, generosity, and kindness. In elevating the tone of their plays, Nicolet and Audinot were endowing them with social utility and toppling the barriers separating popular from elite entertainment. Critics of the time, many of whom had once passed harsh judgment on the "inferior spectacles," perceived and lauded the change. They began to form a phalanx against the attempts of the privileged theaters to keep the popular *spectacles* absurd, episodic, and obscene. If boulevard fare had to exist, and most critics by 1785 shared the view of the police that it did, then its justification and legitimacy would be that it was instructive and edifying. The *Affiches, annonces et avis divers* declared:

> We have said it and we repeat it, since today *spectacles* for the inferior classes of society are necessary, since they have become a necessity for them which can no longer be overlooked, these *spectacles*, without being raised completely to the dignity that reigns at the great theaters (when they do not give farces, be it understood), should at least approach them in decency of sentiments, purity of morals, and the utility of the lessons they can offer.[56]

52. Some people in the government, however, sided with the grand theaters, including Papillon de la Ferté, intendant of the Menus Plaisirs, and the maréchal de Richelieu, Gentleman of the Chamber. See Michelle Marie Root-Bernstein, "Revolution on the Boulevard: Parisian Popular Theater in the late Eighteenth Century" (Ph.D. dissertation, Princeton University, 1981), pp. 63–73.

53. *Sur l'Ambigue-Comique*, p. 38. This anonymous, undated fifty-page pamphlet can be found in BA, RT 2808.

54. Quoted in Jules Bonnaissies, *Les spectacles forains et la Comédie-Française* (Paris E. Dentu, 1875), p. 57.

55. Grimm, *Correspondence*, vol. 14, p. 45 (September 1784).

56. *Affiches, annonces*, 5 July 1785, p. 1812–13.

Even the author of the once critical *Mémoires secrets* was persuaded that Nicolet and Audinot had really changed their ways. Of Audinot, he wrote:

> Before him, upright people dared not go there [to the boulevard theaters]; they were reserved for the rabble, girls of the streets, libertines: buffoonery, indecency, debauchery held forth there. Little by little, he [Audinot] has raised his to a more upright tone. His colleagues are piqued with emulation, and the boulevard has almost become the school of good morals, while the other theaters are degraded.[57]

Yet, for all that, the boulevards remained the boulevards. If the politics of privilege no longer effectively separated popular from elite culture, if that separation was not based on different taste publics or the socioeconomic divide between the upper ranks of society and the lower, and if the theaters used each other's material and eliminated many of the divisions between genres, what, then, was the basis of popular culture? The marketplace itself, as in the heyday of the fairs, was still the decisive factor. The boulevards constituted a counterculture to the officially sanctioned world of court and city. These socially unsegregated lanes of leisure generated their own free-wheeling material and moral nutrients. Eccentric extremes of speech, dress, and manner were permissible. Boulevard culture broke down the social stratification of Parisian society in unwitting prescience of the Revolution. The awesome physical prowess of Nicolet's acrobats communicated the pleasure and the danger of material existence which the boulevards celebrated. Nougaret and Rétif wrote: "The feats of strength that one sees there, the tightrope dancing, the somersaults can provide the lively pleasure that is born of surprise, of astonishment, joined to fear of the danger to which the performer is exposed."[58] Even after they became moralistic, the *spectacles* of the boulevards expressed the culture of the people best in derisive mockery of the world beyond the streets. Humorous satire of the traditional social and cultural order was still the hallmark of the boulevards and their entertainers.

57. Bachaumont, vol. 28, p. 6 (1 January 1785).
58. Pierre-Jean Baptiste Nougaret and Nicholas-Edme Rétif de La Bretonne, *La mimographe, ou Idées d'une honnête femme pour la réformation du théâtre national* (Amsterdam: Changuion, 1770), p. 446.

13

Incendiary Actions

Fires and Firefighting in the Shogun's Capital and the People's City

WILLIAM W. KELLY

About half past the eighth hour [3 P.M.] a fire broke out. . . at a bathhouse in Sakuma-machi. Owing to the strong wind, the area around Izumi-bashi soon burnt to the ground. The fire then crossed the river, and the area around the Benkei-bashi and Shitamachi became a vast holocaust, as bad as the great fire of 1829.

About the seventh hour [4 P.M.] I heard that the Kodenma-chō, Ōdenma-chō, and Abura-machi areas were burnt to the ground, including Chōjiya and Tsuruya. The area west of the Echigoya in Suruga-machi escaped the blaze because the wind was blowing from the north-west, but elsewhere the increasingly high wind fanned it all night. I could not sleep; word came that the flames had spread to Kukagawa, but it was not clear how great the damage had been.

With the fire burning unchecked late into the night, none of us could sleep. Tarō and Ohyaku finally rested at half past the fourth hour [11 P.M.], but Shima [a maid?] and I stayed awake until a little past the ninth hour [midnight]. Sōhaku and Omichi could not fall asleep either.[1]

Edo may have been the most populous and most built-up conurbation of the early-modern world. It was also very likely the most rebuilt metropolis of that era. Fires are, to be sure, a continual public danger in all urban settings, but Edo faced fires that were perhaps unparalleled in frequency and ferocity. Tokugawa Ieyasu formally established his headquarters at Edo in the Eighth Month of 1590. The first recorded fire was the third day of the following month, when the Founder's Hall of Sojoin in Kaizuka (present-day Kōjimachi) was destroyed. A mere ten years later the first major fire swept through half of the new city—including Edo Castle itself—reducing a decade of intense con-

---

1. Quoted in Leon Zolbrod, *Takizawa Bakin*, Twayne's World Authors Series 20 (New York: Twayne, 1967), pp. 126–27.

struction to ashes.[2] Thereafter, with a periodicity that approached the annual round of Edo festivals, the city and its residents were visited by conflagrations major and minor. Indeed, some analysts, such as Nakai Nobuhiko, believe that fires, like festivals and funerals, were conceptualized at the time as spiritually charged *hare* ritual events.[3]

It is no wonder, then, that a fire was known as one of the "flowers of Edo" (*Edo no hana*), the flames and sparks lighting up the city sky like fireworks (or "flower-fires"—*hanabi*—as the Japanese more aptly put it). Edo's fires were likened also to *momiji*, coloring the city with hues as vivid as the fall show of maple leaves, only to leave behind a charred and desiccated wintry landscape. The doyen of post–World War II Edo studies, Nishiyama Matsunosuke, proposed a famous fourfold characterization of Edo as a "city of warriors, men, fire, and forced moves," the fourth chiefly a consequence of the third.[4]

Fires were also called *shukuyū* and *kairoku*, names of ancient Chinese personages that were adapted as appellations for Japanese "fire gods." The *Daikairoku*, a nineteenth-century record of the three great fires of Edo, bespeaks that century's enshrinement of Edo fire folklore. The first of those famous fires—and the most momentous of all Edo blazes—was the great Meireki fire, in the first month of 1657. Also known as the Furisode fire, this was actually two successive conflagrations that destroyed most of Edo, including the castle and its keep, 160 daimyo estates, over 770 bannerman compounds, more than 350 temples and shrines, and nearly 50,000 merchant houses. The number of dead has been estimated at 108,000; the unclaimed were buried in mass graves at a site south of the Sumida River that became Muenji (later Ekōin), a favored site of sumo tournaments.[5] Over a century later, the great Gyōninzaka fire of 1772 burned a path of destruction fifteen miles long and more than two miles wide. The trio was completed by the great Heiin fire of 1806, which started in the southern section of the city and cleared a swath six miles by one-half mile in six hours, claiming 1,200 lives and destroying 83 domain estates, 86 temples, and 530 residential quarters.

Most serious fires started in late winter and early spring, often sparked by cooking fires and heating braziers and then fueled by the seasonal north to northwest winds. Fully half of the recorded Edo blazes occurred in the final and first two months of the old calendar (roughly, the first quarter of the modern year). Often in this season, the wind fanned fires from the higher elevations of Hongō, Koishigawa, Ushigome, and Komagome down into the low-lying commoner wards between Edo Castle and the Sumida River.

2. Ikegami Akihiko, "Edo hikeshi seido no seiritsu to tenkai," in Nishiyama Matsunosuke, ed., *Edo chōnin no kenkyū*, 5 vols. (Yoshikawa Kōbunkan, 1972–1978), vol. 5, p. 95.

3. Nakai Nobuhiko, *Chōnin*, Nihon no rekishi 21 (Shōgakukan,1975), pp. 295–305.

4. Nishiyama discusses these four characteristics in several works; for example, "Zoku: Edokko," in his *Edo chōnin no kenkyū*, vol. 3, pp. 1–27.

5. A book-length study of the fire is Kuroki Takashi, *Meireki no taika*, Kōdansha gendai shinsho 390 (Kōdansha, 1977). See also Ikegami Akihiko, "Meireki no taika," in Nishiyama Matsunosuke, ed., *Edo no sanbyakunen*, vol. 1: Nishiyama and Haga Noboru, eds., *Tenka no chōnin*, Kōdansha gendai shinsho 415 (Kōdansha, 1975), pp. 72–83.

Fire at the bathhouse. Source: Chinka anshin zukan. Courtesy of Kokuritsu Kokkai Toshokan.

Edo Castle suffered major damage seven times after the first serious fire in 1601. As Nishiyama and Nakai note, however, it was the dense downtown merchant and artisan quarters, as well as the theater district, that were the most frequently hit by ruinous fires. Nakai's calculations indicate, for example, that major fires struck this area thirty-one times in the period from 1657 to 1834.[6] Even Nihonbashi Bridge, at the very center of commercial downtown, burned ten times between 1657 and 1858. Although there were periods as long as twenty-five years without a major blaze, there were eight fires in the first eighteen years of the eighteenth century, and nine within twenty-eight years in the early nineteenth century. On average, there was a major conflagration once every six years. Moreover, even apart from the so-called great fires, there were many years when a series of smaller fires did damage just as extensive.[7]

It is no surprise, then, to find that fire prevention and firefighting were prominent in the city bylaws and among the ordinances issued by the city magistrates. Fires placed a heavy financial burden on residents and the shogun's treasury; they influenced building materials, housing form, and urban space; and they figured prominently in the cultural imagination of the Edo populace. The need to rebuild and replenish after a fire created a significant demand for commodity of all sorts, and beneficial effects were felt throughout the national and local economy by major merchants and small artisans alike.

Furthermore, the frequency of arson and of fights at the scenes of fires continued to pose significant threats to urban order. In one famous incident, Bakin's contemporary, the satirist Shikitei Sanba published a thinly disguised fiction about a brawl between two rival fire companies. Angered, a compatriot company of one of those involved in the fray then attacked the houses of both Sanba and his publisher. The city magistrates not only ordered jail terms for the firefighters but also levied a heavy fine against the publisher and sentenced Sanba to fifty days in manacles.[8]

Given fire's multifarious significance, it *is* surprising that the techniques and technology of firefighting changed so little during the two and a half centuries of Tokugawa rule. Throughout the period, firefighting was directed not toward extinguishing the fires in buildings but rather toward limiting the fire's further spread. Thus the roof of a flaming building was ripped off in order to turn the flames upward, and its walls were collapsed inward on all four sides. Meanwhile, buildings surrounding the fire site were torn down to create

6. Nakai, *Chōnin*, p. 304.

7. For example, in 1716, 1717, 1721, and 1771: Yoshiwara Ken'ichirō, "Edo saigai nenpyō," in Nishiyama, *Edo chōnin*, vol. 5, p. 439. This work reorganizes and supplements a massive Taisho collection, *Tōkyō shishikō: Hensai-hen*. The most convenient source for Edo fire statistics, Yoshiwara's chronology gives, for each entry, time and place of the fire's origin, wind direction, and the nature and scope of its destruction. He also indicates any subsequent nicknames and stories about the major fires. In addition, he discusses some of the problems of the statistics, and gives examples of the language and form of the official shogunate fire reports.

8. Robert Leutner, *Shikitei Sanba and the Comic Tradition in Edo Fiction*, Harvard-Yenching Institute Monographs 25 (Cambridge: Harvard University Press, 1985), pp. 29–31.

a firebreak. There were few changes in this kind of "demolition firefighting" (*hakai shōbō*) before the late nineteenth century. Pumps, hoses, and other extinguishing equipment remained crude and largely ineffective. The tool kit for Edo firefighters was primarily that of the building trades: ropes, saws, mauls, and, emblematically, the *tobiguchi*, the famous "fireman's hook," which was associated with the aerial-acrobatic and rough-living roofers (*tobi*) who came to dominate firefighting in fact and in reputation by the mid-Tokugawa period.[9]

In fact, as with other dimensions of societal management, Tokugawa firefighting was marked by a curious combination of technological stasis, organizational transformation, and cultural elaboration. In exploring the place of firefighting in the political processes and cultural productions of Edo, I focus on three moments—in the early seventeenth, early eighteenth, and early nineteenth centuries—when its character fundamentally shifted.

The initial provisions for firefighting in the early seventeenth century reflected the often contradictory ambitions of the early state for its new capital, including the competing demands of military defense and a regulated monumental architecture together with the imperatives of segregated residential space and immiscible social status. The sharp separation of jurisdictions, procedures, and organization only increased the hazards of fire.

In the early eighteenth century, the Tokugawa state was struggling to adjust its administrative procedures and apparatus to the twin realities of a highly commercialized economy and a dense, mobile population in the largest city in the world. Its well-known initiatives of the Kyōhō era (1716–1736), the first of three organized reform programs to be undertaken during the early-modern period, constituted a grand attempt at both renovation and retrenchment, an effort to curb official and warrior class expenditures, raise state revenues, streamline administration, and reassert shogunal prerogatives over warriors' and commoners' conduct. As part of this extensive set of measures, Edo authorities sought to expand the responsibilities of city commoners as residents while restricting their roles and opportunities as merchants and artisans. De-

9. Two developments of note were fire towers and portable pumps. Fire towers (*hinomi yagura*) were first built in 1658; typically, they were about nine meters high, with lacquered, wood-latticed shutters. There was a large drum in the tower, and fire bells were suspended at the four corners. The fire towers that were subsequently built on the daimyo estates and by the entrance gates to commoner wards were slightly shorter and black-lacquered. The daimyo towers used wood clappers, while the towers in the commoners' residential quarters had fire bells. In the Kyōhō era, such fire towers were mandated for every ten residential quarters; quarters without a tower maintained walking watches (*jishinban*). See Nishiyama Matsunosuke et al., eds., *Edogaku jiten* (Kōbundō, 1984), s.v. Ikegami Akihiko, "Hikeshi," pp. 581–82.

In 1764 the shogunate distributed portable pumps known as *ryūdosui* throughout the city. Although these pumps did not help much in extinguishing the main blazes, they were useful in wetting roofs against flying sparks. Nakai cites several documents from officials within the residential quarters who complained vociferously about the pumps; they found them expensive, unreliable, wasteful of manpower, and hard to use in the confusion of a fire site. See Ikegami, "Meireki no taika," pp. 96–97; Minami Kazuo, "Shōbō: Edo machi hikeshi o chūshin to shite," in Toyoda Takeshi et al., eds., *Nihon no hōken toshi*, vol. 2 (Bun'ichi Sōgō Shuppan, 1983), p. 467; and Nakai, *Chōnin*, pp. 306–8.

spite an obvious self-interest in effective urban fire control, Edo residents—
especially property owners and their agents—adamantly resisted the reforms.
They were successful, however, only in mitigating the more onerous demands
of the new system, and by mid-century Edo firefighting was shifting to a
citywide organization of plebeian professionals.

By the early nineteenth century, this transition to a commoner organization
was nearly complete. Fires, both large and small, remained a constant danger
and frequently lighted up Edo's skyline. The squads of brusque, swaggering
roofers and construction workers who fought them were glamorized by a
populace increasingly self-conscious of itself as Edoites. Even the coolies who
assisted the firefighters became colorful elements in the reflexive construction
of an Edo identity. Thus firefighting, in word and deed, was indicative of the
changing political complexion and social arrangements of Edo.

The transformation of firefighting organization was symptomatic of a more
general process—what one may call a negotiated desamuraization of the shogunal capital. That is, firefighting is richly suggestive of the cultural, political,
and economic dimensions of the Edo commoners' reluctant appropriation of
the city as their own.

Status Fears in a New Capital: The Compartmentalization of Firefighting in Seventeenth-Century Edo

From its very beginning, the shogunate feared fires as much for their social
disorder as for their physical destruction. Disorder, in official minds, resulted
from status mixing, and it was exacerbated by Edo's special character as the
capital, attracting commoner migrants and large numbers of warrior contin-
gents from all parts of the country. Misunderstandings and rivalries were
frequent. Arson was a not uncommon means to settle scores, and the swirling
confusion and inflamed passions of fire scenes always threatened to set the
crowds against one another. Ikegami, for instance, cites a 1613 directive (then
reissued in 1616, 1619, 1622, 1625, and 1632) that prohibited the use of samurai
servants for fighting fires in the commoner areas. He interprets this and related
orders as evidence of official fears of another kind of fighting that might break
out at fire sites.

Perhaps this is why, throughout the seventeenth century, there was no
formal citywide organization for fighting fires. Instead, both warriors and commoners were held responsible for firefighting in their respective areas of the city.
The shogunate's principal concern was obviously Edo Castle, and within its
precincts firefighting was handled by its military organization. The senior councilors (*rōjū*) and junior councilors (*wakadoshiyori*) directed the various bannermen
(*hatamoto*) who captained samurai companies. In 1639 the shogunate created
two fire guard positions, one for the castle perimeter and the other for its
interior. Each was given a complement of constables and subordinate patrolmen. The same year it began to make individual daimyo responsible for fire
prevention at particular sites, such as the Tokugawa mausoleum at Momijiyama.

Further steps toward specialized organization were taken in the aftermath of the so-called Oki-chō fire of 1641, which broke out in the residential quarter of that name (in Kyōbashi) and destroyed over half of the city, including 97 commoner neighborhoods and 121 daimyo and bannerman mansions, despite a concerted response by the shogunate; the shogun himself appeared at the main castle gate to direct the daimyo and bannerman squads personally. The inspector in direct charge of firefighting committed suicide. Two years later, the government ordered sixteen lesser daimyo to support four permanent firefighter brigades.[10] They were known as the daimyo brigades (*daimyō-bikeshi*), although their jurisdiction included both commoner and warrior areas. A martial esprit de corps was fostered by colorful uniforms and precision formations when the brigades responded to fires.

This organization, however, proved grossly inadequate in the devastating Meireki fires of 1657. Among the wide range of shogunal reactions was the creation in 1658 of an all-samurai all-Edo fire guard (*Edojū jōbi no ban*, or what came to be known as the "regular firemen," *jō-bikeshi*). Four bannermen were assigned this duty and ordered to establish firefighting headquarters at separate locations around the city. Each commanded 300-man squads and was assisted by six constables and thirty patrolmen. Generally their assignments were to the north and west of Edo Castle, reflecting the direction of greatest danger to the shogun's citadel.[11] The authority structure of the brigades was visible in the processional order. The bannermen wore leather (later heavy patterned-cotton) fire jackets and battle-dress helmets, with protective hoods that fastened under the chin. They rode horses, as did their assistants, who also sported leather hoods and fire jackets. The patrolmen trotted behind, followed by the actual firefighters.[12] While on call, the squads spent their time in a large room at the firehouse. If a night alarm sounded, the foremen awakened the sleeping men by pounding with hammers on the small hollow logs that the firefighters used as pillows. They were a rough lot, heavily tattooed, given to gambling and hostile to townspeople.

Two other types of fire squads developed in this early period. One was based on the shogunate's continued need for daimyo to provide fire guards at strategic sites, especially temples, bridges, castle gates, and granaries. These groups became known as the "dispersed brigades" (*shosho-bikeshi* or *tokorodokoro-bikeshi*). Because the regular firemen and the daimyo brigades responded to the main fire sites, these dispersed brigades frequently had the

10. All of these daimyo had registered domains of less than 60,000 *koku*, and each daimyo had to contribute 30 men per 10,000 *koku*. The four brigades contained 120 men each and were rotated on ten-day duty assignments. The four brigades were reduced to three the following year and several times thereafter the assignments of particular lords were rearranged. See Ikegami, "Edo hikeshi seido," p. 98, for a list of assignments and further details on the 1641 fire.

11. Appointments of six more bannermen raised the total to ten brigades by 1662, leading to the alternate term for the system, the *jūnin-bikeshi*. For details of appointments, locations, and subsequent developments, see ibid., pp. 100–101.

12. Ibid., p. 101.

duty of tracking down flying sparks when their own assigned areas were not threatened.[13]

Apart from the interests of the shogunate, individual daimyo were obviously concerned about fires that started in the commoner neighborhoods surrounding their mansions. Thus in the 1680s a number of major daimyo successfully petitioned for authorization to send squads to fires that broke out near their estates (and after the regular fire squads arrived, to move downwind to track sparks). These new domain lord squads were known as *kakuji-bikeshi* ("individual brigades," also *sanchō-bikeshi* or *kinjō-bikeshi*). In 1717 after a blaze destroyed 72 daimyo mansions and 349 bannerman compounds (in addition to much of the downtown commercial area), the shogunate ordered such units to be formed around all domain estates. Even as it was acceding to this expansion of warrior duties, however, the government was embarking on a new pattern of Edo firefighting, which would eliminate warrior participation and create a citywide commoner organization. The commoners protested, but the new organization was eventually accepted and ultimately celebrated by Edo townspeople.

From Status Anxiety to Fiscal Crisis: Commoner Firefighting and the Kyōhō Reforms

At the same time as it was forming the daimyo *kakuji-bikeshi*, the city magistrates also undertook some tentative measures to systematize commoner units that would prove decisive in transforming the character of Edo firefighting.[14] Initially the magistrates aimed at better organization of the commoners' own firefighting, but they soon went so far as to dismantle the existing warrior units and began to order commoner squads to protect bannerman, daimyo, and shogunal lands and buildings. Seizing the initiative for this major organizational reform was the new city magistrate, Ōoka Echizen no Kami, who took office in the early spring of 1717. Then thirty-one years old, he began what was to stretch to forty-five years of official service, becoming the most celebrated and mythologized city magistrate in Tokugawa history.[15] Ōoka was the principal

13. The first assignments were made in 1639, and by the end of the century, a total of thirty-six units were recorded in the *Genroku bukan*. For details about subsequent reorganizations, see ibid., p. 102.

14. Ibid., pp. 120–37; Minami, "Shōbō," pp. 457–71; Nakai, *Chōnin*, pp. 308–21; Yoshioka Yuriko, "Kyōhō-ki Edo machikata ni okeru sogan undō no jittai: Bōka seisaku o meguru chōningawa no taiō o chūshin ni shite," in Chihōshi Kenkyū Kyōgikai, ed., *Toshi no chihōshi: Seikatsu to bunka* (Yūzankaku, 1980), pp. 108–58.

15. Ōoka served as city magistrate for twenty years and then as a commissioner of shrines and temples for another twenty-five years (1736–1751), until he was seventy-five. For part of that time (1722–1745) he was the rural affairs officer for the Kantō region, and for the entire forty-five years of service, he served as a judge at the shogunate court. His diary for 1737–1751 has been published in Ōishi Shinzaburō and Hayashi Reiko, eds., *Ōoka Echizen no Kami Tadasuke nikki*, 3 vols. (Ōoka Monjo Kankōkai, 1972–1775). See also the biography by Ōishi Shinzaburō, *Ōoka Echizen no Kami Tadasuke* (Iwanami Shoten, 1974).

architect of the Kyōhō reforms, which formed the immediate political context for the major reorganization of Edo firefighting.[16]

The eventual result was a more unified, citywide firefighting system, but the concentration of responsibility on the commoners greatly increased the financial burdens borne by the merchants, who resisted vigorously with many petitions throughout the eighteenth century. Indeed, fire organization proved to be only one of the increased burdens imposed on—and protested by— commoners. Changing policies toward firebreak zones and building codes were also widely—though ultimately unsuccessfully—resisted. The eighteenth-century reorganization of fire procedures and prevention was a protracted and negotiated accomplishment, resisted by a broadly skeptical but increasingly differentiated commoner population.

In addition to the general fiscal crisis of the shogunate, some specific factors lie behind the firefighting reforms that began in 1717, including a string of serious fires of suspicious origin. Nakai Nobuhiko has suggested that directives from the city magistrates to the neighborhood chiefs (*nanushi*) reveal an unusual anxiety among officials. He quotes an early 1717 directive that complained of large numbers of commoner firemen who were increasingly out of control (*wagamama*) and given to extortion and intimidation. The directive worried, too, about an increasing population of unregistered persons (*musatsu no mono* or *mushukunin*), which fueled speculation that the recent spate of fires was due to arson. Later, officials ordered all commoner firemen and unregistered persons to report to the Day Laborers' Exchange; this registration was made the responsibility of the firemen bosses and the firemen recruiters. Subsequent memoranda demanded a citywide inventory of muskets, ordered a review of census registers in commoner neighborhoods, and outlined other efforts to arrest what the government saw as a deteriorating social order.[17]

These actions by the city authorities reveal a concern that they could no longer rely on the merchant and artisan quarters to monitor their own needs. This form of local organization had dated from the great Meireki fires of 1657, when the twenty-three downtown neighborhoods agreed to staff a small rotating fire-duty force.[18] Ikegami discusses at length the subsequent stream of directives from the city magistrates instructing the downtown quarters to organize local duty units and to keep on hand a quota of equipment such as buckets and ladders. His point is a familiar one: the repeated issuance of such decrees only indicates how difficult it was for the shogun's officials to orchestrate and enforce these efforts. The total duty complement was only 167 men, and often, it seems, there were many no-shows. Those sent by the quarters frequently

16. On the Kyōhō reforms, see Tsuji Tatsuya, "Politics in the Eighteenth Century," trans. Harold Bolitho, in John W. Hall et al., eds., *The Cambridge History of Japan*, vol. 4: John W. Hall, with James L. McClain, ed., *Early Modern Japan* (Cambridge: Cambridge University Press, 1991), pp. 445–56. The relationship between the reforms and firefighting is detailed in Nakai Nobuhiko and James L. McClain, "Commercial Change and Urban Growth in Early Modern Japan," ibid., pp. 575–79.

17. Nakai, *Chōnin*, pp. 308–10.

18. Ikegami, "Edo hikeshi seido," pp. 117–18.

included the aged, the infirm, and children. Even the able-bodied adults were unskilled at the necessary roof demolition, and many were quick to flee the fire scene.

Near the end of 1718, then, Ōoka ordered the neighborhood chiefs to organize what became the first citywide fire organization. The essential element in his plan was the requirement that each residential quarter maintain a permanent requisition of thirty men. Whenever a fire was reported, the two quarters downwind of the blaze and the four at its sides were to send their men to the fire site, so that a total of 180 men would be available; a constable and patrolmen would be dispatched from the city magistrate's office to ascertain that the full complement actually showed up. Other conditions included injunctions against fighting with the bannerman and daimyo squads and charges to keep ladders, axes, ropes, firehooks, and other tools on hand and to carry small banners identifying their home quarters.[19]

In an endorsement to the directive, the city elders (*machidoshiyori*) added that only residents of a quarter should be used in its squad. This prohibition on hiring nonresidents is puzzling in view of the fact that the shogunate and daimyo had been using hired firemen for some time. Nakai, though, interprets this directive as another manifestation of the authorities' longstanding view that urban problems were preeminently those of social order. To officials, any local organization should strengthen local self-policing practices.

Ōoka's plan was given official sanction by a late 1718 map drawn up by the city magistrates, who outlined in vermilion the jurisdictions of the new commoner firefighting squads. Weaknesses of the new system were quickly exposed, however, when another major fire in the Second Month of the new year destroyed large sections of the downtown. Responding to subsequent questioning by the city elders, the neighborhood chiefs agreed that the quarter squads were inadequate to extinguish major blazes driven by strong winds. It would be better, they noted, to mobilize several downwind wards to attempt to stop a fire's progress. The city magistrates considered this proposal and ordered some minor adjustments, but did not essentially change the previous arrangements.

Nakai notes, interestingly, that in 1719 individuals twice petitioned to contract for firefighting work. The first petition was a proposal by six men to maintain fifty-five fire watch posts, each staffed by twenty-five men on twenty-four-hour call. Money for their meals and wages would be raised by an assessment on house owners (*iemochi*) within the jurisdictions. The petitioners claimed that they could thus provide far cheaper fire service than assessments under Ōoka's plan. The city magistrates referred the petition to the neighborhood chiefs, who responded negatively. They argued that the existing system promised a faster response time; that it would be too difficult to coordinate responses to multiple fires; that residents who bore responsibility for their own quarters were more conscientious firefighters; and so on. Their opinion car-

19. See ibid., pp. 121–22, for the full text. The two-four system appeared in directives from at least the late seventeenth century.

ried, and the petition was rejected. The second proposal was from two commoners who offered to contract for a 200-man force to track the flying sparks
that were such a problem in urban blazes. This idea, too, the neighborhood
chiefs rejected, on the grounds that the present system was working and the
additional costs would be burdensome to residents.[20]

In fact, the system was not functioning very well, and in the Third Month
of 1720 yet another blaze swept the central wards, destroying about one thousand houses. This disaster strengthened the determination of city officials to
fashion firefighting, as Katō Takashi suggests in Chapter 2 of this volume,
around a direct line of delegated authority that ran from the city magistrates
through the neighborhood chiefs to the residents of the commoner quarters. In
short measure, Ōoka promulgated a reorganization that created the famous
i-ro-ha structure of commoner firefighting. Dividing quarters west of the Sumida River into forty-seven precincts, he mandated a company for each precinct,
to which all constituent quarters were to supply squads of thirty men, led by
the neighborhood chiefs. In practice, each company was formed by men drawn
from about twenty quarters, though some precincts included as few as four
commoner neighborhoods. The precinct companies were named by the forty-
seven characters of the syllabary; hence the new organization became unof-
ficially known as the *i-ro-ha kumiai*. Complaining that there was still confusion
and lack of direction at fire sites as the various groups mixed together, Ōoka
also ordered new company banners bearing rules of conduct written out in
simple language and large company standards, both to be erected to mark the
assembly points for the firefighters.

Still, problems continued to plague the system. In the First Month of 1721,
for example, the magistrates raised the possibility of hiring men to serve as
firefighters. The neighborhood chiefs responded by noting that most squads
were made up of servants (*hōkōnin*) and tenants (*tanagarinin*), a practice that
was not without its costs. They argued that the problem of absences and
incomplete squads occurred largely in quarters that were downwind from a
fire. That is, many servants and tenants were being retained at home or at the
shop to protect family or business property. The chiefs countered with a suggestion that the quotas be reduced to fifteen men per quarter, drawn from
bachelors and the marginal poor, and that only if fire reached the quarter were
the servants to be sent out. When the chiefs brought this proposal before their
own residents, however, it drew many complaints: it was unfair to those
landlords who did not have servants, and it would require the payment of
wage supplements to those who were sent; the result would be as expensive as
a hired squad.

These disagreements continued through much of the decade. The Edo city
administration clearly was moving toward a policy and organization that assigned citywide responsibility to commoner units.[21] City residents, for their
part, resisted the reforms, for various reasons. The *chōnin*—that is to say, the

20. Nakai, *Chōnin*, pp. 313–14.
21. Further evidence can be seen in other directives of the early 1720s that greatly
expanded the commoner units' ability to enter warrior compounds to fight fires—which
previously had been severely restricted. See Ikegami, "Edo hikeshi seido," p. 126.

house owners and their agents—opposed reforms that would increase their financial burden; the propertied benefited from a system whereby all house-holds, from the large houses fronting the main streets to the small back rooms of the menials, rotated in sending out men to the squads. The other ward residents—the tenants and poorer residents—were not well served by the *i-ro-ha* system, but expressed their resistance simply by not showing up for or absconding from fire duty.[22]

At the end of 1729 the city magistrates undertook yet another review of the commoner firefighting organization, and they proposed to group the forty-seven companies into a smaller number of large brigades while halving the quotas of the individual quarters. The new brigades were intended to address the difficulty of collecting firefighters from the wards downwind of a fire; the larger groups were to be a framework for drawing from a wider area to either side and upwind of a fire site. After negotiations, the forty-seven companies were grouped into ten brigades in early 1730 (the number was later reduced to eight), and the quota for each residential quarter was dropped from thirty to fifteen men. Even so, this arrangement still required some 9,378 men—or as Ikegami notes, about 1 in every 50 Edo commoners.[23]

Initially the commoner firefighters were prohibited from responding to fires at samurai dwellings, but as we have seen, this regulation was amended in 1722. Then in 1747 commoner groups were ordered into the Edo Castle pre-cincts to extinguish the embers of a fire in the Second Enceinte, a sanctioned intrusion of symbolic importance. By the late eighteenth century, the common-er firefighters were so superior to the samurai regulars and the daimyo squads that they came to predominate in all city firefighting.[24] As early as 1736 the dispersed brigades were confined largely to fighting blazes within Edo Castle, and in 1828 the samurai regulars too were limited largely to fire duties within the castle compound. Even these responsibilities attenuated, and during the major fires of 1838 and 1844 the great majority of the commoner squads were ordered into the castle compound.

Along with this restructuring, the composition of the squads underwent a fundamental shift in the early and mid–eighteenth century. As we have seen, originally they were formed from residents of the quarters themselves—in particular, the tenants and servants dispatched by the homeowners and their agents; indeed, a common term for the units was "tenant firefighters," or *tana-bikeshi*. The authorities quickly realized, however, that such amateurs were of little use, except for operating the small pumps and hoses; the roof work and demolition required of most firefighters were well beyond their skills. Despite the expenses involved, many squads gradually began to hire local roofers and

22. Ibid., pp. 125–26; Nakai, *Chōnin*, pp. 317–18.
23. Additionally, the sixteen small squads in the districts east of the Sumida River were reorganized into three large companies. See Ikegami, "Edo hikeshi seido," p. 128.
24. This development did not sit well with the remaining warrior squads. Ikegami (ibid., pp. 145–48) discusses an incident in 1782 between a squad of the Satake domain lord and three commoner companies, during which both sides suffered serious injuries. The case came before the city magistrates, who rendered a mixed verdict that somewhat favored the town side.

construction laborers, the so-called *tobi*. It appears that by the 1780s, the *tobi* had become the core of the Edo firefighting squads.

Ikegami cites a document from early 1787 that clearly illustrates this shift. In defense of an official reprimand that they were not supplying their full quotas, a group of neighborhood chiefs described their use of two types of *tobi*. Several "regulars" in each quarter were paid a fixed allowance, and "occasionals" were given temporary allowances.[25] Because they were using such professionals, the chiefs petitioned to halve again their quarters' required quotas. The city magistrates denied this request but did agree that for most blazes the quarters could dispatch half-complements of *tobi*; "tenant firefighters" would be required to respond only to major fires. This concession merely seemed to prompt a series of other requests from various precincts and quarters, pleading fiscal constraints and seeking quota formulas that in one way or another would reduce their requirements. One can see just how far the shift from ordinary residents to the *tobi* had progressed by examining the detailed listings of company compositions in a 1787 document.[26] By the end of the century, a fairly standard and ranked order defined the commoner companies, to which ordinary residents were peripheral. The ranks included the company leader (the *tōdori* or *tobigashira*); the standard-bearer (*matoimochi*); the laddermen (*hashigomochi*); and the ordinaries (*hira ninsoku*), a category that included both regulars and occasionals.[27]

The radical reforms in Edo firefighting were thus generally unwelcomed by the commoners. What might be thought to have provided real self-control over a strategic area of urban life was in fact experienced as a delegation of onerous responsibilities and exactions. These financial burdens on the quarters only increased through the eighteenth century, and they generated sustained opposition to the initiatives of the city magistrates. Especially revealing is a 1767 communication from neighborhood officials to the city elders citing ten reasons for rapidly escalating local expenses, fully eight of which were fire-related:

1. The replacement of ordinary residents in the fire brigades by roofers and unskilled construction workers had required increases in wages.
2. Firefighting expenses that in the past were limited to ladders, jackets, banners, and so forth were now required to cover fire patrols, standards, and other equipment.
3. Expenses were rising for assignments of companies to sites beyond the company boundaries.

25. The wage arrangements actually seem to have varied by residential quarter and period. One local compromise was to finance the regulars from the quarter's budget (assessed on all homeowners) and to pay the occasionals from assessments to all households. See, for example, Yoshioka, "Kyōhō-ki Edo machikata," p. 116.
26. See Ikegami, "Edo hikeshi seido," pp. 133–36. This record includes illustrations of the firefighters' standards and banners. See the color reproduction in Matsunosuke et al., *Edogaku jiten*, pp. 580–81 interleaf.
27. Minami, "Shōbō," pp. 460–64; for the standards themselves, see Nishiyama et al., *Edogaku jiten*, s.v. Ikegami Akihiko, "Kenka," pp. 582–83.

4. Expenses were rising for the labor requisitions by the shogunate for fire-related work, including patrolling of firebreak zones.

5. Expenses were now required for the extra preventive measures ordered by the shogunate, including special fire patrols, extra buckets, and so forth.

6. Fire patrols and special officers had now been made the responsibility of the commoner residential quarters.

7. The two to four fire towers per company that were ordered in 1723 were expensive to build, maintain, and staff.

8. The costs of reconstructing buildings to make them more fire-retardant were enormous.[28]

We may read from this petition the residents' sharp protest to two other fire policy changes that were proving as burdensome as firefighter compensation. The first of these policies was an aggressive expansion of firebreak zones. Since at least the great Meireki fires, the shogunate had asserted the prerogative of claiming urban land destroyed in large fires as "official land" (*goyōchi*). It did not permit reconstruction within these sites. They were to become future firebreaks (*hiyokechi*) and temporary retreats for fire victims, and they were used by the shogunate for such purposes as military practice and hawking. The shogunate actually exercised this prerogative of eminent domain only infrequently in the late seventeenth century. This situation changed dramatically during the Kyōhō decades, however, when the shogunate ordered extensive areas to be set aside in the downtown sections of the city. Yoshioka Yuriko documents the seizure of land in eighty-three quarters in the years 1722 to 1732.[29] In analyzing the particular locations, she found that they were not seen as firebreaks for the commoner residential areas but rather served to protect adjacent shogunal properties, especially its warehouses and rice granaries. Moreover, the shogunate prepared detailed regulations for disposing and managing these firebreak zones that placed onerous responsibilities on bordering residential quarters. As McClain shows in Chapter 5, these neighborhoods were held responsible for keeping the lands clean of debris and for reporting all dumping and any vagrants or other unauthorized entry and use to city authorities. Cleanup and guard costs were to be borne by the quarters themselves. Furthermore, at times of fires, the firebreak areas could be used for temporary refuge, but people were not permitted to bring family or business belongings, nor were the areas to be used for temporary living or storage after the fire.

These and other aspects of the policy prompted a considerable outcry and a large volume of petitions from the affected quarters, which continued through much of the eighteenth century. Yoshioka's detailed study of forty-five petitionary protests suggests that many quarters were able to secure exemptions from

28. Yoshiwara, "Edo saigai nenpyō," pp. 443–44. The two other causes cited by neighborhood officials were the rising costs of day labor and the expenses of disposing of unclaimed corpses.
29. Yoshioka, "Kyōhō-ki Edo machikata," pp. 118–20.

some of the more demanding requirements of management.[30] More important, in the manner of Edobashi, by the early nineteenth century many firebreak lands were simply invaded and appropriated by all manner of commoners and elites. They became important arenas of late Tokugawa popular
culture, frequented by outdoor entertainers and itinerant peddlers, and they
also suffered encroachment by domain lords and temples seeking increasingly
scarce sites for building expansion. McClain shows in Chapter 5 how the
shogunate continued to make its authority felt in Edobashi, but others have
celebrated commoners' appropriations of firebreaks. Hidenobu Jinnai, for instance, has the following to say about Edobashi:

> It is noteworthy that what the bakufu had set aside merely as a fire
> protection area was used by the people for their own purposes, and that it
> assumed a variety of meanings and functions in relation to its new identity
> as an entertainment area. Also significant is its location: the open area,
> bustling with activity, was formed at the base of a bridge, the intersection of
> water and land. In European cities, it was common for the city square to be
> symbolically central and permanent, set off by an imposing cathedral or
> government office building. It is suggestive, therefore, that in the Japanese
> city such a public area formed rather at the nexus of mobility among people
> and things, in a neighborhood filled with spirited activity.[31]

A second area of official concern and reform that drew strong protest from
Edo commoners during the eighteenth century was the effort to enforce fire-
retardant building codes. William Coaldrake has noted that the post-1657
sumptuary prohibition on commoners' use of tile roofs and the continued
reliance on thatch and wood shingles proved a serious fire hazard in the
downtown merchant quarters throughout the seventeenth century.[32] The shogunate's efforts to encourage mud daubing of commoners' roofs went largely
unheeded, and it was only in the 1720s that the magistrates made a concerted
effort to promote use of a new, lighter-weight terra-cotta roofing tile and of
lacquered timbers and clapboard siding.[33] Again, however, the officials encountered heated resistance as commoners protested the costs of such
changes. Yoshioka's study indicates that in the three decades from 1720 to
1750, the city magistrates alternated between exhortation and forced adoption
of these and related measures before eventually compromising with a plan to

30. Ibid., pp. 128–54.
31. Hidenobu Jinnai, "The Spatial Structure of Edo," trans. J. Victor Koschmann, in
Chie Nakane and Shinzaburō Ōishi, eds., *Tokugawa Japan: The Social and Economic Antecedents of Modern Japan*, translation ed. by Conrad Totman (Tokyo: University of Tokyo Press,
1990), pp. 130.
32. William H. Coaldrake, "Edo Architecture and Tokugawa Law," *Monumenta Nipponica* 36:3 (1981), pp. 253–61. Ikegami ("Meireki no taika," p. 94) argues, to the contrary,
that the prohibition of tile roofs was an antifire measure because the collapsing tiles caused
grave injury. This was no doubt the case, but Coaldrake's more general point about the
status symbolics of roofing is more compelling.
33. Coaldrake, "Edo Architecture and Tokugawa Law," pp. 259–61.

require postfire reconstruction in accordance with these codes, compensated with small subsidies and duty exemptions.

In sum, the creation of a citywide commoner firefighting organization in the 1720s was part of a fundamental administrative restructuring of the capital in the late seventeenth and early eighteenth centuries. This effort had been set in motion by the 1657 Meireki fires, then given urgency by the shogunate's increasing fiscal difficulties. It culminated in the Kyōhō reforms of the 1720s, which recognized the commercialization of commoner property and attempted to devolve significant responsibilities on the resident population. The shogun's capital was becoming the people's city, although the people of Edo—never homogeneous and increasingly less so—strenuously resisted the terms by which the shogunate tried to effect this transformation.

From Fiscal Burden to Folklore Emblem: Fighting and Firefighting in Early Nineteenth-Century Edo

It is tempting to view Edo firefighting as a useful metonym of an uneasy triangular balance of political tensions that characterized the capital for much of the Tokugawa period. Despite the usual assumptions of a capital divided roughly equally between commoners and a warrior elite, that elite was in fact continuously divided between the shogunate elite and its supporters and the great majority of domain lords and their retinues, whose interests were more regional than central. It was this shifting triangle of forces that the distinct shogunal, daimyo, and commoner fire squads represented, and the continual altercations between them reflected the antagonisms of this peculiar capital. The commoner squads, for their part, were the pride and the protectors of the downtown residents. Beginning with the Genroku era (1688–1704), they were celebrated in the themes of the plebeian kabuki theaters, and perhaps even inspired the "rough style" (*aragoto*) of performance that the Danjurō line of kabuki actors made into the quintessential Edo stage style. Indeed, the Danjurō family line, the firefighters, and the wharfmen of the Tsukiji fish market were jointly renowned as the "Three Men of Edo," direct spiritual descendants of the roving bullies of earliest Edo, the *machi yakko* and *kabukimono*.

As I have argued, more careful historical analysis does not bear out this inviting model. At all times, though for different reasons, the multiple divisions within the Edo elites and among Edo commoners were as important as whatever solidarities they represented vis-à-vis one another. The institutional developments sketched above indicate that the eighteenth-century decades when Edo firefighting was divided among shogunal, daimyo, and commoner squads was quite brief and transitional. To be sure, fights and rivalries seemed to be an enduring characteristic of Edo firefighting.[34] And the rough-and-ready commoner companies did seem to capture the Edo imagination, at least by the early nineteenth century. The unruly conduct that made the firefighters a

34. On fights, see Ikegami, "Kenka," pp. 582–83; Nakai, *Chōnin*, pp. 304–6; Ikegami, "Edo hikeshi seido," pp. 137–63.

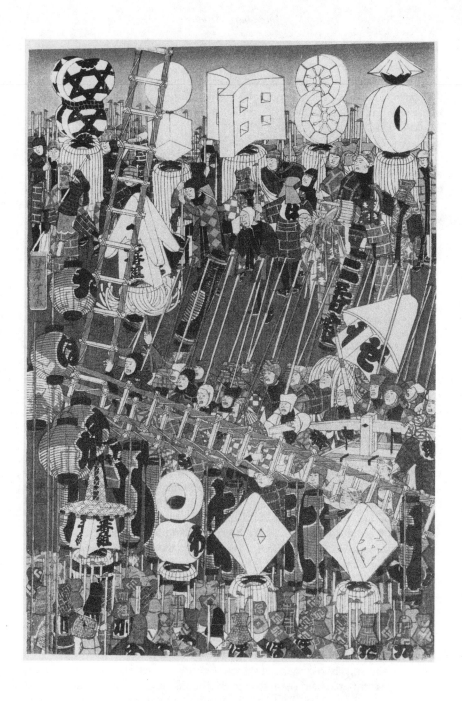

Firemen on review at New Year. Source: Edo no hana kodomo asobi. Courtesy of Shōbō Hakubutsukan.

problem to officials made them a feature of such late Tokugawa kabuki plays as *Kami no megumi wagō no torigumi* and of popular literature such as the Shikitei Sanba story mentioned earlier. The firefighters' argot, their preference for rolling their tongues to trill their speech, and their favorite posture of crouching awkwardly with one heel upon the other, a hand towel tossed casually over the shoulder, were all depicted in the theaters, in storytelling at local vaudeville halls such as those at Edobashi, and in the woodblock prints of these decades.

Yet the popular valorization of the firefighters seems to have been rather specific to the first half of the nineteenth century. It was only then that a lineage of commoner bravado was constructed retrospectively, linking them to the famous bullies of early Edo, the *yakko* and *kabukimono*, and to the quick-tempered foot soldiers jostling and challenging one another around the entrances to the castle.[35] It was during this half-century that the idea of Edo as a distinctive urban society was literally—and dramatically—invented. It was at this moment that the firefighters were included among the *Edokko*, the true sons of the capital. In short, the characteristic development of Edo firefighting in the early nineteenth century was its role in Edo culture-building, its place in an exuberant and proliferating public sphere of cultural productions that claimed a distinctive Edo identity. Their battles, against fires and each other, not only were incidents in the city's everyday life but also embellished events in its public culture. They took their place with the wrestling and freak shows at the Ryōgoku entertainment center, the glitterati tea ceremonies, and other happenings in what Nishiyama Matsunosuke has characterized as a new *kōdō bunka*, or "culture of movement and performance," in Henry D. Smith's felicitous gloss.[36]

Of particular notoriety was a series of early nineteenth-century incidents at the Shiba Shrine, which began with the famous "Me Company brawl" (*Megumi no kenka*) at the end of the 1804 New Year's holidays. On this occasion, a firefighter of that company tried to barge into a subscription sumo meet and was stopped by some of the wrestlers. The confrontation escalated the next day at an outdoor theater event, and it precipitated a fight elsewhere in the shrine precincts between some 381 firefighters and 60 sumo wrestlers. The brawl soon was featured in a kabuki play. Five years later, the shrine was again the scene of a mass fight, this time between two fire squad rivals, the Yo Company (the squad for that area) and the neighboring Ka Company of Yushima. This rivalry apparently reflected larger, enduring animosities, which broke out again at the shrine in the spring of 1811 in violent fighting between firefighters from No. 1 Brigade (including the Yo Company) against large numbers from No. 8 Brigade (including the Ka Company). The fight drew support-

35. Ikegami, "Kenka," p. 582.
36. Smith insightfully discusses the significance of this culture of movement and performance in "The Edo-Tokyo Transition: In Search of Common Ground," in Marius B. Jansen and Gilbert Rozman, eds., *Japan in Transition: From Tokugawa to Meiji* (Princeton: Princeton University Press, 1986), pp. 347–74. Nishiyama develops his concept in several works; see, for instance, his "Edo bunka to chihō bunka," in Iwanami Shoten, ed., *Iwanami kōza Nihon rekishi*, vol. 13, *Kinsei* 5 (Iwanami Shoten, 1964), pp. 161–207.

ers from other brigades as well; in fact, there seem to have been recurring antagonisms between several brigades.[37] Such public brawling led early nineteenth-century Edoites to coin a phrase that lives yet today: "Kaji to kenka wa Edo no hana" (Fires and fights are Edo's flowers).[38]

In Chapter 16 of this volume, however, Takeuchi Makoto suggests deeper reasons for the association of flowers and fights than merely flamboyant and destructive violence.[39] By the early nineteenth century, "fights" (kenka) had developed in official legal parlance the particular meaning of private disputes nonadjudicable in shogunal tribunals; they were specific altercations between commoners. The authorities might apprehend the participants to break up the violence, but under the principle that both sides were presumed to be at fault, the disputants were generally released without punishment (especially if they had caused no serious injuries, loss of life, or destruction of "innocent" property). Moreover, the authorities refused to mediate the dispute itself.

This notion of fights provided a major conceptual opening in the nineteenth century for broad commoner actions that were barely containable by authorities. Throughout the eighteenth century, the shogunate had gradually systematized and strengthened regulations against unlawful assembly and collective protest under the generic term totō, or conspiracy against authorities. Takeuchi's point is that by instituting guidelines to police their own actions and by then insisting to authorities that the actions had been directed at a particular individual (a rice dealer, say, or a landlord), people remained able to take effective collective action against local targets of grievance.

Takeuchi's example of the frustrations of rural officials in the districts around Edo, who in 1805 tried to curb crowd attacks against local elites in actions that officials saw as mimicking those of Edo firefighters, demonstrates the exemplary power of the firefighters' behavior. Without further evidence, however, I am less persuaded than Takeuchi that the Edo firefighters' brawling was the main template for the widespread kenka-style actions of the late Tokugawa period, including the increasing number of violent collective actions in both urban and rural areas. It seems, rather, that the increasing frequency of violence at fires and the apparent inability of city magistrates to contain it were as much a result as a cause of the popular ability to exploit this distinction in shogunal procedure.

Takeuchi's point also helps to explain why Edoites came to be fascinated not only by the violent rivalries among firefighters but also by the increasingly elaborate fight mediations. If officials refused to intervene to adjudicate, disposition devolved to participants and to those whom they might invite to medi-

37. Ikegami, "Edo hikeshi seido," pp. 148–52.
38. Although hardly unique to the late Tokugawa period, the idiom of hana became very popular in the first half of the nineteenth century. It was at that time that the Danjurō line of Edo kabuki actors came to be known as Edo no hana; see Nishiyama Matsunosuke, Nishiyama Matsunosuke chosakushū, vol. 7: Edo kabuki kenkyū (Yoshikawa Kōbunkan, 1987), pp. 35–49.
39. See also Takeuchi Makoto, Edo to Ōsaka, Taikei Nihon no rekishi 10 (Shōgakkan, 1989), pp. 320–22.

ate. Ikegami Akihoko cites Takizawa Bakin's contemporary account of the intricate formality of these procedures for resolving disputes. Bakin describes an enormous mediation ceremony in the early fall of 1818 between two companies of No. 10 Brigade. For the occasion they rented the stately Mikawaya Hall, not far from Ryōgoku Bridge. Members of over half of the Edo companies attended. Some 1,648 persons offered formal presentations, and despite inclement weather, the proceedings continued for the entire day. Even the closing handclapping was done with elaborate protocol in twenty-five rounds. From the crafted mediators' speeches to the clothes and proffered gifts, it was a grand, "stylish" (*iki*), and much-remarked happening.[40]

Such formalities also became increasingly elaborate at the more prosaic level of the townspeople's etiquette concerning fires and their aftermath. The constant danger of small fires in the dense neighborhoods of homes, tenements, public baths, and shops had long prompted local agreements to ensure collective responses from neighbors, to offer assistance in the aftermath of a fire, and to resolve the inevitable conflicts about responsibility. Nakai Nobuhiko has illustrated this process with the agreement among residents of Sawara Hashimoto-chō, which affirmed local protocols for weddings, funerals, fires, and other "ritual" (*hare*) occasions. Its clauses placed a premium on neighborly self-help, disciplined group behavior, and avoidance of contact with outsiders, even persons from nearby quarters. Yoshiwara Ken'ichirō has offered an extended example from a residential quarter in Shinjuku, detailing the local conventions for a range of fire contingencies. They include several levels of compensation for properties demolished to create an emergency firebreak, which varied according to whether the firebreak was necessary, whether the blaze was extinguished before it reached the firebreak, whether the fire jumped the firebreak, and so forth. Yoshiwara also notes the letters of apology that were sent around by the people deemed responsible for the numerous accidental fires in this area caused by braziers, tobacco, foot warmers, and other household items. It is not clear when after-fire condolence visits and gifts became common and expected, but such *kaji mimai*—and the obligatory thank-you gifts for such gifts—figured prominently in the gift exchange registers of all Edo shops by the late Tokugawa decades. Social disorder was as great a concern as physical destruction, and given the extralegal status of fires (except arson), resolution was a local responsibility.[41]

There was therefore a curiously inverse relation between these two emerging emblems of late Tokugawa fires—the rowdy, disorderly, brawling firefighters, whose passions were as inextinguishable as the blazes that attracted them, and the obligatory and ceremonial expressions of sympathy and assistance that attempted to restate orderly relations among neighbors, clients, and

40. Ikegami, "Edo hikeshi seido," pp. 153–54.

41. Nakai, *Chōnin*, pp. 298–304; Nishiyama et al., *Edogaku jiten*, s.v. Yoshiwara Ken'ichirō, "Kaji," pp. 575–76. The *Meguro gyoninzaka kaji emaki*, a late eighteenth-century scroll of a major fire in 1772, has several scenes that depict postblaze condolence gift giving; reproduced in Takahashi Sei'ichirō and Narasaki Sōjū, eds., *Kinsei fūzoku zukan*, vol. 1: *Edo fūzoku* (Asahi Shinbunsha, 1973), pp. 249–63.

business partners. The nineteenth-century culture of Edo fires and firefighting was elaborated on two levels: both through the etiquette of everyday practice, in the commoner neighborhoods and in the shops, and through the more formal productions of popular culture, which were taken self-consciously as a vehicle for and expression of an Edo urban identity. Neither rituals nor reputations, however, necessarily testified to a greater effectiveness of preventive measures or of firefighting itself. Like popular protests, fires seem to have been even more frequent in the nineteenth century, though in both cases, one wonders how much must be attributed to better record keeping.[42] Still, how ever-present a danger in the daily experience of Edoites, fires remained extraordinary events, in their occasional blinding fury and in the extralegal behavior they sparked and permitted. The shifting pattern of response over the Tokugawa centuries is indicative of the degree to which the seventeenth-century shogun's capital had become the nineteenth-century people's city.

This characterization, however, by no means endorses a simple trajectory of progressive empowerment and popular solidarity. To the contrary, the people of Edo were more diverse and more stratified in the nineteenth century than they had been earlier. Both organizationally and procedurally, the shogunal administration had largely divorced itself from direct jurisdiction over fire affairs. Yet this step proved to bring onerous fiscal burdens and complex organizational demands, felt and resisted by all strata of the population, albeit for different reasons. Indeed, the key significance of fire in Edo was the shifting and often unpredictable ways in which it could conjoin and divide the interests of the poorest laborers and the wealthiest merchants, the house agents in the established quarters and the hawkers peddling in parklike fire zones.

Fire was an accidental or intentional act by an individual that immediately became a public event of grave but mixed consequences. The ease of arson and the dangers of urban firefighting subjected residents to the intimidation and even extortion of the firefighters, yet one might easily exaggerate their leverage over the propertied. They were still daily wage laborers and back-alley tenement renters, and they were constrained by the limits of *kenka*-style conduct. All residents, as a fire gained strength and approached their own neighborhood, must have faced the difficult choice of fleeing with their belongings, remaining to try to protect their home or shop, or turning out to help at the main fire site. The conflicts of personal and collective interest were at least as difficult for the managers of the larger shops and businesses; one of the deterrents to sending shop employees to fire squads was that it left the store itself less protected. Detailing procedures of conduct and drilling employees became important to the large houses. The 1768 shop regulations of the Ōdenma-chō cotton merchant Hasegawa had sixty-seven clauses, to be memorized and chanted by all employees. Fully one-quarter related to fire—prevention, safety, and response.[43]

42. Ogi Shinzō, *Tōkei jidai: Edo to Tōkyō no aida de*, NHK bukkusu 371 (Nippon Hōsō Shuppan Kyōkai, 1980), pp. 45–53.

43. Yoshiwara, "Kaji," p. 574; idem, "Edo saigai nenpyō," pp. 445–46.

The greater fire dangers of Edo encouraged the many large Osaka merchant houses to keep their headquarters in Osaka even after the Edo market had eclipsed that of Osaka. They kept minimal stock on hand in the Edo stores. Most also had residential compounds and reserve storehouses on the island of Tsukuda in Edo Bay, which provided shelter for family and employees during and after serious fires, and where building supplies could be stockpiled as a hedge against postfire reconstruction costs. The commodity inflation and labor demands that inevitably followed major blazes obviously could be both costly and profitable to Edoites of all classes and to businesses of all scales, from humble roofers to the local rice dealers and large houses such as Shirokiya.[44] Fire both ruined and enriched individuals and the city. That was the source of its compelling fascination and continual terror. It reflected the commoners' appropriation of urban space and organizational responsibility, but it also inflamed the deep antagonisms that ran through that population.

44. Hayashi Reiko, *Edodana hankachō* (Yoshikawa Kōbunkan, 1982); Yōtarō Sakudō, "The Management Practices of Family Businesses," trans. William B. Hauser, in Nakane and Ōishi, *Tokugawa Japan*, pp. 147–66.

14

The History of the Book
in Edo and Paris

HENRY D. SMITH II

The history of books offers particularly fertile ground for comparison between the capital cities of early-modern France and Japan. The widely heralded accomplishments of the French *histoire du livre*, which has come to
constitute an academic subdiscipline in its own right, offer a rich variety of
methodological and analytical guideposts that may be applied to the case of
Japan, where research in the history of the culture of print remains rudimentary by comparison.[1] In particular, the synthetic work of the 1980s, epito-
mized by the four-volume *Histoire de l'édition française*, provides a lucid
framework for thinking about print culture in long historical perspective,
from its medieval manuscript origins to the mid–twentieth century.[2]

At the same time, the Japanese case offers the opportunity to place the
entire concept of print culture in much broader comparative perspective. To
be sure, the French *histoire du livre* has enjoyed an international leavening
from its early stages, notably through the work of such North American
scholars as Marshall McLuhan, Elizabeth Eisenstein, and Robert Darnton. It
has also served as stimulus for research in neighboring cultures across the
Channel, the Rhine, and the Atlantic. Calls have come forth for specifically
comparative work,[3] yet all such proposals seem to be limited to the familiar
world of Western Europe and North America.

The case of Japan, together with those of China and Korea, enables a
radical broadening of the comparative context of the early-modern history of

1. For one recent survey of *l'histoire du livre*, see Roger Chartier, "Frenchness in the
History of the Book: From the History of Publishing to the History of Reading," *American
Antiquarian Society Proceedings* 97:2 (1987), pp. 299–329. On the Japanese side, the judgment
"rudimentary" should not be allowed to obscure the important work in recent years by
such scholars as Konta Yōzō and Nagatomo Chiyoji.

2. Roger Chartier et al., eds., *Histoire de l'édition française*, 4 vols. (Paris: Promodis,
1983–1986).

3. See, for example, Chartier, "Frenchness in the History of the Book," p. 326; and
Robert Darnton, "Histoire du livre, Geschichte des Buchwesens: An Agenda for Comparative History," *Publishing History* 22 (1987), pp. 33–41.

the book.[4] At the very least, it will force scholars of the "West" to recognize the existence of cultures at the other end of the Eurasian continent, where printing by the eighteenth century was as diverse, as widespread, and as influential as in early-modern Europe. Such recognition has been virtually absent from all that I have so far read. More important, the case of Japan suggests certain variations from Western Europe that can help sort out what is universal in the early-modern culture of print and what is dependent on specific configurations of technology, sociopolitical environment, and international context. In particular, Japan offers crucial variants in the technologies of both writing and printing.

THE BASIC SIMILARITIES

The National Unit

Both France and Japan in the period under question were national units with effective central governments (despite various centrifugal forces at work in each case). Moreover, those central regimes shared a keen interest in controlling the content of printed matter through censorship and systems of permission. The concern and influence of the state over print culture was in both cases reflected in the organization of printing and publishing monopolies that relied on state patronage and sanction. The key contrast was the coexistence in Japan of three wholly separate centers of primary book production—Kyoto, Osaka, and Edo—in contrast to the monolithic role of Paris from the late seventeenth century.

The Role of Church and Religion

Printing in both France and Japan was dominated at the start by religious production, and the subsequent story of the book in both nations is one of gradual secularization. Notable differences exist, to be sure. Buddhism for various reasons relied less than Christianity on printed works to spread its religious message to the common people, and this tendency became more noticeable in various new popular sects of the Edo period. Nor were Buddhist denominations beset by the theological rivalries that found their battle-grounds on the printed page in early-modern France. Hence religious publication seems to have accounted for less of the total in Japan than in France.

Timing and Scale

Japan's "print revolution" occurred a century and a half later than that of Europe, beginning with the introduction (or, more accurately, theft) of the technology of movable type from Korea in the 1590s. The 300-odd titles that

4. The only scholar I have encountered who has insistently called for comparative work across a broad range of cultures is Konta Yōzō, for example in his "Edo no shuppan shihon," in Nishiyama Matsunosuke, ed., *Edo chōnin no kenkyū*, vol. 3 (Yoshikawa Kō-bunkan, 1974), p. 111.

were printed in movable type (first metal, then wood) over the next three decades constitute Japan's incunabula. The break with scribal culture, however, was less sharp than in Europe. Religious texts had been block-printed in Japan since the eleventh century, and movable type offered no radical technological advantage over blocks. Rather, it seems, the cultural situation in Japan was simply ripe for a new burst of printing activity at the time when Hideyoshi's minions brought the new technology back from Korea.

From about 1626, the emergence of commercial publishers in Kyoto dictated a shift from movable type back to the older block technology. The implications of this change were immense, and the reasons for the change are still debated. Some investigators argue, persuasively, that the Japanese writing system favored block composition, both linguistically and aesthetically. Others claim, less convincingly, that block technology was better suited to large editions than movable type.[5] The most important consideration, however, was surely the reduction of the risks involved in estimating the market, since blocks could be stored indefinitely and used at any time to satisfy further demand. A publisher could keep movable-type books in print only by tying up valuable stocks of type.

Commercial publishing grew rapidly in seventeenth-century Japan, first in Kyoto from the 1630s and then in Osaka from the 1660s. Edo was little more than a market for books produced in the Kyoto-Osaka region at that time, but publishing expanded so dramatically there in the mid-eighteenth century that Edo surpassed both Kyoto and Osaka as a publishing center by 1800. The first half of the nineteenth century saw the continued growth of publishing in Edo and the beginnings of publishing in a variety of provincial cities, although the "three great metropolises" of Kyoto, Osaka, and Edo remained dominant.

How does the total volume of printed books in Tokugawa Japan compare with that in France under the ancient regime? The case of France is summarized by Roger Chartier as "between 500 and 1,000 [titles per year] in the sixteenth and seventeenth centuries and only 2,000 at the end of the Ancient Regime."[6] It is much more difficult to estimate the numbers of titles in Japan, where the surviving primary materials are far less plentiful and where quantitative research on books has been minimal. A booksellers' catalogue of 1692 lists 7,200 titles, from which Konta Yōzō estimates a total production over the previous century of 10,000 titles, or some 100 per year.[7] Statistics for the period 1731–1814 from the publishing guilds in Kyoto, Osaka, and Edo

5. Konta Yōzō, *Edo no hon'ya-san*, NHK bukkusu 299 (Nippon Hōsō Shuppan Kyōkai, 1977), p. 25, offers the typical opinion that movable type restricted editions to about one hundred copies. This conventional view is dismissed as a "myth" by Watanabe Morikuni, "Hanmen o yomu—kokatsujiban no insatsu to shuppan," *Bungaku* 45:12 (1981), p. 44. Note also the claim of Tsien Tsuen-hsuin, "Paper and Printing," in Joseph Needham, ed., *Science and Civilization in China*, vol. 5, pt. 1 (Cambridge: Cambridge University Press, 1985), p. 221, that movable type was advantageous in China precisely for large editions.

6. Chartier, "Frenchness in the History of the Book," p. 302.

7. Konta, *Edo no hon'ya-san*, p. ii.

show combined annual totals rising from 360 to over 600 titles.[8] These figures include, however, only the serious academic and religious books known as *mononohon*, excluding the important categories of light fiction and illustrated books (*ezōshi*).

A completely different approach to estimating Tokugawa book production is offered by the *Kokusho sōmokuroku*, the massive bibliography of premodern books first published by Iwanami Shoten from 1963 to 1976 and more recently reissued in a supplemental edition.[9] I have encountered, however, only one effort to use this source as a basis for calculating annual book production, that published by Raymond Nunn in 1969.[10] Using the four volumes that had appeared until that point, Nunn extracted a sample of 669 titles (excluding manuscript sources). Making allowance for the four unpublished volumes of the bibliography, Nunn arrived at an estimated total of 195,000 printed publications for the period 1600–1868. That figure, however, includes later editions of single titles. If such multiple editions are excluded, the total is reduced to just over 100,000, about 30,000 before 1730 and 70,000 after, for annual averages of 236 titles before 1730 and 510 thereafter.

Nunn realized, of course, that many titles did not survive to be listed in the *Kokusho sōmokuroku*, and he attempted to establish a "rate of survival" on the basis of comparison with booksellers' lists. That effort was severely flawed in method, however, and his resulting calculation of 3,172 titles per year (including later editions) for 1600–1730 and 3,235 for 1730–1868 cannot be taken seriously.[11] His effort nevertheless showed a shrewd awareness of the problems involved and provides a starting point for a new estimate based on the same source—an effort that would be greatly facilitated by the computerization of the *Kokusho sōmokuroku*. For the moment, all that can be said is that the estimates obtained by both methods described above, each of which gives about 500 to 600 titles per year for the later Tokugawa period, must fall well short of the actual numbers.

What of the comparison with France? To simplify matters, let us take as comparable periods the 1770s for France and the 1840s for Japan, when the anciens régimes of both nations were on the verge of their final periods of crisis. We may dispense with any correction for per capita differences, since the total population of each nation was in the range of 25 to 30 million persons. Nor, it may be hypothesized, did the average sizes of printed editions differ much—about 500 to 1,000 in both cases. Hence we may

8. See the chart, ibid., p. 93.

9. Iwanami Shoten, ed., *Kokusho sōmokuroku*, 8 vols., rev. ed. (Iwanami Shoten, 1989–1991), supplemented by Kokubungaku Kenkyū Shiryōkan, ed., *Kotenseki sōgō mokuroku*, 3 vols. (Iwanami Shoten, 1990).

10. G. Raymond Nunn, "On the Number of Books Published in Japan from 1600 to 1868," in Harry J. Lamley, ed., *East Asian Occasional Papers*, vol. 1 (Honolulu: Asian Studies Program, University of Hawaii, May 1969), pp. 110–19.

11. For a critical review of Nunn's method, see Robert W. Leutner, "The Japanese Book Publishing Industry—Before and After the Meiji Restoration of 1868" (M.A. essay, Center for Japanese Studies, University of Michigan, August 1970), pp. 4–7.

use the number of titles per year for direct comparison: about 1,500 in France and perhaps 1,000 in Japan. Although it seems likely that the French produced more books than the Japanese, the excess was not so very large.

The crucial similarity, in any event, was not the precise number of books produced but rather the fact that in both nations by the end of the early-modern era printed books had become daily-life commodities. In the administrative capitals of Paris and Edo in particular, every citizen down to the most humble lived in a world saturated with the products of print technology and transformed by their effects.

The Expansion of Readership

In both countries literacy grew steadily, particularly in the last decades of the anciens régimes, thanks to the increase of formal education and to the sheer multiplication of the volume and forms of printed communication. Unfortunately, it is impossible to give comparable estimates of literacy. To begin with, the very notion of literacy necessarily varies because of the contrasting writing systems, and with them the means available to measure literacy. Signatures were not used on legal documents in Japan, nor did the Japanese prepare inventories of wills, so that neither of the critical bodies of evidence used for the study of French literacy are available.

The only attempts at quantifying Edo-period literacy in Western scholarship date back to the 1960s. Ronald P. Dore indulged in some statistical speculation and concluded that by 1868 school attendance (and presumably basic literacy, although he did not claim so) had reached 43 percent for boys and 10 percent for girls.[12] This was a national average, however, so that urban literacy must have been much higher. Herbert Passin gave estimates of breakdown by class that for Edo would work out to about 80 percent literacy for men and 50 percent for women.[13] In Paris, by comparison, 85 percent of men and 60 percent of women were able to sign wills in the late seventeenth century; the proportions rose to 90 and 80 percent, respectively, by the eve of the Revolution.[14] It seems clear that Paris's literacy rate was higher than Edo's at the end of the early-modern period, but they at least remain comparable.

Here, as with the total numbers of books produced, not only are precise numbers unobtainable but they tend to miss the point. As much recent French scholarship has emphasized, people unable to read can still be constantly exposed to printed matter when it is read to them by others—a form of communication that would have been particularly common in such densely settled capitals as Paris and Edo.

12. Ronald P. Dore, *Education in Tokugawa Japan* (Berkeley: University of California Press, 1965), p. 321.

13. Herbert Passin, *Society and Education in Japan* (New York: Teachers College Press, 1965), p. 57.

14. Daniel Roche, *The People of Paris: An Essay on Popular Culture in the 18th Century* (New York: Berg, 1987), p. 199.

THE FUNDAMENTAL CONTRASTS

The Technology of Writing

The Japanese writing system as it had evolved by the time that printing began to proliferate in the seventeenth century is a distinctive variant of the logographic system that Japan borrowed from China in the sixth century.[15] In the intervening millennium, the Japanese had devised a system of phonetic writing in syllabic units known as *kana* that could be used alone for pure Japanese or in conjunction with Chinese characters to indicate pronunciation and to provide the particles and inflections of the Japanese language. This system may sound complicated, but in fact it was even more complex in actual practice. The Japanese devised, for example, two entirely different systems of *kana*, the uses of which were distinguished in elaborate and never clearly formulated ways.[16] And within the more widely used *hiragana* system, variant symbols for given sounds (what are now known as *hentaigana*) were numerous.

Perhaps the reason for this "astonishingly complicated method of making language visible"[17] can be explained, as Roy Andrew Miller has argued, by the fact that the ancient Japanese aristocracy "had in fact little else to do with its time, and so quite naturally it delighted in any device that would make the process as time-consuming as possible."[18] In fact, all writing systems have proved immensely conservative, and the Japanese system as well built up such a weight of traditional attachment that only limited adjustments were made in the interests of readability in the early-modern period. Even books intended for the most popular audiences continued to be written in cursive script, filled with variant characters and making full use of the expressive potential of the writing system itself.[19]

The contrast with France or any other nation of early-modern Europe can be expressed quite simply: Whereas an ordinary modern reader can make immediate and near-perfect sense of any French book of the ancien régime, only a tiny group of highly trained scholars can read cursive printed texts of the Tokugawa period without difficulty; for everyone else, they are virtually illegible. Not all texts were cursive, to be sure: those written in Chinese (or "Sino-Japanese," the Japanese idiom of the Chinese written language) were typically in formal script and can be read today. Or rather, the script can be recognized today, but the meaning will remain obscure for most persons

---

15. For qualifications of the description of the Chinese writing system as "logographic," see John DeFrancis, *Visible Speech: The Diverse Oneness of Writing Systems* (Honolulu: University of Hawaii Press, 1989), pp. 220–26.

16. For a provocative discussion of this issue, see Amino Yoshihiko, "Nihon no moji shakai no tokushitsu o megutte," *Rettō no bunkashi* 5 (1988), pp. 19–57.

17. Geoffrey Sampson, *Writing Systems: A Linguistic Introduction* (Stanford: Stanford University Press, 1985), p. 172.

18. Roy Andrew Miller, *The Japanese Language* (Chicago: University of Chicago Press, 1967), p. 99.

19. For a revealing discussion of one such technique, the use of parallel glosses, see Chieko Ariga, "The Playful Gloss," *Monumenta Nipponica* 44:3 (1989), pp. 309–35.

because the classical Chinese language in which the texts are written is even more distant from modern Japanese than is Latin from modern French.

Because of this fundamental contrast, the very act of reading in early-modern Japan took on meanings it did not have in Europe—or in China, where the writing system was far more straightforward and printed books were uniformly legible. It is not simply that reading was more "difficult" in Japan, although there can be no doubt that mastery required far more time and concentration there than elsewhere; the act of reading Japanese was as much a pictorial experience as a linguistic one. The implications of this contrast for the very concept of literature—a notion that etymologically is bound to the idea of the alphabet—are immense and still inadequately explored by literary scholars.

The political implications of the Japanese writing system are ambiguous, and remain so today despite the substantial simplification it has undergone since Tokugawa times. The complexity of the system encourages reliance on set forms and higher authorities that might provide standards in a sea of tremendous potential variation in writing. Amino Yoshihiko, a scholar of medieval Japan, has argued precisely along these lines, claiming that the writing system imposed by the central elite dictated a uniformity of documentary style in all parts of Japan, thus serving as an instrument of political control.[20] By the same token, however, one might argue that in the Edo period the complexity of the writing system offered a variety of creative modes of expression, a number of them critical of the state. In this as in so many other ways, writing has the contradictory power both to constrain and to liberate.

The Technology of Printing

The use of blocks rather than type for printing in Japan was closely linked to the technology of writing, since the carving of an original block for each page gave complete flexibility of form and hence could perfectly preserve the complexity of the writing system. Formal conventions in the appearance of the printed page evolved, of course, many of them derived from the form of Chinese printed books. But particularly in cursive texts, one can find little that corresponds to Western "typography," since after all there was no type.

Block printing in the East Asian manner and European printing in movable type also involved completely different deployments of capital and systems of labor. Gutenberg's system dictated a primary investment in type fonts and printing presses, with a separate craft required for the manufacture of each. Once this initial equipment was acquired, the entire business of both composition (in effect, the very design of the book) and printing was in the hands of the printing shop (even if the two functions were carried out by different artisans). In Japan, by contrast, virtually no investment in capital equipment was required: the key demand was for skill, acquired only through years of experience. The first skill was that of the calligrapher, who

20. Amino, "Nihon no moji."

drew the image of the page to be reproduced. This was not, however, a specialized craft skill, but rather a talent that was expected of anyone properly trained in writing, requiring only a conventional brush and ink. As such, it was a sector of the printing process that, however crucial, was wholly unorganized and largely anonymous.[21]

The pivotal skill in block printing was that of carving, which required special training over a long period of time (although one does find more and more amateur carvers appearing in the late Tokugawa period, easily spotted by their clumsy work). The carvers were known as *hangiya* (literally, "woodblock workers"), and their enterprise, like that of printers in Europe, involved various skills, with one artisan to prepare the blocks, others to carve different kinds of writing, and others to do the pictures. The carvers were well organized as a separate trade from early in the seventeenth century, although large publishing establishments sometimes maintained their own in-house carvers. In respect to their role in the entire production process, the carver in Japan corresponded most closely to the printer in Europe.

By contrast, the actual printing process was considerably less preeminent in Japan than in Europe. To be sure, it demanded skill, probably more dexterity than the operator of a printing press required, but it needed almost no equipment—just a special tool known as a *baren*, which was used to rub (rather than press) the back of a moistened sheet of paper laid over an inked block. Although a tool of remarkable sophistication in its final stage of development, the *baren* was merely a parcel of the printer's skill, since the printer fabricated it himself, just as the carver made his own knives. As for binding, the final stage of book production, the far more architectonic design of the European book made binding a trade of special importance. In Japan, binding was a relatively simple operation of cutting, pasting, and stitching that could easily be performed in-house by the publisher, typically with female labor.

It is difficult to capsulize the comparative implications of two such widely differing technologies of printing. One commonality deserves emphasis: neither technology changed much at all after its initial establishment, in the sixteenth century in France and the seventeenth century in Japan. The key changes, as Roger Chartier has emphasized for France, were rather in the ways in which labor was organized. At a broader level, however, I propose that the task of comparison can be reduced to two essentials: the calculation of investment risk and the ratio of manual skill to mechanical advantage. Japanese block printing was on both counts relatively more conservative than Western type printing. Given the greater expense of producing a specific book and the added cost of long-term storage, Japanese publishers must have been marginally more disposed than their French counterparts to insist

---

21. The importance of the copyist, known in Japanese as *hanshitagaki*, is emphasized in the round table discussion involving Konta Yōzō, Nakano Mitsutoshi, Munemasa Isoo, and Ogata Tsutomu, and published as "[Zadankai] Kinsei no shuppan," *Bungaku* 49:11 (1981), p. 13.

on books that would be sure to sell, and likely to keep on selling over an extended period of time.

Because of the skill required, the process of production, particularly at the critical stage of block carving, was in the hands of a well-organized band of craftsmen whose training required many years under the supervision of masters. These demands may have made it somewhat more difficult in Japan to disseminate printing skills to the provinces. In France, anyone with access to a printing press and a case of type could produce of a book without a long period of training. Printing in France was thus well adapted to clandestine work, since presses could easily be moved from one place to another. In Japan, by contrast, the technology was centered not in type and machines but in the skill of the workers. Conversely, woodblock printing of crude quality could be fairly easily performed by amateurs, as it often was in the case of illegal handbills.

COMPARATIVE PERSPECTIVES: EDO AND PARIS

The International Book Environment

The book, Robert Darnton has argued, "is international in nature. Despite linguistic differences, customs barriers and ideological policing, books spill over national boundaries and spread the word with profligate abandon."[22] In the early-modern period, this dictum applies more aptly to France than to Japan. From well before Gutenberg, the book in Europe was an international phenomenon, and under the ancien régime, the supply of books from abroad continued to be a critical factor in the circulation of books within France. In particular, books published in French in such neighboring havens as the Low Countries and Switzerland provided a large part of the stock for the clandestine book trade, as Darnton's research has amply demonstrated.[23]

Tokugawa Japan was far more isolated than France, both geographically and politically. We should not imagine, however, that Japan was such a "closed country" that only Japanese-produced books circulated in Edo. On the contrary, Japan enjoyed a steady supply of books from abroad, most of them from China. In 1722, the lifting of the ban on the import of Western books (as long as they did not deal with Christianity) and—more important—of Chinese translations of such books resulted in a steady increase in Japanese contact with books from outside. The impact of these books has been well chronicled in the history of the "Dutch Studies" movement of the late Tokugawa period. Although linguistically accessible only to a small number of scholars and not politically subversive in any direct way, these books had an intellectual impact on Japan that may be compared to the role of books in purveying the Enlightenment in France.

22. Darnton, "Histoire du livre," p. 33.
23. See especially Robert Darnton, *The Literary Underground of the Old Regime* (Cambridge: Harvard University Press, 1982).

Still, it is crucial to remember that international trade in books was far more limited in Japan than in France, for the simple reason that readers in the Japanese language were to be found only in Japan. Thus very few Japanese books were exported, whereas many French books found their way abroad. Similarly, no books in the Japanese language were produced outside of Japan, an effect ensured by the ban on travel abroad. This situation contrasts strongly with the ability of a neighboring French-speaking city such as Neuchâtel to play an important role in the book trade and intellectual life of eighteenth-century France.

Centralization of Publishing Activity

The French pattern of book production differed from that of Japan. For almost two centuries after Gutenberg, printing in France was conducted at a variety of dispersed provincial centers that competed vigorously with one another. Under Colbert in the 1660s, however, decisive measures were taken to end a trade war that severely disadvantaged provincial printers and established virtual monopoly control by the Parisian guild. A small group of master printer-booksellers was able to dominate legal publishing up until the Revolution. Challenges did come from the clandestine market, of course, and there is growing evidence that provincial publishing flourished in the eighteenth century in spite of legal restrictions, but Paris was firmly established as the capital of French book production.[24]

In Japan, the production of books moved rather from the center outward, beginning at Kyoto in the first half of the seventeenth century, then spreading to Osaka and Edo in the second half. With the cultural maturation of Edo in the course of the eighteenth century, the city's share of national book production grew steadily until it finally surpassed the combined production (in titles) of Kyoto and Osaka in the 1790s. Even so, publishing was never so completely centralized in Edo as it was in Paris, nor did the state make any particular efforts to favor Edo publishers over those in other cities. Rather there emerged a kind of functional differentiation that replicated the historical evolution of the publishing industry. Kyoto continued to be the major center for "hard" books, particularly Buddhist and Confucian works, both of which were in Chinese. The Osaka trade focused on practical works, such as home encyclopedias, while the Edo market was more heavily oriented to "soft" books, notably the diverse forms of popular fiction that emerged in the course of the eighteenth century. Much overlap occurred, of course, and the three cities were often in heated competition. Indeed, some of the fiercest interregional rivalries were fought out within Edo, where local publishers competed with the branches of the great Kyoto firms.[25]

Near the end of the Tokugawa period, book production began to grow in provincial cities as well. The largest such center was Nagoya, which by the

24. Robert Darnton, "Reading, Writing, and Publishing in Eighteenth-Century France: A Case Study in the Sociology of Literature," *Daedalus* 100 (1971), p. 228.

25. Konta, "Edo no shuppan shihon," pp. 109–95.

end of the Edo period had nearly thirty bookseller-publishers,[26] but active publishing was also to be found in Ise, Wakayama, Hiroshima, Sendai, Kanazawa, and Nagasaki—all except the first and last of which were castle cities under direct control of daimyo.[27] This provincial activity did not compare in total volume, however, to the production of the three great urban printing centers. Nor should it be imagined that the production of books in Japan was a free market, for one finds here the same pattern as in France: domination by well-established guilds that enjoyed official patronage.

The key commonality in France and Japan was that the production of books was largely in the hands of commercial capital rather than the state. In this respect Japan differed from its East Asian neighbors; in China the imperial government engaged in substantial printing activity, and in Korea almost all printing was under direct state control. The Tokugawa shogunate did engage in some limited printing, but not as a matter of routine: all edicts, for example, were issued in manuscript. The French state, by contrast, directly printed a variety of government documents. Still, in both countries the principal publishing activity was carried on by commercial houses—although typically in close collusion with the state to ensure patronage and to protect their interests. In Edo, for example, certain publishers were given exclusive rights to the printing of calendars, daimyo directories (*bukan*), and maps of the city—perquisites that were essential to long-term survival.

The Organization of Publishing

The study of Edo publishing history remains in its infancy, despite the important work of Konta Yōzō. Part of the problem lies in the paucity of materials: because of the frequent destruction of Edo by fire and of Tokyo by earthquake and war, very few primary materials have survived to document the inner workings of the Edo publishing industry—in contrast, for example, to that of Kyoto, where materials are far more plentiful. It is clear that no amount of research will ever be able to offer the amount of rich detail that we have about publishing in early-modern Paris.

Here only some general observations are possible. In neither country was publishing an autonomous activity; it was always linked with the busi-

26. For a study of Nagoya publishing see Matthi Forrer, *Eirakuya Tōshirō, Publisher at Nagoya: A Contribution to the History of Publishing in 19th-Century Japan* (Amsterdam: J. C. Gieben, 1985).

27. Inoue Takaaki, *Kinsei shorin hanmoto sōran*, Nihon shoshigaku taikei 14 (Seishōdō Shoten, 1981), p. 6, provides statistics by period on the founding dates of all known early-modern publishers, which give a rough indication of the relative scale of publishing in the various cities. The total numbers of publishing houses in each city for the entire Edo period are: Kyoto, 1,733; Edo, 1,652; Osaka, 1,253; Nagoya, 104; Ise, 49; Wakayama, 24; Sendai, 27; Kanazawa, 24; Nagasaki, 21; other provincial, 312. The overall percentage accounted for by the three great cities of Edo, Kyoto, and Osaka is 89 percent. For an interesting case study of one of these provincial centers, see Peter F. Kornicki, "Chihō shuppan ni tsuite no shiron: Nihonkoku Wakayama no baai," in Yoshida Mitsukuni, ed., *Jūkyū seiki Nihon no jōhō to shakai hendō* (Kyoto: Kyōto Daigaku Jinbun Kagaku Kenkyūjo, 1985), pp. 449–66.

ness of selling books. In this sense, both the Parisian *librairie* and the Edo *hon'ya* must alike be translated into English as "bookseller-publisher." Only after the Revolution in France and the Restoration in Japan does one find the emergence of the publisher as an entrepreneur independent of the tasks of physical production and commercial distribution. The bookseller-publishers in both countries were also obliged to deal with the primary craft guilds, those of the printers in Paris and the carvers in Edo.

As suggested earlier, the capital requirements of the publishing enterprise differed in the two nations. In France, the need for capital was divided between the printer, who required such equipment as presses and type fonts, and the publisher, who had to pay both printer and author. In Japan, the capital requirements fell largely on the publisher alone, who commissioned the carving of the blocks, which then became his own capital. In the later Edo period, one does find printers dealing directly with individuals, such as teachers of the arts, who ordered private editions for distribution to students and colleagues.[28] The bulk of publishing, however, remained in commercial hands.

One important calculation for a publisher is always the size of an edition. In France, Roger Chartier notes, printings were usually between one thousand and two thousand copies.[29] The evidence for Japan is far more anecdotal and contradictory, but printings seem to fall into about the same range.[30] Wooden blocks eventually wore down, to be sure, but it seems clear that several thousand decent copies could be obtained from a set of blocks— more than could ever be sold for all but the most popular books.[31] One further imponderable in the Japanese case is the size and number of later printings, which could always be issued as long as the blocks were kept (not always the case: it cost valuable space to store blocks, and there was economic incentive to recycle the wood by planing it for recarving).[32]

Piracy, Copyright, and Author's Rights

Piracy was a common threat to publishers in both France and Japan, and every device was mobilized by the guilds to control it. In the Japanese case, however, virtually no legal protection was offered: it was only under the Meiji state that the concept of copyright was introduced. The forerunner of copyright in Japan was rather the notion of "possession of blocks" (*zōhan*), which came to mean not necessarily physical possession but rather legal

28. This trend is discussed in "[Zadankai] Kinsei no shuppan," p. 14.

29. Chartier, "Frenchness in the History of the Book," p. 315.

30. The evidence is summarized in Nagatomo Chiyoji, "Kinsei: Gyōshō hon'ya, kashihon'ya, dokusha," *Kokubungaku: Kaishaku to kanshū* 45:10 (1980), p. 94. Note also Konta's assumption in *Edo no hon'ya-san*, p. ii, that the average number of copies of each title was one thousand.

31. Forrer, *Eirakuya Tōshirō*, p. 74, deals with the problem of block capacity, dismissing reports of a limit of 250 to 300 copies per block.

32. Nakano Mitsutoshi in "[Zadankai] Kinsei no shuppan," p. 11, notes a report from a Nagoya publisher that whatever the size of the first printing, subsequent print runs were small, about thirty copies, to minimize inventories.

title.[33] It is unclear, however, whether piracy was in fact any more common in Japan than in France, where even in spite of legal copyright protection by the mid-eighteenth century, the illegal reproduction of books was widely practiced.

A related issue is the rights of authors. Here as well, France was far ahead of Japan, as a result of a 1777 law that gave more specific privileges to authors. In Japan, the very concept of the rights of an author was unheard of until the Meiji period. In practice, however, it may be surmised that the actual treatment of authors was not much better in France than in Japan. Roger Chartier notes, for example, that publishers closely controlled authors, and tended more often to pay them in copies of a book than in cash.[34] Robert Darnton, meanwhile, has written of his suspicion that "only a tiny minority of the writers in each country [i.e., Germany and France] could live from their pens."[35] The situation was much the same in Japan, where until late in the Edo period only playwrights were paid for their work. The popular and prolific Santō Kyōden (1761–1816) is often said to have been the first Japanese writer of fiction who was able to make a living by writing.[36]

Censorship and the Guilds

The state in both France and Japan exercised strict and sustained control over publishing from about the same era. In France, a system of close supervision and active prosecution was instituted from the 1660s and continued until the Revolution. In Japan, general control over publishing was first decreed in the Kanbun period (1661–1673), and during the Genroku period (1688–1704) various incidents of the suppression of publication occurred. It was only in 1722, however, as part of the Kyōhō reforms, that a complete system of surveillance and censorship was established.

In both regimes, the biggest threat from printed matter was seen to consist of attacks on the nation's supreme political figure—the monarch in France, the shogun in Japan. The second great concern was heterodox thinking, which in France was conceived in theological terms as doctrines that opposed the Catholic Counter-Reformation, and which in Japan was seen as ideas opposing neo-Confucian orthodoxy—although enforcement of neo-Confucianism did not come until after the Kansei reforms of the late eighteenth century.

The greatest difference in the actual operation of censorship in the two countries was that the shogunate in Japan imposed the responsibility on the publishing guild, whereas in France special government offices were instituted to control the book trade, both through prepublication censorship and

33. "[Zadankai] Kinsei no shuppan," p. 18. In Japanese terminology, a distinction was made between facsimile reproduction (*jūhan*, done by use of actual pages from the book to be copied as the *hanshita* for carving) and approximate reproduction (*ruihan*, done from a new copy of the original made for carving).

34. Chartier, "Frenchness in the History of the Book," p. 315.

35. Darnton, "Histoire du livre," p. 36.

36. Aeba Kōson, "Mukashi no sakusha no sakuryō oyobi shuppan busū," *Aoi* 4 (1910), pp. 1–3.

through police control over illicit publishing. The Japanese system reflects a general preference for indirect control based on the principle of mutual responsibility. In France the guild was involved in the operation of the censorship system, but not to the extent of total autonomy as in Japan.

According to the analysis of Daniel Roche, in France the concern for ideological deviation was balanced by a reluctance to jeopardize the economic interests of the official publishers' monopoly, a reflection of the mercantilist policy of the French state from Colbert on.[37] The Japanese state seems similarly to have always had the interests of the powerful, privileged publishers in mind when it established its control system, but there is little evidence of such explicit financial preoccupation as in France.

It is difficult to compare the precise effects of censorship in the two regimes. Although Japanese scholarship has devoted considerable attention to this particular issue, most of the information comes from government control edicts and from scattered reports of actual works that were banned and authors who were punished; quantitative material is virtually nonexistent.[38] Konta Yōzō has suggested impressionistically that Japan was in general fairly lax in its control of books, particularly in comparison with China, where the mere ownership of proscribed books was punished. Punishment for violation of the publication edicts in Japan, he notes, was never systematic, but rather a matter of simply setting an example now and then (as the shogunate did more than once with Santō Kyōden).[39] It may simply be the case, however, that the system of self-censorship in Japan was in fact effective. It certainly seems to have worked to prevent the publication of any literature that involved outright attacks on the regime. The general absence of seditious publications in Japan, in all but the most indirect and parodic forms, is in striking contrast to the situation in France.

As for France, Daniel Roche has argued, the system of censorship was shot through with ambivalence on the part of the enforcers, particularly in the decades just before the Revolution. In part, this approach reflected a commitment to the prosperity of the publishing industry itself, and in part it was a product of an "ideology of compromise, half-philosophical and half-absolutist," on the part of the censors, who were "men of some education and talent."[40] Yet the number of prisoners sent to the Bastille for book crimes—a total of 941 over the period 1659–1789, he says, for an average of 18 percent of all Bastille inmates—seems vastly in excess of those who suffered for publication-related crimes in Tokugawa Japan.

37. Daniel Roche, "Censorship and the Publishing Industry," in Robert Darnton and Daniel Roche, eds., *Revolution in Print: The Press in France, 1775–1800* (Berkeley: University of California Press, 1989).
38. See Konta, "Edo no shuppan shihon," pp. 109–95; Yoshiwara Ken'ichirō, "Edo hangiya nakama to ihō insatsu: Kasei-ki o chūshin ni," *Bungaku* 49:11 (1981), pp. 138–48.
39. Konta Yōzō in "[Zadankai] Kinsei no shuppan," p. 30.
40. Roche, "Censorship and the Publishing Industry," p. 13. On French censorship see also Raymond Birn, "Book Production and Censorship in France, 1700–1715," in Kenneth E. Carpenter, ed., *Books and Society in History* (New York: R. R. Bowker, 1983), pp. 145–71.

Illicit Publishing

In both France and Japan, the illegal publication of literature that had no chance of approval under the formal censorship system was widespread. The greatest contrasts lay in the locus of such publications and in their content. Many illicit books were shipped to France by publishers outside of the national borders, particularly in Switzerland during the age of the Enlightenment. Japan had no such overseas havens, and illicit publishing had to be carried out virtually under the noses of the men who sought to control publication. That underground publishers were as successful as they were suggests that Konta's hypothesis about the general laxity of publication control in Japan may be correct in this regard as well.

In content, the bulk of illicit literature in the later decades of the anciens régimes appears to have been political in France and pornographic in Japan—although each country seems to have had a good amount of both sorts. Political protest in Japan tended to be expressed in parody rather than outright attack, and was more commonly circulated in manuscript than in printed form. Perhaps the most striking reflection of this contrast was the absence in Japan of any periodical literature, which was of central importance in early-modern France. Comment on current events of any sort, social as well as political, was prohibited under the publishing edicts, so by its very definition "news" was illegal. Simple unlicensed broadsides known as kawaraban did appear to announce major scandals and disasters, but they were irregular and ephemeral. The curiosity of the Japanese public for fuller details about political scandals seems to have been satisfied primarily by the semifictionalized accounts known as jitsuroku ("true records"), which circulated in manuscript form through rental libraries.

Common Reading Facilities

The cities of Paris and Edo offered networks for the shared reading of books, but with spatial and organizational differences. Such facilities were crucial in spreading the influence of print, both through the multiplication of the uses to which single copies of books could be put and through the economic advantages offered to that large majority of the urban population who could not afford the regular purchase of books.

In the early stages of the commercial distribution of books in any culture, lending coexists with selling.[41] At a further stage of development, book lending becomes a specialized service. This stage was reached in Japan about the same time as in Western Europe, in the early eighteenth century. The extensive research of Nagatomo Chiyoji shows the term kashihon'ya (book lender) appearing as early as 1713,[42] and the number of such enterprises in

41. For a good comparative study of lending institutions in a variety of early-modern societies, including China and Japan, see Peter Kornicki, "Kashihon bunka hikakukō," Jinbun gakuhō 57 (1984), pp. 37–57. For book lending in early-modern Europe, see Paul Kaufman, "Some Community Libraries in Eighteenth-Century Europe: A Reconnaissance," Libri 22:1 (1972), pp. 1–57.

42. Nagatomo, "Kinsei," p. 97.

Edo alone had increased to over six hundred a century later, and to eight hundred by the 1840s.[43] One calculation has suggested that the customers of a single book lender would number 150 to 200 households,[44] which when multiplied by several hundred would account for about half of the population of Edo. Studies by Peter Kornicki and others have demonstrated the importance of the late Edo book lender in supplying the readership for certain genres of literature, notably the *yomihon* novels of Takizawa Bakin and others and the *jitsuroku* manuscripts.

However important the book lenders of Edo may have been in spreading the culture of print, they seem to have been lacking in one key element that was conspicuous in Paris: the provision of a common reading space. As Roger Chartier has shown, Paris in the later eighteenth century was provided with a wide variety of facilities for the collective reading of books.[45] In 1784, for example, Paris boasted fully eighteen public libraries (although some were restricted to "men of letters"). Equally important were the *cabinets de lecture*, establishments where for a subscription fee one could go to read journals and books in a pleasant setting. Some of these places were close in atmosphere to literary salons, and many engaged in the lending of books as well. In addition, a large number of bookstalls engaged only in lending.

The *kashihon'ya* in Edo seem to have been purely lending institutions, sometimes at a fixed location but more often, it seems, on a delivery basis. The delivery service was particularly well developed in the daimyo quarters of the city, where large numbers of idle samurai and servants provided a substantial share of the book-lending market. Doubtless customers might read a bit as they browsed at the fixed shops, but the idea of providing a hospitable reading environment was lacking in Japan.

The critical factor behind this spatial contrast probably lies in the absence in Edo of periodical journals dealing with current events, which seem to have been the largest single reason for the *cabinets de lecture* of Paris. Since the appeal of a journal's content faded quickly, it made more sense to go somewhere to read periodicals than to invest in their purchase. It is revealing that when newspapers began to spread in Tokyo in the early Meiji period, there soon appeared public reading rooms of a sort that provide a close parallel to French *cabinets de lecture*.[46] It was also only in the Meiji period that the very idea of public libraries appeared in Japan, an import from the West. The absence of any communal reading spaces in Edo, whether for free public use or for rental, is a revealing mark of the far more privatized nature of the city in Japan than in Western Europe.

43. Peter Kornicki, "The Publisher's Go-Between: *Kashihon'ya* in the Meiji Period," *Modern Asian Studies* 14:2 (1980), p. 331.
44. Kornicki, "Kashihon bunka hikakukō," p. 48, citing a study by Nakamura Yukihiko.
45. Roger Chartier, *The Cultural Uses of Print in Early Modern France* (Princeton: Princeton University Press, 1987), pp. 204–15.
46. Kornicki, "Publisher's Go-Between," pp. 333–34.

Reading Habits

An issue closely related to book lending is the content of popular reading. The Edo book lenders, according to the conventional image, dealt largely in fiction, although Kornicki has mustered evidence to prove that in Japan as in Europe lending institutions circulated a considerable variety of other types of books as well.[47] No studies have been made to show exactly what types of books members of Edo's commoner population owned, and evidence on this score is very sparse. One can only speculate that religious works were less common in Edo than in France, except among members of the various religious movements that emerged in the later Tokugawa period. Not that urban Japanese were irreligious, but at the popular level adherence to religious precepts depended less on the written word.[48]

Another important issue concerning reading habits that emerges from French scholarship is the degree to which books were read aloud or silently.[49] It has been proposed that the way for Gutenberg's invention was paved by a medieval "revolution in reading," in the course of which silent reading gained steady ground at the expense of the "mumbled" (*ruminatio*) style of oral reading. This gradual shift represents the emergence, it is argued, of a freer and more private relationship with the book.

What about Japan? The issue has been addressed for the Meiji period in a perceptive essay by Maeda Ai titled "From Reading Aloud to Silent Reading."[50] Maeda observed that even at the time he was writing, in the early 1960s, one could still hear older people reading newspapers in a "strange singsong" (*iyō no fushimawashi*), and he speculated that the general practice of silent reading may be no more than one to three generations old. He offered various evidence for the pervasive practice of reading aloud in the Meiji period, and noted the clear links between late Meiji fiction (in particular the romances of Tamenaga Shunsui) and such popular arts of oral performance as *rakugo* and *kōshaku*. He contended, along lines proposed by Lafcadio Hearn, that the solidarity of the Japanese household made solitary reading an antisocial act, and suggested that reading aloud to groups helped overcome low rates of literacy.

More broadly, it may be observed that the reading of Japanese tradi-

47. Kornicki, "Kashihon bunka hikakukō," p. 54.

48. A related phenomenon is the decrease in the proportion of Japanese books published in Chinese (that is, *kanbun*). Of early movable-type books, about two-thirds were in Chinese. Statistics provided in Nunn, "On the Number of Books Published in Japan," p. 115, indicate a decrease in the categories "Buddhism" and "Chinese Literature and Thought" from a combined 20 percent in 1600–1730 to 14 percent in 1730–1868. Compare this decline with the decrease in the percentage of French books published in Latin, from 25 percent in 1650 to only 10 percent by the 1660s; a slower rate of decline in Germany provides a better parallel to the Japanese case in the survival of older humanistic learning. See Roger Chartier and Daniel Roche, "New Approaches to the History of the Book," in Jacques Le Goff and Pierre Nora, eds., *Constructing the Past: Essays in Historical Methodology* (Cambridge: Cambridge University Press, 1985), pp. 198–214.

49. I rely here on Chartier's summary in "Frenchness in the History of the Book," p. 312, where further citations are provided.

50. Maeda Ai, "Ondoku kara mokudoku e: Kindai dokusha no seiritsu," in his *Kindai dokusha no seiritsu* (Yūseidō, 1973), pp. 132–67.

tionally involved a pronounced level of orality, typically in sociable settings, along with the strongly visual component imposed by the writing system. Japanese *waka* poetry, for example, was more often recited than read, and was often composed during poetry contests or in linked-verse groups. In the Edo period, printed librettos from the puppet theater served as much as texts for amateur chanters as for enjoyment as silently read literature. Even the reading of Chinese was mastered orally in the chanting of the classics in Edo-period schools. And as Maeda stressed, late Edo popular fiction, with its increasingly vernacular qualities, must have made for good reading aloud in a group. Although none of these observations can be quantified, one does sense that the orality of communication by print was stronger in Edo then in Paris.

The Forms of Print

As a physical presence, the book in early-modern Japan was far less assertive than its European counterpart. The covers were merely extra paper pages, with only subtle decoration and extra thickness for durability. Nothing could contrast more strongly with the architectonic assertiveness of a Western tome, designed like a small piece of furniture and bound in the gilded hide of an animal. The book in Japan was rarely used for display, except for the kind of temporary exhibit that had emerged in the medieval period, in which a precious manuscript would be placed in a decorative alcove or on a special shelf. When not in use, books were laid flat in boxes, which were closed up and put away, in contrast to the European tradition of permanent display in cases.

Inside the covers, Japanese books, particularly in their popular forms, were far more likely to be illustrated than those in France. The wide use of illustrations reflects the ease with which woodblock technology permitted the inclusion of pictures, and it may also be a mark of the high level of visuality of the writing system itself. The invention of multicolor block printing in 1764 led to the steady proliferation of color images in late Edo printed objects, both books and single-sheet prints. The same effect could be obtained in France only by the hand-coloring of each individual page, a process too costly for all but the most luxurious publications. The precise effect of the element of color in the popular print culture of Edo remains a matter for speculation, but at the sensual level it seems to provide a clear contrast to the sober black-and-white pages of French books.

As printing spread in Japan, the opportunities for private publishing multiplied; presumably the same was true of France. Yoshiwara Ken'ichirō provides valuable evidence for such commissioned printing in his account of control edicts in the Bunka-Bunsei period (1804–1830), when the shogunate endeavored to restrict the more flamboyant forms of printing, particularly the use of gilt and large numbers of colors.[51] This period saw a tremendous growth in private orders for printed items on the occasions of all sorts of

51. Yoshiwara, "Edo hangiya nakama to ihō insatsu," pp. 141–48. See also "[Zadankai] Kinsei no shuppan," p. 14.

celebrations and parties, whether as invitations or as gifts for the guests. Men of letters would send specially printed *surimono* as New Year's greetings, *haikai* teachers would commission printed collections of their students' poems, practitioners of the musical and performing arts would print announcements when they conferred an art name on a pupil, and merchants would send out printed placards announcing the opening of a shop. Most of these practices began in the eighteenth century, but they proliferated during the early nineteenth.

At a broader level, late Edo society was flooded with printed ephemera, as was Paris of the ancien régime. The forms varied in accord with customs and technology. Posters were rare in Edo, for example, but placards were legion. It is difficult to offer much in the way of comparison at this stage, except to suggest that Chartier's notion of the "appropriation" and resultant transformation of the forms of elite culture by popular culture offers a persuasive model for the study of printed ephemera in Edo.[52]

One final proviso that may apply to Edo even more than to Paris: as Chartier stresses, the spread of print culture by no means meant the end of scribal culture. Skill in calligraphy was so revered in Japan that writing by hand was an essential accomplishment for anyone with pretensions to literacy. In the very form of printed matter, the distinction between manuscript and book was negligible: block-printed books, after all, are merely facsimiles of handwritten pages. This highly fluid intercourse between manuscript and book helps to explain why few historians in Japan have been able to see the print revolution of the early seventeenth century for the revolution that it surely was.

City versus Country in the Culture of Print

Printing and publishing began in cities and have remained concentrated there to this day. These urban products, however, began to spread to the countryside from an early point. In the case of France, Natalie Davis has argued that the impact was minimal during the first century and a quarter of print: peasants of the sixteenth century had little immediate need for printed books, and oral tradition remained dominant.[53] By the end of the ancien régime, however, things had clearly changed as elite urban culture worked its way down and out. Here again it is useful to borrow Chartier's notion of "appropriation" and to conceive of this process less as the conquest of rural culture by urban print than as the turning of printed matter from the cities to specifically rural ends.

It can only be proposed that the dynamics were similar in Japan: a close study of the process remains for the future. On the one hand, Kornicki has emphasized the importance of late Edo popular fiction in spreading the customs and the dialect of Edo to the provinces, and thus in starting a process that in the modern period might be called the "Tokyoization" of

52. Chartier, *Cultural Uses of Print in Early Modern France*, p. 6.
53. Natalie Davis, "Printing and the People," in her *Society and Culture in Early Modern France* (Stanford: Stanford University Press, 1965), pp. 194–209.

Japan, which continues apace to this very day.[54] On the other hand, the work of Anne Walthall on rural culture demonstrates the many ways in which peasants could indeed "appropriate" urban cultural forms to their own uses, imbuing them with their own meanings.[55]

CONCLUSION

It seems appropriate in conclusion to turn once again to the writings of Roger Chartier, whose thinking has done so much to inspire both the conceptual framework and, on the French side, the particular detail of this chapter. In September 1987 Professor Chartier presented a lecture, "Frenchness in the History of the Book," at the American Antiquarian Society. It is an eloquent plea for the broadening of *l'histoire du livre*, for the use of "Frenchness" as the basis for a new universality and interdisciplinarity in the study of the culture of print. However broad this gesture may have appeared to Professor Chartier's American hosts, the frame of reference remained explicitly and insistently Western. Note, for example, the guarded phrasing of the proposal that "the circulation of printed matter and the practices of reading . . . are at the core of all the major evolutions that transformed European and even Occidental civilization between the end of the Middle Ages and the present day."

We certainly have a long way to go before we can consider dropping the phrase "European and even Occidental" from this sentence. Ultimately, however, we must seek ways to move beyond the explicit and wholly admirable ethnocentrism of Chartier. As the tentative character of all that I have written until now should demonstrate, this is not an easy task. By way of conclusion, then, let me simply turn to the final pages of "Frenchness in the History of the Book" and see what might happen if we dared to add "even in Japanese civilization" to his proposal that "the questions that the history of the book, of publishing, and of reading may reformulate are not themselves enclosed within national territories."

Chartier specifies three "major evolutions" of Western civilization in which print was implicated. The first draws on Norbert Elias's notion of civilization as "the inculcation of new constraints that rein in the emotions, censure impulses, and raise the threshold of modesty." The whole notion of civilization as a system of manners and etiquette will seem immediately relevant to any student of early-modern Japanese culture and its formal obsessions. The linkage with print, however, remains to be probed. It appears on the surface that the tremendous discipline and formalism involved in the mastery of the Japanese writing system imply a case for which Elias's theory works even better than the civilization for which that theory was designed.

54. Karnicki, "Kashihon bunka hikakukō," p. 55.
55. Anne Walthall, *Social Protest and Popular Culture in Eighteenth-Century Japan* (Tucson: University of Arizona Press, 1986).

Second, Chartier proposes, print helps create a *private* sphere of existence, separate from communal controls and state authority. Indeed, Philippe Ariès has argued, print supplies all the necessary conditions for the very notion of privacy, in the "intimate and secret relationship between the reader and his book."[56] This formulation directs our attention to the complex and much-debated issue of privacy in Japan, and urges us to reconsider it in terms of print. One answer may lie in the hypothesis that Japanese culture retained higher levels of residual orality in the face of growing literacy than did European cultures.

Third and last, reading practices are seen as deeply implicated in the creation of a new public political sphere, a space for debate and criticism. This development began in institutionalized forms of sociability in the salons and cafés of the Enlightenment and was made possible by the circulation of the printed word. The case of Japan offers a clear challenge to the universality of this notion, at least in the early-modern period. The Tokugawa polity, in the highly private way in which it defined itself, denied the very possibility of a public political sphere. This definition was challenged by print, to be sure, but in the end the culture of print in Edo shared in the essential privacy of the larger political culture. We are still left with the possibility, however, that the experience with print culture in Tokugawa Japan offered fertile ground for the dramatic emergence of a truly public political sphere in the Meiji period, when suddenly newspapers, journals, and places of public discussion emerged as forums for lively debate over national issues.

The Japanese case thus reminds us that the political impact of print is profoundly ambiguous: it serves both as a device by which the state can control its subjects and as a channel through which the state can be opposed and even toppled. The former effect was more evident in the Meiji Restoration and the latter more obvious in the French Revolution. The line between the two is nevertheless a fine one, and it will require much further thought to decide whether "civilization" in general prefers one side of the line or the other.

56. The words are Chartier's, in "Frenchness in the History of the Book," p. 327.

RESISTANCE

支配反抗

15

Guilds, "False Workers," and the Faubourg Saint-Antoine

STEVEN LAURENCE KAPLAN

The history of work during the ancien régime is not synonymous with that of the guilds, corporations known as *communautés d'arts et métiers*. There were infinitely more workers of all sorts outside the incorporated world of work than within it, in Paris as well as in the provinces. But the social, economic, and political significance of work within the guild system went far beyond the actual territory it encompassed. Indeed, so-called free work, especially in the towns, was almost always regulated in accordance with criteria established by or for the guilds. Within their domains, the corporate communities enjoyed power that was quite extensive; in the eyes of those who did not share it, it was excessive. The system of classification of the guilds implies a world without the least ambiguity. Its frontiers were traced with precision, its rules clearly formulated. In principle, no hidden corners existed, or any open space into which refractory individuals could slide. One could not imagine existing socially or economically outside the categories of the guild taxonomy any more than one could conceive, in a larger context, of achieving salvation through anything but work. The capacity of the guild system to survive and to reproduce itself depended upon its ability to impose respect—for its prerogatives and distinctions, for the canons that governed the labor market and the discipline of workers, and for its monopolies on production, the circulation of goods, and status.

THE THREAT OF THE FALSE WORKERS

One of the most serious threats to the control that the guilds exercised over their social and economic capital came from thousands of infiltrators whom the leaders of the corporate communities denounced as "usurpers," "un-

This chapter is translated by John Merriman from "Les corporations, les 'faux ouvriers' et le faubourg Saint-Antoine au XVIIIe siècle," *Annales E.S.C.*, no. 2, March–April 1988. It appears here by permission.

skilled, unlicensed workers," or "false workers."[1] They set themselves up more or less secretly in rooming houses or simply in rooms, whence derives one of their common names, *chambrelans*. Sometimes these men found sanctuary in one of the enclaves that were privileged juridically or in *collèges*, convents, hospitals, or *grandes maisons*; sometimes they worked under the protection of the various private or seigneurial jurisdictions of the capital. The false workers were journeymen who for various reasons did not want to play the game devised by the guilds, or who were prevented from setting up shop themselves for lack of a regular apprenticeship. In response, they created a world of parallel work, outside the corporate communities; they were considered to be socially illicit, politically seditious, morally corrupt, and technically incapable. The unlicensed workers were taken to be imposters and shammers whose work threatened society in general, as well as the order of guilds, because it was "fraudulent" and "deceitful." They were accused of cheating consumers by providing them with merchandise that was defective, even dangerous. They challenged the masters with dishonest competition, making use of their know-how while offering cheaper prices, thanks to the lower costs of their underground operations. Finally, the false workers undermined the system of subordination erected by the guilds to keep their journeymen in place. They diverted workers from the institutionalized itinerary of apprenticeship and journeymanship, and they offered protection to the workers who had escaped the official labor market.

The policy of the guild system was to suppress such uncontrolled, clandestine work by any and all means. An elaborate series of regulations first struck workers and, secondarily, the masters who facilitated their crime. Guild leaders forbade any unauthorized person "to work in the aforementioned profession in a shop, workshop, or room, even in a bourgeois house,"[2] and they prohibited any master to put out work or to protect unlicensed workers in any way.[3] The false workers benefited from the complicity of the seigneurs of privileged jurisdiction, who reinforced the protection afforded by renegade masters. Moreover, several guilds tried to deny unlicensed workers access to primary materials.[4] By preventing journeymen from having their own tools or from taking tools home from the workshops, a number of guilds refused them the right to an autonomous professional identity (the tools always carrying the name of the master) and, in practice,

1. Many such communities used the formula "false workers": Archives Nationales (henceforth AN), T 1490[4] (silversmiths); Y 15363, 7 April 1748 (tailors); Y 15364, 21 April 1758 (coppersmiths); and deliberation of 23 October 1741, *Statuts et règlements de la communauté des maîtres imprimeurs en taille douce* (Paris, 1754), pp. 66, 72, Bibliothèque Nationale (BN), 8° Z Le Senne 4464.

2. AN, Y 15364, 14 June 1752 (plumbers); arrêt du conseil, 10 November 1750, BN, Inv. F 22466 (saddlemakers).

3. Police sentence 11 December 1733, AN, AD XI 16; arrêt de la Cour des monnaies, 24 April 1717, BN, ms. fr. 21794, fols. 203–4; and arrêt de la Cour des monnaies, 10 December 1703, AN, T 1450 (10), fol. 360.

4. See, for example, the police ordinance of 7 August 1671 and the sentence of the police, 30 September 1732, AN, T1490[10], fols. 252–53.

discouraged them from leaving to set up shop on their own. Another regulation that was widely applied forbade a worker to pick up discarded raw materials, partially to underline his incomplete and dependent status but also to prevent him from taking that step toward the world of uncontrolled work.[5]

The sanctions inflicted on unlicensed workers were severe. The most common was the seizure "of tools, utensils, and merchandise," a devastating, even fatal blow.[6] Such a worker also risked being assessed a fine, including damages and interest. If he could not pay, he might be sent to jail. When the elected governors of the guilds (the *jurés*) thought that an even harsher penalty was necessary, by virtue of alleged "rebellion" against their authority or because of practices considered particularly reprehensible, or when they wanted to set a resounding example, they solicited a royal letter authorizing the imprisonment of the false worker. A certain number of the guilds sought—in vain—to put men who worked in rooms on their own on a blacklist so as to prevent them from going back to the workshop. Others subjected the false workers to a punishment that was even more draconian in their eyes: perpetual exclusion from access to mastership.[7]

There doubtless had been false workers in Paris since the very beginnings of the guild system, but the problem became significantly worse in the eighteenth century because the false workers seemed to proliferate and their capacity to survive appeared to be enhanced. One can, *grosso modo*, divide them into two groups: those who were dispersed throughout the city, most often working in their rooms, and those who were concentrated in (and more or less confined to) well-defined places. Claiming an exceptional "license," the false workers in juridically privileged places sheltered themselves behind particularly imposing ramparts.

In theory outside the jurisdiction of the guilds, these privileged spaces were ancient ecclesiastical fiefs that benefited from a relative extraterritoriality, notably the abbeys of Saint-Germain-des-Prés and Sainte-Geneviève, the cloisters of Saint-Jean de Latran and Temple, the convents of Saint-Denis de la Charte and Saint-Martin-des-Champs. We can also include a certain number of royal establishments (Galeries du Louvre, Gobelins), princely palaces, hospitals (La Trinité, the Quinze-Vingt), and certain *collèges*, although they had quite diverse juridical bases, claims, and

5. Mémoire des maçons, 1720, BN, Coll. Joly 1422, fol. 226; arrêt du Parlement, 29 May 1756, in the *Statuts en l'art de serrurerie* (Paris, 1761), BN, 8° Z Le Senne 8399; Pary, *Guide des corps des marchands et des communautés des arts et métiers* (Paris, 1766), p. 350, BN, 8° Z Le Senne 4485; "Statut des charpentiers," (1763), AN, AD, XI 16.

6. Of course the significance of the sanction varied with the character of the trade. A peddler who lost one or two objects could reestablish himself much more quickly than a watchmaker who lost his workshop or an unlicensed baker whose oven was demolished.

7. *Nouveau recueil des statuts et règlements du corps et communauté des maîtres et marchands tapissiers* (Paris, 1756), p. 191, AN, AD XI 27; "Recueil des statuts des fondeurs-mouleurs," statutes of 1694, art. 16, in *Statuts et règlements de la communauté des maîtres imprimeurs en taille douce*, pp. 82–97; Paul Lacroix et al., *Histoire des cordonniers* (Paris: Séré, 1851), p. 461. Cf. AN, Y 9465A, 29 April 1763.

The faubourg Saint-Antoine. Courtesy of the Bibliothèque Nationale.

practices.[8] But the most powerful of the privileged spaces by far was the faubourg Saint-Antoine: its importance derived from the extent of its territory and from the relatively effective barrier provided by the wall that sheltered it.[9]

THE ROYAL COMMISSION OF 1716

The guilds fought against the faubourg on two fronts. On the ground, they did not hesitate to launch rapid missions into enemy territory to carry out confiscations.[10] On the politico-juridical side of the battle, they did not cease to look for ways to force the faubourg to submit. They won a significant victory in 1716 when the royal council created a commission to study "the daily increase in places claiming privileges and the abuses that result." From the outset the commission thus entirely endorsed the perspective of the guilds: even if certain exemptions could be shown to be well founded juridically, the general interest, it was asserted, should override individual privilege. For the world of work could not do without "statutes concerning the arts, production, and manufactures," and the commission should "propose to the council the means to reestablish among the workers the observation of these regulations."[11]

Before the commission the faubourg Saint-Antoine showed itself to be a special case by ferociously resisting any intrusion (most of the seigneurs and other privileged places capitulated quickly) and by pointing out that the abbess had never possessed rights of police derived from high justice, the prerogative on which most of the seigneurs based their claims to exemptions. Asked to produce her titles, the abbess claimed that all the titles had been pillaged and burned during the civil wars; in any case, she continued, those documents meant nothing because the only title of consequence was the letter of patent from February 1657 in favor of the workers who had been displaced and ruined by the foreign wars and who had taken refuge in the faubourg.[12]

The royal commission sarcastically rejected these arguments, specifying

8. Pierre Vidal and Léon Durin, *Histoire de la corporation des marchands merciers* (Paris: H. Champion, 1911), pp. 104–5; Jean-Louis Bourgeon, "Colbert et les corporations," in Roland Mousnier, ed., *Un nouveau Colbert* (Paris: SEDES/CDU, 1985), pp. 242–44. On the support that the seigneurs of such privileged places gave to their client-workers, see "La requête du seigneur de Loursine" (1682), BN, 4° Fm 8553. On the profits that the prince de Conti took from the Temple, see Edgar Faure, *La disgrâce de Turgot* (Paris: Gallimard, 1961), p. 439.

9. The edict of August 1776 continued to distinguish the characteristics of the faubourgs and other privileged places while trying to bring them together in practice.

10. See the decree of the council of 5 August 1710, annulling the seizure of the joiners: "Etat des dossiers concernant les privilèges," AN, F[12] 781C.

11. "Mémoire sur les privilèges et franchises exercés par les dames abbesse et religieuses de l'abbaye Saint-Antoine par rapport aux communautés des arts et métiers," AN, F[12] 781c; "Extrait général contenant l'état où se trouve l'affaire des privilèges," H 2102.

12. "Mémoire sur les privilèges."

that the abbey did not benefit from the right of high justice, indeed under-
lining that the royal act of 1657 had been only a measure of circumstance
concerning three or four hundred workers and was destined to expire with
the retirement or the death of the last beneficiary. The commission seemed
ready at any time to pronounce against the faubourg, but at the last moment
the abbess obtained a delay, thanks to her friends at court or in the ministry.
The last of these "special favors" dates, it appears, from March 1727; in the
end, the affair appears to have simply died away. [13]

What were the grounds of the guilds' accusations against the faubourg
Saint-Antoine? Their complaints echoed the standard attack on the false
workers, but they were articulated with a special virulence because the
faubourg Saint-Antoine seemed to institutionalize all the abuses and, in a
sense, to offer a genuine alternative model of work. [14] The very size of the
faubourg alarmed the critics: it was a sort of interminable frontier that could
be extended infinitely, seeming "to rise up against Paris to destroy in the end
even the city itself." Without being preoccupied with this paradox, the
guilds described a territory whose population, composed almost uniquely of
unscrupulous people, continued to grow. Its inhabitants were dangerous
because they moved around even if they did not actually change residence;
because they escaped the reassuring classifications and the obligation to
register; because they were, as those who brocaded cloth of gold and silver
put it, "unknowns." Their "prodigious number" struck the glassmakers.
There were more workers without license in their trades in the faubourg,
claimed the makers of gloves, perfume, and stockings, than there were
masters in their communities.

The false workers of the faubourg, according to the tanners, "take bread
from our hands," because they produced for lower costs and then sold for
less. While ruining their masters, who were "reduced to begging," they
cheated the public by committing fraud in fabrication and in marketing.
According to the tapestry makers, these workers did "bad work for derisory
prices" and used "faulty materials." "Without any knowledge" of the arts
they practiced, claimed the glass makers, the false workers produced eyeglasses that irreparably damaged vision. "Wildcat" work that harmed the
stocking makers came from a variety of sources, but the effects were cumula-
tive. On the one hand, four hundred unlicensed workers worked in direct
competition with their trade; on the other hand, false locksmiths constructed tools for the illicit stocking makers and for peasants in the surrounding areas who worked "without control and without discipline." This
community perfectly understood the link between merchant capital, sometimes provided by entrepreneurs who themselves had emerged from the

13. The delays accorded the parties one or two months to produce their titles or face
the loss of the rights they claimed. See, for example, the decrees of the council of 9 August
1717, 28 July 1725, and 11 March 1727, AN, AD XI 10.

14. The following discussion is based on memoranda of various guilds which may be
found in AN, F^{12} 781D and 781E. On the preoccupation of the corporations with the
privileges of the faubourg, see AN F*^{12}207, fol. 130.

world of illicit work, and the proliferation of false workers, who could not themselves, at least in the beginning, purchase looms, tools, or primary materials.

There was another paradox as well. The faubourg attracted a few of the best craftsmen of Paris as well as incompetent workers and troublemakers. The very existence of the faubourg dislocated the corporate systems of control over the labor market. Several masters complained of the lack of workers, who were irresistibly drawn off by the faubourg. Taking journeymen and apprentices themselves, the false workers devised a mode of reproduction that merely aggravated the problem.[15] These false workers, observed the locksmiths, "put themselves in a parallel situation or at the same level with the masters of the Paris trades, yet there is no difference except that the latter are weighed down with public payments and that the former find exoneration on the false pretext that they are tributaries of the abbey."

All the corporate communities feared "the example" of the faubourg, which sapped the bases of subordination. Free to go into the faubourg, journeymen were therefore less docile. In the faubourg, workers gathered openly; some brandished weapons, the glass makers claimed. The arrogance of the people of the faubourg disconcerted the masters, just as the haughtiness of the masters had always tormented the workers. "They fear nothing," declared the embroiderers. In the eyes of the communities, "disorder" and "libertinism" appeared inevitable.

The ideal solution, for the corporations, was quite simple. They wanted to expel all of the false workers from all of the privileged places, and especially from the faubourg Saint-Antoine. Most of the complainants, however, did not entertain any illusions about this prospect: without the power to uproot them, they wished to limit their number and subject them to their authority. The locksmiths and the tanners recommended establishing a ceiling or quota on their number; the stocking makers envisioned a system of registration. Several guilds wanted to force the false workers to work exclusively for masters, an eventuality that other corporate communities did not consider very realistic. Many guilds wanted to prevent the workers of the faubourg from taking on journeymen or apprentices. Everyone wanted to exercise the right to search the faubourg, a brash symbol of guild power and its most efficient expression in this context. To begin searches without warning and without restriction, to examine in order to verify the quality of work and the qualifications of the worker—this would be equivalent to the reconquest of the faubourg by the city, to its quasi-incorporation, to abolition of its extraterritoriality.

The faubourg Saint-Antoine vigorously rejected the provisional conclusions of the commission, which it regarded as nothing more than a

---

15. The master metalworkers, challenging the guilds and the policies of the ministry, complained in 1724 that workers in the faubourg were paid between a third and half of what was paid in Paris. See Police judgment, 16 November 1724, *Recueil des statuts des maîtres chaudronniers*, p. 28, BN, 8° Z Le Senne 4281.

statement of the guilds' "hatred" and "cowardly jealousy."[16] Formally, the faubourg responded in three voices, alternately distinct and convergent: that of the "ladies, abbess, and sisters of the abbey of Saint-Antoine"; that of the "owners of houses in the faubourg"; and that of "the workers of the faubourg." The three voices reflected a careful coordination, without doubt orchestrated by the legal counsel to the abbey, whose hand may be seen in almost all of the formalized petitions. But it appears that he took the trouble to consult the people of the faubourg; there were several assemblies of workers and property owners. In the end, it was the voice of the workers that carried, for it was they who wielded the concession of exemption, the crucial distinction between the faubourg Saint-Antoine and the other so-called privileged places.

The concession dates from two moments in time, the first vague and distant, the second very precise and relatively recent. The king had long ago welcomed "poor workers" to the faubourg, permitting them to work freely there. The privilege had been granted well before the edict of 1581 which "subjected to the corporate system" all of the faubourgs, with the exception of Saint-Antoine, according to its militants.[17] Many workers were presumed to have left their faubourgs then to move to Saint-Antoine, and Henry IV, according to this interpretation, encouraged entrepreneurs to construct buildings and, to this end, solemnly guaranteed the faubourg's exemption.[18]

In 1642 one of the king's favorites, the revenue farmer Charles Moreau, in apparent complicity with the guilds in the city, obtained an edict ordering the incorporation of the artisans and merchants of the faubourg Saint-Antoine. For Moreau and for the crown this was a great financial coup; for the guilds, a nice revenge to be celebrated in the name of the "general rule" of 1581. For the people of the faubourg, it was a diabolical and threatening maneuver against them. The abbess immediately appealed, and the affair dragged on for fifteen years. According to one reading, the application of the edict was suspended during the appeal; according to another, it resulted in a "catastrophe"—the faubourg became "deserted," houses were demolished, hospitals flooded with the down-and-out. The poor were seized by panic or ruined by Moreau's enterprise. But the perseverance of the abbess won out in the end, and the letters of patent of 1657, abrogating the edict of 1642, reaffirmed the faubourg's privilege. A "happy renaissance" ensued. The faubourg again became a beehive; thousands of workers poured in, and hundreds of construction sites signaled a building boom.

16. All the memoranda and formal demands upon which the following discussion is based can be found in AN, F^{12} 781C.

17. One version cited an edict dated April 1597 which "interpreted" definitively the document of 1581 in favor of the faubourg's exemption. But this reading, like others advanced by the faubourg's defenders, was tendentious in the eyes of the commission of 1716.

18. According to Bourgeon, however, in 1637 the faubourg still had only 150 houses and 200 taxpayers—perhaps 1,000 people in all: "Colbert et les corporations," p. 245.

What was the real significance of the letters of patent of February 1657 regarding exemptions from mastership and visits by the governors of the guilds? The law evoked the unwarranted misery of workers uprooted and killed by the war: 1657 was one of the hardest years of the post-Fronde period, and ordinary people suffered terribly. Certainly humanitarian considerations in part motivated the government. As Jean-Louis Bourgeon demonstrates, however, other causes, some of them political, better explain the council's action. Poverty, as a source of disorder, preoccupied the government. Thousands of hapless people were inundating the capital. How could one contain a floating population of the unemployed, impoverished, and delinquent? A two-pronged policy of social control was instituted: on one hand, the lockup, marked by the creation of the Hôpital Général in 1656, and, on the other, an opening up, represented by the letters of patent of the following year. Officials shut away those who were thought to threaten society by idleness; but they also created a vast, unattributed arena of work for the industrious poor, who were much more numerous and who asked only to be able to work. Curiously, the workers and the inhabitants of the faubourg in a written petition at the beginning of the reign of Louis XV described the faubourg of the past as a kind of "great hospital" where the poor of the entire kingdom "were permitted to work without letters of mastership."[19]

Bourgeon thinks that for two reasons "the royal government had deliberately tried to encourage the development of an artisanal pole that would complement and compete with the Parisian center"; that is, to create a body of workers to counterbalance the guild system. First, the Parisian craftsmen had not demonstrated "a perfect monarchical loyalty" during the Fronde; hence it was no longer useful to invest the corporate structure with a monopoly on work. Second, Cardinal Jules Mazarin, the leading figure in the royal government, commanded an entourage that was composed of precocious liberals, businessmen stripped of any a priori fetishism for the guilds and convinced of a pressing need to improve the international competitiveness of the French economy. From this situation two imperatives emerged: first to diversify the types of production, then to put them into fruitful competition.[20]

Thanks to the letters of patent of 1657, the faubourg Saint-Antoine considered itself juridically invincible. The governors of the guilds believed themselves stronger than the king, to whom they denied "the power to establish places of exception," claimed the workers and the inhabitants of the faubourg. Many times during the reign of Louis XIV the trade communities tried to encroach upon the faubourg's exemption, but each time they failed. Such was the experience of the mercers, hatters, watchmakers, lock-

19. "To generous minds, the faubourg Saint-Antoine could have appeared as a gigantic charity workshop," writes Bourgeon, but "those of greater prudence attributed to it responsibility for draining an abscess toward the periphery of the the the city": ibid., p. 246.

20. Ibid., pp. 246–47. Bourgeon's article formulates stimulating hypotheses that must be tested in the archives.

364 *Steven Laurence Kaplan*

smiths, brewers, butchers, saddlemakers, and so forth.[21] In fact, they launched a war of atrophy, taking advantage of the political, psychological, and financial fragility of the union of faubourg forces. They initiated inspections of the faubourg to harass and discourage its workers. They undertook confiscations to force them to go to court. They tried to break their will.

The Ideology of the Faubourg

The accusations directed against the faubourg in 1716 echoed those of 1642; "the workers are unpoliced, unregulated, and cheat the public." Yet the abbess, the property owners, and the workers always accepted the police of Châtelet: "in this faubourg policing is done not by the ministry on behalf of the governors of the guilds but upon the complaints of individuals who find themselves cheated while buying something [and] have the right to go before the commissioners of the Châtelet." As for the charge of incompetence or fraud, that was nothing but "slander." The argument of the workers of the faubourg Saint-Antoine anticipated in a striking way the liberal theses— French and English—of 1776: the market, not the governors of the guilds, is the master and guarantor of the functioning of the economy. If the workers of the faubourg were incapable, "they would have discredited themselves long ago, lost the confidence of the public, and, for lack of sales, would have been forced to leave the faubourg and seek their fortunes elsewhere." Striking proof that their renown had been "justly acquired" was the eagerness of the masters of the trade communities themselves "to have executed by the petitioners the finest products that are ordered in their shops in Paris." The artisans of the faubourg did not have the right to sell or to deliver to the city; only the consumers could freely cross the Rubicon (or rather the Maginot Line) of the guilds. However, individuals clearly had "the freedom not to leave Paris to come to the faubourg and run the risk of being cheated." The public that so intensely preoccupied the governors "is not so poor a connoisseur as one allows oneself to be persuaded: one must listen to its voice in the affairs that concern it, and if [the public] were not more frequently defrauded by the masters of Paris than it was by the workers of the faubourg, then the latter would not have so much business." The market functioned in favor of the public, as the guild monopoly went against its interests. Without the exemptions of the faubourg, "the masters of Paris would be able to sell their merchandise at any price they wanted, because they would no longer have as competitors the skilled workers who provide products at a much better price."

Thus, according to its partisans, the faubourg Saint-Antoine was a sort of utopia, an enclave of freedom (but not of libertinage) in a universe of ob-

21. See, for example, the decrees of Parlement of 18 June 1672, 26 June 1699, and 2 September 1709; and the decree of the Council, 5 August 1710, all in the *fichier desactes*, BN. The struggle lasted over the course of the century (see, for example, the decree of Parlement, 22 February 1759, ibid.).

stacles, inquisitions, and artificial doctrines. A paradox commands attention: It was only in the privileged place par excellence that one could do without the privileges that the "ordinary," dominant places found necessary for their existence. For the people of the faubourg, however, their right not to be Parisians, not to be integrated into the general system of social classification, was indeed a prerogative conferred by privilege. But the petition of the workers shrewdly distinguished their populist, popular privileges from others that were elitist and narrow: "The privilege of the petitioners is not comparable to the privileges granted to the military or religious orders of Paris; the privilege here is not awarded to the abbey of Saint-Antoine to augment the rental revenues of the houses that it owns within its territory, it is not given in consideration of the influence that made possible its acquisition." It was a privilege accorded in a sense to the general interest, a privilege "against mendacity," a privilege extended to "all the poor workers of the Kingdom [permitting them] to exercise their arts and crafts freely."

Let us return to their definition of this privilege, which underlines the great gap that separated the two worlds: it was "freedom from having to acquire mastership" and especially "exemption from the inspections of the governors of the guilds." For the people of the faubourg as for all the false workers, inspection represented nothing less than "slavery." It was the exact opposite of total or uncontrolled freedom. The people of the faubourg reacted to the specter of subordination with the same horror with which the governors viewed the peril of unlimited freedom. It was subjection to injustice, to corruption, to persecution. It was not at all "zeal for the public interest" that animated the governors: "they have no desire to teach the workers of the faubourg the rules of their craft with their inspections; their only goal is to vex and torment the workers by judicial harassment, and to make things so difficult for them that they leave the faubourg and ruin themselves." The governors were liars as well as hypocrites. During each inspection they claimed to find faults in production, even among "our best workers." But it was only a pretext to "seize our tools and our merchandise," to "ruin us" and damage "our reputation." Whereas the governors were "plaintiffs and judges in their own cause," the workers of the faubourg had no possibility of even defending themselves, save in extremis by paying a cash ransom set on a case-by-case basis. In a word, "if the inspection is maintained, the faubourg will become a vast desert." Although this was not a time when statistics would have a strong political impact, the people of the faubourg counted up their moral and demographic losses. In several petitions they referred to "nearly 40,000 workers who live there with their large families and [who] would be forced to leave." Another document affirmed that the artisans of the faubourg "are at least a third as many as those of Paris." Finally, the petition of the workers and inhabitants of 27 June 1727 referred to 10,000 workers, a more realistic but still very high figure.

This marshaling of figures, like the impersonal and self-regulating mechanism of the market, demonstrates the modernity of source of the arguments put forth by the residents of the faubourg. In their brawling, the

366 *Steven Laurence Kaplan*

corporate communities and the faubourg spoke the same language, up to a point. The inhabitants of the faubourg did not contest directly the logic of corporate legitimacy; they merely justified their own exceptional situation. But they quickly moved beyond the traditional discourse. They wanted to shift the discussion from social structure to political economy, from norms and general rules to an emphasis on utility and efficiency, from a passive to an active stance. Their description of the quarter as a new frontier, a kind of economic El Dorado, bespeaks neither self-mystification nor pure propaganda. This was indeed a zone in full expansion, a quite diversified economy, one that entailed much more complicated relationships with the economy and the well-being of the city than the governors cared to admit, at least publicly.[22] The ultimate refutation of the guilds' accusations was the faubourg's dynamism.

The "Sovereign Faubourg" of the Eighteenth Century

The commission of 1716 did not succeed in suppressing or modifying the statutes of the faubourg Saint-Antoine. The commission simply disappeared, probably about 1730. But neither did the faubourg obtain the overwhelming confirmation it desired, although no one could deny its victory. Saint-Antoine was already the "sovereign faubourg," as Balzac would latter call it. Strengthened by its privilege, it continued to welcome workers of all kinds, "false" in the eyes of the guilds, which did not abandon the war but which no longer mounted a great concerted campaign as they had done at the beginning of the century.

We do not have the evidence necessary to assess the development of the district across the century. There was a great deal of building, but then the faubourg was vast. More and more urbanized, it still remained fairly rural, almost like a village in some ways; its population density was low in comparison with the city's. Hundreds of trades were practiced there—351 of them were counted in Quinze-Vingt, the largest of the three revolutionary sections that composed it—but several sectors dominated production. In industry, these were wallpaper, glass, and porcelain and pottery. In some of these enterprises, labor was quite concentrated, but even in "industry" the organization of production inside the workshop remained very artisanal, and an extensive putting-out system often operated in orbit around a major shop. Furniture making dominated the artisanal sector proper, followed by building, metals, clothing, and food production. Here the models of organization varied enormously, ranging from near factories to the solitary shops of the *chambrelans*, as well as such great putting-out operations as those organized in 1790–1791 by the widow Héricourt, who provided work at home for eighty-five residents of the faubourg, including a good many masters of the city who had migrated to Saint-Antoine and who in turn provided work for others.

22. On the physical and juridical growth of the faubourg, see Nicolas Delamare, *Traité de la police*, vol. 1 (Paris: J. et P. Cot, 1713), p. 81.

We find once more in the faubourg practically all the kinds of workers present in the city. Among these "fugitives" were an enormous number of journeymen who had fled the city for various reasons. They sought in the faubourg first of all asylum, then employment. They often found both in the inns that specialized according to trades (much more rarely according to trade and region of origin). The joiners went to Berry, rue de Montreuil, the shoemakers to Pelletier, Grande rue du Faubourg; the bakers to Ordonneau, rue de Reuilly, or to Bonnet, rue de Charonne.[23] Sometimes the homes of real workers' associations (called "clubs" or "exchanges" or "confraternities" or, more rarely, *compagnonnages*), these inns served as offices of information and placement, centers of sociability and mutual aid, and sources of credit.

Some of the fugitives established themselves in the faubourg permanently, either as independents or as wage workers. Others came and went, according to their whims, needs, or circumstances, working sometimes in the city, sometimes in the faubourg. If they were among the many who had not secured written permission to leave their last job (a requirement if one wished to be hired legally), their return to the city had to be secret. But they always could find masters who would take them on. For these very mobile and peripatetic workers, the faubourg was a life raft, a viable and reassuring alternative. When things got hot in the city in 1749 because of a workers' cabal—a sort of strike conspiracy—several journeymen joiners found shelter in the faubourg, working there by the day for about a month.[24] François Albert, journeyman locksmith, found refuge there for several weeks after quarreling with his master.

The great majority of workers who set up on their own remained resolutely *faubouriens* by status and by residence. A few ended up presenting themselves for a mastership: the abbess proudly attested in 1716 to their capacity. Several of the masters eventually returned to the city, but most seem to have held firm to the faubourg. *Chambrelans* proliferated in the quarter. Take the cases of Jacques Demaneon, shoemaker, rue Sainte-Marguerite; Louis Debret, stocking maker, Grande rue; clothmakers such as Dalbin, Bouttemer, and Cournet; and the shoemakers Andrieux and Caron, who worked directly as subcontractors for the city masters.[25] There were also many small employers: the shoemaker Denizart, the cabinetmaker Nocard, the nailmaker Dupon, and the metalworker Gauthier all employed one or two journeymen.[26] Often the distribution of work depended upon certain types of intermediaries, small employers themselves, according to a

23. AN, Y 15365, 12 October 1750; Y 12575, 4 July 1730; Y 10995, 24 May 1753; Y 10993A, 11 May 1750. Such inns also existed in the city (Tourtault and Etard for the bakers, Rousseau for the ropemakers), but they were generally more closely watched by the police, and they were located within the territory of the guilds: Y 15373, 4 March 1770 and 7 May 1775.

24. AN, Y 95233B, 22 November 1749; Y 11004, 6 April 1763; Y 12575, 30 May 1730; Y 15177, 24 June 1783.

25. AN, Y 15363, 16 October 1757; Y 14084, 19 April 1762; Y 9525, 16 April 1766; Y 10995, 11 October 1754; Y 10997, 26 January 1756.

26. AN, Y 14088, 3 February 1761; Y 10994, 27 March, 10 June, and 17 July 1752.

kind of model then found in Lyon. This was the case of a number of joiners of the faubourg who worked for the widow Héricourt and for Henry Mignet, master producer of silk ribbons on the Grande rue, who was a subcontractor himself but who also served as an agent for raw materials for the city. [27] The situation of Etienne Brocher, who produced fine cloth, was somewhat different. He was a work contractor as well as a producer himself, and he was an entrepreneur; among other things, he rented out looms and space in his shop to men who worked for masters in the city.[28] Sometimes the entrepreneur distributed work directly. The enterprises sold directly or were part of a network of subcontractors that was organized in the city by the true capitalists of the trade communities, such as the drapers, stocking makers, and mercers.

The links between the economies of the city and the faubourg often were very discreet yet very extensive. Baking offers a telling example. In 1733, 247 bakers of the faubourg, a third of those who provisioned the twelve bread markets of the capital twice a week, provided 31.4 percent of the bread sold there. A great number of these faubouriens also owned a shop, their number complemented by about a hundred others who baked exclusively for bakeries. Combining production for the market and for the shops, they accounted for 27.4 percent of all the bread officially sold in Paris. In other words, the 500 to 600 masters of the city supplied less than half of the capital's total consumption. Without the faubourg, Paris could not be assured of its daily ration of bread. Given their decisive contribution to the maintenance of public tranquility, these bakers were not considered to be just ordinary false workers. The police obliged the guild to recognize them formally; but at the same time, they had to submit to the inspection of the governors.[29]

The faubourg crystallized certain intracorporative and intercorporative tensions while resolving others. Among the stocking makers, for example, a certain number of "merchants" (masters of one of the so-called six corps) broke their own rules by establishing branches, by subcontracting work, or by practicing in the faubourg and in other privileged places the *Verlag* system, in which the master exercised control over both the acquisition of raw materials and the sales of the final product. On several occasions the corps tried in vain to break their contracts.[30] The ambiguity of the attitude and behavior of many of the members of certain trade communities threatened corporate solidarity with regard to the faubourg—and underlined the im-

27. Raymonde Monnier, *Le faubourg Saint-Antione (1789–1817)*, Bibliothèque d'Histoire Revolutionnaire, 3d ser., no. 121 (Paris: Société des Etudes Robespierristes, 1981) p. 76; AN, Y 14435, 6 February 1787.

28. AN Y 14109, 12 January 1780.

29. See Steven L. Kaplan, *The Bakers of Paris and the Bread Question during the Eighteenth Century*, forthcoming.

30. Ordinance of the regulations of the corporation of hosiery makers, 17 August 1726, BN, Coll. Joly 1732, fols. 183–85. The situation of the hosiers was complicated because the community of master manufacturers of stockings, joined to their own, was largely implanted in the faubourg.

mense complexity of the relationship between the city and faubourg and between ideological-juridical principles and economic practice. In the faubourg, where it is tempting to categorize work in other ways, distinctions were confused not only between master and worker but also among the different professions themselves. The climate was favorable for a war between the masters of various trade communities and between rival guild-institutions. The mercers solemnly denounced those who undertook "their commerce secretly" in the faubourg. But these same mercers, according to the producers of gold- and silver-edged cloth and the master manufacturers of stockings, also secretly employed a great number of workers who produced fine cloth and stockings. The tapestry weavers leveled similar accusations against the mercers, locksmiths, used-clothing dealers, and linen drapers.

ECONOMIC ROLES AND SOCIAL RELATIONSHIPS

The faubourg was welcoming but demanding. To work in the faubourg implied a willingness to renounce, at least provisionally, some deeply rooted ideas concerning social organization. Social relationships did not precede economic ones, as in the guild vision of the world. Much more clearly and frequently than in the city, the economic relationship took primacy. In the faubourg not all people were equal—far from it. But neither was anyone disqualified by lack of a title. There certainly was not total confusion of all ranks, as the governors of the guilds claimed, but one found a mutual tolerance that was necessarily very widely extended, a great flexibility in contacts and exchanges, and fewer barriers to entry than elsewhere.

Struggling to control job placement and to maintain their priority of employment, the journeymen of the city were very corporatist. They tried to stave off competition from the provinces when their own could not find work. But in the faubourg one rubbed up against all kinds of people; no one had to have a license or go through an office to get a job. Bertin, a metalworker, preferred to hire Louis Page, "laborer," rather than a journeymen newly arrived from the city: it was his strictest right to hire whom he pleased, and no one contested it.[31] The cabinetmaker Rigole hired Spiers, known as "the German," a journeymen whom he must have met in the city; but Spiers was obliged to work alongside two young men whom Rigole had trained on the spot.[32]

There were true masters in the faubourg as well; joiners or clothmakers, for example, who had entered the guild. They could play two games: on one hand, fulfilling the most obvious guild obligations, and on the other, making mutual concessions with the faubourg so as to profit from its advan-

31. AN, Y 14435, 31 October 1787.
32. AN, Y 14109, 17 October 1780.

370 *Steven Laurence Kaplan*

tages. Master Chontard, of the guild of cloth manufacturers, had an entire network of subcontractors working outside of his shop (a practice that in no way distinguished him from his colleagues in the city).[33] Denis Devau, master joiner, received the governor of his guild without opposition and paid the fees for inspection, but he hid two journeymen who did not have papers and protected one of his workers who also worked on his own.[34] In the faubourg, however, a journeyman (licensed or not) was often at the same time employee of and competitor with his employer (master or not). Henri Gobert, apprentice carton maker, worked for Pouperon, master on the rue de la Roquette, but also competed with him as a commercial rival.[35] Gerard David, journeyman joiner of the faubourg, fulfilled a contract as a subcontractor for Laisné, a master of the city. But he also worked for other masters, and on his own as well.

Mastership was denigrated and the guilds were detested in the faubourg, but the "noble" work of the city nonetheless retained its reference value. Etienne Brochet, manufacturer of fancy cloth, rue de Montreuil, had nothing to do with the guild, but he did not remain at all indifferent when a competitor, a master from the city, belittled his reputation "before the governors."[36] Certain denizens of the faubourg manifestly suffered from not having a license. To appropriate the title of master in the faubourg was to strain credibility, but dozens of individuals, undertaking all sorts of commerce, baptized themselves as "merchants" without any kind of official justification. Often—but not always—this was the case with second- or third-generation residents of the faubourg, workers who were particularly opulent.[37]

CORPORATE PRACTICES

Empowered by statutes and regulations approved by the Parlement, which authorized or enjoined them to pursue the false workers to the very heart of the privileged places, the guilds did not leave the faubourg in peace. Several of the guilds were particularly active in the hunt for unlicensed workers in the faubourg. The first tactic, and the one with the strongest judicial basis, was the frontier patrol. Strong-minded governors would have liked to erect a sort of iron curtain between the city and the faubourg to prevent the infiltration of merchandise into the capital, as well as the escape of workers from the city to the faubourg. But even in the shadow of the Bastille, the frontier remained completely permeable. On the city side governors or their

33. AN, Y 9525, 26 June 1766.
34. AN, Y 10995, 21 May 1753.
35. AN, Y 10997, 9 May 1756.
36. AN, Y 14109, 12 January 1780.
37. The merchant-baker found himself part of a community in the faubourg. See Kaplan, *Bakers of Paris*. For the case of a merchant-metalworker, see AN, Y 14435, 10 October 1787.

spies watched for the arrival of smuggled goods. "With the goal of surprising the false workers," the governors of the joiners kept the hours of night watchmen (patrolling, for example, from midnight until three o'clock in the morning) and maintained a network of informants among the soldiers of the guard. On 2 July 1759, accompanied by a bailiff and a clerk, two of the joiners' governors watched the Porte Saint-Antoine "to verify various information" and "to observe different wagons and loads of the products of cabinetmakers and joiners that the false workers bring every day into this city, in order to proceed with the confiscation of the said works that are found to be defective, badly made, or not marked with the symbol of a master or of the office."[38] But in practice surveillance proved very difficult and the workers of the faubourgs were clever enough to get around these interdiction tactics.

Several trade communities dared to penetrate the faubourg to carry out inspections of shops, as they did in the city. These guilds took their chances, depending on the lever of intimidation and hoping to create a precedent that the privilege of the faubourg would be obliged to accommodate. The bakers arrived armed with the support of the authorities on behalf of the general interest. The governors had the right to inspect the shops and stocks of the faubourg to examine the quality and weight of the bread. All the journeymen, even those who worked in the privileged places, were required to register in the guild office, and the masters did not have the right to hire workers if they were not registered and could not produce a certificate of leave given by their last master. The governors raided—even at night—the shops and the inns of the faubourg. At the bakery of Ponelle on the Grande rue, for example, they discovered one journeyman with papers and another without them. Ponelle explained that he had not required papers of the latter man because he did not expect to keep him very long. The governors were content to leave after giving a warning; they could have arrested the journeyman on the spot or cited both him and his employer before the police court.[39] Surprisingly, sometimes they uncovered no violations: on 22 September 1772 all of the dozens of journeymen dispersed in twenty-six shops and five inns in the faubourg were found to have the proper papers.[40]

The presence of a certain number of master joiners in the faubourg provided a pretext for governors of the guilds to enter. They frequently did so, but sometimes the reasons were not very clear. For example, they inspected the shop of a master metalworker, Jean-Joseph de Saint-Germain, who exercised the trade of an unlicensed joiner on the rue de Charenton. Instead of telling them that he did what he wanted in the faubourg, Saint-Germain, who was rather upset, confessed that he had come to the assistance of his aged father, himself a false-worker joiner, who had been established for

38. AN, Y 15365, 19 April 1755, 13 September 1756, and 9 July 1759.
39. AN, Y 15378, 10 September 1769.
40. AN, Y 15375, 22 September 1772.

many years on the Grande rue, where he employed three journeymen in a shop with his own name on the sign. The governors "did not intend to prevent the elder St-Germain from taking advantage as an unlicensed worker of the claimed privilege attributed to the said faubourg," but they nevertheless wanted to demonstrate that he could not escape the control of the guilds. Treating him as if he were a master, the governors denounced him for having disobeyed the regulations by opening a second shop, the one operated by his son, and confiscated the son's tools and merchandise.[41] Not all of the interventions by the governors were so complicated. Searching for "defective" furniture, they inspected the shops of the tapestry makers of the faubourg, who often resold the products of the joiners.[42]

The obligation to protect the public remained the strongest argument in favor of such incursions into the faubourg until the Revolution. Citing alleged complaints of cheated consumers in 1783, the leaders of the unified guild of joiners, cabinetmakers, wood turners, and layette makers searched the privileged places, notably the faubourg.[43] The governors of the coppersmiths refused to recognize "the claimed privilege" of the "false metalworkers living in the faubourg." The pretext of their inspections was always "defective" work, but their goal was to chase away their rivals. Like their colleagues the coppersmiths, the governors of the cloth merchants and manufacturers did not admit that one could work outside of the trade community. Louis Segretain, a merchant and manufacturer, rue de Charonne, "has no license," affirmed one governor. But the governors were too clever to base their seizure on this supposition. They arranged, as always when they turned up to observe the workers of the faubourgs, to find "a piece of cloth that was not wide enough."[44] The governors of the light cloth and ribbon makers directly challenged "the right" of the *chambrelans* to do "border work."[45]

Like the false workers in the city, the denizens of the faubourgs opposed the actions of the governors. The first line of defense was juridical and ideological, even political. The workers whose output had been seized claimed the right to work freely in the faubourg, a right of which they were proud. Pierre Lemaigre complained to a police commissioner that governors of the joiners had attacked him "in order to confiscate a desk he had built." His shop was "situated within the territory of the privilege enjoyed by the faubourg Saint-Antoine, a place where the said governors certainly cannot interfere with workers who have the right to work without a license."[46] Another "false joiner worker" of the Grande rue contested not only the

41. AN, Y 15365, 5 May 1750.
42. AN, Y 15365, 27 August 1755.
43. AN, Y 9486B, 30 July 1783. The debate concerning corporate intervention in privileged places remained heated until the Revolution. See, for example, "Mémoire sur les communautés d'arts et métiers," BN, Coll. Joly 1729, fol. 136.
44. AN, Y 9525, April and 26 June 1766.
45. AN, Y 15364, 15 February 1751.
46. AN, Y 10995, 15 September 1753.

confiscation of his output but the very idea of inspection: "The said governors have absolutely no right to inspect anything I do, given that it is by
virtue of not having a license that I can engage in commerce becaues of the
privilege of the faubourg Saint-Antoine." This privilege, he added, as if to
show that he was not without powerful patrons, was "attributed in title to
the abbess of the said faubourg."[47] Sieur Tambrun, *chambrelan* light cloth and
ribbon maker, insisted on his right to "work without being bothered,"
thanks "to the privilege."[48] Michel Daudin, silkworker, rue Saint-Bernard,
recognized that the privilege in his trade had precise limits, but until that
threshold was reached, the governors were not entitled to intervene: "One
had the right to work in the faubourg Saint-Antoine provided that one used
no more than two looms [that could produce light cloth]."[49] We do not know
how many workers had the courage to go so far as Antoine Des Vignes,
combmaker, rue Saint-Sebastien, victim of a confiscation carried out by the
tabletiers (who made fancy boxes, including snuffboxes, and gameboards).
Refusing to seek "an arrangement," he filed suit against the guild, asking
that the confiscation be declared "null, wrong, and damaging." He won, but
instead of receiving the thousand pounds in damages and interest that he
demanded, he got only thirty pounds in addition to reimbursement for what
had been confiscated.[50]

Interrogated by the governors of the saddlemakers, Francois Coeuillet
demonstrated the audacity of a *faubourien*, along with the aplomb of a
merchant-mercer. He knew his rights. He cited the law and his discourse
was precise and manifestly well prepared: "He responded that being domi-
ciled within the limits of the faubourg Saint-Antoine, he had the right to
exercise all sorts of professions in consequence of the letters of patent that
His Majesty accorded in favor of the arts and trades of the aforementioned
faubourg to the abbesses and sisters of Saint-Antoine" in the month of
February 1657, registered by the Parlement in the following month. The case
of Coeuillet is interesting for material as well as ideological reasons. He
would have had a great deal of difficulty starting a business like his in the
city. In two enormous workshops and a large warehouse located behind a
fashionable shop this mercer employed all sorts of workers, painters, saddlemakers, harness makers, and others. The governors discovered an astonishing range of horse-drawn chaises, one-seated Berliners, luxurious carriages, and public vehicles, among a vast quantity of related merchandise.
Coeuillet broke all of the rules of the corporate game—the division of labor,
the respect of limits, the distinction between the right to produce and that to
sell. He anticipated the objections of the governors: "He had the right himself to combine and practice all of the professions of the said faubourg." He
not only had "the right to buy and sell all kinds of merchandise" but also
could produce and repair anything "as a worker of the faubourg Saint-

47. AN, Y 15365, 22 September 1755.
48. AN, Y 15364, 15 February 1751.
49. AN, Y 9525, 17 April 1766.
50. AN, Y 9465A, 3 June 1763.

Antoine," a precious and all-purpose title. We do not know if it was the sheer scope of his claims or of his commerce that most astonished the governors. Even in the faubourg, they insisted, "there really are limits." It seemed to them inconceivable that the status of *faubourien* could so profoundly transform the status of a mercer.[51] If Coeuillet was not a mercer like the others, one must add that a number of his colleagues established in the city circumvented the ban on production precisely by having their work done in the faubourg Saint-Antoine.

Violence offered another means of resistance. Riots broke out quickly in the faubourg. Each time that the governors and the residents of the faubourg clashed, a crowd gathered. The citizens of the faubourg did not hesitate to cross the frontier to join the Parisians in answering the call of a false worker who had been trapped by the wood turners' governors, who incurred several light wounds.[52] In 1721 the commissioner Labbé discovered "a great number of these people gathered in front of the shop" of a joiner, "heated up" against the governors.[53] The governors of the stocking makers provoked "a considerable riot" in 1746 when they confiscated three looms from a stocking worker. The crowd clashed with a troop of guards escorting the governors, hoping to prevent their departure. There were shouts of "thief" and "rabble" against the governors and rocks were thrown at their escort. Toward the beginning of the reign of Louis XV, the producers of frame-made stockings complained bitterly that the people of the faubourgs refused to obey the edicts of the king or submit docilely to "the inspections that the governors should make of their places, for which they are supposed to pay them three sous each week per loom." According to the governors, "these mutinous workers rebelled in the faubourg Saint-Antoine and brought about a gathering of more than four thousand people, who beat the officials of justice with sticks, rocks, and with pieces of glass, leaving several of them dead."[54]

DEBATES AT THE END OF THE ANCIEN RÉGIME

The guilds were not the only foyer of hostility to the privileged places. Even the reformers of the early 1770s, strongly critical of the tyranny and corruption of the guilds, anticipated the end of a system that seemed strongly suspect. One projected law attacked "the false idea that the very place to which they [workers without licenses] go provides a safeguard for their maneuvers, as if they could find in our kingdom any refuge where such bad faith has nothing to fear from our justice." Another measure envisioned a return to the goal of the commission of 1716, enjoining "all those who claim to have the right to produce, sell, and retail merchandise in any place or

51. AN, Y 11085, 24 October 1769.

52. AN, Y 15364, 16 June 1652; Y 12576A, 10 May 1733.

53. AN, Y 12567, 4 October 1721.

54. "Remontrances au conseil pour la communauté des maîtres fabricants de bas au métier," AN, F[12] 781c.

enclosure in our good city of Paris without subjecting workers and merchants to any examination of their honesty and ability, or without subjecting their works and merchandise to any inspection to determine their quality," to present their titles to the ministry within three months of the publication of the measure.[55]

Anne-Robert Jacques Turgot, the controller general and an experienced field administrator closely linked to the physiocrats, solved the problem of the privileged places in one blow by suppressing all corporate organizations, but his solution proved to be fragile. Reestablishing the guilds six months later, the edict of August 1776, an authentic measure of reform, nonetheless was inspired by a narrow vision of coherence through uniformity. The war against the privileged places began again, after a last offer of amnesty and of integration. Either one could pay an annual fee to the government to exercise a profession anywhere in Paris, while submitting entirely to the control of the guilds, or one could find oneself banned from practicing it anywhere in the city or in the faubourgs, including the privileged places.[56] The *faubouriens* reacted with anger: they refused to be treated like ordinary Parisians. While the police sent reinforcements to the Saint-Antoine, the government made a new proposition, one that was hardly more attractive: total assimilation into the structure of the guilds at a reduced price or registration with the office of police in exchange for an annual payment.[57] To force submission, the government threatened to take control of the frontier in order to prevent the sale of the products of the faubourg in the capital. But the government very quickly renounced any attempt to put this measure into effect. It would have required an immense effort, and it did not appear that many of the *faubouriens* would yield to the temptation to exchange liberty for legitimacy.[58]

On the eve of the French Revolution, the guilds renewed their campaign against the privileged places for the last time. The political climate seemed favorable. While defending their own privileges, henceforth represented differently (as rights, properties, police, public control, etc.), the guilds now attacked the "exorbitant" (soon to be denounced as "usurped" and "gothic") privileges of the seigneurs, the protectors of enclaves of unlicensed work. In the "grievance lists" drafted for the Estates General that would inaugurate the French Revolution, the guilds of fashion merchants, florists, starchmakers, wigmakers, and grocers demanded the suppression of all privileged places. As their contribution, the master metalworkers, gilders, and engravers explained the necessity of ending the "local privileges that serve as a place of retreat for the false workers." The traffic of these latter, "so contrary to the exclusive rights of the guilds, harms their commerce, by the diminu-

55. BN, Coll. Joly 1729, fols. 174 and 177.
56. August 1776, Bibliothèque historique de la ville de Paris, fichier législatif.
57. Journal de Hardy, BN, ms. fr. 6682, pp. 301–2 (3 December 1776); declaration of the king, 19 December 1776, AN, AD XI 11.
58. Raymond Monnier believes that numerous *faubouriens* became masters beginning in the fall of 1776: *Faubourg Saint-Antoine*, pp. 69–70.

tion of their production and by the comparison that the unknowing public makes between the price of the defective products that it buys and that which the good worker asks for work of skill and quality."[59]

It was not only the guilds that were interested in the fate of the privileged places. The municipality and the National Assembly were preoccupied with them, for reasons having to do with problems of general policing. In October 1789 the commune of Paris complained that it "found itself hampered in its searches by the respect owed until this moment the so-called privileged places that proliferate in the capital." "The privileged places are society's scandal," proclaimed the deputy Lanjuinais with fervor. His colleague Emmery added, "All places are privileged, or none should be." To ensure the right of discretionary intervention to the authorities, the Assembly declared that henceforth "in all cases where the well-being of the state is compromised, there will be no privileged places."

In fact, three texts, all written at the same time, nicely summarize the debate about the faubourg Saint-Antoine. First, Adam Smith attacked the misdeeds and claims of the guild monopoly, and in particular the idea that there was no good work outside of the community: "The pretense that corporations are necessary for the better government of the trade, is without any foundation. If you would have your work tolerably executed, it must be done in the suburbs, where workers, having no exclusive privilege, have nothing but their character to depend upon, and you must then smuggle it into the city as well as you can."[60]

Turgot took up the same theme in the edict of February 1776, which suppressed the guilds. He vigorously rejected the notion that work outside the guilds was necessarily badly done, dishonest, and dangerous: "In no way does freedom produce bad results in the places where it has been established for a long time. The workers of the faubourgs and other privileged places do not work any less well than those inside Paris."[61]

The last text is part of a series of reports gathered for the defense of the guild system against Turgot's assault. For the masters, freedom would inaugurate the reign of "usury and cheating," of "indifference and negligence," of "anarchy." Without the regulations, the requirements of quality, and the esprit de corps of the guilds, the market would be inundated with fraudulent goods and services, and the social and political order would be undermined by a permanent cabal of workers. Turgot's edict would mean that

59. Charles-Louis Chassin, *Les élections et les cahiers de Paris en 1789* (Paris: Jouast et Sigaux, 1888), vol. 2, pp. 513, 521, 525, 529–32; "Mémoire pour les marchands amidonniers" and "Cahier des voeux et doléances de la communauté des marchandes de modes–plumassières–fleuristes," AN, B III, pp. 602, 624. These works also supply the quotations in the following paragraph.

60. Adam Smith, *An Inquiry into the Nature and Course of the Wealth of Nations*, ed. Edwin Canaan (Chicago: University of Chicago Press, 1976), pp. 144–45. It is interesting to note that this text is quoted in a "petition du corps de l'orfävrerie" to the National Assembly in September 1790 ("'In London,' says Monsieur Smith, 'it is in the faubourgs, exempted from the privileges of the guilds, that one finds the best workers'"): AN, T 1490².

61. Decree of February 1776, BN, Coll. Joly 462, fol. 258.

cooks with neither experience nor conscience would prepare "pernicious stews," symbolically tantamount to the rehabilitation and the victory of the false workers.[62] To put it another way, as the master buttonmakers feared, "all Paris would become the faubourg Saint-Antoine," emblem of all that would signify the end of the guilds.[63]

The Impact of the Faubourg on the World of Work

The revolutionary faubourg did not revolutionize the world of work, but it did jolt it, first of all in psychological terms. For the workers, the faubourg was in the beginning a hope: a new, pioneer quarter that was gently iconoclastic. But it was also a quarter like the others, heterogeneous, full of contradictions. It was the city that elicited its consciousness of being a faubourg, a truly special place, by stigmatizing and besieging the quarter, and by erecting it into an institution. In this sense, the quarter was more an invention of its adversaries than the construction of its own inhabitants. From a charitable project and a speculative venture the faubourg imperceptibly evolved into a political bone of contention, an ideological antithesis, an accidental model of social engineering. It became almost despite itself a subversive space; and almost despite themselves the *faubouriens* internalized a reputation as rebels while projecting a misleading image of unity.

Neither Dantean chaos nor dream world of liberty, the faubourg served as a laboratory for the more or less original experiences of the organization of production. There were two economic results: first, foyers of autonomous innovation developed inside the faubourg; second, an entire network of relations was established with the masters of the city, the indirect repercussions of which were as significant as their immediate results. In the faubourg, one improvised new forms, anticipating the practices of the "Manufactures of Paris" of the time of Jacques-Etienne Bédé.[64] The wholesale merchants themselves had masters and other workers brought in from the outside to work for them, while they developed their own workshops. They combined subcontracting and putting-out manufacture on astonishingly varied scales. They brought together in the same shop workers of many professions. These workshops could hold up to thirty or forty workers, although usually there were fewer than a dozen, often less than half that. In the faubourg there was a dual tendency, at once complementary and contradictory, toward dispersion and toward concentration. Together they bespoke

62. Steven L. Kaplan, "Social Classification and Representation of the Corporate World of Eighteenth-Century France: Turgot's 'Carnival,'" in Steven L. Kaplan and Cynthia J. Koepp, eds., *Work in France: Representations, Meaning, Organization, and Practice* (Ithaca: Cornell University Press, 1986), pp. 190–91.

63. Community of master buttonmakers, "Observations sur le projet de supprimer les maîtrises," BN, Coll. Joly 462, fol. 111.

64. Rémi Gossez, ed., *Un ouvrier en 1820, manuscrit inédit de Jacques-Etienne Bédé* (Paris: Centre de Recherche d'Etude et d'Edition de Correspondances du XIXᵉ Siècle de l'Université de Paris–Sorbonne [Paris IV], Presses Universitaires de France, 1984), pp. 38–42.

the paramount need for of flexibility and adaptation. When necessary, small workshops could join together or link up with larger enterprises, or they could contract to just a single master working in one room. In doing so, they would pay less for rent and avoid the cost of obtaining a mastership. It was, in any case, easier to set up as an independent worker. Furthermore, the distance between worker and entrepreneur was less daunting than that between master and journeyman. Concentration was not necessarily manifest physically, as in the case of the Réveillon manufacturing enterprise, a veritable factory. One master could mobilize twenty *chambrelans*, working alone or with others. Dispersed production could lead to centralized commercialization, through ephemeral consortia or by an entrepreneurial wholesale merchant. On the one hand, such commercialization aspired to regional, national, and even international markets.[65] On the other hand, even while continuing to smuggle merchandise into the city, merchants invited Parisians to make purchases in a primitive version of the department store that brought together the products of various trades.[66]

Largely sheltered from the constraints of the guilds, therefore, hundreds of masters and merchants, entrepreneurs and workers attempted to organize their production and their distribution more rationally, to divide work efficiently, to master the seasonal and cyclical rhythms, to realize various savings in labor and money. Utilizing the space of production and commercialization better than their competitors, the *faubouriens* understood just as well how to use time to their advantage. The masters of the city were jealous of the ability of the faubourg to react quickly to changes in fashion, the caprices of which did not irritate moralists any more than they tormented manufacturers and entrepreneurs. The "freshness" of the merchandise produced by the unlicensed workers embarrassed the urban masters and incited some of them to seek contacts with this illicit production. At the risk of reinforcing the opposition, they were tempted to see in the faubourg the progressive putting into place, even in the seventeenth century, of a protoindustrial organization of work, one that competed with the preindustrial or medieval organization of work, which was lodged in guilds.

But the city could not remain indifferent to this evolution. The competition of the unlicensed workers caused the masters to consider more closely the advantages (and also the disadvantages) of the world of the guilds. In principle, the corporation ensured a privileged if not an exclusive access to raw materials, information, and certain markets. It protected masters against competition that was considered unfair or judged excessive, and against dishonesty. It maintained a certain order, a protocol, and limits. Guarantor of the reputation of a trade, the guild facilitated the sale of mer-

65. See Louis Bergeron, "Paris dans l'organisation des échanges intérieurs français à la fin du XVIIIe siècle," in Pierre Léon, ed., *Aires et structures du commerce français au XVIIIe siècle* (Lyon: Centre d'Histoire Economique et Sociale de la Région Lyonnaise, 1975), pp. 345–46.
66. "Représentations pour le corps de l'orfèvrerie" (c. 1780), AN, T 1490⁴; délibérations, 6 November 1786, KK 1354, fol. 28.

chandise and services: champion of esprit de corps, it functioned like a
family or a firm, considerably reducing the costs of internal and external
transactions.[67] Very often quite specific, these advantages varied from guild
to guild and within a single guild from master to master.[68] As a general rule,
in the domain of economic activity the community engendered and
nourished a sort of collective rent or annuity of advantage. The clash with
the unlicensed workers, in the context of a secular rise in demand, undermined some of these economic benefits. As the faubourg provoked a segmentation of the labor market, it also caused a kind of partitioning in the
way a good number of masters viewed their adherence to the guild: they
remained rigorously masters on the political and social plane, but they gave
themselves considerable latitude on the economic side.

Confronted by the competition of unlicensed workers, concentrated in
the faubourg but also linked to productive ateliers in the city, some masters
refused to be content with the perpetual counteroffensive of their corporation. They turned to unlicensed workers, in Paris and in the faubourg. They
subcontracted production, used the putting-out system, and proposed solu-
tions for the commercialization of production independent of the faubourg.
They rented buildings, lent or leased out tools, including looms, and advanced or sold raw materials. Hundreds of entrepreneurial masters, big and
small, transgressed the guild regulations, all the while remaining deeply
imbued with corporate values. They began to profit from the segmentation
of the labor market. Along with licensed labor, regularly employed, they
began to hire flexible, casual workers, who experienced the alternating se-
quences of employment-unemployment linked to the seasonal character of
work and, more generally, its cycles. In some trades the masters became
aware that they could exercise more control over work done outside their
shops than over work done in them, and thus avoid clashes with their own
mutinous journeymen. Thanks to a good dose of the freedom of the faubourg, they succeeded in modernizing their networks; several of them could
even envision a vertical integration. It could be that it was in the faubourg
that certain new techniques of production were tried. In this sense the
faubourg rendered the corporate structures more supple while at the same
time subverting them. If the corporative system was economically less rigid
toward the end of the ancien régime, its greater flexibility was due, to a great
extent, to the links the masters established with the false workers of the
faubourg and of the city.

One also encountered more flexibility and more improvisation in the
relations between masters and workers in the faubourg. Not that a golden
age of social relations flourished in this enclave. Some employers, masters in
title or not, reproduced the corporative discipline in their shops and com-

67. See Yoram Ben-Porath, "The F-Connection: Families, Friends, and Firms and the
Organization of Exchange," *Population and Development Review* 6 (1980), pp. 1–30.
68. See, for example, the role that the guild of hatters played in the acquisition and
distribution of raw materials: Michael Sonenscher, *The Hatters of Eighteenth-Century France*
(Berkeley: University of California Press, 1987).

plained bitterly about the rise of insubordination. But others profited from the absence of corporate tutelage to define more flexible relations. They came to agreement on the level and the forms of wages, on the cadence of production, and on the length of contract, all without any external mediation. The master could not automatically rely on his hierarchical authority; and the journeyman did not feel himself reduced to the status of a domestic. Despite the conjuncture, neither master nor worker depended exclusively on the other, so they could sometimes realize a true reciprocity of well-defined interests, but not of social roles. A market relationship replaced a judicial relationship. If the first was destined to become more cruel, it was for the time less difficult and less violent than the second.

The faubourg also dislocated the relations of work within the city. The existence of a parallel and contestatory world diminished the value of the capital represented by the mastership, a device of distinction that classified people and controlled life in the world of work. The faubourg broke the control that the masters exercised on their employees, who could now flee with impunity not only a detestable shop but indeed the entire system, the panoptic ambition of which now revealed itself to be derisory. The faubourg proposed not only a temporary refuge but an alternate system of training, a labor market that was both open and flexible, a prospect of lasting insertion and relative independence within that system. One was no longer routinely asked to produce a certificate of discharge given by the last employer, or a license, or a worker's passport. For hiring, the inn replaced the guild office: the former journeyman of the city became a *chambrelan* or small employer, welcoming his former comrades; in this way networks constituted themselves. There were even signs of self-regulation of a corporate character among the workers who were joiners and cabinetmakers, tapestry makers, and metalworkers.[69] The faubourg was no longer just content to welcome outlaws of work; it had emerged as the direct competition of the guilds for Parisian labor.

On the one hand, the crisis of insubordination pushed the masters to a defensive solidarity. It impelled them to reaffirm their attachment to a guild system that had guaranteed their social identity as well as their political and economic security. On the other hand, however, when the masters confronted the specific phenomenon of illicit work, they found themselves divided because they did not all have the same interests. The false workers exacerbated tensions not only within the trade communities, by accentuating the opposition between authoritarian governors and reformist masters, but also between innovators and prisoners of routine, masters who gave primacy to the management of their social capital and those who privileged economic capital. The attitude toward false workers casts into relief the very complicated stratification that existed within the guilds, which were supposed to be united and harmonious.

69. Arrêt de la Cour des monnaies, 18 August 1698, AN, T 1490[10], fol. 63; police decision, 1 August 1691, BN, ms. fr. 21797, fol. 380.

While aggravating tensions within the world of the guilds, the challenge of illicit work probably helped to make the corporate system's recruitment and organization of production more supple. To head off the advance of the false workers, some trade communities coopted them. Others integrated them to compensate for the loss of fallen masters. It is possible that the ease with which some workers could set themselves up in business outside the law deprived the guilds of a sufficient number of candidates for mastership, thereby inducing them to loosen the requirements. It is also possible that some communities concluded that they could protect what was left of their guild monopoly better by a strategy of openness than by one of exclusivity. The study of the false workers reveals that the communities had an admissions policy that was much more nuanced than their liberal critics (and their historians as well) have admitted. The masters believed with reason that "illicit" work reinforced the tendency toward insubordination. But at the same time this parallel world functioned as a sort of a safety valve that reduced pressure by opening a new frontier to journeymen who were frustrated, alienated, or simply ambitious.

The Faubourg Saint-Antoine and the Revolution

In the midst of the Revolution, at the moment of the definitive abolition of the guilds, Jean-Paul Marat echoed the old fears. Friend of the people, he had affection for and honored the glorious faubourg, whose inhabitants were the guarantors of the freedoms won on 14 July. But he was afraid of the faubourg's other face, of its liberal tradition, without daring to admit that a strong link could unite the new liberty with the old. Ferocious enemy of the ancien régime, Marat could nevertheless not accept the end of the old role of work, and he feared, as the enemies of Turgot had earlier, that all Paris might become the faubourg Saint-Antoine: "See the exempt quarters of Paris: the workers who seek only to attract clients through lower prices do not produce quality products. What will happen when this system is that of all workers, when masters will no longer be able to survive the competition, and when the desire to do good work will no longer be nourished?"[70]

The image of the faubourg is double and contradictory: a Parisian avant-garde, martyr of liberty, victorious over despotism; but also the place where disorders began, along with nonconformity—the site of chronic instability. Brought to life during subsequent moments of the Revolution, these two contrary visions reappeared continuously. The myth of the faubourg required the taking of the Bastille—heroic, necessary, unifying, legitimate, never really complete—in order to validate the Réveillon riots (April 1789)— erroneous, divisive, superfluous, ambiguous. The good faubourg would again be the place that received Louis XVI and Marie-Antoinette in its workshops, at the beginning of 1790; the place that in February 1791 sent to the

70. *L'ami du peuple*, 16 March 1791, p. 5n.

Cercle Social, a club that was passably radical, a deputation of citizens carry-ing a crown of oak leaves for the bust of Jean-Jacques Rousseau. The bad faubourg, the one that worried the revolutionaries, was a place that might suddenly change course; a place that, perhaps to exorcise the ghosts of the past, they proposed to rebaptize with "the honorably acquired name of the Faubourg of Glory"; a place that they asked to go back to work again, but calmly. To these fears one must add the hardened hostility of the guilds, which were implicitly suppressed on the night of 4 August but which in fact continued to administer the world of work until their liquidation in 1791, and which abused their new powers. Thus the faubourg, beacon of Parisian liberty, found itself once more excluded and rejected—from the wrong side of the Bastille.

Why was the faubourg Saint-Antoine the revolutionary quarter par excel-lence? It did not become a foyer of revolutionary activity because it was "the traditional center of popular agitation," as George Rudé wrote in one of these teleo- and tautological explanations that do injustice to the best histo-riography of the Revolution.[71] In the eighteenth century, the faubourg was neither the poorest quarter nor the consecrated site of riots.[72] I believe that the explanation is tied to its role as a privileged place: bastion of indepen-dence, center of wildcat work, refuge for all kinds of fugitives, nursery of rooming houses, sanctuary for illegal gatherings. Before becoming a model of popular insurrection, the faubourg was a model (primitive but operation-al) of laissez-faire. It is perhaps in this direction that historians of the Revolu-tion should move. Is it not possible that during the ancien régime the *fau-bouriens* developed a sense of their difference, of their relative autonomy, and a sort of political consciousness vis-à-vis central authority that made them more sensitive to the defense of rights? The daily counterculture of the faubourg, fueled by its ambiguous relationship with the city and with gov-ernmental authority, engendered the spirit of independence that led to its revolutionary vocation. A text from 1817, nostalgic for the world of the guilds and hostile to the Revolution, grasped this link that I have tried to establish:

> At the beginning of our political troubles, where did the factions go to find help? It was not inside the city, where the workers, spread through-out the various professions then organized into guilds, and accustomed therefore to subordination and to order, had behaved with more modera-

71. George Rudé, *The Crowd in the French Revolution* (Oxford: Oxford University Press, 1959), p. 16. On the "revolutionary" mission of the faubourg, also see Rudé, *The Crowd in History (1730–1848)* (New York: Wiley, 1964), pp. 106–7, 115, 174; and *Paris and London in the Eighteenth Century: Studies in Popular Protest*, Fontana Library (London: Collins, 1970), p. 84. See Richard Andrews' sobering evaluation of the role of the faubourg as a permanent center of agitation at the time of the Revolution, "Réflexions sur la Conjuration des Egaux," *Annales ESC*, 1974, pp. 73–106.

72. See Steven L. Kaplan, "The Paris Bread Riot of 1725," *French Historical Studies* 14 (1985), pp. 23–56.

tion and wisdom. It was to these faubourgs, where the guilds did not exist: in the middle of an undisciplined multitude of proletarians, blind artisans of all disorders and crimes. And we have not forgotten the part that the faubourg Saint-Antoine played in the most deplorable excesses of the Revolution.[73]

73. Levacher-Duplessis, *Réponse des délégués des marchands en détail et des maîtres artisans de la ville de Paris aux rapports et délibérations des conseils généraux du commerce et des manufactures* (Paris, 1817), p. 23.

16

Festivals and Fights

The Law and the People of Edo

TAKEUCHI MAKOTO

Tatsuzō: We got together at Ishimidō to put on a "festival of righteous world revival." We wanted to bring relief to those who were suffering so much.

Interrogating officer: What kind of nonsense is that—a "festival of righteous world revival"! You break into the households of respected merchants; smash apart casks of saké. You call that a festival to rectify the world? You have the audacity to claim that your actions stand "apart from the law"?

Tatsuzō: To hoard rice; to take this rice that sustains us in this transient life and squander it on making saké—that is what causes suffering for so many people. . . . We got together in order to make an appeal to this respected merchant, to beg him for some food. None of us ever intended to destroy his shop and home. It just happened that we got into a quarrel with him and a fight broke out.[1]

The interrogation of Tatsuzō took place following a peasant riot in 1836 in the Kamo district of Mikawa province. For all the quick temper displayed by the interrogating officer, both he and Tatsuzō were sparring with cool subtlety. The official was trying to goad Tatsuzō into uttering statements that would permit the government to bring the peasant to trial for his supposed role in the riot, an attack on wealthy rural families who engaged in saké brewing and money lending. Tatsuzō, for his part, was just as eager to keep the interrogation focused on terms and concepts that would justify his actions and absolve him of any responsibility for wrongdoing.

As Katō Takashi points out in Chapter 2, the shogunate had formulated procedures by which commoners could inform higher authorities about per-

---

1. Watanabe Seikō, "Kamo no sawagidachi," in Mori Kahei et al., eds., *Nihon shomin seikatsu shiryō shūsei*, vol. 6 (San'ichi Shobō, 1968), pp. 527–28.

ceived problems and injustices. In Edo, any merchant could submit a petition, a complaint, or an appeal to the head of his five-family group and his neighborhood chief.[2] If the neighborhood chief agreed that there were sufficient grounds for the petition, he would refer it to his superiors, who decided the matter, and all of the parties involved then were expected to defer to their judgment. These were the "rules" from the shogunate's perspective. The government considered any collective act of organized violence to be outside of this protocol. Thus, whenever crowds massed for action in front of a government office, whenever peasants attacked the homes of the wealthy, whenever townspeople ransacked the residence-shops of rice dealers and other well-to-do merchants, all were engaged in illegal acts.

The shogunate usually responded quickly to organized violence: it dispatched police inspectors, rounded up suspects, conducted interrogations, extracted confessions, held trials, and meted out punishments to those it found guilty.[3] At such times, the shogun's officials were most concerned with apprehending the men whom it referred to as "conspirators" (*totō*), the individuals who supposedly planned and led the action. Periodically throughout the Tokugawa period, the shogunate issued proclamations forbidding men to engage in "conspiracies," and it reserved its most terrifying punishments for persons judged to be the instigators of violence. The shogunate cast a wide net in these matters, first by defining as a conspirator any person who, "in whatever matter, arranges an inappropriate course of action through discussions with a large number of peasants"; and then by issuing similar injunctions against cabals in cities.[4] In the case in Mikawa in 1836, the interrogating officer was accusing Tatsuzō of engaging in collective violence, and he was hoping to find a way to label him a "conspirator" as well.

But Tatsuzō had an arsenal of terms that he could deploy in his own defense. He was versed in the fact that certain actions stood "apart from the law" (*hōgai*). According to the research of Hiramatsu Yoshirō, *kenka*—the term included spontaneous quarrels, fights, and brawls—constituted one such sphere of autonomous conduct.[5] Typically, the shogunate refused to adjudicate such incidents. Of course it would investigate any deaths that occurred during violent confrontations and try to bring the responsible party to trial. It also might hold the aggressor liable for medical bills if someone were injured seriously, and on rare occasions it was even known to exile

2. Kimura Motoi, "Chōsan to so," in Iwanami Shoten, ed., *Iwanami kōza Nihon rekishi*, vol. 10: *Kinsei* 2 (Iwanami Shoten, 1975), pp. 213–44. A shogunal ordinance of Meiwa 6 (1769).2 specified that peasants who wished to bring some matter to the attention of higher officials had to do so through the headman and other village officials. See Takayanagi Shinzō and Ishii Ryōsuke, eds., *Ofuregaki Tenmei shūsei*, vol. 1 (Iwanami Shoten, 1976) docs. 3041–42, p. 902. Daimyo issued similar regulations on their domains.

3. For specific examples, see Kimura, "Chōsan to so," and Takayanagi and Ishii, *Ofuregaki Tenmei shūsei*, vol. 1, docs. 3018, p. 891, and 3038–50, pp. 901–5.

4. Takayanagi and Ishii, *Ofuregaki Tenmei shūsei*, vol. 1, doc. 3018, p. 891.

5. Hiramatsu Yoshirō, "Kinsei-hō," in Iwanami Shoten, *Iwanami kōza Nihon rekishi*, vol. 11: *Kinsei* 3 (Iwanami Shoten, 1976), pp. 331–78.

combatants from Edo, although the intent in those cases was less to punish the guilty than to separate enemies in order to prevent vendettas. With these few exceptions, however, the shogunate refused to become mired in private disputes because it was almost impossible to determine who was at fault. It preferred to categorize fights among commoners as "cases of mutual harm," and it almost always left the contending parties to resolve their own differences.

Festivals constituted another autonomous zone of action. Because festivals took place on the sacred soil of the gods, and because so many fights and brawls broke out during the unlicensed moments that always seemed to be a part of commoner celebrations, the shogunate let the people indulge themselves in whatever pleased them during festival days—again, as long as no one was killed or seriously injured. Tatsuzō knew all of this. His verbal jabs (we planned to put on a "festival"; "we got into a quarrel"; it "just happened" that "a fight broke out") constituted a studied defense, a well-organized combination of flourishes designed to parry the thrusts of the interrogating officer. His own actions, Tatsuzō was asserting, were part of a private dispute; they were not subject to review by officials of the state. Technically, he had committed no crime; officially, he ought not to be subjected to punishment.

Very few people who lived in the Edo period ever found themselves in the predicament that Tatsuzō faced in 1836. As the scholar Motoori Norinaga (1756–1833) noted, most commoners who had a petition or legal matter to bring to the attention of the authorities normally followed the "rules" of petition and appeal laid down by the shogunate.[6] They had good reason to do so. Harsh punishments awaited "conspirators," and most persons who turned to violence did so, like Tatsuzō, only as a last resort, only after having made several unsuccessful efforts to resolve the matter through prescribed channels. And like Tatsuzō, most attempted to legitimate their actions, which were patently illegal in the eyes of the authorities, by disguising them as "festivals" or private "fights" that stood "apart from the law." As we shall see, the people of Edo learned these tactics from their confrontations with the authorities during the course of the eighteenth century.

THE GREAT EDO RIOTS OF 1787

An atmosphere of uncertainty embraced the shogun's capital during the spring of 1787.[7] Anne Walthall analyzes those riots in detail in Chapter 17; we need only recall here that after years of calamities, disasters, and poor harvests, the threat to Edo's food supply was reaching unprecedented lev-

6. Motoori Norinaga, "Tamakushige beppon," in Takimoto Seiichi, ed., *Nihon keizai sōsho*, vol. 16 (Nihon Keizai Sōsho Kankōkai, 1915), pp. 19–23.

7. Minami Kazuo, *Bakumatsu Edo shakai no kenkyū* (Yoshikawa Kōbunkan, 1978), pp. 214–45; and my "Tenmei no Edo uchikowashi no jittai," *Tokugawa rinseishi kenkyūjo: Kenkyū kiyō*, 1971, pp. 285–314.

els. In the spring of 1787, in that unfortunate period between annual harvests, rice prices climbed to new heights day by day, and other commodity prices followed suit. Petition after petition traveled from the hands of neighborhood chiefs to higher authorities, urging the government to assist the poor. But these pleas were dismissed, and on the twentieth day of the Fifth Month, Edo's commoners vented their anger.[8]

First the people attacked rice merchants in Fukagawa, on the northern edge of the city, and Akasaka, not far from the shogun's castle. Quickly the violence enveloped all of Edo, from Senju in the north to Shinagawa in the south, and it continued without interruption, day and night, until the evening of the twenty-fourth. During those five days, the authorities did not lift a hand, not even to dispense charity to the poor. Near anarchy prevailed as the rioters attacked not just rice merchants but even the shop-residences of wealthy merchants who were merely suspected of hoarding rice. Finally, late on the twenty-fourth, the shogunate sent out patrols, the feared companies of archers and musket bearers who normally guarded the entrance gates to Edo Castle. That same evening it set up an emergency relief station at Yokkaichi-chō, not far from the main entry gate into Edo Castle, and the riot quieted down.

It is not clear exactly how many persons participated in the riots, but certainly the number ran well into the thousands. Available documents suggest that almost all of them were residents of Edo, members of the city's lower social orders. Especially numerous were day laborers; peddlers who sold fish and vegetables from baskets dangling at the ends of poles they carried across their shoulders; small shopkeepers in the back alleys of the city; and the so-called petty artisans—plasterers, hairdressers, roofers, and those who made paper lanterns, lacquer ware, and footwear for ordinary workers.

It is not known even today whether or not a core group organized and led this large-scale riot. One contemporary chronicler, Sugita Genpaku, observed: "There was no one who could be called a leader. Three hundred people would get together over here, five hundred over there, as the spirit moved them. They beat on drums and rang their bells and gongs. Day and night, ceaselessly, they broke into shops, tossed bags of grain out onto the street, and ripped them open."[9] Although most historians now accept such accounts as reliable, at the time the shogunate was convinced that a cabal of conspirators had stirred up trouble, and it was determined to bring them to

8. The urban masses did not riot only in Edo in 1787. To date, about 500 acts of collective violence have been confirmed in the documents for the Edo period, which lasted about 250 years. Of the nearly 500 cases, 53 broke out in 1787 alone, and of those, 35 were clustered in the Fifth Month of that year. Osaka, Kōfu, Sunpu, Fukui, Wakayama, Yamato Kōriyama, Nara, Sakai, Fushimi, Ōtsu, Nishinomiya, Kōchi, Shimonoseki, Hakata, Kumamoto, and Nagasaki—few cities escaped the tragedy of violence in 1787. See Aoki Kōji, ed., *Hyakushō ikki sōgō nenpyō* (San'ichi Shobō, 1971).

9. Sugita Genpaku, "Nochimigusa," in Mori Kahei et al., eds., *Nihon shomin seikatsu shiryō shūsei*, vol. 7 (San'ichi Shobō, 1970), pp. 68–85.

justice. Investigations began in the closing hours of the riots and continued until the next spring.

After months of collecting evidence and interrogating suspects, the shogunate ultimately decided to punish some thirty individuals. Typical was the fate that befell Hikoshirō, an artisan who was employed in a paper-lantern shop on a back street in the humble residential quarter Fukagawa Rokkenbori-chō. Though the authorities noted that Hikoshirō "lived in poverty and could not support his wife and children," they could not condone his actions. "Despite the fact that pronouncements have been issued from time to time forbidding people to enter into a conspiracy," officials noted when they handed down their judgment, Hikoshirō, "together with Zenpachi and six others, went to the shop of Denjirō to beg for rice." While they were at the shop tempers flared, and "the men stepped into Denjirō's shop and began to smash apart the doors and windows and to destroy his furnishings." This, the authorities claimed, was "an act of insolence against public authority," and they sentenced Hikoshirō to a "severe beating" (*jūtataki*) and "exile, second category" (*chūtsuihō*), banning him forever from Edo and the Kantō region.[10]

Taking Refuge in the Zone of Autonomy

It is astonishing that the shogunate punished only thirty persons for participating in violence that brought thousands of persons into the streets and kept the world's largest city in constant turmoil for five days. In fact, the shogunate's patrols arrested nearly a thousand persons and threw them into the detention center (*rōya*) at Kodenma-chō. But in the end, almost all of those arrested avoided punishment by taking refuge in the zone of private autonomy described by the concept *kenka*. Near the end of the Sixth Month of 1787, Moriyama Takamori noted in his diary, "the authorities arrested a large number of merchants and artisans. It also took into custody a number of rice dealers. But, after deliberations, the officials judged what happened to be a fight, a brawl among individuals. They pardoned them all and released them from detention."[11] Another diarist made the same observation: "By the morning of the twenty-third of the Fifth Month a thousand men were being held in the detention center. . . . But later the authorities decided to label the actions of those arrested as fights, and officials released everyone from detention."[12]

A constellation of factors came together to make possible the transforma-

10. Aoki Kōji, with Hosaka Satoru, ed., *Hennen hyakushō ikki shiryō shūsei*, vol. 6 (San'ichi Shobō, 1984), pp. 245–52.

11. "Moriyama Takamori nikki," ed. Takeuchi Makoto and Asai Junko, in Harada Tomohiko et al., eds., *Nihon toshi seikatsu shiryō shūsei*, vol. 2: *Santo* 2 (Gakushū Kenkyūsha, 1977), p. 146.

12. "Tenmei shichinen teibi gogatsu beikoku futtei ni tsuki Edo sōdō no shidai," Tōkyō Toritsu Chūō Toshokan (Tokyo Metropolitan Central Library).

tion of a mass riot into a series of private disputes that were judged to lie outside the scope of shogunal purview. For one thing, the rioters of 1787 became folk heroes when their actions forced the shogunate to open a relief station that helped the poor, and surely that had something to do with the fact that almost all of them were freed from detention. Of course, those arrested also were fortunate that the resolution of the incident came during a particularly confusing period in the internal politics of the shogunate, when Matsudaira Sadanobu was ousting Tanuma Okitsugu as the head of the board of senior councilors. But most of all, the rioters could thank their own quick wits, their ability to manipulate the "logic of fights" to their own advantage. As another contemporary observer makes clear:

> On this occasion, the people who had been grumbling did not form a gang and commit some act of injustice. . . . That is to say, they had particular rice shops in mind that they wanted to attack and so they made up posters saying that those shops were going to sell rice at especially low prices at such-and-such a time on such-and-such a day. Then, they hung up the posters at various places around the city.[13]

Not all of Edo's commoners were literate, of course, but enough read the posters (or learned their contents from others) so that crowds massed in front of the shops at the appointed times:

> They crowded around and tried to buy rice. The shop owners had not seen the signs, and they had no idea what was going on. Both sides would get to talking back and forth, yelling at each other, and pretty soon a fight would break out. The leaders then gave a signal and their followers would break into the shop and take out the rice. Then everyone joined in, even the ones who had come to actually buy rice.

Although the rioters showed little mercy toward the merchants they despised, they were very disciplined, and they tolerated no looting. After watching a group of demonstrators demolish a number of rice shops in Akasaka, Moriyama wrote in his diary:

> I heard that a great number of rioters demolished several rice shops. The next morning I learned more details about what happened—that more than twenty shops in the Akasaka area had been destroyed totally—and I went to look over things for myself. I walked around the shops located near Akasaka Gate, which guarded a crossing over the moat that surrounded the outer castle grounds, and I saw that the clothing and furnishings from the shops had been thrown out into the street and stomped into the mud and dirt. Rice and soy beans were strewn everywhere. But, I

13. Kanzawa Tokō, "Okinagusa," in Nihon Zuihitsu Taisei Henshūbu, ed., *Nihon zuihitsu taisei*, ser. 3, vols. 19–24 (Yoshikawa Kōbunkan, 1978), vol. 22, p. 180.

was told, none of the rioters removed a single thing from the scene. They were very careful not to start any fires and not to cause any damage to the shops and homes located next to the rice dealers whom they attacked.[14]

Other accounts elaborate on the rules of engagement devised and enforced by the commoners. For instance, not only did the rioters disdain to take home with them any of the food or clothing that they dumped onto the street, but they also prevented looting by others. "If some bystander picks up things that have been strewn on the streets and takes off with them," wrote Santō Kyōzan, "the demonstrators themselves chase after that person, give him a sound thrashing, and bring back the goods he tried to steal. They are acting according to an unwritten set of rules, the same code of conduct that the city's firefighters respect."[15] The discipline that the rioters imposed upon themselves at times could be astonishing: gongs and wooden clappers signaled rest breaks in the action for the crowd that plundered the shop of Yorozuya Sakubei in Kyōbashi.

Clearly the ethical certainty of the rioters lent an air of legitimacy to their actions and magnified their image as folk heroes in the eyes of ordinary bystanders who had turned out to watch the action. Their disciplined behavior permitted them to draw on a legacy established earlier by the city's firefighters. As Santō suggests and as William W. Kelly points out in Chapter 13, the rough-and-ready roofers and construction workers who made up the core of Edo's firefighting forces from the mid–eighteenth century tolerated no looting at the scenes of fires. Yet those same firefighters, when they mobilized to fight a fire, often destroyed the houses of persons they did not like. The chief means of fighting fires at the time was so-called demolition firefighting, in which the firefighters attempted to keep a blaze from spreading by destroying the house on fire, ripping off its roof in order to direct the flames upward and then collapsing the walls inward. At the same time, the firefighting brigades tore down surrounding houses to create emergency firebreaks. The potential for settling old scores was evident to all.

Because the firefighters took an ethical stand against looting at the same time that they engaged in coordinated attacks on people they disliked, it was difficult in the aftermath of a fire for officials to determine if firemen had demolished a house for the legitimate purpose of halting the spread of the blaze or had wrought havoc in revenge for some grievance. Consequently, if some homeowner accused a firefighting brigade of willful destruction, the shogunate was inclined to regard the case as a private fight and not as a matter for the shogunate's courts of justice.[16] The quarreling parties were left to settle their differences through private mediation. The lesson was not lost on Edo's rioters, who also mixed restraint with action, enforcing one set

14. "Moriyama Takamori nikki," p. 146.

15. Santō Kyōzan, "Kumo no itomaki," in Nihon Zuihitsu Taisei Henshūbu, ed., *Nihon zuihitsu taisei*, ser. 2, vol. 7 (Yoshikawa Kōbunkan, 1974), pp. 322–23.

16. Ikegami Akihiko, "Edo no hikeshi seido no seiritsu to tenkai," in Nishiyama Matsunosuke, ed., *Edo chōnin no kenkyū*, vol. 5 (Yoshikawa Kōbunkan, 1978), pp. 91–169.

of laws while simultaneously violating another, masking calculated vengeance as an innocent fight—all so that they too could take refuge in the zone of autonomy.

The style set by the Edo firefighters, it should be noted, had an influence not just on Edo's commoners but also on farmers in the city's hinterland. Take, for instance, the following pronouncement concerning the Kantō provinces issued by the shogunate not long after the Edo riots:

> We have heard that among the peasantry there are some who imitate the behavior of Edo's firefighters. When they bear a grudge against someone, they turn out at a fire and, as a crowd, destroy that person's home. Others take the lead in forming gangs and getting into fights and brawls. Such persons are to refrain immediately from such insolent behavior and are to exhibit civil demeanor.[17]

Naturally, the shogunate tried to curtail the more abusive actions of the unruly firefighters. But it never could succeed in reforming their behavior, as the following report by a patrolman (*dōshin*) to his superior officer shows:

> Firefighters, the construction workers who call themselves the "embankment gang," carpenters, plasterers, roofers, dyers, and the fishmongers of Odawara-chō get into fights among themselves. They conspire and form gangs. They arm themselves with bamboo spears and sharp tools, and then plunder each other's homes and belongings. When this happens, we carry out an investigation and verify the facts, but the leaders of the firefighters or some eloquent person from the neighborhood will mediate between the two sides and arrange an agreeable settlement. As long as no one is killed, the matter does not reach the shogunate's courts.[18]

Such behavior brought despair to the hearts of law enforcement officials. "The twenty-three conspired to start the fight," the patrolman lamented at one point. "How can we ever hope that their demeanor will improve if there are no interrogations, no punishments?"

"Fires and fights are the flowers of Edo," the saying went, and each lighted up the city like the fireworks over the Sumida River, another emblem of commoner culture. But fires and fights had an additional symbolic meaning: each constituted a space "apart from the law." The commoners of Edo who ventured forth into the rioting of 1787 knew this, and in order to escape punishment, they drew a line from their actions back to the legacy forged by the firefighters and construction workers.

17. Takayanagi and Ishii, *Ofuregaki Tenpō shūsei*, vol. 2, doc. 6290, pp. 742–43.
18. Tōkyō Daigaku Shiryō Hensanjo, ed., *DaiNihon kinsei shiryō: Shichū torishime ruishū*, vol. 1 (Tōkyō Daigaku Shuppankai, 1959), doc. 38, pp. 47–48.

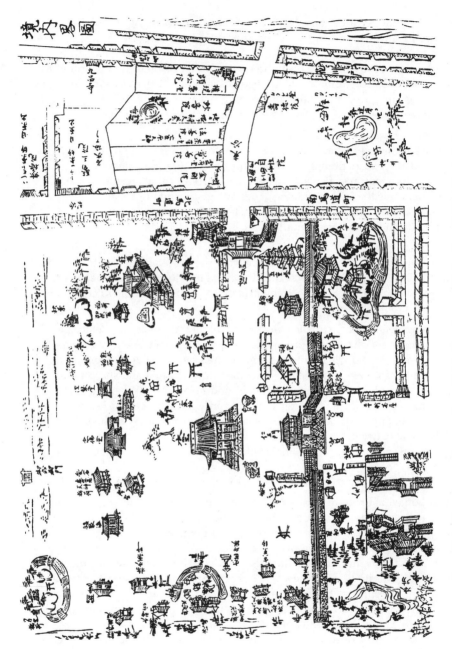

Sensōji and environs. Source: Sensōjishi. Courtesy of Kokuritsu Kokkai Toshokan.

The Sanja Festival

Fights, brawls, and the pillaging of shops were constituent elements of festivals, another space where Edo's flowers bloomed apart from the law. Festivals took place in time and space dominated by the gods; human laws were held in little regard there. No exception was the great Sanja Festival, celebrated at Sensōji Temple in the northern part of the city known popularly as Asakusa, an alternate reading for Sensō. The oral history of Sensōji holds that the temple was founded in the seventh century, when two brothers, Hinokuma no Hamanari and Takenari, were fishing in the Sumida River (then known as the Miyato River) and pulled up in their nets a statue of Kannon, the Buddhist goddess of mercy. The brothers showed the icon to Haji no Nakatomo, a prominent man of the locality (and described as another Hinokuma brother in some accounts), who then constructed a temple and dedicated it to the deity.

By the medieval period, several subsidiary temples and shrines had crowded into the precincts at Sensōji, and merchant quarters had come to line the approach to its main gates. After Ieyasu marched into Edo, the Tokugawa family began to worship periodically at Sensōji, and the shogunate annually bestowed five hundred *koku* of rice on the temple. In addition, the shogunate invested the officials of Sensōji with administrative accountability for twenty-two nearby merchant quarters. The priests discharged this responsibility through two intendants (*daikan*), who dispensed justice and collected dues from the merchants in amounts equal to the taxes that they otherwise would have paid to the shogunate.[19] Three of those quarters— Kita Umamichi-chō, Minami Umamichi-chō, and Minami Umamichi Shinmachi—were located within the official boundaries of the temple complex, and they were commonly referred to as the "internal quarters," or more literally "the quarters within the temple precincts" (*keidaichō*).[20] The remaining nineteen quarters, called the "quarters before the gates" (*monzenchō*), spread out in front of Sensōji and along the banks of the nearby Sumida River. Three of these neighborhoods (Zaimoku-chō, Hanakawado-chō, and Yamanoshuku-machi) were honored as "founding quarters" (*miyamoto sankachō*), a designation that gave them special rights at festivals.[21]

19. Until 1665 Sensōji (affiliated with the Tendai sect) elected its own head priests. After that date, Sensōji was treated as a branch of Kan'eiji, the shogun's main temple. Thus the official chain of administrative command was commissioners of shrines and temples → priests of Kan'eiji → priests of Sensōji → intendants → neighborhood chiefs. For additional details, see my "Sensōji no keidai monzen sekai," in Ogi Shinzō, ed., *Edo Tōkyō o yomu* (Chikuma Shobō, 1991), pp. 168–72.

20. Nishiyama Matsunosuke et al., eds., *Sensōji nikki*, 12 vols. (Kinryūzan Sensōji, 1978–1992), vol. 6, pp. 525–26 (hereafter cited as *Sensōji nikki*). This record of daily events was compiled by the priests at Sensōji from Kanpō 4 (1744) until Keiō 3 (1867). The original manuscript volumes, some three hundred in all, are preserved in a storehouse at the temple. To date, the materials through the early nineteenth century have been published.

21. These three quarters also oversaw affairs in the several villages located in back of the temple that paid annual dues to Sensōji (in lieu of taxes to the government) to support the activities of the temple. See Amino Yūshun, *Sensōji shidanshō* (Kinryūzan, 1962), p. 717.

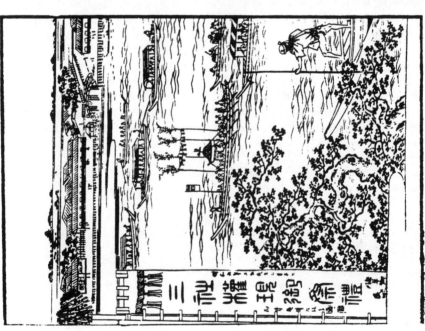

The Sanja Festival. Source: *Tōto saijiki*. Courtesy of Kokuritsu Kokkai Toshokan.

The grandest celebration at Sensōji was the Sanja Festival, a celebration organized by three Shinto shrines erected within the Sensōji complex as places of prayer and worship for the spirits of the temple's seventh-century founders. Each spring, on the seventeenth and eighteenth days of the Third Month, the parishioners of those three shrines joined together to host what became in time one of the three largest, wildest, and most well-attended annual festivals in all of Edo. The celebration took two formats. The "main festival" (*honsairei*) was held in the Years of the Cow, Rabbit, Serpent, Sheep, Chicken, and Boar (the odd-numbered years of the Gregorian calendar), and the "inner festival" (*uchisairei*) was celebrated in alternate years.[22] In either case, the highlight of the festival was the parading on the eighteenth of three giant *mikoshi*, the shrine-palanquins that provided a temporary abode on this special occasion for the spirits of the founding deities. The young men of the three founding quarters carried these *mikoshi*, each of which weighed more than a ton, along a processional route prescribed by tradition. During the inner festival the parade of spirits ran only through the three internal quarters situated inside Sensōji, but in alternate years, during the main festival, the procession wound its way through most (but not all) of the nineteen quarters before the gates, and until the mid–eighteenth century the *mikoshi* were even loaded onto a barge and taken up and down the Sumida River. On those occasions in particular, thousands of spectators turned out to share saké and good times with the often drunken young men who carried the three palanquins on a lurching, frenzied journey.

Private Disputes and the Sanja Festival

Given all of the drinking and excitement associated with festivals, it is small wonder that fights and brawls were commonplace, and it is just as unsurprising that the shogunate adopted a hands-off approach, leaving it to the combatants to resolve their differences on their own. One such incident occurred in 1753:

> Today when the *mikoshi* procession was making its way through Suwa-chō, a large group of bullies appeared. They forced the *mikoshi* and their bearers from their normal course, pushing them into the streets of [Shō-den] Yoko-chō. A quarrel broke out, and then a fight, and a lot of people were injured. Everyone scattered and ran away. Because Seikichi of Suwa-chō and Zenbei of Zaimoku-chō were injured, those two quarters sent in a complaint to the commissioner Nose Higo no Kami. Officials will conduct an investigation and take corrective measures. Moreover, the *mikoshi* was severely damaged. Because the insolent behavior interfered with the use of a palanquin during a festival, the investigation must be thorough.[23]

22. Amino Yūshun, ed. *Sensōjishi*, 2 vols. (Sensōji Shuppanbu, 1939), vol. 2, p. 403. The main festival might be canceled, however, in years of famine or when there had been particularly destructive fires. For instance, it was not held in 1773, 1775, 1777, or 1779.
23. *Sensōji nikki*, vol. 1, pp. 614–15.

Two issues concerned officials and residents of the quarter alike. One was
the matter of who would pay the cost of repairs for the expensively crafted
shrine-palanquins. Even more troublesome was the diversion of the *mikoshi*
from their traditional route. This was the cause of the brawl, which pitted
residents of Suwa-chō, who expected the *mikoshi* to pass through their quarter, against the palanquin bearers from Zaimoku-chō, who had been cowed
into making an unscheduled side trip through Shōden Yoko-chō. Despite
what promised to be a "thorough" investigation, officials ultimately decided
that this was a private fight and the opponents had to settle matters on their
own.

Two other incidents illustrate the jealousy with which parishioners protected the privilege of having the gods paraded through their neighborhoods. In 1757 the residents of Tawara-machi and Sangen-chō, quarters
traditionally not traversed by the *mikoshi*, petitioned to be included on the
processional route. Thereupon the intendants of Sensōji required the residents of Zaimoku-chō, Hanakawado-chō, and Yamanoshuku-machi, the
three quarters that from time out of memory had carried the palanquins, to
put their seals to an agreement to comply with the new routing and to
refrain from getting into any fights.[24]

That directive did not put an end to contention over the routing, however, for several years later representatives of the five-family groups in the
founding quarters sent to the intendants office the following *ukeshōmon*, a
document certifying that a decision made by a superior had been or would
be carried out:

A PROMISE OF COMPLIANCE

As the representatives of the five-family groups, with great respect we
pledge that on the eighteenth day of the Third Month, during the forthcoming festival, the three *mikoshi* will not be carried on a route not specified in the regulations. They will be paraded only within the boundaries
of the internal quarters. Under no circumstances will they be carried
through residential quarters that lie outside of Sensōji's two main gates.
Since temple buildings and offices were damaged during a fire on the
twenty-ninth day of the past month, the *mikoshi* bearers will be especially
careful about their behavior, and they will not get into any quarrels or
fights. . . . Of course, on the day of the procession, the representatives
of the various five-family groups, together with all of the house owners
from the quarters, will accompany the procession of the *mikoshi* so as to
control the bearers and the crowds.[25]

Another kind of private dispute at Sensōji involved forced contributions
to religious causes. According to documentation from the Third Month of
1770:

24. Ibid., vol. 2, pp. 296–97.
25. Ibid., vol. 3, pp. 713–15.

At the time of the festivals for Sanja Gongen and Nishinomiya Inari Shrine, many young people and children from the quarters before the gates are going around soliciting contributions to buy sacred rice wine for the festivals. In particular, they badger the more humble merchants who merely rent shops. If a merchant resists and refuses to make a donation, the youths threaten him and force him to give some money. This has caused a great deal of trouble.[26]

Of particular note here is the phrase "young people and children from the quarters before the gates"; this is the first indication that the actions of the young people whose spirited vigor was so necessary for a successful festival could portend trouble for the community. Later, as we shall see, the forced contributions evolved into acts of violence in which youths ransacked shops whose proprietors were reluctant to donate to the causes the youths espoused.

Collective Violence during the Sanja Festival

Youths from the various quarters around Sensōji seized upon the Sanja Festival as an opportunity to organize acts of collective violence. An entry from the *Sensōji nikki* dated 1796 states that youths from the three founding quarters

frequent archery galleries and teahouses, strutting around haughtily. Moreover, they appear in front of saké shops [and] yell out for drinks and other favors. On top of that, those same young men carry the *mikoshi* during the Sanja Festival, when they mass in front of the houses of merchants who earlier have refused demands. In revenge, the young men break into those shop-residences.[27]

The documentation also makes particular note of the role played by the leaders (*wakamonogashira*) of bands or gangs of youths. The details are not clear, but one probable inference is that a youth leader directed the activities of a loosely organized gang of young men in each quarter.[28] Thus what the officials of Sensōji feared was not the isolated misbehavior of individuals but rather the more sustained and spirited offenses of gangs of young men.

In other parts of Edo, as we discovered earlier, persons with revenge on their minds used fires as a pretext to damage the shops and merchandise of their enemies. But the youths from the three founding quarters at Sensōji did not require a fire; they turned festivals into opportunities to engage in acts of collective violence. In their defense, the youths could claim that they had lost themselves to the moment, given themselves to the spiritual frenzy of the celebration, left themselves and the *mikoshi* in the hands of the gods.

26. Ibid., p. 441.
27. Ibid., vol. 7, p. 666.
28. Further discussion of youth gangs can be found in Tani Teruhiro, *Wakamono nakama no rekishi* (Nihon Seinenkan, 1984), pp. 71–175.

Thus whatever happened reflected the will of the gods; the youths could not be held responsible to worldly authority, and householders who suffered damage could not appeal to the government officials.

The violent actions of the youths from the three founding quarters appears to have escalated during the last decade of the eighteenth century. Moreover, the youths tended increasingly to form themselves into gangs, and they started to use violence for their own ends outside of festival days, whenever it suited their purposes. The officials at Sensōji could not turn a blind eye to such developments, and in 1797 they placed strict regulations on carrying the *mikoshi* during the Sanja Festival.[29] The new regulations consisted of three points. In the first place, they restricted the number of *mikoshi* bearers to thirty youths per shrine-palanquin: a total of ninety bearers for the three *mikoshi*. Second, officials increased the number of persons who escorted the procession. Before 1797, eleven neighborhood chiefs from the quarters before the gates and slightly more than forty men from the residential quarters along the processional route accompanied the young *mikoshi* bearers. From 1797, the government directed that an additional sixty men be added to the escort. In other words, more than one hundred mature men now marched in watch over ninety youths.

Finally, in accordance with a petition submitted by the neighborhood chiefs of the quarters before the gates, city officials agreed to dispatch to Sensōji ten patrolmen (*dōshin*) on the days of the festival to join the escort. The city magistrates routinely had sent two patrolmen to oversee the Sanja Festival from the mid-1750s, when fights first became a problem.[30] Now, in 1797, the leaders of the merchant quarters themselves sought the help of higher officials. Their hope was to bring violence under control; to encompass "within the scope of the law" that rowdy behavior which youths claimed existed in space "apart from the law."

The Outrage of the Young Men from the Founding Quarters

The new regulations imposed on the *mikoshi* procession at the Sanja Festival were a consequence not just of the violence at the festival itself but also of an "outrage" by youths in 1796 that especially alarmed the officials at Sensōji. The head priests at Sensōji had arranged a special display (*kaichō*) of sacred objects brought from Myōzōin, a subtemple within the famous Kitano Tenmangū complex of shrines and temples in Kyoto. The presentation was scheduled to open on the fifth day of the Sixth Month of 1796, and since the general public usually was not permitted to view those icons, officials at Sensōji expected to draw large crowds (and generous contributions) during the special three-month exhibition.[31]

However, when the *mikoshi* bearing the sacred objects from Myōzōin arrived at the entry gates to Sensōji on the third day of the Sixth Month, two

29. *Sensōji nikki*, vol. 8, pp. 156, 410, 660–62.
30. Ibid., vol. 2, p. 295.
31. Unless otherwise noted, the quotations in this section are ibid., vol. 7, pp. 663–86.

days before they were scheduled to go on display, about forty youths from the three founding quarters seized the *mikoshi* and icons and carried them along the regular processional route for the Sanja Festival. It is not clear why the youths took this action; perhaps the officials of Sensōji had slighted them when they planned the exhibition. Whatever the reason, neither the priests of Myōzoin nor the local neighborhood chiefs seemed inclined to bring the youths to heel for their actions. The neighborhood officials surely hoped to keep a low profile after the violence that had marred the festival earlier that year, and the priests of Myōzōin probably feared that any appeal from them to punish the youths would simply jeopardize the safety of their relics.

Within days, however, higher officials at Sensōji caught wind of the incident, and the intendants launched a special investigation. Very quickly the head priests at Sensōji became convinced that the youths who committed this outrage were the same persons who had perpetrated other acts of violence at festivals and intimidated merchants in the surrounding quarters. If they could identify and punish the leaders of this incident, officials believed, they simultaneously could hope to bring a measure of control and order to everyday life in the residential quarters under Sensōji's administrative oversight. The entry in the *Sensōji nikki* for the tenth day of the Sixth Month, for instance, reads: "Youths from the three founding quarters always strut about and bully others. Year after year they carry the *mikoshi* at the Sanja Festival and commit insolent acts of misconduct. . . . We must restore order at this time." Then on the twenty-first, officials admitted that if they overlooked this incident and declined to investigate, "the youths will lose their fear [of us] and will become puffed up with presumption." But, they went on, "with the blessings offered by this occasion, we can bring about peace and order even in normal times." On the twenty-sixth they closed the circle: "The leaders of past incidents are the persons who commanded this unfortunate outrage. . . . We know they ordered this outrage too."

Working on this logic, the intendants of Sensōji ordered the neighborhood chiefs of the three quarters to submit a list of all the youths who had participated in the outrage. The chiefs, however, threw up a screen of excuses and declined to draw up such a list. But the intendants would not give up, and on the twenty-second, after three successive demands from on high, the chiefs presented to the temple officials a list of forty-three participants in the outrage: twenty-five youths from Zaimoku-chō (one later fled the city), twelve from Hanakawado-chō, and six from Yamanoshuku-machi.

Three days later, on the twenty-fifth, the officials of the temple placed another demand on the neighborhood chiefs of the three quarters: identify the ringleaders of the outrage from among the forty-three names on the list. On the twenty-eighth the neighborhood chiefs replied: "We do not know the names of the leaders and so we request that you summon the forty-three youths and ask them yourself." Irked and tired of the delays, temple officials immediately rebuked the neighborhood chiefs for their attitude. At the same time, they handed the chiefs a lengthy roster of "hoodlums" (*warumono*),

rogues whose names had surfaced in previous investigations, and they instructed the chiefs to identify the ringleaders from that list. A few days later
investigators from the office of the commissioners of shrines and temples
turned up the heat by virtually accusing the neighborhood chiefs of malfea-
sance: "If the intendants had not investigated, you would have done nothing. What did you intend—just to let it go as a matter 'apart from the law'?"
The chiefs hardly could resist such intense pressure, and early in the Seventh Month they presented the officials of Sensōji with a report concerning
each person on the list of "Hoodlums."

   On the basis of this information, Sensōji's intendants concluded their
investigative report on the seventh day of the Seventh Month and on the
nineteenth Intendant Kikuchi Sadanoshin announced the following punishments:

> Concerning the outrage committed by the youths from the three found-
> ing quarters upon the arrival of the sacred objects of Myōzōin Tenmangū
> on the third day of the last month, after a report from the neighborhood
> chiefs, the offenders were summoned to appear before the authorities on
> the seventeenth. . . . The following punishments have been decided:
>
> For those persons from Zaimoku-chō judged guilty of misconduct:
>   Banishment; not permitted to visit or reside in the three residential
>   quarters located within the temple precincts   3 persons
>
> For the guilty person from Hanakawado-chō:
>   The same punishment   1 person
>
> For the guilty person from Yamanoshuku-machi:
>   The same punishment   1 person
>
> For the guilty person from Yamanoshuku-machi who committed addi-
> tional serious outrages at the site of the exhibit of sacred objects:
>   Banishment from the nineteen quarters in front of the temple as well
>   as from the quarters within the temple precincts   1 person

Officials "reprimanded" the remaining offenders and confined them "to
their place of residence for three days." In addition, even though the leaders
of the youth gangs did not themselves directly participate in the incident,
officials harbored no doubts that gang members were deeply involved in the
improprieties of the past several years. Thus they banned the gang leaders
from the temple precincts, on the grounds that such a punishment was
"befitting the actions committed in their names." Moreover, on the twenty-
third day of the Seventh Month the temple officials ordered the chiefs of the
three founding quarters to spend "twenty days in house confinement" because of their refusal to submit reports as instructed, a punishment meted
out to the representatives of the five-family groups as well.

Finally, five house owners received punishments because their sons, younger brothers, or shop employees participated in the outrage. As property owners they had neglected their responsibility to control and oversee the persons who were dependent on them; their punishment was house confinement. Any homeowner whose son participated in the outrage was sentenced to ten days, a term reduced to seven days if it was a younger brother or group of shop employees who had joined the incident, and to just five days when a single shop employee was found guilty. From this document we also learn that only three sons or younger brothers of neighborhood chiefs and representatives of five-family groups had a hand in the outrage. Forty of the participants were shop renters, the sons and younger brothers of shop owners, or shop employees.

In all, the resolution of the outrage was swift and severe. Within two months officials had punished more than fifty persons for participating in the incident, or for failure to prevent others from joining the action. In addition, new restrictions on the *mikoshi* processions followed on the heels of the punishments. This sort of determined action, however, did not put to rest certain historical questions. Why, for instance, did Sensōji's officials adopt this stern posture toward youths at this particular time? And what are we to make of the actions of the neighborhood chiefs? Why did they, themselves part of the administrative structure, repeatedly attempt to stonewall higher authorities and cover up for the youths? These questions take us to a broader consideration of youth and their attitudes toward the shogun's laws.

YOUTHS AND NEIGHBORHOOD AUTONOMY

In part, the crackdown against the young men at Sensōji in 1797 was a reaction to escalating violence in the quarters around the temple. Whereas the fights that marred the Sanja Festival at mid-century involved just those young men who were concerned about the processional route of the *mikoshi*, twenty years later bands of youths were using intimidation to compel small-scale merchants to contribute to the youths' favorite causes. Yet even at this date the youths tended to rely on threats and insults; only in the 1790s did the gangs more freely use force and spread fear through the Asakusa area. The sporadic fights of the 1750s were mild in comparison with the more organized and frightening behavior of gangs in the 1790s, when bands of young men "strutted" through the archery galleries and teahouses around Sensōji, demanded "drinks and other favors," and then during festivals attacked the shop-residences of the merchants who refused to bow to extortion. That sort of behavior compelled the attention of the authorities.

But the more determined efforts of the officials at Sensōji to stem violence in their own neighborhoods needs to be placed within a broader, all-Edo context as well. For one thing, officials and residents of the city feared a repetition of the riots that raged over five days in 1787. Then the poorer elements of the city—day laborers, peddlers, small shopkeepers, and petty artisans—ransacked the shops of the wealthy and legitimated their actions by masking them as private fights. The perpetrators of violence around Sensōji in the 1790s also came from the underclasses; they too claimed to act "apart from the law," in this case by disguising gang violence as a festival action associated with the will of the gods. To many observers it seemed that history, if not exactly repeating itself, was making another pass-by in close orbit.

Moreover, by the 1790s youth gangs were emerging as potential trouble-makers in many merchant neighborhoods across Edo, and the shogunate was becoming concerned. The first shogunal law regulating youths in Edo appeared in the spring of 1791 as part of a grand revision of the legal codes during the Kansei reforms:

> Commonly, there are difficult persons in every residential quarter who call themselves "youths" [*wakamono*], and they extort money from land-lords during festivals. Moreover, they make unreasonable impositions on landlords, homeowners, and shop renters for so-called religious contri-butions during the All Souls' Festival [*bon*] in the Seventh Month. They put forth similar demands when sacred objects on loan from other tem-ples are displayed in their own neighborhood temples; whenever be-lievers meet; or when priests circulate subscription lists so as to gather pledges for a specific religious project. The youths harbor grudges against those who refuse to make contributions, and they take their revenge later.[32]

The shogunate acted again in the autumn of 1798 when it issued an edict prohibiting persons from erecting banners, streamers, and paper lanterns inscribed with auspicious sayings during festivals and other celebrations.[33] The reason for this order was clear: "Youths from many quarters go around demanding money to put up large banners, and if someone refuses their demands, a gang gathers and threatens the person."[34] Thus, as the eigh-teenth century drew to an end, the shogunate no longer cared to distinguish between youths who were merely overly zealous in gathering religious con-tributions and the roving gangs who extorted money and gifts from mer-chants. The actions of those who "harbor grudges" and "take their revenge later" seemed cloned from the behavior of those who rioted in the streets in 1787. Everywhere youths stood guilty of disrupting social harmony, and

32. Ōkurashō, ed., *Nihon zaisei keizai shiryō*, vol. 7 (Zaisei Keizai Gakkai, 1922), p. 772. Before this time there were no laws regulating youths; for instance, the word *youths* appears not a single time in the three-volume documentary collection *Shōhō jiroku*, ed. Kinsei Shiryō Kenkyūkai (Nihon Gakujutsu Shinkōkai, 1964–1966), which contains shogu-nal decrees issued from the Shōhō (1644–1648) through the Hōreki (1751–1764) periods.

33. For additional details on this latter phase of the Kansei reforms, see my "Kansei kaikaku," in Iwanami Shoten, ed., *Iwanami kōza Nihon rekishi*, vol. 12: *Kinsei* 4 (Iwanami Shoten, 1976), pp. 1–44.

34. Takayanagi and Ishii, *Ofuregaki Tenpō shūsei*, vol. 2, pp. 714–15.

they became the objects of shogunal suppression. Small wonder, then, that the officials at Sensōji stirred to action during the 1790s, punishing even those youth leaders who had not participated in the "outrage of the three founding quarters." Four years later the authorities at Sensōji again toughened their stand by announcing: "There are to be no leaders of gangs of youths in the quarters before the gates. If anyone poses as such a leader, the neighborhood chiefs of those quarters must submit his name, together with the same particulars that were required earlier concerning the youth leaders of the three founding quarters."[35]

Despite this new resolution on the part of the authorities, however, the neighborhood chiefs often tried to protect the youths, as they did during the "outrage" of 1796. They had several reasons for doing so. Not least was the money the gangs raised for religious purposes. At Nishinomiya Inari Shrine within the precincts of Sensōji, for instance, a bronze torii, the gateway that marks the entry into the hallowed ground of a shrine, bears the inscript "Kyōhō 12 [1727], Eleventh Month." Below are the names of the donors who gave money to construct the torii, and at the very bottom, together with "the parishioners," appears "the youths of the quarters before the gates." Similarly, we can find "the youths" among the contributors for a stone statue of a stylized guardian lion dedicated in the Eighth Month of 1754, and "the youths of Nishi Naka-machi and Higashi Naka-machi" helped to erect a stone shrine fence dedicated in the Second Month of 1807.[36]

Moreover, local officials in charge of organizing the Sanja Festival relied on the youths to take leading roles in ceremonies and to carry the *mikoshi* through the streets. Indeed, as an incident at the Hikawa Shrine in Akasaka demonstrates, a festival could fall flat when youths refused to cooperate. During the Kansei reforms of the late 1780s, shogunal officials decided that lavish, expensive festivals were inappropriate during a period of government fiscal austerity and retrenchment. Consequently, those officials proclaimed that the traditional display of Buddhist lanterns during the Hikawa Festival would be suspended, and they instructed the people to wear simple clothing.

> The youths became angry, and not a single one of them participated in the festival. As a consequence, only middle-aged and older men took part. It was painful to watch. . . . Since the youths did not join in the festival as usual, there were no quarrels, fights, or brawls. But perhaps the gods were not pleased by the absence of the youths, because one of the middle-aged men was injured when the *mikoshi* crashed down on his head.[37]

35. *Sensōji nikki*, vol. 7, pp. 697–98.
36. Amino, *Sensōjishi*, vol. 1, pp. 368, 372–79.
37. Mizuno Tamenaga, "Yoshi no zasshi," in Mori Senzō et al., eds., *Zuihitsu hakkasū*, vol. 9 (Chūō Kōronsha, 1981), p. 313.

No wonder that at Sensōji authorities overlooked the self-indulgent, rowdy behavior of the young men, lest the Sanja celebration too become an uninteresting, unappealing festival of middle-aged men, "painful to watch."

Finally, the leaders of bands of youths helped to preserve harmony and order within their residential quarters by looking after their followers. In addition, the leaders and even individual gang members not infrequently stepped forward to mediate disputes. During the investigation of the outrage of the youths of the three founding quarters, for instance, only one person who did not reside in those three quarters was brought before the authorities. That was Gohei, an employee in a shop located in Minami Umamichi-machi Shin-machi, and Gohei's neighborhood chief, a man named Shōzaemon, went to great lengths to defend him. Shōzaemon's attitude seems surprising at first glance, because Gohei had a reputation as a mean drunk who often got into quarrels and fights, and he had served time in the shogunate's jail for gambling. All the same, his neighborhood chief claimed, Gohei had another side that deserved praise:

> Until now there have been no gangs in the three internal quarters. Whenever anyone in this area gets into a quarrel or a fight, Gohei steps in to settle things peacefully. Before, in the Sixth Month of 1795, Zentarō, an employee in the shop owned by Chōemon in Shitaya Sakamoto-chō, and Yaichi, an employee in the shop of Magoshichi in the same quarter, got into a fight at a teahouse operated by Tashirō in one of the internal quarters. This was a serious matter that ordinarily might have ended up being brought before the commissioners of shrines and temples and might well have resulted in prison terms. But Gohei and Heijirō accepted responsibility for mediating a settlement and everything ended peacefully. After that, the authorities gave the two a reward.[38]

No matter how much higher officials distrusted Gohei and others like him, neighborhood officials relied on such youths to maintain community harmony. In doing so they were able, at least in some limited sense, to isolate their neighborhoods from unwelcome intrusions of state power.

Conclusions

At the beginning of the nineteenth century, Buyō Inshi, another keen observer of the Edo scene, noted:

> The shogunate's proclamations and ordinances are called "three-day laws." No one fears them, and no one pays any attention to them. . . . They are disregarded after that short period of time. In particular, lower officials—indeed, even the great magistrates themselves—are

38. The reward amounted to one thousand *mon* of copper *zeni*, equivalent to approximately one *ryō* of gold at the time. See *Sensōji nikki*, vol. 7, pp. 672–74.

quickly disillusioned, because so many laws and ordinances are proclaimed. Since everyone knows that the government merely issues laws
whenever it feels that it needs them, it is no wonder that the lower orders
do not take the time to learn them, do not obey them. Especially when
you take into account how very difficult it is to make a living in today's
world anyway (and even more so if you observe each and every statute),
then people will not obey the laws, even if they do know them.[39]

The commoners of Edo lived according to their own logic, and many
wanted to police their own neighborhoods, staking out for themselves a
zone of autonomous action. The merchants and artisans of the city had their
own ideas about what constituted fair play and social justice, and their
notions sometimes stood at odds with the shogun's laws, as Buyō suggests.
Thus at times, and particularly during moments of crisis, some people within the community took matters into their own hands, as when they rioted in
1787 to compel wealthy merchants to act benevolently toward the poor. On
other occasions they punished merchants who did not contribute to the
festivities of community life and to religious fund-raising campaigns. City
officials, of course, branded such acts as "conspiracies," and they attempted
to bring the leaders of the cabals before the shogunal courts of justice. By
drawing on a tradition first established by the city firefighters, however,
commoners during the latter half of the eighteenth century were able to
disguise their conspiratorial actions as "fights" or "festivals," thus locating
them in a time and space that stood "apart from the law."

By century's end, some individuals and groups within neighborhood
communities had extended the zone of autonomous action to encompass
additional self-regulating activities, moving beyond those special spheres of
fights and festivals. At Sensōji, leaders emerged who presided over bands of
youth and who looked after the affairs of the members of their gangs, which
themselves had become agents in enforcing norms of community behavior.
Other individuals, such as Gohei, came to play particularly important roles
in mediating disputes within their neighborhoods, settling altercations, disagreements, and fights that otherwise would have had to be turned over to
the shogun's judiciary.

Higher officialdom, however, saw the gangs and their leaders as "outlaws" (*akutō*), and it wished to suppress them. Consequently, each neighborhood chief was caught at the point of collision between the customs and
routines of his community and the laws imposed from above by the shogunate. For most at this time, the solution was to raise the banner of "community solidarity." In this way, the chiefs could hope to control the youth gangs
(who had it within their power to destabilize a neighborhood just as easily
as they could calm its tensions) while at the same time presenting to higher
officialdom a facade of local harmony that would prevent the further penetration of shogunal authority into the neighborhood.

39. Buyō Inshi, "Seji kenbunroku," Kokuritsu Kokkai Toshokan (National Diet Library).

The zones of autonomous action were an integral part of Edo's political landscape, an indication of the way in which the city was ruled both from above and from below. At the end of the regime, this sort of autonomy as exercised by local residents assumed a new dimension of importance, just as Steven Kaplan suggests in Chapter 15 that the independence valued by the workers in the faubourg Saint-Antoine played an important role in the French Revolution. Like the workers in the faubourg, the people of Edo opposed what they considered to be unreasonable intrusions into their lives. Thus arose a tradition of resistance that gathered strength as the nineteenth century advanced, until Japan's commoners became important actors in the drama of mid-century, which led to the overthrow of the Tokugawa shogunate in 1868.

17

Edo Riots

ANNE WALTHALL

Three times, at widely spaced intervals, the populace of Edo rioted. Compare this experience with that of Paris, where contentious gatherings exploded every thirty to forty years.[1] In the First Month of 1733 a single Edo merchant became the object of attack; in 1787 nearly one thousand shops suffered damage; and in 1866 assaults on some two to three hundred buildings climaxed months of unrest. In each case the chief targets were merchants accused of increasing the hardships of the poor by hoarding rice. Despite the often massive destruction of property, in no case was anyone killed, nor did the townspeople confront the agents of the state directly. For this reason, the riots might be interpreted solely in terms of economic problems, but I argue that they invoked issues of power and politics and exposed the contradictory relations between mercantile capital and the state.

The three Edo riots shared certain characteristics. In all cases, the townspeople acted not merely out of hunger but because they held certain expectations of the state, certain assumptions about merchants, and certain values projected onto their own role in society. They expected and welcomed the measures taken by the city magistrates to bring rice into the city during shortages, to distribute it to the poor, or to regulate a fair price for it; and indeed, the townspeople were likely to demand such steps. When they found it impossible to buy rice or when the price they paid was higher than they thought reasonable, they assumed merchants to have selfishly taken advantage of shortages to increase their profits and charged the state with ignoring their hardships. To punish the one and put pressure on the other, the townspeople drew on customary sanctions first forged in Japan's villages.

I thank M. William Steele for his comments on a draft of this chapter.

1. At times contention was more common in modern Tokyo, where there were nine major riots between 1905 and 1918. See Andrew Gordon, "The Crowd and Politics in Imperial Japan: Tokyo 1905–1918," *Past and Present* 121 (1988), pp. 141–70.

The three riots differed, however, in scale, in their settings within the configurations of shogunal politics, and in the kinds of written evidence they provoked. Coming at the end of the series of reforms in the 1720s discussed by Hayashi Reiko in Chapter 9 of this volume, the 1733 riot can be interpreted as a comment on urban policies, particularly as evidenced in the petitions and directives exchanged between the commoners and the city magistrates before the riot. Expanding in the power vacuum left by the fall of Tanuma Okitsugu, the 1787 riot preceded the appointment of the reformer Matsudaira Sadanobu to the position of senior councilor and, according to some accounts, even made his elevation possible. The 1733 riot called forth few reports, but that of 1787 shocked observers all over Japan, from Aomori to Nagasaki, and produced the first pictorial representations of urban conflict. The series of disturbances from 1865 to 1866 demonstrated the commoners' disaffection with the state in light of its obvious helplessness in dealing with the foreign threat and domestic turmoil. In a remarkable series of posters and handbills, commoners insulted their superiors and called for action. Despite official prohibitions, artists graphically depicted destruction.

Rather than emphasize what the rioters did and where they did it, a topic I have discussed before, this chapter examines the documents characteristic of each riot.[2] Like the essays by William W. Kelly (Chapter 13) and by Eiko Ikegami and Charles Tilly (Chapter 18), it analyzes the problems of urban governance from below in order to shed light on how the Edo populace experienced state power. It examines the commoners' perceptions of conflict and its legacy for future action; or to put it another way, how the ways people contended for their interests reflected the spread of literacy and the weakening of state power. In this account, it is important to see neither the state as monolithic nor the commoners as homogeneous. Men who made decisions had their own quarrels, and their vision of the city differed from the visions of the men charged with administering it. The low-ranking samurai intellectuals, who depicted crowd action in the light of their own preconceptions, had more in common with the poor than with their superiors, even though they too belonged to the ruling class. The political agendas of tenants and day laborers differed from those of the wealthy merchants. To account for these riots and to assess their significance, we must examine the factors and documents that pertain to each of them. The Edo riots provide one perspective on the popular reaction to state intervention into urban governance, for as Tilly has written, "popular contention sends political messages other channels do not carry."[3] But in all three cases, that message needs to be defined historically.

2. Anne Walthall, *Social Protest and Popular Culture in Eighteenth-Century Japan* (Tucson: University of Arizona Press, 1986), pp. 141–49, 223. See also Herbert P. Bix, *Peasant Protest in Japan, 1590–1884* (New Haven: Yale University Press, 1986), pp. 112–13.

3. Charles Tilly, *The Contentious French* (Cambridge: Belknap Press of Harvard University Press, 1986), p. 386.

THE 1733 RIOT: PRELUDES TO CONFLICT

Small in scale though it was, the Edo riot of 1733 constitutes a crucial starting point for inquiry into urban conflict. It was not the first riot in the Tokugawa period, but it was the first in the shogun's capital city. Before analyzing the documents that it provoked, however, let us turn to earlier riots—the Japanese term is *uchikowashi*—and the question of whence they came. Why did urban commoners find it appropriate to smash up property rather than take some other form of revenge against hoarding? Tilly points to the importance of understanding how transformations of the state affect popular contention. I argue that it is also necessary to consider the village world where the forms of contention originated.

As late as the 1780s, fully one quarter of the commoners resident in Edo had been born in the countryside, and they carried their traditions with them into the city. Among these traditions were certain community sanctions disallowed by the state but occasionally performed nonetheless. During the long centuries of medieval Japan, when public justice was a legal fiction, communities had defined and enforced socially acceptable standards of behavior for themselves. Crimes that threatened the livelihood of the community's members, especially the theft of food, were punishable by death or the destruction of property. The judgment was not arbitrary; usually taken in a shrine precinct in the presence of the gods and consented to unanimously, it acquired a sanctified power impossible to gainsay. With the imposition of public authority by the Tokugawa shogunate, one effect of concentrated coercive means was to forbid all but the ruling class the right to take life. Other sanctions, less readily detectable, remained. By the eighteenth century the peasants had learned to petition the authorities to redress their grievances; to punish their neighbors they smashed up property, sometimes secretly against an individual or two, sometimes openly in large-scale mass movements. Beginning in Nagasaki in 1713, the urban populace followed their lead.[4]

We know that urban commoners demanded state intervention in the grain market before the eighteenth century, but the documentation is scant. In 1642, for example, the Dutch resident in Nagasaki recorded some news passed to him by his interpreter:

> The price of rice rose extremely high in Osaka, the commoners were unable to feed their families, and many people died of starvation. . . . The poor pushed their way into the magistrate's office to appeal to him to indicate some way for them to survive. He calmed them down, sent a fast messenger to the *bakufu*, opened the storehouses for grains in

---

4. Nagasaki Shishi Nenpyō Hensan Iinkai, ed., *Nagasaki shishi nenpyō* (Nagasaki: Nagasaki Shiyakusho, 1981), p. 50. See also Nishimura Shingon, *Nihon kyōkō shikō* (Osaka: Nishimura Shingon, 1936), p. 360.

Osaka castle, and distributed food to the poor at low prices. In this way
he pacified the rioters.[5]

This, the earliest record of urban unrest in Tokugawa Japan, is cast in terms
of what Irwin Scheiner has called a morality play.[6] The downtrodden but
deserving poor appeal to the authorities for help, and help is given. The
assumption, apparently shared by both sides, is that when necessary the
state will make an effort to help the people.

As far back as the records show, commoners found it appropriate to turn
to the state for relief, an assumption that, according to Steven L. Kaplan
(Chapter 8), they shared with the peoples of Paris. In the Fourth Month of
1675, several neighborhood chiefs in Edo petitioned the on-duty city magistrate: "Because the high price of rice is making survival difficult, please lend
us government rice."[7] Like his counterpart in Osaka thirty years earlier, the
magistrate released 40,000 bales of rice. In 1681 the neighborhood chiefs
petitioned once more, and again the magistrate lent them 30,000 bales of
rice. Whereas in Osaka the poor (vaguely defined) had subverted the status
order by taking it upon themselves to act, in Edo the highest-ranking commoner officials spoke in the name of all the commoners. They continued to
play this role, albeit with increasing difficulty, in the eighteenth century.

The 1733 Edo riot thus incorporated certain assumptions regarding appropriate sanctions and the state's responsibility for the commoners' welfare. In 1713, the year of the Nagasaki riot, the neighborhood chiefs and
townspeople of Edo petitioned the city magistrates not just for relief rice but
for positive measures to bring down prices. They asked the officials to
provide rice gruel for workers on yearly contracts and for short-term laborers unable to procure food for themselves; to allow consumers to buy rice
shipped into the capital by the daimyo of Sendai instead of purchasing it
only through the monopoly merchants; to instruct all daimyo to use rice
brought from their own domains instead of competing with the commoners
for supplies in Edo; and to investigate charges of hoarding. The magistrates
responded that the people who were pushing up the price of rice were
themselves commoners, not the authorities, and what the commoners did to
each other was not the business of officialdom.[8] Despite this plea for coercive intervention into the practices of mercantile capital, the state backed off.

The commoners knew all too well that the magistrates' response was
disingenuous, for in fact the state previously had intervened in the rice
market to raise prices. Since taxes were collected and stipends paid in rice,

5. *Nagasaki Oranda shōkan no nikki*, trans. Murakami Naojirō, vol. 1 (Iwanami Shoten,
1956), p. 166.
6. Irwin Scheiner, "Benevolent Lords and Honorable Peasants: Rebellion and Peasant
Consciousness in Tokugawa Japan," in Tetsuo Najita and Irwin Scheiner, eds., *Japanese
Thought in the Tokugawa Period, 1600–1868* (Chicago: University of Chicago Press, 1978),
p. 50.
7. Quoted in Sasaki Junnosuke, ed., *Hyakushō ikki to uchikowashi* (Sanseidō, 1974),
p. 48.
8. Ibid., pp. 49–50.

the gap between low rice prices and high prices for everything else had caused a financial crisis in ruling-class circles that several measures instituted in the Kyōhō era (1716–1736) were designed to overcome, as Hayashi discusses in detail. In 1724 the shogunate issued regulations to permit a market in rice futures, increased saké brewing to absorb surplus production, stockpiled its own tax rice, encouraged the daimyo to do the same, and asked the townspeople of Osaka to buy more. In 1730 it gave Takama Denbei and seven others the privilege of monopolizing the trade in rice sent to Edo from Osaka.[9] Two years later these measures backfired when a plague of locusts caused crop shortages in western Japan.

The famine of 1732 demonstrated the inability of the state to cope with an emergency.[10] When famine seemed imminent in Edo itself, the city poor, those who rented their shops and rooms, began to insist on a petition to the city magistrates. Under ordinary circumstances, the commoners had to get their demands countersigned first by their landlords and then by neighborhood officials. With starvation staring them in the face, the poor argued that they had no time for such formalities, so on the twentieth day of the Twelfth Month, several hundred landlords gathered before the magistrate's office to appeal directly for a policy to lower the price of rice. Even though the petition was not signed by the proper authorities, the on-duty magistrate accepted it, an unprecedented breach of procedure. He told the townsmen to find out who was suffering and how much, and then to present the results in a formal petition through their neighborhood chiefs.[11] Nevertheless, the magistrate refused to accept the commoners' definition of the crisis: "Raising the price of rice was done out of consideration for the warriors who must sell their stipends in order to live. The more comfortable life becomes for the warriors, the more they will be able to buy from you. Commerce will flourish, and this should not make life difficult for the commoners. . . . We do not understand what your problem is." This attempt to explain supply-side economics did not sit well with the commoners. The exchange of petitions and directives for that year ended with the magistrate's pronouncement: "There is no way for us to lower the price of rice. Tell the people in the merchant quarters to economize."[12]

The commoners refused to believe that the state could not regulate the practices of mercantile capitalists. On the sixteenth day of the First Month of 1733, several neighborhood chiefs announced plans to cook rice gruel for the poor. The next day they petitioned the on-duty city magistrate to lower the price of rice, for they feared that otherwise people might die of starvation.

9. Takeuchi Makoto, *Edo to Ōsaka*, Taikei Nihon no rekishi 10 (Shōgakukan, 1989), pp. 129–35.

10. Estimates of the number of people who died in western Japan range from 12,000 to 969,900. The high figure comes from the "Ryūei nichijiki," in Tōkyō Shiyakusho, ed., *Tōkyō shishikō: Hensai-hen* (hereafter cited as *TS:H*), vol. 3 (Tōkyō Shiyakusho, 1916), p. 716; the lower figure is from Takeuchi, *Edo to Ōsaka*, p. 136.

11. Hara Heizō and Tōyama Shigeki, "Edo jidai kōki ikki oboegaki," *Rekishigaku kenkyū* 127 (1947), p. 25.

12. Quoted in Sasaki, *Hyakushō ikki*, pp. 53, 54.

Clerks in the magistrate's office replied that there was no way to lower the price of rice, and therefore the commoners should stop presenting petitions. On the nineteenth came a petition from the property owners, house and shop renters, and people living in the back streets—the first time that people not of property owner (*chōnin*) status had been listed in an appeal. They complained that "crowds of people were on the verge of starvation," and they proposed concrete measures to lower the price of rice and to make supplies more plentiful. "We humbly request that you not restrict trade in rice to the merchants who have obtained a government monopoly, but to permit trade to be carried out widely. . . . If through your authority the price of rice is quickly lowered, the masses will be grateful to you for being saved." The magistrate once again responded that there was nothing he could do; the commoners should eat rice gruel until prices dropped. The policy of restricting the rice trade seems to have been made at a higher level, by superiors impervious to the commoners' complaints.[13]

While the city magistrates were telling the commoners that the state could do nothing, policymakers were preparing to make changes, at least temporarily. On the twenty-first, the shogunate agreed to permit milled rice to be imported into Edo despite a previous prohibition issued in 1731. It ordered rice stores, monopoly merchants, and samurai with rice stocks on hand to sell them as quickly as possible, but the buyers were not to demand outrageously low prices. The shogunate also announced its own sale of 10,000 *koku* of rice (with plans to distribute the money so raised to the needy), divided 1,071 *koku* among the commoner quarters for charity, and instituted a public works project to clean the moats. On the twenty-third, the city magistrates summoned the neighborhood chiefs to explain how the charity rice would be distributed to the poor and to instruct them to find out how many poor there were. "There is to be no corruption, and any dishonest landlords are to be reported immediately."[14]

The measures taken by the state were too few and came too late to satisfy the urban population. After the twentieth, two to three thousand people went daily to the city magistrates' offices to ask that the merchant Takama Denbei be turned over to them for punishment. At the same time, Denbei appealed to the shogunate to be allowed to sell for less than the current wholesale price the 30,000 *koku* of rice that he had in his storehouse, and officials granted permission on the twenty-third. Denbei's petition, and the fact that he had authorization to wear a sword and to travel in the manner of a samurai, demonstrated that this man was more than a simple rice merchant. He was a government agent, and he knew that the commoners realized this.[15] On the twenty-sixth, room renters and other poor from Hyakugumi-chō demanded that free trade in rice be permitted as soon as possible.[16] That night men gathered before Denbei's gate at Nihonbashi in

13. *TS:H*, pp. 727, 728.
14. Ibid., pp. 718–24.
15. Sasaki, *Hyakushō ikki*, p. 57.
16. *TS:H*, p. 741.

the heart of the city. Shouting, "Give us rice, stop hoarding rice," they stormed the gate until it broke under their weight.[17] The first smashing of property in Edo had begun.

Hara Heizō and Tōyama Shigeki have argued that the Kyōhō period marks the beginning of tremors in the basis of Edo's social organization, exposing, in Tilly's language, the contradictory relations between mercantile capital and state power.[18] Both the reforms launched by the shogun Yoshimune and the 1733 riot can be seen as responses to this contradiction, but I would not want to argue that reforms generated uprisings or that uprisings caused reforms. It seems clear that the commoners attacked Denbei because he had taken advantage of state policies instituted during the reforms, which increased the commoners' suffering to the benefit of the samurai. Furthermore, the riot must not be divorced from the negotiations with the magistrates, negotiations that demonstrated enough support for popular collective action to reduce the risks usually assumed by those who initiated such face-to-face bargaining. Nevertheless, subsequent riots were to show that the relationship between governmental initiative, merchants' practices, and rioting by commoners was much more than a simple matter of action and response. In addition, the commoners' agenda in rioting cannot be completely subsumed under the rubric of political action. Denbei was punished for what he was—an unscrupulous merchant—and the object of attack was mercantile capital as much as state power.

Throughout the Tokugawa period, urban commoners assumed that the state had a role in regulating mercantile capitalism, but they expected to play a part in defining what that role would be. The neighborhood chiefs had their own proposals for what the shogunate could do to guarantee a steady supply of food to the city at reasonable prices; when their efforts failed, the riot constituted a criticism of state-sponsored monopolies in the necessities of life. Yet the 1733 riot annoyed the shogunate more than embarrassed it. In the Second Month of the year, officials told the townspeople that they should be able to survive because rice was coming into the city and public works had been started. "The townspeople of Edo are not so close to death by starvation as are the people of western Japan. . . . Since conditions are the same in Kyoto and Osaka, we will not treat Edo any differently."[19] This policy was to change after the 1787 riot.

THE RIOT OF 1787

The 1780s saw an apparent waning of state power. Governmental initiatives to regulate the spread of commerce, as in the 1781 drive to establish silk inspection stations, were rejected by merchants and peasants alike.[20] When

---

17. Nishiyama Matsunosuke and Takeuchi Makoto, *Edokko no seitai* (Kōdansha, 1975), pp. 76–77.
18. Hara and Tōyama, "Edo jidai," p. 24.
19. *TS:H*, pp. 746–47.
20. Walthall, *Social Protest and Popular Culture*, pp. 80–86, 135–40.

the former strongman Tanuma Okitsugu resigned his position as senior councilor in the autumn of 1786, a vacuum was opened at the top of the government that remained until the next summer, when Matsudaira Sadanobu became a senior councilor. Factional strife within the shogunate was paralleled by waves of peasant uprisings and urban turmoil. The student of Dutch medicine Sugita Genpaku complained that "it is just as though the forces of the ruling authorities decline while those below grab power." These conditions played a large role in the 1787 riot, and the riot in turn became a decisive factor in Sadanobu's rise to power. As Genpaku announced: "Had it not been for the recent riot, the government would not have changed."[21]

This political infighting helps explain the state's ineptitude in responding to the crisis of subsistence in the city. Rumor had it that the shogun had ordered charity rice distributed to the poor, but a member of the Tanuma faction, Mizuno Tadatomo, delayed putting the plan into action.[22] Ōta Nanpo, himself a samurai turned author of literature for a commoner audience, reported that when the shogun asked what was going on, his chamberlain replied that the merchant quarters were quiet; nothing was happening.[23] As they had done before the 1733 riot, the townspeople repeatedly appealed to the city magistrates during the final months of 1786. Besides publicizing reports that merchants had been buying up and hoarding foodstuffs to make exceptional profits, the magistrates simply ordered prices to fall and goods to be released for sale. These directives served only to reinforce the commoners' suspicions that they demonstrated the state's weakness. By 1787 every day saw commoners push their way into the magistrates' offices to appeal for relief, only to receive a scolding and be sent on their way. ("Those below began to revile their superiors.") Then the magistrates forbade any further appeals for aid. According to reminiscences written in 1797 by the doctor and Buddhist priest Kita Yūjun, the magistrate had announced that in previous famines cats had sold for three *monme* apiece, but since he had not recently heard of any cats being sold, conditions could not be all that bad. People complained that "he was all but telling them to eat cats. How could they rest easy if even the magistrates admitted that the government did not have the authority to lower the price of rice?"[24]

Samurai diarists and commentators of the time criticized every measure taken by the magistrates. When officials investigated how much rice the merchants had on hand, the merchants hid their rice in the storehouses of the warriors, shrines, and temples and paid off the investigators. ("Bribes by the wealthy have corrupted the government.") According to one commenta-

21. Sugita Genpaku, "Nochimigusa," in Kondō Heijō, ed., *Kaitei shiseki shūran*, vol. 17 (Kondō Kappanjo, 1903), pp. 687, 720.

22. Tōkyō-to, ed., *Tōkyō shishikō: Sangyō-hen* (hereafter cited as *TS:S*), vol. 31 (Tōkyō-to, 1987), pp. 113–18.

23. Quoted in Nishiyama and Takeuchi, *Edokko no seitai*, p. 99.

24. Minami Kazuo, *Bakumatsu Edo shakai no kenkyū* (Yoshikawa Kōbunkan, 1978), pp. 218, 222.

tor, "In today's world, people with money pay bribes and political affairs in the realm have become as black as night."[25] Another text reported: "While the magistrates spent days deliberating what to do, the people became more and more desperate." In contrast to the rarefied exchanges between magistrates and merchants, bodily functions were invoked to define the poor: "The wives and old women who lived from hand to mouth could not make even enough piss to wet their throats. All they did was wait for death."[26] What better way to make sense of dearth than through the vulgarity that was strictly excluded from official discourse?

In the face of a state unable or unwilling to act and of the common assumption that greedy merchants were taking advantage of the hardships of the poor, is it any wonder that for five days in the Fifth Month of 1787 the commoners rioted? According to a letter sent to Kyoto a few days after the violence subsided: "The riot began because the rioters resented the merchants' hoarding of rice. They did not know what else to do besides wreck those stores." This letter also suggested that the rioters remembered what had happened in 1733.[27] The riot began with demands for charity; only when they were denied did people attack property. Unlike the 1733 riot, which concentrated on one merchant in the heart of the city, the 1787 riot erupted in areas where the poor lived, in Asakusa, Honjo, and Fukagawa. The first incidents occurred at night, but when officials did nothing, riots continued in broad daylight. Then they spread through Yotsuya and Aoyama to Shinbashi, Kyōbashi, and Nihonbashi. The only merchants to escape damage were those with a reputation for virtue and those who distributed charity as soon as the rioters appeared.

In their reconstructions of the riot, many commentators emphasized the role of mythical or semimythical figures. In his diary entry for the twenty-second day of the Fifth Month, Moriyama Takamori, a shogunal official, reported seeing "an unshaven youth of seventeen or eighteen and a man of unusual strength."[28] "He was not an ordinary man!" another diarist exclaimed. "Was he perhaps a *tengu*?" He was refering to the apparitions, at once half man and half bird, who simultaneously could destroy the world of the Buddhist law and act as representatives of the mandate of heaven by encouraging good and chastising evil. A purveyor to temples, Kameya Rōfu, also wondered whether the man was a *tengu* and mentioned a priest of superhuman strength as well.[29] Kita Yūjun wrote: "I saw a tiny youth with the strength of a sumo wrestler." By 1825 Takizawa Bakin had decided that the youth must have been either a *tengu* or Yoshitsune, the legendary

---

25. *TS:S*, p. 113.

26. Quoted in Minami, *Bakumatsu*, pp. 220, 223.

27. Ono Takeo, ed., *Nihon keizai kikinshi* (Gakugeisha, 1935), pp. 198, 202. Another suggestion that the events of 1733 had not been forgotten comes from Takizawa Bakin, who reported that "old people still told of that riot": *TS:S*, p. 229.

28. *TS:H*, pp. 773–74.

29. *TS:S*, pp. 110, 148–51.

twelfth-century warrior hero.[30] In 1846 the novelist Santō Kyōzan remembered "a beautiful youth and a strong man who flew about like a veritable Hercules." This depiction of the heroes became increasing popular in the latter part of the Tokugawa period.[31] These figures, summoned up to explain acts of destruction, were remembered when the commoners rioted in 1866.

Depictions of mythical figures provided a way for the Edo populace to draw on its symbolic world to explain what had happened and to legitimize the riot. As violence grew beyond all imagining, the rioters themselves claimed that *tengu* had appeared. In various accounts, messengers of the gods, Benkei (Yoshitsune's faithful companion), violent gods, Kongorikishi (the Japanese Hercules), a "white-haired old man," and a "giant priest" helped the crowd or led it to acts of destruction. The variety of these symbols suggests that for the rioters their contents were not fixed. The rioters mobilized beliefs in monsters, legendary figures, and the protective deities of the Buddhist law to construct a representation of their actions and an explanation of the riot in terms that went beyond a simple response to dearth and greed.

Warriors, too, explained the riot in terms of supernatural agency. The Mito retainer Tsuda Nobuhiro wrote in 1811: "This was not something that could have been done by human hands alone. The King of Heaven aided the people." In 1831 the shogunal retainer Yamada Katsuraō wrote that "what heaven mandates is truly frightening," and his remarks echoed those of other commentators. These notions were used to criticize the Tanuma faction and to cast its policies as the primary cause for the riot. Uezaki Kyūhachirō wrote a letter to the shogunate complaining that Tanuma had instituted policies in accordance with his own greed, so "people in the world have no choice but to do likewise. Morality declines, and since heaven and humans are united, yang and yin naturally become unbalanced, crop failures follow, and then there are riots." Yamaguchi Shirōemon argued that "owing to bad policies, the riot was a calamity that arose naturally out of the deeds of heaven."[32] Whereas the commoners personified the supernatural as active creatures engaged with the populace, the warriors explained the riot in more abstract terms and treated the crowd as a natural force.

One significant depiction of the riot appeared in a penny novel (*kibyōshi*). Set in the Kamakura period (1180–1333) to evade government censors (a standard device of writers when they dealt with contemporary issues), the

---

30. *TS:H*, pp. 792, 794.

31. Santō Kyōzan, "Kumo no itomaki," in Nihon Zuihitsu Taisei Henshūbu, ed., *Nihon zuihitsu taisei*, ser. 2, vol. 7 (Yoshikawa Kōbunkan, 1974), pp. 322–23. In 1847 a friend of Kyōzan's, Saitō Hikomaro, wrote: "A big strong priest of over forty and a beautiful youth of twelve or thirteen flew about like birds. What kind of gods could they have been?" The next year Saitō Sachinari reported: "A big youth flew around like a bird. It was said he was very beautiful"; and in 1868 Kitamura Kaki wrote: "Two men were particularly impressive leaders. One was a big youth, the other a big priest of superhuman strength": *TS:S*, pp. 254, 240, 259.

32. *TS:S*, pp. 93, 156, 252, 255, 588, 66.

story has two titles, suggesting at least two editions. Its plot turns on a pun between *kome* (rice) and *kame* (tortoise), a transgression of the grammatical order that reveals a materially satisfying countermeaning.[33] Like epics and tales, it begins with a villain, Mannenya Kakuemon, who promoted tortoise cuisine, then cornered the market by buying tortoises directly from the sea god and storing them in the dragon palace, a representation of the merchants who had been accused of hiding rice in the mansions of the daimyo. Even the shogun's retainers had gone beyond the bounds of common decency in hoarding rice.[34]

This text contains one of only two pictorial representations of the riot, albeit as an allegory. By his promotion of tortoise cuisine, Kakuemon had angered the turtles. "There is no way we can bear this. We are already on the verge of starvation," they complained in a quotation taken directly from what rioters said to the shogun's police.[35] The pictures draw on a repertoire of comic and vulgar images "that stand against the serious and oppressive languages of official culture."[36] They subvert both the meaning of the riot and the social order it overturned by doubling symbolic inversion.

Another depiction of the riot took the form of a parody. Written by a low-ranking samurai intellectual and published in 1789, it satirized contemporary politics and society with Emperor Daigo (885–930) cast in the role of the shogun and Sugawara no Michizane (845–903) as Matsudaira Sadanobu. Its field of vision was wider than that of the penny novel about militant turtles, encompassing the eruption of Mount Asama in 1783, crop failures, famine, and drastic increases in food prices as well as the riot, but it reversed the meaning of these events by portraying them as the blessings of benevolent rule. (Mount Asama emitted money; beggars dressed in fine brocades.) In the scene depicting the riot we find the comely, strong youth mentioned in so many accounts of the riot and another reference to the mythical *tengu*, allusions that situate this book firmly amid the rumors and reports of its time. Peddled through the streets of Edo, it achieved tremendous popularity before the government ordered its sale stopped.[37] Taken as a whole, it exposed the growing disdain for administrators and policymakers on the part of the Edo populace.

The 1787 riot differed from that of 1733 not only in scale and location but in its political implications and the volume of comments on it. Had it not come at a critical juncture in shogunal politics, it probably would not have attained the size or notoriety it did. It proved to be a tremendous embarrass-

---

33. This definition of the pun comes from Peter Stallybrass and Allon White, *The Politics and Poetics of Transgression* (Ithaca: Cornell University Press, 1986), p. 10.

34. The text of this book can be found in *TS:S*, pp. 261–78. A detailed discussion of it is in Minami Kauzo, "Tenmei Edo uchikowashi no kibyōshi," *Nihon rekishi* 453 (1986), pp. 69–75. Yamada Tadao also discusses the text in "Seiji to minshū bunka," *Rekishi hyōron* 465 (1989), pp. 36–37.

35. *TS:S*, p. 275.

36. Stallybrass and White, *Politics and Poetics*, p. 10.

37. Koike Masatane et al., eds., *Edo no gesaku ehon*, vol. 3 (Shakai Shisōsha, 1982), pp. 180–212.

Will the tortoise storehouses be rebuilt?

Having quickly reached a decision, the horde of turtles vied to be first in smashing Mankaku's store to smithereens. Every member of the household ran away.

Turtle at far right: "How mean to have done such hoarding. Just look at how high tortoises have become."
Turtle at bottom right: "What a mess, what a mess."
Turtle at far left: "I'm going to pluck your balls right out of your arse. Lightning will strike me dead before I let you go."
Man on ground: "Forgive me, forgive me. I'm so sorry for what I did."

It would be better to get some use out of him before he gets hurt.

Woman at left: "How horrible."

Source: Atara ni tateru ka kamegura. Courtesy of Kokuritsu Kokkai Toshokan.

ment for the shogunate, erupting as it did "at the shogun's knees," and one
of the first reforms enacted by Matsudaira Sadanobu was the institution of
the city savings association (*machi kaisho*), which, as Katō Takashi shows in
Chapter 2, provided loans to the poor at low rates of interest. Sadanobu also
encouraged the economic development of the Edo hinterland.[38] In 1837,
when riots swept the rest of the country, the city savings association distributed rice and money to the poor. Tilly and Kaplan suggest that the French
monarchs distrusted Paris and kept it at arm's length—one reason, perhaps,
why Paris saw so many more contentious gatherings than did Edo. As Katō
points out, a great deal of shogunal governing energy centered on Edo
alone. In making a serious effort to export subsistence crises to rural areas,
the shogunate gave priority to Edo. It was not an accident of history that five
thousand incidents of popular contention erupted in the countryside and
three hundred in other urban areas between 1600 and 1868, while between
1787 and 1866, Edo remained relatively quiet.

THE 1866 RIOT

By 1866 the people of Edo found that their world had become vastly more
complicated than it had been in the eighteenth century. The steady drain of
the country's silver in the seven years since trade began with the West
forced prices up and the value of copper coins down. As early as 1861 the
government found it necessary to issue charity rice to day laborers, peddlers, unemployed artisans, and even some property owners. It also loaned
money to its own retainers. Then, in preparation for its expedition against
the dissident forces of Chōshū domain, the shogunate and its allies bought
up all the supplies they could, driving prices still higher. By this time the
publishing industry had so far expanded and literacy had so greatly increased that the populace was both better informed about what was going
on and much more likely to comment through anonymous broadsheets
(*kawaraban*) and posters.

The coming of the barbarians provoked tremendous, if unauthorized,
discussion. Government records, samurai's letters, merchant's diaries, and
artists' prints considered these great events from all possible angles. The
makers of broadsheets had a field day depicting the hairy foreigners and
their interactions with the samurai, who were hard put to figure out how to
deal with them. Widely distributed, these early newspapers provided more
information than the shogunate's censors could control. As M. William
Steele has written: "Edo commoners knew well that the warriors lacked the
means to drive the foreigners away and poked fun at their helplessness."
They expressed their scorn in such verses as the following: "In ancient times
it was the Gods of Ise who frightened away the Mongols; now it is the Lord

38. For a treatment of Sadanobu's reforms as they pertained directly to Edo, see Her-
man Ooms, *Charismatic Bureaucrat: A Political Biography of Matsudaira Sadanobu, 1758–1829*
(Chicago: University of Chicago Press, 1975), pp. 88–91.

of Ise [the senior councilor Abe Masahiro] who is frightened."[39] The prohibition on reporting contemporary events had became a dead letter.

Abetted by news of foreign ways and the rise in prices, the spread of xenophobia contributed directly to political criticism. The low-ranking samurai on fixed salaries hated foreign trade, they hated the authorities who had allowed it, and they hated the merchants who got rich from it. During the early 1860s posters complained of the difficulties of making a living when prices were so high, demanded charity, and threatened the merchants engaged in foreign trade with the punishment of heaven. In the Third Month of 1865 a poster criticized trade with foreign countries, called for the removal of the barbarian-suppressing shogun who could not suppress the barbarians, and urged that the barbarians be expelled.[40] This direct attack on the shogun himself went unpunished.

The riot of 1866 was preceded by a phenomenon unknown during the negotiations between city and shogunal officials in 1733 and 1787: posters appeared urging the poor to take action. For a year the threat of riot, of *uchikowashi*, was publicized in the city streets. In the Fifth Month of 1865, a poster found near a guardhouse at Shinbashi proclaimed: "Since the price of rice keeps rising, the poor have a hard time making a living, and they are suffering hardships. We are now telling the rice shops that we are going to smash up property because we will starve to death if prices rise any higher. Sympathizers should gather at the signal at Yanagihara." It was signed "The leaders of the poor in Kanda and Asakusa."[41] Whoever made this poster obviously expected it to be seen not just by officials of the shogunate and the merchants against whom it was directed but by at least some of the people who might be inclined to riot.

This poster and others like it contributed to popular agitation during the next month. One day in Akasaka and Shiba, "fourteen or fifteen children wearing martial attire gathered here and there. . . . They waved paper streamers and flags, carried toy spears, swords, and guns, and beating drums and blowing conch shell trumpets they marched through the streets gathering adherents as they went."[42] This farce may have recalled the legend of the youth who led the 1787 riot. The shogunate certainly disapproved, for it issued a directive forbidding such behavior. A few days later posters appeared criticizing the rice wholesalers and money changers and the officials who supervised them. By thus inflaming popular sentiment, the broadsheets helped to keep pressure on the state.

Confronted by these tokens of popular unrest, the government did its best to get food to the needy. It permitted free trade in rice and other grains, thus ending once and for all the monopolies enjoyed for so long by the privileged wholesalers. In the Sixth Month, the city savings association fol-

39. M. William Steele, "Goemon's New World View: Popular Representations of the Opening of Japan," *Asian Cultural Studies* 17 (1989), p. 82.

40. Minami, *Bakumatsu*, p. 268.

41. Yoshiwara Ken'ichirō, *Edo no jōhōya* (Nihon Hōsō Shuppan Kyōkai, 1978), p. 205.

42. Ibid., p. 207.

lowed orders to sell parched rice cheaply, but this measure was not univer-
sally praised. A graffito found posted on its wall used puns to criticize the
policy's mean-spirited intent: "Here is the city saving association [*machi
kaisho*]/mistakes they made [*machi gaisho*] in their desire to save the people:
wanting money, they sold five *go* [of rice] for one hundred [*mon* of silver]."[43]
Later that year, the shogunate commended merchants who had distributed
rice to the poor. These merchants had started their charity drives in 1860,
partly out of sympathy for the poor but partly out of fear of the consequences if they failed to help them. At the end of 1865, the shogunate
reiterated its permission for free trade in rice and distributed relief rice
itself.[44] Concern about what the poor might do had obviously exercised the
merchants and the state long before the riot.

By 1866 a wide variety of groups were making threats against mercantile
capital and defying the power of the state to stop them. Shortages arising
from the conflict between the shogunate and dissidents in Chōshū domain
continued to push prices higher, and merchants appeared to be hoarding
rice in hopes of making even greater profits. In the Second Month an inflammatory poster appeared on the wall of a rice warehouse in Kobune-chō:

> The price of rice has gotten really high, and if it goes higher, the entire
> city undoubtedly will be rocked by a riot. The people pushing up prices
> are to be investigated and condemned to death immediately. There are
> rumors that some people are hoarding rice. They will be punished in the
> same way. We volunteer our hearts and lives to carry out the retribution
> of heaven in order to save the people.
> [Signed] The righteous of the realm[45]

By calling for heavenly retribution and asserting their own righteousness,
the people who wrote this poster claimed legitimacy for their proposed
course of action, an assertion of virtue that denied the state's monopoly on
violence. The signature suggests that it was written by imperial loyalists,
perhaps even Chōshū sympathizers. Certainly it was in the shogunate's
interest to brand these posters the work of agents provocateurs, but they
also imply that low-ranking samurai and the urban poor had common interests.

Low-ranking samurai and the urban poor may have had similar problems, but they did not always embrace a common perception of proper
remedies. Inflammatory posters soon threatened the members of the ruling
class responsible for preserving law and order. In the Fourth Month another
poster found in three places between Gofuku-chō and Asakusa gave exact
instructions for the riot and designated specific targets:

43. Ibid., p. 208. See also Minami Kazuo, *Ishin zen'ya no Edo shomin* (Kyōikusha, 1980),
p. 150.
44. Yoshiwara, *Edo no jōhōya*, pp. 208–9; Minami, *Bakumatsu*, pp. 270–71.
45. Minami, *Bakumatsu*, p. 271.

On the fifth night of the Fifth Month, everyone must come to the place listed below carrying mallets, fire axes, and six-foot poles. If anyone mingles with us who appears to be a samurai or who carries even one sword, he will be killed as soon as he is spotted. . . . We will smash up all the government purveyors, then all those who deal in foreign goods . . . and after that we will treat all the houses of the patrolmen [dōshin] at Hatchōbori the same way.

Just a day later, another poster bluntly castigated the policemen:

FROM ONE HUNDRED RIGHTEOUS TOWNSPEOPLE:

The policemen currently making emergency patrols are exceedingly corrupt. Without any investigation they arrest the townspeople and severely interrogate them, they demand excessive bribes, and they extort money by tying people up in ropes. This has nothing to do with the administration of the city, and henceforth they will be punished.[46]

These posters promised attacks not merely on the traditional enemies of the poor, the privileged merchants, but also on those who made profits from foreign trade and even the lowest-ranking government servants. In plain and angry language that contrasted sharply to the flowery language employed by "the righteous of the realm," these posters explicitly rejected samurai interference on either side.

The 1866 riot in the Fifth Month did less property damage than the one in 1787 (only 226 stores were attacked), but it lasted longer. With the exception of Yotsuya, Kanda, and a few other places mentioned in 1787 records, the riots erupted in the suburbs, well away from the traditional city center. Perhaps in Nihonbashi the poor had received allowances from wealthier neighbors and suffered stricter supervision by the shogun's officials. Again merchants who had reputations for providing charity escaped damage, as did those willing to be generous when confronted by the crowd. In addition to the rice stores, many pawnshops, saké shops, and offices of merchants who had become wealthy from foreign trade suffered the most. According to the diary of one neighborhood chief, the rioters were samurai, townsmen, and servants, but equally noteworthy was the presence of large numbers of teenagers, and some boys as young as twelve. One record mentioned that a priest and a youth with an unshaven forehead joined the crowd; another reported a youth of fifteen or so who flew over the rooftops in a manner that recalled the reports of the 1787 riot.[47]

The measures taken to suppress the riot were even less effective than those deployed in 1787. When children attacked one store, spectators urged them on while the patrolmen remained hidden in their guardhouse, like the watchman in the Kurosawa film *Yōjimbō*. Four days after the riot began,

46. Ibid., p. 272.
47. Ibid., pp. 214, 280.

the city magistrates issued a directive forbidding people to gather to watch the rioters. One patrol grabbed some spectators, but a troop of samurai who happened by criticized them for not arresting the rioters instead. In the ensuing melee, one patrolman was killed. According to a satirical verse: "Not one rioter has yet been arrested; only the spectators get caught."[48] The next day the shogunate stationed troops at four places in the city, and the head priest at Kan'eiji in Ueno distributed over 1,500 *ryō* in gold coins to the poor. A sign hung outside the gate at one city magistrate's office compound read: "This government is all sold out." Another claimed: "Owing to high prices, goods are in short supply, and able officials are all sold out."[49]

The increase in literacy in the nineteenth century was matched by the breakdown of state control over the written word, so that by the 1860s the unspeakable was spoken, the unnameable named. One broadsheet represented the riot as a battle between the lord of greed and the poor, with the poor marching forward pulling a cart filled with bales of rice. It claimed that an evil general had tormented the city by driving prices so high that no matter how hard the poor worked, they had nothing to eat, a moral judgment that clearly placed virtue on the side of the rioters.[50] Other pictures were even more graphic, showing the rioters tearing up roofs, pulling down curtains, opening drawers to spill their contents in the street, and ripping open bales of rice. The owners cringed and threw up their hands in dismay while outside beggars scraped up the rice to carry it off. Scenes only alluded to 1787 were now clearly pictured.

The contrast between the representations of the 1787 and 1866 riots suggests a weakening of the coercive power of the state to censor forbidden subjects. In the allegory of the militant turtles, the author used the "cheerful vulgarity" of the powerless as a weapon against the pretense and hypocrisy of the powerful, a mockery of conventional behavior also exposed in the parody.[51] In both cases the dismal official word was transformed into the laughter of the folk. This representation of commoners' actions allowed the authors, in many cases low-ranking samurai, to insulate their perception of the riot from any assessment of its significance. They simply stood back and joined in the laughter. On another level, allegory and parody constituted appropriate means for representation because no publisher would have dared issue a realistic depiction of the riot in the 1780s. The illustrations of 1866 were much more serious. Stripped of any metaphorical mask, the enthusiasm of the crowd burst forth in all its immediacy. It had become news, a project that flattened out symbolic undertones to make the representation itself apparently transparent. The state's control over the written

48. Minami, *Ishin zen'ya*, p. 156.
49. Minami, *Bakumatsu*, p. 284; idem, *Ishin zen'ya*, p. 157.
50. Nishimaki Kōsaburō, comp., *Kawaraban shinbun: Edo Meiji sanbyaku jiken 2: Kurofune raikō kara Toba Fushimi no tatakai*, Taiyō collection 2 (Heibonsha, 1978), p. 133.
51. Stallybrass and White, *Politics and Poetics*, p. 18.

Edo riots at the end of the Tokugawa period. Source: Hasegawa Shinzō, *Jikken garoku.*

word had so far declined that the dissemination of information for its own sake had become possible.[52]

Even after the riot, contention between the state and the commoners continued to plague the city. In the Eighth Month the shogunate made a survey of the destitute, dividing them into three grades and promising relief only to the very lowest. The other two grades, constituting some 80 percent of the poor, remained unaided and unhappy. A poster found on the gate at the Kanda Myōjin shrine on the thirteenth day of that month announced that this was "an evil policy designed by disloyal, unrighteous, and wicked officials."[53] According to one report, an impoverished metalworker said that "although everyone in the quarter wants to buy the cheap relief rice, only four or five families are allowed to do so. Since it is well known that we are really poor, this policy must have been made by the devil."[54]

The sickly Iemochi died late in the Eighth Month at the age of twenty-one, and the shogunate scheduled his funeral rites for the next month. In accordance with traditional practice, the shogunate directed the townspeople to observe public silence until the completion of the rites on the twenty-third. Instead, the poor set up camps in temple precincts as bases from which they launched marches through the surrounding neighborhoods to requisition food to be cooked and distributed to their families. To the beat of drums and with flags and streamers announcing "the sufferers of such-and-such residential quarter" or "the destitute of such-and-such a neighborhood," they thronged before the houses of the rich clamoring for alms. Some were so desperate that they even approached the daimyo. One group shouted at some Americans: "We are suffering hardships because trade with the barbarians has forced the prices of commodities to rise." Women and children threw stones to chase the foreigners down the street.[55] The shogunate did nothing, even to enforce its own ban on noise.

Inflammatory posters helped maintain the atmosphere of unrest. On the seventeenth, one broadsheet written almost entirely in the Japanese syllabary accused the merchant Surugaya San'emon of hoarding rice: "He is so greedy that he has given not one *mon* in alms, and he is the most outrageous person in the world because he locked up his rice and pretends he has none."[56] The next day a poster criticized by name a commissioner of finance (*kanjō bugyō*):

Among the government officials are many bad people. Oguri Kōzuke no Suke and his colleagues think it is fine that prices rise. . . . Since we have

52. In an important article, Miyachi Masato calls attention to the tremendous increase in the diffusion of political information in the 1860s and its contribution to the creation of a national identity: "Fusetsudome kara mita bakumatsu shakai no tokushitsu: Kōron sekai no tanshōteki: seiritsu," *Shisō* 831 (September 1993), pp. 4–26.
53. Yoshiwara, *Edo no jōhōya*, p. 217.
54. Minami, *Ishin zen'ya*, p. 160.
55. Minami, *Bakumatsu*, p. 297; idem, *Ishin zen'ya*, p. 166.
56. Minami, *Bakumatsu*, p. 289.

no other way to save our lives, we are . . . going to attack the Oguri
mansion in Surugadai. Then we will kill his evil henchmen, save all the
people from disaster, dispel our rage, and make the name of the Edokko
[children of Edo] known throughout Japan. If anyone hides, may he be
visited by the punishment of heaven.[57]

Like the earlier posters promising vengeance against the shogunate's patrolmen, this one focused the commoners' wrath on the ruling class, but a
commissioner of finance was a much more important official. Calls for his
head would be like demanding death for the secretary of the treasury.

The winter of 1866 brought desolation, starvation, and relative quiet to
the streets of Edo, but the criticism of government officials continued.
"When we heard the directives in previous years, prices fell, but when the
authorities lie, the world will collapse."[58] By 1867 the shogunate had decided to withdraw the expeditionary forces sent against Chōshū. One parody pointed to the power vacuum sensed by the populace:

The judges for the spring of 1867:

The Emperor:	There is no sign from the emperor's palace.
Public Authority:	The shogun has no power.
Great Councilor:	There is no one to be great councilor.
Senior Councilor:	The senior councilors have no perseverance.
Benevolence:	Benevolence has no heart.
The Daimyo:	The daimyo have no money.[59]

Regardless of whether the commoners saw this ditty in satirical terms, and
regardless of whether they had any alternative to propose, this parody
exposed the moral, financial, and coercive bankruptcy of the state.

In his study of early nineteenth-century English country tunes and the
peasant folk songs of Vietnam from the 1920s and 1930s, James C. Scott has
argued that songs often give the oppressed an outlet for their frustrations. In
the absence of more obvious signs of rebellion, a mockery of deference in
one's behavior and the creation of divergent values in jokes and songs
signify a symbolic withdrawal from elite values in the commoner population. The more bitter the song and the darker the humor, the more alienated
the singer from the ruler.[60] Japanese commoners too mocked customs of
deference and made jokes about officials, but what they criticized was the
officials' hypocrisy, not the basic values that both professed to respect.

The commoners' disaffection worried the state. It is debatable whether

57. Ibid., p. 296.
58. Ibid., p. 297.
59. Yoshiwara, *Edo no jōhōya*, p. 221. For an example of songs of parody in a regional
castle town, see James L. McClain, "Failed Expectations: Kaga Domain on the Eve of the
Meiji Restoration," *Journal of Japanese Studies* 14:2 (1988), pp. 426–27.
60. James C. Scott, *The Moral Economy of the Peasant: Rebellion and Subsistence in Southeast
Asia* (New Haven: Yale University Press, 1976), pp. 234–39.

the riots and political commentary of 1866 exerted a decisive influence on the flow of events leading to the Meiji Restoration, but surely they should not be ignored. Katsu Kaishū wrote to Matsudaira Yoshinaga: "It is difficult to know when the lower classes will rise, but it appears that they become more discontented daily. This is really frightening." The lord of Nagoya warned that the expedition against Chōshū was impossible given the extreme prices for food, the natural disasters evident everywhere, and the sight of domestic unrest even at the shogun's knees. As Hara Heizō and Tōyama Shigeki have pointed out, one reason for the lack of major warfare between shogunate and imperial forces was the fear not only of foreign intervention but of domestic turmoil.[61]

CONCLUSIONS

A comparison of the three Edo riots provides one perspective on how the city changed. The 1733 riot exposed the strains produced by mercantile capitalism unhelpfully and imperfectly regulated by an absolutist state. Compounded by natural disasters, these strains also played a key role in 1787. By then, however, the spread of literacy and a crisis of political leadership threatened the state's control over the dissemination of information. This weakening of state power, however, should not be seen as linear, continuous, or smooth.[62] After 1787 the shogunate briefly reasserted its censorship of politically sensitive materials, and it even managed to reform its coercive control over Edo with enough success to prevent any riots during the 1830s, a decade otherwise famous for social turmoil. By 1866, however, it had become obvious that the state's regulation of the economy made both less effective in dealing with the foreign intrusion. The failure of the state apparatus was nowhere more visible than in its inability to suppress unrest or to channel the flow of information.

The three riots can be studied not only in terms of action as texts but also as the occasions for textual representations of commoners' views of their relations with the state. In both 1733 and 1787 this relationship was contested with no noticeable politically transformative effects, but in 1866, when antagonisms had sharpened, the riots became part of a broader struggle that had actual and symbolic dimensions. There is a difference, in other words, between castigating officials as useless or corrupt and announcing that the state is bankrupt. During the 1787 riot, the subordinate classes became the objects of a gaze that constituted itself as "respectable and superior by substituting observation for participation";[63] that is, the way intellectuals talked about the crowd buried its transgressions against

61. This point and the Katsu quote can be found in Hara and Tōyama, "Edo jidai," p. 32.
62. Charles Tilly makes this point in reverse for the growth of state power in early modern France: *Contentious French*, p. 6.
63. Stallybrass and White, *Politics and Poetics*, p. 42.

authority under the rhetoric of a morality play. By 1866, voices that spoke for the crowd and voices that spoke to the crowd exposed the contingent, particular basis of state power.

Like Paris, Edo lived under what Kaplan has called the tyranny of grain. Bottlenecks in the distribution system caused either by state policy or by the excesses of mercantile capitalism easily magnified the effect of crop failures on the supply of basic foodstuffs. Yet the two cities were also different. Whereas in France the purpose of riots was to seize grain, in Japan the intent was to shame and punish the wrongdoers—the theft of property was expressly forbidden. Whereas women were the "conventional agents of legitimate subsistence insurgency" in France, in Japan they usually remained on the sidelines.[64] They commented on the action, but they did not participate. The shogun and his officials lavished much lively concern on Edo, whereas the French king mistrusted Paris and kept his distance. To the end of the Tokugawa period, the shogunate insisted that at least some of its taxes be paid in rice to be stored in the city, and the reforms launched by Matsudaira Sadanobu included measures to protect the urban population against future shortages; such measures were notably lacking in Paris. It is small wonder, then, that Edo saw many fewer contentious gatherings than did Paris.

64. Steven Laurence Kaplan, "Provisioning Paris: The Crisis of 1738–1741," chap. 8 in this volume; Anne Walthall, "Devoted Wives/Unruly Women: Invisible Presence in the History of Japanese Social Protest," *Signs: Journal of Women in Culture and Society* 20:1 (Autumn 1994), pp. 106–36.

18

State Formation and Contention in Japan and France

Eiko Ikegami and Charles Tilly

In his masterly, prophetic *City in History*, Lewis Mumford laid out a grand scheme for the analysis of any city, anywhere. The scheme addressed a question that combined morality, politics, and sociology: Can urban growth continue indefinitely without destroying human existence? Mumford spoke—nay, intoned—vivid, angry answers. "If we would lay a new foundation for urban life," he wrote,

> we must understand the historic nature of the city, and distinguish between its original functions, those that have emerged from it, and those that may still be called forth. Without a long running start in history, we shall not have the momentum needed, in our own consciousness, to take a sufficiently bold leap into the future; for a large part of our present plans, not least many that pride themselves on being "advanced" or "progressive," are dreary mechanical caricatures of the urban and regional forms that are now potentially within our grasp.

Mumford went on to strike memorable metonymies: the masculine spear for hunting bands, the feminine container for Neolithic villages, their union for the first cities. "The city, then," he declared, "if I interpret its origins correctly, was the chief fruit of the union between neolithic and a more archaic paleolithic culture."[1]

After abandoning his gendered metaphors, Mumford pursued their logic through his grand panorama of Western urban history. Two dimensions defined Mumford's scheme: the expansion of productive means and the concentration of political power. Below a threshold combining minimum levels of production and power, only villages and bands existed; an urbane thinker such as Mumford could find no place there for his way of life.

---

1. Lewis Mumford, *The City in History: Its Origins, Its Transformations, and Its Prospects* (New York: Harcourt, Brace & World, 1961), pp. 3, 27.

Beyond some maximum combination of production and force, bread, circuses, and conquest spelled the end of civilized existence. Between those limits, an excessive emphasis on force created the vainglory of the Baroque City, an excessive emphasis on production, the all too human filth of a Coketown. A modest balance between production and political power, according to Mumford, caused the small-scale humanity of the classical polis and of the medieval city. Since Mumford never quite explicated his analytic argument, he did not spell out its implications for the formation of states. Most of the time, he treated forms of rule as outgrowths of the prevailing technology, especially the technology of war. But the logic of his analysis clearly pointed to alternate trajectories of state formation, depending on the prevailing combination of production and power.

In a Mumfordian mood, at a Mumfordian scale, let us undertake a comparison of collective action in Edo (Japan's, and perhaps the world's, largest city) and Paris (France's dominant metropolis) during the seventeenth and eighteenth centuries. More precisely, our analysis concerns popular contention: the ways in which ordinary people made discontinuous claims—demands, attacks, petitions, expressions of support, and so forth—on other people, including authorities. How and why did French and Japanese patterns of contention vary and change? In particular, how did transformations of the two states affect popular contention?

Let us formulate an argument, more or less Mumfordian, on the basis of European experience over the long run. We can see later whether the argument helps make sense of Japanese experience. We will argue that:

1. Cities grow up chiefly as repositories, users, and distributors of concentrated capital, both commercial and industrial.
2. States grow up chiefly as repositories and users of concentrated coercive means, especially in the form of organized armed force.
3. The character of states varies systematically as a function of (a) the relative predominance of concentrated capital and of concentrated coercion in their territories and (b) the absolute scales of capital and coercion.
4. Relations between holders of state power (rulers, for short) and manipulators of capital (capitalists, for short) vary from city to city and within the same city as a function of the relative predominance of capital and coercion in the city at a particular point in time.
5. Until the last century or so, the expansion of state power almost anywhere in the world entailed, and resulted from, the accumulation of greater and greater coercive means, especially in the form of war and preparation for war.
6. Any ruler accumulating coercive means has two basic alternatives:
    a. Seize or coopt existing means of coercion by such devices as drawing armed vassals into state service. This alternative, feasible only where concentrations of coercion in such forms as private armies already exist, tends to create organizationally bulky states with extensive patrimonialism and significant limits to centralization.

b. Draw revenues from the subject population, its goods, or its commerce, and convert those revenues into the means of war. Pursued in a coercion-rich environment, this alternative tends to generate extensive resistance on the part of magnates and populace alike. If successful, it tends to create a centralized bureaucratic state. Pursued in a capital-rich environment, this alternative tends to produce an organizationally flexible state in which capitalists wield great power.

7. The forms and intensities of popular collective action depend on the process of state formation the ruler chooses. To the extent that a ruler pursues a fiscal (rather than a coercion-seizing) strategy for the expansion of military power, popular struggle takes the form of resistance to taxation and of attempts to withhold valued goods, especially food, from the national market.

So, at least, we argue. We will explore the argument's application to seventeenth- and eighteenth-century Edo and Paris. The two cities illustrate different combinations of coercion and capital in the creation of national armed force, and consequently—if the argument is correct—different patterns of popular struggle.

CAPITAL AND COERCION

Let us elaborate the argument before moving on to Edo and Paris, beginning with some critical terms. We should interpret *capital* generously, including any tangible mobile resources and enforceable claims on such resources. Capitalists, then, are people who specialize in the accumulation, purchase, and sale of capital. *Coercion* includes all concerted application, threatened or actual, of action that commonly causes loss or damage to the persons or possessions of individuals or groups who are aware of both the action and the potential damage. (The cumbersome definition excludes inadvertent, indirect, and covert damage.) The means of coercion center on armed force, but extend to facilities for incarceration, expropriation, humiliation, and publication of threats.

Different combinations of capital and coercion create differing social relations among cities and within cities. As a first approximation, we can think of capital and coercion as producing analytically separable sets of connections among cities, often the very same cities; although the idea sounds odd, it is no stranger than the recognition that a set of friends who do many things together form one configuration when they engage in athletic activity and quite another when they engage in gossip. On the side of coercion, we can define a hierarchy and a set of connections with respect to state power, in which command of force cascades downward from a seat of the national state. On the side of capital, we posit a hierarchy and set of connections with respect to trade and wealth, in which goods, services, and money flow up and down in relations of unequal resources.

Cities often occupy disparate positions in the two hierarchies: a great commercial center is not always a major locus of state power, and vice versa. Within such cities, broadly speaking, relative position within the two hierarchies affects the relative power of capitalists and state officials. In the fortress towns of uncommercialized regions, agents of the state predominate. In commercial metropolises that do not happen also to be regional capitals, merchants overshadow state officials. In a city that occupies equally high (or low) positions in both hierarchies, capitalists and agents of the state confront each other on more equal terms. When a city's relative position is changing in either direction—through quick commercialization, for example, or a rapid expansion of state power—struggle intensifies as the less favored party and its allies seek to maintain their position and the more favored party tries to take advantage of its newfound strength. Thus interactions between capital and coercion affect both the quantity and the quality of local struggles.

Cities and states (that is, capital and coercion) cross dramatically in the effort to build the means of war. War is the costliest and most wasteful activity humans ever carry on. War also creates states.[2] The warmaking ruler's problem is straightforward: to extract the means of war from a limited territory, population, and set of resources, when the people involved are reluctant to yield the necessary resources.[3] All rulers solve the problem, to the extent that they do, through some combination of two strategies: seizure of existing coercive means, and taxation and borrowing to cover the cost of creating or purchasing coercive means. The combination of strategies that actually works depends on the social environment. Where some concentration of coercive means in the form of militias, private armies, smaller kingdoms, and the like has not already been built up, rulers have nothing to coopt; and where the economy is not relatively commercialized and capital already somewhat concentrated, attempts to tax and borrow produce meager returns.

Even where it is feasible, each strategy generates its own political problems. A ruler who seizes existing coercive means by such steps as incorporating private armies into national forces receives willy-nilly the prior organization and leadership of those means; in general, he must concede substantial power and autonomy to warlords, regional magnates, and the like. The continued existence of such powerholders sets severe limits to the central state's expansion and offers a basis for resistance and rebellion against the ruler's demands. Even as Tokugawa shoguns drew the daimyo into their net, they found they had fished whales they could not maneuver at will. The fiscal strategy, however, also entails built-in costs: it necessarily lends power to those who possess and manage money, and they soon become indispensable for credit, the organization of extraction, the production of military goods, and the purchase of those goods for national armed forces.

2. Charles Tilly, *Coercion, Capital, and European States* (Oxford: Basil Blackwell, 1990).
3. Margaret Levi, *Of Rule and Revenue* (Berkeley: University of California Press, 1988).

At the extremes, the coercion-intensive cooptative strategy produces massive landlord-run state bureaucracies like that of Russia, while the capital-intensive fiscal strategy produces piratical merchant-led cartels like that of Genoa. In between the two extremes runs a path of state formation through capitalized coercion: the creation, often unwitting, of a substantial centralized state through the checking of capital by means of coercion, and the ringing of the masters of coercion with capital. Within Europe, Britain and France represent different variants of that path. These alternative paths of state formation have strong implications for popular collective action, especially in the form of uprisings, resistance movements, and other forms of open, large-scale contention. Because collective action is costly and risky, most people do not act together on their common interests most of the time. Popular collective action becomes more likely (1) where people who share an interest already have strong links through day-to-day social organization such as work or kinship, (2) where action by visible outsiders manifestly threatens shared identity or even survival, (3) where political entrepreneurs have effectively organized a significant part of the interest-sharing population, and (4) where protective coalitions with other groups reduce the risk of acting together.

Different paths of state formation cause different combinations of these conditions to prevail at different times. To the extent, for example, that rulers pursue a fiscal strategy for the expansion of military power—especially in conditions of weak commercialization—popular struggle takes the form of resistance to taxation and of attempts to withhold valued goods, especially food, from the national market. The less commercial the economy is, the more frequently the goods in question will already be committed to local ends, and the more intense the resistance to their taxation, requisitioning, or forced marketing will be.

State formation is by no means the only process that generates popular collective action. In the European experience, the creation of capitalist social relations through such means as enclosure of common land incited at least as much resistance as the imposition of state power. In Tokugawa Japan, not only heightened taxation but also protoindustrialization and fluctuations in the food supply shaped major forms of popular struggle.[4] Nor did all confrontations between state and citizens result from the expansion of state power; authorities often acted on behalf of other interests—merchants, landlords, churchmen, and others. Nevertheless, when we compare the Japanese and French experiences, it is useful to single out state formation and its influence on popular collective action. In both places, the two centuries before 1800 saw major changes in state power that strongly affected the interests of ordinary people. Japanese and French changes in state organization differed distinctively. They should therefore, in principle, have produced characteristically different patterns of contention. That is our problem: Did they?

4. James W. White, "State Growth and Popular Protest in Tokugawa Japan," *Journal of Japanese Studies* 14:1 (1988), pp. 1–25.

CITIES AND STATES IN FRANCE AND JAPAN

When Tokugawa Ieyasu became lord of the Kantō plain in 1590, Edo stood only at the sixth level of Japanese towns—an intermediate marketing center with fewer than 3,000 residents and no significant administrative functions. Within a few decades the city housed some 100,000 people and bade fair to become the national capital in fact if not in name. By 1700 it approached 1 million inhabitants, stood at the peak of one of Asia's two greatest urban hierarchies, and could well have been the world's largest city.[5] During the eighteenth century, Edo's population leveled off at something more than 1.2 million. Paris began the same period with about 220,000 residents, arrived at 500,000 toward 1700, and then grew slowly to about 640,000 by 1794, only to fall to about 580,000 in 1806 as the revolutionary and imperial wars took their toll.[6]

During the later eighteenth century, France's urban hierarchy resembled Japan's, but France had distinctly more market centers and fewer very large cities. Speaking of his levels 3 to 5 (from low-level administrative centers with 3,000 to 10,000 inhabitants to elevated administrative centers and major ports with 30,000 to 300,000 inhabitants), Gilbert Rozman remarks:

> Inhabited by roughly three-quarters as many persons as Japan, France had almost precisely three-quarters as many cities at each of these levels. In contrast, at levels 1 and 2 France was far behind, with fewer than one-third the population of Edo, Osaka, and Kyoto. This deficit was in large part compensated for by the fact that French level-3 cities were more populous than Japanese counterparts and France had many more level-6 central places. Despite its smaller population, France had about 400 more central places than Japan.[7]

The contrast suggests a more extensively commercialized economy in France than in Japan, an even greater geographic concentration of governmental power in Japan than in France.

Despite the reputation of seventeenth-century France as the citadel of absolutism, more detailed histories seem to confirm the contrast. In France an extensive commercial network grew up long before the national state laid down anything like a regular administrative grid. The administrative regularization appeared especially with the imposition of resident intendants and their subordinates under Mazarin and Colbert; from that time onward, the top-down hierarchy only grew. By disarming the civilian population,

5. Gilbert Rozman, *Urban Networks in Ch'ing China and Tokugawa Japan* (Princeton: Princeton University Press, 1973), pp. 286–88.

6. Jan de Vries, *European Urbanization, 1500–1800* (Cambridge: Harvard University Press, 1984), p. 275; Bernard Lepetit, *Les villes dans la France moderne (1740–1840)* (Paris: Albin Michel, 1988), p. 450.

7. Gilbert Rozman, *Urban Networks in Russia, 1750–1800, and Premodern Periodization* (Princeton: Princeton University Press, 1976), pp. 237–38.

limiting private violence, destroying private fortresses and armies, encouraging noble families to reside in cities, and drawing new nobles disproportionately from city-dwelling mercantile families, seventeenth-century kings extended the network of top-down control. Louis XIV's Versailles embodied that trend. His rapid expansion of the state's warmaking capacity, furthermore, multiplied governmental agents, even if many of them retained considerable independence as a result of having purchased or leased their offices by means of substantial cash advances to the crown. After a turbulent period in which militias, provisional committees, and roving representatives of the central government played significant parts, the Revolution spun a web of administrative centers over all of France. Evidence assembled by Bernard Lepetit supports the analytic separation between two hierarchies among the same French cities. Lepetit's factor analysis of information concerning the 215 largest cities in 1780 distinguishes the clusters of variables shown in Table 18.1.

The variables in each of these clusters vary together. Cities that have their own newspapers are also much more likely to have their own *parlement* and university, and cities that have direct access to the sea (marine navigation) are also much more likely to have regularly scheduled transport both within the city and from the city to Paris. However, the relationship between having a newspaper and having marine navigation is significantly weaker, and the presence of a merchants' consulate, a royal court, or a high level of income from the octroi (city customs levy) is tied more or less equally to the administrative and mercantile variables.

If the summary we offered earlier is correct, we should expect to find that between 1600 and 1800 (a) relationships within each cluster, and especially the administrative cluster, grew stronger; (b) relations between population size and variables in the administrative cluster likewise grew stronger; (c) relations between population size and variables in the mercantile cluster grew weaker; (d) relations between variables in the two clusters grew weaker. So far no one, not even Lepetit, has amassed the evidence required to test these hypotheses. Pending collection of the essential evidence, they

TABLE 18.1
Variables characteristic of French administrative and mercantile centers, 1780

Administrative center	Mercantile center	Both types of city
Intendant	Postal service	Merchants' consulate
Bishopric	Public transport	Level of octroi
Bureau de la Ferme Générale	Chamber of Commerce	Chambre des Comptes,
Collège	Marine navigation	Cour des Aides
University	Connections with Paris	
Parlement		
Local press		

SOURCE: Bernard Lepetit, *Les villes dans la France moderne (1740–1840)* (Paris: Albin Michel, 1988), p. 151. Each variable represents either presence/absence or a simple three-step measure of intensity, weighted for the city's size.

seem reasonable guesses about the French urban system's changing character.

Medieval Japan and France had much in common. Both had a decentralized power structure, a system of vassalage, and a feudal mode of production. They diverged radically, however, with respect to the position of cities. With few exceptions (such as Sakai at a brief moment in the sixteenth century), Japanese medieval cities did not achieve an impressive degree of autonomy. But Japan's corporately structured villages were much more autonomous, and often successfully resisted feudal exploitation. Japan entered the seventeenth century with a considerably thinner commercial network than France's. Under Tokugawa control, it experienced impressive administrative concentration. Political centralization, in turn, stimulated further commercialization of the economy, as a national-scale market economy developed. This concentration of political power during the formation of the Tokugawa state prompted a remarkable growth of cities, especially Edo. Tokugawa Japan apparently followed a much more "coercion-intensive" path than did contemporary France. But the Tokugawa state cannot be understood only in terms of centralization. Tokugawa state formation adopted a distinctive way of consolidating landlord power; this trajectory affected the relationship between coercion and capital thereafter.

THE TOKUGAWA STATE

Battles among warlords racked Japan from the outbreak of the Ōnin War in 1467 to the last great battle of the Osaka summer campaign in 1615. The decisive victories of the Tokugawa family and its allied daimyo in these wars resulted in the establishment of the Tokugawa shogunate. Behind the glorious battles among warlords was a far-reaching social reorganization that suppressed numerous popular contentious movements. This process overcame the defensive capacities of villages and religious institutions; it also demilitarized the nonsamurai population. Tokugawa state formation stands as the world's classic case of statemaking through the monopolization of violence.[8]

A student of Western history might expect that after such decisive military victories, the Tokugawa regime would have established a strong centralized political system, restricted the daimyo's influence, and directly controlled villages throughout the country. History, however, did not unfold that way. The Tokugawa regime did develop a much more sophisticated and centralized apparatus than its predecessors. But that is just one side of the story. The Tokugawa shogunate did not create such institutions as a national standing army, national taxation, and a centralized police system to undertake direct surveillance of individuals. The strength and durability of the

---

8. Fujiki Hisashi, *Toyotomi heiwarei to sengoku shakai* (Tōkyō Daigaku Shuppankai, 1985); Takagi Shōsaku, " 'Hideyoshi no heiwa' to bushi no henshitsu," *Shisō* 721 (1984), pp. 1–19.

Tokugawa system owed much to its complex, integrated, yet decentralized power structure, which was flexible enough to absorb various levels of contention without causing any threat to the central government.[9]

The Tokugawa state reorganized three relationships: (1) between the central authority (the shogunate) and regional powerholders (daimyo); (2) between the military powerholders (i.e., the shogun and the daimyo) and their respective samurai vassals; and (3) between villages and samurai authorities. On every level the independence enjoyed by subordinates during the medieval period diminished under Tokugawa rule. The Tokugawa regime successfully established its claim to act in the name of *kōgi*, public authority, thus elevating itself above lesser political powers. Daimyo were no longer equal allies or enemies of the Tokugawa family, but became subjects under Tokugawa control. The compulsory alternate residence system (*sankin kōtai*), plus frequent expropriation and relocation of daimyo domains in the early Tokugawa period, intimidated the regional lords and effectively reduced the daimyo's independence, transforming them from autonomous warlords to a warrior elite who lived in Edo every other year. Indeed, the daimyo became so convinced of the shogunate's military might that they made no attempt to challenge the Tokugawa hegemony until the very end of the period.

The story, however, has another side. Within the Tokugawa system, daimyo retained considerable freedom to govern the subjects of their own domains. The shogunate never established a standard, centralized fiscal system for the entire country, and daimyo never paid taxes to the shogun. Taxes from the shogunate's own territorial holdings financed the central government. Daimyo also retained their own independent judicial systems, as well as administrative control over their samurai subordinates. When the situation could not be controlled by a single daimyo's power, or a daimyo's policy contravened the shogunate's interest, the central government intervened.

As for relations between samurai and the state, during the medieval period samurai and their bands of armed followers had been relatively independent, self-armed mounted warriors; under the Tokugawa regime they lost much of their proud autonomy and found themselves incorporated into the state system. The state forced them to live in castle towns, cut off from direct control over their land. Instead, the samurai received heritable stipends and engaged in various administrative jobs under the daimyo or shogunate government. As a result, during the Tokugawa period an interesting division of residence arose: those who were armed (the ruling samurai class) lived in cities, and unarmed farmers populated villages.

When it came to relations between the samurai and villagers, the so-called self-governing villages (*sōson*) of the medieval period had been much more independent and self-armed. Medieval villages paid taxes collectively

9. Eiko Ikegami, *The Taming of the Samurai: Honor, Individuality, and Statemaking in Japan* (forthcoming, Harvard University Press).

to their lords. Armed villages led by samurai-farmers often formed contentious movements that constituted the most serious threat to ruling feudal
authorities. The Tokugawa system incorporated villages much more firmly
into the state and eliminated their self-defense forces. Still, villagers themselves, not samurai officials, established the traditions and social context in
which peasants lived out their daily lives. Moreover, since villages were
collectively responsible for paying taxes, they had, by extension, bargaining
power with samurai authorities.

STATE AND CAPITAL IN TOKUGAWA JAPAN

The Tokugawa political system supported ongoing expansion of a large-scale
market economy and long-distance commodity exchange. The extensive
economic development of the sixteenth and seventeenth centuries, a result
of the expansion of arable land, produced a surplus in villages.[10] The structure of the Tokugawa-daimyo state system also promoted the formation of a
national market. The shogun's and daimyo's finances depended on tax revenue paid in rice, which they sold in the market to gain cash. Long distance
trade also grew with the expansion of the urban population in consumption
centers. By the late seventeenth century a national market economy flourished. Commercialization brought a lower relative price for rice and a higher
price for other commodities, a situation that adversely affected rice-
dependent daimyo finances. Daimyo started to borrow money from merchants in order to meet the growing expenses of urban life.

Nevertheless, no European absolutist state was more successful than the
Tokugawa in blocking increased bourgeois influence on the government.
How was this possible? In the relationship between capital and coercion in
Tokugawa Japan, three points stand out. First, the Tokugawa state emerged
as a garrison state at a time when the impulse of commerce was still weak;
by European standards, cities did not develop much independence. The
remarkable expansion of a commercial economy came only after the establishment of the Tokugawa state. To be sure, during the last stages of the
Warring States periods, when the scale of battle enlarged, some merchants
were able to provide warlords with weapons and other resources. But this
brings us to the second point. With the pacification introduced by the Tokugawa shoguns and the virtual withdrawal of Japan from international
trade, this generation of merchants lost the opportunity to grow further.
Because of the war's cessation, the shogunate and daimyo continued to
adapt the old system that defined the provision of arms as the responsibility
and obligation of every samurai, according to the stipend he received from
the lord. Thus the lords' peacetime military expenditures remained small. In
Europe, by contrast, after the monarchs achieved pacification within their

10. Ōishi Shinzaburō, *Edo jidai* (Chūō Kōronsha, 1977); Matsumoto Shirō, "Genroku
Kyōhō no seiji to keizai," in Matsumoto Shirō and Yamada Tadao, eds., *Genroku Kyōhō-ki no
seiji to shakai*, Kōza Nihon kinseishi 4 (Yūhikaku, 1980), pp. 1–35.

domains, they continued to wage international wars and compete with one another in the world market. In the process of continuing to build up a strong military-fiscal machine, the rulers of the European states provided opportunities for merchants to expand their incomes and other resources, and thus to expand their power in the political sphere. Had the warlords of sixteenth-century Japan carried their warfare into the seventeenth century, or had Japan been subject to the vagaries of a less protected geopolitical context that made isolationism less feasible, the relationship between the state and capital in early-modern Japan might have been very different. The contributions of businessmen to the fiscal growth necessary to sustain large-scale warfare, as well as their potential involvement in international trade, might well have empowered the Japanese merchant class and allowed it to intervene in the political process. In reality, however, without the opportunity to engage in the lucrative business of war, merchants were unable to break through the Tokugawa system of domination.

Third, Japan imposed a policy of strict status demarcation which segregated merchants from the political process. Sons of Japanese merchants, unlike their European counterparts, had little opportunity to trespass their status boundary through marriage, education, or the purchase of estates. Their inferior status was reinforced by the regulation of such symbolic means as dress codes and enforced humility in the presence of samurai officers. This does not mean, however, that the Tokugawa state repressed commercial activities. Rather, the Tokugawa state actually promoted the exchange of rice and goods on a large scale. Moreover, merchants were much freer than farmers to accumulate wealth. Individual samurai, furthermore, had no right to engage in commercial activity under Tokugawa rule. Samurai could not increase their economic edge by taking advantage of expanding capitalist development. The implementation of a strict status system avoided the creation of an entrenched class with both economic and political power.

As a consequence of top-down political pressure for revenues, eighteenth-century Japanese commercialization was almost comparable to that of France. But this commercialization occurred after state formation that had taken an extremely coercion-intensive path. The military and political origins of many cities, the virtual closing of Japan to international trade, the concentration of the samurai population in cities, and the segregation of the bourgeoisie from the political process all contributed to the construction of cities in which the administrative position prevailed over commercial activity. Edo represents the typical case of coercion's predominance in cities.

HYPOTHESES

Our earlier reasoning suggests that we should find significant differences in the collective actions of the common people of seventeenth- and eighteenth-century France and Japan, including those in the two countries' dominant cities, Paris and Edo. What should we expect? In principle, merchants should have had greater incentive and capacity to act against extensions of state power in France than in Japan, while the self-governing tradition of Japan's villages, with their social networks facilitating collective action, gave them an obvious advantage. Changes in the way peasants were taxed should have generated more popular resistance in Japan than in France. The pyramidal yet decentralized Japanese state system allowed the central government to avoid being the direct target of contention. Japanese peasant movements, according to this reasoning, would have had a serious disadvantage in mobilizing samurai and merchants, while French popular action would have had a greater potential to form alliances across state boundaries.

What of Paris and Edo themselves? We should likewise find some characteristic differences in popular collective action, attributable to the fact that the relative commercialization of France should have given merchants and other bourgeois of the capital greater power vis-à-vis royal officials than their Japanese counterparts had. We might reasonably expect Parisian merchants to bargain and resist royal demands more effectively, to be more readily available as patrons of popular demands and resistance, and yet also (as powerholders in their own right) to be more common objects of popular demands. With the movement of significant parts of the state apparatus and personnel to Versailles, we should detect a further strengthening of the merchants' and bourgeois' position in the city, and increasing difficulty in the royal officials' efforts to enforce the king's will without bourgeois collaboration. At the Revolution, however, we should notice some redressing of the balance, as the central organizations of a rapidly expanding state proliferated in the city itself.

Edo was the most politically constructed, top-down city of the Tokugawa regime. We might reasonably expect the merchants of Edo to have resisted the ruler's control less effectively than their Parisian counterparts. The large samurai population of Edo may have produced more effective control over the civil population. What could be expected from the subsequent development and rapid commercialization of the Tokugawa economy? Because of the continued predominance of coercion over capital in the political arena and the fact that the shogunate was not very successful in extracting taxes from the flourishing commercial sector, it is difficult to imagine that merchants could have directly and effectively opposed governmental demands. At the same time, with the expansion of the laboring population in increasingly commercialized Edo, the supply and price of food could present more powerful incentives for contention by and among the poorer classes.

Paris, 1600–1789

From a wide variety of archival materials, contemporary periodicals, and other publications, we have assembled a catalogue of "contentious gatherings" (CGs) that occurred in the Ile-de-France and four other French regions from 1600 to 1984.[11] A CG is an occasion on which a number of people other than government employees and officials—we used an estimated ten or more participants as a rule of thumb—gathered in a publicly accessible place and made claims that, if realized, would bear on the interests of at least one person outside their number. "Claims" run the range from direct attacks (verbal or physical) to humble petitions to expressions of support. CGs include almost all events for which observers used the current equivalents of such words as *riot, disturbance, demonstration, march,* and *movement,* plus a number of authorized assemblies and celebrations in the course of which someone made claims.

The catalogue of CGs has a strong bias toward events that somehow engaged royal authority; it greatly underrepresents conflicts in labor and commodity markets. Nevertheless, it captures the larger events in those categories, and provides a broad picture of change in the larger events over the two centuries that concern us. Let us adopt a fairly mechanical procedure in presenting the events: breaking up the two centuries into five forty-year periods, characterizing the CGs in each forty-year span, then providing more detail on one or two events in each period.

1600–1639

The period featured attacks on Protestants and peripheral events of noble-led rebellions, victory celebrations, acclamations of the king, processions, battles of youth groups, and duels or other combats between gentlemen in which their retinues joined. At the arrival of news (on Sunday, 26 September 1621) about the death of the (Catholic) duc de la Mayenne during the siege of (Protestant) Montauban, "the populace" attacked the carriages of Protestants, fought with city archers, broke through the guards at the Porte Saint-Antoine, stormed out to burn the Protestant church in suburban Charenton, sacked the house of the church's concierge, then returned to the central city four hundred strong, bearing an improvised white flag.[12]

1640–1679

In Paris the struggles of the Fronde formed the high point of contention. On 26 August 1648, for example, royal forces arrested Broussel, leader of the opposition in the Parlement of Paris opposition to royal demands for revenue to support France's expanded participation in the general European war of the time. People threw up barricades through much of the city and broke the doors and windows of houses whose owners refused to place themselves under arms for the popular cause. A pamphlet of the time reports that when the troops started to take Broussel away, "the people rose; increasing little by little as they followed the carriage and shouting in confusion that the guards were taking their liberator to jail, and that they would have to free

---

11. See Charles Tilly, *The Contentious French* (Cambridge: Belknap Press of Harvard University Press, 1986) for details; the bibliography contains a selected list of sources.
12. *Le Mercure François* 7, p. 851.

442   *Eiko Ikegami and Charles Tilly*

him."[13] The period also saw more attacks on Protestants, commemorative processions, public celebrations and mournings, deputations, presentations of petitions to the king, acclamations of royalty, resistance to the exactions of troops and tax collectors, seizures of prisoners from police, the throwing up of neighborhood barricades at rumors of threats to the Parlement, fights around the naming of parish priests, rentiers' assemblies, expulsions of tax collectors, assemblies to demand reduction of taxes, gatherings around public figures to demand succor or redress, and the sacking of the houses of unpopular figures. On 1 June 1645, in a typical conflict, residents of the faubourg Saint-Denis fought the efforts of salt-tax guards to search for illegal salt, so the king sent two hundred French guards and another two hundred Swiss guards to "break up the sedition, disperse the people, rescue the salt-tax officers and archers from the people's hands, seize and arrest those who are assembled and put them into the hands of the Lieutenant of the Grand Provost of France, whom His Majesty enjoins to execute them on the spot if they are involved in the sedition and resisting His Majesty's forces."[14]

1680–1719

Events of this period include church assemblies for Gallican rights, public celebrations, attacks on Protestants, Protestant resistance to forced conversions, secret Protestant assemblies, assaults on unpopular figures in the street, battles between rival student groups, brawls between soldiers and civilians, attempts to resist arrest and to free prisoners, resistance to tax collectors, attacks on food merchants, seizures of food and grain, struggles between smugglers and customs officers, and public assemblies to request abatement of taxes, protest hunting privileges, and oppose governmental regulation. On the side of resistance to taxation we find an event near the chief Parisian food port on 22 March 1714. The collector of excise sent agents to collect delinquent taxes from two Swiss guards doubling as wine merchants, who denied that they owed anything and returned to their wagons. "There," goes the police report,

> they whistled several times, which instantly brought more than forty armed persons out of nearby cafés and other places in addition to those who were already on the spot. With that assistance they took away the wine the agents had seized. Mr. Aunillon says that could have had terrible consequences if they had not held the agents back. He notes in his

13. *Relation: Relation véritable de tout ce qui s'est fait & passé aux Barricades de Paris, les vingt-sixième, vingt-septième & vingt-huitième d'Aoust mil six cens quarante-huit* (1648), Bibliothèque Historique de la Ville de Paris. See also Jean-Louis Bourgeon, "L'Ile de la Cité pendant la Fronde," *Paris et Ile-de-France* 13 (1963), pp. 23–144; Jean-Pierre Labatut, "Situation sociale du quartier du Marais pendant la Fronde parlementaire (1648–1649)," *XVIIe siècle* 38 (1958), pp. 55–81; A. Lloyd Moote, *The Revolt of the Judges: The Parlement of Paris and the Fronde* (Princeton: Princeton University Press, 1971), pp. 151–53; Roland Mousnier, *Paris capitale au temps de Richelieu et Mazarin* (Paris: Pédone, 1978), pp. 258–72.
14. Bibliothèque Nationale, Fonds Français 18432.

letter that two hundred armed persons joined the mob, and many of them had pocket pistols.[15]

As for seizures of food, a report of 6 April 1709 offers a good example: "This morning in the market of the faubourg Saint-Germain," it says,

> a large troop of women, who people said were wives of soldiers in the Royal Guards but among whom many others mixed in, took all the bread from two bakers in the presence of three agents of the Châtelet and a Guards sergeant. The agents said what they could to stop the violence, but the women ignored them and the crowd didn't stop until all the bread was gone and they had to get away to save the bread they had taken.[16]

In both these CGs, characteristically, the threat of violence was serious but the actual use of force slight. Much more often than members of the general public, in fact, agents of authorities initiated the use of force.

1720–1759

The CGs of this period spread over an even wider range: public celebrations, strikes, demonstrations of workers against masters, resistance to police action (e.g., removal of vagabonds), runs on financial institutions, protests against public policy, attacks on unpopular figures in the street, sacking of houses or other premises of public enemies, battles between rival groups of youths, deputations, interventions by spectators at public punishments (including executions), retaliations against plaintiffs in cases of excessive punishment, resistance to arrests, tributes to public heroes (including imprisoned criminals), resistance to tax collectors, seizures of food, attacks on bakers and other food merchants or their premises, public assemblies for the purpose of legal contestation, and funerals of public figures.

Resistance to taxation and seizures of food continued in this period, but let us focus on two other standard events: struggles between masters and ordinary workers and interference in the state's repression. In the Parisian baking industry, masters and ordinary workers struggled throughout the century to determine who would control hiring and firing. The clerk of the master bakers' guild acted for them in this regard, and attracted the journeymen's hatred for his pains. "On Monday, May 28, 1742," Steven L. Kaplan reports,

> Estienne Berton, master baker and the guild's chief clerk, entered a bar to have a drink and look for a workman needed by one of his confreres. He apparently went up to five bakers' assistants in the garden. They beat him with mop handles and canes, "breaking his head." Later they man-

---

15. Archives Nationales, G[7] 441; for the frequent civilian employment of troops garrisoned in Paris, see Jean Chagniot, *Paris et l'armée au XVIIIᵉ siècle: Etude politique et sociale* (Paris: Economica, 1985).

16. Archives Nationales, G[7] 1647.

handled another baker who was Berton's friend, whom they had mistaken for the guild's second clerk. Two days later Berton died of his injuries.[17]

Among popular attacks on arresting officers, an event of 28 March 1749, will illustrate what was often at issue:

> This morning G. Delacroix, brigadier of the poorhouse archers, passing through the rue Dauphine with his brigade, arrested a beggar, who by shouting and resisting aroused the populace to the point that for his security and to avoid the mistreatment the crowd was ready to deliver, they had to release the beggar. As he passed in front of Auger's hat shop, someone threw several potfuls of water and urine on him from the windows of the second and third floors, which incited the populace to gather again and throw stones.[18]

With Protestants largely fled or underground, religious issues figured less acutely in 1720–1759 than they had done in the turbulent forty years after 1680. But questions of justice—including popular reaction to unjust state action—acquired a new prominence.

1760–1799

CGs up to 1787 or so featured strikes, mocking and insulting gatherings, fights among groups of young men, brawls between rival groups of workers, group kidnapping, resistance to arrests and other police actions, opposition to controls within trades, appeals for authorities' intervention in trades, attacks on blacklegs, seizures and destruction of grains, assaults on food merchants and their premises, public celebrations, acclamations of or attacks on public figures, burning or burying in effigy, battles between smugglers and excise officers, schoolboys' rebellions against discipline, theater brawls, disputes over religious ritual and privilege, and assemblies to send petitions or deputations to authorities. Then, with the great mobilization against royal authority that became visible in 1787 and turned revolutionary a few years later, the tempo of popular collective action accelerated enormously.

The politically oriented popular collective action we commonly associate with the Revolution actually became fairly common in the few years before 1789. At the dismissal of Chief Minister Etienne Loménie de Brienne (26 August 1788), law clerks from around the Palais celebrated:

> In the evening, all the young people from around the Palais started to shoot off rockets and firecrackers in the Place Dauphine, which was illuminated for the most part, as was the rue de Harlay. The mounted watch

17. Steven L. Kaplan, "Réflexions sur la police du monde du travail, 1700–1815," *Revue historique* 261 (1979), pp. 46–47.
18. Arlette Farge, *Vivre dans la rue à Paris au XVIIIᵉ siècle* (Paris: Gallimard/Julliard, 1979), p. 149.

gave up, leaving the youths to have their fun, and they enthusiastically burned the effigy of the fired chief minister, who had been, people said, molested in the gallery of the Château of Versailles when leaving the king and again in the streets of that city right after the news of his firing spread.[19]

Nevertheless, the law clerks' revenge was lethal only by proxy. The next year Parisian crowds much more frequently took the law into their own hands, and they wrought popular justice against enemies of the people. An extraordinary profusion of demonstrations, processions, ceremonies, and attacks continued for four years until, with the Terror and subsequent repression, Revolutionary authorities reasserted the state's claims to a monopoly over the use of violent action.

This quick *tour d'horizon* necessarily falls far short of a comprehensive survey of Parisian contention. Yet it suffices to show the significance and vehemence of popular challenges to royal power within the capital, and it demonstrates the continued salience of royal taxation as a stimulus to collective action, the rising importance (from the 1690s onward) of struggles over the much-strained food supply, the complicity or alliance of merchants and bourgeois officials in popular resistance to royal actions, and the virtual disappearance of great lords as major actors in the city's struggles after the Fronde. The largely effective seventeenth-century royal campaign against Protestants, who were once an important mercantile presence in Paris, likewise removed them both as crucial actors and as objects of collective abuse by ordinary people. Royal cooptation of the nobility and the movement of royalty to Versailles left the city an arena of confrontation among workers, merchants, royal officials, municipal officers, and repressive forces in a variety of alliances. The revolutionary transformations of the state likewise transformed popular collective action in Paris.

Some of the recurrent conflicts, it is true, had little or nothing to do with transformations of the state; the repeated attacks on public enemies and the struggles between masters and journeyman had their own logics and rhythms. Even there, however, the state sometimes occupied a central position; the widespread actions against suspected kidnappers of children in the 1750s began with the rumor that royal agents were collecting vagabonds for shipment to French colonies.[20] Again, the clerks of guilds exercised their disputed control over the labor market by royal sanction.[21] Above all, the record of Parisian popular contention shows us a city in which the agents of the state constantly confronted both bourgeois and workers, but were unable to impose anything like absolute order on either one. To that extent, the Parisian experience conforms to the models we sketched earlier.

19. Bibliothèque Nationale, Fonds Français 6687, journal of the bookseller Hardy.
20. Jean Nicolas, "La rumeur de Paris: Rapts d'enfants en 1750," *Histoire* 25 (1981), pp. 20–28.
21. Kaplan, "Réflexions sur la police."

EDO, 1600–1800

In postwar Japan large-scale efforts to excavate local documents have produced remarkable advances in the study of Tokugawa collective action. Aoki Kōji produced an impressive compilation of conflicts occurring between 1590 and 1877.[22] He found records of 6,889 collective movements, including 488 urban riots, 3,189 internal village conflicts, and 3,212 peasant *ikki*— actions of protest addressed to samurai authorities.[23] Aoki's list, like the compilation for France, includes a wide variety of contentious events, from petitions, complaints, and disputes to rebellions and riots. Since Aoki himself was oriented toward quantitative study, and since he classified his data both by region and by form of action, both Japanese and Western scholars have found his compendium to be an invaluable guide to contention in Japan.

Aoki's work, however, is not above criticism.[24] Following the standard distinctions made by other Japanese historians, for example, Aoki distinguished between *murakata sōdō* (village conflicts), in which the protesters' targets were fellow villagers, and actions directed at samurai authorities. The main problem with his classification stems from the complexity of contention. Quite often an event simultaneously included both conflicts among villagers and accusations against outside political authorities. Yet, in spite of such difficulties, Aoki's inventory of protest gives us valuable evidence about long-term trends.

The forms and causes of Tokugawa collective action shifted significantly during the seventeenth and eighteenth centuries. If our reasoning is right, those changes should correspond to the shifting relations between coercion and capital. Japanese historians generally agree on four peaks in the tide of Tokugawa contention: the Kyōhō era (1716–1736), the Hōreki through Tenmei periods (1751–1789), the Tenpō decades (1830–1844), and the final years of the Tokugawa era.[25] The changing nature and causes of collective action across the four periods reflected the far-reaching structural changes brought about by socioeconomic integration through commercialization. One obvious sign of this change was an increase in urban contention. According to Aoki's categorizations, before the Kyōhō era only 3.4 percent (23 of 699) of all conflicts were urban, whereas after 1716 15.3 percent (465 of 3,024) of all contentious events took place in cities. The record includes just three major conflicts in Edo: in 1733, 1787, and 1866. It has often been pointed out that subsistence crises caused by substandard rice harvests were major causes of

22. Aoki Kōji, *Hyakushō ikki sōgō nenpyō* (San'ichi Shobō, 1971).

23. Not all *ikki* were violent or illegal; some groups, for instance, organized themselves to submit legal petitions to higher authorities. Since the publication of Aoki's compendium in 1971, many new conflicts have come to light, but they have not yet been integrated with Aoki's original data. See Aoki Kōji, with Hosaka Satoru, ed., *Hennen hyakushō ikki shiryō shūsei*, 13 vols. (San'ichi Shobō, 1979–1985).

24. William W. Kelly, *Deference and Defiance in Nineteenth-Century Japan* (Princeton: Princeton University Press, 1985).

25. Kodama Kōta et al., eds., *Nihon rekishi taikei*, vol. 3 (Yamakawa Shuppan, 1988).

TABLE 18.2.
*Conflict events in Edo and other regions of Japan, 1590–1877,
by type of event (percent)*

Type of event	Edo region		Other regions	All Japan	Number of events
	Core[a]	Periphery[b]			
Appeal to higher authority	1.4%	3.6%	8.0%	7.8%	558
Orderly petition or complaint	1.4	4.2	7.9	7.7	553
Village conflict	66.7	73.7	44.9	46.3	3,329
Disorderly gathering	1.4	3.9	6.4	6.3	451
Destructive riot	2.9	3.2	6.4	6.2	447
Urban conflict or riot	18.8	5.8	7.1	7.1	511
Other	7.2	5.5	19.3	18.6	1,335
All events	99.8%	99.9%	100.0%	100.0%	7,184
Number of events	69	307	6,807	7,184	

[a] Katsushika, Ebara, Toshima.
[b] Shimōsa Katsushika, Iruma, Saitama, Adachi, Tama, Tachibana, Tsuzuki, Niikura (Niikura had no events).

all these uprisings and that urban food shortages were common to the four peak periods of general contention. But poor harvests surely occurred long before the eighteenth century. Most likely eighteenth-century Japan saw social conditions emerging that linked subsistence crisis with increasing contention. What mechanisms might produce such an effect?

From tabulations of Aoki's data that James W. White generously made available to us, we have constructed two tables that help to distinguish between actions in Edo's core region (the city itself and three adjacent districts) and events that took place on the city's periphery (eight surrounding districts). Table 18.2 shows that village conflict—a classification that includes ostracism, boundary disputes, struggles over water or fishing rights, and so on—occupied a much larger share of all events in the Edo region, especially on its periphery, than elsewhere in Japan; two-thirds or more of all conflicts in the Edo region fell into this category, whereas for the rest of Japan the proportion was 45 percent. In a similar tabulation made by Aoki himself (but with different regional divisions) 63 percent of the events in the Kantō region (including Edo) and 52 percent of events in Kinai (including Osaka and Kyoto), which experienced early commercialization, were village conflicts, whereas in the rest of the country the proportion was 40 percent. We could reasonably speculate that the presence of capital stimulated conflict in villages where commercial agriculture flourished.

During the second half of the Tokugawa period, not only did the number of *ikki* increase (see Table 18.3), but their scale and intensity grew as well. Rarely observed in the seventeenth century were violent actions that involved the destruction of shops and property (*uchikowashi*, with the most common targets being rice shops and the shop-residences of privileged merchants), but such attacks became prominent around the middle of the

TABLE 18.3.
Rural conflicts as proportion of all conflicts in Edo core and periphery, 1590–1877

Period	Core	Periphery	Total	Number of events	
				Region	Core
1590–1599	—	0.0%	0.0%	1	0
1600–1640	—	33.3	33.3	3	0
1641–1680	0.0%	92.3	85.7	14	1
1681–1720	87.5	70.0	75.0	28	8
1721–1760	71.4	91.3	88.6	53	7
1761–1800	78.6	76.7	77.2	57	14
1801–1840	75.0	67.1	68.9	103	24
1841–1877	33.3	70.6	65.8	117	15
				376	69

eighteenth century.[26] In spite of the increasing intensity of conflict, however, nonviolent peasant petitions and appeals continued to be major tools of opposition. Meanwhile, village conflicts also increased significantly during the eighteenth century. A change in the nature of village conflicts in the period suggests structural changes within villages.[27] Despite the conspicuous general growth of contention in the late Tokugawa period, people rarely confronted the central government directly. These patterns are curious from a comparative perspective; the historical sequence that caused the change requires close examination.

Early Tokugawa Period

In the early seventeenth century, collective action often was led by wealthy farmers (*dogō*), men who previously had been village-based samurai but who, for one reason or another, preferred to stay in the villages as cultivators to becoming daimyo vassals resident in the emerging castle towns. Facing now a potential decline in their financial lot as well as in social status, these men organized subordinate villagers and engaged in violent confrontations with authorities. Riots were usually triggered by new policies such as cadastral surveys, by which the daimyo hoped to assess more accurately the productive capacity of village lands, to impose new taxes based on that evaluation, and to disarm elite peasants. Resistance often was vehement, but the wealthy farmers and their plebeian allies could not defeat the landlord class, which consolidated its strength under the Tokugawa regime. Unlike the previous regime, furthermore, the Tokugawa authorities tamed religious institutions so that they could not provide institutional or ideological support for resistance. With the collapse of the Shimabara rebellion in the 1640s, which was led by wealthy farmers who had embraced the Chris-

26. Itō Tadashi, "Hyakushō ikki to 'minshū jichi,'" in Rekishigaku Kenkyūkai, *Kōza Nihon rekishi*, ed. Nihonshi Kenkyūkai, vol. 6: *Kinsei* 2 (Tōkyō Daigaku Shuppankai, 1985), pp. 79–114.

27. Aoki Michio, "Murakata sōdō to minshūteki shakai ishiki," ibid., pp. 267–308.

tian faith, the resistance from this wealthy rural substratum virtually disappeared.

During the second half of the seventeenth century, as the daimyo established more complete political control over their realms, each domain constructed its own semi-autonomous political economy. Villages in any one daimyo domain usually fell under the same tax system and were subject to the same administrative policies. By the late seventeenth century each daimyo's territory also formed its own marketing system, which, although dependent on an emerging national market, was also semi-autonomous. In such an environment, peasant movements no longer proceeded village by village, but often involved alliances of many villages within a single domain.[28] In 1686, for example, about two thousand peasants of the Matsumoto domain assembled in the castle town and demonstrated for five days against a new method of taxation introduced by the lord. Though the leaders were executed, the daimyo ultimately had to accept the peasants' demands. The majority of events, it should be noted, were less confrontational. Peasant leaders usually first submitted petitions to the authorities. When peasants found the lord's agent in the local area powerless or corrupt, they appealed directly to the daimyo, and when their lord did not accept their demands, they sometimes appealed all the way to the shogunate. Lawsuits in Edo became common practice for peasants.

The transformation of contention in the seventeenth century resulted largely from the development of the Tokugawa system of political domination, including the reorganization of villages. The opposition by the former samurai turned peasants was an obvious case. The decline of their personal domination in villages, the removal of the samurai class from the land, and the daimyo projects that increased the amount of arable acreage all contributed to the growth of a class of independent peasants who cultivated small plots of land. Gradually these peasants became the chief actors in Tokugawa contention. The formation and maturing of the Tokugawa state shaped the seventeenth century's contentious movements.

Later Tokugawa Period

During the late seventeenth century, commercial agriculture began to develop on an increasingly large scale in the region around Osaka and Kyoto. By the eighteenth century, impulses toward commercialization were observed everywhere in Japan, promoting far-reaching structural change. The socioeconomic changes that seriously affected collective action included (1) the emergence of price problems, (2) the deterioration of shogunal and daimyo finances, (3) the nationalization of the Tokugawa economy, which often resulted in distribution problems, (4) the penetration of commercial agriculture into rural areas, displacing subsistence farming, and (5) the develop-

28. Hosaka Satoru and Asami Takashi, "Ikki to uchikowashi," in Aoki Michio et al., eds., *Ikki*, vol. 2: *Ikki no rekishi* (Tōkyō Daigaku Shuppankai, 1981), pp. 235–82; Saitō Jun and Yoshitake Keiichirō, "Hyakushō ikki," ibid., pp. 181–234.

ment of stratification among commoners, marked especially by the emergence of urban and rural laboring classes.

These five interrelated factors called up new responses from the state. A general decline in the price of rice during the eighteenth century, for example, eroded the economic base of the samurai. Occasionally, however, rice prices suddenly climbed steeply, inviting the outrage of urban and rural workers, who were vulnerable to high prices. In spite of such far-reaching structural changes, the Tokugawa state itself did not change fundamentally. The shogunate and daimyo continued to depend primarily upon rice taxes for their revenues, for instance, and the merchant class remained excluded from the political process. But the shogunate and daimyo responded to ongoing commercialization. The shogunate, for example, attempted to extend its control over commercial activities, sought to extract more taxes from commerce, and searched for ways to control commodity prices and the supply of rice. Thus the evolving interaction between capital and coercion shaped important aspects of collective action.

Signs of changes in collective action appeared during the Kyōhō era in the early eighteenth century, which in particular witnessed an increase of intense contention on lands under direct Tokugawa control. At this time the shogunate came to recognize its serious financial difficulties. Tokugawa house lands had been taxed at lower rates than daimyo domains, and those rates even decreased during the seventeenth century. The decline began to maker serious inroads cut into shogunate revenues, and the concurrent fall in the price of rice further weakened the shogun's economy. The eighth shogun, Yoshimune, launched a reform program that included various measures to increase tax revenues. Predictably, it evoked peasant opposition. In 1720, for example, several hundred peasants in Aizu Minamiyama Okurairi rushed to demand decreases in taxes, the ending of rice shipments to Edo, and the dismissal of local officials.[29] In 1725, ten villages in Tajima Asako made a forceful appeal outside of prescribed channels (*gōso*) to the shogunate in Edo. In 1729, some 2,400 peasants of Iwashiro demanded a decrease in taxes and accused local officers of tyranny. The incident shocked the shogunate. Since the shogunate's rural intendants commanded just a small military force, the movement was suppressed only after neighboring daimyo dispatched their samurai to support the shogunate's troops.[30] Meanwhile, the scale of contention in daimyo domains also continued to grow; sometimes more than 10,000 peasants joined at a time. Not only did contentious actions became larger and more violent, but in another conspicuous change that characterized the eighteenth century, demonstrators frequently destroyed the houses of wealthy commoners who were seen to be taking unfair advantage of the changing economic structures.

It was in this context that the first major urban conflict hit Edo. In 1733 western Japan suffered serious famine. The shogunate responded by order-

29. Itō, "Hyakushō ikki to 'minshū jichi.'"
30. Saitō and Yoshitake, "Hyaushō ikki."

ing rice grown in northeastern Japan to be sent to the troubled region. Normally, however, rice from the north was sold in Edo's markets, so while the shogunate's actions helped commoners in western Japan, rice prices in Edo leaped dramatically. In reaction, as Hayashi Reiko and Anne Walthall show in greater detail in Chapters 9 and 17, some 1,700 angry Edo residents attacked the shop of one of the city's largest rice dealers, Takama Denbei, whom they blamed for the rise in price.

The second peak of contention, observed in the decades of the 1750s through the 1780s, reveals a more far-reaching penetration of commercialization into rural Japan. Villagers sometimes formed networks of contentious actions that crossed the political boundaries of domains. This phenomenon arose less in protest against rice taxes (which were determined by the domain rulers) than in response to the continued spread of trade and commercial agriculture. Such movements appeared most often in two advanced regions, the area surrounding Osaka and Kyoto, on the one hand, and Edo's hinterland, on the other. In both regions the shogunate administered its own extensive, multiple holdings, but they were interspersed with territories of the shogun's vassals and with daimyo domains. These areas were very advanced commercially, but thinly staffed with coercive forces.

In 1781 an extraordinarily large number of peasants joined in collective action in the Edo hinterland. Their anger was triggered by the shogunate's attempt to introduce silk trade centers in the Kōzuke and Musashi regions and to impose new taxes. Silk producers petitioned the shogunate to abrogate the new policies and simultaneously attacked the houses of silk dealers who favored the establishment of such centers. In all, sixty-seven merchants' houses were demolished, and the shogunate was obliged to rescind its plans.[31] The shogunate's new determination to resolve its own financial difficulties by increasing exploitation of commercial opportunities generated widespread resistance. Contention centering on commercial agriculture continued to grow throughout the remaining years of the Tokugawa period.

Collective action in the late eighteenth century also became more urban and more closely bound up with problems in the rice distribution system. In the spring of 1787, uprisings of the urban poor erupted in major cities all over Japan, including Edo, Osaka, Kōfu, Sunpu, Fukui, Wakayama, Nara, Sakai, Fushimi, Ōtsu, Amagasaki, Hiroshima, Shimonoseki, Hakata, and Nagasaki. Within a month, merchant shops were destroyed in more than thirty incidents. The Edo riot, described by Takeuchi Makoto in Chapter 16, was the most violent; nearly a thousand shops suffered damage. The high price and short supply of rice in Edo—the immediate factors behind the violence in the city—were not simply the consequences of a poor harvest, but rather resulted from the nationalization of the Tokugawa economy. During the famine of 1783, the daimyo domains in northern Japan experienced major peasant uprisings because their lords continued to send rice to Osaka and Edo, despite local shortages. Three years later, in the face of another bad

---

31. Hosaka and Asami, "Ikki to uchikowashi."

harvest, those domains forbade the shipment of local rice to outside markets. This action forestalled peasant hostility, but it resulted in shortages in Edo, where an increased number of laboring poor were hurt by rising prices.

By 1787 the structure of Edo's population had changed considerably since 1700. At century's end the city harbored a large number of migrants from surrounding rural areas who came to Edo in search of jobs as day laborers. Moreover, labor relations within the city had greatly changed as increasingly casual arrangements replaced traditional long-term employment or hereditary subordination. The system of social control in Edo did not accommodate itself to this change. The city's senior administrators continued to rely on neighborhood chiefs and other local officials in the merchant and artisan quarters to control this new, young floating population. But as Takeuchi shows, such a task often was beyond the skills of the chiefs, and the day laborers played a major role in the riots of 1787.

From the late eighteenth to the first half of the nineteenth century, the number of urban and peasant riots continued to increase, many of them centered on the issue of rice prices. Reflecting the expansion of commodity production all over Japan, however, conflicts related to commercialization of the economy became more salient. In this period the daimyo aggressively promoted the production of several kinds of commodities in their domains in order to increase their revenues. The shogunate also strengthened its control over the commercial sector of the economy. Its action resulted in conflicts between the privileged merchants in urban centers who monopolized the trade of a certain commodity, on the one hand, and rural producers and nonprivileged merchants, on the other. In the Osaka area, to cite but one example, nonprivileged merchants and producers of cotton and vegetable oils initiated large-scale petition movements.[32] They mobilized men from 1,307 villages and appealed directly to the shogunate to abolish the monopoly claimed by certain Osaka merchants. The movement was organized strategically, and the protesters patiently used all possible legal measures at their disposal.

The late eighteenth century also saw a significant increase in village conflicts as ordinary peasants filed numerous lawsuits citing the conduct of village officials. Reflecting the conflicts stimulated by capital, these lawsuits largely addressed economic issues.[33] In this process, inheritance of official posts within the village often was replaced by more egalitarian annual rotation or by an election system.[34] These village conflicts reflected the development of a new socioeconomic stratification stimulated by rural commercialization. The increase in village conflicts threatened the shogun and daimyo, who expected village officials to act as their agents in subjecting citizens to state control.

32. William B. Hauser, *Economic Institutional Change in Tokugawa Japan: Osaka and the Kinai Cotton Trade* (Cambridge: Cambridge University Press, 1974), pp. 84–97; Aoki, "Murakata sōdō."

33. Aoki, "Murakata sōdō."

34. For one instance, see Thomas C. Smith, *The Agrarian Origins of Modern Japan* (Stanford: Stanford University Press, 1954), chap. 12.

During the Tenpō era, collective action exploded all over the country. In 1833 and 1836 Japan suffered extremely poor harvests. The further penetration of a commercial economy into villages during the nineteenth century mobilized rural people who did not themselves produce rice and subsistence crops. To confront the serious unrest caused by the shortage of food supplies, local daimyo further strengthened their control over rice distribution. The shogunate's priority, in sharp contrast, was to bring enough rice into Edo to avoid a repetition of the 1787 attacks on merchants. Though the administration managed to prevent riots in Edo at this time, other areas experienced serious contention, which usually included the destruction of merchants' houses.[35] Aoki's compilation shows that the number of peasant and urban conflicts reached their highest frequency during the period surrounding the Tenpō famines.

Toward the end of the Tokugawa regime, contention once again appeared all over Japan. Political chaos spread as the shogunate increasingly proved itself incapable of responding effectively either to the threat of Western imperialism or to hostile daimyo. In the midst of such confusion and disorder, major struggles hit Edo again in 1866. These popular actions did not, however, result directly in the collapse of the Tokugawa regime. With a few exceptions—most notably the rebellion led by Ōshio Heihachirō in 1837—urban and rural movements failed to mobilize the samurai class, and they did not mesh with ongoing political conflicts between the shogun and the daimyo. Nor did wealthy privileged merchants confront the state.[36] It was the movement led by hostile daimyo that eventually toppled the regime.

Conclusions

Commercialization in a strong state created through coercion provided the critical conditions for the evolution of struggle in Japan. The frequency of peasant discontent and acts of collective violence during the Tokugawa period should surprise those Western readers who still cling to an image of a peaceful, controlled society derived from excessively culturalist—even Orientalist—interpretations of the Japanese experience. Upon close examination, it is true, one is impressed with the mostly nonconfrontational nature of these popular actions. Peasants certainly demonstrated forcefully and presented demands in castle towns, but they seldom attacked daimyo's

35. For a specific case, see James L. McClain, "Failed Expectations: Kaga Domain on the Eve of the Meiji Restoration," *Journal of Japanese Studies* 14:2 (1988), pp. 423–28. Harold Bolitho discusses the reforms in "The Tempō Reforms," in John W. Hall et al., eds., *The Cambridge History of Japan*, vol. 5: Marius B. Jansen, ed., *Japan in the Nineteenth Century* (Cambridge: Cambridge University Press, 1989), pp. 117–67.

36. Matsumoto Shirō, "Bakumatsu ishin-ki ni okeru toshi shihai no jōkyō to uchikowashi," in Sasaki Junnosuke, ed., *Murakata sōdō to yonaoshi*, vol. 1 (Aoki Shoten, 1972), pp. 69–108; Satō Shigerō, "Ishin henkaku to jinmin tōsō," in Aoki et al., *Ikki*, vol. 5: *Ikki to kokka* (Tōkyō Daigaku Shuppankai, 1981), pp. 45–98.

castles. Throughout the period, protestors rarely confronted the authority of the shogunate directly. Usually they asked humbly for the authorities' understanding and repeated their petitions. In this regard, Japanese claimants differed significantly from their French counterparts; French people more often resisted the central state's demands, and France's regional powerholders more often leagued with ordinary people in that resistance.

Why this difference? Although Japanese villagers knew that they lacked powerful allies and that the state's retribution could be terrible, their submission was not simply a sign of weakness. It reflected an accurate understanding of the Tokugawa state. The state consisted of an integrated but decentralized structure of power in which various levels were incorporated, and contenders took advantage of those complex layers. It was wise to respect the authority of the shogunate, as it might serve as the court of last resort. Indeed, upon direct appeals from peasants the shogunate often punished greedy lords or dismissed local officials. In daimyo domains, by the same token, local officers were condemned first, as were local wealthy commoners, but the actors often strategically avoided attacking the lord directly. Despite the conventional form of address in commoners' petitions, "With fearful mind we humbly submit . . . ," participants in popular movements followed rational, calculated strategies. For two and a half centuries before the fall of the Tokugawa regime the complex structure of the Japanese state was thus able to absorb various levels of contention before they became critically threatening.

The history of Japanese contention, then, appears to support our model. Struggles during the first half of the Tokugawa period, it seems, were largely coercion-led—related directly to the development of the Tokugawa state system. The movement in the second half responded more strongly to the growth of commercialization and the state's response to the new situation. The growth of capital did not lead Japan to the French path, however, because it occurred within the constraints set by the prior formation of the state. In France, extensive commercialization before state power became concentrated and centralized had put in place a partly autonomous network of cities, a bourgeoisie with some independent bases of power and some forms of alliance with landlords, and a peasantry that had its own capacity to form alliances and resist state expansion. Although plenty of French struggles pitted peasants against merchants and other bourgeois, France stood apart from Japan in the varied and widespread resistance to demands from the state. Ultimately, though the French state did eventually gain power over its competitors, it did so only at the cost of extensive concessions to its citizens. The French Revolution marked the most dramatic moment of a struggle that extended over several centuries. In France and Japan, in Edo and Paris, alternative articulations of capital and coercion produced significantly different forms and transformations of popular contention.

19
Visions of the City

JAMES L. McCLAIN AND UGAWA KAORU

The essays in this volume weave a tapestry whose motif portrays not one Edo and not one Paris, but many. Kings and shoguns, aristocrats and samurai, high government officials and lowly functionaries, lawyers and clerks, wealthy bourgeois and impoverished outcasts, prosperous grain merchants and humble artisans, false workers and members of the construction trades, Shinto priests and worldly cardinals, prostitutes, beggars, and street performers—all of those people and more inhabited the two great capitals, East and West. In a multitude of separate ways, the people of Edo and Paris formulated visions of the city in which they lived, of what it was and what it ought to be, of what it had been and of what it might become. At times those various conceptualizations were radically at odds, one with the other, and at times they were in congruence. Abstraction was the starting point for action, the nebulous from which specific policies, plans, and modes of behavior took shape as each social group, each person, sought to fabricate a concrete urban reality that exemplified a particular idealization of the city. The dynamics of historical change gathered energy from the fashioning and the implementation of those sometimes complementary, frequently competing visions, so that Edo and Paris became cities that belonged to everyone and were the singular possessions of no one.

In general terms, the visions of urbanism in Edo and Paris can be separated into two broad categories: the city from above and the city from below. Surely the most powerful view of the city from on high was the idea of a monarchical, shogunal capital as articulated by the Bourbon and Tokugawa rulers. Examples of how the kings and shoguns changed the face of Paris and Edo fill the pages of this volume. As McClain and Merriman show in Chapter 1, Ieyasu's chief concern during his first decade in Edo was to build an impregnable military stronghold. To this end he summoned to Edo the architects, builders, lumber dealers, and construction workers who could erect great stone walls, frame imposing entrance gates, and gouge out a protective network of canals and moats. Around his citadel he gathered his vassal bannermen and housemen, who became some of Japan's first urban samurai. Present at the very moment of the city's creation, Ieyasu molded Edo's physical design in ways that did much to determine the contours of the city's future growth.

Yet it is also important to remember that after Ieyasu was appointed shogun in 1603, his vision of Edo changed. Military concerns, though still present, receded to the background as Ieyasu and his successors increasingly committed themselves to building a city that embodied the splendor of Tokugawa political pretensions. Thus, when they imposed upon the daimyo the requirement to spend alternate years in Edo, the shoguns also authorized, in fact compelled, the regional lords to construct elaborate mansions in the city. The appearance of those opulent residences (so grand that William H. Coaldrake refers to them as "palaces") helped to define an elite architectural style that made manifest the power, wealth, and dominance of Japan's class of military lords, and their location at the foot of Edo Castle enhanced Tokugawa standing in the eyes of all by identifying the shogun as the master of the nation's elite. The early Tokugawa shoguns expanded upon this theme by constructing imposing office buildings and indulging themselves, as Coaldrake also shows, in displays of monumental architecture such as the great mausoleum at Zōjōji.

Henry IV and his successors, of course, were no less eager to stamp their imprint on Paris. Not long after the Bourbon king captured Paris from his rivals, Roger Chartier writes, Henry authorized the construction of the Place Royale and the Place Dauphine, developments that contained shops, residences, and aristocratic mansions. Later Louis XIII lent his seal of approval to the development of the Ile Saint-Louis, and to this new Paris Louis XIV contributed the Invalides, great boulevards, public fountains, and triumphal arches at Saint-Denis and Saint-Martin. As in Edo, the buildings announced the ruler's claims to ultimate political supremacy and symbolized the grandeur of absolutist power.

King and shogun, however, envisaged Edo and Paris as more than physical monuments to authority; the attributes of rulership, the imperatives of early-modern absolutism in France and Japan, also demanded that their capitals be well ruled, that order be imposed upon the population as well as upon the landscape. In Edo, that meant building an administrative system where none had existed before, and Katō Takashi describes the complex structure of offices that the first three shoguns, and especially Iemitsu, devised in order to govern Edo. In addition, the new state imposed legal codes, organized police forces, appointed judicial officials, and built prisons. In Paris, too, the kings attempted to extend their control over what William Beik calls a "diverse and unruly society." One way they did so, as both Beik and Sharon Kettering demonstrate, was to put a rein on the prerogatives of the well-entrenched, traditional elites, dominating the Hôtel de Ville and infiltrating the Châtelet so that officials of those two agencies cantered more in accordance with the royal will. And like the Tokugawa shoguns, the Bourbon kings created new administrative structures: the appointment of lieutenants general of police from the 1660s dramatically expanded the circumference of royal authority.

Another aspect of the city from above emerges from the essays on provisioning by Hatano Jun, Hayashi Reiko, and Steven Laurence Kaplan. The engineering hand of shogun and monarch could be seen clearly in the measures taken to provide water to the cities. In Edo the government initially assumed the chief responsibility for designing and constructing a system of canals and sluices that brought water into all sections of the city, whereas in Paris the crown installed pumps along the Seine to move water to public fountains that supplemented an already large number of private wells. Both the Bourbon and Tokugawa regimes, Hayashi and Kaplan agree, preferred to rely on market mechanisms and the dictates of supply and demand to provision the capitals with foodstuffs. Yet each government also advocated a "capital-first" policy that inspired it to maintain an infrastructure of roadways and shipping facilities that permitted merchants to go about their business; to regulate guilds and protective merchant associations so that they did not conspire to put their own interests above those of the public (or the state); and to intervene in the market during times of crisis.

Without denying the formidable intentions of the Tokugawa shoguns and Bourbon kings, many contributors to this book also provide rich detail about the host of important ways in which Edo and Paris were shaped from below as well as from above. The chapters by Jurgis Elisonas and Robert M. Isherwood bring to life the vitality of the street entertainments and theaters of the urban commoners, while Henry D. Smith II extends our view into the world of print and reading. McClain shows how the merchants and artisans of Edobashi transformed the use of space within their neighborhood, creating a residential quarter that was radically different from what officials had planned, and several chapters demonstrate how the state's reliance on indirect rule ceded to the people within the merchant quarters of Edo and Paris the prerogative to supervise activities important to their lives and livelihoods, as they managed the water supply, fought fires, and built and repaired bridges. At times, as Kaplan and Takeuchi Makoto show in their essays on the faubourg Saint-Antoine and Asakusa, residents of some quarters even were able to carve out for themselves quasi-autonomous zones of work and self-policing.

While the forces from above and below gave shape and texture to life in Edo and Paris, other chapters in this volume also make clear that just as there was neither one Edo nor one Paris, neither was there a single "above" or a single "below." The state was not monolithic, in either France or Japan. Many persons of diverse social groups played roles in governing and managing the cities. As might be expected, their views were not always in congruence, and their disagreements, too, affected life within Edo and Paris. Examples are plentiful. In Edo the city elders sometimes clashed with the senior councilors about how space ought to be used (and won their points); on other occasions the senior councilors and city magistrates pressed their aspirations upon subordinate functionaries, as when the up-

per echelons of the administrative pyramid decided that commoners ought
to fight fires and maintain the water supply system. In Paris, differences of
opinion among elites, as Chartier shows, determined the pace and direction
of the city's physical expansion; and so segregated were the administrative
jurisdictions in Paris that many urban services would have come to a standstill were it not for the efforts of the "middle men" described by Sharon
Kettering.

Neither did Edo or Paris have homogeneous populations. Wealth, status,
occupation, gender, age, and any number of other attributes divided the
populations and multiplied their visions of what the city ought to be. Paris's
social elites did not look with favor upon the vulgarities of boulevard life,
and many commoners at Edobashi criticized the entertainers who invaded
their neighborhood. Samurai favored high rice prices and a well-organized
distribution and sales system for the stipend grain that they sold for cash
income; but Edo's commoners banded together to demand (unsuccessfully)
the abolition of monopoly privileges for rice dealers in the hope that freer
competition would lower retail prices for the staff of their daily life. Paris's
great merchants jealously guarded their time-honored privileges, and Kaplan's false workers fled to Saint-Antoine, where they might ply their trades
as they pleased. The youths of Asakusa imposed their version of neighborly
obligations on the families within their residential quarters, and the neighborhood chiefs had little choice but to shield them from higher authorities.
Aristocrats and daimyo lived on great estates, existing in splendid isolation
apart from the urban masses; the poor huddled on crowded back streets or
congregated on the fringes of the two cities, creating a sense of neighborhood and community that brought meaning to their lives.

The governing officials and the ordinary people within the two cities
resorted to a variety of techniques to quiet the differences among themselves and to reconcile the competing visions of urbanism that emerged
from above and from below. Coercion and persuasion anchored the opposite ends of the spectrum that defined the options available to government.
The impulse toward arbitrary, unilateral action by the Bourbon monarchs
and Tokugawa shoguns was apparent at several junctions: when they imposed taxes and other levies; when they committed their country to war, or
closed its borders to nearly all foreign intercourse; and when they comman-
deered land for government offices and works of monumental architecture.
More frequently, however, authorities in Edo and Paris preferred to rely on
persuasion, which often enough involved bestowing privileges on certain
groups. In France, as William Beik shows, the crown regularly dispensed
special considerations and granted concessions to aristocrats and other urban elites in exchange for obedience, and the Tokugawa shoguns made their
bid for loyalty from below by extending any number of prerogatives to their
samurai retainers and to valued merchants, such as those who marketed the
state's tax rice.

People reacted to this mix of coercion and persuasion in a variety of
ways. At times the people living in Edo and Paris simply capitulated to

initiatives from above. Acquiescence perhaps bloomed most readily in two environments: wherever the state resolutely decided that it was necessary to advance a particular policy, casting itself as a juggernaut that could be resisted only at unacceptable cost, and wherever one or more idealized views of the city from below appeared to be in harmony with the vision authored on high. The expropriation of land for the shogun's use and for defensive purposes and the issuance of legal codes and royal letters of patent took place within the boundaries of a coercive environment. A concordance of visions could be seen in many other corners of the two cities: guilds and protective associations in both Edo and Paris were only too happy to accept special prerogatives; Parisian real estate developers usually liked the fit of their speculative hand to the glove of royal privilege; aristocrats and daimyo discovered that benefits granted by the autocratic state enhanced their own social and economic standing in the capital cities.

At other times, residents of Edo and Paris responded to initiatives from above (or launched their own attempts to define the city from below) by inviting negotiations with the authorities. This was the case at Edobashi, where, as McClain shows, merchants submitted a continuous stream of appeals and petitions to officialdom. Like water running over a rock, those proposals eventually wore down the resistance of the state, and the residents of Edobashi were able to persuade officials generally to accept their vision of how the quarter ought to be developed as a residential, commercial, and religious center. Hatano Jun and William W. Kelly also highlight the negotiations that went on between the authorities and the people (as well as among various factions within the commoner population), although the results differed from those at Edobashi. As part of the "negotiated desamuraization" of Edo, Kelly explains, the state wished to offload the expenses and obligations for protecting the city from fire onto the shoulders of merchant and artisan families, a move that the commoners initially resisted but finally came to accept. The state also succeeded in persuading the merchants and artisans of Edo to assume responsibility for maintaining the water supply system, and eventually the people even celebrated their drinking water as another of the wondrous "flowers of Edo." The essays in this volume also provide numerous examples of negotiation and compromise on the French side: the crown, aristocrats, and ecclesiastical communities, for instance, ultimately worked out an accord to reconcile diverse claims to urban space, and the provost of merchants and other business leaders accepted lesser administrative roles in return for assurances about the perpetuation of commercial privileges.

The course of negotiated autocracy, however, did not always run smoothly. At times competing visions of the city were too far apart for easy resolution and negotiations broke down. When that happened, people frequently resisted the state. One form that opposition might assume was noncompliance (in a sense, another negotiating tactic), as when kabuki and puppet theaters in Edo and Nicolet's performers on the boulevards of Paris simply ignored regulations that displeased them or found ways to comply technically with the decrees of government while evading them in spirit. The youths of Asakusa routinely disregarded government decrees intended to curb their self-policing activities, just as the false workers of Saint-Antoine refused to bow to pressure from above, preferring to relocate themselves in a space where they could enjoy a degree of autonomy to work at their crafts as they saw fit. Other examples readily come to mind: merchants who withheld grain from the market in violation of government decrees to sell stockpiles; woodblock printmakers and bookseller-publishers who routinely circumvented censorship guidelines; commoners charged with firefighting responsibilities who simply declined to show up for duty.

Often mild acts of resistance served to reopen the negotiating process. What happened next depended on how shrewdly the opposing sides marshaled their arguments and on how forcefully the state wished to press its case. In the instance of firefighting in Edo, authorities eventually got their way, but publishers and the denizens of the boulevards and amusement centers in both Edo and Paris never were inclined to docilely place their toes along the line prescribed by the law. In a few instances resistance escalated into violence, the most radical tactic available to the people of Edo and Paris. As the essays by Anne Walthall and by Eiko Ikegami and Charles Tilly show, such acts were rare, but they did succeed in delivering a strong message, and they could have an impact on state policy: the decision to give priority to provisioning the capital in time of famine (however late and reluctantly officials came to that position in the case of Edo) was clearly a response to real or threatened violence from below.

The direction of change in early-modern France and Japan was toward expanded state power and the concomitant emergence of a large-scale administrative capital that formed the combined political, economic, and social nucleus of each nation. But the variety of competing visions of the city and the manner in which issues of contention were resolved also reveal significant and instructive variations between the two countries concerning styles of urbanism and absolutist governance. At the heart of those differences is the perception, shared by many of the contributors to this volume, that the Tokugawa shoguns wielded greater power than did the Bourbon kings. "No European absolutist state was more successful than the Tokugawa in blocking increased bourgeois influence on the government," Ikegami and Tilly argue, and Beik seconds that notion when he notes that "the king seems to have had to do much more accommodating" than the shoguns.

If the Bourbon kings stood on a less stable pedestal than did the Tokugawa shoguns, perhaps it was because they never won for themselves, not even in the Fronde, a victory of the magnitude of Sekigahara, where Ieyasu dispatched the daimyo coalition of western Japan and confirmed his position as the most powerful warrior lord in Japan, ready to accept the mantle of shogun. Nor did Henry IV or any of his successors ever experience the sense of completion that Ieyasu must have felt after his successful campaigns at Osaka in 1614–1615, when he confirmed his hegemony in the most unequivocal way possible, by putting the last of his serious rivals, and many of their wives and children as well, into their graves. Those great victories gave the Tokugawa family enormous leverage over the remaining daimyo of Japan and secured for the shogun direct control over nearly one-quarter of the productive capacity of the country. The Bourbons, by way of a sharp and telling contrast, never had enough men under arms to permit themselves to exercise undisputed hegemony over more than a few provinces of France at a time.

Those differences in armed strength and coercive potential held important consequences for the exercise of authority. Unable to exert total control over the countryside, for instance, the kings never found a way to dominate France's systems of economic production either, and their attempts to expand royal revenues were hindered, at times crippled, by the privileges of town, church, and aristocrat. Moreover, the Bourbons, as Beik reminds us, experienced considerably more frustration than did the Tokugawa family in trying to rule through a bureaucracy. The shogun theoretically was free to appoint and dismiss his senior officials at will, and he could hold them directly accountable for the actions of lower-level urban administrators such as the city magistrates. France's kings, however, were hard pressed to find the economic resources to support an extensive state apparatus, and partly as a consequence of their limited revenues, they also had difficulty recruiting a body of officials who could be relied on to carry out royal commands. To compensate for their weak fiscal base, for instance, the kings multiplied the number of government agents during the seventeenth and eighteenth centuries, yet many of those appointees retained considerable independence from the crown because they had purchased or leased their offices.

Contrasting configurations of state power also led the two regimes to adopt different sorts of "capital-first" provisioning policies. Quite clearly, the Bourbons were particularly concerned with feeding Paris's commoners, whose wrath they truly feared, especially after young Louis XIV's panicky and humiliating flight from the city during the Fronde demonstrated that the crown could not always trust its own ability to suppress popular discontent. The Tokugawa regime, too, went to considerable lengths to create mechanisms to supply water, food, and other essentials to all of Edo's residents, but within that framework it paid particular attention to the needs of the samurai estate. The water supply network, as Hatano describes it, was systematically planned to meet warriors' requirements first, and when food shortages threatened the capital, the shogunate gave priority to the interests of its samurai followers by supporting the price level of stipend rice even though that move brought additional hardship to the city's commoners and twice in the eighteenth century incited them to violence. The reasoning of the shogun is not difficult to follow: the Tokugawa hegemony—the shogun's ability to dominate the daimyo and to impose his will within his own domain—rested fully and entirely on the loyalty of his warrior followers.

Other differences existed between shogun and king. Because they shared borders with contentious European rivals, for instance, the Bourbons never could master the international balance of power, whereas the Tokugawa shoguns effectively isolated their island nation from foreign threat, thereby saving themselves the enormous sums that the French kings spent on foreign adventures. The Bourbons sought to satisfy their never-ending need for funds for military expeditions by selling offices, farming out taxes in return for cash advances, confirming guild power in exchange for payments to royal coffers, and installing municipal officials who agreed to ply the crown with loans, gifts, and generous tax receipts. This set of practices represented one of the negotiated compromises that defined Bourbon absolutism. In some ways, the intermediaries drew close to the crown because they relied on regime-backed coercion to help them make collections from subjects and creditors. But by the same token, the ultimate price of cooperation by the middlemen and agents was an eventual attenuation of state power as the intermediaries grew stronger, made the crown dependent on them for credit, and limited the king's capacity to extract revenues from an expanding economy.

Of great significance as well was the fact that the two administrative capitals had different histories. Edo, for all practical purposes, was a new city, clay for the Tokugawa to mold. Paris long had been France's leading city, home to powerful ecclesiastical, seigneurial, and bourgeois populations whose special rights, sanctioned by tradition, created an intricately textured urban environment where the Bourbons' best hope probably was to make peace with a preexisting society that zealously guarded its traditional privileges. Perhaps for that reason, the Tokugawa shoguns demonstrated a greater ability to dictate the use of space than did the Bourbon kings. No royal monument dominated the Paris cityscape in anything like the way the walls and towers of the shogun's castle loomed over Edo, and no Bourbon could have seriously considered trying to impose on Paris the status-determined residential patterns that colored every map of Edo. Nor, for that matter, does one need a rich imagination to picture the clamor and dissension that would have arisen had Louis XIV ever contemplated the sort of massive relocation of religious institutions and merchant neighborhoods that Tokugawa Ietsuna so effortlessly decreed in the wake of the great Meireki fires in 1657.

Also affecting the course of statemaking East and West was the fact that Paris had already established itself as a major center of European trade and economic exchange before Henry IV founded the Bourbon monarchy, whereas Edo's rise from commercial insignificance during Ieyasu's lifetime to a dominant position within Japan's national economy took more than a century to complete. In Paris, the prominence of entrenched commercial interests leads to the familiar point: from the very beginning the Bourbons had little choice but to rule through negotiated compromise. In Japan, the graph plotting the relationship between commercial change and the trajectory of absolutism is amenable to more ambiguous readings. Looked at from one perspective, the shogun's enormous wealth, a consequence of Ieyasu's great military victories, seems to have given the Tokugawa regime economic leverage of the sort the Bourbons could only dream about. The Tokugawa family, after all, directly controlled extensive and rich agricultural lands, a resource that permitted the shogun to provide generous annual stipends to his warrior followers. Because that stipend rice, together with the shogun's own tax rice, was almost always sufficient to feed Edo in normal times, the Tokugawa shoguns enjoyed a degree of independence from the market and the merchant estate that the Bourbon kings could never know (as was evident in the shogunate's actions during the dearth of 1732–1733).

But, as several of the chapters of this volume demonstrate, the nature of Japan's economy also imposed constraints on state power. In the first place, Edo's residents demanded more than just rice, and many of those other commodities (as well as a portion of the capital's rice as things eventually turned out) had to be produced or grown in western Japan and shipped through Osaka and Kyoto. Thus the shoguns needed to provide an infrastructure that would shape and support an integrated national marketing structure. In the end, the Tokugawa regime could not escape some dependence on the market and the merchant estate. As the commercial economy grew during the course of the seventeenth century, Japan's shoguns, like the kings of France, found it advantageous to negotiate a symbiotic relationship with merchants, bartering privileges for cooperation from the commercial sector so that Edo would be adequately provisioned. The diffuse nature of Japan's newly emerging marketing system imposed another limitation on Tokugawa power. While the shogunate directly administered Osaka and Kyoto, its touch fell but lightly on the merchants in those major commercial centers (in the early nineteenth century perhaps only three thousand samurai resided in Osaka, whose total population numbered nearly a third of a million persons). Small wonder, then, that many of the great entrepreneurial families such as the Shirokiya and Mitsui preferred to keep their business headquarters in western Japan, where they might evade some of the more direct consequences of shogunal authority.

Finally, different articulations of state power with commercial growth resulted in contrasting modes of collective violence. In France, as Ikegami and Tilly argue, contentious movements tended to be directed against the demands of the central state. That was largely because extensive commercialization before 1600 had put into place a network of partly autonomous cities, brought into existence a bourgeoisie that enjoyed an independent basis of power and which could strike alliances with landlords, and produced a peasantry capable of forming its own coalitions. Japan represents a somewhat different model. While acts of collective violence in reaction to the expansion of state power typified the first half of the Tokugawa period, struggles by Japanese commoners in the second half of the period—when the riots in Edo occurred—responded more strongly to the growing commercialization of the economy and to the way state policies contributed to that process. However, because the most advanced stages of commercial growth took place only after the regime had already developed its instrumentalities of political control (creating what Ikegami and Tilly call a "coercion-intensive" environment), the number of violent movements were comparatively few. Moreover, because people feared the state's retribution and because they could hope to appeal to the shogun and his very highest officials as courts of last resort, in Japan more often than in France protest was aimed at the lower levels of state authority, or at merchants who were seen as the recipients of state-sponsored privilege (as was the case in the Edo riots of the eighteenth century).

As intriguing as those contrasts are between governance and urbanism in France and Japan, they specify differences of degree and magnitude, not of kind. In the end, the distinctions serve to remind us of the strong similarities in the historical processes that were at work in early-modern France and Japan. In both societies the trajectory arched toward absolutism. Each regime strengthened its top-down governing hierarchy, regularized an administrative apparatus, issued laws in its own name, fashioned police forces loyal to crown and sword, disarmed the civilian population, claimed a monopoly on the use of force and violence to resolve disputes, reached out to grasp new tax revenues, and built (or remodeled) a capital city that would make its authority manifest. Yet, while absolutist state power was growing, neither Tokugawa shogun nor Bourbon king ever became omnipotent. The circle was not closed; absolutism was not made whole; and indirect rule emerged as a defining component of the early-modern state in both France and Japan. The ordinary residents of Edo and Paris represented powerful constituencies who had their own visions of how they wanted to live. They could mobilize themselves in an effort to bring their abstractions to reality, and they represented formidable obstacles to state policies that threatened their interests. More often than not, the state negotiated and compromised, and in the end the people of Edo and Paris created their own cultures, defined popular etiquettes, appropriated space for their own use, and helped to manage the neighborhoods they inhabited.

When Henry IV turned to organizing the growth of his capital, Chartier observes, he faced a task of daunting complexity, for Paris was a city where "history had imposed its own heritages" and where "traces of the accumulated past" were too deep to be effaced. Surely that was so, but just as undeniably, the Bourbon kings and Tokugawa shoguns imbued Paris and Edo with new "heritages," evident in the modern cityscape. The Louvre and Edo Castle, impressive spans across the Seine and Sumida rivers, triumphal arches and shogunal mausolea greet visitors to today's Paris and Tokyo and recall for them the grand building projects of the absolutist masters of the early-modern period. But any tour of the modern capitals will turn up other traces of the "accumulated past" as well. A warehousing company in business yet today at Edobashi; fireworks over the Sumida River on a hot summer's evening, and the Boulevard du Temple where Nicolet's theaters flourished; furniture workshops in the faubourg Saint-Antoine, and the shouts of the *mikoshi* bearers at the Sanja Festival, still celebrated each spring at Sensōji—all pay tribute to the richness of the past, to Edo and Paris, to cities and power and the people who brought life to these two great metropolises.

Glossary

baillage court A royal court situated in a provincial town or city with local jurisdiction similar to that exercised by the Châtelet in Paris

bakufu 幕府 The shogunate; the house government of the Tokugawa shogun, who presided over the affairs of the nation

bannermen *See* hatamoto

bourgeois In Paris, nonnoble urban property owners who had been resident in the city for at least a year and who paid taxes

buke shohatto 武家諸法度 Regulations defining the conduct of the daimyo lords and the direct retainers of the shogun; included restrictions on marriage, the naming of heirs, and construction of castles; promulgated in 1615 and revised periodically thereafter

bushi 武士 A warrior, samurai

cabinet de lecture A reading room; an establishment where for a subscription fee one could read journals and books

cens Quitrents; a seigneural tax

chambrelan A "false worker," especially one who operated out of a one-room shop

Châtelet The major royal court below the Parlement of Paris, with extensive jurisdiction over police matters; oversaw the law courts and prisons of Paris and regulated commerce on hand

chigyō 知行 Fief; territory granted by a lord to a personal retainer, who exercised fiscal and administrative prerogatives over the holding

chōnin 町人 (1) Merchant and artisan property owners; that is, persons who were entitled to possess, rent out, sell, and bequeath specified parcels of land, who paid taxes and levies on those plots, and who were members of five-family groups and eligible to serve as neighborhood chiefs; (2) merchants and artisans in general; (3) all nonsamurai who lived in cities

city magistrate *See* machi bugyō

commissioner of building *See* sakuji bugyō; voyer de Paris

commissioner of engineering works *See* fushin bugyō

communautés des arts et métiers Guilds; closed corporations of masters and artisans

conseil de police A special council established by Louis XIV in 1666 to oversee the policing of Paris

contrôleur général Controller general; head of superministry whose functions touched on taxation, finances, the economy, public works, and public order

corps de ville The collective government of a French town, consisting of various appointed magistrates and elected councils

daikan 代官 Intendant; a rural official of the shogunate who collected taxes and enforced laws: reported to the commissioners of finance (*kanjō bugō*)

daimyō 大名 Territorial lords who ruled over holdings with an assessed productive capacity of 10,000 or more *koku* of rice

daimyō-bikeshi 大名火消 Samurai firefighting squads that the shogunate instructed sixteen daimyo to organize in 1643

dizainier An officer in the Parisian citizen militia who administered a residential quarter on behalf of the city

échevin An executive member of a municipal government

Edodana 江戸店 The Edo branch outlets of merchandisers whose headquarters were located chiefly on the Kyoto-Osaka region

Edozu 江戸図屏風 A set of folding screens painted to depict Edo in the years before the Meireki fires of 1657, most likely in the early 1630s

elder *See* toshiyori

false worker *See* faux ouvrier

faubourg A suburb; an extension of the city beyond its walls

faux ouvrier "False worker"; a person who worked outside of the guild system

five-family group *See* goningumi

Fronde A civil war from 1648 to 1652 in which noble and regional factions fought the French crown

fudai daimyō 譜代大名 "Allied lord"; a daimyo who was elevated to that status by the Tokugawa family or who, as an independent lord, allied himself with Ieyasu before the battle of Sekigahara in 1600

fushin bugyō 譜請奉行 Commissioners of engineering works; oversaw projects that involved extensive engineering work, such as the construction and repair of castle walls and moats; appointments were made regularly from 1653

gachigyōji 月行事 A representative of a five-family group; maintained contact between the group and the neighborhood chief

généralité Royal tax district

gō 合 *See* koku

gofunai 御府内 The "lord's city"; Edo

gokenin 御家人 Housemen; direct retainers of the shogun who staffed lower offices within the shogunal bureaucracy and did not have the privilege of personal audiences with their lord

goningumi 五人組 Groups of landowners in a residential quarter; established by the shogunate and charged with making certain that its members and their families obeyed the law and paid taxes

hairyō yashiki 拝領屋敷 The residential estates and mansions of daimyo in Edo

Halle, La The central market of Paris

hangiya 版木屋 Artisans who carved the wooden blocks used in printing

hatamoto 旗本 Bannermen; direct retainers of the shogun who had the privilege of personal audiences with the shogun and were granted annual stipends (*karoku*) or fiefs (*chigyō*) whose annual productivity was assessed at not more than 10,000 *koku*; were appointed to administrative positions such as city magistrate (*machi bugyō*) and commissioner of engineering works (*fushin bugyō*); numbered approximately 5,200 families in the early eighteenth century

hinin 非人 A category of outcasts who begged and developed a variety of street performances; some were employed to guard criminals and to dispose of corpses

hirokōji 広小路 A "widened street"; a firebreak

hon'ya 本屋 Bookseller-publisher

Hôpital Général A charity hospital

hôtel A townhouse or mansion of an aristocratic family

hôtel de ville City or town hall; seat of municipal government

housemen *See* gokenin

ikki 一揆 A temporary informal union of commoners, organized to protest government policies

jō-bikeshi 定火消 "Regular firemen"; "bannermen firemen"; an all-samurai, all-Edo fire guard organized in 1658

junior councilor *See* wakadoshiyori

jurés Elected governors of guilds

kaichō 開帳 A special display of a temple's most sacred icons (usually kept from public view)

kamigata 上方 The cities of Osaka and Kyoto and their extended hinterlands

kanjō bugyō 勘定奉行 Commissioners of finance, who supervised tax collection and the shogunate's budgets; appointed regularly from the 1640s; reported to the senior councilors

Kansai 関西 (1) All of Japan west of the Hakone barrier in Sagami; (2) the region around Kyoto and Osaka, including the traditional prefectures of Ōmi, Yamashiro, Tanba, Tango, Izumi, Kawachi, Yamato, Kii, Ise, Iga, Tajima, Settsu, Harima, and Awaji

Kantō 関東 (1) Eastern Japan from Shinano and Tōtōmi to Shimotsuke and Hitachi; (2) the seven provinces immediately to the east and north of the Hakone barrier (Hitachi, Shimotsuke, Kōzuke, Musashi, Shimōsa, Kazusa, and Awa), to which Sagami is sometimes added to make the *Kantō hasshū,* the Eight Kantō Provinces

karoku 家禄 A heritable annual stipend granted to samurai families

kashihon'ya 貸本屋 Booklender; a shop or peddler who lent out books for a fee

kawaraban 瓦版 Broadsheets; single-page printings of the news of the day, sold in the merchant quarters from the 1820s

Kinai 畿内 The provinces of Yamato, Yamashiro, Kawachi, Izumi, and Settsu.

koku 石 A measure of volume equal to approximately 50 bushels; divided into 10 *to* (斗), 100 *shō* (升), and 1,000 *gō* (合)

kōsatsu 高札 A signboard where the shogunate posted official notices and proclamations

laboureur A peasant engaged in commercial agriculture, especially prominent in the Paris supply system

letters patent A form of royal legislation, signed by the king and used for municipal purposes

librairie Bookseller-publisher

lieutentant général de police The official who exercised general policing responsibilities in Paris in conjunction with the Châtelet and a variety of other authorities; oversaw sanitation, the control of diseases, the water supply, building regulations, prices, fairs and markets, and sumptuary regulations

lods et vents Levies imposed by seigneural property owners, including the king, on the transfer of land and buildings

machi-bikeshi 町火消 The commoner, all-Edo firefighting force created in 1718

machi bugyō 町奉行 City magistrates; samurai officials who exercised general responsibility for administering the merchant and artisan residential quarters in Edo; reported to the senior councilors

machidoshiyori 町年寄 City elders; merchant officials appointed on a hereditary basis to assist the city magistrates

machi kaisho 町会所 The city savings association, established by the shogunate in 1792; made grants and loans to poor commoners; funded by levies on merchants' residential quarters

maire Mayorship; the head of a town's governing council (*see* échevin); in 1692 Louis XIV sold these posts as venal offices in many towns

metsuke 目付 Inspectors who maintained surveillance over bannermen and housemen

monme 匁 *See* ryō

nanushi 名主 Neighborhood chiefs; assisted the city elders

ninsoku yoseba 人足寄場 Workhouses established in 1790

ōmetsuke 大目付 Inspectors general; maintained surveillance over daimyo and officials of the shogunate; appointed on a regular basis from 1632

parlement The highest royal court in a French province; dispensed "sovereign" justice and registered royal laws; the Parlement of Paris covered two-thirds of the kingdom

parlementaire An officeholding judge in a parlement

présidial A royal appeals court situated in jurisdiction between the baillage courts and the *parlements*

prévôt (1) Provost, executive official of Paris; (2) a provincial police official

prévôt des marchands Provost of the guilds (in Paris); as head of the *échevins* presided over the Hôtel de Ville; held jurisdiction over the river transportation system that was designed to channel goods to the capital

prévôté Provostship; military police of a province

procurator general *See* procureur général

procureur général An official appointed by the king to represent royal interests in Parlement; supervised networks if administrative and judicial officials

quartenier An officer in the Parisian citizen militia who administered a *quartier* on behalf of the city; superior to *dizainier*

quartier A residential quarter, district, or neighborhood

reibyō 霊廟 Mausoleum

rōjū 老中 Senior councilors; these officials constituted the highest policy-making board in the shogun's bureaucracy, with authority to issue laws and regulations concerning the imperial court, daimyo, and lesser officials; supervised important subordinate officials such as the city magistrates and commissioners of building; the first appointment to this post was made in 1623 and the office was institutionalized in the 1630s; appointments were made from among *fudai daimyō*

rōya 牢屋 *See* rōyashiki

rōyashiki 牢屋敷 The shogunate's prison and detention center

ryō 両 A unit of value for coinage; the standard gold coin issued by the shogunate, the *koban* (小判), was equivalent to one *ryō* in the early seventeenth century and contained almost exactly fifteen grams of gold, although it was periodically devalued thereafter; the shogunate fixed the exchange rate of 1 *ryō* of gold at 50 (later 60) *monme* (匁) of silver or 4 *kan* (貫) of copper coins (*zeni*銭)

sakuji bugyō 作事奉行 Commissioners of building, appointed (permanently from 1632) to preside over all aspects of shogunal building projects; reported to senior councilors

samurai 侍 (1) A warrior with the rank of bannerman or higher; (2) a warrior above the bottom rank; (3) any warrior

sankin kōtai 参勤交代 Alternate residence system; the requirement that daimyo reside periodically in Edo (generally every other year) and that their legal wives, immediate heirs, and appropriate retinues of service personnel reside in the city at all times

seii-taishōgun 征夷大将軍 A military figure appointed by the emperor from the eighth century; the shogun claimed the right to administer the affairs of the samurai class from the medieval period; the Tokugawa expanded the powers of the office so that the shogun became a national hegemon; the Tokugawa shogun received pledges of loyalty from all daimyo and served as head of his house government (*bakufu*), which administered the affairs of the nation

senior councilor *See* rōjū

shō 升 *See* koku

shogun *See* seii-taishōgun

shogunate *See* bakufu

shosho-bikeshi 所々火消 The "dispersed brigades"; firefighting squads organized by the daimyo in the seventeenth century, on instructions from the shogunate, to protect strategic sites such as temples, bridges, and granaries

to 斗 *See* koku

tobi 鳶 The roofers and unskilled construction workers who came to form the core of Edo firefighting squads

Tōhoku 東北 Northern Japan; the region generally encompassed by the traditional provinces of Dewa and Mutsu

tokorodokoro-bikeshi *See* shosho-bikeshi

toshiyori 年寄 Elder; the highest official in the shogunate before being replaced by the senior councilors in the 1630s

totō 徒党 "Conspirators"; persons who planned and led illegal actions, especially actions that included collective violence

tozama daimyō 外様大名 "Outside lord"; a daimyo who achieved that status independently or by alliance with Oda Nobunaga or Toyotomi Hideyoshi

uchikowashi 打ち壊し Attacks by commoners on the property of wealthy merchants

voyer de Paris Official in charge of maintaining public buildings in Paris; held final and sole authority to approve or disapprove all building projects

wakadoshiyori 若年寄 Junior councilors; the (usually) three to five officials appointed from 1633 (except for the period from 1649 to 1662) to constitute the
second most important board in the shogun's bureaucracy; supervised lesser
officials such as the *metsuke*

yashiki 屋敷 *See* hairyō yashiki

yōjōsho 養生所 An infirmary and convalescent center established for poor merchants and artisans

zeni 銭 *See* ryō

Contributors

WILLIAM BEIK has made his scholarly reputation through his studies of municipal governments in prerevolutionary France. His widely acclaimed *Absolutism and Society in Seventeenth-Century France: State Power and Provincial Aristocracy in Languedoc* (Cambridge University Press) was awarded the Herbert Baxter Adams Prize by the American Historical Association. He is currently working on the culture of urban protest in seventeenth-century France and is a co-editor of the multivolume series New Approaches to European History (Cambridge University Press). Professor Beik teaches at Emory University.

ROGER CHARTIER has written widely on the cultural practices of ancien régime societies, particularly the history of the book and the history of reading. His most recent publications in English translation include *The Order of Books, Readers, Authors, and Libraries in Europe between the Fourteenth and Eighteenth Centuries* (Polity Press), *The Culture Origins of the French Revolution* (Duke University Press), and *Cultural History: Between Practices and Representations* (Polity Press and Cornell University Press). His work has appeared in Japanese translation as *Dokusho no bunkashi* (Shin'yōsha). Professor Chartier is Directeur d'Etudes at the Ecole des Hautes Etudes en Sciences Sociales, and he has been a Visiting Professor at the Newberry Library, University of Chicago; Yale University; University of California, Berkeley; Cornell University; and Johns Hopkins University.

WILLIAM H. COALDRAKE received his doctorate from Harvard University in the history of Japanese architecture and holds the Foundation Chair of Japanese at the University of Melbourne. He has worked extensively in the restoration of historic temples and castles, an experience that formed the basis for his *The Way of the Carpenter—Tools and Japanese Architecture* (Weatherhill). Professor Coaldrake has taught at Sophia University, the Smithsonian Institution, and the Oriental Institute of the University of Oxford. His Oxford lectures are to be published under the title *Architecture and Authority in Japan*.

474 *Contributors*

JURGIS ELISONAS is Professor of History and East Asian Languages and Cultures at Indiana University. He is the author of *Deus Destroyed*, an extensive look at the image of Christianity in early-modern Japan, and the co-editor of *Warlords, Artists, and Commoners*, a collection of essays on Japan in the sixteenth century. The two chapters that he contributed to volume 4 of the *Cambridge History of Japan* are a monographic study of Japan's foreign relations at the dawn of the early-modern age. He wrote this chapter while he was a Fellow at the Research Institute for Humanistic Studies, Kyoto University.

HATANO JUN teaches at Nippon Kōgyō University and is a specialist in historical architecture. Professor Hatano has supervised the reconstruction of several historical buildings in Japan and important Buddhist monasteries in Nepal. He has also designed exhibits for the National Museum of Japanese History and the newly opened Edo · Tokyo Museum. Professor Hatano's publications include *The Royal Buildings of Nepal* (Nippon Institute of Technology), *The Royal Buildings and Buddhist Monasteries of Nepal* (Nippon Institute of Technology), and several journal articles on the construction of waterways and the provisioning of water to Japanese castle towns.

HAYASHI REIKO is best known for her work on early-modern economic history. Her books include *Edo ton'ya nakama no kenkyū* (Ochanomizu Shobō), *Edodana hankachō* (Yoshikawa Kōbunkan), and *Shōnin no katsudō* (Chūō Kōronsha). More recently Professor Hayashi has been engaged in research on Japanese women and contributed "Chōka josei no sonzai keitai" to volume 3 of Joseishi Sōgō Kenkyūkai, ed., *Nihon joseishi*. She teaches at Ryūtsū Keizai University.

EIKO IKEGAMI was born and educated in Japan, where she received a B.A. in Japanese literature. After working for the *Nihon Keizai* business newspaper, she came to the United States on the Fulbright program and completed a Ph.D. in sociology at Harvard University. She is currently Assistant Professor of Sociology at Yale University and is the author of *The Taming of the Samurai: Honor, Individuality, and State-Making in Japan*, forthcoming from Harvard University Press.

ROBERT M. ISHERWOOD received his doctorate from the University of Chicago and has written extensively on the topic of music and politics. His most recent books are *Farce and Fantasy: Popular Entertainment in Eighteenth-Century Paris* (Oxford University Press) and *La Musica al Servizio del Re. Francia: XVII Secolo* (Società editrice il Mulino). He is Professor of History at Vanderbilt University.

STEVEN LAURENCE KAPLAN is Goldwin Smith Professor of European History, Cornell University. His two-volume *Bread, Politics, and Political Economy in the Reign of Louis XIV* was published by Martinus Nijhoff in English and by Librairie Académique Perrin in French. Professor Kaplan has also authored *Provisioning Paris: Merchants and Millers in the Grain and Flour Trade during the Eighteenth Century* (Cornell University Press) and edited *Understanding Popular*

Culture in Early Modern Europe (Mouton). He is the founder and editor of *Food and Foodways: Explorations in the History and Culture of Human Nourishment*.

KATŌ TAKASHI is a graduate of Waseda University and a leading expert on the political history of Edo. His most recent publications include the documentary compilations *Hyōryū kidan* (Kokusho Kankōkai) and the five-volume *Edo chōkan* (Tōkyōdō Shuppan). His "Edo meisho annai no seiritsu" appeared in Takizawa Takeo, ed., *Chū-kinsei no shiryō to hōhō* (Tōkyōdō Shuppan) and his "Nihon kinsei no kyodai toshi" in Hikaku Toshishi Kenkyūkai, ed., *Hikaku toshi no tabi: Jikan · kūkan · seikatsu* (Hara Shobō). Currently Mr. Katō serves as Specialist on Cultural Properties for Kita Ward in Toyko.

WILLIAM W. KELLY is Professor of Anthropology at Yale University. He is the author of *Deference and Defiance in Nineteenth-Century Japan* (Princeton University Press) and his recent articles include "Finding a Place in Metropolitan Japan" in Andrew Gordon, ed., *Postwar Japan as History* (University of California Press) and "Japan Debates an Aging Society: The Later Years in the Land of the Rising Sun" in Lee Cohen, ed., *Justice across Generations: What Does It Mean?* (Public Policy Institute). Professor Kelly has received numerous grants for research in Japan and currently is working on the topic of Japanese baseball.

SHARON KETTERING is Associate Professor of History at Montgomery College and is the author of *Judicial Politics and Urban Revolt in Seventeenth-Century France: The Parliament of Aix, 1629–1659* (Princeton University Press) and *Patrons, Brokers, and Clients in Seventeenth-Century France* (Oxford University Press). Professor Kettering has published numerous articles on patronage, most recently "Patronage in Early Modern France," *French Historical Studies* 17:4 (1992) and "Brokerage at the Court of Louis XIV," *Historical Journal* 36:1 (1993).

JAMES L. McCLAIN is Professor of History at Brown University. He is the author of *Kanazawa: A Seventeenth-Century Japanese Castle Town* (Yale University Press) and recently has contributed "Cities and Commerce in the Seventeenth and Eighteenth Centuries" (with Nakai Nobuhiko) to volume 4 of the *Cambridge History of Japan*; "Matsuri to kokka kenryoku" to Hikaku Toshishi Kenkyūkai, ed., *Machi to kyōdōtai* (Meicho Shuppansha); and "Bonshōgatsu: Festivals and State Power in Kanazawa" to *Monumenta Nipponica* 47:2 (1992). Professor McClain has been an Invited Research Scholar at the Research Institute for Japanese Culture, Tōhoku University, and a Visiting Sangyung Scholar, Yonsei University.

JOHN M. MERRIMAN did his undergraduate and graduate work at the University of Michigan and is Professor of History at Yale University. His books include *The Margins of City Life: Explorations on the Nineteenth-Century Urban Frontier* (Oxford University Press; French translation forthcoming from Editions du Seuil), *The Red City: Limoges and the French Nineteenth Century* (Oxford University Press; French translation by Belin), and *The Agony of the Republic: The Repression of the Left in Revolutionary France, 1848–1851* (Yale University Press). He has also edited several volumes, including *French Cities in the Nineteenth Century* and *Consciousness and Class Experience in Nineteenth-Century Europe*. Professor Merriman is completing the two-volume *Modern Europe since the Renaissance*, to be published by W. W. Norton.

HENRY D. SMITH is Professor of History at Columbia University. His current research deals with the visual culture of the city of Edo-Tokyo, in particular the role of color woodblock prints. His most recent books are *Ukuyo-e ni miru Edo meisho* (Iwanami Shoten) and *Taizansō and the One-Mat Room* (ICU Hachirō Yuasa Memorial Museum).

TAKEUCHI MAKOTO teaches at Tōkyō Gakugei University and is a foremost urban historian of the Tokugawa era. His studies focus on commoner culture in Edo, and his principal publications include *Kyokutei Bakin* (Shūeisha), *Edo to Ōsaka* (Shōgakukan), and *Bunka no taishūka* (Chūō Kōronsha). Professor Takeuchi contributed numerous entries to the *Edogaku jiten* (Kōbundō), and he is a co-editor of *Edo-Tōkyōgaku jiten* (Sanseidō).

CHARLES TILLY is University Distinguished Professor at the New School for Social Research and directs the Center for Studies of Social Change. His recent books include *European Revolutions, 1492–1992* (Blackwell), *Coercion, Capital, and European States* (Blackwell), *The Contentious French* (Harvard University Press; French translation by Fayard), *Big Structures, Large Processes, Huge Comparisons* (Russell Sage Foundation), and *As Sociology Meets History* (Academic Press).

UGAWA KAORU received his undergraduate and graduate educations at Rikkyō University, where he is a professor in the Faculty of Economics. He is a specialist in premodern English economic and urban history, and his publications include *Ingurando chūsei shakai no kenkyū* (Seikyōkai Shuppan) and *Ingurando shakai keizaishi no tabi* (Nihon Kirisuto Kyōdan Shuppankyoku). Professor Ugawa is the founder of the Comparative Urban History Association and edits its journal, *Hikaku toshishi kenkyū*.

ANNE WALTHALL is the editor and translator of *Peasant Uprisings in Japan: A Critical Anthology of Peasant Histories* (University of Chicago Press) and author of "The Life Cycle of Farm Women in Tokugawa Japan" in Gail Bernstein, ed., *Recreating Japanese Women, 1600–1945*; "The Family Ideology of Rural Entrepreneurs in Early Nineteenth Century Japan," *Journal of Social History* 23:3 (Spring 1990); and "Japanese Gimin: Peasant Martyrs in Popular Memory," *American Historical Review* 91:5 (1986). She is Professor of History at University of California, Irvine.

Index